Deadball Mayhem

Scoundrels, Scandalous Behavior, and Tragic Events

Ronald T. Waldo

Mechanicsburg, PA USA

Published by Sunbury Press, Inc.
Mechanicsburg, Pennsylvania

SUNBURY PRESS®
www.sunburypress.com

Copyright © 2025 by Ronald T. Waldo.
Cover Copyright © 2025 by Sunbury Press, Inc.

Sunbury Press supports copyright. Copyright fuels creativity, encourages diverse voices, promotes free speech, and creates a vibrant culture. Thank you for buying an authorized edition of this book and for complying with copyright laws by not reproducing, scanning, or distributing any part of it in any form without permission. You are supporting writers and allowing Sunbury Press to continue to publish books for every reader. For information contact Sunbury Press, Inc., Subsidiary Rights Dept., PO Box 548, Boiling Springs, PA 17007 USA or legal@sunburypress.com.

For information about special discounts for bulk purchases, please contact Sunbury Press Orders Dept. at (855) 338-8359 or orders@sunburypress.com.

To request one of our authors for speaking engagements or book signings, please contact Sunbury Press Publicity Dept. at publicity@sunburypress.com.

FIRST SUNBURY PRESS EDITION: February 2025

Set in Adobe Garamond | Interior design by Crystal Devine | Cover by Lawrence Knorr | Edited by Sarah Peachey.

Publisher's Cataloging-in-Publication Data
Names: Waldo, Ronald T., author.
Title: Deadball mayhem : scoundrels, scandalous behavior, and tragic events / Ronald T. Waldo.
Description: First trade paperback edition. | Mechanicsburg, PA : Sunbury Press, 2025.
Summary: Mayhem and tragedy prevailed throughout baseball's Deadball Era while scoundrels committed egregious acts that adversely affected the game. From the tragic suicides of Win Mercer and Chick Stahl to hurler Eddie Doheny's mental breakdown on the eve of the 1903 World Series and nefarious behavior by Rube Waddell, *Deadball Mayhem* chronicles many of these key moments and stories from baseball's history.
Identifiers: ISBN 979-8-88819-283-2 (softcover).
Subjects: SPORTS & RECREATION / Baseball / General | SPORTS & RECREATION / Baseball / Essays & Writings | SPORTS & RECREATION / Baseball / History.

Designed in the USA
0 1 1 2 3 5 8 13 21 34 55

For the Love of Books!

Contents

Acknowledgments v
Preface vii
Introduction x

CHAPTERS

1. Mike Donlin: Alcohol, a Nasty Temper, and Deplorable Behavior 1
2. Win Mercer: The All-American Boy's Dark Side 28
3. Ed Delahanty: Reckless Behavior Assists the Cruel Hand of Fate 54
4. Eddie Doheny: Breakdown on the Eve of the First Modern World Series 80
5. A Heated Rivalry: Fred Clarke versus Frank Bowerman and "Hey Barney" 107
6. Rube Waddell: Straw Hat, or Compromised by Gamblers? 135
7. Chick Stahl: Failure Not an Option to the Fragile Mind 163
8. The 1908 National League Pennant Race: Chaos, Protests, and Bribes 191
9. Ty Cobb: Fearless Grit and Determination, with a Confrontational Mindset 219
10. Tigers Solidarity, Carl Mays, and Ban Johnson: Players Strike, a Deserter, and Baseball's Czar 247
11. Mayhem and Tragedy in the Deadball Age 275
12. Baseball's Dawn Turns to Morning 303

Notes 312
Bibliography 356
Index 365
About the Author 378

Acknowledgments

I want to take an opportunity to acknowledge those individuals who made it possible to write this book. First, I offer my extreme gratitude to author and baseball historian Steve Steinberg, whose critical and gracious assistance corroborated and clarified certain points regarding baseball player Mike Donlin's family history. Thank you very much, Steve. Since authoring a book and having it published is a team effort, I want to extend my sincere thanks to those at Sunbury Press Books who have aided in completing this edition regarding baseball history and my two previous books. I am truly appreciative of the hard work, diligence, and professionalism courtesy of Lawrence Knorr, Sarah Peachey, and Crystal Devine at Sunbury Press.

Finally I wish to extend a gracious thank you to family and friends who have supported my craft for these many years. Extending beyond this, I am also grateful for baseball history lovers everywhere, whose enthusiastic interest in learning about past eras motivates me to continue this path, writing about the days of yesteryear related to the great diamond game

Preface

Baseball's Deadball Era functioned as a rich and fertile ground for growing the game once the twentieth century arrived with endless possibilities. Players' diamond exploits defined the era and left a lasting mark throughout baseball history. The game's greats became the first class of elite icons, paving the way for others. Moments and events during the Deadball Era shaped the game and assisted it in prospering and thriving. Major league magnates, possessing tremendous intuition and understanding that baseball's popularity hinged on making the ballpark experience as joyful and pleasing as possible, worked hard to improve the diamond product and build new, beautiful palaces that housed their teams. In conjunction, they reaped rich financial benefits when their clubs proved successful in contending for pennants. Problems arose whenever all the levers of power within the diamond structure did not interact smoothly and cohesively.

At times, pain and adversity littered prosperity's path as baseball surged onward in the Deadball Era. This book examines some of the agonizing and nefarious moments from that period. Mayhem reared its ugly head as scoundrels engaged in shameful behavior, which blemished the game. Calamity and misfortune also prevailed, as stress and pressure related to baseball, and outside forces, led to the demise of a handful of that period's most popular and accomplished ballplayers. The gravity of one's responsibilities went beyond diamond performers, causing even one league executive to commit a tragic act. However, good usually conquered evil, and baseball flourished amidst the conflicting emotions of sorrow and joy borne out of these diamond incidents and events.

A host of books related to the topics and players covered in this work offered guidance and supplied critical research pursuant to undertaking this project. The bulk of information I cultivated came from articles in various newspapers, the *Sporting News*, and *Sporting Life*. Through exposure to a treasure trove of data for this project, each chapter possesses extensive footnotes offering a path to the information I utilized to author this book. I also tapped into websites thanks to membership through the Society for American Baseball Research where both authors and individuals who love baseball history gain access to the stories and opinions from long ago, during any diamond era.

Regarding the topics for each of this book's chapters, I possessed a fundamental understanding of the person covered in that section and all the momentous events behind why I selected the individual as a subject. Through authoring this book, I learned so much more about these players, managers, owners, and league executives that I previously did not know. This gave me a renewed insight into the Deadball Era, especially related to some of the players I have written about in past books. As an author, I always wish to expand my horizons while working on a project, and I look forward to learning new things or discovering different angles or snippets of information related to a certain topic. I possess a strong passion for baseball history and always enjoy coming across newfound material when joyously delving into the research and writing processes.

I feel that exposure to fresh and exciting tales is the sheer beauty surrounding baseball history. New discoveries are always present at the beckoning call, and a wealth of unearthed findings await. I certainly gained knowledge in different areas of the Deadball Era through authoring this book. Hopefully, acting as a literary guide, readers will experience the same pleasure while traveling down this historical baseball road I have mapped out, covering a glorious period from over a century ago.

Introduction

Throughout baseball history, different moments and events have aided in defining a specific period. This holds true for baseball's Deadball Era, covering the years from 1900 through 1919. Over that span, some of the game's greatest performers graced the diamond and established credentials from which later contemporaries received comparison. Although baseball slowly transformed from its rowdier stigma of the 1890s to a purer version where those in charge championed a clean and fair approach, it took years of challenging work to eliminate entrenched, tough, hardened ideals. The despot's day in the sun continued while the clean-shaven collegiate product attempted to put a dent in the past diamond generation's way of thinking. The battle to extricate the seedy element's tentacle-like grasp from the game proved a long and hard one that no group or person could accomplish in short order.

The premise of this book is to examine some of that era's scandalous incidents and the scoundrels who perpetrated events that interfered with the baseball hierarchy's hopes and aspirations of achieving a pristine sport, which appealed to people of all ages and social standing. When planning to cover twenty years of the grand game's history, I focused on making thoughtful decisions about which players and events to include in the work. New York Yankees/Highlanders first baseman Harold "Hal" Chase certainly could have received a chapter dedicated to his behavior as a player and a manager throughout the Deadball Era, but he did not make the cut. I decided that other actions, including Mike Donlin's many alcohol-induced indiscretions, the charge that quirky Philadelphia Athletics southpaw hurler Rube Waddell might have faked an injury after gamblers paid him off not to participate in the 1905 World Series, and Ty Cobb's attack on a Cleveland hotel house detective and a New York Highlanders fan, warranted stronger consideration.

The same holds true for my selections regarding tragic events from the Deadball Era. I deliberated including the sad tale of New York Giants pitcher Arthur "Bugs" Raymond, who died at thirty under strange circumstances on September 7, 1912. So, too, did I consider the stories of Boston Beaneaters catcher Martin "Marty" Bergen murdering his family and then committing suicide on January 19, 1900, along with the double-life of player, manager, umpire, scout, and college coach Arthur Irwin, who killed himself on July 16, 1921, leaving behind two wives and families. These two dreadful incidents did not make the grade since Bergen's act occurred nineteen days into the start of the twentieth century, and Irwin's demise happened in the 1920s. Other sad tales rose to the forefront above these two unfortunate events.

I have included the tragic suicides of George "Win" Mercer, Charles "Chick" Stahl, and Harry Pulliam in the book. Marty Bergen's heinous act is mentioned in the Stahl chapter since the two played together with the Boston Beaneaters. Win's situation proved intriguing since he demonstrated qualities that rooters viewed as the antithesis of the rough-and-tumble rowdy when he debuted as a major leaguer in 1894. Win exhibited the boy-next-door persona, loved and adored by fans, teammates, and opposing players. Considered the National League's handsomest player, Mercer frequently pitched on Ladies' Day at home as a member of the Washington Nationals since female patrons worshiped the young man. In the cases of Chick and Win, baseball's pressure and stress from independent forces led them to tragically end their lives. Extreme anxiety and nervousness caused National League president Harry Pulliam to do the same in 1909.

The book also covers the human mind's fragile state in the chapter about Pittsburgh Pirates southpaw twirler Edward "Eddie" Doheny, who suffered a nervous breakdown on the eve of the 1903 World Series against the Boston Americans. To a lesser degree, the situation surrounding Boston Red Sox hurler Carl Mays deserting his club in 1919 came about from becoming mentally and emotionally overwhelmed by too many unfortunate incidents in his life. Mental state was a key component that led to former star outfielder Edward "Ed" Delahanty's accidental death in 1903. That particular year supplied many tragic moments for baseball lovers following the fortunes of their favorite clubs or players. To this day, mysteries still exist surrounding the reasons behind these players' actions. I present information regarding the unanswered questions and allow the reader to reach conclusions based on that data and form their own opinions.

On occasion, mayhem and chaos burst forth during the Deadball Era. Gamblers influenced events, and power struggles occurred between those who owned the clubs and those who presided over the leagues. Concerning American League president Ban Johnson, who some believed ruled that organization like a dictatorial autocrat, brave souls did challenge his authority while standing on their principles. Just as teams engaging in thrilling pennant races and players performing incredible feats galvanized paying clientele, confrontation also aided in baseball's growth during this period. Good and bad moments defined that era; shameful behavior and unfortunate events counterbalanced the positive atmosphere, ushering in a new brand of baseball in the twentieth century.

CHAPTER 1

Mike Donlin

Alcohol, a Nasty Temper, and Deplorable Behavior

Throughout the early years of baseball's Deadball Era, rough-and-tumble players exuded their influence upon diamond events. Steeped in traditions established by their predecessors in the 1890s, these bastions of the confrontational approach, carrying aggression's torch, strongly counterbalanced those who believed the game's ultimate survival and long-lasting popularity rested through a civilized tone. Although many of these "rowdies," as people referred to them, left that side of their personality on the baseball field, some ballplayers carried this persona into their everyday lives. In the case of one individual where endless talent abounded, the situation proved quite vexing when poor behavior circumvented athletic ability. Those who followed baseball never questioned Michael "Mike" Donlin's capabilities as a diamond performer. Conversely, the lethal combination of alcohol and bad temperament at times smashed such skill and talent like a wrecking ball.

Mike Donlin was born in Peoria, Illinois, on May 30, 1878. The Irish Donlins relocated back to Erie, Pennsylvania, where Mike's father, John, worked as a railroad conductor.[1] Sadly, disaster and devastation followed the family in this dangerous industry. A calamitous tragedy occurred on Monday evening, June 29, 1885. Mother Maggie Donlin, nurse Sarah "Sadie" Mahoney, and two of the family's children, a ten-year-old boy and a ten-week-old baby girl, occupied a freight train traveling west along the Nickle Plate Road. The train made a scheduled stop at a station near East Springfield, Pennsylvania, leaving several empty cars and the caboose sitting on the trestle near J. M. Strong's grist and saw mills, which stood eighty feet above Crooked Creek. Maggie, Sadie, and the two children occupied the caboose. Since the engine's detachment occurred for switching purposes, brakeman John Feltis signaled with a flag to another freight locomotive that followed them on the Nickel Plate Road.

Unfortunately, the oncoming locomotive closed in quicker than anticipated. Feltis ran to the back of the train, entered the caboose, and yelled, "Run for your lives! There's a train close upon us!" The terrified women looked out and saw the advancing freight train bearing down upon them. The brakeman hurriedly escorted Mrs. Donlin, holding her daughter, and Mahoney, to a flat car attached to the caboose. Although John Feltis instructed the young boy to follow his mother, the ten-year-old son remained in the caboose. Sensing the impending danger, the moving locomotive's engineer quickly threw the engine into reverse and jumped off, followed by the fireman. With momentum slightly altered enough, when the locomotive struck the stationary train's caboose, the impact did not shatter it but sent it crashing into the flat car. The collision's force caused the flat car to double like an oxbow, breaking the couplings at one end and throwing it over the trestle's edge, partially teetering, while the wreck tossed all four people toward the creek beneath the bridge.

John Feltis and Sadie Mahoney suffered profoundly serious injuries.[2] Initially, telegraph wires forty feet below the bridge halted Maggie Donlin's plummet. Maggie tightly clutched the baby girl in her arms as she remained suspended for an hour by wires that cut deeply into the flesh and stripped it away from the ribs. The telegraph wires finally gave way, and Mrs. Donlin fell to the bottom. Luckily, the child's dress caught on overhanging tree branches. When rescuers reached the baby girl, they discovered she only had a broken arm.[3]

Maggie suffered a badly shattered arm and internal injuries, and several ribs tore loose from the breastbone during her ordeal. Physicians held out no hope for recovery. Mike Donlin's mother died on July 1, and the family held her burial in Erie the following day. An article in the *Conneautville Courier* about this tragic train wreck mentioned Maggie as Conductor Donlin's wife. It also chronicled that the ten-year-old son survived the accident. The story did not verify whether John Donlin happened to be working as this train's conductor.[4] Days after the tragedy, an updated Erie dispatch identified an injured brakeman as Thomas Fahey, and professed that Sadie Mahoney might be scarred for life because part of her face was torn away resulting from the fall off the trestle.[5]

The railroad curse claimed another Donlin on August 12, 1890. Michael's uncle, James Donlin, an Erie & Pittsburgh Road line conductor, died at the Conneautville Station in Pennsylvania. The locomotive where he functioned as the conductor stopped that afternoon at the station to take on additional cars. While this procedure occurred, James assisted, standing on the main track with his back toward the engine. Although the whistle blew, indicating backing,

Donlin did not realize the danger. A tender (coal car) struck James, knocking him to the tracks. As the engine moved in reverse, the back wheels ran over Donlin, killing him instantly and almost severing his head.[6]

On January 6, 1894, John Donlin, who had worked on the Erie & Pittsburgh Road and the Nickle Plate Road, died at St. Vincent's Hospital in Erie while a doctor administered anesthesia before performing surgery.[7] Previously, John and James's father, Michael Donlin I, died on March 15, 1875, when a train engine ran over him and mangled his body. A switch-tender for the railroad, Michael had decided to hitch a ride on the engine at Cherry Street in Erie to take him toward his home for dinner. The locomotive stopped along the way at a roundhouse to add empty cars. When the train started moving again, Donlin either clumsily exited at that point or fell onto the tracks in front of the oncoming engine.[8]

Following his mother's death in 1885, young Michael Donlin moved in with another Irish family named the Murphys, who treated him like their own son.[9] Although this kindly family took him in, Mike spent much of his time as an orphan on Erie's streets. He contracted tuberculosis as a youngster and later found work selling candy on the area's railways.[10] To improve his poor health, Donlin traveled to California's warmer climate as a teenager. Playing baseball in the mild weather quickly restored Mike's vigor and vitality as he gained power and speed as a player despite his slight build.[11]

In 1899, Donlin achieved star status in the California League, pitching for the Santa Cruz Beachcombers/Sand Crabs. With Santa Cruz that year, Mike won a significant percentage of his games on the mound and did fine work at the plate while playing other positions, leading the league in hitting. Before the 1900 campaign started, *St. Louis Republic* sportswriter John B. Sheridan's article affirmed he first heard about Mike's exploits while the St. Louis Perfectos played a series in Baltimore against the Orioles the previous spring. A wire from Sheridan's newspaper claimed Perfectos manager Oliver Wendell "Patsy" Tebeau expressed interest in securing Donlin. While dining with the writer following a tough 4–3 loss at Union Park on May 31, 1899, Tebeau denied having any such inclination. All parties placed Mike on the back burner until the *Sporting News* started printing favorable stories about the player.[12]

Editor Alonzo Joseph "Joe" Flanner of the *Sporting News* received a tip from one of his correspondents about this Santa Cruz southpaw pitcher who possessed a sizzling fastball and was a hard-hitting outfielder. Upon receiving the information, Flanner enthusiastically shared it with Frank Robison, St. Louis's part-owner.[13] According to John Sheridan, the editor also forwarded the statistics and scores to Patsy Tebeau, offering powerful testimony supporting Mike Donlin's hitting prowess. These figures so impressed the Perfectos' manager that he wired the correspondent in California to inquire if Mike would be interested in signing with St. Louis while also asking about salary demands. Following a one-day delay, Tebeau received a reply from the telegraph company, informing him they could not forward his message because that person currently languished in a Santa Cruz jail. Patsy wired back to deliver it anyhow.

In his piece, Sheridan wrote that this message reached the agent at the jail, who then sent for Donlin. Mike requested a big salary, and it cost the Perfectos $600 to purchase him from Santa Cruz. Patsy oversaw the negotiations through this incarcerated individual. Each time St. Louis's skipper sent a wire to the California city, Donlin traveled to the jail to consult with the correspondent. In the end, both sides agreed on terms, and Tebeau paid a fancy price for an individual he had never seen play a game while no scout made a recommendation. It turned out that the jailed correspondent never watched Mike on the diamond, either. Donlin befriended the journalist in California when he got into trouble, who then authored glowing endorsements about his baseball talent due to that tight bond.

John Sheridan wrote that this correspondent, who also happened to be a ballplayer, first-class journalist, and former United States soldier, eventually received freedom for his offense, which occurred through drinking too much liquor.[14] However, Sheridan's account proved inaccurate. The correspondent did not reside in jail during these negotiations; instead, Mike Donlin had run afoul of the law. Mike cooled his heels in a jail cell for engaging in a brawl. Impressed with his baseball potential, Frank Robison bailed Donlin out of jail and purchased him from Santa Cruz. Shortly after he joined the Perfectos, Mike called on Joe Flanner at the *Sporting News'* office in St. Louis. The ring of honor on the headquarters' walls contained photos of iconic diamond performers Edward "Ed" Delahanty, Denton "Cy" Young, Hugh "Hughie" Jennings, John "Mac" McGraw, Charles Comiskey, and Jesse Burkett. Donlin fervently gazed at this galaxy of late nineteenth-century icons before posing a question to Flanner.

"Say, Joe," blurted out Donlin, "where is my picture?"[15]

In his first game as a Perfectos team member on July 19, 1899, Michael relieved starter John William "Willie" Sudhoff after he faltered against the Boston Beaneaters at South End Grounds. Although Boston secured an 8–1 victory, Mike did impressive work on the mound for St. Louis.[16] Donlin also played shortstop when sickness sidelined veteran Edwin "Ed" McKean. After a sensational showing in his first game at that position, Mike performed wretchedly the following day, making numerous erratic throws. Although he struggled at first base when installed there, St. Louis's fans screamed in protest whenever Patsy Tebeau did not pencil the youngster into his starting lineup. In the rooters' eyes, smacking the leather viciously around the ballpark more than made up for Donlin's defensive shortcomings.[17] Playing the outfield eventually suited Mike best, as he appeared in 66 games and batted .323 during his rookie season.

Decades after Donlin's debut, Boston Red Sox part-owner James Aloysius Robert "Bob" Quinn offered his opinion in 1926 on the type of player he wanted when building that club. Quinn hearkened back to 1899, when the cocky youngster from Santa Cruz first joined St. Louis, and Mike and manager Patsy Tebeau did not hit it off.

"Men like Mike Donlin—they are of the kind," said Quinn. "Mike had the ideal temperament, coupled with his native ability. He had been with St. Louis only two days when Patsy Tebeau, his manager, called him to one side and informed him, briskly: 'Say, bud, you're altogether too fresh to suit me, see?'

"Mike glared back at him challengingly. 'Oh yeh! Well, listen, you'll have to get used to me. I'm gonna be around here a long time!'"[18]

Mike Donlin's native ability never came into question, although people could certainly subject his temperament to scrutiny. Donlin acquired the nickname "Turkey Mike" due to his red neck and manner of strutting about with supreme confidence. Abrasive attitude and sureness in his ability aside, one incident involving Mike did not make headlines until the Perfectos finished a one-day trip to Cincinnati on August 6, 1899. According to a newspaper story from his old haunt in Santa Cruz, as the squad waited that Sunday night for a Baltimore & Ohio train at Grand Central Depot to take them back to Pittsburgh to resume a series, Donlin and catcher Freeman Osee "Schreck" Schrecongost engaged in a vicious fight. Several teammates and bystanders intervened to stop the fracas before one of the players became seriously hurt. The newspaper claimed Schrecongost got the worst of the brawl before it abruptly ended.

This article asserted that bitter feelings had existed between the two Perfectos' team members for several days. In the Sunday afternoon game at League Park, which the Cincinnati Reds won, 4–2, Mike made two powerful laser throws toward home plate while playing first base. Both tosses came in low and struck Osee on the shins. When the team traveled back to the hotel by omnibus after the contest, Schreck made a sarcastic remark about fresh kids with $10,000 arms and two-cent heads who broke into the league before they knew the first rudiments of the game. Donlin immediately jumped to his feet and threatened to throw Osee out of the vehicle. Cooler heads prevailed. The two players did not clash again until later, upon departing Cincinnati, when they placed their baggage in the train's sleeper car. After doing so, Schrecongost approached Mike and said something to him in a muffled voice.

Donlin quickly turned around and fired out his right fist, striking the St. Louis catcher's jaw with so much velocity that he crumpled to the ground. Osee regained his footing and lunged toward Mike, who, for a second time, dropped his teammate with a single punch. Schrecongost arose once again, and each man started exchanging fierce blows. Realizing Donlin had bested him thus far in this scrap, Osee attempted to grab a weapon of opportunity when it presented itself. Schreck lifted a nearby coupling pin before his rushing opponent could prevent the catcher from picking it up. Just as Osee prepared to smack Mike over the head with this weapon, players and bystanders witnessing the confrontation rushed in and stopped him. Perfectos team members commandeered the two men and escorted them to the train as it pulled out of the depot.[19]

Shortly after various newspapers chronicled this incident, Mike Donlin stated during an interview that the article about his fight with Osee Schrecongost happened to be a fake story. Mike added that he and Schreck considered each other the best of friends who would never contemplate engaging in a tussle. Considering Donlin's claim, feisty veteran St. Louis catcher John "Jack" O'Connor's comment four days after the incident happened seemed interesting. He applauded the youngster's fierce nature while engaging in a bout where Jack dismissed the notion that Osee did the bidding of teammate Jesse Burkett.

"If Burkett had any trouble with Donlin, he is just the man to settle it right there," said the great catcher on the night of August 10. "As for getting Schreck to do his fighting, that is rubbish. I think everyone knows that you have got to do your own fighting in this world, and if you cannot do it, you will not find fellows standing around to do it for you. I figure that Schreck, who is a big kid, got to joshing Donlin too much and that Mike, who is a hot-tempered fellow, took a punch at him without thinking."[20]

O'Connor's comment about a plausible reason for Mike Donlin punching Osee Schrecongost seemed dubious when another team member offered the incident's genuine version. This player stated that Schreck and Jesse Burkett engaged in a scrap after the catcher ridiculed the veteran outfielder, causing him to lose his temper. The individual qualified that the two had been good friends before the fight and became even better buddies after the altercation. This Perfectos squad member felt compelled to offer the true account because of the ridiculous stories published by newspapers regarding Burkett's envious feelings toward Donlin.[21] After the 1900 baseball campaign concluded, Mike offered his version of what happened on August 6, 1899, to a *St. Louis Globe-Democrat* reporter, refuting that he had knocked Osee out by smacking him over the head with a coupling pin.

> I never figured in that trouble at Cincinnati at all; Schreck did, but he was far from being vanquished and would have been given a sure decision had [boxing referees] Charley White, Joe Stewart, or George Siler been around.

It happened about 11 o'clock one night while we were waiting in the depot for a train to [Pittsburgh]. Burkett and [Roderick "Bobby"] Wallace were sitting on the steps of the train, reading a paper, when Schreck came along and looked over their shoulders.

"Playing the role of Johnny Butt-in, eh?" ejaculated Burkett.

Jesse gave Schreck one of his hard looks, and the big fellow walked away. He came back to the gang who had seen it all, and asked what he should do.

"Burkett and I'll never get along," he said. "He don't seem to like me, and is picking on me all the time."

"Go back and call him," cried one of the bunch. "If you don't, he'll continue bulldozing you the rest of your life. Call him good, and after it's over he'll be your friend."

Now, Schreck is rated as about the strongest player in the business since Ed McKean and [William "Bill"] "Scrappy" Joyce have passed away [from playing baseball], and they don't make many better little fighters than Burkett. The upshot was that Schreck walked back to where Burkett was still resting, slapped him on the back with one hand, tore the paper out of his hands with the other, and then asked him to explain himself.

"No explanation coming," replied Burkett. "You're a pretty fresh kid, and I guess I'd better give you 'yours' now as well as any time."

So saying, Jesse shot out his right for the jaw. But Schreck blocked it, sent his right over to the mark and Jesse brought up against a long line of freight trains. He came rushing back, got "copped" again and then retired for the night.

We were off for [Pittsburgh] with everybody wondering how Burkett and Schreck would take things the next day. At breakfast Schreck was on hand first and was quickly followed by Burkett. Jesse walked right over to where Osee was sitting, extended his hand and said: "Old man, I was in the wrong. Take my hand." This Schreck did, and the two are the firmest sort of friends now. Burkett is plugging Schreck for the team next year, and as he played great ball for Buffalo in the American [in 1900] I guess he will be back and hold onto his job.

Donlin further explained that when newspapers carried the incorrect story about him whipping Schrecongost in a fight, the entire team, especially Jesse Burkett, experienced a good laugh. As a result, Schreck became quite bitter toward Mike. Throughout St. Louis's entire road trip, Osee irked Donlin when he continuously introduced him to friends in the same manner.

"Shake hands with Mr. Donlin," Schrecongost constantly repeated. "He's a member of our club, the fellow, you know, who the papers say licked me in Cincinnati. Why, he can't lick one side of me, and that report was a 'bloomer.'"

Over time Mike grew tired of Schreck's constant overcompensation to correct a false media narrative while the catcher introduced Mike to others. Finally, when the Perfectos reached the final leg of their road trip in Philadelphia, Donlin decided to take one punch at Osee the next time he made that remark, even if the catcher killed him. Sure enough, Schrecongost went through the entire proclamation on the first morning in the city shortly after eating breakfast at the hotel while addressing someone he knew, as Mike stood close by. Donlin concluded the story for this pundit by describing what happened after Schreck included the fight tale in his greeting to that friend.

> "I can't lick one side of you, you overweight minor leaguer! I'll show you." And away went my right for Osee's chin. It landed full on the mark, but didn't make the slightest impression, and away I darted from the hotel as fast as my legs would carry me. Schreck was after me, but I soon had him distanced, and he went back to the hotel. I hugged the outskirts of the town until after luncheon, and when it was getting close onto time to take the bus for the ballpark I called the hotel up from a drugstore and asked the clerk to send Schreck to the phone. I felt pretty safe, being at the other end of the wire, with him, not having the slightest idea how near or how far I was from him.
>
> He was at the receiver in a few minutes, and before he had time to say a word I exclaimed: "My name's Donlin. You're not mad, are you? Let me come back to the hotel, dress and hold my job."
>
> "Sure," came his response, and with many misgivings I hurried back to the hostelry. Schreck was there to greet me, and, extending his hand, said, "What's the use of us scrapping, Mike? We're teammates, ain't we?" We remained fast friends, he cut out that paragraph in his introductory remarks and I hope when we begin operations next spring Schreck will be one of us.[22]

Although Mike Donlin had not fought Osee Schrecongost at the Grand Central Depot in Cincinnati, he did punch his teammate while the club played in Philadelphia. Regarding the 1900 season, Donlin figured in other cases involving a confrontation or a threat of violence. On the diamond, Donlin appeared in 78 games for the St. Louis Cardinals and batted .326. Remaining on the field for his team served as Mike's big problem. On June 25, the *St. Louis Dispatch* reported that a nasty cut to the ballplayer's face, suffered during an encounter the previous day, confined him to his home.²³ The *St. Louis Globe-Democrat* reported that around 3 A.M. on Sunday, June 24, Mike and another player, believed to be pitcher August "Gus" Weyhing, became entangled in an altercation with two other gentlemen. The Cardinals' players had been relaxing in a saloon located at Eighteenth Street and Washington Avenue in St. Louis.²⁴

According to a *St. Louis Republic* article, Donlin and another man, whom they did not identify as Weyhing, traveled downtown on Saturday evening to see off Johnnie Murphy, nicknamed "Jockey" Murphy due to his former involvement in horse racing, at Union Station. Murphy's train departed St. Louis at 11:20 P.M. After Jockey's train left the city, Mike and his companion played a few games of billiards at an establishment near Union Station before starting home. Before calling it a night, the pair decided to stop at a saloon at Eighteenth Street and Washington Avenue for a drink. Upon entering the tavern, they walked near two other individuals partaking in alcohol. Donlin invited the two strangers to join them, and they accepted. The group consumed a few more drinks before Mike made some remarks in jest about the red whiskers of the older gentleman from this duo.²⁵

An article in Santa Cruz's *Evening Sentinel* reported that when commenting on the elderly man's profuse whiskers, Donlin said, "What a treat for the wind," and "The old boy's got his face fenced in." Wishing to avoid trouble, the old gentleman left the tavern while his youthful companion, who possessed curly red locks, followed close behind. This newspaper, which suggested Gus Weyhing accompanied Mike that night, claimed both ballplayers felt good but were sober and only wished to enjoy a quiet time at the establishment.²⁶ An eyewitness to the encounter offered insight for the *St. Louis Republic* article. This individual, while stating that none of Donlin's remarks appeared malicious or taken out of context by the red-whiskered gentleman, told the reporter what he witnessed once Mike and his friend left the establishment.

> They went out of the saloon and stood on the sidewalk. As they were about to depart Donlin again spoke jokingly of the elderly stranger's whiskers. This time the man grew angry and called Donlin down. Donlin laughed and again cracked a joke about the whiskers, running his fingers through them as he did so.
>
> Then the man, who was about 45 years old, hit at Donlin, but missed him. Donlin did not hit back, but caught the man's arm and gave him a push away, saying: "None of that. What's the matter with you?" Just then the younger man leaped at Donlin from behind and slashed him along the face. Donlin turned around with a cry and started for the fellow. As he did so he was cut again and again. He grabbed the fellow's hand, after several

vain efforts, but the knife cut his fingers and he had to let go. In fact the cuts in his fingers rendered him powerless.

By this time he was a sight to see. His face and clothes were covered with blood that flowed from his wounds in streams. He was fighting mad and eager to get at his assailant. But the fellow, after Donlin was obliged to loose his grip, dashed across Washington Avenue and down Eighteenth Street toward Olive [Street].

Donlin's companion tried to come to his rescue, but the elderly man with the beard which gave rise to the trouble held him off. The affray was on and over in a few seconds. Donlin was quite badly cut. He asked to be taken to a doctor, and they took him to the City Hospital. The cutting took place on the sidewalk outside of the saloon.

While Donlin might have left the stranger's whiskers out of the discussion, I thought that what was said by the ballplayer did not call for a fight. The man had red whiskers and seemed to be very proud of them. Donlin called them "chin willies," "lilacs," and "grass." That was all.

The eyewitness concluded by stating Mike Donlin did not act offensive, while the man who sliced his face happened to be about thirty years old, small, and of slight build.[27] Upon arriving at St. Louis's City Hospital, a doctor dressed the wounds on Mike's face, neck, and hands. Someone at the medical establishment immediately recognized him as a St. Louis Cardinals ballplayer. Donlin's companion refused to offer his name when asked. The person believed to be Gus Weyhing falsely identified himself as John Jones, a blacksmith.[28] Hospital employees also notified police, and two detectives arrived. They detained Mike and his friend for two hours to answer questions before allowing them to leave. The *St. Louis Post-Dispatch* reported that St. Louis police assigned two detectives, Thomas "Tom" McGrath and Louis "Louie" Ziegler, to the case.[29] A story in the *St. Louis Globe-Democrat* claimed that Detective Ziegler and Detective William "Sport" Brady drew the duty to investigate this matter.[30]

On the night of June 24, 1900, a *St. Louis Republic* reporter arrived at the boardinghouse where Donlin lived. Mike, his face swathed in cotton covering cuts on the neck and cheek as he lay in the warm room, fanned away flies while reclining. The reporter hoped to elicit Donlin's side of the story regarding the incident. Mike held forth his bandaged hand and smiled grimly before commenting to the reporter.

"You want me to tell you how this happened," he said. "Well, old fellow, I am sorry, but I really cannot talk about it. It would not make it any more creditable to me or do any good. I acted foolishly, and I got mine. I will keep my mouth shut and take my medicine. I have been a fool and I cannot unmake myself by talking. You will not hold me discourteous for refusing to talk to you? When a fellow makes a fool of himself the best thing he can do is to keep a shut mouth. While I do not think I earned this, I got it and have got to stand it."

Although he did not discuss the particulars to the reporter behind someone slashing his face with a knife, such an approach might not be feasible when confronting St. Louis manager Patsy Tebeau. That same night, Tebeau declared he knew about the incident but would not take action until he heard Donlin's side of the story.[31] Some press members felt Patsy could administer severe discipline by suspending Mike for the season's duration. These same diamond experts surmised Tebeau had soured on the young player.[32] A column in the *St. Louis Republic* laid bare for the public what they considered Donlin's most significant faults in tenuous situations:

> Personally he is a well-meaning, excellently disposed boy, but he lacks sense and is overmuch inclined to convivialism and low company, which is a very unfortunate thing. He has a penchant for engaging in disreputable street brawls. Several of these have been aired in the public prints, and many more have been suppressed. It is a very unfortunate thing for the boy, in spite of his seeming readiness to act the rowdy, is really a very nice and likeable young man of fine disposition and excellent parts. His extreme youth—he is but 21 [Mike turned 22 on May 30, 1900]—and naturally high spirits allow him to do many foolish things which he will deeply regret when older.[33]

On June 26, Mike Donlin surprised his teammates by showing up at the club's morning practice before their game that afternoon against Cincinnati at League Park. Although Mike's sliced hands remained bandaged, the young player told his Cardinals brethren that he planned to return to his outfield post as soon as he could grip a bat.[34] Those pondering Pasty Tebeau's reaction to Donlin's mishap should have focused more on the manager's feelings about his job. On August 19, 1900, Tebeau resigned as St. Louis's manager. Fans had anticipated this action for some time.[35] Patsy first debuted as a player in 1887 with the Chicago White Stockings. After joining the Cleveland Spiders in 1889 and spending one season playing for that city's Infants' Players League entry in 1890, he returned to the National League a year later when the organization folded. Gaining experience managing the Infants for part of 1890, Spiders ownership selected Tebeau to run the show in July 1891, and he continued as their field boss until taking over St. Louis's reins in 1899.

After the Reds defeated St. Louis at League Park, 8–5, on August 19, ownership held a meeting at the club's office. During this conference, attended by representatives from St. Louis's daily newspapers, magnate and team treasurer Edward C. Becker, and co-owner Martin Stanford "Stanley" Robison, brother and organization president Frank Robison announced Tebeau had resigned. He added that after much persuading, third baseman John McGraw agreed to manage the squad for the season's duration. At 10 P.M., press members spotted Frank and business manager Louis "Louie" Heilbroner chatting in the Southern Hotel's rotunda.[36] When the National League eliminated four baseball franchises and contracted down to eight teams after the 1899 campaign ended, with the Baltimore Orioles' squad where McGraw performed as a member for eight seasons, one of those axed, he shifted over to St. Louis. Reluctant at first to move since John owned a prosperous Baltimore saloon along with teammate Wilbert Robinson, he eventually signed a Cardinals contract paying him $10,000 for one year.[37]

When reading the morning newspapers on August 20, John McGraw expressed indignation at the articles claiming he acquiesced to Frank Robison's wishes and agreed to manage St. Louis. On the contrary, McGraw had declined to accept the job on numerous occasions. When John arrived at League Park that afternoon for the first time in a week after missing games due to illness, he watched the contest versus Cincinnati from the clubhouse since he still did not feel fit enough to play. John chatted with a *St. Louis Globe-Democrat* reporter as Louie Heilbroner oversaw things from the dugout.

"To say that I was surprised when I picked up the morning papers and saw that I was credited with having accepted the management of the St. Louis club is putting it mildly," McGraw told the reporter. "How the story originated I did not know, but I have since learned that Mr. Frank Robison informed the members of the press as a body that such was the case. Why he issued that statement I cannot say, as he knows that I have steadfastly refused the position. Mr. Robison has been after me continually for the past several weeks with flattering offers to serve, but I turned them all down."

McGraw added that when Frank Robison pressed him to accept the managerial post on August 13 to replace Patsy Tebeau, who committed to resigning, he offered up other potential candidates, including Heilbroner. On Sunday morning, August 19, Robison called on John in his hotel room and stated he planned to accept one of those suggestions, naming Louie to manage the Cardinals. After McGraw told his boss he made a wise choice, Frank asked John if he would help Heilbroner attend to his duties. Within his capacity as team captain, McGraw heartily concurred, agreeing to select the lineup and batterymen for each game. He also replied affirmatively when asked if Louie should sit on the bench, since John felt the dugout was the proper place for a manager.[38]

Patsy Tebeau had written and handed in his resignation ten days earlier, but Frank Robison refused to accept it. After St. Louis finished in fifth place in 1899 with an 84–67 record, Patsy fell on hard luck one year later. His club occupied seventh place while fashioning a 42–50 record when he resigned. Tebeau had amassed a great fortune through playing baseball and other interests. He partnered with Scrappy Bill Joyce to open a saloon in St. Louis. While the establishment did tremendous business, it adversely affected the players who frequented the bar. The excessive alcohol consumption did more harm than good.[39] When Patsy announced his intentions to the press, the former pilot declared he was through with baseball for life and laughed at reports regarding him taking a position with another team.

"I've been in baseball plenty long enough and have laid away enough money to satisfy the wants of my family the remainder of their lives," said Tebeau. "When I offered the Robisons my resignation I made up my mind that I would never go back into the game. I've had my day and now pass the game up to others."[40]

Shortly after Tebeau cut ties with the St. Louis Cardinals' organization, an anonymous player offered insight into the squad's unsettled climate. This individual claimed that, contrary to published comments by the management hierarchy, harmony did not exist within the club. He alleged that ownership froze Patsy out while John McGraw enjoyed no real authority. The team member qualified that John possessed responsibility but not power, that Tebeau decided everything and always dictated his wishes directly to the players and not through the Cardinals' team captain. The anonymous individual also accused team members from the McGraw clique of not offering their best diamond effort. He reasoned that although Tebeau voluntarily resigned, in a sense, factors forced that decision upon him. According to this person, under the dynamic that existed, with John out on the field participating in games, Patsy happened to be useless occupying a seat on the bench.[41]

The new hierarchy, with Louie Heilbroner as St. Louis's skipper, drew an unfavorable reaction in one instance from the resident team member who exhibited a bad temper. When Mike Donlin took his place on the diamond, he performed magical feats. Fans remained in awe long after Mike crushed a mammoth home run to the clubhouse at League Park on August 26, 1899, against Philadelphia Phillies hurler William "Bill" Bernhard. Another time, Brooklyn Superbas pitcher Joseph "Joe" McGinnity used a novel approach when facing Donlin in a game. Brooklyn held a three-run lead in the ninth inning, with two outs and Cardinals runners occupying every base as Mike strolled to the plate. Rather than take a chance on Donlin crushing one of his offerings and winning the game, McGinnity intentionally walked St. Louis's slugger and forced in a run. This strategy proved prudent as Joe retired the next batter to end the contest.

Unfortunately, Donlin spent too much time on the bench because of confrontations with umpires and other indiscretions. John McGraw devised a plan, hoping to secure Mike's services.

"Mr. Heilbroner," said McGraw, "I think we would win a lot more if we could keep Mike in the game. Can't you do something to stop his fighting with the umpires?"

McGraw set the trap, gauging Louie's reaction to his question. The diminutive Heilbroner, who stood four feet eleven inches, quickly rose from the bench.

"I'll stop him!" emphatically remarked Heilbroner. "The next time he is put out by an umpire I'll plaster a fine on him."

Louie's chance came before St. Louis played their game that afternoon. When umpire Henry "Hank" O'Day walked over to the Cardinals' dugout to receive the batting order, Donlin greeted the arbiter with a snide remark.

"So you are here, are you, you blind old robber?" inquired Mike.

"Yes, I am here, Mr. Donlin, and you are out of the game before it starts," retorted O'Day.

"That will cost you exactly $100, Donlin," interposed the dignified Heilbroner.

"What's that?" screamed Donlin.

"You're fined $100 for getting put out of the game," replied Louie.

"I am, am I?" questioned Mike. "You little shrimp, I'll show you."

Mike immediately grabbed Louie with one hand, lifting him off the ground.

"Take the cover off the water bucket, Mac," Donlin told John McGraw. "I am going to drown this insect of a manager."

Louie Heilbroner wisely remitted the fine. He only lasted through the remainder of the 1900 season, running things from the Cardinals' bench.[42] John McGraw played just that one campaign for St. Louis, opting to jump to the American League, which offered new opportunities as a major organization after operating as a minor league in 1900. McGraw accepted terms as a player, manager, and owner for the new Baltimore Orioles' entry in 1901. Once the 1900 campaign ended, Mike Donlin traveled to California and played winter baseball in Santa Cruz. Fans in that city started a subscription plan, hoping to raise enough money to convince Mike to abandon the Cardinals and suit up in California next year. Donlin also made a trip to San Diego, California, so a physician could operate on his scarred face. The cosmetic surgery almost restored Donlin's countenance to its former beauty.[43]

McGraw initiated a hostile recruiting drive, courting National League players to join the Orioles at higher salaries than they currently received. When he returned to Baltimore on March 28, 1901, John possessed the signed contracts of Mike Donlin and Pittsburgh Pirates third baseman James "Jimmy" Williams to play for the Orioles. While talking to the press, McGraw snapped his fingers and laughed when someone suggested that Brooklyn Superbas manager Edward "Ned" Hanlon and other National Leaguers considered forcing any players McGraw had signed to return to their previous clubs through court action.

"Every man I have signed," said Mac, "will play on the Baltimore team, and they will report here next week. On April 5, the opening exhibition game will be played with Yale."[44]

Days earlier, Baltimore's manager had inked both men to contracts while they did preliminary training in Hot Springs, Arkansas. St. Louis owner Frank Robison expressed shock over Donlin's desertion, since he believed the outfielder had committed to playing for the Cardinals in 1901. Robison stated Mike arrived in Hot Springs on March 21 to utilize the benefits of the area's mineral springs baths, leading him to believe the player's presence there meant he planned to join the Cardinals once spring training started. Donlin had attempted to jump the club once before, claiming he signed a deal to play for the Southern California Winter League's team in San Jose, California. John McGraw's smooth-talking manner swayed Mike to abandon St. Louis and join the Orioles.[45]

In his bulletin regarding National League business, president Nicholas "Nick" Young classified Mike as property of the Cardinals' organization based on a contract he signed for the upcoming season. Outraged over the situation, St. Louis team treasurer Stanley Robison declared Donlin had agreed to a contract one month ago. Mike responded that he did not consider himself bound by this agreement because he did not know how baseball's conditions and climate might develop and progress.[46] Strangely, Donlin indeed agreed to an old contract months earlier and received advance money from the Cardinals' organization. Later, when sent a second contract approved by the Protective Association of Professional Baseball Players, Mike declined to sign this document. Frank Robison countered in writing to Donlin, "If you do not intend to play in St. Louis, return money advanced." When Mike complied with this demand, he felt it eliminated that obligation and freed him to sign with John McGraw. Donlin also declared he had always desired to play in Baltimore.[47]

Mike Donlin thrived playing for John McGraw and the Orioles in 1901, appearing in 121 games and batting .340. In a flash, before the 1902 campaign started, Donlin recklessly threw away all his progress.

At noon on March 12, 1902, Mike entered a Baltimore saloon on Howard Street and started consuming beer. He remained in the establishment until 11:30 P.M. At some point during this drinking spree, Donlin switched from beer to a beverage called absinthe, which the United States later banned for a while because of its perceived hallucinogenic nature. After an employee threw Mike out of the tavern, he staggered across the street to the Academy of Music.[48] A musical version of *Ben Hur* had just finished at the theater.[49] Before the company's performers exited the extravagant gothic cathedral structure, Donlin entered the hall and urinated on some artificial palm trees in the lobby.[50]

Different versions of what happened after Mike exited the theater found their way into print. According to an article in Chicago's *Inter Ocean* newspaper, Donlin struck Miss Minnie Fields of the *Ben Hur* company in the face two times as she walked across the street with a female companion.[51] The *Boston Daily Globe* stated Mike assaulted Miss Fields, an actress and chorus girl in the production. While walking with Margaret Kingston to the boardinghouse where they both lodged, Donlin struck Miss Fields with a vicious blow to her face, lacerating her cheek. As Minnie staggered, Miss Kingston screamed, and Mike punched Fields a second time, causing her to fall to the ground. At this point, a young man rushed to the scene who immediately recognized Donlin before the Orioles' team member quickly fled. Mike's friends claimed the ballplayer attacked the actress by mistake while taking a swing at another individual who dodged the maneuver.

Minnie, a resident of Washington, D.C., could not perform in the production the following evening due to shock from the ordeal.[52] An article in the *Washington Times* also confirmed Fields lived in that city. Their prose mentioned that Kingston, a fellow actress, happened to be her roommate at the Baltimore boardinghouse. This publication wrote that as the two women crossed the street toward their residence at 11:30 P.M., a man who had been lounging on the pavement walked up to them and struck Minnie with a forceful blow that cut her cheek. After Kingston screamed before the perpetrator hit Fields a second time, a man standing nearby, identified by the newspaper as Ernest B. Slayton, answered the distress call and ran over to the scene. He seized the individual, whom he recognized as Mike Donlin, and became involved in a scuffle before the ballplayer broke away and sprinted into a neighboring saloon.[53]

The establishment that Donlin entered in retreat happened to be the Diamond Café, owned by teammates John McGraw and Wilbert Robinson.[54] A police officer arrived where the assault occurred shortly after Mike fled and assisted the barely conscious Fields. Although extremely frightened, Kingston suffered no injuries. A crowd gathering at the scene initiated an unsuccessful search of the saloon. Witnesses stated Donlin had been periodically hanging around the Academy of Music's stage door entrance earlier in the evening. People connected to the company declared that neither actress counted Mike as an acquaintance. Fields, a small, delicate-looking girl of quiet manners, had been part of the *Ben Hur* production since it originated in New York City.

The publication also reported that contrary to an initial bulletin regarding Donlin fleeing to Philadelphia, Pennsylvania, people spotted him with friends in Washington on March 13. Efforts by newspaper journalists in that city to elicit any information from Mike about the assault proved fruitless. Donlin suggested that after visiting several of his old baseball friends, he planned to leave Washington around midnight.[55] Baltimore Police Justice Harry Goldman approved a sworn warrant for Mike's arrest relative to committing such a brutal and unprovoked attack. Coincidentally, Justice Goldman also worked as the Baltimore Orioles' team secretary.[56] Conflict of interest issues did not enter the equation. Wilbert Robinson stated Donlin had abstained from drinking for several weeks before he attended a ball a few nights prior that started him on an alcohol binge.[57]

On March 14, Orioles ownership, through manager John McGraw's order, expelled Mike Donlin from the team because of his reprehensible behavior.[58] Club officials declared that under no consideration would they allow Mike to rejoin the squad. They also referred the case to American League president Byron Bancroft "Ban" Johnson. Different individuals connected to baseball believed Johnson might permanently block him from playing in that organization.[59] Ban heartily concurred regarding the action taken by Baltimore's management and sympathized with the club owners. Johnson then gave a brief response when asked by a reporter if another American League team could pick up Donlin.

"I do not think any other American club will want him," replied Johnson.[60]

John McGraw initially wired from Hot Springs, recommending the Orioles indefinitely suspend Mike, acquiescing to the citizenry's demands.[61] Ban Johnson also sent a message to McGraw while still in the Arkansas town, informing the manager that he had banished Donlin from the American League. Upon returning to Baltimore on March 21, John testily said he did not know any details about the incident involving Mike Donlin and Minnie Fields, and expressed no interest in receiving that information.[62] Baltimore police's entire detective department remained on high alert searching for Donlin and requested assistance from law enforcement authorities in nearby cities to be on the watch for this fugitive.[63]

On Saturday evening, March 15, local police arrested Donlin in South Washington after the baseball player became involved in a disturbance on a streetcar where he reportedly acted as a peacemaker.[64] When press members questioned him about the assault on Minnie Fields, Mike alleged that he possessed no knowledge of anything he had done that evening and could not account for his arrival in Washington. Donlin then offered a vitriolic remark as he sneered at a reporter who inquired if the player wanted to make a statement.

"You people have already said enough about me," replied Donlin. "I have nothing to say to any of your kind. Be sure and mention the brilliant capture."[65]

Sergeant Thomas Hogan of the Baltimore Police Department escorted the prisoner back to that city.[66] Around midnight on March 16, the two men started their journey by train. Upon arriving, Sergeant Hogan took Mike to the Northwestern Police Station. Donlin was released after James Carey, a plumber, posted the $1,000 bail.[67] The detective returned to Washington on the morning of March 17 and attempted to visit Minnie Fields at her residence at 933 O Street Northwest to receive assurance that she would testify as a witness against Mike.[68] Fields's relative, Mrs. Pierce, informed Sergeant Hogan that the actress was in Baltimore, where a doctor attended to her injuries. The *Washington Times* printed news received from Boston, Massachusetts, regarding a proposition originating in Baltimore about a plea settlement in the case. Mart Lowe, a representative for the Klaw & Erlanger Theatrical Exchange, which produced and booked *Ben Hur*, wired that they planned to prosecute Donlin to the limit of the law.[69]

Michael Donlin appeared before Justice Harry Goldman for his arraignment on the afternoon of March 17. Minnie Fields attended, willing to share her version of the attack, if needed. Fields wore two veils. When the actress lifted the outer one, people in the courtroom clearly saw the visible injuries to her face. Donlin's counsel waived an examination of the cases regarding the assaults on Minnie and Ernest B. Slayton. Judge Goldman sent the matter to a grand jury and set a $1,000 bond for each assault charge. The court informed witnesses present for the arraignment that the grand jury might call them to issue statements and testify.[70]

On March 18, these witnesses appeared before the grand jury. After convening and hearing testimony, this body handed down two indictments against the ballplayer for alleged "night assault." The grand jury decided on these charges pursuant to a Baltimore statute related to assaults committed on the highways or at places of public resort or amusement between the hours of 6 P.M. and 6 A.M. when an individual committed that attack without provocation. If convicted under this law, it carried a penalty of not less than a $25 fine and one month's imprisonment for a person, or up to two years in a penitentiary. Washington's *Evening Star* reported that Mike's counsel would request an early trial date.[71]

Two interesting side stories resulted from Donlin's highly publicized attack on the actress and Slayton, and his subsequent arrest and trial. On March 19, the *Pittsburgh Press* printed an article proving Mike did not know the meaning of "loyalty" and "gratitude." Upon receiving a large salary boost before the 1900 season when playing for St. Louis, Donlin approached owner Frank Robison shortly after the campaign started and told him that his brother had gotten into serious trouble in Chicago, Illinois. This resulted in the sibling's court trial, a guilty verdict on the charge, and a prison sentence. Vouching for the youth's innocence, Mike declared he could prove this point if given a little time.

The Cardinals' owner hired a lawyer to reopen the case, and in the end, Donlin's brother gained his freedom. Although the fight for justice proved a long one, Robison, well acquainted with Illinois Governor John R. Tanner, succeeded in getting the convicted family member pardoned. Frank paid all the legal fees and for numerous trips to Chicago and Springfield, Illinois, to secure the young man's freedom. Despite this great expense, Robison never asked Mike for any money. Donlin cried when he thanked the owner for his help and generosity. Mike told Robison that throughout his time playing baseball, he would never consider doing business with another magnate, no matter how much money somebody offered for his services. The following spring, after borrowing $100 and receiving the cost of railroad transportation from the Cardinals' organization to travel to Hot Springs, Donlin acted the ungrateful turncoat when he signed to play for John McGraw's Baltimore Orioles. He never notified St. Louis's owner about his desertion, leading Frank to refute newspaper stories detailing this treachery.

"It's all a mistake," Robison said at the time. "I know Mike, and I know he will be here reporting day."

Of course, this turned out to be untrue, as Donlin never paid back the borrowed money or reimbursed the price for a train ticket.[72] A second intriguing story related to this case surrounded the incident's main victim. In an article appearing in their newspaper on March 15, 1902, the *Washington Times* identified Minnie Fields as a well-known resident of that city, since she had prominently figured in a suit pending before the Supreme Court of the District of Columbia for the past two years. Local attorney Thomas M. Fields filed proceedings against her, asking the court to restrain Wilhelmina A. E. von Olsen from claiming to be his wife. He also requested the cancellation of a marriage certificate purporting to represent their legal union.[73]

This litigation had been ongoing for some time as stories about Thomas M. Fields's pending case in Washington's Equity Court against Wilhelmina A. E. von Olsen, alias Minnie Roberts (Robert), appeared in that city's newspapers in 1898. The husband wished to have annulled a marriage certificate that Minnie exhibited as evidence of the nuptials. Thomas also asked the court that she desist promoting herself as Mrs. Fields.[74] In answering this charge, the defendant claimed she had been legally married to Thomas in Baltimore on October 5, 1887, by Reverend Henry S. Clogg. She also stated the complainant committed bigamy when he wed Theresa Agnes Burke on July 9, 1896. Minnie commented that her husband believed a fire at a storage warehouse in

Washington destroyed the couple's important paperwork, including a marriage license. Unknown to him, she possessed those documents.[75]

The fire Minnie Fields alluded to happened shortly before 2 A.M. on July 25, 1894, at the George W. Knox Express Company. Quick-moving flames reduced the four-story stables and warehouse to a pile of charred bricks and timber.[76] Three firefighters died, a dozen persons suffered injuries, and over two hundred horses burned to death in the stables while individuals whisked one hundred and fifty animals to safety. Initial estimates placed the cost of property damage at more than $250,000.[77] A further odd twist finalized the case of *Thomas M. Fields v. Wilhelmina A. E. von Olsen*. In April 1903, District of Columbia Supreme Court Justice Ashley Gould signed a decree prohibiting von Olsen from calling herself or proclaiming to be Fields's wife. Justice Gould also ruled the marriage certificate canceled and ordered her to surrender it to the court. The case had come before Justice Andrew C. Bradley in 1902, who decided in Mrs. Fields's favor. Justice Bradley died that spring before he could sign the document related to this ruling, thus requiring his colleague to hear the case.[78]

The *Washington Times* only connected Minnie Fields as the same person victimized by the brutal attack at the hands of Mike Donlin and a defendant in the suit filed by attorney Thomas M. Fields in a District of Columbia court that one time. No further mention meant the publication made a mistake or dropped it for another reason. Whatever the case, some newspapers started referring to the actress and chorus girl as Mamie Fields. On March 19, 1902, Donlin's trial started in criminal court, with Judge Albert Ritchie presiding. The grand jury had levied two indictments for night assault against Mike, who pleaded guilty to the second count of each, charging him with common assault. Several people testified, including character witnesses who offered glowing references for the baseball player.

Miss Fields and Ernest B. Slayton testified as the prosecution's only witnesses.[79] Slayton worked as a broker in Chicago.[80] He also resided at the same boardinghouse where Minnie lived.[81] Fields wore a gray suit and hat with a bon and muff of light-colored fur. The discoloration on Minnie's face became more evident when she lifted her dotted veil. Fields expressed no animosity toward Donlin as she testified, explaining the course of events that happened at 11:30 P.M. on March 12, 1902, across from the Academy of Music.

> I had been at the Academy Café, Franklin Street, with Miss Margaret Kingston. We left there about 11:25 o'clock and went across the street to the Academy of Music, as I wanted to use the long-distance telephone to Pittsburgh. We found the Academy closed and started to cross Howard

Street again to join Mr. Slayton and Miss Helen Bogart. We were all going to Gordon's for supper. Just as we came up to Mr. Slayton and Miss Bogart, somebody behind me said something, which I did not understand. I turned to Miss Kingston and asked what the man had said, but she did not know, either. Mr. Slayton said to the man, "Just pass on; you don't know these ladies." Thereupon Mr. Slayton was knocked down and then I was struck. Both my eyes were blackened, my teeth were loosened and my nose was bruised. I don't know who did it. I fainted and afterward went to my home in Washington.

While answering a question posed by State Attorney Robert M. McLane, who prosecuted the case, Minnie said her face became so swollen from the force of the blow administered by Mike that the *Ben Hur* company management did not recognize her. She then included a comment about the attacker.

"I don't know Donlin," she added. "He must have crossed the street behind me."

Judge Ritchie inquired about what Mike Donlin had said to the two actresses before committing his violent offense. Too reluctant and embarrassed to repeat the vile remarks, Fields whispered the comments to McLane, who then communicated them to the court. Minnie said that before Donlin spoke to Mr. Slayton, the ballplayer examined him from head to toe and said, "I recognize you." More abusive language followed. Miss Fields believed Ernest had searched out a police officer when Mike punched him.

Ernest B. Slayton's testimony corroborated what Minnie Fields said under oath. Besides sporting a discolored eye, Slayton complained about a cut on the back of his head he received while falling and hitting the pavement during the fracas with Donlin.

"I was standing on the side of the street opposite the Academy with Miss Bogart," Mr. Slayton said, "and I saw Miss Fields and Miss Kingston crossing. I noticed a man following them and he seemed to be in a hurry to catch up with them. I supposed at first he was connected with the *Ben Hur* company. I heard him using profane language, but I could not understand what he said. As he was about to take hold of Miss Fields, as I thought, I said to him, 'Please pass on; you don't know these ladies. Don't molest them.' I don't know what he said to Miss Fields."

Slayton then declared that he started talking to the two ladies, with his back to Mike, when he heard Donlin say, "I can size you up," before the ballplayer spewed more foul epithets. At this point, the situation escalated.

"Just as I was turning my head Donlin struck me and knocked me down," continued Slayton. "I was dazed, but I got up quickly and I heard Miss Kingston say, 'There he goes.' An officer then came up and Miss Kingston said Donlin had gone into a saloon and she would go there with the officer and pick him out among a hundred men. Donlin did not appear to be drunk."

Mike Donlin took the stand as the defense's first witness. Mike addressed the court by stating that he was twenty-three years old and unmarried, and that police had never arrested him before—a mistruth—before the defense counsel asked the player to relate what he recalled from that night.

"I remember nothing at all of it," said Donlin. "I was under the influence of liquor and lost my head. I don't remember going to Washington. When I read in the papers there what I had done I wanted to come back, but I was ashamed to do so. I registered in Washington under my right name. I had not drunk liquor for four weeks before that day. I started to drink about noon. I don't remember seeing the ladies. The accident would never have happened had I been in my right mind."

When cross-examined by Robert M. McLane, Donlin told him he had been at the Rathskeller saloon under the Academy of Music and did not remember how he ended up in Washington. Neighborhood bartenders Stewart McGinnity, Thomas Ratty, Michael Ratty, and others substantiated Mike's intoxication claim. These witnesses also declared Donlin had a reputation as a drunkard. Thomas Ratty testified that Donlin had requested a glass of water at the Rathskeller for irrigation purposes when urinating on the artificial palm trees in the Academy of Music's lobby near the Academy Café. Mike's attorneys, William F. Campbell and Robert W. Beach, begged for clemency and mercy from the court.

Campbell stated that while intoxication acted as no excuse for such a crime, the testimony showed no premeditation or deliberation existed. Beach said that had Donlin been sober, he would never have committed such a heinous act. In discussing the punishment their client had already received, the two lawyers cited that the Baltimore Orioles released him, meaning Mike could not collect his $2,800 salary for playing baseball in 1902. They also declared Donlin supported his younger brother and sister. Once the trial concluded, Judge Albert Ritchie sentenced the defendant, who had entered a guilty plea, to six months in jail and a $250 fine. Judge Ritchie addressed the court before announcing his decision.

"This young man," Judge Ritchie said, after hearing the testimony, "seems to have borne a very good reputation prior to this offense, but he has committed most aggravated assaults. It is probably true that he would not have done what he did if he had not been intoxicated. People on our streets, however, and women especially, must be protected against the acts of intoxicated persons as well as against the acts of those who are sober. Giving full consideration to the previous good character of the traverser and the fact that he committed the assaults while drunk and that he now regrets his actions, I will pass sentence commensurate with the offense."

After receiving his punishment, authorities took Mike Donlin to the sheriff's office, where he waited several hours until a van took him and other prisoners to a jail. The fine imposed by Judge Ritchie also carried a $10 court costs fee. If Donlin paid the fine within five months and exhibited good behavior while incarcerated, he could then gain early release.[82] Mike accepted the sentence with palpable indifference.[83] Baltimore's baseball organization also suffered a huge loss due to Mike's behavior, since it deprived them of a star player and the $500 the club advanced to him.[84] Friends in high places immediately started working to get Donlin released from prison. In April, Reverend J. D. Boland, a priest at St. Vincent de Paul Catholic Church and a stockholder in the Baltimore Orioles' club, started a petition to Maryland Governor John Walter Smith, pleading that the young man suffered sufficient punishment and should gain release before his sentence expired. Other well-known individuals from the city joined in requesting that Governor Smith pardon Mike.[85]

In early May, California League representatives took a different stance than these Baltimore gentlemen. Since the American League had disqualified Donlin and the Senior Circuit deemed him a deserter, the California League hierarchy declared Mike would be ineligible to play for any of that organization's clubs.[86] This decision ended up moot. On May 20, 1902, Donlin signed a contract in jail to play for the Cincinnati Reds once he gained his freedom.[87] Reds owner John T. Brush agreed to pay Mike a $3,000 salary.[88] Upon reaching this agreement, Donlin also consented to leading a temperance life in the future.

People connected to baseball spoke up in support of Mike after he inked this deal. On May 23, umpire Joseph "Joe" Cantillon, who had worked in the American League in 1901 and performed as a National League arbiter one year later, praised Donlin. After the previous two campaigns ended, Cantillon oversaw barnstorming excursions to the West Coast involving major league all-stars. Joe remarked that Mike participated in both tours and described him as one of the easiest men to handle on the team. Brooklyn Superbas manager Ned Hanlon also weighed in on some of Donlin's misfortunes.

"Mike is a great little ballplayer," declared Ned Hanlon, "and he has been as much sinned against as sinning."[89]

Efforts by Baltimore's influential citizens to expedite Mike's advance release from jail bogged down. Murkiness also existed over how former Orioles teammate Joe McGinnity's effort to raise the $250 to pay Donlin's fine had evolved. On June 24, according to the *Pittsburgh Press*, the whole situation wreaked havoc on Mike, both physically and mentally. He deeply felt the disgrace of his actions, knowing his siblings missed receiving necessary financial assistance. These factors preyed on his mind so much that the ballplayer became sick. Donlin, whose weight dropped to 125 pounds, underwent treatment in the prison's hospital for various ailments.[90] On August 20, 1902, Mike gained his release from jail after serving a five-month sentence for assaulting Minnie Fields.[91] Weeks before joining the outside world once again, Donlin vowed that, since alcohol had caused his many problems in life, especially whiskey, he planned to refrain from drinking in the future.[92]

Mike Donlin arrived in Cincinnati to join the Reds on August 25. Mike claimed he never felt better or stronger in his life. Donlin declared he would be ready to play regularly shortly and had engaged in four days of demanding work at Oriole Park in Baltimore to prepare for his return. When Mike called on the Burnet House, a Cincinnati hotel, he received a warm greeting from New York Giants and Philadelphia Phillies team members, who also wished him good luck.[93] Donlin appeared in his first game as a pinch hitter for the Reds on August 26 against the Giants and took his position as the club's starting left fielder the following afternoon. Mike appeared in 34 games for Cincinnati in 1902 and batted .287. Donlin sizzled at the plate the following year for the Reds, hitting .351 in 1903. Although Mike possessed a lusty .356 average in 1904, he ran afoul with Cincinnati management. His pledge to stop drinking alcohol turned out to be nothing more than a hollow promise.

On July 6, Reds manager Joseph "Joe" Kelley suspended Donlin because of drunkenness. Following the game against the St. Louis Cardinals on July 4 at League Park, Mike started a Fourth of July celebration that included alcohol and extended well into the next day. When Cincinnati prepared to leave the St. James Hotel and travel to the ballpark on July 5, Donlin remained missing. A sudden thunderstorm made the field unplayable, leading Cardinals club officials to postpone the contest. Later that day, Kelley saw Mike staggering along Broadway, exhibiting a wobbly gait. Donlin had not been in good graces with management for some time.[94] One of Mike's closest friends called on Kelley and told him the outfielder pledged he would never drink again. Other National League owners approached the organization's president, Harry Pulliam. They suggested that the Senior Circuit banish Donlin as the American League had done in 1902, prompting Reds owner August "Garry" Herrmann to offer a dissenting view.

"That is going too far," declared Herrmann. "They don't hang men for getting drunk."[95]

On August 7, 1904, Cincinnati traded Mike Donlin to the Giants for fellow outfielder Harry McCormick, who the Reds then shipped to the Pittsburgh Pirates for outer gardener James "Jimmy" Sebring.[96] Mike flourished under manager John McGraw and became the most popular baseball player in New York. Donlin batted .356 in 1905 and experienced a highly rewarding season in 1908, when he hit .334 and drove in 106 runs. Alcohol's demon still caused problems for Mike. On February 8, 1906, Donlin traveled by train throughout New York, from the Big Apple to Troy, with some teammates and other baseball players for a banquet and a series of indoor games. After the train left Poughkeepsie, these individuals became boisterous and rowdy. The train's conductor claimed that when he instructed them to cease such detrimental behavior, Mike struck him in the face.[97]

When the locomotive reached Albany, police arrested minor league players Walter Bennett and John J. McGrath for intoxication and disorderly conduct. They also detained Mike Donlin on the charge of assault with a deadly weapon. Mike had drawn a loaded pistol on a porter, who, in his statement to law enforcement, claimed this party of players started drinking when the train left Grand Central Station in New York City.[98]

On April 10, 1906, Donlin married actress and vaudeville performer Mabel Hite.[99] When a holdout in 1907 caused Mike to miss the entire baseball season, he remained with his wife on the vaudeville circuit by accepting a position working for the Whitney Theatrical Company that employed Hite.[100] After Donlin returned to the New York Giants in 1908, the spouses performed together in the one-act play *Stealing Home*, which opened at Hammerstein's Victoria Theatre in October. Sadly, this marriage ended due to tragic circumstances. On October 22, 1912, Mabel died in New York following a lengthy battle with cancer.[101]

Throughout Mike and Hite's marriage, the baseball player strived to exude more maturity and engage in grounded behavior, although poor habits related to alcohol occasionally reemerged. When New York owner John T. Brush only offered Donlin a $6,500 salary to play in 1909, while he wished to receive $8,000, Mike retired and performed vaudeville skits with his wife full-time until 1911.[102] On the night of September 11, 1909, Donlin became involved in a fight shortly after 11 P.M. with lawyer Edward N. Danforth on the sidewalk in front of New York's Knickerbocker Hotel, where the ballplayer and Mabel lived. New York's *The Sun* claimed that when Mike, his wife, and another woman exited a taxicab and prepared to enter the hotel, Danforth, while walking hurriedly with Edward C. Brannon, insulted and bumped into Hite.

The attorney denied making a disparaging comment and said he accidentally ran into her. Officer Hassenmuller arrested the two men and drove with all involved parties to the nearby police station in a taxicab. Subsequently, when police only booked Mike upon their arrival at the Tenderloin Police Station, Danforth offered to post Donlin's bail. At this point, theater mogul and real estate speculator Felix Isman arrived to pay the fee guaranteeing Mike's release. The lawyer then scolded the retired ballplayer for recklessly reaching an inaccurate conclusion.

"The trouble with you, Donlin," said Mr. Danforth, "is that because you are a great ballplayer you think you own the earth. You acted in a hasty manner and did not wait to see what the facts really were."

"Well, no man can insult my wife," replied Donlin.[103]

Mike Donlin arrived in his automobile at the Jefferson Market Court on September 12, accompanied by Mabel Hite and three friends. Mike and his entourage took their seats in the courtroom and waited an hour before Magistrate Moses Herrman commenced the proceeding. Silence prevailed when Judge Herrman called out Edward N. Danforth's name. Upon realizing Danforth was not present, the magistrate considered issuing a subpoena compelling him to come to court until Edward's lawyer, Leonard Snitkin, informed the jurist his client did not wish to press charges. Judge Herrman immediately dismissed Donlin's case. While returning to his automobile, Mike offered a statement to press members covering this hearing, detailing what had occurred on Saturday night at Long Acre Square.

"We were driving up to the Knickerbocker in this machine [not a taxicab as originally reported] when a fellow on the curb called out to my wife, 'Hello dearie,'" said Donlin. "As soon as the car stopped I ran back to him—the man proved to be Danforth—and said, 'What do you mean by insulting my wife?' He answered me with a blow on the nose and I hit him back."

Upon scrutinizing his face, reporters internally verified that Donlin had told the truth, since marks on his nose proved that allegation. Noticing these journalists examining his face for corroboration, Mike added one final comment.

"I guess the other fellow has some too," continued Mike. "It's a good thing for him that he did not come to court, for I should have made a counter charge against him."

Because Edward N. Danforth failed to appear in court, the true story behind who was at fault never entered the record.[104] While Danforth's point at the police station about his antagonist believing he owned the earth due to performing as a great baseball player appeared valid, another possibility existed. Through time, a chivalric Mike Donlin, defending Mabel Hite's honor, had finally evolved to where he now understood how civilized men treated a woman. However, the baseball player and actor needed to do more work when it came to coexisting with his fellow man. On this occasion, alcohol played no part in the dispute for a change.

*While playing for the National League's St. Louis baseball club, **Mike Donlin** became involved in different altercations on the diamond and in public. One of those incidents occurred in front of a St. Louis saloon on the morning of June 24, 1900, when a confrontation resulted in a young man cutting Mike's face and neck with a knife. Donlin jumped to the American League's Baltimore Orioles in 1901 and batted .340 for manager John McGraw's squad. On March 12, 1902, while in a drunken state, Mike assaulted actress Minnie Fields on a Baltimore street following the conclusion of a performance of* Ben Hur *at the Academy of Music. Police arrested Donlin after he fled to Washington, D.C. A trial led to his conviction on the charge and a five-month prison sentence. (Courtesy of the Library of Congress).*

CHAPTER 2

Win Mercer

The All-American Boy's Dark Side

In an era when most baseball players acquired the stigma as rowdy and incorrigible, or, even worse, undesirable from a social standpoint, a perception existed of the true gentleman as a pure anomaly, not attached to the game during the late nineteenth century and Deadball Era. Diamond rooters also viewed performers possessing an unruly and raucous personality as unshaven and rough around the edges regarding physical appearance. To the delight of baseball fans, especially female clientele, rare exceptions existed where an individual combined charming behavior, an athletic physique, and dashing good looks. Throughout that period of baseball history, handsome pitcher George Barclay Mercer surpassed all others, exuding a gentlemanly demeanor and captivating charisma on the diamond. Sadly, as is the case regarding mere mortals, flaws remained hidden from the public.

Born on June 20, 1874, in Chester, West Virginia, to Jacob and Margaret "Maggie" Wells Mercer, George moved numerous times during his childhood. The Mercers first relocated to Wheeling, West Virginia.[1] The young man and his family eventually settled in East Liverpool, Ohio, where he started exhibiting baseball prowess on sandlot fields, like West End Park.[2] Mercer signed his first professional contract in 1893 to play for the New England League's club in Dover, New Hampshire, after gaining a solid reputation as an accomplished pitcher in East Liverpool.[3] George posted a 20–13 record for Dover, supported by a 2.05 ERA. Following that campaign, Mercer hooked up with the organization's Fall River Indians.[4] While on a trip to Maine in the summer of 1893, hoping to secure baseball talent for the Washington Nationals, Gustavus "Gus" Schmelz, who managed that National League squad in 1894, scouted George.

According to Dover pilot Frank Leonard, Gus watched Mercer pitch against the club from Portland before offering him $900 over six months to play for Washington. Feeling such an amount was too low, the hurler declined to sign. After working in exhibition games for Fall River in 1894, skipper Mike McDermott offered George a $1,000 salary for five months. Inclined to accept this deal, Mercer contacted Schmelz and signed with the Nationals when Gus tendered a proffer of between $1,200 and $1,500 a year.[5]

George did not experience immediate major league success. The nineteen-year-old hurler lost his first nine decisions pitching for Washington in 1894, tossing six complete games during this baptism under fire. Mercer did not garner his first big-league victory until he defeated the Louisville Colonels, 12–2, on May 29 on the Boundary Field home grounds.[6] George ended up going 17–23, supported by a 3.85 ERA in his rookie campaign, as the Nationals finished eleventh in the twelve-team National League with a 45–87 record. Mercer also exhibited great aptitude as a batter, hitting .291 in 1894.

Viewed by many, especially female rooters, as an Adonis on the baseball diamond and a regular fashion plate away from the ballpark, George Mercer had acquired a nickname years prior that endured throughout his career.[7] George earned the monikers "Win" and "Winnie" early in his baseball profession. Years after his major league debut, a scribe for the *Pittsburgh Commercial Gazette* wrote in 1901 that the sobriquet came about due to fans yelling during a hotly contested, critical game, "Win, Mercer! Win, Mercer!" W. A. Calhoun, former Ohio Valley League president and an individual privy to baseball affairs in that state, wasted no time refuting this false assertion regarding Mercer's moniker. He fired back at this Pittsburgh newspaper writer,

> Allow me to give the baseball public a correct version of Pitcher Mercer's sobriquet "Win" in place of the wonderful "pipe" or "jag" given out by your correspondent in your Saturday edition. The writer knows the baseball history of Mercer perfectly, having seen him play probably every game he ever played in with local teams, and it was afterward my good fortune to pick "Win" out as a "comer," and by the aid of Manager Frank Leonard, now of Syracuse, to introduce him to professional baseball in the [New England] New York League.
>
> Mercer's full name is [George] William Barclay Mercer, and his sobriquet of "Win" came about through an odd series of changes. Mercer came to East Liverpool from a West Virginia farm, and at that time was, as a boy, very much of a "yap." He found employment in the potteries here and was in the line of an old custom here to have a nickname and was christened "Virginia," which in time became "Virgin," and this was later

cut to "Gin," which in time became "Win," the writer, with several others, being responsible for the last change, which was soon extended to "Winnie." This was soon turned into "Winifred" by eastern baseball writers, and as Winifred B. Mercer, East Liverpool's star twirler has achieved a worldwide fame. To address this king of the diamond properly, write his name plain William Barclay Mercer, and you will make no mistake.[8]

Washington Post sportswriter Joe Campbell constantly reinforced the "Winnie" nickname of the curly-haired twirler in his articles.[9] Besides portraying a matinee idol on the bump, Win also successfully played other positions as his career in Washington evolved. Known as an astute student of the game who combined handsome features, superb natural ability, and a keen intellect, Mercer developed a devastating pitch while playing for the Nationals. He perfected a "slowball" that baffled opposing batters. A precursor to the changeup we know today, Win maintained that he learned to throw a baseball this way with the same arm movement as his fastball, which kept batters guessing at the plate.

"The ball when delivered as a 'slowball' does not revolve and to the batter appears as big as a balloon," Mercer once described the pitch to a Washington sportswriter. "Accordingly the man at the plate strikes at it with a mighty effort and he succeeds in only making a popup which can be easily handled from the infield, if he hits it at all."[10]

Win Mercer experienced a tougher season in 1895, going 13–23, buttressed by a 4.42 ERA. Washington improved slightly in the standings, finishing in tenth place with a 43–85 record. Mercer achieved superstar status in 1896 when he anchored the Nationals' staff by posting a mark of 25–18, with a 4.13 ERA. The fact that Washington only secured 58 victories made his performance even more remarkable. When arriving at Washington's Boundary Field for preliminary training on March 31, Win showed no ill effects after suffering from smallpox in the off-season.[11] Stricken with varioloid months earlier in late November, some reports claimed Mercer appeared close to death at his East Liverpool home. These rumors proved untrue, as health officials established a stringent quarantine in mid-December.[12]

On December 19, 1895, Dr. Charles O. Probst of the Ohio State Board of Health visited the quarantined Mercer residence in the company of Dr. Charles B. Ogden. After examining Win, Dr. Probst stated the pitcher was recovering nicely and that the disease's scabs had started to fall off his body. The health official also confirmed that one of Mercer's younger brothers took ill, suffering from varioloid.[13] When Win reported for duty at the home ballpark in March, no scars resulted from this winter ordeal. His face appeared as smooth as ivory, containing a hue comparable to the marble cast of Apollo Belvedere.

Mercer still possessed that shock of coal-black, crimpy hair that earned him the admiration of ladies who attended games. He remained the same good-looking young fellow that counted every man, woman, and child in Washington among his friends. Upon his arrival, the strong, sturdy, healthy youngster made a bold prediction that became true in 1896.

"Just watch me this season," said Mercer.[14]

That spring, the attractive youngster obtained an honor befitting a diamond icon. Besides providing the usual attraction for female fans at Boundary Field when he pitched against the Cincinnati Reds on May 26 in a losing effort, 18–5, the band performing at the contest played the "Win Mercer Caprice" as one of its numbers throughout the afternoon. Composer N. Dunning had recently written and dedicated the song to Washington's baseball club.[15] At some point during Mercer's sensational breakout season, Cleveland Spiders manager Patsy Tebeau sneeringly referred to the Nationals' crack hurler as an incredibly lucky individual. Tebeau also considered Win's 1896 performance a fluke. Sportswriter Joe Campbell refuted this claim, offering evidence proving Mercer rightfully obtained his status as a true student of the game whose solid pitching resulted from careful study and observation.

After the season ended, Phil Wagner, superintendent at Boundary Field and brother of Washington owners George and Jacob Earl Wagner, shared a story with Campbell. In early November, while inside the ballpark's home dressing room, Phil came across a memorandum book that offered insight into Win Mercer's knowledge regarding National League batters. The information inside this book proved teammate Eugene "Gene" DeMontreville's claim that Win happened to be a student of the game. This booklet's structure resembled the shape of a railroad advertisement, with pages for notes. On the inside cover, Win had inscribed, "If I'm lost return me to Win Mercer, East Liverpool, O., or Washington, D.C., care National Baseball Club."

In a concise, clerical hand, Mercer wrote the names of prominent National League diamond performers under headings penned in red ink, reading "Player" and "Remarks." The word "Player" appeared on the left side at the top of the page, with "Remarks" on the right side of the ledger. This list contained the names of 150 major league ballplayers. People unfamiliar with baseball lingo would have been confused over Win's blunt, brief comments about his colleagues that included slang phrases known only to those within the diamond profession. Phil Wagner explained this dope book during an interview with the *Washington Post* correspondent.

> But it don't puzzle me, for I had seen that book before. Mercer used it during the season of 1895. It is a tab he kept on the players in the

other league clubs. This interesting tab of Mercer's tells the peculiarities of the batsmen and the names of the heavy hitters, such as Delahanty, Burkett, Jennings, and Keeler. Opposite the name of the Phillies' slugging left fielder [Edward "Ed" Delahanty] is the significant note: "Can hit anything; mix 'em up on him and take a chance." Jesse Burkett follows Delahanty, and these remarks are tabbed at the right of Jesse's name: "Hits high and low ones; ain't stuck on speed. A slow curve sometimes fools him."

Here are a few selections from Winnie's roster of batsmen: "[Adrian 'Cap'] Anson—He'll kill a high ball; get 'em around his knees and over; don't waste any time in passing them up to Anson; slow in meeting a hurried delivery. [Hugh 'Hughie'] Jennings—Has no preference; likes speed; mix 'em up on him. [William 'Bill'] Lange—Death to a low, speedy ball; keep it around his neck; can't hit a high slow curve, but can cop speed; a good waiter. [Dennis 'Dan'] Brouthers—Likes 'em waist high and likes speed. [William 'Bill'] Everitt—Can hit 'em at any altitude, but prefers low ones with speed in 'em. [Jacob 'Jake'] Stenzel—Mix 'em on him and he'll get twisted. [John 'Jack'] Doyle—Will hit anything, and a good waiter. [Louis 'Lou'] Bierbauer—Peculiar; likes 'em low and over the outside corner; keep a slow curve opposite his neck. [Michael 'Mike'] Tiernan—Very yellow on a high curve if used in mixing 'em up; a good waiter." A careful inspection of Mercer's dope will admit of but one inference, which is that Delahanty is the best natural batsman in the league.[16]

Shortly after the 1897 baseball campaign started, Win Mercer offered insight on one of the players in his dope book that Phil Wagner hadn't shared. In an interview, Win bestowed the utmost esteem upon star Baltimore Orioles outfielder William "Willie" Keeler as a player and a person.

"The most scientific batsman I ever pitched to is Willie Keeler," said Win Mercer. "At least 90 percent of the batsmen have their weaknesses, but Keeler is flawless. He can smash a slow curve and he can bat out speed. Nothing is impossible to him—curves, speed, height, or anything else—and with all his great talent as a fielder and batsmen, he's a modest, unassuming little gentleman."[17]

Acting as one of Washington's workhorses along with pitcher James "Doc" McJames, Mercer fashioned another grand season for the Nationals in 1897, posting a 21–20 record, supported by a 3.18 ERA. Win also continued functioning as an asset on the home grounds and at opponents' ballparks when clubs held Ladies' Day. After winning two contests in a three-game set against the Pittsburgh Pirates at Exposition Park, Mercer pulled down critical duty when Washington opened a series against Cincinnati on July 15. Since it was

Ladies' Day at League Park, Reds officials assigned Win to work one of the gates so women could gaze at the "Apollo of the Potomac" as they entered the facility.[18] Although fans viewed Mercer as a scholar and a gentleman, the twirler sometimes displayed a confrontational attitude toward authority while sticking up for and believing in righteous diamond justice.

On September 13, Win took the bump as the Nationals opposed the Reds at Boundary Field. Mercer did not remain in the game awfully long, due to his intolerable language toward umpire William "Bill" Carpenter over what the hurler perceived as unfair calls on some pitches.[19] Since Win felt the umpire became insufferable due to calling a couple of good pitches balls, an inevitable confrontation occurred when the hurler finally lost his temper.[20] In the third inning, Mercer engaged Carpenter to question one specific poor decision by the arbiter.[21] As the little umpire passed Win to take his position behind the mound, Washington's pitcher pulled a pair of blue glasses out of his pocket and offered them to Bill, who ignored this action. When Mercer opened the eyewear and attempted to place it on Carpenter's face, the umpire realized he needed to defend his dignity by ordering the matinee idol out of the game and to the bench.[22]

The Nationals' manager, team captain, and outfielder, Thomas "Tom" Brown, attempted to pacify the arbiter as Winnie mocked leaving the contest. Carpenter rejected Brown's plea, and the manager summoned Doc McJames to take Mercer's place on the mound. Cincinnati won the game, 2–1, when McJames forced home a run in the seventh inning by walking four consecutive batters. A crucial decision by Bill in this frame did not endear him to Boundary Field's fans. When Reds catcher William "Pop" Schriver stepped up to the plate, Washington's manager and pitcher decided to intentionally walk him. Understanding this strategy, Pop stepped out of the box and swung at an offering. Nationals catcher James "Deacon" McGuire called this breach of the rules to Carpenter's attention, but the umpire ignored his complaint. When Schriver left the box again but did not attempt a swing at the next pitch, Bill called him out. Following a brief argument between Carpenter and Pop, the umpire reiterated his decision.

Manager William "Buck" Ewing and other Cincinnati team members calmly engaged Bill and explained why he ruled incorrectly. After considering the matter, Carpenter reversed his decision, which impacted the game's outcome.[23] Bill ended the contest after eight innings on account of darkness.[24] As Carpenter walked off the field at the game's conclusion, a faction of patrons accosted the arbiter over his inferior performance that afternoon. Already unhappy over the umpire banishing their heartthrob from the contest, many female patrons could not contain their disgust over his deplorable seventh-inning reversal. An article in Washington's *The Times* chronicled what happened when the umpire attempted to exit the premises.

> The male portion of the spectators might have felt like mobbing Carpenter, but they refrained from becoming violent.
>
> Not so, however, with woman. Crowding around the place where the umpire comes into the grandstand, they awaited him with drawn parasols and upraised fans. Just what the language was like would be rather hard to translate, but no sooner had Carpenter started for the office than he was assailed with whatever the women had in their hands. One used her fist, and was not slow in telling her companions that she came near hitting him on the solar plexus.
>
> The umpire was too manly to turn upon the women, and made rapid strides for the office.[25]

One month before the 1898 campaign started, the *Evening Star* speculated that manager Tom Brown would select Win Mercer to start the opening game against the Baltimore Orioles; health permitting and his arm's condition being sound. The newspaper also reasoned that to alter his pitching style and leave Orioles batters guessing, Win might abandon the slowball and utilize an arsenal of speedy benders. The *Evening Star* admitted Mercer had improved upon that slowball and happened to be as good in the spring as at any other time of the year, where opposing hitters found him almost invincible during the season's first month. Nationals owner Earl Wagner appreciated the fact that Win always proved a willing worker, assisting the club whenever needed.

"That boy is a credit to the game as well as to himself," said Earl Wagner. "I have always paid him the limit and a bonus besides. No matter how many games he has pitched, be it three or four a week, I have yet to ask him to go into the box that he has refused, but instead has replied with a cheerful smile that he was willing to go in, and would do his best. He has never given me any trouble whatever; is a thorough gentleman, and I consider him the star twirler of the National League."[26]

Even the spirit of the National League's conscientious star twirler, as his boss categorized him, could break because of inferior performance. The Washington Nationals performed miserably in 1898, finishing in eleventh place with a 51–101 record. Washington went through four managers, as Tom Brown, Jack Doyle, Deacon McGuire, and Arthur Irwin all took turns running the squad. Win's work also suffered, as he fashioned a 12–18 record, while his ERA ballooned to 4.81. On September 10, an article in the *Evening News Review* newspaper, from his hometown of East Liverpool, suggested this could be

Mercer's final season with the Nationals. Many of his friends viewed this favorably since Winnie might end up with a better club that supplied solid support when he pitched. This article also included some comments from Washington's *Sporting Life* correspondent.

This writer contended Win had made some rash statements to a Cincinnati baseball scribe about working on a championship team. The *Sporting Life* writer mused that his ambition could become true by moving to another organization after the season closed, while also mentioning the hurler would not garner such a big salary with a different team. Amid murmurings that Mercer's better days had passed, Washington's pitcher declared he could still perform at an elevated level. A Pittsburgh publication reported that Win's services still remained in great demand. The Nationals' organization had rejected a deal from the Boston Beaneaters, who won the National League pennant in 1898, involving fellow pitcher Frederick "Fred" Klobedanz. Washington preferred selling Mercer outright to Boston for $3,000.[27]

Winnie remained with Washington in 1899 and went 7–14, supported by a 4.60 ERA, as the club executed another dismal season by once again finishing in eleventh place. Their 54–98 record left them 49 games behind the pennant-winning Brooklyn Superbas. After the campaign ended, speculation raged concerning the National League eliminating four teams. The Nationals happened to be one of those clubs receiving consideration. Although uncertainty prevailed throughout the early months of 1900, Washington management sent out notices to its players, telling them to report to that city on March 19 so they could travel to a spring training location in the South not yet selected. The organization also understood Mercer might report several days early. Following Earl Wagner's visit to Pittsburgh, Pirates owner and former Louisville Colonels magnate Barney Dreyfuss commented on March 1, 1900, regarding why he believed the National League would consist of eight teams for the upcoming season.

> Earl Wagner was here Wednesday. He said that there was sure to be ten clubs. For years I have made it a point to play any card that Wagner is on as a loser. I still think that is a good idea. I have coppered his declaration. Watch if I do not come out O. K.
>
> Did you notice that Wagner said that while he had signed Mercer to a contract last fall, he now declares that he signed him to another contract yesterday? What would be the use of signing Mercer again if he was going to play with the Washington club in the league the coming season? Did you notice that Mr. Wagner went out and signed [Washington star outfielder John "Buck"] Freeman and others for the Boston club? Eight clubs is my pick. Baltimore will be glad to get out when the time comes.[28]

Dreyfuss possessed clear foresight into the National League's destiny. On March 8, a committee established months earlier at the National League meetings to examine contracting from twelve clubs to eight, recommended eliminating Washington, Louisville, Baltimore, and Cleveland from the organization. The following day, the league's owners unanimously agreed to this proposal. Each of the discarded clubs received various amounts of monetary compensation. The Nationals requested a stipend of $46,500 as payment but received $39,000, as the organization shaved off $7,500 because the Wagners had sold three players to Boston. This settlement also called for placing Washington's remaining players in a league pool for selection by other clubs.[29]

With respect to two former star Nationals players, the committee placed a $2,500 price tag on first baseman Dennis "Dan" McGann and stipulated that no club could purchase Win Mercer for less than $2,000.[30] Owner Andrew Freedman brought Win aboard to play for his New York Giants in 1900. Viewed as a "live one" and the "distinguished hurler," fans and writers felt the Giants made an astute move because Mercer possessed great fielding ability, did stellar stickwork, and joined the conversation as one of the league's swiftest base runners.[31] The hurler signed a three-year deal paying him $3,500 per season.[32] With Washington in 1899, Win also played third base besides pitching and batted .299 in 417 trips to the plate. In 1898, Mercer had wielded the cudgel for a mark of .321. For New York, the versatile performer appeared in 33 games on the mound in 1900 and contributed in 48 contests playing four other positions. Win went 13–17, backed by a 3.86 ERA on the bump, and batted .294 that campaign.

Mercer only lasted one season playing for the Giants. Freedman tended to be obdurate, alienating his players and managers. A single season of dealing with Andrew's autocratic methods proved enough for Win, who once told New York's magnate exactly what he thought of him regarding how Freedman oversaw the organization. Other options became available for Mercer because Ban Johnson's American League planned to elevate that organization to major status as direct competition to the National League in 1901. Since Johnson placed a team in Washington, it seemed Win could be the perfect fit in the city where he had garnered so much fame if he decided to jump leagues.[33] This grand reunion occurred when manager James "Jimmy" Manning revealed on March 23 that he signed Mercer to pitch for the Senators. Many of Washington's rooters expected this announcement to bring joy and excitement to their brethren who had watched Win for so many years.

Every citizen in the city who loved baseball embraced the return of a dependable and solid pitcher, a decided favorite of female fans who always clamored to watch their beloved on Ladies' Day and happened to be the most popular player ever to don a Washington uniform. Manning finally closed the deal after several days of negotiations with Mercer.[34] Weeks after the season started, newspapers reported the Senators' organization had agreed to pay Win $3,600 to play for them in 1901.[35] Mercer's return to the town where he previously experienced his greatest glories did not end up as a triumphant homecoming. Illness hampered Win throughout the campaign and hindered his ability on the mound. Although Mercer desperately wanted to help the squad, Washington's club directors sent the fan favorite home to East Liverpool numerous times throughout the season to regain his health.[36]

Win Mercer appeared in 24 games on the mound for the Senators, posting a 9–13 record, supported by a 4.56 ERA. Within a utility capacity, the versatile Win also saw time at every position in the field, other than second base and catcher, and batted .300. At one point in the campaign, Jimmy Manning had to clarify that the club did not hand Mercer his outright release after the pitcher alleged this to be the case upon the organization sending him home for a rest.

"Mercer became disheartened over his showing," said Manning, "and gave out the report that he had been released. I have persuaded him to go home for a week or two and get a good rest, and when in condition rejoin the team. I still believe Mercer a first-class ballplayer and a great pitcher when in condition, but handicapped as he was with an injured limb, it was simply impossible for him to do good work."[37]

Illness and an arm injury proved too great an obstacle for keeping the once-happy relationship between Win and Washington baseball thriving. When the season ended, Mercer joined a barnstorming squad of American Leaguers that played games as they traveled across the country to California. For this team, called the All-Americans and organized by American League umpire Joe Cantillon, Win primarily pitched and played second base. When the entourage reached St. Louis, Mercer traveled to Chicago and conducted an all-day conference on November 7 with league president Ban Johnson and White Sox owner Charles Comiskey about playing for that club if the Senators granted his release. Afterward, Win admitted Comiskey made him a tempting offer regarding suiting up for the White Sox.[38] Because of his bad luck the previous season and a disagreement with Manning, Win drew that coveted release from his old club, making him a free agent.[39]

Still unsigned in early December, St. Louis Browns owner Matthew "Matt" Killilea offered his potential intentions surrounding Mercer while talking with a journalist from the *St. Louis Globe-Democrat*.

"If no one has signed Win Mercer," said Mr. Killilea, "a good thing has been overlooked. I consider him a good pitcher and one of the best all-round men that ever walked on a ball field, and if he is still unattached I am willing to offer him a berth with the St. Louis club."⁴⁰

Win and his barnstorming teammates experienced a harrowing moment on December 19 when the train that carried them to their next destination in California wrecked. Although Mercer and the other All-American players escaped unscathed, three railroad crew members died in the accident.⁴¹ While the club played in California, rumors abounded that James Calvin "Cal" Ewing, owner of the California League's Oakland Clamdiggers, offered Win a berth to manage and act as team captain for his squad in 1902. Hometown friends believed Mercer appeared ready to accept the post, since he wired family in East Liverpool to have his clothing shipped to Oakland. Letters that Win wrote to buddies in the east indicating his interest in playing for Ewing, who gave a one-month deadline for deciding, appeared genuine. In a game in Los Angeles, Win made one of the most remarkable catches ever witnessed in Southern California while playing right field. Mercer enjoyed California and the state's baseball fans loved him.⁴²

Ultimately, Win again cast his lot with the American League in 1902. While playing out West, Mercer agreed to terms to join Detroit after conducting negotiations with new Tigers manager John Francis "Frank" Dwyer. On a visit to Chicago, Dwyer received positive scouting reports from Joe Cantillon and Tigers outfielder James "Jimmy" Barrett, who declared that Win pitched as well as he had done any time over the past few years while playing with the All-Americans. On Sunday, January 26, White Sox skipper Clark Griffith informed Frank he intended to capture Mercer for his squad the following day once the ballplayer returned from California. That night, an anxious Dwyer did not go to bed. Instead, he remained awake, went to the railroad station, and waited for the train bringing Winnie to Detroit. Once the diesel locomotive arrived, Frank commandeered Mercer and presented him with a contract. Win signed the document to play for Detroit after 2 A.M. on Monday.⁴³

Before the season started, Mercer's former Giants teammate, catcher Frank Bowerman, visited Detroit on March 2. While talking with other players at the Griswold Hotel, Bowerman praised the Tigers' new pitcher. Frank dismissed a suggestion regarding Win's baseball ability declining. Bowerman added that he expected Mercer to perform as one of the best pitchers on Detroit's staff. Frank then bestowed massive credit to Winnie for his instrumental tutelage, teaching Christopher "Christy" Mathewson how to become a better hurler with New York in 1900. Although Mathewson did little while making six appearances after joining the club that summer, Bowerman contended Mercer's guidance and helpful suggestions transformed Christy into a capable player at the professional level.⁴⁴ The result of Win's one-on-one instruction led to a breakthrough campaign for Mathewson in 1901, when he posted a 20–17 record, backed by a 2.41 ERA.

Mercer rebounded solidly in 1902, fashioning a 15–18 record, with a 3.04 ERA. Once again, Win played for a second-division team, as Detroit came home seventh in the American League race by going 52–83. On August 29, Mercer commented that owner Barney Dreyfuss would lose two-thirds of his Pittsburgh Pirates club due to American League defections in 1903 following a raid by high-ranking league officials the previous week. The hurler continued that his prediction would receive validation at an organizational meeting in October, with the announcement about these individuals playing for a new American League team in New York.[45] Win ended up a bit ambitious in his forecast, as five Pirates joined New York: pitchers John "Jack" Chesbro and Jesse Tannehill; catcher Jack O'Connor; outfielder Alfonzo "Lefty" Davis; and infielder William "Wid" Conroy.

When the 1902 campaign ended, Mercer received the honor of managing an aggregation of star American League players called the All-Americans in a postseason series against Pittsburgh, who claimed their second consecutive National League pennant.[46] As Win concentrated on running this all-star club, newspapers stated that when Tigers owner and team president Samuel F. Angus announced his squad's roster for the upcoming season, it would include the title of manager next to Mercer's name. Frank Dwyer, who piloted the team in 1902, expected to remain through the fall and winter to handle outstanding matters that needed attention. Press members suspected for two months that if Dwyer no longer held the position, Win was Angus's logical first choice to succeed him. Although not ready to make an official announcement regarding the appointment, Samuel hoped to finalize everything shortly after Christmas when Mercer returned to Detroit. Win also signed an agreement to coach the University of Michigan's baseball team before the upcoming major league season started.[47]

During an interview while in Pittsburgh with the All-American baseball team, Win Mercer adamantly denied stories about him agreeing to manage the Detroit Tigers in 1903.[48] While in the Smoky City, Ban Johnson also commissioned Mercer to oversee some critical league business. On the morning of October 7, 1902, a young Pittsburgh capitalist secured an option on five acres of land, located thirteen minutes from the downtown courthouse and accessible to seven streetcar lines. One hour after making the purchase, this individual wired Johnson, proposing utilizing the property for a possible American League franchise ballpark. The league president instructed Win to examine the grounds. After looking over the land the following Wednesday morning, Mercer wanted to leave a check with the businessman. The real estate entrepreneur refused, requiring Johnson to come to Pittsburgh and personally close the deal. Win wired the league boss and urged him to complete the transaction since it offered the chance of a lifetime to compete head-to-head with the Pirates in that city.[49]

That opportunity never occurred as Ban Johnson did not place an American League franchise in Pittsburgh. Due to the success of their barnstorming tour one year earlier, after the All-Americans participated in the postseason series against the Pirates, they started another cross-country journey playing baseball. A squad of All-Nationals joined the excursion, with Mercer serving as treasurer of this aggregation referred to as the "Tourists."[50] Since he debuted with Washington in 1894, the public adored Win and placed him on a pedestal as their favorite. However, unbeknown to many rooters, the pitcher participated in an addictive activity away from the diamond. Mercer gained a reputation among other baseball players as the "highest roller" within the gambling realm. His pursuit into this world proved a glaring weakness rather than a vice. Win found himself unable to resist participating in anything containing an element of chance, which greatly appealed to the hurler.

Mercer could not watch people playing poker or a game of craps without betting on the turn of a card or a toss of the dice. Winnie did not gamble for monetary gain but rather for the love of a game of chance.[51] Players and sportswriters categorized Mercer as baseball's biggest gambler. Besides participating in shooting dice, Win habitually bet on the ponies. At times, Mercer wagered $500 on a horserace or craps while exhibiting no more emotion than he did when calmly facing a batter with two men on base and no outs. He always exhibited unflappable nerve while gambling.[52] During his travels with the Tourists, Win won $500 participating in a craps game in Indianapolis, Indiana.[53] While shooting dice in Louisville, Kentucky, he cleaned out all other participants and ruled as the big winner in a game in Toledo, Ohio.[54]

A bizarre incident with an indirect connection to Mercer's gambling habit occurred while the Tourists stayed in Sacramento, California. On November 30, unknown nefarious individuals attempted to defraud Win and his teammates out of the money they had earned on this successful barnstorming trip.[55] Bad actors, obviously aware of Mercer's proclivity for betting at the racetrack, attempted to swindle the Tourists' treasurer out of $5,000.[56] Shortly after most members of the two squads left the Golden Eagle Hotel for Oak Park, where they played a game that afternoon, clerk Louis "Lew" Wilcox encountered a young boy wearing a messenger's cap who rushed into the hostelry. The youngster approached Wilcox and handed him a note addressed to J. W. Wilson, the Golden Eagle Hotel's proprietor, which read:

"Mr. J. W. Wilson—Send me the envelope I have in the safe. One of your 'good fellows' is making quite a money talk out here, and I'll either make him put up or shut up. Wrap it in a piece of newspaper and tell the young man to hurry back.—WIN MERCER."

The clerk, familiar with Win Mercer's signature, believed this request appeared legitimate.[57] Wilcox handed over the fattest of the two envelopes in the hotel's safe.[58] This huge error turned out to be a blessing. Unknowingly, Wilcox gave the young boy a package containing the Tourists' railroad tickets for future travel.[59] Fifteen minutes later, a second messenger appeared carrying the envelope.[60] He returned the wrong package containing railroad tickets before handing the hotel employee the following message:

"Mr. Wilson—Can't call a bet with railroad tickets. This fellow means business and has his money up. [Cleveland Broncos hurler Adrian 'Addie'] Joss says to send his sack out. Rush the kid back before the game is over. Wrap it up well.—MERCER."[61]

At this point, Lew Wilcox became suspicious, so he asked former Pittsburgh Pirates pitcher Jack Chesbro, who happened to be sitting in the hotel office, to take the money out to the ballpark.[62] Chesbro agreed to the clerk's request, transported the money to Oak Park, and found Mercer and Addie Joss had not requested the cash be delivered to them. Win's envelope contained $5,000 and Joss's $600.[63] The hotel notified police, who examined the forgeries and started an investigation.[64] Weeks after Mr. Wilcox thwarted this swindle, which could have caused devastating repercussions for the two barnstorming baseball clubs, newspapers reported on Mercer's desire to wear a Cincinnati Reds uniform in 1903 while playing for manager Joe Kelley. Months earlier, while Win and Frank Dwyer conducted a recruitment trip in Cincinnati for their team, Kelley offered the pitcher a liberal amount of money to sign with his squad. Mercer listened and confessed that no contractual obligation bound him to Detroit next year. Winnie then failed to attend a scheduled appointment with Joe before leaving the city.

On December 26, Cincinnati owner and team president Garry Herrmann received a telegram at his office from Norris "Tip" O'Neill, one of the directors for the California tour involving Win Mercer. The message, a belated Christmas wish from a baseball standpoint, read, "You can sign Mercer. Wire him Langham Hotel, San Francisco." That afternoon, Herrmann wired the following response to O'Neill in San Francisco, "Pending negotiations, the Cincinnati club has agreed to make no further efforts toward securing additional players."[65] Garry did not plan to approach or procure any players from the American League due to ongoing peace negotiations between that organization and the National League. Herrmann intended to diligently adhere to a truce agreed upon by both leagues.[66] A settlement meant no more players jumping between leagues, looking to improve their monetary climate. The previous June, Win had requested his release after receiving a lucrative offer to captain and manage the California League's Los Angeles club.[67] In the end, he remained with the Tigers.

Detroit Tigers ownership received a reassuring message from Mercer in California. In ten eloquent words leaving no doubt as to his intentions in 1903, Win wired, "O'Neill nor I know nothing about wire sent to Herrmann." While attending the peace conference in Cincinnati, where both leagues hammered out an agreement to coexist as equal institutions, Samuel Angus stated that although still unofficial, Win would function as player and manager for Detroit in 1903. In this press statement, Angus declared Mercer had already started planning for spring training and possessed full authority to select a location to hold that session.[68]

In the end, the baseball players' westward excursion was jinxed with injuries. After the group arrived in Los Angeles, catcher Michael "Mike" Kahoe of the All-Nationals fell down a pair of stairs. Hurt so badly by this mishap, Kahoe could not play for two weeks. When the squads reached Sacramento, Willie Keeler became another casualty when he fell out of a buggy during an accident. Joe Cantillon, manager of the All-American club, also endured an injury because of this unfortunate incident. The *San Francisco Call* reported that Keeler's problem at first appeared minor. When the pain intensified, he consulted a physician, who, after an extensive examination, diagnosed a broken bone in his back. The doctor advised Willie to return home to Brooklyn, New York, and rest over fear that he might not appear again on a baseball diamond.[69]

The *Sporting News* claimed Keeler suffered from a horrible arm injury. On December 29, Willie, accompanied by Cantillon and outfielder Duff Cooley, left the entourage in San Francisco and traveled back East. Joe enacted a hasty departure to address business in Chicago after receiving word about his brother becoming severely ill.[70] In his absence, Cantillon delegated the burden of responsibility to Win for overseeing the All-Americans' affairs. Other injuries plaguing the club included second baseman Jimmy Williams hurting his ankle in Sacramento, illness forcing Cooley to return to Boston, Massachusetts, outfielder Tully "Topsy" Hartsel spraining his wrist and missing two weeks of action, and utility player Charles "Charlie" Dexter suffering a broken collarbone that confined him to his hotel room. Kahoe also endured another physical hindrance when a foul tip tore open his hand.[71] Each of these unfortunate diamond outcomes paled in comparison when press outlets revealed life-altering, tragic news.

A report over the wire from San Francisco on January 13, 1903, shocked the baseball community. The sad and depressing dispatch stated pitcher George Barclay "Win" Mercer had died due to asphyxiation that morning in his room at the Occidental Hotel. Even more alarming to those who knew him was the fact that Mercer had voluntarily ended his life by committing suicide.[72] Upon finding out this horrible news, his friends could only justify the act in their minds due to Win suffering from temporary mental derangement. The *San Francisco Call* pieced together all the information surrounding the tragedy in an article on January 14.

According to this publication, Mercer left the Langham Hotel, where the remainder of the team lodged, at 9 P.M. on Monday, January 12, and checked into the Occidental Hotel. Win registered at the hostelry as George Murray from Philadelphia, Pennsylvania. This newspaper's account claimed that at 1 A.M., hotel workers Henry Cassen and W. H. Van entered the premises using a pass key after detecting a strong gas odor coming from Mercer's room.[73] An article appearing in the *Salt Lake Herald* that same day alleged the night watchman, while making his rounds and smelling gas seeping from Win's room, broke down the door after knocking and receiving no response from inside.[74] Their version of the event proved identical to what the San Francisco publication had reported one day after the ballplayer's death.[75] Both sources of information offered consistent details regarding what these employees discovered.

The *San Francisco Call* reported that Cassen and Van found Mercer lying dead on the bed. So determined to guarantee he successfully brought about his own demise, Win had connected a long rubber hose to a gas jet in the middle of the room. Mercer had placed the other end of that hose in his mouth between clenched teeth.[76] Adorned in his night clothes, Win's coat and vest covered his head.[77] The player piled the clothing over his head to ensure the deadly fumes did their job. On a nearby table rested various letters the despondent athlete had written before committing the deadly act, revealing his identity. The first, written to his mother, Mrs. Maggie Mercer in East Liverpool, offered some insight into his suicide.

> Dearest Darling Mother: I do not want to break your heart, but I am afraid I will by committing the act which I am about to commit. I think I am doing the right thing, dear mother; so please forgive me. Women have gotten the best of me, but I forgive them, even though they are my downfall. God bless them! Well, dear mother, I must say goodbye forever; please forgive me, dear mother, and brothers—I love you all and am sorry to leave you.
>
> Again I say goodbye to mother, Howard, Ross, Clifford, Hazel, Robert and all my dear uncles and aunts and cousins. From WINNIE.

Win Mercer penned a second letter to his sweetheart back in East Liverpool, Miss Martha C. Porter:

> With tears streaming from my eyes I pen these few lines to you, the dearest and sweetest little girl in the whole world.
>
> The act which I am about to commit is simply terrible, but I cannot help it, dearie. I am to blame, nobody else, so I am going to face it as rigid as I have many other wrong acts.
>
> Please forgive me, dear Martha. I love you to the last. Oh, if I could only kiss you once more I would be satisfied to go. Good night to your father, mother, Itha, John, and my dear old pal, Harry. I am sorry to leave you, but I think it is best that I should go. Your unfortunate. WINNIE.

Norris "Tip" O'Neill, manager and facilitator connected to the baseball barnstorming tour, was the third person close to Mercer who received a final message.

> Dear Norris: Please pardon me for the act I am about to commit. God only knows that I am sorry to do it, but I think it best that I should.
>
> A word to my friends: Beware of women and a game of chance.
>
> Well, my dear old pal, with tears in my eyes I say goodbye forever. I wanted to do right. Please forgive me, dear old friend.
>
> You will find two sacks of money in the safe; also sixty-three in my trousers pockets.—WIN.[78]

Win Mercer also left a note for one final individual, which read, "Tell Mr. Van Horn, of the Langham Hotel, that Winnie Mercer has taken his life."[79] Win and his fiancée, Martha Porter, from one of the most prominent families in the Ohio Valley, planned to get married in the spring. The beautiful romance between these two had been ongoing for seven years. Mercer supported his mother for many years by sending her monthly checks. He had also purchased a wonderful home for his mom and provided her with a comfortable bank account.[80]

Maggie Mercer and her husband, Jacob, had divorced several years before. Win's father, who currently lived in Harrisonville, Ohio, did not find out about his son's death until January 19.[81] Mercer's mother idolized her son, who did not drink and saved his money. When friends and family first received news of Win's suicide in San Francisco, they did not believe it. The family only realized the information to be true when East Liverpool Mayor William C. Davidson received a special telegram from San Francisco verifying Mercer's death and asking him to break the sad news to his mother.

Mrs. Mercer was devastated after hearing confirmation of Win's death. A powerful bond and attachment not always witnessed between mother and son existed between the two.[82] Maggie lived in Detroit while her child pitched for that team but did not like the city and returned home. Brother Ross had worked at the Griswold House billiard room in that city the past summer.[83] He also operated a pottery business back home in Ohio, in which Winnie owned a half-interest. Mrs. Mercer had recently built a new residence in Hancock County, West Virginia, near East Liverpool, and resided there. Besides his mother and Ross, brothers Robert, Howard, Hazel, and Clifford survived Mercer. On Friday night, January 16, family and East Liverpool friends sent a letter to San Francisco's chief of police, George Wittman, asking him to conduct a thorough investigation regarding the circumstances surrounding Win's death.[84]

George Y. Travis, manager of the East Liverpool baseball squad that Mercer had played on as a youngster, the hurler's friend and Washington Senators first baseman George "Scoops" Carey, and numerous individuals from the Ohio town requested that San Francisco law enforcement investigate the matter. Maggie Mercer and others believed someone murdered her son. She claimed somebody forged the letters Mercer allegedly wrote. Initial information about the one penned to her made the false claim that Win had a sister in his farewell to family members (possibly a mistake by newspapers due to the name "Hazel" regarding his brother). Mercer's mother also declared her son never signed correspondence "Winnie." The family surmised that the nefarious people who had attempted to swindle him and the Tourists out of a hefty sum of money at Sacramento's Golden Eagle Hotel in December demonstrated that enemies existed who wished to harm him.[85]

San Francisco police responded the following day, stating they found no basis or foundation for the theory alleging Win Mercer's murder, and insisted he committed suicide. Law enforcement positively verified that he wrote all the letters. They also possessed a statement from a druggist who identified Mercer as the purchaser of the rubber hose used to commit the deed. The apothecary clearly recalled selling that item to the baseball player.[86] On January 21, a San Francisco coroner's jury issued a suicide verdict related to Mercer's death.[87] Family, friends, fellow players, and baseball fans all pondered potential reasons for Win taking his life. The letters attributed to Mercer offered some clues into his state of mind by mentioning "women" and "games of chance" in a negative connotation. While searching for answers in his *Detroit Evening News* column, sportswriter Frank Cook related a conversation between him and Win in 1902. Cook did not know if a failed love affair had shattered Mercer's life, although the pitcher once said he expected to go back home and get married when his baseball career ended.

"The Detroit girls don't suit, then, Win?" asked the writer.

"Not so long as there is one down home," Mercer answered with a peculiar smile.[88]

Twenty-two-year-old James Sidney "Sid" Mercer offered more insight into the possible reasons for Win's suicide in his tribute column that appeared in the January 18 Sunday edition of the *St. Louis Republic*. Mercer shared his connection to Winnie as a third or fourth cousin, but had never experienced the pleasure of meeting the pitcher. Sid talked openly about Win's gambling weakness. Concerning his distant cousin's health issues while playing for the Washington Senators in 1901, after pitching in a tough game on the home grounds, he suffered a hemorrhage in the clubhouse once the contest ended. The hurler later asserted that if ever to suffer that type of affliction again, he would kill himself. Sid added that as the Tourists traveled to California in 1902, during a stopover in Las Vegas, New Mexico, Win visited his brother Clifford. Suffering from tuberculosis—or consumption, as referred to at the time—Clifford had moved there for the beneficial effects of the warm, dry climate.

The trip depressed Win Mercer, who feared soon succumbing to this disease he deeply dreaded. Lastly, Sid Mercer talked about an unfulfilled romance between Win and a Pennsylvania girl from a wealthy family. Winnie deeply admired the lady, who shared mutual feelings toward him. Sadly, the young girl's parents disapproved of the relationship and sent her away to an eastern school. According to Sid, whether this permanently ended the romance, Win never seemed the same again.[89] Winnie's teammates on the tour alleged that while he had usually appeared rational, they felt the pitcher had become slightly demented before he killed himself. Most of the two teams' members agreed Mercer had not acted naturally for some time. This appeared more noticeable to those who met him recently after not seeing the ballplayer for a while. These individuals assessed that a strange look in Win's eyes indicated the young man suffered from intense mental strain.

Mercer's note warning friends about games of chance, and the fact that he frequently gambled on the ponies at racetracks, indicated the young man might have been despondent over suffering heavy monetary losses. His fellow players confidently expressed that falling into debt gambling could not have been the impetus behind Win taking his own life. These teammates claimed Mercer had lost big in the past and still maintained a cheerful demeanor. An acquaintance of Win's saw him on the afternoon of January 12 at a racetrack. This individual witnessed Mercer place a losing wager of $100, who bet even on the horse Seize to show. Seize finished fourth. The acquaintance did not know of any other bets Win might have put down that afternoon.[90]

Newspapers started carrying stories about Win Mercer using $3,000 or more of the Tourists' purse earned on this barnstorming trip as his personal gambling fund. Although Win's friends would not admit he embezzled the money because of accrued debt, they acknowledged the hurler had gambled heavily on the trip. When the All-Americans and All-Nationals reached California, they showed $8,000 on the positive side of the ledger, and each player had drawn a $250 bonus.[91] Weeks after his suicide, the *San Francisco Bulletin* reported Mercer had lost an estimated $4,000 to $5,000 visiting racetracks to bet on horses. From the beginning, the hurler's touring teammates adamantly declared no money was missing from their accounts and Win did not owe them a cent. For those aware of Mercer's penchant for gambling, they knew it was not unusual for him to bet as high as $300 on a single race. The article alleged these players kept the truth a secret out of respect for Win's family. Detroit owner Samuel Angus also denied the publication's claim that Mercer had misspent his team's funds.

While on the barnstorming trip the previous winter, Win won a considerable amount of money gambling. He also worked extremely hard for the two baseball clubs, making the tour a financial success. This resulted in his fellow players giving him a beautiful present as a token of their appreciation. When Joe Cantillon started organizing the excursion to California in 1902, he called on Mercer first because of his sterling executive capability. On the afternoon before committing suicide, Win supposedly lost all but $63 of the Tourists' funds.[92] Friend George "Kid" Speer, a member of the American Association's Milwaukee Brewers in 1902, called Mercer a true gentleman in every sense. Kid strongly condemned stories about the Tourists' treasurer being short in his accounts. Speer affirmed that, if true, it would not have caused him to commit suicide.[93]

While the main point of the *San Francisco Bulletin*'s article focused on the allegation that Win stole money, it also specified that his teammates could offer no rational explanation for the pitcher's action, other than constantly worrying about his health and believing the onset of tuberculosis had occurred.[94] This explanation matched one of the possibilities Sid Mercer raised in his column. Willie Keeler also corroborated this sentiment regarding Winnie's grave concern after visiting Clifford in New Mexico.

> While we were in New Mexico with the All-American and All-National combination, last fall, Mercer visited his brother, who has been there for three years for his health. When "Winnie" saw the hopeless condition of his brother, who is troubled with a pulmonary disease, he was shocked, to say the least, and the possibility of the disease being hereditary and perhaps permeating his own system preyed heavily on his mind. He became melancholy, and frequently expressed the fear that he would eventually become a victim, too.
>
> We told him that he was an athlete and in perfect health and in other ways tried to make him forget his delusion, but it seemed to grow on him. When I left the coast, however, he seemed to have regained his composure,

and I thought no more of the matter. The news of his death came as a shock to me. I have no doubt that worrying over the possibility of his being taken down like his brother brought on insanity and death. Winnie pitched brilliant ball on the trip, his slow delivery working beautifully against the fast pitching of [William "Bill"] Donovan and [Jack] Chesbro, and I was confident that he would experience his best year as a pitcher next season. He had a bright future before him.[95]

On the evening of January 13, 1903, the players that remained in California met at the Langham Hotel to discuss how they wanted to proceed following the death of a diamond comrade. The group decided that for the purpose of necessary practice, by playing regular contests on Thursday, Friday, and Saturday, they would then hold a final benefit game on Sunday, January 18, 1903, to collect money for Win's mother.[96] The contest, played in San Francisco, and won by the All-Americans, 5–3, raised $1,500 for Maggie Mercer.[97] Two of the Tourists' members, Cleveland pitcher Addie Joss and former Detroit teammate and outfielder Richard "Dick" Harley, slated to play for the Chicago Cubs in 1903, accompanied Mercer's body to East Liverpool for the funeral.[98] On the evening of January 19, Harley shared some thoughts regarding his intimate friend and close companion while talking about Win with a reporter from that town's *Evening News Review*.

"Winnie was the greatest pitcher in the business, bar none," said Harley. "He was never known to be other than a perfect gentleman, on the field and off, and he won friends in every town he visited. He probably did not fully realize the great extent of his popularity, but if he did it did not change him in the least. He was always the same big-hearted, manly fellow, ever ready to do a kindness to a stranger as well as a friend."

Dick declared that baseball fans considered Win their idol. Harley also revealed Mercer received one of the highest salaries in either major league when Samuel Angus chose him to manage Detroit. While praising his good friend, Dick shared that Win always took young players under his wing and constantly offered encouragement while reprimanding veteran diamond performers who attempted to blame misplays on these novices. Harley added that as peace discussions began between National and American League officials, Mercer worried about the Tigers' club losing some star ballplayers. When prospects started looking favorable for Detroit as the two organizations decided on assigning disputed players, Tourists team members kidded outfielder Samuel "Sam" Crawford, in Win's presence, that he better behave since his manager stood nearby.[99] When Harley eventually returned to his hometown of Philadelphia after attending Win's funeral, he offered further comments regarding the pitcher's tragic suicide.

The death of Mercer was a shock to every one of us. He was one of the finest fellows I ever traveled with. Win always was ready for a joke or a good time and made friends with everyone he met on the trip.

None of us could account for his action, and I guess his death always will remain a mystery. For a few days before he committed suicide Mercer complained of pains in his head, but we thought nothing much of this at the time. He gave none of us an inkling of his intention, except that he acted a little queer the day that he took his life. His accounts were all straight to the penny. Indeed, even the last day of his life he looked up each of the boys and gave him $30, the amount coming to each man from the game the previous afternoon.

From a financial viewpoint the trip was a success. After having a good time and visiting many points of interest, we cleared more than $550 each over and above all expenses.[100]

Although Dick Harley categorized this barnstorming excursion as a success and a fun time, an editorial column in the *Pittsburgh Press* on January 19 disagreed. This article wrote, "The calamity which befell the roving ballplayers in the death of Winnie Mercer at San Francisco last Monday night should be a lesson to all barnstorming clubs." The column claimed that temptations placed before Mercer could only have occurred on such a trip, where no authority figure guided these men, and, according to the *Washington Post*, discipline proved very lax. It also stressed that baseball players, under pressure throughout a long major league season, needed time to rest and decompress. The *Pittsburgh Press* cited the many injuries suffered during this trip before decreeing that these athletes owed it to the employers that paid their salaries to be in shape when the bell sounded on another season in April.[101]

In the wake of Win Mercer's death, Tigers owner Samuel Angus hired Edward "Ed" Barrow, who managed the Eastern League's Toronto Maple Leafs in 1902, to oversee Detroit. On January 12, Angus had sent a message to Mercer, that he never received, regarding the Cincinnati peace commission awarding disputed outfielder Sam Crawford to the Tigers and confirming the club's claims to pitcher Bill Donovan and shortstop Norman "Kid" Elberfeld. Win had recently sent a telegram to the owner, voicing his pleasure over Detroit remaining in the American League. Samuel expressed shock when news reached him about Mercer's death.

"I regarded him as a peerless pitcher," said Angus, "and it was a delight to sit in the stand and see a man combine brains and brawn in winning his games. Because of his great tact I thought that this year he would get the best possible results from the players, because they liked him in the first place, and in the second they looked up to him because of his superior mentality."

Win's death hit Frederick "Fred" Postal, owner of the Washington Senators' squad the twirler played for in 1901, as hard emotionally as Angus when finding out the terrible news. Postal said that while he had been disappointed with Mercer's showing in 1901 and did not care much for him by the conclusion of that campaign, his opinion changed when learning that the fault did not lie entirely with Win.[102]

At East Liverpool's First Presbyterian Church, a large crowd attended Mercer's funeral on January 21, 1903. On the breast of Win's body, lying in the casket, rested a bunch of roses bearing "Martha," the gift of his fiancée and the daughter of S. H. Porter.[103] The church auditorium's small size proved insufficient to accommodate all who wished to witness the service. The previous evening, hundreds of people braved the rain for the viewing at the Mercer home.

Beautiful floral tributes included those from his mother and brothers, and K. T. & K. Pottery, where Win once worked.[104] Magnificent flower arrangements from local businessmen, baseball enthusiasts, and friends and associates from his youth surrounded the coffin.[105] Mercer's oldest East Liverpool buddies donated a floral tribute design consisting of a green baseball field with white flowers acting as the bases.[106] Mourners started filing into the church prior to 1 P.M., and the building was filled well before the funeral started, leaving many people unable to gain access.[107] Those who stood outside in the rain entered to view the body after the final benediction.[108] Reverend Dr. Milton Butler Pratt, one of the individuals who officiated the ceremony, gave a stirring sermon. Reverend Pratt said that up until the day he died, Win tenderly cherished his mother. According to the minister, whenever the pitcher wrote home, he did so to send Maggie Mercer a message of love. When encountering someone from East Liverpool during the season, Mercer always anxiously inquired about his mother's welfare.[109]

Following the mass, a funeral procession traveled to the twenty-eight-year-old pitcher's final resting place at Spring Grove Cemetery.[110] Almost one month after Win Mercer's death, Cincinnati owner Garry Herrmann made a startling comment while talking with St. Louis Cardinals president Frank Robison. Herrmann intimated that the tragic outcome might not have occurred if Win had signed to play for the Reds.

"Do you know," remarked Herrmann to Robison, "that I feel that Win Mercer would have been alive today had I answered that telegram that Tip O'Neill sent to me about Christmas time? There was some reason for Mercer trying to get away from Detroit. It may never come to light, but that O'Neill feeler was not a 'kid,' but was on the level. No one tried harder to sign Mercer last fall than Joe Kelley and I. We were on his trail for a couple of nights, but failed to locate him, and he left town without our getting to do any business with him."

Frank Robison responded that after the Washington Nationals suffered the fate of contraction following the 1899 season, he gladly would have taken Mercer instead of the $5,000 share of the National League's obligation owed to him.[111] While Garry Herrmann only made a supposition behind the reason for Win committing suicide, a sportswriter shared some revelations about the pitcher's gambling habits more than four years after his death.

Versatile writer Clarence L. Cullen, who covered horseracing for Washington's *Evening Star*, gave readers a glimpse into Mercer's obsession with betting on the ponies in his Sunday article from August 4, 1907. Referring to Win as "Romeo," another nickname he carried while playing for the Nationals, Cullen explained that the hurler caught the horse bug early in his baseball career. The writer also declared that those familiar with these facts concluded this obsession did more to damage his career and contributed to his death more than anything else connected to the handsome, splendid ballplayer.

Cullen wrote that Mercer possessed broad knowledge about all the horses, studiously consumed the information and dope, and always paid attention to the educated money. Despite all these advantages, Win usually did not experience success at the racetrack. Clarence said he encountered Mercer about twenty times at tracks around the National League circuit, including the Benning Race Track in Washington. In all those instances, Cullen only saw Win cash in a winning ticket once. Even on that occasion, bad luck plagued Mercer, who had played a three-to-five parlay on a particular horse to win. His selection finished in a dead heat with another stallion who carried forty-to-one odds. Since the owners of the two horses decided against a runoff, the racetrack split the tickets, and Win received less money back than he placed on the bet.

Clarence also cited one instance in 1898 when a wager affected Win's performance on the mound. According to the writer, before pitching against the New York Giants at the Polo Grounds one afternoon, Mercer decided to place a bet at the track on the Brooklyn Handicap. Before the game started, Winnie told Cullen he liked Sly Fox to win the big race and would send $200 down to the track as a wager on the three-year-old horse. Mercer pitched brilliantly through the first five innings, not allowing New York to record a hit. As Win prepared to start working in the sixth frame, somebody in the press box using a megaphone related to him the news regarding Ornament winning the Brooklyn Handicap, and that Sly Fox, who led throughout most of the race, finished third. Win had only selected his horse to win and not place. As Mercer prepared to pitch, Clarence noticed from the press box a dejected look on the hurler's face as his hand shook while fiddling with the baseball. The Giants scored six runs that inning, and the ruined pitcher's day concluded when he exited the contest at his own request.[112]

When recalling this incident surrounding the Brooklyn Handicap, Clarence Cullen experienced a memory lapse while thinking back nine years. On May 28, 1898, jockey Ted Sloan rode Ornament to victory in the Brooklyn Handicap horse race at the Gravesend Race Track as Sly Fox finished third.[113] That Saturday afternoon, Win Mercer started for the Washington Nationals against the Pittsburgh Pirates at Exposition Park rather than facing New York as Cullen claimed. Mercer only lasted three innings, allowing Pittsburgh to build up an 8–0 lead, en route to a 9–7 victory.[114] Win certainly did not pitch brilliantly before receiving unwelcome news about the horse race, as alleged by the sportswriter. Mercer could have placed a bet with a bookie ahead of the event and experienced a dreadful day pitching because of its result. Another possibility existed that Cullen confused the racetrack when discussing a game with Win working on the mound at the Polo Grounds, or he mixed up the years and horses when talking about a poor wager the hurler made regarding the Brooklyn Handicap.

The studious and cerebral Win had kept a book on the strengths and weaknesses of opposing hitters.[115] According to former Washington teammate Scrappy Bill Joyce, hardnosed John "Jack" Glasscock, who played for the Pittsburgh Pirates when Mercer broke into the National League, also possessed a ledger containing an enemies list. Joyce explained that in one game between the two teams, Win struck Glasscock, also known as "Pebbly Jack," with a painful pitch to the ribs. Thinking this purposeful maneuver personal, Jack wrote in his little book, "Mercer—Get him."

> This meant that Glasscock would not rest until he had turned some trick on Mercer—something to even up matters. From that time until the fag end of the season Glasscock waited patiently, seeing Mercer play many times, but he never got a chance. His observation of Mercer was such as to make him believe that he could not play dirty ball and one night Glasscock walked into a Pittsburgh hotel where Mercer was stopping and said: "Win, I guess you didn't mean to hit me with that ball. I'll wipe it off."
>
> True to his promise Jack pulled out the book and drew his pencil through Mercer's entry. It was the only score ever wiped off quietly by Jack Glasscock.[116]

In a tribute to Win Mercer days after his death, the *Pittsburgh Dispatch* wrote that the ballplayer proved as game as D'Artagnan of *The Three Musketeers*, loved from Portland, Maine, to Portland, Oregon, and handsome as a fairy tale prince.[117] Dick Harley had guessed Mercer's death would always remain a mystery.[118] While fear, pressure, and guilt brought about unspeakable circumstances, no mystery existed regarding the love and admiration Winnie received from his diamond peers and baseball fans.

*Throughout his time playing for the Washington Nationals from 1894 to 1899, female fans considered pitcher **Win Mercer** the handsomest ballplayer in the National League. Win, who acquired the nicknames "Romeo" and "Apollo of the Potomac," frequently pitched on Ladies' Day at the Boundary Field home grounds. Besides possessing dashing good looks, Mercer performed as the Nationals' staff ace for many campaigns and became the league's preeminent student of the game during that time. Sadly, underlying problems related to health concerns, a gambling habit, and women, led Win to commit suicide in his San Francisco hotel room on January 12, 1903. For the second straight off-season, Win had traveled with a team on a barnstorming tour that concluded in California. (Courtesy of the Library of Congress).*

CHAPTER 3

Ed Delahanty

Reckless Behavior Assists the Cruel Hand of Fate

Throughout baseball history, blessed patrons watched numerous brother combinations pull off amazing exploits while entertaining them at the ballpark. Many of these individuals—including Paul and Lloyd Waner, Joe and Luke Sewell, and Joe, Dom, and Vince DiMaggio—possessed star quality throughout their diamond eras. Well before these iconic men pulled on a major league uniform, a group of brothers from Cleveland, Ohio, established the standard regarding family dominance within the sport. From 1888 through 1912, a Delahanty performed at the big-league level, courtesy of five brothers cavorting on the diamond. Of those five siblings, and most other major leaguers during his career, Edward "Ed" Delahanty left all contemporaries in the dust, combining raw power and an uncanny ability to hit any type of pitching while establishing the gaudiest batting numbers of that period. Unfortunately, demons lurking below the surface brought about unfortunate circumstances for one of the most accomplished individuals to ever play the game.

Edward James Delahanty was born in Cleveland on October 30, 1867, to parents James and Bridget. Ed's parents had immigrated to the United States from Ireland near the end of the Civil War. Throughout his youth, Delahanty's father worked in various blue-collar occupations offering low pay while his mother converted their large home into a boardinghouse to bring in extra cash from paying guests. Like many other youngsters, Ed and his brothers enthusiastically played baseball on local ball fields and grew to love the sport in which they excelled.[1] Following a stellar and successful Cleveland sandlot career, Delahanty signed his first professional contract with the Ohio State League's

Mansfield club in 1887. Ed batted .351 for Mansfield before moving on to the Tri-State League's Wheeling National Citys/Nailers in 1888. In 21 games with Wheeling, Delahanty posted a .408 average before the National League's Philadelphia Phillies purchased him on May 21.

Baseball lifer William Henry "Harry" Wright managed the Phillies in 1888. Upon joining Philadelphia, Ed acted like a swaggering, brash youngster who cocked his cap to one side of his head, wore stiff-collared shirts, smoked the best cigars, and chewed a superior tobacco brand. Delahanty struggled in his first major league season, hitting .228, while appearing in 74 games. Throughout this rough campaign, Ed fumed and fretted over his inferior performance, never hesitating to engage in severe self-criticism regarding his diamond work. Wright's patient and compassionate approach assisted Delahanty in tempering such harsh self-evaluation. Following his 1889 season with the Phillies, Ed played for the hometown Players League's Cleveland Infants one year later. Patsy Tebeau, third baseman for Cleveland's Brotherhood of Professional Baseball Players organization entry in 1890, marveled at Delahanty's ability to smash wasted offerings from opposing hurlers all over the ballpark.

"If you let that bat-mad galoot step into the ball he'll knock its cover off," said Tebeau while declaring that the most dangerous thing to throw Ed was a wild pitch.

Ed Delahanty, later known as "Del" or "Big Ed," returned to the Phillies in 1891 after the Players League folded. Throughout that decade, Delahanty gained a reputation as a deadly hitter. Patsy proved correct in his assessment of Ed's proficiency in hitting wild pitches. Using a long, heavy bat, Delahanty took tremendous swings utilizing his broad shoulders and powerful hands. He deftly stepped forward to reach outside pitches, swatting the baseball like a kid attempting to pick the cherries off the farthest end of a tree limb. Ed frequently struck inside pitches off his shoe tops over the fence. Delahanty readily admitted he could have been an even better hitter by showing restraint and exhibiting plate discipline.

"If I could only hold myself like that old crab, Cap Anson," Delahanty said, "I would bat better than he ever did. But I can't. When the ball seems to me to be coming to my liking, I am going to belt it. I don't care where it comes, I'll either hit it or miss it, and if I miss it, God knows that I'll miss it by enough."

One time, in a game against St. Louis in 1892, Browns third baseman George Pinkney experienced a rude awakening when Ed pulled the unexpected. Figuring him to bunt, Pinkney suffered a broken ankle when struck by a blistering drive off Delahanty's bat with velocity resembling a projectile shot out of a cannon. Ed occasionally tore the shoes off opposing infielders with his sizzling line drives.[2] Used primarily as an outfielder as his major league career progressed, although he played other positions, Delahanty loathed a manager asking him to bunt. Once, Harry Wright signaled Ed to bunt and sacrifice a runner. When the opposing twirler fired an offering toward home plate, the pitch looked so tempting that Delahanty took a mighty cut and drove the sphere out of the ballpark for a home run. Laughing as he reached the dugout, Ed encountered his unhappy manager.

"That'll cost you $15, Del," said Wright.

"What for?" inquired the amazed player.

"For not bunting," answered Harry.

Astounded by Wright's response, Delahanty remained speechless. Following this incident, Ed faithfully obeyed all future orders from the boss. Nobody found out if Harry remitted the fine.[3]

In 1893, Delahanty experienced a breakout season for the Philadelphia Phillies, hitting .368 and leading the National League in home runs (19) and RBIs (146). The following year, Ed batted .405 and drove in 133 runs. At 5 P.M. on October 10, 1894, Del married Miss Norine Thompson, who lived in Philadelphia.[4] Ed continued his assault on league pitchers in 1895, hitting .404, smacking 11 four-baggers, and driving home 106 runs. The following season, Delahanty highlighted his power-hitting prowess through a historic performance on a sweltering summer afternoon.

On July 13, 1896, in a game between the Phillies and Chicago Colts at West Side Grounds, temperatures reached ninety-five degrees in the ballpark's grandstand. In another section, where only three red-headed male fans sat, the mercury approached 115 degrees. The boy selling soda pop profited due to the 1,000 spectators seeking respite from the heat and quenching their thirst. Both squads, pining for cooler weather, did not use the full allotted practice time before the contest. As the affair progressed, a cool breeze offered some relief for the diamond combatants. Although Chicago won the game, 9–8, Ed Delahanty owned Colts hurler William "Adonis" Terry. In five plate appearances, Delahanty blasted four home runs and connected for a single against Terry.[5] In this one-man show, Ed accounted for seventeen total bases. His scorching single also knocked over Chicago shortstop William "Bill" Dahlen.[6]

Regarding his four round-trippers, Delahanty blasted a pitch into the bleachers, crushed another one out of the ballpark over the scoreboard, and forced stalwart Colts outfielder Bill Lange to futilely chase his other two drives, which resulted in inside-the-park home runs. Before Ed came up to the plate for the final time late in the game, Chicago skipper Cap Anson threatened his team. Anson gave strict orders that if the bases were not empty when Delahanty batted, he would fine the entire squad the price of three meals based on the exorbitant rates establishments had used when that city hosted the World's Fair in 1893. Cap's directive proved effectual, as no Phillies occupied the bags when Big Ed blasted his final home run out of the lot.[7] Delahanty connected against Adonis's first pitch. The baseball soared out to left field, hit the clubhouse roof, and bounced off another part of the structure.[8] As darkness descended after the game ended, a legion of small boys searching behind the clubhouse still had not found the baseball.[9]

Ed batted .397 in 1896, led the National League in RBIs (126), and tied Scrappy Bill Joyce in home runs (13). Even when Delahanty saw a drop by hitting only .334 in 1898, he still paced the circuit with 58 stolen bases. Del experienced the best season of his career in 1899 when Philadelphia's star performer batted .410, smacked nine four-baggers, and drove in a league-leading 137 runs. While Ed played for Philadelphia, Colonel John I. Rogers was the acting club president, owning the franchise with partner Alfred "Al" Reach. Many Phillies players perceived Rogers as a tightwad during his tenure running the organization. Thus far, Delahanty had earned no more than the National League maximum of $2,400 per season. His highest pay boost during the past eight seasons amounted to a measly $200.[10] Ed finally saw a significant salary bump when Philadelphia's baseball organization paid him $3,000 in 1900.[11]

Throughout the 1890s, people living in Cleveland adored their hometown hero. Local kids, hoping to achieve remarkable things in baseball, idolized Delahanty. Thomas "Tommy" Leach, who debuted with the Louisville Colonels and starred for the Pittsburgh Pirates during the first decade of the twentieth century, corroborated this lionization of the diamond icon. Although Leach categorized Ed as his hero, he sometimes tired of his father constantly expounding about the Phillies' outfielder's greatness.[12] However, biographer Jerrold Casway alleged Delahanty became gruff and stubborn when things did not go his way. Casway added that Ed's self-centered attitude sometimes alienated teammates because he cared more about personal accomplishments than the club's success. The author maintained that Ed acted like an overgrown spoiled child who depended on strong women in his life. Jerrold reasoned this included Delahanty's domineering mother and manipulative wife, whose attention he urgently needed during rough times despite resenting this reliance on them.[13]

Ed became disenchanted with the Phillies during the 1901 campaign. On June 20, Philadelphia purchased former Baltimore Orioles standout Hughie Jennings from the Brooklyn Superbas. Delahanty exhibited unhappiness when manager William "Bill" Shettsline appointed Jennings team captain, meaning the club's longtime star would now take orders from a younger player. On the evening of August 12, Washington's *Evening Star* published a story regarding Senators manager Jimmy Manning raiding Philadelphia's club and signing players for the 1902 campaign to play on that American League squad. The article named Ed as one of the individuals preparing to switch leagues. Such a move appeared plausible since Manning and Delahanty had long enjoyed a warm, personal friendship. When questioned on the matter by a sportswriter, Jimmy adamantly denied he was dickering with Phillies team members. A journalist for Philadelphia's *North American* disputed this notion.

"Of the list of Quakers likely to jump or considering offers Delahanty is said positively to have signed to play left field and captain the Senators," wrote the Philadelphia sportswriter. "There is no loud talk about it, but the tip is given out on the quiet."[14]

The American League's emergence in 1901 as a feasible, major-league alternative to the long-standing National League intrigued players within the senior organization, feeling jilted financially by their current employers. Ten days after the first report about a raid involving Phillies team members, Philadelphia's *The Times* reported Ed Delahanty had received a guaranteed $4,000 contract to suit up for Washington in 1902.[15] Besides pledging his allegiance to the American League, Delahanty happily worked as a recruitment officer for the new organization, extolling its virtues within the landscape of better financial opportunities. For several weeks in August, rumors abounded about Cincinnati Reds team members succumbing to big promises of lucrative deals while ignoring past contractual obligations. These reports also claimed Ed functioned as a liaison between the American League and Cincinnati's players.

Following the morning contest of a Labor Day doubleheader on September 2 against Philadelphia at National League Park, Reds team members met at their Bingham House Hotel lodging. After the first game concluded, Delahanty quickly dressed and exited the grounds before his teammates to visit the Bingham House Hotel and conduct discussions with Cincinnati players Jacob "Jake" Beckley, Frank "Noodles" Hahn, William "Bill" Fox, John Dobbs, and Dick Harley. Newspaper stories alleged Ed made overtures to these five individuals regarding where they planned to play baseball in 1902. The reports could not verify what type of offers Delahanty made or if any players accepted the proffers. Each team member unequivocally denied signing a contract to play in the American League. Although Delahanty also vehemently refuted claims that he, too, planned to jump to Ban Johnson's organization, his actions contradicted that assertion.[16]

Such denials appeared hollow since his conduct involving the Reds' players was not an isolated incident. While Philadelphia visited Pittsburgh for a July series against the Smoky City baseball club, Ed coordinated a meeting with Pirates first baseman William "Kitty" Bransfield in his hotel room. Following this conference, Delahanty hustled Bransfield to see American League agent and *Philadelphia Inquirer* sportswriter Frank Hough. After listening to both men and telling them he would consider their offer, Kitty re-signed to play for the Pirates in 1902.[17] When the 1901 campaign ended, Ed, Hough, and a Pittsburgh reporter snuck around the Smoky City hoping to entice local players to consider switching their loyalties and playing for the American League.[18]

When it came to the possibility that seven Phillies team members could ignore their contracts and jump to the rival league, John I. Rogers professed to be an agnostic since he knew nothing about these potential desertions except published newspaper accounts. Bill Shettsline stated that while unaware if any of his players cast their lot with the American League, everyone had previously signed standard National League contracts binding them from year-to-year to play for Philadelphia.[19] Ed Delahanty suited up for the American League's Washington Senators in 1902. Delahanty experienced a solid season at the plate, hitting .376 and leading the circuit in batting. This supreme achievement meant Del had led both major leagues in that department.[20] The Senators could not capitalize on Ed's batting proficiency, finishing sixth in the pennant race with a 61–75 record. Good friend Jimmy Manning ended up not managing Washington in 1902. Manning retired from that position before the season started when his stock option as partial owner expired. Thomas "Tom" Loftus replaced Jimmy to steer the Senators' craft.[21]

Despite Delahanty's success that season, living in the nation's capital and the lucrative guaranteed contract did not realize his preconceived lofty standards.[22] On December 3, 1902, a press dispatch sent from Washington alleged Ed, along with pitchers Albert "Al" Orth and John "Happy" Townsend, had agreed to play for the National League's New York Giants in 1903. According to this story, Delahanty, who habitually bet on the ponies, went broke at the Aqueduct Racetrack in Queens, New York. Claiming to be unable to procure advance money from Senators ownership, Ed jumped at the first proposal made by John McGraw that offered $2,000 ready cash upfront. McGraw reportedly acquiesced to Delahanty's demand of $6,000 to play for the Giants in 1903. Ed also requested Orth's and Townsend's inclusion in the deal.[23]

McGraw substantiated this story by stating he possessed signed contracts from all three players. Orth denied signing any such document from his home in Lynchburg, Virginia.[24] Al then made an unexpected trip to Washington, where he once again reiterated not reaching an agreement to suit up for New York in 1903. Orth also claimed he had seen neither Delahanty nor the Giants' manager since the season closed.[25] Townsend wrote a letter to Senators management refuting this report, adding that he planned to faithfully fulfill the two-year contract the pitcher had signed before the 1902 season.[26] When New York owner John T. Brush returned to New York from a western trip, he confirmed having signed contracts in his pocket, including one with Ed's John Hancock on a document. None of these were agreements from Washington's two hurlers, meaning Al and Happy proved truthful in their denunciations.[27]

From New Orleans, Louisiana, Ed Delahanty followed the path of his two teammates, denying he reached terms with the Giants.[28] Del readily admitted that John McGraw had attempted to do business with him on numerous occasions. Ed also confessed he might not play for Washington in 1903. The star player claimed McGraw offered a one-year contract paying him $7,000, which Delahanty unabashedly rejected without considering the proposition. Ed then asked New York's pilot if he could receive authorization from ownership to go any higher regarding his salary. When John answered negatively, Delahanty replied that he would not conduct any further business with the Giants' representative until the club met his closing price of $10,000 a year.[29]

Washington Senators owner and president Fred Postal expressed shock and disbelief over reports that the defending batting champion might desert his team. Postal confirmed that Ed, short on funds, had requested a salary advance in November. The team president sent Delahanty $1,000; a $600 advance of money owed him in 1903, and $400, the final installment of his 1902 salary, due to him in February. Upon sending the cash, Postal heard nothing further from his player.

"If Delahanty has deserted us I don't believe that I will ever trust the word of a baseball player again," said Postal. "He is signed to a two-year contract of the most binding type, and has promised me repeatedly that he will be with the club next year, in spite of offers he has received from other teams. He is one of the last men on earth I would have suspected of treachery, and his loss, if the story is true, will be a severe one. Townsend we won't miss any, and Orth will be easily replaced. Neither of the men is in the class with Delahanty."

Club attorney Wilton J. Lambert planned to utilize the courts if any of these three players accepted money from the Giants, thus breaching their contracts with the Senators.[30] Postal's kneejerk reaction seemed a bit meanspirited regarding Al Orth and Happy Townsend since both men proved faithful and did not engage New York's operatives. Del proved to be a different story. William F. H. Koelsch, the Giants' correspondent for *Sporting Life*, reported that John T. Brush had signed Ed to a three-year contract, paying him $8,000 each season he played with New York. Efforts to improve the club had been a two-pronged attack, as John McGraw did the talking to potential players while Brush then acted on bringing the strongest diamond performers into his stable.[31] Weeks after issuing various denials regarding the possibility that he could abandon his teammates and fans in Washington, Delahanty finally admitted to agreeing to play for the Giants. Ed articulated from New Orleans about how things stood on December 22.

I have no reason to fear the American League, and I have been assured by McGraw that Colonel John I. Rogers will not enjoin me from playing with a National League club other than Philadelphia. That is all cut and dried. While I hate to cut loose from so good a fellow as Manager Tom Loftus, at Washington, I am anxious to help New York beat out the Pittsburghs and Cincinnatis for the 1903 pennant. If the two leagues declare peace it will not affect me in any way as regards salary, as I have mine fixed as far as the next three years are concerned.

I am to receive without qualification $8,000 a year for that time from McGraw, and the first year's salary has been paid me in full. The rest has been placed in a New York bank, subject to my check, at dated intervals, and I am in no way concerned with which way the wind goes. I get the money whether I play or not, and that settles the question, no matter what proceedings may follow. I might be enjoined from playing with New York, but I will get my salary, nevertheless. When this contract wears out I will be satisfied to quit the game and follow the turf to campaign a string of racers.[32]

Such an arrangement established a sweetheart deal for an individual who did not care about anyone but himself. Unfortunately, a desire by the National and American leagues to end their long war over players undermined Delahanty's plans. At 2 A.M. on January 22, 1903, at the Grand Hotel in Cincinnati, Ohio, every National League owner ratified a peace agreement previously reached by the two organizations.[33] When both parties initially hammered out the pact on January 10, a committee tasked with settling who owned the rights to disputed players awarded Ed to the Washington Senators.[34] Shortly after the committee adjudicated this matter, American League president Ban Johnson sent a telegram to Delahanty in New Orleans, which read, "Come on, Del; we want you." Upon hearing the news, Ed readily admitted he would play for Washington in 1903, although the star player had signed with the New York Giants and received $2,500 in advance money as part of that deal.

"I don't intend to return a cent of that $2,500 either," declared Delahanty. "My contract was a special one, which provided for a certain sum a year, even if prevented from playing by injunction or unforeseen debarments."[35]

While discussing Ed Delahanty's total disregard for "honesty" and "integrity," an article in the *Buffalo Enquirer* claimed that due to his attitude about the advance money, players of Del's ilk discredited the game. This editorial pulled no punches, declaring that the sooner these individuals drifted out of the game, the better. The newspaper's article also branded Mr. Delahanty as not above the courts, and just possibly, a few months in jail for obtaining money under false pretenses might curb his arrogance and teach him a valuable lesson.[36] John

McGraw and John T. Brush certainly possessed dirty hands in this matter. New York's two baseball representatives cleverly utilized the fact that Ed had tumbled into heavy debt due to gambling losses. Vulnerable because of this dire situation, Delahanty proved an easy mark when McGraw made his attractive offer. In a way, the fresh money supplied by John and Brush assisted in feeding Ed's gambling habit.[37] Delahanty seemed more resigned to his fate of playing baseball with the Senators in 1903 through force.

> I suppose I'll have to go back to the Washington Club in 1903, but that is not a cause of complaint from me, for I was treated well there, and I guess if I deliver the goods I'll have no trouble. A ballplayer's standing is dependent on what he does on the ball field, and I propose to do my best for Loftus, and if I have good luck in batting, I'll fare all right. I felt to better myself, not because I was dissatisfied or was anxious to be on Brush's payroll, or to be under McGraw's management.
>
> I wanted the money and got it. I will not return the advance money to [New York Giants team secretary Frederick "Fred"] Knowles, McGraw, Brush or to any club's agents. My contract was a special one and called for so much a year, even if I were prevented from playing by injunctions or unforeseen debarments. I'll play with Washington again, but the New York advance money is in my kick to stay. I will not leave New Orleans until the race meeting closes and will begin to play ball in the practice games here early next spring. I'll be in shape to deliver the goods when I join the Senators.[38]

Catcher and utility player Alexander "Broadway Aleck" Smith, who played for the Baltimore Orioles in 1902, spent time with Del at the New Orleans racetracks, betting on the horses. Smith offered his opinion concerning the winners and losers regarding baseball's peace agreement.

"I knew it would come, sooner or later," said Smith, "and as usual the player will get the short end of it. Peace means increased attendance in all the cities. It is a good thing for the magnates but hard for the players."[39]

When Smith arrived in New York on February 26 after spending the entire winter down South with Delahanty and his wife, Norine, he commented on where things currently stood regarding his friend.

> Delahanty told me that if he could not play with the New York Club he would give up the business. "I will not play in Washington, and that settles it," said Dell, and I know that he means it.
>
> Delahanty has been in New Orleans with his wife this winter, and has had his ups and downs in betting on the ponies, but he is far from

being broke, as has been reported. I feel sure that he will not pay back the $4,000 advanced him by the New York Club just for the sake of getting into the game again.⁴⁰

Inconsistencies certainly existed when people exhibited no inhibition in throwing money around. One newspaper report claimed Senators president Fred Postal had actually advanced $1,600 to Ed Delahanty, split up over two checks. Ed cashed the first one for $600. Possibly due to concentrating on wagers at the racetrack or receiving a hefty sum of money from the Giants, Delahanty forgot to deposit the bigger check in the bank. Realizing the canceled check had not come back, Postal notified his bank that he wished to stop payment. Fred then alerted Ed of his action, sarcastically informing him in a message that he did so out of the goodness of his heart since possessing too much money corrupted many young men.⁴¹ Understanding that the strained relationship between Washington's ownership and Delahanty might be irreparable, Detroit's rooters clamored for him to join the Tigers, prompting Postal to issue a statement.

"Personally I am just as sore on Delahanty's actions as any man would naturally be when an employee deserts him the way Delahanty left me," explained Postal. "He would leave a big hole in the Washington team, though, and I would hate to let him go unless we could get a good man to take his place in the outfield."⁴²

Things became clearer as the Senators prepared for spring practice in the nation's capital before the 1903 campaign commenced. On March 19, Washington's owner received a telegram from Ed in New Orleans, stating he wanted to confer with manager Tom Loftus. Some in the press believed this indicated that an anxious Delahanty desired to resolve the controversy over his contract. Others felt Ed planned to play for New York.⁴³ One day after Fred Postal received this correspondence, Loftus explained that three scenarios existed regarding Ed performing on the diamond in 1903. None of them included suiting up for the Giants.

> There are only three possibilities. Delahanty must play with the Washington Club, keep out of baseball entirely, or I must get his equivalent if he plays elsewhere.
>
> Under any circumstances, if he plays baseball again in a major league he must report to me in Washington. Then I will listen to any proposition McGraw or anybody else sees fit to make toward buying his release.
>
> But really there is little chance of Del wearing any other uniform than the Washington one this year. I have ordered him to report to the

Washington Club next Monday [March 23] and have quoted the expulsion article of the constitution to him.

I have no doubt that he will come and report. Then if he wants to play in New York and that club offers sufficient inducements I may consider the deal.[44]

Ultimatums pulsated front and center, especially from those in positions of authority, whose words carried weight regarding baseball policy. While Tom Loftus declared what he expected from Delahanty, the presidents of the two major organizations, Harry Pulliam of the National League and the American League's Ban Johnson, held a conference on March 20. This session's focus encompassed a discussion of Ed's case and that of shortstop George Davis, who hoped to return to the Giants after spending one year with the Chicago White Sox in 1902. Delahanty and Davis became tethered together regarding their grievances since the peace agreement committee overseeing disputed players awarded George to Chicago. President Pulliam articulately expressed his organization's position on this issue.

"Neither man will be eligible to play in the National League until he has been released from his obligations with the clubs holding a contract with him," said Pulliam. "The fact that George Davis is now practicing with the New York club or the fact of any litigation friendly or otherwise between Davis and the New York club will not operate to change the attitude of the National League in this matter until it is decreed by a court of last resort that this position of the National League shall be changed. Then and not till then will it change."

American League president Ban Johnson echoed Harry's stance on this important subject, where unity proved essential for all parties to maintain a peaceful relationship.

"The American League has no intention of allowing any person, be he player, manager or club owner, to violate the peace agreement in any way," said Johnson. "George Davis must fulfill his contract with the Chicago American League club and play there, and the same applies to Delahanty and the Washington American League club. They must fulfill their obligations as decreed by the joint peace committees and if they do not they cannot play baseball anywhere and will be out of the game for good."[45]

A united front by leaders of both leagues made it difficult for disloyal players to do as they pleased while ignoring their contractual obligations. Magnates offering support for these directors also left few options for men like John T. Brush, John McGraw, George Davis, and Ed Delahanty. Cincinnati president Garry Herrmann adamantly declared his Reds would refuse to take the field if Davis and Delahanty appeared with New York.[46] Chicago president James

"Jim" Hart later concurred with Herrmann's sentiment, proclaiming the Cubs would not play if the Giants insisted on using George or Ed.[47] Loftus talked about Delahanty near the end of March, explaining the player must first report to Washington and make himself look good to the manager. Tom added that before considering any potential trade to another team, Del needed to exhibit good faith with the Senators.

Loftus also took a shot at McGraw and Brush, saying they did not seem to understand that the two leagues now worked together and no longer fought as bitter enemies. Tom also reminded baseball fans of what New York's magnate said when owners reached the peace agreement, "You can make me swallow it, but you can't make me say I like it." Loftus reasoned that the Giants' management hierarchy would wake up before the season opened.[48] The New York Highlanders, slated to play their inaugural American League campaign in 1903, positioned themselves to be one of the clubs pursuing Ed's services. Highlanders president Joseph Gordon expressed confidence in Delahanty playing for his team.

"There is little doubt in my mind that we will secure Delahanty," said Gordon, "although the deal may cost us a little more than $10,000."[49]

When these negotiations started between Ed and New York manager Clark Griffith, some press members felt Ban Johnson should order all discussions to cease between the two parties. This group of sportswriters, who deemed Delahanty a despicable contract jumper, staunchly felt clubs should follow the peace agreement to the letter of the law. This left Ed with no alternative other than playing for Washington. If not the case, when it came to the American League's image, these scribes reasoned it made more sense for Del to join the Giants rather than the Highlanders.[50] Tom Loftus constantly reiterated that Delahanty must play for the Senators, or he would be inactive. Following a delay because of a railway accident in Georgia, Ed reached Washington on March 21 and registered at the Hotel Oxford. When interviewed after his arrival, Delahanty declared he would not remain idle since playing baseball proved a grand profession while also vowing to give consummate effort for whatever team ended up securing his services.[51]

One report claimed Ed Delahanty's weight ballooned to 250 pounds during the off-season. While Ed pondered playing on the Pacific Coast as a solution to his problem, he asserted that the process of getting into condition would not occur before positively knowing his destination as a player in 1903.[52] On April 11, Loftus and Delahanty got together and patched up their differences, leading to the announcement that the "King of Swatsville" would don a Washington uniform. Press members also understood that Ed planned to repay the advance money John T. Brush gave him.[53] Considering his present physical condition and weight, Delahanty appeared at a distinct disadvantage compared to his teammates.[54] Before talking with Tom, Ed had sat in the comforting shelter of the clubhouse for the past two to three weeks watching his colleagues smack the horsehide all over American League Park as they prepared for the upcoming baseball campaign. The Senators' skipper appeared pleased after the two men settled all their disagreements.

"I know the value of Delahanty as much as anyone," said Loftus. "There are better fielders and better baserunners, but where can be found his equal with a bat? I was offered $5,000 for Delahanty, but the Washington Club is not in the selling business now. He is worth just as much to me as to any other club. With Delahanty back in the fold, the Washington team is particularly well fortified with utility men."

Washington's correspondent for the *Sporting News*, John F. Luitich, reported that Senators ownership and Ed had reached an agreement regarding paying back the $4,000 advance money owed to the New York Giants.[55] On April 19, 1903, one day before the American League season started, Ban Johnson arrived at National League headquarters and delivered a $4,000 check for Harry Pulliam so the Senior Circuit's president could give it to that organization's New York club. Senators ownership agreed to pay back half the obligation while Ed retained $2,000 of the advance sum and received the $4,000 in salary agreed upon when signing a two-year contract with Washington prior to the 1902 campaign.[56] Based on some reports that the Senators agreed to pay Delahanty $6,000 to play for them in 1903, in a roundabout way stretching accounting methods, Johnson included one-third of that money in the check he gave to Pulliam.[57] Ban offered a brief explanation of how this process played out.

"I received the $4,000 from the management of our Washington Club and left it at Mr. Pulliam's office to be forwarded to the New York National League Club," explained Ban. "Delahanty is now free and clear to fulfill his contract with the Washington Club, and he will play on the Washington team during the entire season. No matter how tempting the offers may be to secure his services elsewhere, none of them will be entertained."[58]

While taking the high ground, Ban Johnson's pie-in-the-sky thinking only worked when dealing with a compliant individual. On the other hand, this was not the case when it involved a disgruntled, overweight, and out-of-shape ballplayer who could earn more money and improve his financial stability by playing for a different team. Shortly after the season started, Del worked out an arrangement to join younger brother Thomas "Tom" Delahanty on the Western League's Denver Grizzlies. Ed planned to jump Washington and leave for Denver on Friday night, April 24. Fearing such a move could bring condemnation from baseball's big dogs, Western League and Minor League

Association officials burned up the wires sending messages to one another.[59] National Association of Professional Baseball Leagues secretary John H. Farrell judiciously reacted to a very problematic dispatch from Western League president Michael Sexton.

"Delahanty, of Washington, accepted terms with Denver and wants to report there now," read Sexton's message. "Shall I permit deal to go through or stop it? Answer quick."

John H. Farrell promptly replied to Michael Sexton's critical inquiry.

"Stop it by all means," responded Farrell over the wire. "We should not embarrass the discipline of the major leagues in this, their most important case, nor deprive the Washington Club and the American League of one of its most valuable assets—Player Delahanty. We expect fair treatment from the American and National leagues. Piracy and honesty never entered into partnership."[60]

Playing for Denver might have proved a much better option for Ed Delahanty rather than sticking it out with the hapless Senators. After starting the season 4–3 in their first seven games at American League Park, the club embarked on a month-long road trip that proved disastrous, as Washington posted a 6–20 record while away from home. When the team played in New York, a sportswriter witnessed Delahanty staggering down a street drunk. While away, Ed also visited his sick wife, Norine, in Philadelphia.[61] During this road trip's initial stages, Washington's *Evening Star* wrote that many fans thought Delahanty resembled a professional fat gentleman who escaped from the circus.[62] This excessive weight proved a detriment, as the former star player struggled at the plate and in the field due to his lack of conditioning.[63]

Although his batting average plummeted to .225 following a game against the Boston Americans at Huntington Avenue Baseball Grounds on May 4, Ed rebounded at the plate. Delahanty went 2-for-4 two days later versus Boston and then combined to go 9-for-27 in the next two series against Philadelphia and the St. Louis Browns, pushing his average up to .282. Because Ed injured his back while playing in St. Louis, manager Tom Loftus did not use him in a series against the Chicago White Sox. When Loftus sent Del up to pinch hit in the contest versus Cleveland on May 19 at League Park, Naps hurler Clarence Eugene "Gene" Wright easily retired him on a harmless groundball. After the game, Tom sent Ed to Mount Clemens, Michigan, where the benefits of that resort's hot baths and spring water could help drop some of his excessive weight and round the player into shape.[64] Delahanty returned to the starting lineup on May 29 and went 2-for-3 at the plate as Boston defeated Washington, 7-2, at Huntington Avenue Baseball Grounds.

Unable to play up to his capabilities because of carrying extra weight and being out of shape, Ed became sullen and melancholy. Delahanty also professed unhappiness over Loftus moving him from his regular left field position to the right garden while inserting Albert "Kip" Selbach in the veteran player's old spot. Initially, Ed balked at the move, causing Loftus to assert his authority, a tactic that eventually led Del to accept this change.[65] Delahanty objected to the switch since his new position placed him in the sun field at American League Park. Ed also loafed on many occasions in right field. In a home game against St. Louis on June 4, the Browns scored six runs off Senators hurler Case "Casey" Patten in the fifth inning. Of the five hits Patten allowed that frame, three were easy flyballs to short right field that Delahanty should have reached without exerting much energy.[66]

Dissension crept into the Washington team members' mindset as dissatisfaction and malaise gripped the squad. Ed certainly did not love his job. A beacon of hope extinguished as quickly as it had started burning brightly. News of a potential trade involving the Senators sending Delahanty and first baseman Scoops Carey to the Highlanders for first baseman John Ganzel and second baseman Jimmy Williams briefly delighted the struggling ballplayer.[67] Unfortunately for Del, the deal never occurred.

The next ensuing road trip following a two-week homestand spelled more disaster for the lowly Senators, who occupied last place in the American League when they opened a series against St. Louis on June 19 at Sportsman's Park. This game, which the Browns won, 4–0, embarked Washington on an eight-game losing streak. Manager Tom Loftus, feeling pressure over his squad's abysmal diamond performance, lost his composure during the contest against the Browns on June 20. When Tom started heckling St. Louis's Jesse Burkett as he batted, the player asked umpire Thomas "Tommy" Connolly to force the Senators' skipper to shut his mouth. Connolly refused. Unable to endure the insults any longer, Burkett challenged Loftus. The two men engaged in a pushing match, as Tom later termed it, which evolved into a scrap.

Immediately after the game ended, Browns owner Robert Hedges offered his opinion about this unseemly incident. Although Hedges did not defend Burkett, he declared that Loftus, the manager and partial owner of a major league baseball club, did not deserve any consideration, even from the most despicable specimen of humanity living. Loftus had used atrocious, indecent language in the dispute. Robert also alleged Tom attacked his player while in an inebriated condition. That night, a *St. Louis Star* reporter visited Loftus at his room in the Southern Hotel. The manager's face and nose remained puffy from the earlier skirmish, although he had partaken in a cold plunge in icy water, hoping to reduce the swelling. Tom told the pundit Jesse must have been crazy for singling him out since everybody on Washington's bench had shouted at the Browns' outfielder. Loftus then refused to divulge any other details and asked the sportswriter to excuse him and not press the subject further.

"It is useless to say anything now," continued Loftus, "the affair was bad enough without making it any worse discussing it."

That same evening, the entire Senators' squad sat outside in front of the hotel, discussing their manager's dilemma. This affair cast a deeper gloom on team members than the misery that already existed. On June 23, upon reviewing the umpire's report regarding this incident, Ban Johnson suspended Loftus for five days, fined Jesse $50, and severely reprimanded Connolly for allowing the pushing match to morph into a full-blown fight.[68] Things had already started eerily for the players when the club traveled to St. Louis. Ed Delahanty drank heavily on the train. After consuming so much alcohol, Ed's demeanor took a morbid shift as he started talking about death. His teammates did not place much credence in Delahanty's mood, although they were fully aware of his personal problems. Some suspected marital issues and Ed's jealous nature toward Norine.[69]

When Washington arrived in Cleveland on June 25 for the third leg of their western swing, Delahanty went 1-for-4 at the plate as the Naps defeated the Senators, 4–0, at League Park. Following that afternoon's game, Ed visited his mother, sister, and two younger brothers at his parents' home. After spending time with his family, Del went on a drinking binge, leaving him in no condition to play the game against Cleveland on June 26. Ed did not report to the hotel where the team stayed as expected. Instead, Delahanty's sister called the suspended Tom Loftus and told him her brother was sick. Consequently, Loftus found out drunkenness acted as the true culprit for Ed's condition.[70] When the Senators' players returned to the hotel following their 1–0 defeat at the hands of the Naps, Ed was traversing the city, having a good time with alcohol as his companion.[71] Washington's *Sporting Life* correspondent, Paul W. Eaton, described the situation regarding Delahanty.

"When the club reached Cleveland, June 25," wrote Eaton, "Del proceeded to do a sensational tank act, and was soon filled with enthusiasm, and he doesn't take his with sugar in it, either, as was shown by his making several scenes and threatening other players and himself with a knife."[72]

Eaton also alleged that Ed had not been prone to excessive drinking before this season. The sportswriter declared such conduct in 1903 became an uncontrollable habit of indulging well beyond anything considered good or healthy for the player. Eaton supposed heavy gambling losses or the situation regarding the peace agreement not allowing Delahanty to play for the New York Giants might explain his alcohol-induced, erratic behavior over the past few months.[73] Delahanty may have also believed his station in life related to that second point could change. The Detroit Tigers traded shortstop Kid Elberfeld to the New York Highlanders on June 10. This maneuver brought about a policy change by National League president Harry Pulliam. On June 26, Pulliam issued a statement regarding his reversal in allowing George Davis to play for the New York Giants.

According to Pulliam, after the two major leagues reached peace in January and the player dispersal committee awarded Del, Davis, and Elberfeld to their American League clubs, Giants owner John T. Brush appealed this ruling on the grounds that no such agreement had the right to invalidate a legal contract. In March, when Highlanders president Joseph Gordon expressed interest in acquiring Ed and George, Harry discussed the matter with Ban Johnson. Following their discussion, the heads of each respective league decided it would be unfair to take players away from New York's National League entry and allow them to play for their American League counterpart. Within this discussion, Pulliam and Johnson agreed that none of their clubs should trade the three disputed players throughout that campaign. Harry, reasoning the American League broke this bond of trust when Detroit shipped Kid to New York, withdrew his objection and permitted Brush to play Davis until the other organization could exhibit just cause contrary to his decision.[74]

Davis appeared in four games for the Giants from June 26 through July 1. Federal Judge Edward B. Thomas stopped this venture by issuing a temporary order restraining George from playing with any team other than the Chicago White Sox. A court agent served Davis with this injunction while enjoying a day at the Brighton Beach Race Course at Coney Island, New York.[75] After only seeing action in those four contests in 1903, George remained on the sidelines throughout the campaign's duration and returned to Chicago in 1904. This scenario impacted Ed Delahanty's shameful behavior. Ed missed the doubleheader split between the Naps and Senators at League Park on Saturday, June 27. Under the watchful eye of teammate James "Jimmy" Ryan, Delahanty appeared sober as the team traveled across Lake Erie by boat to their next destination in Detroit to play the Tigers.[76] Ryan had encouraged Ed to make the trip by boat train, feeling a night on the lake would do him good and lift his spirits.

When Washington arrived in Detroit, Delahanty continued drinking.[77] Ed's state once again rendered him unable to compete on the diamond. Aware that Del's debilitating condition was leading him to ruin, Senators players started chiding their teammate over his conduct.[78] They also noticed a darker, deeply despondent tone that included morbid remarks, leading teammates to feel he should never be alone. Acting on this notion, a team member always remained with Delahanty.[79] Ed also continued suffering delirium tremens, a condition seen in chronic heavy drinkers dealing with alcohol withdrawal, causing extreme perspiration.[80] Suspicious of his teammates' intentions, Delahanty once again threatened them with a knife before breaking down from fatigue, his quivering body drenched in sweat.[81]

Washington club officials summoned Del's mother, Bridget, and two brothers to Detroit. With assistance from a doctor, family members calmed down Ed in his room at the Oriental Hotel.[82] Following an intervention by loved ones and teammates on Tuesday, June 30, Delahanty promised to abstain from drinking alcohol and took a temperance pledge. Ed remained sober on Wednesday and most of Thursday as the Senators finished their series versus the Tigers.[83] Before deciding to reform his life, Delahanty and his mother went to a local Catholic church and received counseling from a priest. After this mediation, Ed promised to treat his teammates and manager with respect and dignity while vowing to no longer touch red eye whiskey.[84] Delahanty felt embarrassed and humiliated when a Detroit newspaper printed an article on July 1 about signing the pledge to cut out alcohol following a confrontation with his mother.[85]

Before Ed promised to take a sobriety pledge, a Detroit friend acted as his companion while he caroused about town. This person later said that the situation involving Kid Elberfeld moving over to the New York Highlanders and Harry Pulliam allowing George Davis to play for the New York Giants convinced Del it shattered the peace agreement to pieces. This caused Ed to firmly believe John T. Brush and John McGraw might be willing to allow him to join the Giants at a salary that paid him more than he earned with Washington.[86] On July 2, Senators third baseman William "Bill" Coughlin searched for Delahanty so he could return a diamond ring that his teammate allowed him to wear on the trip. While on this road excursion, Ed sported expensive jewelry that included rings, pins, and diamonds belonging to a Washington jeweler, who entrusted the ballplayer with selling some of these items to team members.[87]

That afternoon, Detroit defeated the Senators, 1–0. Ed Delahanty did not accompany his teammates to Bennett Park for the game. The schedule called for the entire club to depart that city at 10:30 P.M. from the railroad station and travel back to Washington. When the squad returned to the Oriental Hotel, upon inquiry, a clerk informed them Ed had departed the premises that afternoon.[88] Delahanty left behind his Senators uniform in the hotel room.[89] Before checking out, Del wrote his wife, Norine, asking her to leave Philadelphia and meet him in Washington. He also talked about a lapsed accident insurance policy that named his five-year-old daughter, Florence, as the beneficiary.[90] Ed then hustled to the railway station, purchased a ticket for New York, and exited Detroit on the 4:25 P.M. Michigan Central Railroad train, expecting to arrive in Buffalo, New York, at 9 P.M. Delahanty had not alerted his teammates to his intentions and left some personal items behind with his uniform.[91]

In his message to Norine, Ed stated that he expected to reach Grand Central Station in New York City the following morning. Delahanty wore a fashionable blue suit for this journey.[92] In the letter to his wife, Ed also mentioned that he wished the train jumped the tracks and crashed.[93] Before corresponding with Norine, Del possibly broke his temperance pledge. Part of the train ticket package included a Pullman berth, a benefit that also allowed the privilege of using the dining car, where they served alcohol and tobacco. Initially, Ed behaved, quietly sitting in the dining car, stewing over his plight, smoking a cigarette, and ordering a drink of whiskey to calm the nerves. The tranquility did not last long, as Delahanty's behavior quickly aggravated the train's conductor, John Cole.[94]

According to Cole, Del caused trouble through various disturbances. The conductor claimed Ed consumed five drinks of alcohol in the dining car, pulled two travelers out of their sleeper berths, and threatened him with a straight razor.[95] Cole's account stipulated Delahanty terrorized passengers with this open blade.[96] Ed also constantly rang the train's service bell, which further peeved the conductor. Delahanty smoked one cigarette after another in the dining car, which, according to Cole, rules prohibited. After the conductor talked with Ed about this matter, he stopped smoking. John once again confronted the ballplayer when a porter refused to serve him any more alcohol. A troubled and angry Delahanty then caused a commotion by breaking his glass. Cole told Ed he needed to pay three dollars to replace the glass and alerted him that the ballplayer must abide by Canadian law since that happened to be where the train traveled at the time. Delahanty replied that he did not care if the train was in Canada or Hell. The conductor then ordered Ed another whiskey.[97]

Ed Delahanty became obedient and fell asleep in the dining car. When the train reached Bridgeburg, a town near Fort Erie, Ontario, Delahanty awoke from his slumber in a disoriented state. Believing the locomotive had arrived at its Buffalo destination, Ed rushed to his sleeping berth to retrieve his bag. Unfortunately, the aisleway's poor lighting caused Del to enter the wrong berth. Amidst the confusion, Ed and other individuals exchanged angry words. Alerted to the disturbance, John Cole arrived to find Delahanty involved in a physical confrontation with a porter and two other conductors.[98] Tired of his behavior and antics, Cole expelled Ed from Michigan Central Railroad Train No. 6 for drunkenness and left him at the Bridgeburg depot.

The conductor did not follow proper protocol since John Cole should have turned Delahanty over to a constable as Canadian law dictated. As the train crossed the International Railway Bridge above the Niagara River toward Buffalo, Ed started following as it disappeared into the distance. This was illegal; safety rules did not permit pedestrian traffic on the bridge.[99] The *Washington Times* reported that before his removal, an error regarding Delahanty's purchased ticket revealed that the ballplayer traveled on the wrong Pullman with a one-way voucher to take him in the opposite direction he wanted to go, which a ticket puncher discovered when confronting him.¹⁰⁰ Realizing he needed to reach his next destination to meet with manager John McGraw before the Giants left New York and embarked on a western road trip, Ed forged onward by foot at 10:55 P.M.¹⁰¹ Delahanty started walking across the single-track railroad structure on the Canadian side of the Niagara River that widened to about one-half mile at that point. The bridge did not include a footwalk.

While on the bridge, Ed encountered watchman Samuel "Sam" Kingston, who stopped him from continuing his trek. A verbal dispute ensued, followed by a scuffle. When the brief fracas ended, Kingston placed Delahanty's hat on his head by mistake, rather than his own.¹⁰² The employee later alleged the draw of the bridge had been opened to allow a ship to pass through.¹⁰³ According to Sam, following this altercation, Ed started running toward the American side of the bridge when his attention became diverted elsewhere. Kingston claimed Delahanty either fell or jumped into the river, calling for help several times after splashing into the water before the current swept him away.¹⁰⁴

Unaware that his player had met a tragic demise, manager Tom Loftus lashed out at Ed on the evening of July 4, following the Senators' 10–3 victory over Cleveland that afternoon in their first contest after returning from the long road trip. Up to this point, Loftus only knew that Del had deserted the club. Tom, not sure of his whereabouts, exclaimed Ed had been useless to the squad throughout their recently completed western swing.

"I am tired of being a good-fellow now," said the manager, "when he turns up he will be disciplined, and severely at that. I don't care to discuss the matter too freely now, because Mrs. Delahanty is here, and is deeply mortified over her husband's conduct, but wait?"

The heavy tone while concluding his remark for the press indicated that such punishment might be severe.¹⁰⁵ Before Big Ed's disappearance, Loftus suspended him without pay until he worked himself into proper condition for playing good baseball.

Norine Delahanty arrived in Washington on July 3 to meet Del. Extremely distressed over her husband vanishing, Norine telegraphed various people attempting to establish his whereabouts. Tom also made numerous inquiries to several places. Mrs. Delahanty and Ed's family in Cleveland feared something horrible happened to him.¹⁰⁶ Following a request from Washington chief of police, Major Richard Sylvester, Marshal Samuel Trew of Mount Clemens started a fruitless search for Delahanty in his town.¹⁰⁷

All involved parties finally found out the heartbreaking news about Ed Delahanty. On July 7, Loftus received a letter from John K. Blunett, district superintendent for the Michigan Central Railroad. In this correspondence,

Blunett explained the problems conductor John Cole experienced with an unruly passenger on a train that traveled to Buffalo on the night of July 2. Following ejection from the train, the district superintendent explained, the traveler in question experienced a confrontation with a bridge tender on the International Railway Bridge and then fell or plunged into the Niagara River. Although Blunett could not positively identify Delahanty based on encounters with witnesses that fateful night, the Michigan Central Railroad company possessed the suitcase he had left behind. It contained complimentary pass No. 26 to enter Washington Senators home games at American League Park. The district superintendent hoped the baseball club could identify this individual and convey his death's unfortunate circumstances to the family.[108]

Blunett also sent a similar letter to M. S. Johnson, a Washington tailor. The district superintendent wrote that the valise left behind by an unruly passenger contained a suit of clothing made by Johnson for E. J. Delahanty of the Washington club. Blunett requested verification from this individual that he had tailored the suit. Upon receiving this letter, Johnson notified Tom Loftus that he designed this clothing item for Delahanty. Given this new evidence, Loftus, concluding Ed had met an untimely end, notified his wife, Norine, who became devastated over her husband's death.[109] The Michigan Central Railroad superintendent also received the address of Delahanty's family from the tailor. He then wrote to Norine Delahanty, informing her of the circumstances involving what happened on the night of July 2, stating he believed her husband had fallen off the bridge and drowned.[110] The Senators' organization verified they had issued baseball pass ticket No. 26 to Del. In the eyes of Washington's manager and players, this offered conclusive proof that Delahanty had died.[111]

Upon receiving the news that Ed had drowned, brother Frank Delahanty, who played for the New York State League's Syracuse Stars, left at noon on July 8 to travel to Buffalo.[112] From there, Frank linked up with brother-in-law Edward J. Maguire and uncle J. E. Croke, a Buffalo Exchange Street broker, in Fort Erie. Once there, they joined forces with Police Chief Richard Griffin to investigate the affair. The party immediately searched out sixty-five-year-old bridge watchman Sam Kingston, who related his first-hand account regarding Ed Delahanty to family members.

According to Kingston, after conductor John Cole banished Ed from the Michigan Central Railroad train, the traveler seemed intent on reaching Buffalo and catching another Pullman to Washington to keep an appointment to meet his wife. Sam affirmed the two crossed paths when Delahanty walked on the bridge. While flashing a lantern on the ballplayer's face to see if he could identify him, Kingston asked this individual if he possessed a pass to use the bridge. The bright light immediately angered Delahanty, leading him to fight with the security guard, who perceived the ballplayer did so in self-defense. The two men scuffled back and forth on the bridge three spans away from the open draw, where the ship, *Ossian Bedell*, from nearby Grand Island, New York, passed through.

During the battle, Ed's smashed hat landed on the bridge's floor. Delahanty finally gained an advantage when Sam fell and caught his feet between two railroad ties. Ed broke free and started running away. He did not move toward the open draw three spans away but rather bolted laterally toward the edge of the bridge and fell into the water on the structure's north side. Kingston's version of the story differed from his original claim, where the guard initially stated that the famous ballplayer fell through the open draw of the bridge.[113] Brother-in-law Edward Maguire took notice of this point while discussing discrepancies in the two versions. Maguire also mentioned the discussion he, Croke, and Frank had with Cole.

"Kingston in his first story said he saw Eddie come on the bridge," said Maguire. "Now he says he saw him after he was on the bridge; again at first Kingston said there was a tussle, now he says there was no tussle. Another thing we learned, too, is this: Kingston says Eddie was drunk. Conductor Cole, of the Michigan Central Train, said he was crazy. In fact, we have learned quite a few things. Conductor Cole told me he did not put Eddie off the train in the wilderness because he pulled women out of the berths in the train. The conductor said it was not until Eddie began to attack people with a razor that he was put off. I know positively Eddie never carried anything but a safety."

Maguire and Frank Delahanty refuted the narrative that Del had started drinking because of jealousy toward his wife. They also denied that Ed left his mother, Bridget Croke Delahanty, destitute, but they suspected the possibility of foul play involving Washington's player. Frank quickly took aim at who he believed owned responsibility for the unfortunate course of events that occurred.

"I have some suspicion about how Ed went off that bridge," said Frank Delahanty. "The poor fellow's dead now, and he can never tell his side of the story, but the others (Delahanty would not mention the names of the persons to whom he referred) can tell just what they please. You can say this much for me—that the railroad is responsible for Ed's death. They had no business putting him off where they did. Even if he killed a man they should have brought him to Buffalo and turned him over to the police. If he was drunk and disorderly aboard that train they should have taken care of him. He drank and paid for the whiskey they sold him, and it was their whiskey he got drunk on. Then why didn't they carry him here?"[114]

Although the three relatives believed Sam Kingston's story, two of these individuals did not hesitate to lay fault at the feet of the Michigan Central

Railroad. Uncle J. E. Croke echoed Frank Delahanty's sentiment, expressing indignation while talking with a *Buffalo Courier* reporter.

> From all I have been able to learn, Eddie was all right when he got on the train at Detroit. He went in the buffet car and I know from railroad employees he sat in there for four or five hours spending his money and drinking. They sold him the drinks, but when he became intoxicated and boisterous they ejected him from the train. I wouldn't care if they had brought him across the river to Buffalo and then put him off, but they had no right to put him off in the wilderness.
>
> When he was good enough to spend his money on the train they should have been good enough to care for him. And, furthermore, if he was bad enough to have to be put off the train, he was bad enough to be put into the custody of an officer. If they had carried him to Buffalo he could have been arrested. Arrest would be preferable to allowing a man to get killed.

The uncle also added that although Ed Delahanty possessed a diamond stud worth $600, two diamond rings on his fingers, and others in the vest pocket valued at $2,000 while also carrying $200 in cash, he did not believe these valuables figured in his death. J. E. Croke, Edward Maguire, and Frank Delahanty made their statements once the trio arrived in Buffalo after leaving Fort Erie. In conducting a rigid investigation with Chief of Police Richard Griffin through interviewing numerous witnesses, the three family members concluded nobody murdered Ed Delahanty, and he did not commit suicide.[115] Each of these relatives believed the railroad company liable for what happened, since Delahanty would have lived on if employees had tolerated his behavior until the locomotive reached Buffalo.

On July 9, a body believed to be Del's washed up in the lower gorge of the Niagara River. Authorities immediately notified the ballplayer's relatives.[116] Some rivermen found the body in a whirlpool near where the *Maid of the Mist* sightseeing boat docked. Ed's body had gone over Niagara's Horseshoe Falls, stripped of all clothing except his shoes, stockings, and necktie due to the waterway's powerful current.[117] Delahanty's body appeared bloated and badly mangled. The *Maid of the Mist*'s propellor had possibly almost completely severed off one of his legs. M. A. Green, a stockholder in the Senators' club, identified Ed's body at the village of Niagara Falls through his teeth, two crippled fingers, and clothing. Local authorities immediately shipped the remains to Washington. That same morning, Green also positively identified the luggage left on the train as belonging to Del. The Pullman Company sent these personal effects to Norine Delahanty.[118]

Ed Delahanty's body arrived in Cleveland on July 10. A viewing occurred at his parents' home. On Saturday, July 11, the funeral service took place at the Church of the Immaculate Conception. Monsignor Thomas P. Thorpe, who officiated the funeral mass, spoke of Delahanty's admirable disposition and unstained character. Once the service ended, eight pallbearers, including New York Giants manager John McGraw, carried the casket to the hearse, taking Ed to his final resting place at Calvary Cemetery.[119] Delahanty's death left his wife and daughter in a destitute situation. Although Ed held membership with the Fraternal Order of Eagles, Erie Lodge No. 42, in Philadelphia, he had been negligent in paying dues. Norine would receive no benefits unless the organization's members started their own collection.[120]

Friends and fellow players of the former baseball icon started raising money for a fund to benefit Norine and Florence. Washington manager Tom Loftus decreed that individuals send all charitable contributions care of him at the Hotel Oxford.[121] Twenty-four years old at the time of her husband's death, Mrs. Delahanty sued the Michigan Central Railroad in court for their reckless disregard on the train that night. On May 4, 1904, a jury awarded Norine $3,000 and Florence $2,000. Unfortunately, after the railroad company appealed this judgment, a Toronto, Ontario, appellate court overturned the original decision. Lack of funds prevented Mrs. Delahanty from challenging that verdict.[122] When rivermen discovered Del's body on July 9, the $200 in his pocket when leaving Detroit and diamonds valued at over $2,000 belonging to a Washington jeweler were missing. Law enforcement surmised these items forever lost, because the river's strong current tore Delahanty's clothing off his body.[123]

Upon recovery of Ed's body, Tom Delahanty, who played for the Denver Grizzlies, believed beyond a doubt it was his brother's, although he had received a telegram confirming a sighting in Indiana. Tom based this on a positive identification from J. E. Croke through Del's pinky finger and teeth filled with gold. From Denver, the younger Delahanty talked of someone murdering his brother since he always wore two rings and a large diamond stud on his tie. Neither item turned up with the body despite authorities recovering that tie, minus the diamond.[124] Former Philadelphia Phillies teammate William "Bill" Hallman appeared to agree with Tom, finding it unfathomable that Ed could have drowned.

"Ed Delahanty was almost as skilled as Paul Boyton [an accomplished swimmer and adventurer from that period] in the water," said Hallman. "He was a miraculous swimmer, and I cannot understand how it was he drowned when he fell from the railroad bridge near Kingston. I fear foul play. I know well the bridge in question. At the point Ed fell off, there is a fall of not more than 30 feet to the water. Del—even if he was intoxicated, poor fellow—would have sobered up enough by the fall to have paddled to shore. He and I had many swims together in the Delaware River, and the Atlantic Ocean. He could outswim me or any other player in the profession. In fact, there were but few men in the country who were as much at home in the water as he was. I have seen him do all kinds of tricks in the Atlantic Ocean even when it was at its worst."

Obviously, Hallman had Sam Kingston on his mind when referring to Bridgeburg as Kingston, Ontario. While Billy vouched for Delahanty's prowess as a swimmer, he did not mention if that expertise included drunkenness while navigating the Atlantic Ocean or suffering from inebriation if finding a thirty-foot drop from a bridge while diving into the Delaware River. Bill continued by declaring he had seen Ed one week before his death. To Hallman, the iconic ballplayer, nattily attired and adorned in $1,500 worth of sparkling diamonds, never looked more prosperous in his life. Bill asserted Del told him he no longer experienced financial difficulty, before saying, "I'm solvent again."[125]

As had been the case months earlier regarding Win Mercer's suicide, mystery shrouded Ed Delahanty's tragic death. One distinct difference did exist. While Mercer legitimately exuded the boy-next-door persona, Delahanty became rough around the edges, especially when consuming alcohol. Despite this noticeable contrast, the tragic deaths of these popular, star baseball players did hold two interesting links.

*In the 1890s, Philadelphia Phillies outfielder **Ed Delahanty** gained status as one of the National League's supreme batters. He led the circuit in hitting in 1899 and then paced the American League in 1902 after jumping to the Washington Senators. Suffering heavy losses that winter while gambling at New Orleans racetracks, Ed signed a lucrative deal to play for the New York Giants in 1903, although still under contract with Washington. After the two leagues reached a peace agreement in January, Delahanty became disgruntled when a committee tasked with ruling on disputed players awarded him to the Senators. On July 2, 1903, while walking along the International Railway Bridge after conductor John Cole expelled Ed from a Buffalo bound train, the ballplayer fell into the Niagara River and drowned. (Photo in the Public Domain).*

CHAPTER 4

Eddie Doheny

Breakdown on the Eve of the First Modern World Series

Two links existed between the Win Mercer and Ed Delahanty tragedies in 1903. These individuals enjoyed wagering on the ponies and reveling in games of chance. In both cases, a desire to place bets at numerous racetracks plunged Mercer and Delahanty into debt. Coupled with pressure and subsequent stress related to maintaining the lofty expectations as diamond performers and human beings established by others, such an obstacle brought about heartbreaking consequences for both men and their families. Sportswriter Paul Eaton reported that during the off-season prior to the 1903 baseball campaign, Delahanty lost $4,000 in one day while placing wagers at a New Orleans horse racetrack.[1] In attempting to convince Ed to abandon the Senators and sign with New York, Giants manager John McGraw engaged the ballplayer in discussion on one occasion at the Benning Race Track in Washington, D.C.[2]

As he did in his column that appeared in the *Evening Star*'s Sunday edition on August 4, 1907, turf writer Clarence L. Cullen examined Ed Delahanty's penchant for playing the ponies and Win Mercer's poor luck at the racetrack. According to Cullen, when he first encountered Delahanty in Washington following his disastrous winter gambling in New Orleans, the writer claimed Ed appeared to be a most melancholy man when they shook hands. Clarence concluded Delahanty had arrived in no condition to play baseball, overdrawn to the hilt and attempting to grab as much money as possible from two different organizations. The winter itinerary had led Ed to grow well above his playing weight. Cullen declared that once games started, Delahanty looked lethargic, could not catch his breath while running, lost his sharp batting eye, and, most importantly, displayed no love or passion for his work. Clarence concluded his article by affirming that those who knew Ed believed he would still be alive and well four years later if not for his gambling addiction.[3]

As the sports world mourned the losses of two popular players because of tragic circumstances, the Pittsburgh Pirates battled to secure their third consecutive National League pennant while under the leadership of skipper Fred "Cap" Clarke and owner Barney Dreyfuss. In 1901, Pittsburgh won their first flag in franchise history when they posted a 90–49 record and finished 7 ½ games ahead of the second-place Philadelphia Phillies. One year later, the Pirates obliterated the rest of the league in 1902, fashioning a flashy 103–36 mark that allowed them to pace the runner-up Brooklyn Superbas by 27 ½ games. Following this phenomenally successful season, Clarke lost star hurlers Jesse Tannehill and Jack Chesbro, who defected to the American League's New York Highlanders.

The National League race proved much tighter in 1903 as the Giants and Chicago Cubs offered formidable opposition to the Pirates. Dreyfuss and the Buccaneers' manager brought in numerous youngsters to replace Tannehill and Chesbro, along with veteran twirler William "Brickyard" Kennedy. The bulk of the hill work fell to stalwart hurlers Charles "Deacon" Phillippe and Samuel "Sam" Leever. For most of the season, these two mound bulwarks received solid support from southpaw pitcher Edward Richard Doheny (pronounced Dorney), who had joined the club in the summer of 1901. Regrettably, Doheny started suffering from mental illness as the campaign progressed, leaving him unable to help his teammates as they battled to capture the National League flag. Ultimately, an unforeseen catastrophic event cast a deep pall on another productive season and ended a baseball career.

People referred to Edward Doheny as "Ed" and then "Eddie" when he played for Pittsburgh. Doheny's Pirates teammates nicknamed the hurler "Irish" because of his heritage.[4] Ed was born to parents James and Mary O'Connor Doheny on November 24, 1873, in Northfield, Vermont. Doheny received his education at Northfield High School and Norwich University.[5] Ed gravitated toward baseball at an early age and quickly learned the game's nuances. He mastered the art of curving a baseball and threw left-handed, a commodity during that era. Becoming a pitcher best suited the youngster's talent. Doheny experienced success and gained a considerable reputation hurling for several amateur clubs and the Norwich nine in his hometown. Upon accepting his first professional assignment in 1894, Ed looked to pitching for a club in Farnham, Quebec. In 1895, Doheny hooked up with Vermont's St. Albans baseball squad. As Ed's status rose while on the bump for St. Albans, he attracted the attention of many major league managers.[6]

Although Doheny exhibited bouts of wildness on the mound, his ability and potential teased admirers. One of those devotees was Howard L. Hindley, a dispatcher on the Central Vermont Railroad and later as the editor of the *Rutland Herald*. Hindley referred to Ed as the "man with the iron arm." Howard fell so much in love with Doheny's talent that he sent a letter to Boston sportswriter and New England League president Timothy "Tim" Murnane, praising the young hurler. When the Boston Beaneaters made a trip to New York in 1895, Murnane and a press colleague visited Giants owner Andrew Freedman. Desirous of bolstering his pitching staff, Freedman asked Tim if he possessed any knowledge regarding a good southpaw pitcher he might purchase. After frankly replying negatively, Murnane pulled out Hindley's letter from his pocket.

"Here is a letter from a fan up in St. Albans, Vermont, who says that there is a pitcher working for the St. Albans Club in the Northern League who is a wonder and fit for the big league," said Murnane. "You might take a chance and give him a trial. It will not cost you a cent except car fares and expenses."

"I'll do it," exclaimed Freedman, "and if he makes good I'll give you $100."[7]

Near the end of the 1895 campaign, Ed Doheny received a brief trial with the Giants. Doheny proved unimpressive, tossing three complete games, losing each start, and posting a 6.66 ERA while exhibiting wildness by walking 19 batters. Ed did a little better for New York in 1896, going 6–7, supported by a 4.49 ERA. Inferior support behind him from a second-division club contributed to some of those defeats.[8] For part of that year, the Giants farmed out Doheny to the Atlantic League's New York Metropolitans, along with fellow twirlers Miles Standish and James "Cy" Seymour.[9] Ed soon found that toiling for an owner like Freedman could be unbearable. Hurler Win Mercer only tolerated playing one season for the Giants in 1900 because of a strong aversion toward Andrew's tyrannical approach overseeing his baseball empire.[10]

Andrew Freedman became the Giants' majority owner at the beginning of 1895. Baseball writer John B. Sheridan referred to Freedman as corrupt political boss Richard Croker's henchman when it came to New York's Tammany Hall machine. Sheridan alleged that Andrew's chief motivation was grabbing as much money as he could while owning the Giants. To achieve this, Freedman abused players and managers, tormented umpires, and scorned any fellow owners or league officials who stood in his way. Shortly after the 1901 baseball season ended, Andrew devised a failed scheme to turn the National League into a syndicate corporation. Under this plan, Freedman proposed receiving 30 percent of the organization's profits. Fellow magnates friendly to the Tammany Hall man would reap 12 percent for their trouble, while Chicago's, Philadelphia's, and Pittsburgh's owners could count on only getting 8–10 percent.[11]

Before the 1897 baseball season commenced, Ed Doheny participated in a blessed event regarding his brother Daniel. Ed stood as Daniel Doheny's best man at the brother's wedding in Copperfield, Vermont, on January 27 to Mary O'Sullivan of St. Albans. Reverend Joseph Paquet officiated the ceremony held in Copperfield's Catholic church. The newlyweds left immediately for their honeymoon after the mass ended. Sister Kathleen Doheny played the organ and sang "Ave Maria" during the wedding ceremony. Nellie O'Sullivan acted as Mary's bridesmaid.[12]

Giants manager Scrappy Bill Joyce selected Doheny to do the honors in both the 1897 campaign's initial tilt and at the Polo Grounds' home opener. Against the Philadelphia Phillies at National League Park on April 22, Ed suffered a 5–1 defeat. In the April 26 contest at the Polo Grounds versus the Washington Nationals, umpire Thomas "Tom" Lynch ended the diamond clash in the tenth inning, with the score tied 3–3, when a rainstorm, wind, and darkness rendered it impossible to continue.[13] New York's newspapers felt Doheny did fine work in both outings, especially in the game versus the Senators.

"Young Ed Doheny," wrote New York's *The Sun*, "the Vermont boy, was the hero, and he deserved all the praise he received, for he pitched a truly magnificent game and should have carried off a victory at that. Doheny's left-handed delivery was a complete enigma, and with anything like clean support the Washingtons would have had a hard time to escape a shutout."

The *New York Herald* equally praised the hurler's performance against Washington.

"Doheny's pitching," wrote the *New York Herald*, "in the face of his miserable support, was simply grand. It stamps him as one of the 'gamest' young pitchers who ever faced a batsman. It was his good work alone which saved the team from defeat long before the ninth inning."

In another article, the *New York Press* commended both Ed Doheny and Win Mercer for their performances on the mound in the contest between the Giants and the Nationals on April 26.

"Doheny and Mercer were the respective pitchers," stated the *New York Press*. "Both pitched a strong game. The New York southpaw again furnished evidence that in him the club has drawn one of the richest pitching prizes in recent years. The difference between Doheny and Mercer was that Mercer was afforded superb support from his fellow Senators, while the backing up which the Giants gave Doheny was as far removed from superb as Hong Kong is from Hoboken [New Jersey]. Yet, in face of the most disheartening support, Doheny did well to the end."[14]

Ed picked up his first victory of the 1897 season on May 4, defeating Washington, 6–1, at Boundary Field. Doheny baffled the Nationals' batters throughout the afternoon, effectively throwing curveballs that kept opposing players off balance when hoping to secure a clean hit.[15] New York manager Scrappy Bill Joyce quickly became a true believer regarding Ed's vast potential. *Washington Post* sportswriter Joe Campbell also fell into that camp and agreed with the assessments various New York newspapers made following Doheny's first two campaign appearances.

> The Green Mountain south paddle, Doheny was a case of what [National League umpire] Tim Hurst calls the "verdant tissue," otherwise "green goods," for the unsophisticated senators yesterday. In his repertoire Doheny has a choice assortment of the green stuff and the elusive brick of gold in the shape of kinks and shoots. This trick lay out of the Vermonter is calculated to make many a major league batsman look like a Rueben from Booblsville ere the champion season is over.
>
> Doheny is as stocky of anatomy as a chunk of green mountain granite, with his liberal swath of chest and a port side wheel that's as cunning as any south-sided running gear in the league, and this doesn't bar [Frank] King Killen, [Theodore "Ted"] Breitenstein, Bill Hill or Danny Friend. Doheny has speed to burn and a curve that ducks up to the rubber and breaks in front of the plate like the twinkling balls from a Roman candle.[16]

Although Ed received shoddy support from his teammates behind him, the southpaw hurler struggled with command and exhibited wildness. Through his first seven starts, Doheny issued 36 walks, hit six opposing players with offerings, and tossed four wild pitches. Ed also fanned 32 batters, tops among all hurlers on the Giants' staff.[17] While still hindered due to control problems, Doheny seemed destined to experience a breakout season in 1897. Unfortunately, a problem rose to the surface, preventing this from happening. On June 12, New York's baseball organization announced their decision to fine and suspend Ed without pay for insubordination. Doheny displayed insolence when Andrew Freedman took it upon himself to circumvent manager Scrappy Bill Joyce's duties by verbally reprimanding the pitcher.

Rumors abounded that Ed did not enjoy a harmonious relationship with his teammates. The fact that Doheny happened to be a pleasant young man did not deter a clique on the Giants' club from disliking him. Some sportswriters believed this explained why he received feeble support when working on the mound.[18] Freedman determined the suspension would last until he felt Ed had received sufficient discipline. Andrew expressed disdain over his player exchanging harsh words with him during a recent game.[19] *Sporting Life* correspondent

William F. H. Koelsch, who covered the club for that publication, reported Doheny had recently been prone to acting arrogantly and quarreling with several team members. He identified George Davis and Cy Seymour as two of those players. Koelsch also confirmed Ed had threatened to assault Seymour. The scribe claimed management suspended Doheny for two months.[20]

Shortly after receiving his reprimand, Ed Doheny signed a contract to play on a baseball squad in Corning, New York, for the campaign's duration. This act directly defied Freedman and the organization since the club indeed suspended the hurler for two months. Subsequently, because Corning played in a league that did not fall under the umbrella of Major League Baseball's National Agreement, Andrew could not utilize the courts to prevent Doheny from joining that squad.[21] Ed ended up returning to Vermont, hoping to earn money playing baseball while suspended without pay by New York. Doheny joined a squad from Barre, infusing a degree of superiority to the club. He dominated the St. Albans' team in a contest on July 2. Barre went undefeated for the week ending in June and beginning in July, including impressive wins in a doubleheader over a club from Montreal, Quebec. Barre secured the morning game, 11–4, and conquered the boys from Canada, 14–9, in the afternoon affair. Like all other players on this team, Ed only received expenses for his efforts.[22]

Expressing hope over acquiring the New Englander, Boston offered to trade veteran catcher Charles "Charlie" Ganzel to the Giants for Doheny.[23] As Ed's punishment neared its end, New York's *The World* commented on August 9 that once the hurler rejoined the Giants, fans and press members hoped he might start piling up victories. Although Doheny looked to be in peak condition, some people wondered if the hurler would possess a proper state of mind upon returning to the club due to believing the organization had treated him unjustly. The newspaper concluded Ed would pitch his arm off to prove a point before adding that few club executives suspended a star pitcher at a season's critical juncture to assuage upset feelings.[24]

Doheny never appeared in another game during the 1897 campaign. When rooters and writers questioned why Ed did not return to the lineup, manager Scrappy Bill Joyce explained the southpaw hurler suffered from poor health.[25] Doheny started ten games before his suspension, completed each mound assignment, and posted a 4–4 record, supported by a 2.12 ERA. The Giants placed third in the National League race with an 83–48 mark, leaving them 9 ½ games behind the pennant-winning Beaneaters. In the off-season, Ed kept busy refereeing wrestling matches in Vermont, including a big event at the Blanchard Opera House in Montpelier on December 18.[26] Doheny saw more action on the mound for New York in 1898 but did not expand on his immense success in limited duty one year earlier. Ed started 27 games, made one relief appearance, and posted a 7–19 record, braced by a 3.68 ERA. Accusations regarding poor performances and a lack of support from his teammates continued festering.

On June 9, the Chicago Orphans defeated the Giants, 10–8, at the Polo Grounds. Doheny's mound work that afternoon proved an interesting exercise of contrasts, as he pitched erratically at times and dominated during other points in the game. Ed walked seven batters and tossed five wild pitches. He also struck out twelve Orphans players. Chicago committed five errors in the contest, while New York accounted for seven miscues. This comical diamond burlesque exhibition took three hours and eight minutes to complete.[27] Doheny missed time in late July and early August when a sizzling drive struck his pitching hand and drove a ring into his finger. Ed returned to his Northfield home to recuperate.[28] Upon Doheny rejoining the club in late August, fans lamented the fact that the Giants' diamond execution proved substandard when the southpaw pitched.[29]

The actions of these teammates, who supposedly had Ed Doheny's back when he worked on the mound, thrust the young man from Vermont into the limelight because of their egregious behavior. On September 2, Pittsburgh defeated New York, 5–4, at Exposition Park. During the game's initial stages, an insurrection occurred against manager Scrappy Bill Joyce.[30] After only pitching one inning, starter Amos Rusie complained of feeling sick and declared to his manager that he could not continue in the contest.[31] Rusie did a superb job that first frame, easily retiring the Pirates. Amos felt ill in the top of the second inning while running to first base. For the following ten minutes, Pittsburgh's next batter stood waiting as two of Joyce's players refused to obey his directives.[32] After Rusie informed him that he could not continue, Scrappy Bill ordered George Jouett Meekin to replace him. Meekin balked, claiming he suffered from a bad arm.

Joyce then gestured to right fielder Cy Seymour to come in and work on the rubber. Seymour gestured negatively, planted his feet firmly in the turf, folded his arms, and refused to budge from that spot. Scrappy Bill looked around desperately for another solution before he trudged out to right field accompanied by second baseman William "Kid" Gleason and shortstop Jack Doyle, who the Giants had recently re-acquired from Washington for $2,000. When the three men reached Cy, he, too, grumbled about having a sore arm and refused to pitch. Exposition Park's fans started to hoot and holler as Joyce disconsolately turned back toward the diamond. Understanding these two Giants players had staged a mutiny, the spectators yelled insolent questions like, "Who is the manager of the team?" Noticing the deep despair on his manager's face, Ed Doheny jumped off the bench and rolled up his sleeves.[33]

Although Doheny had pitched the previous afternoon, he walked up to Scrappy Bill and offered his services in the box. Pittsburgh's crowd cheered at the plucky hurler's dedication and desire to help the skipper in his time of need. When asking Meekin to replace Amos Rusie and then arguing with Jouett when the twirler refused, Joyce exclaimed it would be unfair to use Ed on consecutive days.[34] Doheny entered the fray without warming up, leading him to walk three Pirates batters in the second inning and hurting New York's chances for victory.[35] Ed pitched a solid game from that point forward. Regrettably, that wildness and his teammates' usual ineptitude in offering support aided Pittsburgh's victory. Regarding the mutiny, one story claimed Doyle opposed Scrappy Bill and aspired to replace him as the squad's captain and manager.[36]

Exhibiting loyalty to a manager many players had turned against did not help that individual in his teammates' eyes. The inclination of Doheny's diamond brethren to not hustle when he eagerly took his turn in the rotation and performed diligently for the Giants compounded this matter. When Ed opposed the Baltimore Orioles at the Polo Grounds in the second game of a doubleheader on September 13, he lost the contest, shortened to seven innings, 5–0. Three days later, Pittsburgh defeated him, 6–0, on the home grounds. New York's *The World* harshly criticized the performance of Ed's teammates in both contests. The newspaper commented that Doheny pitched marvelously against the crack Orioles unit, who struggled to handle his wicked curveball. In the first inning, Baltimore tallied four runs on one scratch hit. The Giants mounted no semblance of a counterattack because they batted and fielded poorly.

Four thousand spectators in attendance at the Polo Grounds took notice of who deserved the blame for this defeat. While showing their general disapproval for most of the squad, the crowd heartily cheered Ed as he walked off the field when an inning ended, or took his turn batting. *The World* called the disgraceful display by other team members one of the plainest cases of a "throw down" in the annals of baseball history. The publication also commented on a noticeable falloff in attendance when Doheny pitched since rooters surmised a loss, likely due to his diamond brothers mailing in their effort, either on purpose or because of disinterest. Concerning the contest against Pittsburgh, this newspaper declared the Giants could only muster six hits, despite an ordinary outing by Pirates pitcher James "Jim" Gardner, before effusively praising Ed.

> It was different with Doheny. He pitched fine ball, probably better than any other twirler on the New York's staff could have done. He also fielded his position well, and, in fact, did everything in his power to win the game. His comrades, apparently, were not with him, and as it was an impossibility for one man to beat nine others, the record of poor Doheny was again besmirched by another defeat.
>
> Even the Pittsburgh players would admit that with any kind of support behind him, Doheny would have won a victory.

The publication then pointed out different moments in the game where the Giants could have pushed some runs across the plate. Critics chalked things up to nothing more than careless baserunning. In his only game with New York, John "Jack" Gilbert cracked a single and then remained planted close to the bag at first, rather than taking a typical lead. When Kid Gleason struck his standard pop fly to the outfield, Pittsburgh's Patrick "Patsy" Donovan muffed it on purpose and forced Gilbert at second base. John "Jack" Warner then connected for a single, moving Gleason to second. As Donovan bluffed throws twice to catch Jack or Kid napping, Warner foolishly started for the keystone sack, and Patsy easily threw him out. In the ninth inning, New York loaded the bases with one out. Those three runners remained cemented to the bags as the Giants' final two batters lofted harmless pop flies *The World* article claimed the players appeared to strategically place, thus ending the team's chances.[37]

The cancer infecting this club ran deeper than a group of players disliking Ed Doheny, so they offered him abysmal support. Consequently, these individuals eventually pushed back after newspapers constantly roasted them for their attitude and performance. In the middle of September, the local press reported that third baseman Frederick "Fred" Hartman abandoned the team and returned home to Pittsburgh. Some stories alleged Fred revolted against receiving a fine, while others stated he left to tend to a sick child. Newspapers also claimed management had fined Jouett Meekin, Amos Rusie, Michael "Mike" Grady, Kid Gleason, Jack Doyle, and Mike Tiernan. Each of these players scoffed and laughed over such ridiculous rumors. Manager Scrappy Bill Joyce denied the notion that dissension existed on the New York Giants.

The case regarding Hartman's situation appeared legitimate. Due to illness, Tiernan, who had not maintained a good relationship with Joyce, retired from the club for the remainder of the campaign. Tales contended that Mike and Scrappy Bill had not coexisted in harmony for some time, and this tension led to the development of an anti-management clique. Such stories in the press affected attendance, as rooters remained away from the ballpark because of insinuations about team discord. Regarding a conspiracy existing whenever Ed Doheny pitched for New York, fellow hurler Jouett Meekin, one of the game's most popular players, made his feelings known on the subject.

"I have been accused by certain so-called critics of being in a conspiracy to drive Eddie Doheny off the New York Club," said Meekin, "I can say that I have roomed with Eddie for a long time, in the spring at Lakewood [New Jersey], and on all the trips, and I know that there is absolutely nothing in the talk. It is a mighty strong accusation to make against a ballplayer, and I do not believe that any experienced writer without prejudice would make such a charge as has been made against the New York players. The team has made eight or nine errors behind me on several occasions and yet no one thought of accusing the team of throwing me down. I see the smart ones say that I have been fined, and yet when I got my check last week it was for the full amount."

The players' philosophy seemed to be that negative press fomented the home fans into a frenzy, causing them to roast and heckle Giants team members at the Polo Grounds. This reception resulted in nervousness on the diamond, triggering the squad to commit four critical errors as they did when Ed Doheny pitched against Baltimore on September 13.[38] When reading the tea leaves surrounding Meekin's comment, the team did not play boneheaded baseball when Ed pitched because they detested him, it only occurred since the Giants were not particularly good. New York's final place in the 1898 National League standings substantiated this theory, as the club finished seventh with a 77–73 record. Scrappy Bill Joyce briefly relinquished his duties on June 10 as Cap Anson managed the squad for a month. Before the 1899 season began with John Day, and later Frederick "Fred" Hoey at the helm, New York sportswriter William F. H. Koelsch stated Doheny looked to be in great shape and could return to the form exhibited two years earlier until suspension and sickness sidelined the pitcher.[39]

Ed battled gallantly for an awful team as one of New York's three mound workhorses in 1899. Doheny posted a 14–17 record, supported by a 4.41 ERA, as the Giants finished in tenth place with a dreadful 60–90 mark, leaving them 42 games behind pace-setting Brooklyn. Ed also experienced a wonderful moment in his personal life by marrying Katherine O'Sullivan, from St. Albans, on June 5, 1899.[40] Before the 1900 campaign started, mixed messages appeared in print regarding Doheny's intentions. One story, commenting that Ed had not agreed to salary terms, claimed the hurler grew tired of playing for the Giants and would welcome a trade to another club.[41] This imagined stance became moot when Doheny signed a contract on March 15 for the 1900 season.[42]

That year, New York reached a new low in the reconfigured eight-team National League. The Giants found a place in the basement, posting a 60–78 record and finishing 23 games behind the pennant-winning Superbas. Ed Doheny experienced the worst season of his career, going 4–14, with a 5.45 ERA. Poor work in the field by teammates because of inadequacy or disdain for the hurler aided the St. Louis Cardinals in their 6–1 victory over Doheny at League Park on June 30. Although Ed gamely fought onward, mesmerizing St. Louis's batters with his curving shoots, eight errors by colleagues made this a futile exercise. New York only connected for two hits against Cardinals pitcher James "Jim" Hughey. An article in the *St. Louis Republic* acknowledged that such a grand showing by a pitcher usually resulted in a win nine out of ten times.[43]

George Davis managed the Giants for a full season in 1901 after replacing Buck Ewing overseeing the club the previous summer. Despite Doheny's indifferent showing in 1900, Davis re-signed the pitcher. Ed now realized what many sports journalists had suspected for years. The southpaw hurler believed he never received good support when pitching, owing to efforts from a certain clique that did not like him and hoped he failed.[44] Ed struggled for New York as the season progressed. His erratic work did not please George, who expressed no jubilation with his staff in general. Davis planned to send Ed home once new pitcher William "Willie" Mills joined the club on July 11.[45] Rumors pointed toward skipper John "Bid" McPhee picking up Doheny for his Cincinnati Reds.[46] On July 18, New York newspapers announced that George released Ed to add catcher Broadway Aleck Smith to the roster.[47]

After toiling for a second-division team throughout most of his major league career, Ed Doheny received a stroke of good luck. As the Pittsburgh Pirates prepared to embark for St. Louis on the evening of July 25, manager Fred Clarke told reporters at the train station that he gave veteran shortstop William Frederick "Bones" Ely his unconditional release. To keep the Pirates at the sixteen-player roster limit permitted by the league, Fred also announced Doheny's signing.[48] Eddie reported to Pittsburgh on July 27 with instructions to work out every day at Exposition Park until the Pirates returned from St. Louis.[49] Doheny looked fantastic in practice and appeared to be mastering the overhead style of delivery Clarke wanted him to utilize.[50]

Eddie made his first appearance for Pittsburgh in relief against St. Louis on August 5 at Exposition Park as the Cardinals throttled the Pirates, 20–6. At noon on August 7, Pittsburgh's management hierarchy reluctantly handed Doheny his notice of release, effective in ten days. The club did not want to make the move but needed to clear space on the sixteen-man roster to add a catcher. The Pirates' manager hoped they could bring Eddie back into the fold later. Fred selected Doheny to start that afternoon's contest versus St. Louis. Eddie pitched brilliantly, resulting in constant applause from Exposition Park's fans. Through the first five innings, the Cardinals connected for only three hits off the southpaw hurler.[51] Doheny tossed a complete game as Pittsburgh garnered a 9–3 victory. Eddie pitched marvelously in his next start on August 11, defeating Chicago, 5–1, at West Side Grounds.

On August 17, Pittsburgh released infielder Lewis "Lew" Carr. Management executed this transaction for the sole purpose of re-signing Doheny, which officially occurred on August 19. Upon Carr's release, Eddie left with catcher Charles "Chief" Zimmer to join their teammates in St. Louis as the squad continued a brief western jaunt.[52] Doheny finally found baseball nirvana in the Smoky City, posting a 6–2 record with the Pirates in 1901, backed by a

2.00 ERA. Eddie suffered one setback when the club traveled through the east in September. On September 12, Doheny and third baseman Tommy Leach returned to Pittsburgh while the team continued a series against Brooklyn. Fred Clarke sent Leach back home to improve his health and temper. Eddie made the trip to the Smoky City because he injured his pitching arm dealing with a broken door at Washington Park.

While entering the ballpark before the game on September 11, Doheny found the entrance to the visiting team's dressing room barred. Taking matters into his own hands, Eddie calmly busted open the door with his left arm. Doheny exited New York before hearing from Superbas owner and president Charles Ebbets regarding monetary compensation for replacing the door.[53] When it came to benefits, fellow National League owners looked at the Pirates' roster with longing eyes. Many teams, devastated by American League raids, particularly expressed interest in syphoning off some of Pittsburgh's excellent pitching talent for their clubs. In January, a newspaper report claimed Clarke planned to help the depleted Cardinals by allowing them to grab Eddie and fellow hurler Edward "Ed" Poole. On January 11, 1902, before leaving Pittsburgh to go hunting, Fred reacted to this false narrative about the Pirates' baseball organization acting as Good Samaritans.

> Not a player has been let out. I received a letter from President Dreyfuss telling me that if I wanted to make any changes in the team for 1902 I had better go to the league meeting in New York with him, otherwise there would be no necessity of my leaving Kansas [Fred's off-season home in Winfield] until after the holidays.
>
> That happened in November, and I replied promptly, declining the invitation with thanks, but I did not stop at that, but made it as plain as I knew how that, while I did not want any new men, I did want to take every one of the old bunch to Hot Springs [Arkansas] in April.
>
> "Don't allow the smooth men at the meeting to tell you any fairy stories," I wrote to President Dreyfuss. "You know them. They will try to convince you that Pittsburgh is too strong and will have a walkover in the next race unless you part with some of the players. That is all rot. Baseball is too uncertain to make it possible for anybody to tell six months in advance how any team will size up on the field."
>
> President Dreyfuss knows the game, and I suppose he would have held on to his players even if I had not warned him, but the developments at the meeting proved that I had made a good guess. The very first move the magnates made was to attempt to frame a deal for getting some of the Pirates. President Dreyfuss wisely declared out of that game. I don't

know much about the political moves of baseball, but I do believe that Pittsburgh is in a position where it can afford to stand pat. For that reason not a player will be released, and any rumors to the contrary while this war lasts may be put down as false.[54]

Protective of his players like a mother bear to her cubs, Fred offered an understatement when he indicated Pittsburgh was in a position where it could stand pat. None of the National League's other seven clubs offered a challenge as the stocked Pirates cruised to the pennant in 1902. Fred had at his disposal a stable of five exceptional pitchers: Jack Chesbro (28–6, 2.17 ERA), Deacon Phillippe (20–9, 2.05 ERA), Jesse Tannehill (20–6, 1.95 ERA), Eddie Doheny (16–4, 2.53 ERA), and Sam Leever (15–7, 2.39 ERA) offered outstanding options. Eddie might have piled up more victories if not for spraining his ankle while playing with his son, Edward Michael Doheny Jr., in their New York hotel room during the team's September eastern excursion. This injury caused Doheny to miss the remainder of the campaign and a postseason series against a team of American League All-Stars.[55] Eddie's final mound appearance occurred on September 6 when he defeated New York, 9–3, at the Polo Grounds.

While Fred Clarke lost Jack Chesbro and Jesse Tannehill from his staff when the two hurlers decided to cast their lot with the American League's New York Highlanders in 1903, he still expressed supreme optimism regarding the Pirates claiming a third consecutive National League pennant. Clarke's comment from the previous year about uncertainty making it impossible to tell how a team might size up on the field six months down the road proved truly prophetic as the current pennant race progressed. Once the season started, *Sporting Life* correspondent A. R. Cratty wrote that Eddie Doheny, fellow pitchers Frederick "Bucky" Veil and William Kennedy, also known as "Perk" besides "Brickyard," and first baseman Kitty Bransfield, decided to live at the Monongahela House throughout the year. The four players found it more appealing to stay in a hotel rather than a cheap boardinghouse. They also felt the location appeared good since visiting squads usually lodged at this establishment, meaning veterans like Doheny and Kennedy could renew acquaintances with former mates.[56]

The 1903 season evolved into a battle between Pittsburgh and New York. During a game involving the two teams in front of a large crowd at the Polo Grounds on May 18, Eddie Doheny exhibited unusual behavior at his old stomping grounds. The Pirates defeated the Giants, 3–2, in a highly contentious game. The Polo Grounds' faithful expressed displeasure with Doheny's tactics in the contest, as rooters felt he plunked Joe "Iron Man" McGinnity and Dan McGann in the back with pitches on purpose.[57] Eddie won by maintaining his composure on the mound while getting into tight jams throughout the contest. Bleacher fans and New York's team members working the coaching lines constantly harassed Doheny to rattle the pitcher and throw him off his game. Incessant complaining by managers Fred Clarke and John McGraw to umpire Robert "Bob" Emslie sometimes made the proceedings tedious.[58]

Things took an ugly turn in the seventh inning when Pittsburgh batted. Eddie stepped up to the plate with a teammate on base and smacked a towering pop fly on the infield.[59] McGinnity and Giants catcher Frank Bowerman drifted over to catch Doheny's popup.[60] Umpire Emslie immediately called Eddie out based on the infield fly rule from that baseball era. Nevertheless, Doheny ran to first base, carrying his bat. About halfway down the line, Eddie tossed the bat aside, almost hitting Bowerman as he danced and fumbled about attempting to catch the pop fly. Not realizing the umpire had already called Doheny out, spectators started heckling the prince of the mound they once cheered, feeling he attempted to interfere with New York's catcher. This reception angered Eddie, who foolishly responded by bowing to the rooters in mock courtesy. This only aroused the fans to express their contempt even more.[61]

In the bottom of the seventh inning, Pirates shortstop John "Honus" Wagner interfered with Joe McGinnity at second base as he attempted to hustle to the next station. Although Joe reached third base, McGraw argued with Emslie that the arbiter should permit the runner to continue home since he believed his player would have scored if Wagner had not pulled such a deceitful ploy.[62] Later, the umpire called Fred Clarke out for alleged interference on the base paths when Bowerman clumsily executed another play. Once the game concluded, about one thousand disappointed and angry patrons stormed the field surrounding Pittsburgh's players and threw stones, but before any Pirates team members suffered an injury, police arrived and escorted them to the clubhouse.[63] A group of police officers had taken up a strategic position as a precautionary maneuver to aid Doheny once the contest concluded.[64]

Pittsburgh sportswriter A. R. Cratty stated Eddie Doheny devoutly practiced his Catholic faith, came from a deeply religious family, and never missed church services. Two or three brothers had entered the priesthood, and a sister followed her calling as a nun in a convent. Cratty also claimed Eddie belonged to a secret society connected to his church and happened to be a powerful representative of that group. In every city Doheny visited, faithful members called on him. The dozens of police officers that rallied by his side at the Polo Grounds included many of this religious fraternity's members who proudly upheld an obligation to assist others belonging to their sect.[65]

Because of this diamond battle's raucous nature, National League president Harry Pulliam watched the following day's game between Pittsburgh and New York on May 19 from owner John T. Brush's private Polo Grounds box.[66] Pulliam used to be Barney Dreyfuss's right-hand man within the Pirates' organization after they shifted from the Louisville Colonels in December 1899. He'd been voted to the position of president, secretary, and treasurer by National League magnates on December 12, 1902.[67] Prior to the contest's start, a reporter asked Clarke to comment on a story out of Pittsburgh that the team captain and manager exhibited signs of experiencing a nervous breakdown.

"You can't say it too strong for me," said the captain. "There is absolutely no truth in it, and I can't for the life of me think how such a story gained circulation."

Before the clash began, Pulliam announced through his secretary that he had suspended Eddie Doheny for three games without pay due to the player's rowdy behavior the previous afternoon.[68] The league president later clarified this news release, asserting he did not suspend Doheny for throwing his bat but issued the punishment because Eddie gossiped after the game ended. Exhibiting that Harry did not favor Brush's boys, he walked up to George Van Haltren before the contest on May 20. He informed the Giants' outfielder about his sentence for inciting the crowd during New York's 4–3 victory over the Pirates the previous day.

"You are out of the game for five days," said Pulliam. "Your sensational methods of holding up [Giants third baseman William 'Billy'] Lauder's injured finger during yesterday's game so that the spectators could see the bloody bandage is a thing we don't want in baseball, and I intend to make an example."

Harry Pulliam then lit a cigar and turned his back on Van Haltren.[69] That same day, prior to action starting between these two rivals, a prominent Pittsburgh piano manufacturer sent a telegram to New York, declaring he would stand for Eddie's lost salary during the three-day suspension if the pitcher agreed to fight the case in court.[70] This entrepreneur and devoted Pirates fan alleged Pulliam had no right to suspend Doheny until umpire Bob Emslie wrote his report on the matter.[71] Such passion by the rooting populace inspired Clarke.

"There you are," said Fred Clarke. "You see how our city backs us up. We don't ask any favors, only a fair deal. Play the game is our motto."[72]

Playing the game became difficult for one club member as the 1903 campaign moved into the summer. As Pittsburgh traveled through the east during a June road trip, Clarke, Honus Wagner, Sam Leever, and Deacon Phillippe conducted a meeting one morning with Barney Dreyfuss in his room at the Waldorf-Astoria Hotel while the squad lodged in New York for two scheduled series.[73] During this conference to discuss the team's situation, Phillippe mentioned that Eddie Doheny had been acting strangely lately, appearing aloof and withdrawn. Dreyfuss asked the hurler if he felt Eddie might experience a mental breakdown. Deacon responded that he felt concerned over his teammate's behavior. Barney thanked Phillippe for his candor on the issue, stating Clarke had also recently offered an opinion on the subject. Dreyfuss then stated he hoped a situation did not arise like the one involving Detroit's Win Mercer earlier that year.[74]

During this road trip, the Pirates' players enjoyed the presence of Eddie's precocious toddler son, Edward Michael O'Sullivan Doheny. Doheny declared the boy attached his wife's O'Sullivan birth name all by himself without prompting from the parents. Little Eddie, loving red, offered advice one day to his father.

"Say, Pop," shouted Eddie Jr., "take off that blue tie and get a red one."[75]

Deacon Phillippe's concerns proved well-founded as Pittsburgh started another road trip in Cincinnati on July 26 after the Pirates played two games against St. Louis at Exposition Park. Doheny improved his record to 12–6 by defeating the Reds that Sunday afternoon at Palace of the Fans, 5–2. Barney Dreyfuss later stated Eddie exhibited signs of insanity in Cincinnati when the pitcher claimed a local shoemaker intended to kill him.[76] On the evening of July 27, while eating dinner with some teammates, Doheny threw a plate at an imaginary policeman that only existed in his mind.[77] This response resulted from Eddie's delusion that police detectives constantly followed him, a fear he complained about to manager Fred Clarke numerous times. On the morning of July 28, Doheny confronted Clarke and said he could not stand it any longer and planned to return home to give these detectives the slip.

Fred argued with his player over this point. Eddie readily admitted the Pirates' organization treated him royally, and he fostered no reason to exhibit a disgruntled attitude. Following lunch, Doheny did not comment on his intentions while playing a game of billiards with Clarke. When the two finished, Eddie bid Fred and the other team members a fond farewell. Further efforts by Pittsburgh's skipper failed to convince Doheny to remain with the club. He left for the railroad station and boarded the Big Four train at 2 P.M. bound for Boston, Massachusetts.[78] When Eddie arrived in Boston that night, he telegraphed his wife, Katherine, at their home in nearby Andover to meet him there. She caught a train to the city on the evening of July 30, and the couple arrived in Andover on the morning of July 31.[79]

Doheny had been taking care of himself and was one of the easiest men on the squad for Clarke to manage. Some of Eddie's close friends suggested summer's heat adversely impacted the hurler's mind. On the evening of July 28, Fred positively admitted he believed Doheny suffered from mental issues and affirmed that the southpaw could not rejoin the club.[80] Upon Clarke informing the entire squad about Eddie's condition, they mourned over the popular hurler abandoning them while laboring under a mental hallucination. Every team member on friendly terms with Doheny expressed sorrow over hearing the news, although each one had commented on his strange behavior the past week. Clarke wired Barney Dreyfuss in New York for instructions on procuring Eddie's replacement. Fred commented on the morning of July 29 about altering plans to take a break at his ranch in Winfield, Kansas.

"I had intended leaving for Kansas next Sunday to take a rest," said Clarke, "but since this occurrence I fear it will not be politic for me to leave the team. Someone must be in charge who cannot only direct the affairs of the playing aggregation, but who at the same time can devote himself to gathering new players. We certainly need some help, and I am keeping my eye open for any good men I can find."

Fred also stated he did not feel discouraged despite this new development and injuries to various Pirates players.[81] When Clarke alerted Dreyfuss that Doheny had deserted the squad, Pittsburgh's owner stated he could not discuss particulars about the matter until he interacted further with his manager.

> If it is true that Doheny is mentally deranged, I am certainly sorry to hear of it. Doheny has taken the best care of himself this season, and has pitched good ball. He has given up his old companions, and has been living a life that would tend to keep him perfect physically. He has been saving money, besides, and was apparently happy and contented. Fred Clarke told me that there was something wrong with the pitcher before the team started West, but I laughed at him. Now it seems that Fred was right.
>
> But we must not allow one man to hurt the team's chances of winning another pennant. I have notified Fred Clarke to begin at once a skirmish for another pitcher to replace Doheny, and have offered several suggestions as to where one might be secured. That is the way we work it in Pittsburgh. I watch the dope and keep tab on the players' records. But I never sign a player without allowing Manager Clarke to have a look at him and make the selection. No man plays on the Pirate team with whom Clarke is not personally satisfied.[82]

Some of Barney Dreyfuss's comments indicated Eddie Doheny previously had a drinking problem, which the player eradicated by eliminating bad companions and remaining in fine shape. When interviewed by the press, team secretary William H. Locke, who traveled with the team on their road trip, stated that while he did not know whether Eddie Doheny might receive permission to return to the club, he concurred that Barney Dreyfuss would not interfere with whatever decision Fred Clarke reached. Locke affirmed Doheny should receive punishment, but the severity of the reprimand rested with Clarke. William worried that welcoming Eddie back with open arms might set a bad precedent and embolden other players to take a vacation during the season. Locke stated he had no idea why Doheny left the team while the official failed to convince the pitcher to stay with the club. William also categorized anybody who thought Fred and Eddie had engaged in a stormy confrontation as delusional.[83]

Doheny's decision to abandon the team created huge problems for the Pirates' pitching staff. Hurler Deacon Phillippe needed to take a week off in August to rest an injury. Phillippe wrenched his hip while pitching in the second game of a doubleheader against Philadelphia at Exposition Park on July 4. When Deacon, who resided in Pittsburgh's East End neighborhood, stopped at team headquarters, he talked about Eddie and admitted to feeling sorry his teammate acted the way he did. Phillippe added he imagined Doheny's behavior indicated the hurler's mind troubled him.[84] When Eddie reached Andover, he issued a statement to the press on July 31 during an interview with a reporter, offering context regarding his decision.

> I will report back to the Pittsburgh team August 10, if I do not before that time. I came home to rest for a few days; that is all. Sometimes a good deal is made of a small matter. I was feeling sick and decided to come home. I had no trouble with the manager or any member of the team; it was simply the way I felt that made me decide to come home to Andover and rest. I may go back in three of four days, but, as I have already stated, I shall report to the team on August 10, anyway.
>
> When I left I had no intention of not going back, and don't understand how that impression got abroad.[85]

Ralph S. Davis declared in the *Sporting News* that some people did not believe Eddie suffered from mental issues. They thought Doheny deserted the Pirates over unhappiness about his teammates not offering ample support when he pitched. Davis scoffed at this suggestion, citing Eddie's fine record thus far in 1903. The writer also affirmed Barney Dreyfuss functioned as more than Doheny's friend. The owner also happened to be a confidant. Davis revealed that while playing for the Giants, Eddie engaged in a wayward lifestyle that was not conducive to playing good baseball. Doheny allowed social pleasures and alcohol to rob him of critical energy and vitality. When Eddie joined Pittsburgh, he suddenly made more money than he needed to live on and feared the temptation to spend it foolishly by wasting it chasing bad vices.

Doheny arranged for Dreyfuss to pay him a specific amount of money during the baseball season and keep the hurler's remaining salary until the campaign closed. Barney then invested that stipend, which gained the highest profit return and allowed Eddie to save money. To Ralph, this friendship proved that no clash occurred between the two men, contributing to Doheny leaving the club. Davis also declared that every team member expressed sincere regret about Eddie's decision, while the scribe rejected a local sportswriter's silly notion that the Buccaneers bring back southpaw twirler Jesse Tannehill as a replacement. Dreyfuss certainly had no interest in having a contract-jumping traitor once again on his team.[86] Rumors abounded that Pirates officials would allow Doheny to return, alleging Fred Clarke happened to be angry when making his initial comment on this topic after the pitcher returned home.[87] As he alluded, Clarke also left for his Kansas farm to help mend fraying nerves, leaving Honus Wagner in charge of the team for two weeks.[88]

When Clarke arrived back in Pittsburgh on August 7 after resting in Winfield, Pittsburgh's manager found two letters awaiting him. One sent by Mrs. Katherine Doheny stated that her husband's health had improved rapidly since returning home and that he planned to report to the team without delay. The following was the second correspondence Fred received from Dr. Edward C. Conroy of Andover, dated August 1.

"I have attended Mr. Edward Doheny since he came home," wrote Dr. Conroy. "He is suffering from a mild form of nervous prostration. His condition is improved since you saw him. This improvement is in no small part owing to his being kept absolutely quiet. In a week he will be able to be with you again."

Fred expressed happiness upon reading these messages from Mrs. Doheny and Dr. Conroy.

"The letters about Doheny were good news to me," said Clarke. "It pleases me to learn that Eddie is improving and that he had an excuse for leaving us. All of the boys will be glad to see him. He is a good pitcher."[89]

Clarke wired Eddie, telling him to rest a few more days and then meet the team in New York when they started a series against Brooklyn on August 12. The doctor's explanation about Doheny's condition proved sufficient for Fred. Had Clarke found that a vexed Eddie deserted over some incident, Pittsburgh's manager would not have allowed him to return. Fred vowed that Doheny's teammates would gladly welcome him back.[90] This assessment appeared accurate when Eddie rejoined the squad in Boston on August 15 at a critical time because Deacon Phillippe continued to suffer from a bad back. The *Pittsburgh Press* reported that Doheny, appearing of sound mind and body, exchanged affable greetings with his teammates, donned his uniform, and accompanied the squad to South End Grounds. Eddie seemed in good spirits and happy to be back, flashing smiles when he arrived at the team hotel.[91]

Such a rosy narrative conflicted with other newspaper accounts. The *Buffalo Morning Express* reported that Pirates players gave the truant hurler a cool reception when he rejoined the club. This publication also alleged Doheny was unpopular with team members, and his stunt in Cincinnati had caused him to fall deeper out of favor. Upon Eddie rejoining the club, many players notified Clarke they did not want to share a room with him.[92] When it came to Pittsburgh's newspapers, some carried water for the Pirates' organization while others preferred performing the mortal enemy role. The contention that several team members did not want to join Doheny as his roommate possibly correlated to a story pitcher Bill Kennedy shared with them shortly after Eddie returned to Andover.

Kennedy had suspected Doheny suffered from mental problems before the Pirates embarked on their western trip. Many weeks earlier, Eddie scared Bill one night at the Monongahela House where both players lived. According to Kennedy, a pounding on his apartment door awakened him in the middle of the night. When he arose from bed and opened the door, Bill saw Doheny standing in the hall, wearing his night robe. Eddie immediately confided to his teammate that he had just received an electric shock through an apartment wall.

"I'll wager," said Eddie to Bill, "that they're trying to work a panel game on me."[93]

A panel game usually involved at least one woman conning a male tourist by inviting that unfortunate individual to come and stay at her home. While the mark slept, a second criminal, using a panel in the wall, robbed the victim.[94] Kennedy escorted Doheny back to his apartment, searched the room where Eddie slept to investigate any wires that might have shocked him, but found nothing. Although Bill contemplated many things internally about this incident, he did not share the story about his midnight experience until after Eddie departed for home.[95]

Fred Clarke selected Eddie Doheny to pitch the second game of a doubleheader against Boston on August 15 at South End Grounds. The Beaneaters defeated the Pirates, 8–5, as Eddie exhibited rust and wildness the entire contest. Doheny issued six walks, hit three batters with pitches, and threw wildly on a play at first base. Although Eddie's teammates freely smacked Boston pitcher Charles "Togie" Pittinger's offerings for twelve hits, the Pittsburgh hurler's inconsistency proved too great an obstacle to overcome.[96] Doheny struggled while attempting to round into shape. Despite many subpar performances, Eddie reeled off a four-game winning streak after he suffered defeats in the first two outings following his return. Things coalesced in the final two starts of that stretch, as Doheny defeated St. Louis, 3–0, on August 30, and beat Cincinnati, 6–3, on September 3, to raise his record to 16–8.

All this progress evaporated the morning of a Labor Day doubleheader versus the Chicago Cubs on September 7 at Exposition Park. Eddie pitched abysmally, lasting only two innings on the hill before Clarke replaced him with rookie hurler John Gustav "Gus" Thompson after the Cubs scored five runs on four hits and four walks.[97] Although Chicago knocked Doheny out of the box, he avoided taking the loss as Pittsburgh grabbed the lead before Thompson surrendered seven tallies in the seventh inning. The Cubs won the contest, 13–8. After the game, some reporters alleged Fred relieved Eddie for indifferent playing. On Tuesday, the southpaw twirler disappeared. Some of his friends advanced sickness as the reason; others alleged the ballplayer spent the day consuming too much wine. Doheny did not reappear at Exposition Park until Friday, September 11, as the Pirates prepared to play Philadelphia.

When it became apparent that Pittsburgh and the American League's Boston Americans would win pennants in their respective organizations, Barney Dreyfuss and fellow magnate Henry Killilea agreed to play a postseason series to determine baseball's supreme champion. This majestic World Series now appeared in jeopardy due to Eddie's behavior and Pirates shortstop Honus Wagner's addition to the squad's injury list.[98] Dreyfuss was concerned that Doheny displayed too much intensity while working on the mound. Stress also appeared prevalent, leading him to fight with opposing players and sometimes his own teammates. He continued to act distant and exhibited the glassy-eyed stare of a person trapped in his own alternate reality. Some fans and writers believed Eddie's fervent desire to win caused this behavior.[99]

Following what ended up as his last appearance of the season against Chicago, Doheny angrily complained of substandard defensive work by his teammates. On September 12, he argued with the Pirates' owner. When questioned on the matter by *Pittsburgh Daily Dispatch* sportswriter Frank McQuiston, Dreyfuss stated Eddie did not pitch a good game on Labor Day. Following that poor outing, management accused him of not being in proper condition, which Doheny denied. Eddie's wife, Katherine, came to Barney's office on September 8 and informed the magnate that her husband suffered from an illness. Dreyfuss then told McQuiston that Doheny made his first appearance at Exposition Park in days on Friday.[100] Due to becoming an extremely sick man, Eddie's brother and Catholic priest, Reverend P. J. Doheny, arrived in Pittsburgh on September 21 to be at the pitcher's bedside.[101]

Father Doheny immediately took his brother, who exhibited extremely poor health, back home to Andover. According to scribe A. R. Cratty, Eddie Doheny had genuinely wished to lead an exemplary life after suffering his first lapse in over a year drinking alcohol. Cratty proclaimed that in this instance, Eddie's efforts at ceasing too suddenly after succumbing to liquor damaged his nervous system. As the Pirates prepared to play Boston in the 1903 World Series, Fred Clarke found himself in a bind regarding pitching options. The manager did not count on Doheny's availability. Sam Leever, who went 25–7 with a league-leading 2.06 ERA in 1903, dealt with a sore pitching arm. Trainer Edward "Ed" LaForce hoped to have the salary wing in decent shape for Sam's first World Series start. This left reliable Deacon Phillippe as Clarke's only viable choice against the Americans.[102] Deacon rewarded his manager's confidence in him by defeating Boston in Game One on October 1 at Huntington Avenue Baseball Grounds, 7–3.

Phillippe did gilt-edged work for Pittsburgh against the Americans. He started five games, completed each outing, and went 3–2, supported by a 3.07 ERA. Unfortunately, no other Pirates hurler secured a victory in this best-of-nine series versus Boston. Pittsburgh's manager initially had only planned to use Deacon in four games. Positive expectations before Game Two on October 2 in the Americans' home ballpark regarding Leever's arm after endless massaging by LaForce proved foolish. Sam seemed in fine shape before taking the hill and looked sharp while warming up.[103] That crispness abandoned him once the game started. Leever lasted one inning, as Boston scored two runs off the hurler en route to a 3–0 victory as Americans pitcher William "Bill" Dinneen allowed three hits. Sam possessed no speed, could not snap off curveballs, and lacked control. Rookie hurler Bucky Veil relieved Leever in the second frame and pitched well.[104]

The Pirates secured Games Three and Four behind Phillippe's stout pitching. Deacon defeated the Americans, 4–2, at Huntington Avenue Grounds on October 3 and beat Boston on October 6 at Exposition Park, 5–4. The Americans exacted revenge in Game Five the following day, breaking open a scoreless game in the sixth inning against Buccaneers pitcher Bill Kennedy and cruising to an 11–3 victory. Before Game Six at Exposition Park on October 8, Sam Leever, whose arm had been in bad condition for some time, asked Fred Clarke to allow him to face Boston.[105] Although Leever exhibited more resolve and pitched better than in Game Two, the Americans won, 6–3, as poor support by teammates contributed to the loss.[106]

A dispute arose between Clarke and Boston skipper James "Jimmy" Collins prior to Game Seven, scheduled for Friday, October 9. That afternoon, Fred announced the contest's postponement due to chilly weather. This decision did not please Collins since the Americans' organization had made travel plans to leave by train on Friday night and return to Boston to finish the World Series. He also felt the dreary, gloomy weather could work to his club's advantage with Denton "Cy" Young on the hill, utilizing his speed. Jimmy searched out Clarke at Pittsburgh's team headquarters to voice his displeasure.

"What's the matter with you people?" he inquired angrily of Clarke.

"Nothing," replied the Pirates' manager, "but it's too cold to play."

"We're willing to take a chance," replied Collins. "What's the use of waiting a day. It is likely to be just as bad then. We want to finish these games here and get away. I think it's a shame."

Cynics supposed that Fred had also postponed the game to allow an extra day's rest for hurler Deacon Phillippe.[107] If this idea entered Clarke's calculus, it did not matter, as Boston defeated Pittsburgh in Game Seven on October 10 at Exposition Park, 7–3. The Americans now led four games to three as the World Series shifted back to Boston. In an article in the *Pittsburgh Press* on October 11, sportswriter Ralph S. Davis declared that because of Eddie Doheny's inexcusable conduct this season, management should never permit him to return to the club.[108] Throughout the World Series, Doheny scrutinized each game and felt anguish when the Pirates lost.[109] To lift the twirler's spirits, Eddie's teammates shipped his uniform to Andover. Unfortunately, this kind gesture confused Doheny, who thought the club no longer needed him.[110] While intended to cheer up her husband, Katherine Doheny said it broke the ballplayer's heart and depressed him, leading Eddie to believe his baseball career had ended.

Eddie also blamed Dr. Edward C. Conroy for not allowing the southpaw twirler to join his teammates while playing games in Boston because of his condition.[111] Although Doheny experienced hallucinations and exhibited paranoia, suffering a nervous breakdown because of his intensity while pitching, the ballplayer had not yet committed a violent act. On Saturday evening, October 10, Dr. Conroy arrived at the residence to visit his patient. Eddie informed the physician that he no longer required his services.[112] Dr. Conroy initially thought Doheny joked about dismissing him.[113] The medico quickly realized the ballplayer's profound seriousness when Eddie tossed him out of the house headlong through the door. Dr. Conroy summoned Andover Chief of Police William L. Frye. Following a discussion between the two, they decided that faith cure doctor and nurse Oberlin Howarth should attend to Doheny.[114] Howarth managed to quiet Eddie, who slept peacefully throughout the night.[115]

At 7 A.M. on Sunday, while something diverted Oberlin's attention elsewhere, Doheny suddenly jumped out of bed and hit his nurse with a cast iron stove leg (or stove poker). Howarth immediately crumpled to the floor as Eddie continued raining blows on him with the weapon. A deep gash opened in Oberlin's head, causing a stream of blood to flow. Katherine Doheny hurriedly ran out of the house and cried for help. Neighbors heard her screams and rushed to the home to assist, finding Eddie in the doorway brandishing the bloody weapon. Chief of Police Frye and Officer George W. Mears arrived at the scene.[116] Doheny, dressed in his night clothing, defied their attempts to capture him, threatening to kill the first man who tried. After the crazy madman kept the crowd at bay for an hour, Frye and Mears caught Eddie off guard and overpowered the athlete.[117]

Authorities found Howarth lying on the floor in a pool of blood. Despite the attack's brutality, law enforcement and medical personnel considered his injuries serious but not life-threatening. Upon police arresting Doheny, Judge Andrew C. Stone ordered physicians to conduct a thorough examination. The doctors pronounced him insane and committed Eddie to an asylum in Danvers, Massachusetts. Chief Frye and Officer Mears escorted Doheny to the institution at noon on October 11.[118] Regarding the sensational nature of newspaper stories, Mrs. Doheny refuted the claim that police officers needed to overpower her husband. Katherine's account surrounding Eddie's attack on Oberlin Howarth differed from the story perpetrated by the press.

> Ed blamed the doctor for keeping him out of the Pittsburgh-Boston series, and after a mad outbreak over the loss of Saturday's game he chased the doctor when he called. After that he seemed to cool down, and I went to another part of the house. I soon heard a scuffling and other sounds of fighting in my husband's room, and, catching my baby, I ran there. As I threw open the door I saw my husband standing over Mr. Howarth, who had evidently been knocked down by Mr. Doheny, who was standing over him with something in his hands, and, I suppose, was about to hit him again. Baby screamed and I cried, "Eddie! Eddie! Don't do that!" He turned and looked my way with eyes that did not seem right, then he dropped whatever he had in his hand, and when I asked him to go back to bed he did so quietly. Then I ran and called in the neighbors to help Mr. Howarth. The story that the officers had to come in and overpower my husband is not true. When they came to take him away to the asylum he went with them, harmless as a child.

According to the initial diagnosis from doctors at the Danvers State Hospital, they expected Eddie Doheny to recover his reason following treatment. Due to inclement weather, baseball officials postponed the game between Boston and Pittsburgh at Huntington Avenue Baseball Grounds on Monday, October 12. After a long discussion with Barney Dreyfuss, manager Fred Clarke called all team members over to a small corner of the Hotel Vendome to discuss the unfortunate turn of events regarding Eddie.

"Boys," said Clarke, "I'm going down to see Mrs. Doheny and her little baby [three-year-old Eddie Jr.]. Will you stand by me in what I do?"

Every player responded resoundingly, "Yes." Clarke should have been resting in his hotel room because of a leg injury, but he braved a rainstorm to travel twenty-four miles north to Andover by train. While there, Fred experienced a comforting talk with Mrs. Doheny. Dreyfuss and the entire club decided to care for both Doheny and his wife financially.[119] Katherine also gave Clarke an envelope related to her husband for Pirates second baseman Claude Ritchey, who took it back to Boston with him and left it at the hotel lobby's desk.[120] On October 13, Boston claimed the title when they defeated Pittsburgh in Game Eight, 3–0, at Huntington Avenue Baseball Grounds.

As the Pirates' players dejectedly entered the Hotel Vendome following the contest, still wearing their uniforms, they quietly walked to the desk for their room keys. The clerk handed Ritchey the letter his manager had brought back from Andover the previous day. When Claude opened the envelope, two one-dollar bills fell out. The letter, written in a beautiful feminine hand penned by Katherine Doheny, read, "Eddie said he owed you $2 and asked me to pay you. Here it is." A lump rose in Ritchey's throat before he handed the letter to Fred Clarke. After reading the correspondence and somberly returning the note to Ritchey, Fred said, "Poor Eddie." Katherine's letter explained that as authorities prepared to escort her husband on the trip to Danvers, Doheny made a lucid comment about his only outstanding obligation.

"I owe only $2; that to Claude Ritchey," said Eddie. "Won't you pay him?"[121]

Barney Dreyfuss graciously split up the $21,000 he earned as his share for Pittsburgh playing Boston in the World Series and gave the money to his players.[122] This meant Pirates team members received their regular salary and a bonus. In turn, the players kindly agreed to give Mrs. Doheny a full share and a private purse they collected among themselves.[123] Sadly, the early prognosis by physicians at Danvers State Hospital proved ambitious as Eddie did not respond to treatment. On February 20, 1904, devoted Pirates fan Tom Quill, known throughout other National League cities, stopped at Pittsburgh's baseball headquarters. Seeing Deacon Phillippe there, he asked about Doheny.

"I am afraid that there is no cure for poor Ed," remarked Phillippe. "I had hoped for the best, but it does not look promising."

Tom grieved upon hearing such gloomy news. Quill then shared a tale from the previous summer when he was with Eddie at the Monongahela House. Tom explained that Doheny seemed in bad shape from the effects of stimulants and attempted to hurt a newspaper reporter the pitcher considered his bitterest enemy. When Quill pleaded with Doheny to retire to his apartment, the frenzied ballplayer suddenly lunged at him. Tom barely dodged Eddie's frantic maneuver. Quill told Phillippe and others at the office that this incident convinced him Doheny had become insane.[124]

On March 3, Dreyfuss received word that Eddie Doheny would no longer be able to play baseball.[125] Shortly after hearing this regrettable news, Pittsburgh's owner announced he planned to pay Doheny's salary for the 1904 campaign to his wife.[126] On May 22, Barney received a letter from one of Eddie's brothers. The correspondence related the heartbreaking news that the hurler's mental condition had not changed, and specialists at the asylum held out no hope for recovery.[127]

Before the 1905 season started, Katherine Doheny wrote Dreyfuss to update him on her husband's status. Mrs. Doheny's letter stated Eddie showed no improvement, did not recognize friends, and would never regain his reason.[128] Sadly, Doheny spent the remainder of his life institutionalized. On December 29, 1916, forty-three-year-old Edward Richard Doheny died at the Medfield State Hospital in Massachusetts from pulmonary tuberculosis. Besides serving as a devoted member of the Catholic Church throughout his life, Eddie belonged to the Brownson Council, No. 419 Knights of Columbus in New York City.[129]

Following the announcement of Doheny's death, Ralph S. Davis wrote in his *Pittsburgh Press* column on January 3, 1917, that if the southpaw hurler had not suffered a mental breakdown in 1903, the Pirates might have defeated the Boston Americans in the World Series. Davis also vividly recalled an incident from early that season. A Pittsburgh scribe, now deceased, had criticized Doheny regarding the twirler's performance in a game. That night, Eddie seized a shotgun with the intention of shooting this sportswriter. People apprehended Doheny when he tried to enter the office where the reporter worked, subdued the ballplayer, and took the shotgun from him. Ralph reasoned Eddie suffered from insanity at the time.[130] In a year of tragic events, the man with the iron arm became the third and final casualty from what proved to be a lethal period in baseball history.

*Following hurler **Eddie Doheny**'s exceptional start to the 1897 season, New York Giants owner Andrew Freedman suspended and fined him on June 12 for insubordination. Although the punishment lasted two months, Eddie did not return to the lineup that year due to illness. During his time with the Giants, New York's newspapers constantly authored stories about Doheny's teammates offering substandard performances on purpose when he pitched. After the Giants gave Eddie his unconditional release on July 18, 1901, he signed with the Pittsburgh Pirates a week later. As the Pirates battled in 1903 to represent the National League in the first modern World Series against the Boston Americans, Doheny, believing detectives tailed him and a Cincinnati shoemaker wanted to murder the pitcher, suffered a nervous breakdown. (Courtesy of the Michael T. "Nuf Ced" McGreevy Collection, Boston Public Library).*

CHAPTER 5

A Heated Rivalry

Fred Clarke versus Frank Bowerman and "Hey Barney"

A contentious rivalry emerged in the National League during the Deadball Era's infancy. In 1902, the New York Giants finished in the league's basement, while the Pittsburgh Pirates cruised to their second consecutive pennant. With feisty John Joseph "Muggsy" McGraw arriving on the scene for the Giants that summer, things tightened up in 1903 as New York became Pittsburgh's primary challenger for National League honors. From 1901 through 1905, one of these clubs copped the organization's flag before the Chicago Cubs wedged their way into the conversation when discussing baseball's greatest teams. An old-school diamond renegade who utilized any tactic if it meant bringing home a victory, the Giants' new skipper came from a class of rowdies that dominated baseball in the 1890s.

Although Pirates manager Fred Clarke embraced such practices to a lesser degree, club owner Barney Dreyfuss strived for a clean baseball environment that excluded rowdyism and the rough-and-tumble tactics lauded by athletes of the previous generation. Understanding the game's growth and prosperity hinged on producing a diamond product that appealed to all members of society, Dreyfuss strongly advocated cleaning up baseball. His goal's significance centered on making it more appealing to female clientele. While Barney exhibited a virtuous stance and upheld high moral standards, his temper sometimes supplied a roadblock toward those aspirations. When two squads battled for every inch of diamond turf to win a championship, these conflicting philosophies caused immense confrontations. In the process, physical clashes occurred, tarnished reputations rose to the forefront, and league jurisprudence received harsh scrutiny.

Dreyfuss's and McGraw's connections to baseball existed for many years before this heated rivalry was forged like molten steel in a Pittsburgh mill. Bernard "Barney" Dreyfuss was born on February 23, 1865, in Freiburg, Baden, an area of Europe that later became part of Germany. At seventeen, Dreyfuss immigrated to the United States.[1] His father, Samuel Dreyfuss, had lived in the United States for several years before returning to his country of origin. Dreyfuss received an education in his homeland and worked at a bank in Karlsruhe before traveling to America.[2] Upon reaching this new land of hope and opportunity, Barney settled in Paducah, Kentucky, where relatives lived. Once there, the young man worked as a clerk on a steamboat that transported goods along the Tennessee River.[3] Dreyfuss quickly found another job as a laborer for the Bernheim Brothers distillery.[4] Shortly after joining Bernheim, the company promoted Barney to bookkeeper.

Before long, Dreyfuss rose to head accountant. Barney, exhibiting an interest in baseball, joined an amateur squad in Paducah and played second base. In time, Dreyfuss became the club's manager and led the team to diamond success.[5] Barney operated this thriving club for four years.[6] After the company promoted Dreyfuss to credit manager, Bernheim Brothers moved their business to Louisville, Kentucky. Once there, using money he diligently saved, Barney purchased stock in the American Association's Colonels baseball club. Organizational officials, recognizing the young man possessed brilliant savvy within many aspects of baseball's front-office machinations, appointed Dreyfuss as the team treasurer in 1890. In 1896, four years after Louisville joined the twelve-team National League, Harry Pulliam assumed the post as club president.

Before the 1899 campaign started, team secretary and treasurer Barney Dreyfuss gained controlling interest in the Colonels and switched positions in the management hierarchy with Pulliam.[7] Dreyfuss paid $50,000 to become the majority owner of Louisville's baseball franchise.[8] Understanding that contraction seemed a distinct possibility after the season ended, Barney searched for ways to remain connected to the game at this level since the National League would likely select the Colonels as one of the clubs they eliminated from the organization. On December 8, 1899, Dreyfuss partnered with co-owners William Kerr and Philip Auten of the Pittsburgh Pirates' franchise through a blockbuster arrangement. As part of this epic deal finalized at Kerr's Arbuckle Building office in downtown Pittsburgh, the Pirates received stellar players Fred Clarke, Honus Wagner, Claude Ritchey, Tommy Leach, Deacon Phillippe, and George Edward "Rube" Waddell from the Colonels. The new ownership trio named Clarke, who had overseen Louisville since 1897, to manage Pittsburgh in 1900.[9]

When the board of directors held their annual meeting of the Pittsburgh Baseball Club on December 10, 1899, in Jersey City, New Jersey, they elected

Barney Dreyfuss president and Harry Pulliam team secretary.[10] Following the consummation of this deal, a Louisville inhabitant told William Kerr and Philip Auten that although Barney performed his duties in a dedicated, hustling, hard-working manner, he did not like others usurping his authority. Differences of opinion emerged amongst the ownership group as the successful 1900 season on the field and financially progressed through the summer.[11] Because of this contentious atmosphere, Kerr and Auten relieved Pulliam of his duties months after the campaign ended.[12] Barney, angry over the partners firing his friend and trusted assistant, lashed out against William and Philip. This response led Kerr and Auten to determine they needed to remove Dreyfuss as president at the next board of directors meeting.[13]

Barney engaged in various deft maneuvers to avoid receiving his walking papers. Since the situation had grown so fragile between the two parties, Dreyfuss issued an ultimatum to his colleagues in early 1901 that they either purchase his stock or sell their club options to him. At the beginning of February, Barney bought out his partners. On February 18, 1901, Dreyfuss became the organization's majority owner when he paid $66,150 to purchase the stock options held by William Kerr and Philip Auten.[14] In gaining control of a franchise whose diamond future looked bright, Barney needed to get down in the mud and fight dirty to maintain his position as the Pirates' magnate.

John McGraw traveled a different road to prominence within Organized Baseball. McGraw was born on April 7, 1873, in Truxton, New York.[15] John's mother, Ellen, died from diphtheria when he was eleven.[16] McGraw's father, John Sr., frequently remained away from home due to earning $9 each week, working sixty hours on a maintenance crew for the Elmira, Courtland, and Northern Railroad. One evening, when the father happened to be home, a neighbor called at the house demanding money to replace a window his son broke while playing baseball. Following a beating from John Sr. over the property damage, young John packed up his belongings and gained refuge with Mary Goddard, who operated a nearby Truxton hotel.[17]

John D. O'Connor and his wife later helped look after and care for John, known as Jack, during his youth. In an interview with *New York Daily News* sportswriter Harry Forbes in 1938, O'Connor said McGraw loved playing baseball as a youngster and constantly participated in games at a lot across the street from their residence. Due to robust devotion to the game, young Jack usually missed lunch, prompting Mrs. O'Connor to make sandwiches to send to the field. Because of a deep dedication to his diamond craft, McGraw refused to eat. The youth became so angry that he did not go home at dinnertime.[18]

In 1890, at seventeen, John signed his first professional contract with a club in Olean, New York, from the New York-Pennsylvania League. That winter, he joined a squad managed by Al Lawson, representing Ocala, Florida, on a baseball tour of Cuba. One year later, in 1891, McGraw pulled on a uniform for the Illinois-Iowa League's Cedar Rapids Canaries. While there, manager William "Billy" Barnie of the American Association's Baltimore Orioles scouted and signed John to play for his team. That off-season, McGraw made a second trek to Cuba, this time on a club overseen by "Honest John" Kelly of Mobile, Alabama. After the American Association folded following the 1891 campaign, John remained with the Orioles as a member of their National League squad in 1892. Pegged as a second baseman before Ned Hanlon took control as Baltimore's manager that summer, McGraw saw time at shortstop in 1893 until Hanlon's keen baseball mind and sharp eye for talent recognized the little infielder's endless possibilities and installed him as the Orioles' permanent third baseman in 1894.

John became a fixture at that position and a baseball star. He saw limited action in 1896 after contracting typhoid fever while Baltimore traveled through the South on their spring training trip. The illness so incapacitated McGraw that it took him until 1898 to recapture his strength and previous skill level.[19] For seven consecutive seasons starting in 1893, John topped the .300 mark each year in batting, with his highest average of .391 coming in 1899. The Orioles also captured National League flags for three straight campaigns from 1894 through 1896. When McGraw first broke into the professional ranks, he was reticent, lacked a formal education, and exhibited little polish as a ballplayer. Through arduous work and dedication, McGraw studied and improved himself rapidly as a diamond performer and a member of humanity. During the winter, John attended college to improve his standing in society.[20]

He also evolved into one of the game's firebrands, exhibiting no reservations over assaulting opposing players, umpires, or occasionally even Baltimore team members because of a burning desire to win. Although loathed by individuals from other clubs, McGraw's teammates and friends embraced him. Prior to the 1900 baseball season's start, National League owners agreed to eliminate the Orioles, along with Louisville, the Washington Nationals, and the Cleveland Spiders. Following the league's reduction to eight teams, the St. Louis Cardinals purchased John and former Baltimore catcher and friend Wilbert Robinson.[21] Before league officials eliminated these four clubs, the Pittsburgh Pirates' Barney Dreyfuss had commented to a *Pittsburgh Leader* sportswriter about the prospect of John joining the team he now owned.

"Great player as I recognize McGraw to be," said Barney Dreyfuss, "I wouldn't have him on a team of mine. He is one of the sort who always keep a team in trouble. Off the field McGraw is a model. In action, he is as near crazy as a sane man can get."[22]

Both players objected to their St. Louis transfer, while six Cardinals team members who once played for Cleveland considered these former foes enemy intruders.[23] Following one season in St. Louis, McGraw and Robinson organized a new Baltimore franchise and placed it in the American League, which planned to operate in direct competition with the established Senior Circuit in 1901.[24] Although committed to playing baseball for the Orioles in 1901, Cardinals owner Frank Robison forwarded contracts to John and Wilbert in February for the upcoming season. McGraw laughed when he heard the news, having not yet seen the document that Robison wished him to sign.

"That's the best ever," ejaculated the Baltimorean. "I haven't seen the paper yet, but understand that 'Robbie' [Wilbert Robinson] has forwarded it to me at the Springs [Hot Springs] and I guess it is there waiting for me. So he offers us the same salary as we received last year? That is indeed kind of him, but we will have to decline and hold the contracts as souvenirs."[25]

Frank Robison honestly did not grasp these two players' true intentions since John had held a conference with New York Giants owner Andrew Freedman at the end of December. On January 2, 1901, newspapers reported McGraw had traveled to New York to meet with Freedman, who also happened to be a member of the National League's Board of Directors, besides overseeing the Giants. Scribes speculated John would drop the idea of joining the American League and reach an agreement with Freedman to play for and manage the Giants. Such a preemptive strike appeared logical since the older baseball body realized Baltimore could be a beautiful harvesting ground for Ban Johnson's organization if the league president received staunch support from McGraw and the other Orioles' owners.

John returned to Baltimore on January 1 after celebrating the previous night with New Year's Eve revelers at Herald Square in the Big Apple. McGraw had held discussions with New York's magnate on December 29, 1900. Whether Muggsy received an offer to bring him into the fold remained uncertain. Such a move would be a major coup for the National League to strike a blow against their new nemesis. McGraw offered little information about the meeting while talking to a reporter on the night of January 1.

"You know any man is liable to run over to New York without telling the world all of his business," said McGraw. "I want to state emphatically that I am considering no offers from the persons mentioned by rumor as making them. I am with each passing day more than ever with the American League and have the fullest faith in its success."

This journalist then shared a dispatch Ban Johnson sent from Chicago that evening. The American League president stated that even if McGraw did desert because of negotiations with Andrew Freedman, it made no difference to his organization's plans moving forward. After reading the message, John offered a comeback.

"Certainly my desertion, if I contemplated such a thing, would make no difference," responded John. "Mr. Johnson understands me thoroughly, however, and he knows as well that I am in the American League to stay as he does that I am not so important a person as to be able to wreck a league. I will also say that I am not negotiating with Mr. Freedman or anybody else with reference to deserting the American League."

Ban Johnson also confirmed John McGraw had written to him about Andrew Freedman requesting a conference. Ban wired back and advised John to go to New York and talk with Freedman if he desired. Johnson felt confident McGraw's loyalty would remain with the American League cause, no matter what extravagant monetary inducements he might receive to join the Giants. On the other hand, Ban believed that if John did bolt, it would at least occur at a point before the season rather than once the league started playing games.[26] Whatever love that initially existed between these two strong-willed individuals quickly dissipated once the 1901 campaign began. It appeared quite plausible that Johnson, dedicated to eliminating rowdiness and umpire baiting from his organization, might clash with the confrontational McGraw, whose main concern centered on his self-interests.

Baltimore's manager and the league president became involved in a heated dispute in June over which American League team owned the rights to first baseman Hughie Jennings, John's former Orioles teammate in the 1890s. On June 17, McGraw mentioned his correspondence with Jennings, where Hughie, property of the Brooklyn Superbas, corroborated Muggsy's belief that Baltimore possessed first claim to his services. John also declared Ban lied when the league official told Hughie the Orioles had waived his rights to Connie Mack's Philadelphia Athletics.[27] Johnson referenced Mack's entitlement when ruling on June 16 that Jennings's rights belonged to his club. McGraw responded by declaring Hughie would arrive in Baltimore in three days to play for the Orioles. John accused Ban of attempting to weaken his team, while also threatening a court injunction to protect his interests.[28] One day later, Chicago White Sox magnate Charles Comiskey offered his support for Johnson's judgment.

> Connie Mack has the prior claim over McGraw, and, in my opinion, President Johnson is right in ruling that Hugh Jennings must go to Philadelphia if he plays in the American League.
>
> At the time all of the managers were making up our lists of four National Leaguers that we were to claim, McGraw had his limit of four—[Samuel James Tilden "Jimmy"] Sheckard, [William "Bill"] Keister,

Robinson and himself—and [Frank] Foutz, his first baseman, not only claimed, but signed, and all the rest of us had not yet to go after the ones we wanted. Jennings was then claimed by Mack, and, in spite of the fact that McGraw may now need him more, I believe it is only fair to give him to Philadelphia, and that's where he will go when the thing is once settled.[29]

The meeting that Comiskey alluded to had previously occurred in Chicago, where managers selected the four National League players each wanted to claim as owning their rights. John McGraw rejected Ban Johnson's assertion that he did not permit individuals at the conference to sign any of these men without first gaining the league president's authorization. McGraw admitted he did not wire Ban to seek approval when affixing Mike Donlin's and Jimmy Williams's signatures to contracts at Hot Springs. John also revealed the franchise representatives at this conference decided to change the initial agreement of limiting each club claiming three players up to four. McGraw accused Chicago, Philadelphia, and Boston of not living up to this pact, as they each signed seven or eight National League players.[30] Ultimately, Hughie Jennings played for the Philadelphia Phillies in 1901 after Brooklyn sold him to that club.

This animosity festered throughout the summer between the two. While John did not readily admit that he planned to part company with Johnson next year, a *Baltimore American* sportswriter interpreted this as the case following an interview with the Orioles' skipper at the end of July. In turn, Johnson, whose executive ability made National League owners envious, accused McGraw of attempting to wreck the American League. Ban's resolve appeared unbreakable, considering his statement on July 29, 1901.

> I cannot and will not state definitely that Baltimore will not be in the American League circuit next year, but I will say this: We have our eyes on other cities that are much better than Baltimore. They are better baseball towns and we can place a better team in any of them. You know that in running a big league you must have several strings to your bow. You must always be prepared for just such moves as this one of McGraw's.
>
> As you can readily see, it is lucky now that we have another city in the East where a good club may be placed and where it is sure to make money and plenty of it. Baltimore is not such a great baseball town. There are many better.
>
> And as to McGraw, he's a traitor and a man who would not hesitate to throw down his best friend. His actions in starting a movement with a view before him of breaking up the league proves this. But we were

ready for him. I found out what he was a long time ago, and as soon as he started his game he was headed off.[31]

According to Ban Johnson, John McGraw seemed dedicated to sabotaging potential American League prosperity while indicating he planned to utilize this same tactic by moving the Baltimore franchise and thus eliminating Muggsy. The Orioles finished fifth in the 1901 American League race, posting a 68–65 record. McGraw did not sound like a disgruntled player, manager, or owner in December, when he spoke positively of Johnson and the league.

> Ban Johnson, president of the American League, has shown himself broad-minded and liberal. He wants the interests of the game advanced and is ready for any fair, amicable settlement between the leagues. [Albert "Al"] Spalding [who experienced a brief tenure in 1901-02 as National League president] and Johnson have both shown that they want to keep the game popular and to obliterate partisanism.
>
> I do not anticipate any change in the American League circuit. We are all right as we are.
>
> The American League has now nearly if not its full quota of the best players in this country, and they are fairly well distributed among the clubs.[32]

Baseball lovers could interpret such a statement in two ways. John either appeared genuinely happy with his current situation, or, in playing the long game, he greased the wheels in case an opportunity arose to return to the National League. In August 1901, White Sox manager Clark Griffith criticized Johnson for considering a policy of banning players like Baltimore's Joe McGinnity, who he suspended indefinitely for spitting in umpire Tommy Connolly's face. In condemning this approach, Griffith declared that Joe Cantillon and John "Jack" Sheridan constituted the only good arbitrators out of the five Ban employed.[33] In the summer of 1902, McGraw confronted the bad umpire whose face had received a spray of McGinnity's spittle one year earlier.

In a game against Detroit at Oriole Park on May 24, John viciously attacked Dick Harley when the Tigers' player spiked him in the left knee on a play at third base. That evening, McGraw called on team doctor Standish McCleary to attend to his severe injury. The physician applied disinfectant to, cleaned, and stitched the wounds. Unfortunately, the knee became infected.[34] McGraw missed over a month away from the club and did not return to the starting lineup until June 28, when Baltimore played the Boston Americans on the home grounds. A problem arose in that game's eighth inning when the Orioles'

Cy Seymour cut the base upon returning to second after discovering a teammate had retreated to third. Americans shortstop Alfred "Freddy" Parent, realizing Seymour cheated, yelled to third baseman Jimmy Collins to throw him the baseball. Once he possessed the sphere in his hand, Parent tagged Seymour, and Tommy Connolly called the runner out for not sprinting on the basepath when making his trek back to the keystone sack.

John McGraw ran out to vociferously argue with Connolly over his decision. The umpire ordered McGraw off the field before banishing him to the clubhouse for such abusive behavior. When John refused to leave, Tommy awarded the game to Boston, 9–0, by forfeit. Excellent police presence prevented any of the three thousand spectators angry over this outcome from accosting Americans team members and subjecting them to bodily harm.[35] On June 30, Ban Johnson announced he indefinitely suspended McGraw and Baltimore outfielder Joe Kelley for their on-field conduct two days earlier during the contest against Boston. Johnson sent each ballplayer a letter notifying them of his decision, based on harassing an umpire they had attempted to drive from the league for the past two seasons. Ban explained his assessment of another blemish on the game by somebody from the Orioles' organization.

> I have had time enough since I returned from the North to make a thorough investigation of this Baltimore trouble and I am convinced that Umpire Connolly was absolutely right. He knew what he was doing, because he knew the rules, and I am glad he maintained his position and humiliated Mr. McGraw.
>
> I have received his report in the affair, and have compared it with reports which have come to me. I find that it is correct, and I shall stand by Connolly.
>
> When McGraw protested vigorously against a decision he rendered, and in doing so used insulting language, Connolly ordered him off the field. He refused to go, and then Kelley, the other prime disturber on the Baltimore team, began to hurl insulting and highly abusive language at him.
>
> In order to maintain his dignity as an official of the American League there was nothing for Connolly to do but forfeit the game to Boston.

Johnson added that he did not know how long the suspensions might last since the pair had committed other offenses in 1902. Ban also stipulated that disturbers like McGraw and Kelley needed to learn to keep their place on American League diamonds. Johnson concluded that Orioles fans had grown disgusted over such abrasive tactics.[36] Considered rabble on the diamond and a traitor working behind the scenes to push a personal agenda to the greatest advantage, McGraw finally gained his freedom from a league president he perceived as oppressive. On July 7, 1902, Giants officials announced that John left Baltimore to take over as New York's National League club manager.[37]

After Ban Johnson had berated, suspended, and fined him on numerous occasions, McGraw finally broke free and voluntarily severed his American League ties. Due to John's vindictive nature, many friends believed New York's new skipper would do everything within his power to disrupt Ban Johnson's organization and bring it crashing down in ruins.[38] Those supporting John speculated his move back to the National League could spark an escalation of the bitter war between these two major league institutions. Critics emphasized the American League should receive congratulations for eliminating a detrimental, unseemly character. These individuals also felt that Giants owner Andrew Freedman would tire of Muggsy's ways and the impending problems resulting from his diamond approach.[39] Following an organizational meeting on July 8, Baltimore vice president Sydney S. Frank commented on the formal action regarding McGraw's request to grant his release.

"The club has formally granted McGraw the release he asked for," said Frank. "In view of the fact that he was not in harmony with the president of the organization of which the Baltimore club is a part, it was not to the advantage of the club to retain him. The meeting was perfectly harmonious, and there is still the utmost good feeling on both sides. McGraw has now no interest of any kind in the Baltimore club. He has sold his stock, amounting to $6,500, to Mr. [John J.] Mahon [the Orioles' team president]. No director has yet been elected to succeed McGraw, but Kelley and Robinson will succeed him as joint managers, with equal authority. The Baltimore club will receive no bonus from the New York club for the release of McGraw, as has been reported."[40]

According to a July 9 article in New York's *The Sun*, this move ended up as a contingency plan on John's part after he could not realize his original intention. The newspaper claimed that if a scheme McGraw initiated weeks earlier had succeeded, he would not have signed to manage the Giants. Two months earlier, John concluded that no matter which league fielded a team in Baltimore, baseball appeared destined to fail in that city. Fan apathy caused a huge problem, although, over the winter, John had assembled a roster of players whose combined salaries reached $50,000. McGraw unsuccessfully warned rooters that money would be unavailable to pay these salaries and expenses if the Orioles did not garner their box office support. This article also revealed Ban Johnson hoped to ruin the Baltimore club so he could transfer the franchise to New York, which then benefited the entire American League.

The Sun reported that John McGraw almost outmaneuvered Johnson, placing a team in New York. On June 4, McGraw received information while spending an afternoon at Brooklyn's Gravesend Race Track about the availability for purchase of a vacant lot on Manhattan Island. This plot of land maintained borders to the west at First Avenue, to the north at 113th Street, to the south at 111th Street, and to the east by the East River. John immediately consulted Frank Farrell, who owned racehorses and had become known as the "Pool Room King." While in the presence of this journalist from *The Sun*, John told Farrell about the property, who agreed to secure a lease if the grounds for a potential ballpark remained available.

"Farrell stands ready to back me for any amount," said McGraw to the reporter at the time, "and if we can get a ground we will put Freedman out of business. Baseball has been bad in Baltimore, and we intend to dump that city as soon as we can make arrangements to come to this city."

Upon investigating this property's status, the interested party found New York City officials had condemned it and intended to use it for a public park. Orioles team president John J. Mahon, who was also Joe Kelley's father-in-law, arrived in New York on June 8 only to find the lot was unavailable. Frank Farrell, John McGraw, and Mahon then discussed viable alternative options above the Harlem River. To become connected to baseball, Frank appeared agreeable to paying $30,000 a year to lease a plot of land and alleged he would purchase the Baltimore franchise for $50,000. Realizing they might lose their American League franchise in 1903 since Ban Johnson desired to place a club in New York, Orioles ownership planned to unload their highest-priced players to the top bidders. Influential people in Bronx Borough strongly desired an American League club in that area.

This newspaper reporter confirmed that McGraw did not consider making a deal with Andrew Freedman until finding out that he and his investors could not secure the Manhattan Island property. Like Freedman, Farrell wielded immeasurable power within Tammany Hall's councils.[41] Frank did become one of the New York Highlanders' principal owners when the club debuted in the American League in 1903, under the guidance of pilot Clark Griffith. McGraw took some final parting shots before rejoining the National League. John criticized Johnson for exhibiting partiality to certain teams and owners while also alleging to know intimate details about the American League's dire financial situation. Baseball experts connected to the organization pushed back against this assertion, claiming such a comment clearly validated that McGraw possessed limited knowledge of league affairs.[42]

Shortly after joining the Giants, McGraw added some familiar faces to his roster. On the night of July 16, the Baltimore Orioles' majority stockholders conducted a critical meeting that sent ripples throughout baseball. President John J. Mahon—representing John, current Orioles manager Joe Kelley, and team captain Wilbert Robinson—sold 201 shares of the franchise's stock to Andrew Freedman and Cincinnati Reds owner John T. Brush for a price rumored as high as $50,000. Once both sides consummated this deal, attorney and facilitator Joseph C. France, who represented Freedman and Brush at this conference, shifted pitchers Joe McGinnity and John "Jack" Cronin, first baseman Dan McGann, and all-purpose player Roger Bresnahan to New York. Joe Kelley and Cy Seymour moved on to play for Cincinnati. Ban Johnson had known two days earlier that Kelley, expected to become the Reds' new manager, planned to desert the Orioles.

Since Baltimore no longer employed enough players to field a team, the St. Louis Browns secured the game on July 17 at Oriole Park through forfeit. Under the American League constitution's rules, when this type of event occurred, it meant the Baltimore franchise also forfeited their right to continue operations. As per this charter rule, Johnson gained authority to assume control of the club and bring in new players to finish out the campaign's schedule. Second baseman Jimmy Williams and outfielder Kip Selbach, undoubtedly the Orioles' top ballplayers, demonstrated no intention of deserting since the club currently employed them on two-year contracts. While McGinnity waited at the station to board his train for New York, the hurler wore the appearance of somebody realizing he became mixed up in an unethical operation.

Had Cincinnati's and New York's baseball magnates restocked the Orioles with minor leaguers after purchasing the franchise, they could have dealt a more lethal blow to Ban's organization.[43] Instead, these two moguls seemed satisfied with their short-term personal gratification by tearing apart the carcass and leaving only the bones. Purchasing the Baltimore Orioles proved nothing more than a means to funnel the squad's best players to New York and Cincinnati. On August 11, 1902, John T. Brush severed his ties as the Reds' owner when a group of individuals led by Garry Herrmann finalized a deal to buy that baseball franchise.[44] Brush did not remain retired from baseball leadership as a magnate for long. On the evening of September 29, Andrew Freedman announced from the Fifth Avenue Hotel in New York that he chose the former Cincinnati front office executive, who owned a block of stock in the Giants, to replace him as club president.

"I take pleasure in announcing that John T. Brush," said Freedman, "chairman of the Executive Committee of the National League and the former majority owner of the Cincinnati National League club, will succeed me as president of the New York baseball club at a not far distant date, and that Mr. Brush will also secure sufficient stock to place him in a position of controlling interest in the National Exhibition Company, New York Baseball Club."

Freedman shared that his many other business interests made it impossible for him to devote the necessary time to running the New York Giants' baseball operation. Andrew revealed that while he received many flattering offers to purchase his majority interest in the club, the magnate chose Brush as his successor after considering him for more than a year because of John's commitment to the National League's success. Such a change could not happen while Brush owned the Reds. John cleared this hurdle when he sold the club to Garry Herrmann. Freedman expressed confidence that through combining the holdover players and any additions Brush might make to the roster, Giants fans should be excited over watching a high-quality diamond product in 1903. Andrew remained as a stockholder within the organization.[45]

New York's new leadership team of John McGraw and John T. Brush set their sights on transforming the Giants into a National League powerhouse. No longer having Ban Johnson to engage in heated battles, McGraw needed to turn elsewhere to discover a brand-new adversary. John found a worthy antagonist in the Pittsburgh Pirates, who claimed their third consecutive league flag in 1903. To McGraw, no individual connected to the Pirates' organization was off limits, not even owner Barney Dreyfuss. New York exhibited that they would be a powerful force, rather than an also-ran as in the past, by posting a 15–5 record in their opening 20 games of the 1903 campaign. A huge salvo of animosity between the Giants and Pittsburgh occurred during a series at the beginning of June between the two clubs at Exposition Park. After losing the first contest on June 1, 10–2, the Pirates blanked New York in the next two games.

Pittsburgh defeated the Giants, 7–0, on June 2. Pirates batters barraged New York hurler Luther "Dummy" Taylor for 14 hits in the contest. During the game, umpire James "Jim" Johnstone banished burly Giants catcher Frank Bowerman from the field for arguing with him over balls and strikes. Bowerman watched the remainder of this diamond clash from the grandstand as Jack Warner took his place behind the plate.[46] Once the game concluded, Fred Clarke walked up to Warner and quoted Frank commenting earlier from the grandstand, saying, "If I was catching Pittsburgh would not make so many hits." Clarke then hinted that Bowerman held an extremely low opinion of Jack's catching ability. This infuriated Warner, who refused to speak to Frank for the remainder of the road trip.[47] When Jack approached Bowerman about these comments, in which his teammate referred to him as a third-rate catcher, while the club traveled by train to Chicago after leaving Pittsburgh, New York's sturdy backstop denied making such statements.[48]

Warner also engaged John McGraw over Frank's despicable attitude. McGraw severely reprimanded Bowerman before the catcher offered another denial and replied, "I'll bring Clarke face to face with you and prove he is a liar."[49] That opportunity occurred when Pittsburgh made a trip to New York near the end of June to play a series at the Polo Grounds. Upon arriving at the ballpark before the game on the afternoon of June 26, the secretaries of each team, Fred Knowles from the Giants and the Pirates' William Locke, accompanied Fred. As he approached the gate, Clarke noticed several New York players milling around the entrance. The fact that three of them started following Fred as he advanced toward the gate indicated that what was about to happen definitively qualified as a premeditated and carefully considered action. Frank Bowerman, one of the players standing near the entrance, greeted Locke before confronting Clarke.

"Hello, Fred," he said, holding out his hand for a cordial shake. "May I speak to you a few minutes."

"Certainly," replied Clarke, who smiled good-naturedly as he returned the grip.

The two ballplayers walked into a nearby ticket office, accessible since one of the two barred doors happened to be open. After Fred entered, Frank swung the door shut. Since a person could only open these doors from the inside, Bowerman maintained absolute control of the environment to execute his vile plan. Once inside, Frank accused Fred of falsely repeating a remark to Jack Warner attributed to him about not showing capability when working with one of the Giants' hurlers.

"You are wrong, Frank," replied Clarke. "I know you made the statement, but I did not tell Warner."

"You lie!" shouted Bowerman, who uttered a vulgar insult for effect.

Following his comment, the angry ballplayer landed a fierce punch against the unsuspecting Clarke's face. This room's size worked to Frank's advantage since it was only five feet wide and most of that area contained desks. The force of this first blow knocked a surprised Fred into a corner, where, with arms pinned at his side, he remained at the mercy of his much larger assailant. Bowerman placed his knee on Clarke's stomach and, with a free hand, hammered away at Pittsburgh's helpless manager for several minutes. Fred never had an opportunity to land even one punch. Hearing the commotion, Locke found a police officer, but New York's Roger Bresnahan, in the ticket office before his teammate accosted Clarke, calmly blocked the doors and refused the law enforcement representative access. Realizing he had inflicted enough damage, Frank walked out of the office unscathed. Battered in this brazen attack, a hurting Fred already could not stand upright after pitcher Frederick "Fred" Mitchell drilled him in the stomach with a fastball the previous day in a game against Philadelphia.

Without taking measures to patch up his battered face, Clarke left the ticket office shortly after Bowerman and hurried to the clubhouse, put on his uniform, and played left field for the Pirates that afternoon.[50] Giants management announced before the game started that they did not plan to punish Frank for instigating this fight.⁵¹ When Fred emerged after receiving a ruthless thrashing, he sported a black eye, a badly swollen jaw, and several abrasions on his face. One thing that led to Bowerman losing control was when Clarke refused to face Jack Warner and John McGraw as he belligerently requested.⁵² Warner happened to be one of New York's team members who waited outside the ticket office while Frank confronted and then assaulted Pittsburgh's manager.

Different opinions existed regarding league punishment for Frank Bowerman. Some ballplayers reasoned that because the confrontation did not happen on the diamond and the two combatants wore street clothes at the time, everybody should treat it as a private matter. Others understood that since National League president Harry Pulliam earnestly championed clean baseball, he needed to act to protect the game.⁵³ Giants hurler Christy Mathewson pitched masterfully in the actual contest, defeating the Pirates, 8–2.⁵⁴ While encountering Pittsburgh's manager at the Hotel Marlborough on the morning of June 27, a *Pittsburgh Press* correspondent wrote that Fred was not in very good shape and possibly could not play in that afternoon's contest.⁵⁵ Clarke suited up as the Pirates turned the tables and beat New York in eleven innings, 4–2.

In a column for the *Pittsburgh Press*, sportswriter Ralph S. Davis condemned Frank Bowerman for his cowardly behavior. Davis reasoned Frank, who he referred to as "Brutal" Bowerman, should receive severe punishment for attacking Fred Clarke. While possibly subject to criminal law in this case, Ralph believed discipline from Bowerman's employer was necessary, although the sportswriter did not think John T. Brush or John McGraw intended to follow this course.⁵⁶ In an article for the *Sporting News*, Davis called Frank irresponsible and, like Philadelphia Athletics hurler Rube Waddell, lacking gray matter of the brain and submitting to his lower instincts when aroused.⁵⁷

Angry Pirates fans denounced Bowerman's behavior. A wire from Greensburg, Pennsylvania, claimed Frank never became involved in scraps with players who possessed equal physical stature.⁵⁸ On the evening of June 27, Barney Dreyfuss traveled to New York to thoroughly investigate Bowerman's malicious attack on Fred Clarke. Initially, Dreyfuss refused to believe the story possessed truth and declined to take any action until first finding out all the facts. The correspondence he received from Clarke that afternoon before leaving Pittsburgh corroborated the confrontation's veracity. Barney categorized the assault as uncalled for and a result of a plot by Giants players to weaken his club. Dreyfuss was incensed that New York's club officials permitted the catcher to play in the game on June 26 and that team secretary Fred Knowles announced the organization would take no disciplinary action against Frank.

"Section 28, of the constitution of the National League, specifies," Dreyfuss said, "that club owners can punish either managers or players for disorderly conduct, intoxication, *et cetera*, either on or off the field. The failure on the part of the New York Club officials to take action in this matter plainly shows that it must be sanctioned by them. I intend to make a thorough investigation of the case, and someone will suffer, if the charges are proven, and I have not the least idea now that they are not correct. I cannot state what this action will be, but I will certainly protect myself and my players from such ruffianism."[59]

On July 14, 1903, Harry Pulliam notified Frank Bowerman that he had fined New York's catcher $100 for attacking Fred Clarke.[60] Pulliam rendered this monetary penalty after mulling over testimony he gathered on the incident from Clarke, Bowerman, and William Locke. In Frank's statement to the league president, he admitted to striking the Pirates' field leader. As a basis for issuing the fine, Pulliam referenced a section of the National League constitution, which stipulated that the league punish a player for assaulting another individual on or off the field. Bowerman could continue playing until the fine was paid by a determined date or if he decided to appeal the case before the league's Board of Directors.[61] Frank had five days to make the payment if he did not petition the board for a hearing. Harry conducted this investigation after Dreyfuss brought the matter to his attention.

The first game of the return engagement between these two clubs at Exposition Park occurred on July 15. Pittsburgh management arranged for extra police officers at the ballpark to protect Bowerman in case bleacher section rooters decided to inflict their own justice on the catcher for his June attack against Fred Clarke. Although police presence for Frank's benefit rattled him, his four runs batted in played a huge part in helping the Giants secure a fourteen-inning victory over the Pirates, 6–3. The heavy police presence on the field and officers escorting Bowerman to the team's omnibus after the game ended prevented any violent outbreaks.[62] Of course, mental stress strongly prevailed as rooters hissed and jeered when Frank walked from the diamond to take his place in the cab. This heckling continued throughout the four-game series. Bowerman, who had played for the Pirates in 1898 and 1899, alienated so many local patrons that even his Pittsburgh friends for many years turned to enemies.[63]

After losing the first contest on July 15, the Pirates claimed the series' final three games. Christy Mathewson went the route, beating Pittsburgh in the opening affair. On the morning of July 18, John McGraw reiterated his intention to start Mathewson in that afternoon's final game, which Pittsburgh's newspapers had printed while discussing the prior meeting between these rivals. Pirates officials anticipated a large Saturday crowd at Exposition Park, eager to watch Christy on the mound. For fifteen minutes before the contest started, Mathewson threw warmup tosses to Frank. At the same time, fellow hurler Roscoe Miller loosened up with one of New York's other catchers in case anything happened to Christy. When Bowerman finished this task, he looked around the ballpark and noticed a huge crowd gathering to view the diamond festivities. A cowardly yellow streak overcame Frank. The catcher approached John McGraw and told his manager he feared playing. Alluding to how the fans treated him in the previous games, Bowerman informed McGraw he could not face these angry rooters.

Since Christy Mathewson excelled on the mound when Frank worked behind the plate, John scratched his star hurler from the lineup and opted to use Miller. When the Giants took the field, ten thousand enthusiastic fans immediately noticed Christy did not join them to pitch, although along the path leading to the visitors' bench, it said, "Mathewson will pitch tomorrow," placed there on Friday. Fans in the grandstand booed Roscoe and yelled things like, "Take him out," "Put Christy in," "We came to see Mathewson pitch," and "Where's Mathewson?" Fans did not realize Bowerman's faintheartedness acted as the reason for Christy not pitching. If so, things could have gone far worse for the catcher, who looked sullen and glum as he walked off the field under police protection when the contest concluded. Some scribes declared McGraw should have insisted that Bowerman, who only appeared in the series' first game, work behind the plate despite lacking nerve. A New York sportswriter stated Mathewson ought to have pitched since John had announced him as the starter.[64]

Two revelations occurred much later, adding further context to a probable reason behind Frank Bowerman's assault on Fred Clarke. According to a story from November 1904, John McGraw noticed acrimony among his squad after New York played their early June series the previous year in Pittsburgh. Players formed cliques and stared rudely at other team members not in their group. Silence prevailed when they rode to the ballpark in the omnibus, and pregame practice appeared dull and lifeless. When the club reached Chicago, John realized the problem stemmed from Fred Clarke's comment to Jack Warner about Bowerman criticizing his teammate's ability. Half the club took Jack's side in the dispute while the other team members stood in Frank's corner. Exhibiting the brilliance and tactical genius of an army general, McGraw instigated his grand plan by confronting Bowerman about slighting Warner by saying, "If I was catching there, that run would have never come in."

"Did you make that crack?" McGraw asked.

"Mack," protested the big catcher. "that's the meanest lie that ever was told, and I told Jack Warner so; but he don't believe me."

"All right," said McGraw. "That's all that I wanted to know. Now, just keep quiet and do the best you can until we get home."

The day Pittsburgh arrived in New York, John called Frank aside before the series' first game on June 26.

"Frank, have you got a good right swing?" inquired John.

Bowerman smiled grimly before forming a firm fist rivaling that of Hercules. During the winter months, Frank lived at a lumber camp in Michigan, spending time fishing, hunting, and chopping down trees. This physical specimen could be the perfect muscle to execute his boss's grand vision.

"Well, it's up to you then," advised McGraw, "to put life in the team. Don't lose any time."

Frank fully understood these instructions and accosted Fred Clarke that afternoon. The incident had the positive effect New York's manager hoped for, as his players exhibited more fire and passion in that game and beyond. Bowerman and Warner also rekindled their friendship, yelling pet names at one another while working the coaching lines that day. When questioned about the incident after it happened, John responded briefly.

"There's more than one way, of putting life in a ball team," replied John McGraw.[65]

Another newspaper story, printed in the *St. Louis Globe-Democrat* on June 18, 1905, offered insight into why friction existed between these two ballplayers. According to Frank, the problems started in 1899 when Clarke played for Louisville and he performed as a Pirates team member. Bowerman told the sportswriter that six years earlier, catchers usually stood back behind home plate when no opposing runners occupied the bases. Fred had developed into an expert bunter who often utilized his speed to reach first base. Frank devised a method to circumvent this strategy by running toward the dish when Clarke bunted the baseball. This maneuver did not thrill Fred since it eliminated a key component in his arsenal if discovered by other teams.

In a game between the two clubs, Clarke laid down a bunt, turned around, and threw his bat at Bowerman to stop him from running to grab the ball. The wooden cudgel struck Frank's throat and almost knocked him unconscious. Angry over this cheap tactic, Bowerman grabbed the bat and chased Fred. Frank caught Clarke at first base and struck him with the bat. Police officers rushed onto the field to avert a riot. The following day, Bowerman encountered Fred under the grandstand and punched him in the jaw. A few months after the season ended, when Pittsburgh's ownership group of Barney Dreyfuss, William Kerr, and Philip Auten named Clarke to manage the Pirates, Fred could not allow Frank to remain on his club and shipped the catcher to the New York Giants.[66]

John McGraw continued imposing his will on members of the Pittsburgh Pirates. Even John's pugnacious nature did not exempt the person at the top of the organizational chain of command. The Pirates claimed the 1903 National League pennant and then suffered defeat at the hands of the Boston Americans in the first modern World Series. During Game Two at Huntington Avenue Baseball Grounds on October 2, which Boston won, 3–0, boxer James "Gentleman Jim" Corbett and a small party of people sat in the front row of the same ballpark box as Pirates owner Barney Dreyfuss and his Pittsburgh friends. Understanding that Barney possessed a reputation as quite the gambler, Corbett's group attempted to make some small wagers as the contest progressed, but to no avail.[67]

This betting stigma cropped up once again before the 1904 season started. New York sportswriter Joseph "Joe" Vila reported that Highlanders owner Frank Farrell had chided Dreyfuss over a comment he made about the American League no longer existing by summer. Farrell then offered to bet Barney any amount of money on this proposition. Dreyfuss's enemies constantly leaked fabricated stories about him placing bets. On March 2, 1904, a newspaper printed the false tale that Barney made a wager with John McGraw over Pirates hurler William "Doc" Scanlan winning more games that season than Giants pitcher Leon "Red" Ames. Dreyfuss denied each of these gambling accusations while also claiming he never made the comment attributed to him about the American League's demise, or that the Highlanders' magnate even engaged him on the topic. Pittsburgh's owner responded to a *Pittsburgh Press* correspondent about such stories that injured Barney's reputation and hurt his feelings.

> Of course I know where these stories come from, but I do not care. I will attend to my business just the same. As a matter of fact, I very seldom make a bet on any matter pertaining to baseball. Once in a while I wager a hat or suit of clothes with some fellow magnate on some proposition, but that is more in fun than any other way.
>
> I do not make baseball bets, because I believe it is a bad thing for the sport. I do not like to have my players wager on the result of games or on the outcome of the league race, hence I do not set them the example. I could have won all kinds of money the last three seasons had I cared to back my Pirates to the full extent of my confidence in them, but I steadfastly refused to bet. Mark you, I do not mean to infer that I never bet, but not on baseball.[68]

Prior to the 1904 season's start, McGraw declared that Pittsburgh could not win the pennant again because they only possessed two prize pitchers, Deacon Phillippe and Sam Leever. John reasoned no club could secure the flag with only two good hurlers. If so, his Giants would have taken home first-place money in 1903 because of Christy Mathewson and Joe McGinnity. McGraw announced that he now possessed a deeper staff than the previous year.[69] John's prognostication proved accurate, as the Pirates' three-year reign atop the mountain ended in 1904. New York won the pennant with a 106–47 record, while Pittsburgh finished fourth, fashioning a mark of 87–66.

The Pirates added a third capable starting pitcher when they purchased Patrick "Patsy" Flaherty from the Chicago White Sox on June 6. A native of Carnegie, Pennsylvania, and Honus Wagner's childhood friend, Patsy had come to Pittsburgh once before as part of the Louisville consolidation until the organization shipped him to the Eastern League's Syracuse Stars in 1901.

Flaherty posted a 19–9 record for the Pirates in 1904, supported by a 2.05 ERA. A Giants player subjected the mild-mannered pitcher to despicable abuse while working the first game of a doubleheader at the Polo Grounds on August 16. Using vile and vulgar language, New York's Joe McGinnity constantly berated Patsy. Usually one of the coolest and calmest among Pittsburgh's squad members, Flaherty's blood started boiling, causing him to lose his temper. Patsy began moving toward McGinnity, but Pirates first baseman Kitty Bransfield grabbed the hurler before he could inflict any physical damage on his foe and turn the diamond into a battlefield. After the game ended, Flaherty informed the press of the outcome had Bransfield not intervened.

"If I had got to McGinnity," said Patsy, "I suppose I would have drawn a suspension sentence covering the remainder of the season."[70]

Due to the schedule pitting these two squads in a home-and-home series of games, fans at Exposition Park voiced their vehement displeasure with this event, still fresh in their minds, when Joe McGinnity took the mound in the initial contest of a twin bill on August 23.[71] This contentious, ill feeling between these bitter adversaries reached its apex shortly after the 1905 campaign started. Pittsburgh and New York opposed each other for the first time during a series beginning at the Polo Grounds on May 18. That afternoon, the Pirates battered Christy Mathewson and the Giants, 7–2. At one point in the game, Mathewson stopped and talked to John McGraw while coming in from the field after an inning ended. According to McGraw and several spectators, Pirates hurler Michael "Mike" Lynch made a remark from the visitors' dugout.

"Keep the big quitter in there, McGraw; don't let him get out of the game as he once did before," said Lynch.

At the time, neither John nor Christy resented Mike's comment.[72] However, McGraw displayed his combative nature to intimidate home plate umpire Bob Emslie. Once Pittsburgh grabbed the lead for good in the fourth inning, John ratcheted up the abuse. Bob, who the *Pittsburgh Press* referred to as "Vacillating" Emslie, quietly withstood the barbs coming from New York's skipper and the Polo Grounds' spectators. Bob offered no response and seemed to enjoy McGraw calling him a fat-headed bum. When Emslie angered John in the second inning, New York's skipper stoked up the crowd against the umpire, yelling to rooters, "I'd as soon have Barney Dreyfuss umpire as Emslie; it would be all the same thing." Late in the game, McGraw became more vicious and tried all types of maneuvers to hinder the Pirates' momentum, but none of these tricks worked. When the contest ended, a Pittsburgh fan walked up to Fred Clarke.

"Why don't you let your men kick a bit?" asked this rooter. "McGraw's men kept up a running fire all afternoon at Emslie."

"It's all right," replied Fred. "I promised Harry Pulliam I'd try to obey the rules, and that is what I am doing. But I had one of my men take written notes of all that transpired, and I made a few mental notes myself. I did not do that for nothing. I am keeping track of everything, and President Pulliam is going to learn all I can tell him about the matter. I am tired, taking everything from the umpires, when McGraw does as he pleases."[73]

Clarke inferred John's bullying tactics worked since National League umpires sometimes appeared reticent to confront the bombastic manager. Although the Giants cruised to an easy 7–1 victory over the Pirates on May 19, McGraw continued being a nuisance to Vacillating Emslie, who once again withstood the abuse like a true gentleman. During the contest, John attempted to include three old, worn practice baseballs by giving Bob a batch to use for game action. When Emslie tossed the three soiled balls back to New York's bench, Muggsy once again threw them in the umpire's direction. Bob secured the baseballs until the frame ended and then handed them back to McGraw, who immediately held the spheres up for the crowd to inspect, hoping this galvanized the partisans to harass the arbitrator.[74] As John walked back to the dugout, a grandstand fan offered a suggestion.

"Why don't you get another umpire, Mac?" asked the supporter.

"I would as soon have Barney Dreyfuss umpire this game," answered McGraw.[75]

Unlike the previous day when John McGraw made a similar remark, Barney Dreyfuss attended Friday's game, sitting in a Polo Grounds box with a male and a female friend from Pittsburgh.[76] Witnesses within twenty feet of McGraw when he offered this opinion for the second consecutive afternoon vowed that no profanity accompanied his comment.[77]

The largest barrage of fireworks occurred when these two squads played on May 20. The Giants drubbed Mike Lynch for four runs before Fred Clarke relieved him with Charles "Charlie" Case in the fifth inning, and held on to defeat the Pirates, 5–4. Remembering Lynch's comment from two days earlier, John verbally engaged Pittsburgh's twirler from the coaching line as the pitcher walked to the bench following a tough inning.

"Stay in the game today, you big quitter, and take your medicine," shrieked McGraw. "You'll get it good and plenty."

After Joe McGinnity retired the Pirates in the next frame, Clarke walked alongside McGraw on his way to the outfield. The respective managers became involved in a heated discussion, leading Fred to threaten John for roasting Lynch. This shouting match almost transformed into a physical confrontation. Frenzied patrons urged Frank Bowerman to join in and help his boss, but the catcher ignored the goading and walked back to New York's bench. Umpire Jim Johnstone separated the two men and ordered McGraw off the field. John argued this decision, but Johnstone refused to change his mind. John finally withdrew to a closet adjacent to his squad's dugout and closed the door behind him. Pittsburgh's players felt this did not suffice, leading Johnstone to respond, "He's off the grounds and that settles it." The arbitrator also refused to banish Clarke, although the Polo Grounds' patrons enthusiastically implored him to apply equitable justice.[78] Through a wire he sent to the *Pittsburgh Press* after the game, Fred explained what might happen in the future due to this encounter with McGraw.

"If ever McGraw repeats the words he said to me on Saturday," stated a steamed Clarke, "he and I will fight, as sure as I am living, and I will land hard on him if I start. Had he not been removed from the grounds just when he was Saturday I am sure he and I would have come to blows. The way he talked to Mike Lynch was simply scandalous. He called him all the vile names in the category and a few that I have never heard before."[79]

Upon leaving the field after the umpire expelled him from the contest, McGraw walked under the grandstand and prepared to access the Polo Grounds' clubhouse. While standing on the clubhouse balcony, John noticed Barney Dreyfuss below him, observing the game from the ballpark's entrance. McGraw decided to continue behaving in a derogatory manner at the Pittsburgh owner's expense.

"Hey, Barney!" yelled McGraw.

Dreyfuss offered no response before John snidely repeated this greeting and asked a question aimed at badgering the highest authority of his baseball club's major adversary.

"Is that bet you made with Shad Gwilliam [an individual connected to amateur baseball in Western Pennsylvania with a gambling reputation] in Pittsburgh of $700 to $400 on the Pittsburgh series on the level?" inquired John. "If it is on the level, I'd like to have a piece of it."

"I don't think you are on the level," replied Pittsburgh's president.

"Oh I'm not, eh, but I haven't got any bookmakers chasing me," answered McGraw.

Witnesses who overheard this exchange swore that John did not accuse Barney of influencing National League umpires. Dreyfuss made a final threat as he walked away from the scene.

"Wait till I get you and I'll get you right," said Dreyfuss.[80]

Some people felt John McGraw used the gambling angle while berating Barney Dreyfuss since the Pirates' magnate had previously questioned his integrity. As ammunition before the season started, Dreyfuss cited a story floating around at the time that in March, John had reneged on paying off several markers with New York bookmakers before leaving for Hot Springs. McGraw denied this accusation in the spring.[81] Joe Vila, who covered the Giants for the *Sporting News*, commended umpire Jim Johnstone for removing disruptive elements from the field during this game. Vila commented on another flow of abuse spewing from rowdy John. Joe also praised Johnstone for expelling Christy Mathewson, swelled head and all, along with loud catcher William "Boileryard" Clarke. According to the correspondent, Clarke earned his salary by yelling like a mad bull on the coaching lines and urging the hoodlum element in the stands loyal to McGraw's cause to commit deeds of disorder and unsportsmanship.[82]

Feeling John had unjustly and shamelessly impugned his character and stripped him of dignity in public, the pious Dreyfuss addressed the matter with league president Harry Pulliam. On May 22, 1905, Barney delivered a letter to Pulliam, filing a formal complaint regarding how New York's manager treated him on May 19 and 20. While discussing the first offense on May 19, Dreyfuss charged that as he sat with friends in a Polo Grounds box, McGraw offered personal references and sneering remarks about the magnate umpiring the series' remaining games. Barney then took John to task for his behavior toward him on May 20, as he viewed the game from the ballpark's entrance with some friends. Dreyfuss mentioned that Johnstone removed John from the game for using bad language and Pittsburgh's president ignored McGraw when shouting from the clubhouse balcony, "Hey, Barney!"

Barney alleged he did not respond until John insisted on making a wager. According to Dreyfuss, after telling McGraw he wanted nothing to do with him, the Giants' skipper accused him of being crooked and controlling the umpires. Barney concluded the letter, begging Harry to take steps to protect visitors at the Polo Grounds from John McGraw's abuse.[83] Pulliam swiftly responded to his former boss's charges. On May 27, Harry notified John through correspondence that he had suspended New York's manager from all ball field privileges for fifteen days and fined him $150. The punishment started that day and concluded after the Giants played Pittsburgh at Exposition Park on June 10. This penalty applied to the first count of Dreyfuss's formal accusation relevant to May 19. Pulliam decided a trial conducted by the league's Board of Directors should rule on the second, more serious allegation that McGraw had accused Barney of crookedness and manipulating National League umpires.

Harry settled on the first charge because he believed it fell under his purview when it came to disorderly and disgraceful diamond conduct. He stipulated that this fine and suspension constituted separate issues from the hearing before the Board of Directors. Secretary Fred Knowles, of New York's baseball team, declared too much one-man power existed in the National League, and the organization should return to the old executive committee, which existed in 1902. Pulliam responded that the league had thrived since he became president in 1902, and all eight teams combined recorded record gate receipts in the first 15 games of the 1905 campaign.[84] Besides receiving a fine and remaining on the sidelines for fifteen days, under National League rules, the Giants' organization could not pay John McGraw his salary while incarcerated.[85]

The entire situation infuriated McGraw, who believed Harry and Barney worked in concert to help Pittsburgh and hurt New York. John believed blatant bias existed as Pulliam, who Dreyfuss had employed for many years in Louisville and Pittsburgh, bowed to his puppet master pulling the strings.

> Pulliam plainly showed the animosity in the matter when he published the original charges by Dreyfuss without even taking the trouble to read the charges before they were rushed into print.
>
> On top of that he imposes an unheard penalty on me for alleged disrespect of his patron saint, Dreyfuss. He deprives my team of my services for two weeks on the eve of the first western trip, which will be a crucial test of the championship, and in addition he calls the Board of Directors together to try me on an absurd charge of lese majeste [an offense for insulting the dignity of a monarch or ruler], it being asserted that I accused Dreyfuss of crookedness. I have not done so, but others have and when he brings me before the Board of Directors there may be some developments that Dreyfuss does not anticipate.
>
> So far as I can see Pulliam and Dreyfuss feel that it would be a good thing to drive me out of baseball, and then the Pirates would have the thing all to themselves. They have a guess coming.[86]

John McGraw exhibited a narcissistic demeanor, suggesting the New York Giants could not function without his services. Regarding McGraw's accusation that Harry Pulliam informed the press about his punishment before alerting him to the charges, the league president could not avoid following this path. When Barney Dreyfuss visited Pulliam's New York office to levy his complaint, *The Sun* journalist William B. Hanna accompanied the Pirates' owner. Hanna's presence forced Harry to send copies of these charges to all the area newspapers so *The Sun* could not scoop their competition.[87] Intending to fight this injustice, McGraw suited up in uniform at the Polo Grounds on May 27 but did not appear on the field. John received a letter from his sister, Mrs. Margaret McGraw Bowker, who lived in Fulton County, New York.

McGraw's sibling wrote to the Giants' manager about their sixty-year-old father, John Sr., dangerously ill at her home. John took an early train that evening to his sister's residence.[88] McGraw briefly remained away from the club to visit his sick father.[89] Upon finding out Pulliam had appropriately responded to his complaint, Dreyfuss pleasantly smiled.[90]

"John McGraw, manager of the New York team, must answer to the directors of the National League for his unprovoked attack on me," said Dreyfuss. "The time has come when the leader of the Giants must be put on the rack for his conduct. He has been defiant to the rules entirely too long. It's amazing the way he runs things at the Polo Grounds. Umpires seem to be afraid of him. He browbeats them as in the old Baltimore days, and gets away with the tactics."

Barney also declared the league needed to rule on McGraw's habit of sneaking into his little closet near the bench after an umpire sent him off the field at the Polo Grounds. Dreyfuss alleged a passageway under the grandstand led to the clubhouse, where John had cut holes in a partition so he could coach his squad from that conning tower.[91] The National League Board of Directors met in Boston on June 1 to decide on the second charge brought forth by Barney. Two board members, Dreyfuss and John T. Brush, could not preside over the hearing because of their link to the complaint. The body also might force Boston Beaneaters president Arthur Soden to recuse himself since he owned minority stock in the New York Giants' organization. This left Chicago Cubs president James Hart as the only body member unconnected to the case.[92] Regardless of how the board decided, Barney pondered filing a lawsuit against John McGraw and held a long conference with Pittsburgh's former city district attorney, Clarence Burleigh, on May 27.[93]

Dreyfuss's friends advised the Pirates' owner not to attend the hearing in Boston since they believed he would not receive a fair deal. Barney felt it his duty to be there because he owed it to baseball to stand by these charges.[94] In the end, these friends' assessments proved quite accurate. All the involved parties experienced a long day on June 1. Since John T. Brush missed the midnight train from New York to Boston, the Board of Directors rescheduled the meeting for 2:30 P.M. This session did not start until 3 P.M. Before the meeting commenced, Harry Pulliam objected to lawyers Cornelius Sullivan of New York and Boston's George W. Anderson representing John McGraw. The board overruled the league president. Dreyfuss spoke first, relating his version of the events on

May 19 and 20 while also supplying the only corroboration he possessed, a sworn statement by William "Billy" Murray, manager of the Eastern League's Jersey City Skeeters.

Once Barney finished speaking, McGraw presented his side of the case to the board members. John admitted he talked to Dreyfuss but never called him a crook. He said that Pittsburgh's magnate yelled back at him about not being on the level.[95] Regarding the second time he shouted to the crowd on May 19 about just as soon having Barney umpire that game, McGraw declared he did not know Dreyfuss happened to be sitting in the stands.[96] John also admitted to referring to Dreyfuss on May 18, while others heard him do so on May 19 and 20.[97] McGraw confessed he had asked Barney about some markers New York bookmakers held against him. Seven people—including Harry Stevens, scorecard entrepreneur and concessionaire for many major league baseball clubs, actor Louis Mann, and a New York City police detective—spoke as witnesses on the manager's behalf. John's attorneys wanted to introduce further affidavits, but the board deemed it unnecessary. The members adjourned to secretly weigh the testimony. At 8:30 P.M., Pulliam offered the official statement on this decision.[98]

The Board of Directors exonerated John McGraw since, in their minds, Barney Dreyfuss failed to sufficiently prove the Giants' skipper had insulted him from the Polo Grounds' clubhouse balcony. The members then harshly censured Dreyfuss for not possessing sufficient evidence to call the board together after levying such charges.[99] The entire board did vote, as Arthur Soden and James Hart sided with John T. Brush, vindicating McGraw.[100] In reprimanding Barney, Hart said, "We were trying the wrong party."[101] After helping gain absolution for his manager of any wrongdoing related to Dreyfuss's second charge, Brush fought to have Harry Pulliam's sentence of a fine and a fifteen-day suspension reviewed. Pulliam refused to consider the motion. When New York's magnate appealed to the chair and asked for a vote regarding his request, the tally ended up three-to-one supporting Harry. Chicago's president and Soden sided with Barney, favoring the league president. Brush offered his impression once the meeting concluded: "McGraw has been fined and suspended and he knows not what crime he is accused of. Dreyfuss had absolutely no case against him. It was absurd."[102]

The Giants' owner contended Pulliam had no authority under the National League's constitution to punish John McGraw pursuant to his alleged action on May 19 since no umpire removed the pilot from that game.[103] In his original ruling, Harry stated he fined John because umpire Jim Johnstone had banished him from the contest on May 20.[104] Barney Dreyfuss did not have much to say after the board members rejected his complaint.

"What's the use of it?" Dreyfuss asked reporters. "I got licked, and I'll take the medicine."[105]

When Barney arrived back in Pittsburgh on June 3, he demonstrated no inclination to criticize his fellow directors. Dreyfuss revealed that he always believed a meeting of the board needless since Harry Pulliam possessed the authority to discipline McGraw for repeatedly violating league rules. He also claimed John's two lawyers and Brush coached witnesses, not under oath, to support the Giants' manager.[106] Barney did not hold the Board of Directors responsible for rebuffing his claim because they based their decision on shameful lies. Dreyfuss announced he did not bring individuals to corroborate his testimony because he came armed with the truth. Barney ridiculed the parade of opposition witnesses, especially the comical performance of a comedian who testified, whose theatrical tone proved quite amusing. Barney told of withstanding everything that happened, other than a patronizing comment, courtesy of Harry Stevens. Dreyfuss said he wanted to die when Stevens approached him and said, "Barney, old boy, I'm still your friend."[107]

Barney concluded his comments by telling press members he closed the book on this incident and had no intention of pursuing it any further.[108] John T. Brush planned to take a different approach and secure total victory in the John McGraw case, as this intense rivalry between these two diamond entities raged onward.

On June 2, 1903, the Pittsburgh Pirates defeated the **New York Giants** at Exposition Park, 7–0. After umpire Jim Johnstone banished New York catcher Frank Bowerman from the field for arguing balls and strikes, he watched the remainder of the contest from the grandstand. When the game ended, Pirates outfielder and manager Fred Clarke approached Jack Warner, who replaced Bowerman, and quoted Frank as saying from the grandstand, "If I was catching, Pittsburgh would not make so many hits." When the two clubs met at the Polo Grounds on June 26, Bowerman asked Clarke if he could talk to him and proceeded to brutally attack Pittsburgh's manager in a small ticket office. In this photo of the 1904 New York Giants, Frank Bowerman is the third from the right sitting in the bottom row. (Photo in the Public Domain).

CHAPTER 6

Rube Waddell

Straw Hat, or Compromised by Gamblers?

From New York Giants owner John T. Brush's perspective, condemnation by the National League's Board of Directors against colleague Barney Dreyfuss of the Pittsburgh Pirates ushered in the first phase of absolute justice regarding the suspension and fining of his manager, John McGraw. Early on June 2, 1905, McGraw's supporters and friends, hoping to see the punishment overturned, besieged league president Harry Pulliam at his Boston hotel.[1] That same day, attorney John J. Ward, on behalf of Brush and the National Exhibition Company, the official legal name for the Giants' ownership consortium, filed an injunction in a Boston court, asking to restrict Pulliam from collecting the $150 fine he imposed. This suit also requested Harry immediately lift McGraw's fifteen-day suspension.

In this injunction, New York's ownership, headed by Brush, alleged that according to the National League's constitution and bylaws, Pulliam acted illegally since John did not receive due process through a hearing. They also declared in the suit that the league president seriously impaired McGraw's rights and those of the Giants' organization while causing irreparable harm to the baseball world.[2] Massachusetts Superior Court Judge Henry Newton Sheldon ruled quickly on June 5, granting a temporary injunction against Harry Pulliam, preventing him from enforcing the suspension and fine recently levied on John McGraw. This injunction also restrained National League umpires from refusing to allow McGraw to enter a major league baseball field within his capacity as New York's manager.

Understanding this verdict allowed him to return to his post, John suited up that afternoon for the game against the Boston Beaneaters at South End

Grounds. Judge Sheldon explained that he based his decision on Pulliam having no right to suspend John without proper proof under Rule 28 of the National League's bylaws.

"Unless Pulliam had seen the misconduct for himself, which he did not," said Judge Sheldon, "he should have given McGraw notice of charges against him, which he did not, and consequently the court renders null and void the action of Pulliam in this case."

A second hearing on the issue could occur when New York appeared in Boston in September to play the Beaneaters. Although the court's ruling could be viewed as binding in only Massachusetts, McGraw felt this decision set a legal precedent if he decided to take similar action in other states.[3] In an ironic twist, John T. Brush was the impetus behind amending the Fleischmann clean-ball law Harry Pulliam utilized within the league constitution to render his judgment. Because of his players' and manager's rowdy behavior in 1904, Brush secretly requested altering the statute, which previously only called for a suspension without any monetary punishment. The Giants' owner believed adding a fine as a tool for the league president should deter future undesirable conduct. Brush had asked Harry not to attach his name to this legislative endeavor since he felt it might infuriate the individuals on his club the new rule targeted.[4]

Harry Pulliam interpreted that Judge Henry Newton Sheldon's decision rendered the Fleischman resolution as dead since the National League had not properly re-enacted it when adopting a new constitution in the past. Pulliam felt this verdict encouraged rowdyism in professional baseball. Harry announced that upon returning to his New York office, he planned to vote for remitting any previous fines doled out against players under the Fleischmann provision, where the penalty exceeded ten dollars, the amount permitted before triggering an individual's right to appeal that ruling. Eight players convicted of rowdy diamond conduct fell under this criterion, including Honus Wagner and Otis Clymer of the Pirates, and the Giants' Dan McGann.[5] Harry cited fairness as his reason for reversing previous penalties.

"As long as I am president of the league, there cannot be one law for John McGraw and another for Dan McGann," said Pulliam.

Cincinnati Reds magnate Garry Herrmann also thought the Board of Directors should instruct these players' employers to repay salary withheld during their suspensions, however organizations did not always comply with this rule.[6] Pulliam stated publicly that Judge Sheldon's verdict satisfied him, and he planned to fully adhere to the decision.[7] Barney Dreyfuss found John T. Brush's hypocrisy astounding since in 1902, as chairman of the league's executive committee, he handed the Pirates' Honus Wagner a twenty-day suspension for throwing a baseball bat at umpire Tom Brown during an argument in a game. Brush based his ruling on what he read in a morning newspaper. Later, upon receiving Brown's incident report, where the umpire stated Wagner did not commit this alleged offense, the executive committee chairman lifted the suspension after it sidelined Pittsburgh's player for five days. In an article he penned, Dreyfuss exhibited no surprise over Judge Sheldon issuing a preliminary injunction.

"Just what I expected," wrote Dreyfuss. "Baseball law and civil law conflict in many ways, and when McGraw went into court with the plea that he had been fined and suspended without first being given a chance to present his side of the case, I knew that the injunction would be granted, for the very foundation of law is that every person charged with an offense is entitled to a fair and impartial trial before being adjudged innocent or guilty. But in baseball we must have laws of our own, without which it would be impossible to maintain an organization like the National League. Certain powers are vested in our president, and every player signing a contract knows that he is amenable to our laws, and that unless he lives up to the same, our president has the right to impose a fine or order a suspension."[8]

Although Barney exhibited a strong understanding and pride in the innocent until proven guilty model, a bedrock of jurisprudence in the United States, this did not mean the Pirates' owner had forgotten the disrespectful way John McGraw treated him. Bitterness abounded when the Giants arrived in Pittsburgh for a four-game series that started on June 7, 1905. As the crowd filed out of Exposition Park after the two squads played the series' final contest on June 10, Brush walked up to Dreyfuss and held out his hand.

"Come, Barney," said Brush, "let's shake hands. It's all over now and I must confess that our treatment in this city was more than I could have been led to expect."

John T. Brush smiled as he tried to make amends. On the other hand, Barney Dreyfuss wore a scornful look of disdain as he firmly told Brush to go to hell. Then, in a scathing tone, Dreyfuss informed New York's owner of what he really thought of the entire McGraw situation and his colleague's role in the sordid affair. When Barney finished offering his blistering opinion, he turned away, walked to the clubhouse, opened the door, and slammed it behind him. Brush remained motionless, exhibiting a dazed look on his face. This ended up being the only time these two magnates interacted throughout the four days, as John had wisely avoided Barney on all previous occasions while in the city. Brush proved accurate in his statement to Dreyfuss since the organization and Pirates baseball fans at the ballpark treated the Giants courteously throughout the four-game series.[9]

Amidst all the turmoil and legal ramifications, New York claimed their second consecutive National League pennant, posting a 105–48 record and finishing nine games in front of second-place Pittsburgh. In the second installment of the modern World Series, the Giants opposed Connie Mack's Philadelphia Athletics, who claimed the American League pennant following a spirited battle with the Chicago White Sox. One year earlier, John T. Brush had refused to play this postseason series when it appeared the rival New York Highlanders might lock up the league flag. Believing that winning the National League championship was baseball's greatest honor, Brush disqualified the Highlanders for belonging to a minor league.[10] Although the defending World Series champion Boston Americans secured another American League pennant, New York's owner remained steadfast, declaring the National League constitution did not stipulate the organization's champion should place baseball's highest honor on the line against a club representing an inferior minor league.[11]

In October 1905, Barney Dreyfuss did not plan to attend any games of the World Series he helped create in 1903. As Garry Herrmann traveled east by train with Julius Edgar "J. Ed" Grillo, a sportswriter and current owner of the American Association's Toledo Mud Hens, to view World Series contests, they visited Dreyfuss at Pirates headquarters during a layover in Pittsburgh while waiting to catch their next train.

"Going on for the game?" asked Herrmann shortly after calling on Pittsburgh's owner.

"I should say not," replied Dreyfuss. "They would 'kid' me to death in New York if I did. They'd have 'Hey Barney' signs displayed everywhere, and as I'm one Dutchman who appreciates the difference between fame and notoriety, I don't make the trip."[12]

If Barney happened to be a fan of stout pitching, he missed one of baseball history's greatest mound performances in the 1905 World Series. In each game, the winning hurler tossed a shutout. New York easily prevailed over Philadelphia, four games to one, to wear the crown as world champions. Pitcher Christy Mathewson capped a skillful effort by claiming the fifth and deciding game for the Giants, 2–0, on October 14 at the Polo Grounds. Mathewson also secured victories in Games One and Three over the Athletics. Effortlessly and with pinpoint precision, Christy mowed down Philadelphia's batters, tossing three complete games and not allowing a run to cross home plate, while the Athletics only touched him for 13 hits in 27 innings pitched. After the final contest ended, disappointed American League president Ban Johnson lamented Philadelphia's defeat and offered reasons for their World Series loss. One of Ban's explanations centered on the actions of the Athletics' star southpaw pitcher.

"Perhaps the defection of Rube Waddell discouraged the players," said Johnson.[13]

When it came to raw baseball talent, unbridled enthusiasm for engaging in numerous activities, eccentric behavior, and a propensity for causing his managers grief, few players rivaled George Edward "Rube" Waddell. In the battle for diamond supremacy against New York, Waddell performed the noncombatant role for mysterious reasons. Two factions clung to different narratives explaining why Rube could not compete in the 1905 World Series. One account offered another example of Waddell's reckless behavior when engaging in childlike antics, while a separate story chronicled nefarious intentions perpetrated by the sporting world's slimy underbelly.

On October 13, 1876, Rube Waddell was born on a farm near Bradford, Pennsylvania. A precocious youngster who exhibited a free-spirit personality at an early age, Rube loved fire engines, fishing, and playing baseball. At three, Waddell ran away from home to sleep at a local firehouse.[14] Waddell's lineage included a mix of Pennsylvania Dutch heritage with a dash of English ancestry.[15] Because he possessed so much lightning and thunder in his powerful left arm, young Rube's friends expressed reluctance over playing catch with him since the tosses stung their hands. In 1896, Wesley Baker, a traveling salesman (referred to as a drummer during that period), became stranded in Prospect, Pennsylvania, while peddling his goods throughout Western Pennsylvania. Baker watched Waddell pitch in a game for a local team and immediately recommended his purchase to the ownership of a club from Franklin, Pennsylvania.[16]

As a teenager, Rube frequently pitched for different teams in Butler County and the surrounding area. At twenty, Waddell became involved in one of those situations that epitomized his later exploits as a major league hurler. In 1897, manager Thomas H. George secured Rube to pitch for his club at Volant College in Lawrence County, Pennsylvania. Waddell entered the learning institution on May 8 and remained there until June 23. Although he attended the college solely because of his baseball prowess, the hurler took language classes to justify his academic admission.[17] Rube earned two dollars a game pitching for Volant College. Waddell worked about two or three times each week for the university nine while also offering his services to a squad in Greenville, Pennsylvania, for the same number of contests.[18] A decade after Wesley Baker first witnessed Rube pitch, a correspondent originally from Sharon, Pennsylvania, who worked for the *Plain Dealer* in Cleveland, Ohio, related in 1906 an incident where highwaymen (thieves that robbed people along a roadway) kidnapped the southpaw twirler.

According to this sportswriter, a baseball team from Mercer, Pennsylvania, wanted Waddell to pitch in one of their championship games on the same day he was scheduled to work for Volant College. A group of Mercer's ballplayers decided kidnapping Rube was the best method to guarantee their man pitched. These individuals disguised themselves as highwaymen and waited along the roadside to intercept Waddell as he traveled to Volant College's game. When

Rube finally arrived at the ambush point in his horse-drawn buggy, he happily leaned back in the vehicle, whistling "The Turkey in the Straw." Upon reaching the conniving ballplayers, the pseudo-highwaymen surrounded Waddell before one person pointed a loaded revolver at the twirler.

The kidnappers ordered a frightened Rube to throw up his hands. One of the fake highwaymen bound Rube's hands before they rode to Mercer to a hidden location, where he remained sequestered until right before gametime. Waddell's captors told him he would receive his freedom and earn one dollar if he pitched the championship game that afternoon. Since it was too late to reach Volant College in time for their contest, Rube agreed to pitch for Mercer and easily vanquished the opposing team. When Waddell returned to Volant the following day, he experienced a tough time trying to explain to manager Thomas H. George that highwaymen had kidnapped him.[19] This little incident established a precedent for the various unique situations Rube sometimes became involved in, whether due to his own actions or unforeseeable outside forces.

Waddell's ability quickly attracted the attention of those connected to Major League Baseball. In the spring of 1897, Pirates manager and outfielder Patsy Donovan invited Rube to Pittsburgh for a tryout. Donovan also asked Waddell to join him and other players at breakfast before showing what he could do on the mound. Rube never received an opportunity to pitch, as Patsy immediately released him. After asking Waddell to sit next to him during the meal, the hurler's incessant blathering grated on Donovan's nerves and made him decide against bringing Rube into the fold.[20] Although Waddell did not receive an opportunity to pitch for his hometown squad, he still realized the dream of playing big league baseball. The Louisville Colonels expressed a deep interest in acquiring Rube.

Colonels manager Fred Clarke had heard about Waddell's pitching exploits. Clarke contacted Rube and offered him a contract. Waddell wired back, demanding he receive $25 for each game he pitched. Fred responded that Louisville would willingly pay him $500 for the remainder of the season. Elated over receiving so much money beyond his wildest dreams, Rube gladly accepted these terms.[21] Pitching for a club in Evans City, Pennsylvania, at the time, Waddell received instructions from Colonels management to join the team at their hotel in Washington D.C. Rube finally reached the nation's capital after midnight on September 8. He immediately trekked to the hostelry, entered the establishment around 2 A.M., walked up to the night clerk, introduced himself, and demanded a room. Since the clerk did not recognize Rube, who brought no luggage, the hotel employee expressed reluctance to assign the pitcher a room.[22]

Rube Waddell responded by asking for manager Fred Clarke's room number. In 1915, Pittsburgh Pirates shortstop Honus Wagner, who played for Louisville in 1897, related how things progressed after this original standoff between the hotel clerk and Rube, who became adamant about speaking to Clarke.

"Really, I don't think you'd better waken Mr. Clarke at this hour," the clerk told Waddell. "I'm sure he'd not welcome you, for he doesn't like to be bothered once he goes to bed. I'll fix you up with a room, and you can see him early this morning when he gets up."

"No, I'm positive he wants to see me tonight," Rube replied. "He told me to look him up as soon as I reached Washington. I'm the new pitcher, and he wants to be sure I've arrived."

Waddell's persistence paid off. The desk clerk acquiesced and gave the new pitcher his boss's room number. Rube trudged up the stairs, found the room, and started banging loudly on the door. After a few minutes of continuous pounding, Fred Clarke awakened from his sleep and loudly demanded to know who dared to disturb his rest.

"It's me, Rube Waddell, your new pitcher," shouted Waddell through the keyhole.

"Well, tell the clerk to give you a room and I'll see you in the morning," yelled Clarke.

"Not on your life," answered Rube through the keyhole. "Must see you now or I'll take the first train out of this burg."

Realizing that Rube happened to be a first-class hurler, Fred did not want to lose the services of a valuable player. Clarke crawled out of bed, opened the door, and allowed Waddell to enter his room. For the next thirty minutes, Fred sat in his nightshirt, listening to Rube tell him about his amazing pitching expertise and how the southpaw twirler would win the pennant for Louisville by himself if Clarke allowed him to work in every game. Fred started wondering if he might be up all night, listening to this mound prodigy brag about his ability. Figuring Waddell a nut, Clarke framed up a plan that would allow him to get some sleep while also playing a joke on the other Colonels' team members. Fred gave Rube the room numbers for every player on the squad.

"Go around, wake the boys up, and introduce yourself," Clarke said. "I know the fellows will be glad to meet you."

Waddell gleefully started on his journey and Clarke returned to bed, chuckling over the mutiny that likely followed when this new pitcher disturbed every Louisville player. An hour later, Fred slept soundly once again when another horrible pounding on his hotel room door awakened him a second time.

"Who's there?" thundered Cap.

"It's Rube Waddell, your new pitcher," came the reply.

"Well," replied Clarke, "you go back to wherever you came from or go to bed—one of the two. I'm not going to allow any 'nut' living to wake me up all hours of the night, no matter how good he can pitch."

"Yes, Mr. Clarke," said Rube, "but I just wanted to tell you that I've met all the boys except the one in Room 128, and I can't wake him up. I thought possibly something was the matter with him and you ought to know about it."

When sharing this tale, Honus Wagner claimed outfielder William "Dummy" Hoy, a deaf-mute, occupied Room 128.[23] This proved impossible unless Rube Waddell telekinetically transported himself to New York, where the Cincinnati Reds happened to be involved in a series with the Brooklyn Bridegrooms. Hoy played for the Reds in 1897 and did not join Louisville until 1898. That afternoon, Rube Waddell, who did not get any sleep because his engagement with every new teammate lasted until 4 A.M., started against the Baltimore Orioles at Union Park on September 8.[24] Rube pitched well in his major league debut, but tough luck allowed Baltimore to win the game, 5–1.[25] Waddell's only other appearance on the mound for Louisville attracted equal attention for his behavior when working the first base coaching box, along with what he did while pitching.

On September 15, the Colonels finished a series against the Pittsburgh Pirates by playing a doubleheader at Eclipse Park. Fred Clarke missed the twin bill since he attended a friend's wedding in Chicago, Illinois. First baseman Perry Werden managed the squad in Clarke's absence.[26] While coaching at first base during the second contest so Werden did not have to deal with him in the dugout, Rube taunted Pirates starting hurler Emerson Pink Hawley.

"Yer thinks yer ther handsomest Pink in ther business, don't ye," yelled Rube, "cause yer got $10 for pitchin' for Mars [Pennsylvania] against Butler?"

Hawley answered this heckling by straightening up and firing a strike past Louisville's batter, his way of affirming that he happened to be the handsomest Pink in the business. The enthusiastic Waddell interpreted this as a response from his adversary.

"Dere's odders," Waddell informed Hawley.

In the sixth and seventh innings, an exuberant Rube started panting on the coaching lines from yelling and performing all types of gymnastic maneuvers. Pittsburgh's players valiantly attempted to respond to Waddell's antics. Patsy Donovan made a sarcastic remark as he trotted in from the outfield at the end of a frame. Gesturing wildly, Rube followed Patsy and dished out harsh verbal abuse as his rebuttal. Unable to tolerate such behavior, Donovan turned away. This caused Waddell to double over on the ground, mimicking a snake, before he and Eclipse Park's crowd roared with delight. Umpire John "Kick" Kelly reprimanded both teams, saying, "Boys, this won't do; you must stop." The ballpark's spectators loved and appreciated Rube's hijinks. When Werden sent Waddell to the mound in the fourth inning, Fred Clarke's nut did not appear exhausted from his workout thus far as a coach.

Rube's offerings puzzled the Pirates' batters. When Pink Hawley stepped up to the plate in the seventh frame, Waddell fanned him on three pitches. After Rube vanquished Pink, Pittsburgh's twirler walked over to the mound and offered his hand to the Colonels' hurler. Waddell accepted this kind gesture, shaking Hawley's hand, bowing, and exclaiming, "Thank yer." Although the Pirates won the game, shortened to eight innings, 8–2, Rube baffled Pittsburgh's hitters after he entered the fray.[27] Clarke exhibited deep displeasure when he returned from Chicago and heard about Rube's behavior.[28] Fred, also unhappy with his new hurler's propensity for drinking alcohol, fined Waddell $50 for that indiscretion.[29] Louisville decided to farm out Rube to the Western League's Detroit Tigers in 1898.

Waddell experienced a rocky time while playing for Detroit. On the day Frank Graves resigned as the club's manager in May, Tigers owner George Vanderbeck decided to devote more attention to maintaining team discipline. Rube became one of Vanderbeck's first casualties in this new atmosphere. After finding out Waddell had pitched for a team from the Delray neighborhood in Detroit, the owner slapped a $25 fine on his player.[30] In 1906, *Detroit Times* sportswriter Paul Bruski explained what happened that year when Rube, upset over how Vanderbeck treated him, wandered to a different baseball destination. Bruski shared an account from an old rooter of a Detroit City League club, called the Rayls, when discussing how Waddell became a hero in Canada.

One May morning, Rube Waddell evaded his handlers, who kept an eye on the pitcher's activities, and stopped in a Michigan Avenue saloon owned by local sportsman and businessman Fred Striker. When he entered the establishment, Rube spotted several Rayls team members carrying their grips to depart by train for Chatham, Ontario, to play a special contest on May 24, celebrating the birthday of England's Queen Victoria.

"Hello, boys," offered Rube. "Whither away?"

"To Chatham, fond sir, to play ball on the Queen's birthday," responded Rayls manager Fred Atkinson.

"May I go with you?" Waddell cordially asked. "The Queen is a lady I've always had a great admiration for."

Rube happily made the trip to Chatham with Atkinson's baseball club. When the train stopped in Windsor, Ontario, Waddell had enough time to find a place selling large firecrackers. Starting the birthday celebration to honor Queen Victoria early, Rube placed a lighted firecracker in the train conductor's coat pocket and fled before it exploded. He also periodically tossed them out of a train window among crowds at various stations along the way. Waddell threw a firecracker into the check room of the hotel where the team lodged as the players dressed for this festive game. According to the old Rayls fan sharing this story, once Rube took the mound against Chatham on May 24, 1898, he struck out 27 batters. In his newspaper article, Paul Bruski wrote that when Chatham came to bat in the bottom of the ninth inning, with the Rayls holding a commanding lead, Waddell engaged in a legendary exploit that people continued discussing throughout his career.

> Rube took the firing line and looked over the field. Then he turned to the first baseman and called to him, beckoning. Swelled up with pride at the distinction, the player advanced.
>
> "Stand here," said the Rube. Then he called the second baseman, and stood him beside the other.
>
> One after another player was called and assigned a place in a semi-circle round the box. Only the catcher stood in his correct position. The crowd, mystified, held its breath. Something was going to happen. All was ready.
>
> Rube struck out the three batters on nine pitched balls and the game was over.[31]

Waddell enjoyed Chatham so much that he briefly remained in the Canadian town and pitched for their team. In a doubleheader against a squad from Dunnville, Ontario, on June 22, 1898, Rube started both games and fanned 37 batters.[32] In the twin bill's nightcap, Waddell secured a 5–0 victory for Chatham and struck out 20 Dunnville players.[33] News of such scintillating performances convinced George Vanderbeck that he needed to persuade Rube to rejoin Detroit, but the hurler did not intend on returning to his former club.[34] Exhibiting his nomadic nature, Waddell wandered back to Western Pennsylvania and pitched for a baseball team in Homestead. On August 10, Rube received a letter from the management of the Western League's Columbus Buckeyes/Senators, inquiring if he might be interested in joining that squad if they obtained his release from Detroit. Abandoning all hope of convincing Waddell to return to their club, the Tigers offered to trade him to Columbus.

Rube wired back that playing for Homestead kept him content, and he planned on finishing the season with them.[35] This satisfaction did not last long, as Waddell abandoned Homestead's squad in September and joined a team near his home in Butler, Pennsylvania.[36] Although Rube had traveled many miles pitching for numerous baseball squads, the Louisville Colonels still included him on their reserve list for 1899.[37] Waddell accompanied the Colonels on their spring training jaunt to Thomasville, Georgia. According to Louisville catcher Malachi Kittridge, Rube made a bad first impression when the Colonels opened the season against the Chicago Orphans on April 14 at Eclipse Park. Barney

Dreyfuss invited eminent Louisville lawyer, former local club co-owner, and onetime American Association president, Colonel Zachary "Zach" Phelps, to address the team before the game.

When Colonel Phelps's longwinded speech meandered on past an acceptable amount of time, Rube Waddell spoke up, telling the bloviating barrister he had made a hit but should cease to give Dreyfuss and Pulman (referring to Harry Pulliam) a chance to talk. The lawyer responded by categorizing Rube as the freshest thing that ever went unsalted.[38] Such an attitude did not paint a rosy picture for Waddell remaining with the Colonels. Columbus finally got their man, and Louisville sent him to the Buckeyes/Senators, hoping Tom Loftus and George Tebeau could harness Rube's mental aptitude so his natural ability blossomed. Early in the season, the franchise shifted from Columbus to Grand Rapids, Michigan, and became known as the Furnituremen. As skipper, Loftus worked wonders developing Waddell's potential. Toiling in the two cities, the southpaw hurler went 26–8 and fanned 200 batters.

Milwaukee manager Connie Mack witnessed Rube pitch for the first time in 1899 when he tossed a two-hit shutout against the Brewers/Creams and recorded 13 strikeouts.[39] Louisville team secretary and treasurer Harry Pulliam arrived in Grand Rapids on August 6, hoping to secure Waddell from Loftus for the remainder of the season. Although Pulliam offered $500 for Rube's services, Tom declined, affirming that the Colonels had loaned the twirler to Grand Rapids for the campaign's duration and could not recall him until the Western League's season concluded. Loftus had no intention of allowing a grand drawing card like Waddell to work his magic in another baseball city.[40] Harry traveled to Michigan, anticipating Tom would accept this payment since it happened to be the first stage of a much larger transaction.

Louisville hoped to finalize a deal discussed a week earlier with Brooklyn manager Ned Hanlon regarding selling Rube to the Superbas. When first approached about this prospect, Loftus demanded a financial inducement and a pitcher from Brooklyn's roster. All parties understood the Colonels' organization accepted responsibility for paying to guarantee Waddell's release from the Furnituremen. Since the negotiating factions only met one of Tom's two demands, he balked over allowing Rube to leave Grand Rapids. Hanlon exhibited no inclination toward giving away a pitcher at the present time. Although negotiations reached an impasse, Ned remained confident Waddell would join the Superbas since he declared the hurler rightfully belonged to his club because Louisville agreed to the deal. Hanlon also clung to the pipedream that Brooklyn might acquire versatile Honus Wagner and third baseman Tommy Leach from the Colonels.[41]

Once Rube Waddell's obligation to the Furnituremen concluded, he joined Louisville for the remainder of the season. Rube continued his excellent execution on the mound by going 7–2 for the Colonels, supported by a 3.08 ERA.[42] On December 8, 1899, Waddell returned to the bosom of his hometown when parties from the Louisville and Pittsburgh organizations finalized a considerable deal that transferred the Colonels' top players to the Pirates. Ownership named Fred Clarke to manage this new powerhouse aggregation, while Barney Dreyfuss became a partner by purchasing a sizeable portion of stock in Pittsburgh's club.[43] Rube experienced a rough 1900 season playing in his backyard. Although the hurler only posted an 8–13 record for the second-place Pirates, he led the National League with a 2.37 ERA. Waddell's main problem stemmed from his behavior, leading to clashes with Clarke.

On July 7, 1900, Pittsburgh's newspapers reported that Fred had suspended Waddell indefinitely without pay.[44] Clarke doled out this punishment for a host of misdeeds. One reason Fred decided on this suspension arose from hearing numerous accounts regarding Rube's drinking excursion the previous day.[45] A second, more egregious breach of conduct led Clarke to take punitive action. For many evenings, Waddell had participated in pickup baseball games in front of his Meyran Avenue boardinghouse in Pittsburgh's Oakland neighborhood. While catching in one of these scrub games, Rube stoved his finger.[46] Unhappy over receiving yet another fine and suspension while playing baseball and needing to earn a paycheck, Waddell jumped the Pirates and pitched for a club in Punxsutawney, Pennsylvania.

Eager to add pitching depth to his Milwaukee club in the American League minor organization, Brewers manager Connie Mack traveled to Pittsburgh and gained permission to sign Rube. Waddell initially declined the offer to pitch for Milwaukee when Mack called him on the telephone, claiming he enjoyed playing in Punxsutawney because the fans liked him and catered to his wishes. Connie continued sending messages over the wire for two weeks, finally convincing Waddell to join the Brewers.[47] Rube pitched magnificently for Mack, became a fan favorite, and helped the Brewers gain ground on the first-place Chicago White Stockings. Waddell garnered national attention when he won both games of an August doubleheader over Chicago, claiming the first seventeen-inning contest and securing the nightcap shortened to five frames.

After reading about Waddell's impressive performance versus the White Stockings, Dreyfuss wired Connie that he wanted the twirler returned to Pittsburgh, a request certainly within the owner's right since Rube still belonged to the Pirates. Mack responded that Barney should send somebody to get him.[48] Fred Clarke tasked catcher Chief Zimmer with traveling to Indianapolis, Indiana, where Milwaukee currently played, to retrieve Waddell.[49] Rube finished that season with Pittsburgh before this relationship became unsustainable shortly after the 1901 campaign commenced. When the St. Louis Cardinals defeated Waddell in his first start on April 23 at League Park, 10–4, Clarke did not appear upset, blaming the lousy spring training weather for this inferior performance.[50] Fred's patience did not last long. Rube saw action three days later in a practice game against Pittsburgh College (Duquesne University).[51]

Following this warmup contest, as the Pirates prepared to play their home opener against St. Louis at Exposition Park, Waddell opted to travel home to Prospect, enjoying the company of friends in his favorite taverns and saloons along the way. Rube's father, John Waddell, brought the missing ballplayer back to Pittsburgh on May 1. Clarke sent him to the firing line that afternoon against Chicago.[52] Rube performed horribly, allowing five runs, three hits, and four walks before Fred replaced him with Jack Chesbro in the first inning.[53] Chicago defeated Pittsburgh, 8–3. Hours after the game against the Orphans ended on May 2, Clarke stormed into Barney Dreyfuss's office and demanded the Pirates' owner remove Waddell from his team.[54] In 1910, Dreyfuss explained that after failing to sell Rube to the Boston Beaneaters when the 1900 season ended, he finally worked out a deal with Chicago in 1901 that only cost their manager, Tom Loftus, a cigar.

> We were about tired of Waddell and his peculiarities and when Boston made us an offer of $1,500 we accepted. But Rube kicked; he wouldn't play with Boston under any circumstances; so the deal was off.
>
> A little after, Tom Loftus, then managing the Chicago [Orphans] Americans, came to me and asked what I would take for Waddell. "I'll take that toby you're smoking," I replied and immediately the deal was made.
>
> Waddell was informed of his sale and when he and Loftus came together he inquired as to salary. The sum mentioned was $300 less than we were paying him, but after Loftus had told Rube what a great pitcher he was, et cetera, George Edward just fell all over himself to sign a contract.
>
> After this laborious task was completed, Rube looked up and said: "Say, Barney, there's one thing I forgot. I'll have to have half the money paid for my release; if I don't get it I won't play!"
>
> When I told him that the "purchase price" was a Pittsburgh toby, Rube felt pretty bad. But you couldn't feeze [faze, or frighten away] him—he demanded the toby and got it.[55]

Rube Waddell posted a 14–14 record pitching for Chicago, supported by a 2.81 ERA. After abandoning the club with one month remaining in the campaign, Rube joined a squad of National League players traveling to the West Coast with their American League counterparts for a barnstorming tour.

Upon receiving adulation from California rooters, Waddell signed a contract to play for the California League's Los Angeles club in 1902. Connie Mack, who now managed the Philadelphia Athletics of the American League, an institution currently thriving as a major league entity, had not seen Rube since their time together with Milwaukee. Desirous of bringing the sturdy southpaw into the fold, Mack wired Waddell in Los Angeles to travel east and join his Athletics. Following assistance from league president Ban Johnson and the Pinkerton Detective Agency, Connie finally secured Rube for his team.[56]

Although Waddell did not pitch his first game for Philadelphia in 1902 until June 26, the stalwart hurler performed brilliantly for Mack. Rube posted a 24–7 record, backed by a 2.05 ERA, as the Athletics claimed the American League pennant by going 83–53. Johnson also played a pivotal role in Waddell's success. While pitching for Louisville, Pittsburgh, and Milwaukee, Rube proved erratic, some days performing as a world beater while, on other occasions, opposing players fattened their batting averages against him. Inconsistency arose when those working the coaching lines for the opposition used aggressive verbal tactics to throw Waddell off his game. When Rube joined Philadelphia, Ban directed his umpires to protect the southpaw twirler. Johnson instituted a rule stipulating that no coachers had permission to speak to Waddell. When offenders addressed Rube, umpires banished them to the bench. Chicago White Sox pitcher and manager Clark Griffith received such treatment twice for opening his mouth during the second game of a doubleheader at South Side Park on August 28.[57]

Rube still suffered severe consequences for unacceptable behavior. Waddell claimed 21 victories for the Athletics in 1903. However, the star hurler, earning a $3,500 salary playing for Philadelphia, left the club three times, drank heavily throughout the campaign, and broke many team rules. Connie Mack's patience finally reached the breaking point while the squad played a late-August series in Cleveland against the Naps. None of his teammates saw Rube for three days after they arrived in Cleveland on August 22. Scheduled to pitch on August 25, Waddell finally appeared at the team's hotel at 5 A.M. Upon hearing about his pitcher's unacceptable conduct, Mack informed Rube that the Athletics no longer required the rebellious ballplayer's services.

Connie instructed Rube to turn in his uniform and go wherever he pleased. Mack suspended Waddell indefinitely. At first, Rube refused to believe he received his walking papers before begging Connie for one more chance. Mack remained resolute and firm.[58] Suddenly having free time, Waddell could now fully concentrate on immersing himself in acting on the stage in a production titled *The Stain of Guilt*.[59] While talking with Philadelphia's *North American* sportswriter Charles "Charley" Dryden, Connie declared that Rube's frequent club rules violations had exhausted his patience.

"I've paid his hotel bill, and now I'm done with Waddell," said Mack. "Also I notified the hotel people that should he order a room, they must look to him for pay. Waddell will not be taken home with the club. Moreover, I've notified the presidents of minor league towns where Rube plays with *Stain of Guilt* not to let him pitch. I've stood a great deal of nonsense from that great southpaw, and if I put up with any more of it the public will begin to think I'm as bad as he is."[60]

Mended fences allowed Rube Waddell to return to Philadelphia in 1904. Waddell exhibited mature behavior throughout the year, posting a 25–19 record and recording 349 strikeouts, a single-season, modern-era mark that stood until the Los Angeles Dodgers' Sanford "Sandy" Koufax fanned 382 batters in 1965. Regrettably, this newfound appropriate comportment did not continue during the off-season. One positive event occurred when Rube suffered through a rough year in 1903 because of self-inflicted circumstances. On June 3, 1903, Waddell wed for the second time when Reverend John Arba Marsh, pastor at the High Street Baptist Church, officiated his marriage ceremony to twenty-three-year-old milliner May Wynne (Wyman) Skinner (May Ross) in Lynn, Massachusetts. Miss Skinner met Rube through the pitcher's friend and her family member Philip "Phil" Poland, who played baseball for a club from Milton, Massachusetts.[61] The couple exchanged wedding vows at Poland's home.

May became acquainted with Waddell during the summer of 1902, when she by chance attended a game between the Athletics and Boston Americans at Huntington Avenue Baseball Grounds. At the time, Miss Skinner did not appreciate or admire baseball. Her friends noticed May's interest in the game increased after Poland introduced the young woman to Rube. From that point forward, she attended most of the games Philadelphia played in Boston.[62] Following the conclusion of the 1904 baseball season, a strange arrangement transpired between Waddell and his wife. They did not live together most of the time, as May Waddell resided in Lynn, while Rube dwelled nearby with her parents at their home in Peabody, Massachusetts. A problem arose on February 8, 1905, between Waddell and May's father, Edward Ross, during a dispute about a board bill.[63]

Rube drank heavily that afternoon and embarked with an expressman for the Ross residence as it started to turn dark.[64] Waddell arrived back at his father-in-law's home shortly after 6 P.M., went to the room where he slept, packed his trunk, came downstairs, and told Mr. Ross he planned to live with his daughter in Lynn. When Edward inquired about Rube's board bill since the ballplayer had not paid one cent since he started residing at the home in December, Waddell became enraged and argued with his father-in-law. During the confrontation, Rube grabbed a flatiron near the stove and attacked Mr. Ross. Subjected to Rube's relentless battering against his body with the weapon, Edward's face became badly lacerated and torn, the scourge knocked out six teeth, and May's father suffered contusions on his stomach and limbs.

Sensing her husband was in severe trouble from the brutal pummeling unleashed on him by their son-in-law, Mrs. Ross grabbed a broom and attempted to help her spouse. Waddell, emitting a savage growl, picked up a heavy kitchen chair and smacked Mrs. Ross with it, knocking her to the floor. As she lay dazed on the kitchen floor, the family's large Newfoundland dog, devotedly protective of the woman, entered the fray. The animal lunged for Rube's throat, but he pulled away and hurled the flatiron at the angry beast. Upon leaping at Waddell a second time, the dog sunk its fangs deep into the hurler's left arm. Using his powerful right fist, Rube propelled the canine away from him and drove it out of the house. During this struggle, Edward Ross regained his faculties and ran from the dwelling, screaming, and the shrieks alerted neighbors. Waddell then picked up his trunk, walked outside, threw it in the waiting express wagon, jumped aboard, and rode to Lynn.[65]

Edward Ross hustled over to Copeland's Store to inform Constable Fred S. Copeland that Rube Waddell had assaulted him. Copeland immediately notified Captain John C. Keazer of Peabody's police department about the crime. Besides tearing into Rube's arm with its teeth, the Newfoundland dog also shredded his trousers in the tussle. Pedestrians who passed the express wagon as it traveled along Lynn Woods Road toward Lynn affirmed they heard Waddell complaining about the severe pain related to the dog bites and witnessed blood flowing freely from his wounds.[66] Peabody police sent out a bulletin to neighboring cities and towns to take Rube into custody for attacking his wife's parents.[67] That town's law enforcement body also issued a warrant for Waddell's arrest on an assault charge.[68]

When Rube reached Lynn, he trekked to the post office pharmacy. Once inside, Waddell asked the clerk to dress his hand, explaining that a dog had bitten him. The Newfoundland's teeth lacerated his left arm near the wrist so badly that the clerk refused to attend to the pitcher's wounds and advised him to seek a doctor's care. Rube responded by pouring peroxide on the bitten area to prevent blood poisoning. As Waddell stared at his mangled limb, he remarked, "There's my $4,500 hand gone to hell." Upon inquiry by curious Lynn citizens, they found Rube did not visit the offices of any neighborhood physicians.[69]

Rube Waddell's lazy lifestyle had become a source of consternation for Mr. and Mrs. Ross. Each day, Waddell rose from bed at 10 A.M. before partaking in a modest breakfast of a roll and coffee. Rube saved his voracious appetite for dinner, when he consumed food in a manner that made Edward Ross nervous. In between meals and after supper, Waddell lazily sat smoking his pipe. A shave in front of the kitchen mirror followed engaging in his final tobacco pleasure of the day before retiring. The only time Rube did not loaf was when his father-in-law accepted a contract to cut wood for a neighboring farmer. The two men received $1.25 a cord for the job, and Waddell never stopped talking about performing sweaty manual labor that placed him in the lumberjack class. While living in Peabody, Rube's social life consisted of sitting on a cracker box in Copeland's Store afternoon and night, regaling the locals about his pitching exploits.[70]

Edward Ross declared that he wanted Rube Waddell arrested for breaking his jaw and beating his wife, expecting it to occur when the ballplayer reported to Philadelphia in March.[71] From the home of relatives in Lynn, May Waddell announced she decided to seek a divorce from her husband. May had not seen Rube since he fled Peabody. She considered the attack on her parents the final act in a series of inexcusable incidents Waddell perpetrated against her family. May and other Lynn citizens believed Rube traveled to Philadelphia.[72] Waddell briefly spent time in Lynn where, on February 4, he had heroically assisted a shop owner in that town.

While walking along Union Street with friend Phil Poland that Saturday at 4:30 P.M., the two noticed a commotion at a nearby business. A blaze had broken out in Mrs. M. F. Patten's flower shop. Despite another fire causing severe damage to this establishment five days earlier, the owner opened, hoping to garner some weekend business. Mrs. Waldron oversaw operations that day, working with nine-year-old stockboy Willie Hooley. Although Mrs. Waldron warned Hooley to be careful while working and avoid bumping into the large oil stove used for heating the store, the young boy accidentally knocked it over while carrying three good-sized pasteboard boxes. The fire's quick acceleration, fueled by the oil, frightened the woman and young lad.

When Waddell and Poland arrived on the scene, smoke and flames poured out of the building. Quickly assessing the situation, Rube ran into the establishment, lifted the flaming stove from the floor, ran out of the store into the street with the heating apparatus as it was about to explode, and tossed it into a snowbank. Waddell hustled back inside and pulled a portiere (curtain) from its fastenings to extinguish the remaining burning oil on the floor and around a door's woodwork.[73] For a third time, Rube sprinted back into the store, which also functioned as a millinery, grabbed a bundle of burning lingerie, and carried the clothing out. Although Waddell suffered severe burns on his face and hands, he did not seem bothered by this inconvenience.[74] Rube's courageous behavior afforded him material when talking with friends that evening.

"I just pitched up that oil stove," said Waddell, "gave it a sort of spitball twist, and sent it clean over the home plate into a snow heap. It was just a little practice for my arm, that's all."[75]

Waddell arrived in Philadelphia on February 11, 1905. The pitcher expressed surprise when confronted by a correspondent for the *Sporting News*, who went by the penname Veteran (the alias used by Philadelphia sportswriter Horace Fogel), and questioned about reports from Lynn that he had assaulted his in-laws. Rube refuted accounts that he injured Edward Ross using a flatiron and needed to fend off an attack from the family dog.

"Nothing in that yarn," said Rube. "You see, my arm is all right and that no dog has bitten me. Now, you don't suppose I would do such a foolish thing as pitching flatirons at the heads of my wife's parents, do you? Why, that's foolish nonsense."

Given Waddell had done foolish things in the past, using that as part of the argument regarding his portrayal of a false accusation was disingenuous. The sportswriter felt that since Rube arrived in Philadelphia so suddenly and unexpectedly, the Lynn reports possessed truth because it appeared the hurler fled some trouble. The *Sporting News* correspondent also surmised Connie Mack would need to flex his diplomatic powers to fix the situation so Waddell could pitch in Boston in the upcoming season. Veteran wished someone had soundly thrashed Rube in one of these physical confrontations to knock some sense into the hurler.[76] This report proved accurate about Mack's persuasive powers. Connie pleaded with Peabody Police Chief Michael H. Grady, promising to produce Rube when desired if he agreed to hold the warrant until after the 1905 season concluded. Although Chief Grady acquiesced to this request, Mack purposefully did not inform Waddell, who offered contrition to the police official and promised to behave in the future.

Over time, Edward Ross became less dedicated to having the court prosecute his son-in-law.[77] The two men settled their differences, leading to a discharge of the case when Rube appeared in Peabody's police court on January 8, 1906. The judge tossed the case when nobody answered the assault complaint against the famous baseball player.[78] While Waddell no longer needed to worry about spending time in jail, a huge problem related to the previous baseball campaign still hung over him like a huge, dark cloud. Statistically, Rube fashioned one of the best performances of his career during the 1905 season, posting a 27–10 record, supported by a 1.48 ERA. Waddell also fanned a league-leading 287 batters. Throughout the campaign, Philadelphia engaged in a tight battle for the American League pennant with Chicago.

On July 7, the Athletics defeated Boston in ten innings on the Columbia Park home grounds, 2–1. Charles "Chief" Bender replaced Rube on the hill in the seventh frame when a line drive struck his left hand.[79] Waddell's next start occurred against the Cleveland Naps at League Park on July 13. Although still nursing his injured pitching hand, Rube engaged in stupid behavior after the club left Philadelphia to travel by train to Cleveland. When the locomotive stopped at St. Marys in Elk County, Pennsylvania, where family members lived, Waddell abandoned his teammates. Once St. Marys' baseball enthusiasts realized Rube had arrived in town, they persuaded him to play for the local team against a neighboring squad. The citizens wished Waddell to pitch, but he played first base because of his injury. Rube heartily enjoyed himself, participating in a meaningless game while suffering from a sore pitching hand that could further sideline him if aggravated.

"It was one of the best games I ever played," said Rube. "We started at 2:30 in the afternoon and quit at 6:30, seven innings having been played. We won, 36–23, and I hardly had a chance. The outfielders got all the putouts."[80]

This reckless decision by Rube Waddell paled in comparison when conflicting stories of the hurler either acting stupidly or with nefarious intent rose to the surface. On September 5, Waddell lost a thirteen-inning affair against Boston at Huntington Avenue Baseball Grounds, 3–2. When Connie Mack selected Rube to start versus the Americans on September 8, the southpaw pitcher only lasted two innings before James "Jimmy" Dygert made his major league debut as a replacement. Following this outing, Waddell, complaining that his left shoulder bothered him, did not appear in another contest for weeks. When the Athletics reached New York for a series against the Highlanders after finishing a week-long homestand on September 16, hope existed that he might work in one of the games. Mack intended to use Rube when he felt confident his player's left arm had rounded into decent enough shape to work on the hill.

Waddell's keeper, Frank Newhouse, also traveled with Philadelphia's squad. A trainer for boxers and baseball clubs who performed muscle rubbing, Newhouse's primary job regarding Rube surrounded carrying his money and handing it out in lesser amounts when necessary. While Frank vigilantly attempted to prevent Waddell from turning to alcohol's dark side, these two individuals worked out a great system whenever they walked into a saloon. According to other Athletics team members, when the pair ordered two drinks, Newhouse consumed both while Rube wiped his mouth with the bar towel.[81] Frank also massaged and rubbed Waddell's arm and shoulder muscles each day after suffering the injury. Coolly smoking cigarettes when Newsome worked on him, Rube never winced when receiving physical therapy. According to Frank, an individual suffering from this type of shoulder sprain usually could not withstand treatment without grimacing or flinching.[82]

A sensation that rocked baseball explained why Rube Waddell appeared content whenever Frank Newsome massaged his damaged shoulder. When the Athletics reached New York, people in that city talked about nothing but a series of articles written by sportswriters Charley Dryden of the *North American* and Horace Fogel, who worked for Philadelphia's *Evening Telegraph* as a sports editor. These two pundits alleged sinister parties from New York tampered with Waddell by attempting to bribe him not to participate in the upcoming World Series, provided the Athletics won the American League pennant and opposed the Giants. Within their articles, Dryden and Fogel quoted Connie Mack and other players as believing Rube had faked his shoulder injury for weeks to engineer a grandstand ploy as he did on numerous occasions in the past.

Familiar with this behavior, team members paid no attention to Waddell and his issue since the players felt they could win the pennant without him. Their main criticism against Rube stemmed from him deciding to pull such a stunt with so many doubleheaders scheduled down the homestretch. Upon arriving in New York, Connie Mack and his squad expressed shock and outrage when hearing rumors about gamblers corrupting their teammate, which had been the common topic of discussion in that metropolis' taverns, sporting resorts, and other public places for the past week. Bookmakers brazenly approached Athletics players and correspondents traveling with the club, offering to make wagers that Rube did not pitch in any World Series games.

A disgusted Mack immediately challenged his compromised pitcher. Before a doubleheader against the Highlanders at American League Park on September 19, Connie ordered Waddell to wear his uniform for preliminary practice. After coming onto the field, Rube refused to participate, claiming his shoulder bothered him. Mack asked Waddell how much longer he planned to keep up this lame shoulder business. Prior to Wednesday's contest on September 20, while standing in uniform on the diamond during pregame practice, Rube picked up a stray baseball used by others and fired it back to his teammates standing sixty feet away. Waddell later grabbed a bat during the practice session and swung it above his head for a long time, imitating a juggler performing tricks. Connie sarcastically reminded the hurler that no man with a sore shoulder could have pulled off either feat.

According to Dryden and Fogel, some of Rube Waddell's teammates told them they did not believe the pitcher's story about how he injured his left shoulder. One explanation alleged that Waddell had participated in horseplay on the train station platform during a stopover in Providence, Rhode Island, as the team traveled back to Philadelphia from Boston, and bumped into the side of a Pullman sleeper. The other account claimed Rube fell over some baggage in the aisle of the sleeper. Team members trusted that nothing ailed Waddell, but none had witnessed either occurrence.[83] Rube immediately denied the accusation that he sold out to gamblers for the purpose of not participating in the World Series. To back his claim, Waddell offered $1,000 to any individual who could prove this false allegation and another $1,000 to meet the man face-to-face who had the nerve to ask him to lose.[84] On the afternoon of September 22, Rube issued a statement to the press, denouncing this charge.

> I have not been approached by anyone with a view of crippling my team. I want all I can to land the pennant, and while I am suffering with a sore arm, will go in the box tomorrow if Mack wants me to, and I will pitch my arm off to help the team out. The rumors that I am lying down on Manager Mack are pure rot.
>
> I have worked hard with the other members of the team to bring this world's championship to Philadelphia. I'll win every game I pitch from now on, and will also beat the Giants when we meet in the World's Series.[85]

Rube's left shoulder, the one he reportedly injured during a sleeper car scuffle by tripping over a teammate's grip, exhibited a slight mark, indicating bruising. Regarding a sprain, his shoulder experienced no swelling. The *Los Angeles Record* reported that a physician examined Waddell's shoulder and found nothing wrong. This newspaper also wrote that a club attaché, who preferred anonymity, intimated parties had tampered with the hurler to keep him out of the World Series.

"It might be worth $10,000 to some people," said this man, "to have Waddell on the bench during the postseason games."[86]

Rube Waddell had not appeared in a game since leaving the contest against Boston in the third inning on September 8, complaining of a sore arm. Up to this point, club doctors could not definitively diagnose Rube's ailment. On September 28, these physicians ordered X-rays on both the shoulder and the arm.[87] Some writers and baseball followers suggested rheumatism might be the culprit. Amidst intense scrutiny surrounding his motive behind remaining sidelined, Waddell entered the game in the eighth inning as a reliever against the Detroit Tigers on September 27 at Columbia Park. The crowd's rousing cheers were the only positive takeaway regarding this futile endeavor. Attempting to throw a combination of fastballs and curveballs, with an occasional slow pitch, Rube gave a pitiful exhibition on the bump.

When placing a little speed on the ball, Waddell failed to throw the sphere over home plate while curves bounced harmlessly in front of a batter. The only time Rube fired a toss straight and true, Tigers left fielder Matthew "Matty" McIntyre blasted a single. After throwing seven pitches, Waddell exited the contest in favor of Chief Bender. Nobody cheered as he walked off the diamond. These dejected rooters wondered if Rube's left arm had forever lost its speed and cunning. After the game ended, Connie Mack issued a dire statement to the press about Waddell's status moving forward.

Waddell is done for this year. He may do us some good next season, but he won't this fall. I am convinced that the "Rube" has rheumatism in his left shoulder, and if I am correct he may never be able to get back to his old-time form. Some people have been "roasting" Waddell, but I can't do so when I feel certain that he has not been "faking" about the extent of his lameness. Waddell practiced before the game and his arm seemed to be working well after he had thrown many balls. While the game was going on his left arm stiffened up somewhat, and when he went into the game it was useless. From the way the "Rube's" arm acts I am convinced that the trouble is rheumatism in the shoulder.

The trouble probably started the night we were returning from the last Boston trip. The boys got to smashing straw hats, and Waddell appointed himself a committee of one to attend to [Philadelphia pitcher Andrew "Andy"] Coakley's hat when the latter joined us at Providence. When Waddell tried to get Coakley's hat there was a scrimmage. The hat was in Coakley's grip, which Andy threw at "Rube." The grip struck Waddell on the shoulder and left a bruise. At that time Waddell was covered with perspiration and he must have got a cold in his shoulder while cooling off at the Providence station.[88]

Curiously, according to some newspapers, Rube complained about a sore arm after leaving the contest on the afternoon of September 8 against Boston before the train station incident involving Andy Coakley. Although Connie Mack officially articulated the company line, a huge question still lingered in the minds of baseball fans and scribes. Did horseplay over a teammate's etiquette faux pas wearing a straw hat past the acceptable date for such fashion end Rube's season, or had gamblers paid him to fake an injury? Team captain and third baseman Lafayette "Lave" Cross unequivocally stated that on behalf of the Athletics players, they expressed no anger toward Waddell and did not mistreat him over his perceived injury.

Philadelphia *Sporting Life* correspondent Francis C. Richter reported that while working out before a home game against Chicago on September 30, Rube felt something snap in his left shoulder. Suddenly, Waddell could manipulate his arm without experiencing any pain. Mack personally caught Rube and became cautiously optimistic when the southpaw twirler's arm exhibited excellent speed. Hope existed that Waddell might receive another chance to pitch, although Connie would wait to use him until his club clinched the American League pennant.[89]

Rube Waddell experienced results like the fiasco against Detroit when working in the regular season's final series against the Washington Senators at

American League Park. Rube proved ineffective after relieving Coakley, tossing six innings on October 6. One day later, Waddell started the first game of a doubleheader and only lasted one frame, allowing two runs. Rube did not appear in the World Series versus the New York Giants. American League fans expressed displeasure over Philadelphia not maintaining the level of play they exhibited throughout the campaign when opposing the Giants. Rooters also believed those responsible for such a deterioration in performance should suffer the consequences and receive punishment.

Unexpectedly, at the Polo Grounds before Game Two of the World Series on October 10, 1905, Waddell announced his arm appeared strong once again and had recovered its former power and effectiveness. For the second time, Connie Mack worked as Rube's catcher in a practice session and declared to newspaper journalists that the southpaw hurler never had better control or possessed more tantalizing speed. However, Mack's lack of trust and confidence in Waddell caused him to keep the star pitcher out of Philadelphia's lineup. This dearth of faith indicated Connie might discard Rube during the off-season, with the Boston Americans as a trade partner. Baseball's National Commission also pondered investigating the matter due to American League president Ban Johnson's extreme dissatisfaction over Waddell's conduct.[90]

Throughout the winter, individuals connected to Organized Baseball supported both narratives about Rube's reason for missing the World Series. Near the end of December, American League umpire Francis "Silk" O'Loughlin offered his impression on why Rube could not pitch against New York.

> Well, Rube lost his chance of being the big hero by playing the schoolboy act. When the Philadelphia club was coming home from Boston on its last trip, I believe, he and Coakley got to fooling. Coakley tried to bar the door of the car on Waddell. Of course, the Rube wouldn't stand for it, and he threw his shoulder heavily against the door. Rube felt his shoulder give on him, and to make it worse, he caught cold in it. That did settle it.
>
> When the world's championship series came along, Rube was in a bad way. He wanted to pitch in the games the worst way, and he did everything he knew to put himself right. When the doctor told him that his case was hopeless, his heart was broken. No pitcher ever lived who loves the applause of the multitude and the limelight more, and to have led Connie Mack's Quakers against the Giants would have been the event of his life.[91]

Inconsistency seemed evident as someone presented another version of what happened when Rube Waddell and Andy Coakley engaged in train depot foolishness at the beginning of September. In his column for the *Pittsburgh Press*, sportswriter Ralph S. Davis declared that if Waddell indeed took money from gamblers, the National Commission should drive him out of baseball through permanent banishment.[92] West Coast newspaper stories supported the assertion that gamblers had compromised Rube and enticed him to fake an injury. On January 18, 1906, after a reader sent the newspaper a clipping from an article on this subject, sportswriter Bozeman Bulger of New York's *The World* classified such talk as pure nonsense. Regarding assertions that the National Commission contemplated acting against Waddell, Bulger stated that this body did not even discuss the issue during a recent meeting. Bozeman shared a conversation between him and Rube while investigating the story one week before the 1905 World Series started.

"I saw Waddell on the street and he was almost in tears because of his inability to pitch," wrote Bulger. "He said that Pitcher Coakley, in a scuffling match on the train, had struck him on the arm with a dress suitcase and hurt the muscle. Anybody who saw Waddell and heard him talk could not believe him guilty of the charge. Again, what incentive was offered for him to be crooked? If a gambler wanted to cinch the games for the Giants what could have been his object in buying off Rube Waddell, who had not been able to pitch for several weeks?"[93]

Longtime career minor leaguer and former Pacific National League umpire William "Wild Bill" Setley held a dissenting view. On April 4, 1906, while passing through Denver, Colorado, on his way to Galveston, Texas, Setley weighed in on what he believed were the facts surrounding Waddell's case.[94] Wild Bill declared he possessed proof that Rube received a big monetary consideration in exchange for not playing in the 1905 World Series against the Giants.

> I saw a letter from Waddell written to a player on the coast in which the Rube used the words, "I got mine, old pard, and it was something over $10,000, too," in referring to his failure to pitch for the Athletics in the series.
>
> Rube declared in the letter that a syndicate of New York gamblers and stock brokers had made up a purse for him, but that [John] McGraw of the Giants knew nothing about the deal. Several of the players were on, however, Rube said, and bet heavily on the series.[95]

When Wild Bill Setley revealed this information, Rube Waddell prepared to play the 1906 baseball campaign with the Philadelphia Athletics. Although Connie Mack had expressed suspicion and skepticism regarding Rube's shoulder injury the previous September, he still welcomed the iconic hurler back to the club for another season. Optimism reigned shortly after players reported to

Montgomery, Alabama, for spring training, as Waddell's pitching arm appeared sound once again. Mack reasoned that Rube, wanting to rehabilitate his reputation with the public, would experience a banner year and restore his previous prestige.[96] Although Waddell's record dipped below the .500 mark to 15–17, he posted a 2.21 ERA and paced the circuit for the fifth consecutive season with 196 strikeouts.

While Rube's winning percentage tumbled in 1906, he also received a deep slash to his pocketbook, courtesy of the courts. On May 10, Philadelphia's desertion court ruled that Waddell had to forfeit half the yearly baseball salary the Athletics paid him to his second wife, May. This decision revealed Connie had sliced Rube's yearly stipend down to $1,200, meaning May received $600 in support through this legal edict. Waddell also proclaimed that when the pitcher gave his wife the $1,200 he had saved to tide them over through the winter months, she absconded with the funds and never gave him a penny.[97] The loss of $1,200 in 1905 offered plausibility to the claim gamblers had approached Rube and corrupted his mind. When two Philadelphia sportswriters first broke the bribe story in September 1905, scribe Horace Fogel persisted as the most adamant of the two men about Waddell's unsavory conduct.[98]

Besides working for Philadelphia's *Evening Telegraph*, Fogel had also briefly managed the New York Giants at the beginning of the 1902 campaign. On November 26, 1909, Horace and a group of partners paid $350,000 to purchase the Philadelphia Phillies' franchise. The new ownership syndicate elected Fogel president at an organizational meeting in Camden, New Jersey.[99] Horace's time at the helm proved short-lived. On October 17, 1912, Fogel received notice from National League officials regarding charges against him that owners would address during an official hearing when the body met in New York on November 26. Horace responded by sending league president Thomas "Tom" Lynch correspondence expressing defiance over the right of league officials to try him for making statements relative to National League baseball concerns. Fogel denied the assertions that he had earlier stated the league conducted a crooked race in 1912 and that Lynch and his umpires worked in concert with the New York club's interests. Supposedly, Horace further declared that these parties had fixed it so the Giants secured the pennant.[100]

In a sudden move, Horace Fogel resigned from his position during a session of National League magnates on November 26 before these individuals considered the charges against the Phillies' former president.[101] As someone connected to baseball through different avenues, Fogel fully knew of different skeletons in the grand game's closet. In September 1920, as newspapers dissected the activities of a Chicago grand jury amid accusations that Chicago White Sox team members had conspired to throw the 1919 World Series against the Cincinnati

Reds, Horace rattled some of those bones. Fogel had rehashed previous times when gamblers infiltrated baseball's orb, including Rube Waddell's suspicious behavior fifteen years earlier.[102]

Regrettably, Waddell could not challenge these accusations and defend himself since the great pitcher had died on April 1, 1914, in San Antonio, Texas, from tuberculosis.[103] During a newspaper interview on September 29, 1920, Horace offered his account of what had occurred in 1905 as the Philadelphia Athletics battled for the American League pennant, hoping to meet the New York Giants in the World Series. Fogel declared that a trio of New Yorkers, headed by Timothy P. "Little Tim" Sullivan, a Tammany Hall politician and prominent gambler, had approached Rube with their scheme to assist the Giants.

> Rube Waddell was permitted to remain in Organized Baseball for five years after it was established that he had been reached in 1905.
>
> The Athletics were in Boston when "Little Tim" Sullivan; a crony of his named Ryan, a gambler, and a third party whose name has escaped me at the present time came to Boston and talked with Waddell. They met him in a room in a hotel, and offered him $17,000 not to appear in the 1905 World's Series against the Giants. He was paid $500 at the time and promised the rest after the Series if he did not pitch.
>
> Waddell accepted the first payment and agreed to go through with it. On the train from Boston to Philadelphia, Waddell and other players were skylarking, and during the fun Waddell presumably tripped over a valise owned by Andy Coakley. He asserted at that time that his pitching arm had been badly injured, and this was believed to be true until the rumors reached the other players of the deal in Boston.
>
> When the series opened at New York [Game Two on October 10, 1905], Waddell was taken by three Athletic players—Harry Davis, Topsy Hartsel, and Lave Cross, as I remember it—to a room in the Marlborough Hotel. An osteopath was summoned to examine the pitching arm, which Rube claimed was so badly injured. The osteopath examined it, and after he had trapped Rube into a certain number of false statements, and finished his examination, he turned to the other players and said: "There is nothing the trouble with his arm." Harry Davis, I understand, rushed at Waddell and was going to punch him, but was restrained by the other men present.

Horace Fogel declared that after covering some of these details in an article in 1905, Rube Waddell had threatened retaliation against the newspaper for smearing his reputation. Fogel also alleged that under duress, Waddell later confessed to his crime and revealed those involved, including Little Tim Sullivan. Upon hearing about Horace's claims on the night of September 29, 1920, Philadelphia manager Connie Mack responded that he knew nothing about the former scribe's charge regarding gamblers previously influencing Rube. Mack also displayed ignorance over Waddell confessing to the alleged plot and Organized Baseball not expelling him for life after making this admission.[104] Mystery prevailed over what really happened regarding Rube during the latter stages of the 1905 baseball campaign. In the end, either childlike behavior over a straw hat or an appalling disregard for his faithful employers by a corrupt adult vanquished Major League Baseball's iconic pitcher during his hour of glory.

Throughout **Rube Waddell**'s career with the Philadelphia Athletics, manager Connie Mack (shown in this photo) dealt with many incidents involving the eccentric hurler. In 1905, Mack needed all his virtuous patience to handle a situation as the Athletics battled to represent the American League in the World Series against the New York Giants. Two questions arose over a shoulder injury sidelining Waddell near season's end. Did Rube injure his arm while engaging in tomfoolery with teammate Andy Coakley at a Providence, Rhode Island, train station? Or did gamblers, backed by Tammany Hall politician Timothy "Little Tim" Sullivan, pay Waddell not to participate in the 1905 World Series? During a newspaper interview on September 29, 1920, former Philadelphia sportswriter Horace Fogel declared that gamblers had compromised Rube fifteen years earlier. (Courtesy of the Library of Congress).

CHAPTER 7

Chick Stahl

Failure Not an Option to the Fragile Mind

For ballplayers and managers, pressure and the inherent mental strain from working hard to succeed on a baseball diamond has left some of those heavily invested in the fight battered and bruised. While many connected to the game in the past thrived within this environment by turning around and using it as a positive force toward achievement, others succumbed, unable to deal with the intense stress and anxiety. This feeling sometimes proved a double-faceted heavy burden during the Deadball Era since many players also managed major league clubs during that period. The desire to receive constant fan adulation added another layer, along with the responsibility of displaying their talent at the highest standard and accomplishing remarkable things while overseeing an entire team. Sadly, a minority of individuals wilted under the burden of pleasing those who adored and cheered for them. Most importantly, these baseball icons struggled to find satisfaction within themselves.

Although a baseball player may exhibit a smile on the outside, this does not mean conflict and struggle is not lurking below the surface, slowly eating away at him. When it came to possessing a happy-go-lucky, pleasant demeanor during the Deadball Era, few surpassed outfielder Charles Sylvester Stahl, who played for Boston's clubs in both the National and American leagues. Stahl, nicknamed "Chick" as a youngster and shortened to "Chic" at times by newspapers in his hometown of Fort Wayne, Indiana, displayed a cheerful personality and always appeared ready with a joke or quip. Despite this jovial exterior, a dark contrast within Chick's inner soul and mind led to an all-too-common tragic outcome relative to that era.

Charles Sylvester Stahl was born in Avilla, Indiana, on January 10, 1873.[1] His parents, Reuben and Barbara Stadtmiller Stahl, moved the family to Fort Wayne when Charles was an infant.[2] The Stahls came from German heritage and practiced Catholicism.[3] During his childhood, young Stahl earned an education at various cathedral learning institutions in Fort Wayne. In his leisure time, he assisted his father, a carpenter, and learned to play baseball on the local sandlots. Charles sharpened those skills by participating in pickup games on Hamilton's Fields before developers used that property to build residential homes. Stahl quickly exhibited skill dominating the game because of his athletic prowess and gained recognition playing for the local Brunswick squad. In 1889, he became a Pilsener club member in Fort Wayne's City League.[4]

Besides performing as one of Pilsener's two hurlers, Charles also played the outfield and gained a reputation as a hard hitter within the organization. He rose to a status known in the baseball world as a "comer." Because of Stahl's pleasant and cheerful nature, he took nothing seriously. Regardless of the team's fortunes, he seemed a good-humored philosopher who laughed whenever he encountered hard luck.[5] Charles also branched out beyond his home surroundings to cultivate his talent and reputation as a ballplayer. In 1889 and 1890, he spent time playing for a squad in Paducah, Kentucky. Stahl's diamond journey took him to Kalamazoo, Michigan, in 1893.[6] Charles's work as an amateur ballplayer garnered attention, leading him to earn an engagement in 1895 when Decatur, Indiana, organized a salaried club.[7] This team included many well-known players from the northern part of that state.[8]

Shortly after joining Decatur, Stahl accepted an offer to play for the Virginia State League's Roanoke Magicians.[9] Signed to pitch, Charles performed most of the time as an outfielder due to his proficiency with a bat.[10] Stahl went 8–11, supported by a 3.16 ERA while toiling on the mound, and finished the year as Roanoke's second most-accomplished hitter behind infielder Richard "Dick" Padden, with a .311 batting mark.[11] After the campaign concluded, the Eastern League's Buffalo Bisons drafted Charles to play for them in 1896.[12] Once that season began, Stahl batted at a ferocious pace for the Bisons, wielding the stick at a .328 clip in 121 games, supported by 135 runs scored, 28 stolen bases, 27 doubles, 23 triples, and 6 home runs. At this stage in his life, Charles possessed the attributes of a trim athlete in impeccable condition, and a well-educated young man who always dressed stylishly. A true gentleman on the field, Stahl became a favorite among Buffalo's fans.[13]

Female patrons particularly showed infatuation over Chick Stahl. During a game on July 7 at Olympic Park II, a young lady presented Stahl with a beautiful floral arrangement. Chick blushed when prompted to take a bow and make a speech to commemorate the moment. The crowd eventually coerced

Stahl to doff his cap three times. That night, Bisons team members paraded all over the city wearing the flowers in their buttonholes.[14] The woman who gave Chick the magnificent roses performed for a local opera company where he had made a big impression with many young ladies. Teammate Joseph "Joe" Herndon reasoned Stahl's dashing good looks were the reason behind the gravitating attraction.[15] When the season ended, the Wilbur Opera Company announced they hired Stahl to play leads and high comedy parts while traveling with the group over the winter. One critic, questioning Chick playing leads since he could only perform as a ballplayer, surmised the job came about because of a relationship with the "flower girl" in the opera company.[16]

Stahl prepared to play the biggest role of his baseball career in 1897. Following that stellar season with Buffalo, Boston Beaneaters manager Frank Selee purchased Chick from the Bisons to perform a utility role behind projected starting outfielders Frederick "Fred" Tenney, William "Billy" Hamilton, and Hugh Duffy. The Beaneaters' organization did not divulge the price they paid to add Stahl to the club's reserve list. Writers speculated that the Bisons might have received $500 since the club needed an influx of cash.[17] The Washington Nationals originally drafted Chick after the 1896 season concluded but decided to waive their claim to him. Boston gladly secured the promising young player.[18] Stahl grabbed a starting position in the Beaneaters' outfield in 1897, prompting Selee to move Tenney to first base.

Chick sizzled during his rookie campaign in the National League, appearing in 114 games and batting .354. Stahl impressed both rooters and sportswriters from the outset as crowds on South End Grounds' home turf and visiting ballparks anxiously looked forward to catching a glimpse of this novice baseball prodigy. When Boston appeared in the nation's capital at the end of April, *Washington Post* scribe Joe Campbell bestowed praise and accolades upon the speedy outfielder.

> The Boston club has a budding phenom in Stahl, the young right fielder, who came within an ace of being a Senator. In fact, he was drafted last winter by [Washington owner] Earl Wagner. Mr. Wagner, however, had so much faith in the fleet-footed [Nationals outfielder William "Billy"] Lush that he waived claim to Stahl, who was immediately snapped up by Selee.
>
> Stahl is a natural batsman, with a pugnacious attitude at the bat and a good eye. Both Wagner and [Washington manager Gus] Schmelz regret that they overlooked Stahl, whose release could not be purchased from Boston for any reasonable amount, nor is there a player on the Washington team, barring, perhaps, one of the pitchers, who would even be considered by Selee in any possible deal for Stahl.[19]

The pitcher Joe Campbell alluded to also praised Chick Stahl when the Nationals played a series against the Beaneaters at South End Grounds in August. Stahl's performance thus far as a major leaguer impressed staff ace and student of the game Win Mercer, who conveyed his sterling opinion when interviewed by a *Washington Post* writer days after losing to Boston, 8–0, on August 18.

"One of the freest natural batsmen I have ever encountered is Chick Stahl, the laughing Hoosier, of the Boston team," said Winnie Mercer. "Stahl can hit a low curve, a wild pitch, a fastball, high or low, and how are you going to beat that combination? In last Wednesday's game at Boston I sent a slow drop ball to him, and he assassinated it. Next, I tried him on a speedy one over the inside corner and high, and he dropped a single into short right field. The next ball he hit was a wild pitch a foot out. That's what you call versatile hitting."[20]

Boston claimed the National League pennant in 1897, going 93–39 and outdistancing the second-place Baltimore Orioles by two games. The Beaneaters then succumbed to Baltimore in the postseason Temple Cup, four games to one. Chicago's *Inter Ocean* believed Chick Stahl deserved a large share of Boston's pennant glory. The newspaper felt that without him, the Beaneaters would have been hard-pressed to match up against Orioles star outfielder Willie Keeler during the regular season and Temple Cup games.[21] Boston grabbed the bunting once again in 1898, going 102–47 and outpacing Baltimore by six games to lead the National League. Stahl's stellar rise to prominence continued as he batted .308 for the Beaneaters, while third baseman Jimmy Collins experienced a monster season, hitting .328, driving home 111 runs, and pacing the circuit with 15 home runs.

A confrontation between two players almost sabotaged Boston's flag glory. On July 28, at the Southern Hotel when the club played in St. Louis, the dining room's headwaiter escorted rookie hurler Victor "Vic" Willis that morning to eat breakfast at the same table as catcher Martin "Marty" Bergen. When Willis sat down, Bergen, dealing with mental problems and still irked over the pitcher's attitude toward him the previous night on the train, demanded Willis move to another table. When Vic refused, Marty slapped him across the face. Other players and hotel employees interceded before the situation escalated. A staff member tipped off a reporter about the incident. When the scribe approached Frank Selee regarding the dispute, the Beaneaters' skipper convinced the writer to withhold the story until the season's end because of Boston's involvement in a hot pennant battle.[22]

Following the campaign's conclusion, Chick, while visiting Buffalo, shared a tale from his days playing baseball in Fort Wayne that offered a glimpse into his humorous personality. The story involved friend and current Washington hurler John "Cy" Swaim and George Tebeau, who managed the Western League's Columbus Buckeyes/Senators for part of 1898.

> I was Cy Swaim's catcher once in an exhibition game at Fort Wayne. We were short of a backstop, and George Tebeau stuck me behind the pad because I used to catch occasional games in our spring practice. Cy's full arm swing, that windmill of his, confused me when the base runners on the other team tried to steal a base. I could nail a runner at third once in a while, but on the throw to second Cy's pile-driver shape loomed up before me and balked my throw. So I fixed it up with Cy to give him a tip every time I was in the act of throwing to the second sack.
>
> "When I yell, 'low bridge,' Cy, you duck and don't feel afraid that I will nail you," said I. At the first yell of low bridge I fired away. But Cy forgot to duck, and the ball collided with his Adam's apple, bounced off into foul ground, and the base stealer ran to third. When Cy recovered he sauntered up to the home plate and threatened to make a whisk broom of me. "See here, Chick," said Cy, "don't give me any more of that low bridge business and make me look like a Rube. I won't stand for it. I have a young lady friend here—that one with the yaller dress up there in the stand—and if you keep yelling low bridge at me you will queer me with the lady."[23]

Although the Beaneaters slid down to second place behind the league-leading Brooklyn Superbas in 1899, Stahl enjoyed a sensational season, hitting .351, banging out 202 hits, and scoring 122 runs. Chick's ball-hawking skills amazed fans at South End Grounds fans when Boston defeated Cincinnati, 8–2, on June 3. In the eighth inning, the Reds' Elmer Smith stepped up to the plate and squarely met pitcher Edward "Ted" Lewis's offering with his bat. The screaming drive headed to the farthest corner of the lot near the right-field bleachers, never rising more than ten feet the entire time. Fans expected the smash to reach a plot of grass close to the fence. Stahl immediately sprinted like a greyhound toward the baseball's destination. Chick traveled about forty yards before leaping into the air and extending his right hand to its fullest length. He barely reached the sphere and hung on, although momentum dictated the ball jarring from his glove. The crowd heartily cheered for five minutes, having witnessed a splendid fielding display by one of the game's fastest men.[24]

Shortly after the season ended, National League president Nick Young categorized Stahl as one of the organization's best seven or eight free hitters. An article in the *Fort Wayne Sentinel* marveled at Chick's consistency as a batter since he did not experience ebbs and flows but offered a steady and superb performance each day. His fielding and throws from the outfield also received special attention in Associated Press dispatches throughout the campaign. The local newspaper reasoned the hometown boy, who quickly rose to become one of the National League's most valuable players, deserved to receive the salary limit permitted in 1900.[25] On the morning of January 15, 1900, Stahl left his off-season home in Fort Wayne and traveled to South Bend, Indiana. Over the next few weeks, Chick coached Notre Dame's baseball team, teaching the university boys strategy and fundamentals while also rounding them into shape for the upcoming season.[26]

While Chick Stahl worked diligently with Notre Dame's ballplayers, the Beaneaters' baseball family suffered a severe tragedy. On the morning of January 19, at the family home in North Brookfield, Massachusetts, referred to as "Snowball Farm," catcher Marty Bergen, dealing with severe psychological problems, murdered his wife and children with an ax. After executing this dastardly deed, Bergen committed suicide by cutting his throat in front of a mirror so brutally that it nearly severed his head. Marty killed his thirty-one-year-old wife, Harriet Gaines Bergen, first before murdering his five-year-old daughter, Florence, and two-year-old son, Joe.[27]

Boston experienced a rough season in 1900, sliding to fourth place with a 66–72 record. Chick maintained his excellent consistency, batting .295 and driving in 82 runs, good for second on the team. The fact that Stahl played at such an elevated level proved amazing, since he battled malaria for a good portion of the season. He contracted the illness while the club traveled through Louisville early in the campaign. Despite the affliction troubling him the entire summer, Chick remained in the lineup.[28] When the Beaneaters' season concluded, Stahl, along with teammate and friend Jimmy Collins, spent eleven days at Mount Clemens, Michigan, utilizing the therapeutic benefits of that area's hot mineral baths.[29] Chick arrived in Fort Wayne on the afternoon of October 25 to spend the winter in his hometown. Stahl announced that the time spent in Mount Clemens proved beneficial, and he felt better after engaging in extended treatment for malaria.[30]

Shortly after arriving home, Chick found himself entangled in legal trouble. On December 3, a local newspaper reported that Fred W. Roebke, a Fort Wayne constable, filed suit against Stahl and Fred Schwartz for $1,000 in personal damages. Roebke alleged that the two defendants tossed and rolled him about while goofing around in pretended sport to cause severe injury. Regarding criminal proceedings, Chick and Schwartz appeared in court, where Justice of the Peace Louis P. Huser levied fines against the two gentlemen for their conduct.[31] The off-season became more intriguing for Stahl and Boston's baseball faithful when the star outfielder flexed some free agency muscle within an environment briefly existing during that era. It is likely that while spending time with friend Jimmy Collins at Mount Clemens, the two discussed this burning issue.

On March 4, 1901, a dispatch from Cleveland, Ohio, claimed Chick Stahl had signed a contract to play for Boston's new American League team. That day, Connie Mack, Hugh Duffy, and Jimmy Collins conferred with league vice-president and Boston owner Charles Somers and Cleveland Blues club magnate John Kilfoyl in that city. American League president Ban Johnson chose Mack to manage the Philadelphia Athletics while he selected Duffy to oversee the Milwaukee Brewers. Johnson also recruited Collins to play for and manage the organization's Hub entry. Following this meeting, as Jimmy prepared to leave for his Buffalo home, he offered a brief comment to the press.

"I have signed to play with the Bostons," said Collins, "and shall have a team that will be first-class in every particular."[32]

While striving to build a first-class club, it made sense that Collins wanted his friend and stalwart outfielder Chick Stahl to join him. Besides residing in Buffalo, Jimmy played for the Bisons in 1893 and 1894. On March 4, Stahl officially inked his signature to a contract, making him a member of Collins's American League team.[33] Chick arrived in Buffalo on March 29, while Jimmy returned to the city a day later so the two could leave for Charlottesville, Virginia, that night for spring training. After talking to both men at the Hotel Iroquois prior to their departure, a reporter for the *Buffalo Evening Times* declared Stahl still wore that same beautiful smile and appeared better looking than the day he left Buffalo to join the Boston Beaneaters. Chick commented that he had practiced in Fort Wayne the past two to three weeks in warm and pleasant weather, a stark contrast to Buffalo's winterlike atmosphere.[34]

A *Buffalo Enquirer* sportswriter, who used the pen name Hotspur, also interviewed Stahl before he traveled to Charlottesville. The scribe mentioned the hope of Boston Beaneaters' ownership enticing Chick to return to their club. The magnates exuded confidence since hurler Bill Dinneen decided to go back to the Beaneaters after agreeing to a personal contract with Charles Somers to play for his squad. Bill reneged on that deal and signed a second document with the National League team. Stahl offered his opinion on futile attempts by his former employer, desiring him to follow in Dinneen's footsteps.

> Ever since it was given out that I would play with the American League team in Boston instead of with the National League team the directors of the latter club have been trying to gain my consent to jump my contract and sign with them. Since they secured Dinneen they have been even more lavish in their telegraph expenses. However, they might just as well let good enough alone, for I will never play with the National League again. I have cast my fortunes with the American League and have signed a contract to play for Jimmy Collins. I will not break the latter, and I will

certainly play with his team if I am well and in sound state of mind when called upon.

I am of age. I know what I am doing. I am no traitor or coward, and I will play with Boston this year, but, as stated before, in the American League Club.

Chick's explanation about age tamped down any notion that Jimmy Collins had influenced or coerced him into reaching this conclusion. Collins, who happened to be standing nearby, offered a poignant comment in front of Hotspur.

"That's right; stick, Chick and we will make you a manager next year," laughingly replied Collins.[35]

As the club finished preparations in Charlottesville on the eve of the opening game against Baltimore at Oriole Park on April 26, Chick Stahl once again reiterated his commitment to remaining in the American League.

"I see some people have an idea that I am weakening and it would not take much to induce me to go back on my contract with Somers and rejoin the National League," said Chick. "As far as weakening is concerned and going back to the National League, I want it understood that I am with the American League as long as it exists and I can play ball and all the money the National League could scrape together could not induce me to return to its ranks."[36]

Stahl's bitterness toward his former club centered on their signing two pitchers for the upcoming season, although both individuals had inked deals to play for the American League in 1901. Chick refused to talk to these two hurlers, Dinneen and Vic Willis, for jumping back to the National League. Stahl declared he would never play for the Beaneaters' triumvirate again, consisting of ownership partners Arthur Soden, William Conant, and James B. Billings, even if he needed to quit playing baseball. These magnates persisted, and one of the directors held a three-hour conference with Chick at a Boston hotel in late August and then offered a three-year contract paying the outfielder $10,000. Since Stahl resembled a good listener during this meeting, the three owners appeared optimistic. They also did not object to welcoming back Jimmy Collins but realized such a gambit was pointless.[37] Chick offered a statement after the long talk with this agent did not budge him from his position.

"Jimmy Collins could get $10,000 in a minute to play with the Nationals," said Stahl. "My price is $20,000, and then I would retire."[38]

The Boston Americans finished second in the American League race in 1901, posting a 79–57 record that left them four games behind the pace-setting Chicago White Sox. Once the campaign concluded, Stahl and Collins spent a few days relaxing in Buffalo. On October 11, Jimmy left his home and traveled to Cleveland to confer with Charles Somers about the club's inaugural season and preparing for next year. Collins affirmed that following a slow start in 1901, the Americans struck their stride, boosting his players' confidence and rendering their early problems a distant memory. Jimmy said that although the team expressed joy over placing second, they strived for bigger things in 1902. Before Chick left for Fort Wayne on the same day Collins embarked on his trip to Ohio, a *Buffalo Morning Express* sportswriter interviewed him.

> The National League magnates of the Boston club have not given up all hope of winning Collins back. Just before we started for Buffalo I received word to meet an emissary of theirs at a certain place, and when I went there he said that there was $14,000 for Collins and $10,000 for me to return to the old club, and he said that the figures offered Collins might be raised. Those are salaries that would make one feel like a bank president. But I am satisfied with my present berth, and I know that Collins is.
>
> Why, when I first started in the baseball business $15 was bigger to me than the baker wagon going along there, for I remember that when the season was over and I wanted to take one of the old uniforms home with me to practice in the spring, Jack Rowe [Chick's former Buffalo manager] told me that I could by depositing $15. That was too much money, and the uniform did not go with me. So long as this war keeps up the men will get good wages, but look out for a drop.[39]

During the off-season, Chick Stahl oversaw the operation of a saloon he owned in Fort Wayne. Utilizing the appeal connected to his status as a star major league baseball player for publicity purposes, Chick stood around the bar looking pleasant while watching the cash register.[40] The location of Stahl's establishment proved a key point regarding a near brush with death for the Americans' outfielder.[41] On the evening of January 26, 1902, Miss Louise "Lulu" Ortman, a jilted lover, attempted to shoot Chick with a concealed weapon. Ortman intended to kill Stahl for casting her aside and devoting his attention to another woman.[42] Lulu, an attractive twenty-two-year-old girl who dressed impeccably, worked as a stenographer for the Kennedy Lumber Company. Her father, Henry Ortman, owned a well-known Fort Wayne cigar manufacturing company. Ortman had carried the revolver with her since the previous Wednesday, but an opportunity did not present itself until four days later.[43]

Different versions surrounding details of the incident appeared in local newspapers. One account claimed Lulu's intimate friend informed Fort Wayne Police Superintendent Homer A. Gorsline of her intentions. This version alleged that Gorsline overpowered the scorned woman as she drew the revolver, disarmed the perpetrator, and escorted her to police headquarters.[44] Another narrative asserted one of Stahl's friends alerted the police superintendent to possible trouble.[45] An article vowed Ortman fired one shot from the gun that barely missed striking Chick's head.[46] A conflicting explanation reported Stahl grabbed his former sweetheart's arm before she could fire the weapon, and a crowd of bystanders held Lulu until a law enforcement official arrived on the scene to arrest her.[47] The *Fort Wayne Journal-Gazette* offered the most concise article chronicling her desire to end Chick's life.

According to this publication, Lulu L. Ortman attempted to end Chick Stahl's life at 7 P.M. on January 26. Lulu arrived in this area of town that Sunday afternoon, walked into Granneman's Drugstore, and sat at a table with a view of the street. After remaining there for some time, Ortman briefly left the drugstore before returning later that afternoon. Although Lulu never explained why she loitered at this business, a close observer could have detected a tint of anger on her face rooted in vengeance. Around 7 P.M., Stahl and a friend walked past Granneman's Drugstore. Without saying a word to those inside, Ortman rushed out of the pharmacy, confronted the ballplayer, and demanded an explanation for his behavior regarding their relationship.

Chick refused to talk to the woman in public, so the two walked west, where they stopped after about one hundred feet from the street for more privacy. Once they reached this spot, Lulu reached for a revolver concealed in the folds of her dress. Chick, using his swiftness and strength as an athlete, grabbed the gun away from the infuriated woman. Superintendent of Police Homer Gorsline, who witnessed this scuffle, walked up to the pair and investigated the matter. All three individuals journeyed to the police station, where Gorsline held Ortman in custody, pending a hearing. The issue resulted from trouble Lulu and Chick experienced some time ago.

Stahl courted Ortman before a misunderstanding occurred. Chick broke off their relationship and sought the companionship of a different woman in another part of Fort Wayne. Lulu did not appreciate Stahl dumping her for another girl. Ortman told police officers that she purchased the revolver the previous Wednesday and carried it with her, awaiting a chance to use it upon meeting her recreant lover. Lulu affirmed a commitment to killing Stahl because he no longer loved her. Chick had little to say other than he planned to file charges the following morning in police court. Ortman's father, the cigar factory owner, refused to post bail, stating his daughter declined to listen to his opinion on the matter and that he planned to allow the law to follow its due course. This headline referred to Stahl as "Chic" rather than "Chick."[48]

Besides pressing charges, Chick told police officers that the girl possessed no valid reason to attempt to murder him.[49] The misunderstanding leading to this disagreement centered on Lulu Ortman's claim that Stahl had agreed to marry her and later reneged on fulfilling this promise.⁵⁰ This story had a peculiar twist. On January 29, the *Fort Wayne Journal-Gazette* printed a small article claiming they had misrepresented the girl's family connection. Because of annoyance to Henry W. Ortman and his family, the newspaper wrote that this cigar manufacturer, renowned for creating the "Pearl" and "H. O." cigars, was not Lulu's father. Confusion existed since Henry W. happened to be a business mogul manufacturing cigars and the father of a daughter employed as a stenographer. The *Fort Wayne Journal-Gazette* revealed the arrested woman's dad happened to be another man named Henry Ortman, who operated his business on a different street.⁵¹

Law enforcement officials released Lulu Ortman from custody on January 27, 1902, when Chick Stahl did not appear in court to file charges that Monday morning. Some stories reporting this unexpected turn of events now referred to the free woman as Lulu Ortmann, rather than Ortman.⁵² Whether Ortman, or Ortmann, with a spelling change possibly rooted in the supposition that two cigar makers named Henry existed, Lulu eventually moved to Chicago.⁵³

Following a tumultuous winter back home, Chick once again performed steadily for Boston in 1902, appearing in 127 games and batting .323. The Americans finished third in the American League race with a 77–60 record, leaving them 6 ½ games behind pennant-winning Philadelphia.

Chick Stahl's 1903 campaign saw a division into two categories: a challenging few beginning months fraught with injury and a jubilant moment of championship glory. Stahl's problems started in early May when he suffered an injury while the club played in Detroit.⁵⁴ After being unable to participate for several games, team officials announced Chick had received care in St. Louis for a crippled knee.⁵⁵ On May 24, after Boston defeated Chicago at South Side Park, 7–0, Jimmy Collins added that Stahl had also suffered an injury to muscles in his stomach.⁵⁶ Amidst these health issues, Chick's father, Reuben Stahl, died in Fort Wayne on May 28, 1903.⁵⁷ During his physical and emotional ordeal, Stahl lost twenty pounds.⁵⁸

When the Americans arrived in St. Louis to begin a series on May 20, Chick consulted former city health commissioner Dr. Max C. Starkloff about his health situation. Dr. Starkloff performed two painful operations. The physician expected his patient to make a speedy recovery. Dr. Starkloff believed that if no further complications arose, Stahl could start playing for Boston once again in June.⁵⁹ Chick wanted to rejoin his teammates in Detroit on June 23, but the medico advised further caution to his patient. Dr. Starkloff offered assurances that Stahl would return to the lineup shortly.

"Stahl will come around all right," said Dr. Starkloff. "He hurt himself last season and suffered another injury this year that put him to the bad. He has an abscess. I think it will heal readily, and he ought to be back in the game when the Bostons get back again for the games of July 4 with St. Louis."

Although Chick possessed the appearance of a sick man, lacking color in his face, Dr. Starkloff remained confident that good nursing would restore him to health.[60] Stahl made his triumphant return on July 14, going 1-for-4 as the Cleveland Naps defeated the Americans in a twelve-inning affair at Huntington Avenue Baseball Grounds, 4–3. Although Chick's final .274 batting line was the lowest of his major league career, team glory superseded personal goals. Boston cruised to the American League pennant, posting a 91–47 record that put them 14 ½ games ahead of the second-place Athletics. The Americans topped off their exhilarating 1903 season by defeating the Pittsburgh Pirates, five games to three, in the inaugural modern World Series. Stahl appeared in all eight games and hit .303 against Pittsburgh.

Chick beamed with pride when he arrived in Buffalo at the end of November to visit his friend Dr. A. E. Campbell of Parkside Avenue. While discussing Boston baseball on November 29 with a reporter, Stahl enthusiastically praised local hero Jimmy Collins for his fine generalship as the club's manager and captain. Chick also declared that every team member would be ready to fight to the finish in 1904, playing for a man they loved and adored.

> Jimmy Collins is the greatest baseball general of them all. He has a system combined with open personality which has simply had to win. The boys on the Boston team swear by Collins and it is to this fact—the confidence which he enjoys of the entire team—which has made the teamwork of the Bostons a by-word in the baseball world during the past year.
>
> The "hit and run" and the double steal tricks, so successfully worked by [Patsy] Tebeau in his palmy days, have been combined and improved by Collins until the method has become invincible. Collins has been compared to Tebeau in this respect and the odds are all in favor of the Bison by a long way. His polish and gentlemanly tactics have been effective even where Tebeau failed.
>
> Collins has been loyal to his players, fought for them, and is simply one of us. He has carefully watched over the work of the team and, while always on the lookout for the interest of the owners, he has never been guilty of any deal which would make him unpopular with his men.
>
> Collins's methods are all his own and while all the boys are familiar with them, the team has not given the secrets away. This is what has placed the Bostons on a pedestal which has been the envy of the big league. Collins is a born leader of men on the diamond, and next year will see his talented team just where it is this year—at the top.[61]

After a spirited fight with the New York Highlanders, Boston claimed their second consecutive American League pennant in 1904. The Americans posted a 95–59 record, while the Highlanders finished 1 ½ games behind with a mark of 92–59. Boston did not receive an opportunity to appear in the World Series since the New York Giants' management refused to play a club that belonged to an inferior league. Chick Stahl appeared in every game for the Americans, batted .290, and tied for the league lead in triples with teammate Buck Freeman and the Washington Senators' Joseph "Joe" Cassidy, blasting 19 three-baggers. Expectations ran high for a three-peat in 1905. On March 8, Chick arrived in Buffalo as Jimmy Collins's guest before the two embarked for spring training in Macon, Georgia. That afternoon, the two buddies walked arm-in-arm, eliciting smiles and handshakes from friends and acquaintances. Stahl, looking physically well after resting over the winter, offered his impressions about the upcoming season.

"We are out for another banner, just as well as Buffalo," said Stahl, "and we expect to do the act with less toil than was required last season. We look for Myron Grimshaw [Boston's rookie first baseman who played for Buffalo from 1902 through 1904] to make good. If he does not, he will be among the few who have been graduated from the Bisons that have failed."[62]

For the first time since the American League became a significant institution on equal par with the Senior Circuit, the Americans failed to join the pennant conversation. Boston came home in fourth place in 1905 with a 78–74 record as Connie Mack's Philadelphia boys secured the bunting. The campaign was difficult for Stahl, as his batting average plummeted to .258. On the eve of the season opener, as the Americans stopped in Montgomery, Alabama, during their exhibition tour, Collins gave Chick and shortstop Freddy Parent a day off because of injuries. Stahl suffered from a gimpy hip, while Parent experienced a stiff and sore back.[63] Chick's batting average languished at .211 following his first two at-bats against the St. Louis Browns at Sportsman's Park on May 23. Boston's manager pulled his friend from the game in the fifth inning after the Americans loaded the bases and sent Kip Selbach up to pinch-hit. Selbach promptly smacked a two-run single to center field that aided Boston's 5–3 victory.[64]

After this contest ended, Jimmy Collins announced Kip would play center field until Chick Stahl rounded into shape. Newspapers from St. Louis reported Stahl was a sick man and under the care of a doctor in that city.[65] Stahl returned to the Americans' starting lineup on June 7. When the club could not play a scheduled July game against Chicago at South Side Park because of rain and wet grounds, Chick took advantage of the off day and traveled to Fort Wayne to handle a business proposition. Stahl, aspiring to become a baseball magnate, wished to be part of a group that purchased the Central League's Fort Wayne Railroaders, which had recently suffered from mismanagement. Previous owner Isadore "Izy" Mautner, a very unpopular magnate with league officials, announced he could not complete the campaign as promised under an early-season agreement. The league, as their prerogative, seized control of the franchise.

A vigorous fight started regarding the disposal or sale of the club. Fort Wayne businessmen desired to secure the franchise, and many believed Chick's inclusion in the process was a perfect fit. Stahl told these entrepreneurs he would only join a consortium if permitted to purchase a large slice of the franchise. Although all parties eventually agreed on this point, the negotiations took so long that, in the meantime, Central League officials approved relocating the team to Canton, Ohio. The only option Chick and his partners maintained surrounded buying another franchise in the future. Fort Wayne's citizens would express great interest in supporting a club owned by a local hero like Stahl. While things had not worked out on this occasion, Chick contemplated applying for another franchise in 1906.[66]

From the standpoint of just playing the game, Chick Stahl rebounded for Boston in 1906 and stood out above all other teammates. Stahl appeared in every contest for the Americans and batted .286. Unfortunately, the club collectively performed miserably, finishing in the American League basement with a 49–105 record, leaving them 45 ½ games behind the pennant-winning White Sox. A big problem existed regarding manager Jimmy Collins. Despite earning an $8,500 salary in 1906 to perform his dual functions for the organization, Collins shirked that obligation. Unable to take his position at third base as the campaign progressed due to a knee injury, Jimmy ignored responsibility rather than devote all his energy to running the club and exhibited little interest in the organization's affairs.[67]

The Boston Americans' ownership had undergone many transformations over the past few years. In 1902, Charles Somers, who also acted as the American League's vice president, sold his interest in the Boston franchise to Henry Killilea and dedicated his attention to overseeing the Cleveland Naps, a club he also owned. A father and son tandem purchased the Americans' franchise from Killilea in 1904. Charles H. Taylor, a Boston publisher, and his son John I. Taylor took control of the team, assuming the president's title within the organization. Collins abandoned the squad on several occasions in 1906, which the Taylor ownership duo initially ignored. Instead of always performing his diamond duties, Jimmy relaxed on a beach in Nantucket, Massachusetts.

When Collins returned after one of these absences, Huntington Avenue Baseball Grounds fans roasted him with unpleasant remarks. In one game, when the overweight ballplayer smacked a long drive, he could not stretch the safety into a double due to being out of shape. On another occasion, while coaching third base, Jimmy sent a runner home that had no chance of reaching the plate safely. The crowd harshly jeered Boston's manager after this boneheaded decision and when he struck out in another contest. Although Collins's physicians insisted his knee had healed sufficiently to allow him to return to third base, the player refrained from entering a contest other than to pinch-hit. Jimmy also did not inform the club about his involvement in a runaway horse incident while traveling in a carriage at Nantucket on August 26.[68]

Following their 9–3 loss against Cleveland at Huntington Avenue Baseball Grounds on August 28, Americans team secretary and treasurer Hugh McBreen announced the organization had indefinitely suspended Collins for absenting himself from the team without permission. This decision surprised teammates Buck Freeman and Bill Dinneen, who did not realize such a problem existed. Like many fans, Freeman believed attending to some club business explained Jimmy's absence. Charles Taylor made a brief statement when pressed by media members.

"What is there to say?" responded Taylor. "I cannot see that there is need to say anything in this matter. This is not a first offense. Mr. Collins has now twice left the club without permission and he has also absented himself once or twice on the road without leave. I have no idea where he has gone. He has been treated with every consideration."[69]

At 5 P.M. that same day, league president Ban Johnson boarded a train in New York, bound for Boston. Upon arriving at 10 P.M., Johnson conducted a meeting with Charles Taylor at the Algonquin Club.[70] When interviewed after these two baseball power brokers engaged in their conference, Johnson detailed the situation surrounding Jimmy Collins's indefinite suspension.

> The suspension of manager Collins was not a surprise to me. The Boston club could not have taken any other course, and it is to be regretted that this action was not taken at an earlier date.
>
> When a club manager neglects his charge, a state of demoralization at once pervades a team, and all chance for its success is destroyed.
>
> The Boston club has shown great forbearance in its dealings with Mr. Collins, and it is beyond me to explain why he should so grossly betray the confidence and trust reposed in him.
>
> When he signed with the Boston club this spring he was generously treated in the matter of salary, and I can safely say there was not a ballplayer in the American or National league so handsomely compensated. Mr. Collins was given absolute charge of the club and money was always

at his command to purchase players where it was impossible to improve the team.

Weeks ago it was apparent that manager Collins had lost all interest in his work, and didn't seem to care a rap about the success or failure of the club that had been placed in his charge.

Ban Johnson added that several weeks ago, he engaged Collins in a discussion and attempted to alert the manager to his duties regarding the Americans. That intervention proved unsuccessful. Johnson also praised Boston's performance on their recent western road trip, crediting Chick Stahl regarding the squad's proficient work. Ban admitted that he regretted Jimmy's present predicament due to his splendid character traits.[71] Americans team officials had expected Collins to suit up and play in the game against the Naps. Instead, he remained in Nantucket. The Taylors also announced Stahl would take over the squad as interim manager and captain. Chick's first job under this title involved informing his good friend that ownership had suspended him. When approached by a scribe that evening in Nantucket, Jimmy refused to discuss his punishment.[72] Boston posted a 14–26 record with Stahl at the helm in 1906.

One week after the campaign ended, Chick became ensnared in an unfortunate incident in Buffalo. Stahl traveled to his old stomping grounds to meet with twenty-three-year-old Hattie Burnett, who resided in Buffalo with her grandmother, Martha Stephens. Hattie was also the daughter of Charles Burnett. The attractive and highly intelligent young lady resided with the grandmother since she did not have a good relationship with the father's second wife, whom he married following her mother's death. After talking with Chick on a matter, Miss Burnett drank poison early in the morning on October 12 while in his company in the waiting room of the Erie Railroad Depot at Michigan and Exchange Streets. Buffalo police detectives Thomas Flesh and John Murray happened to be standing nearby when Hattie drank the small bottle's contents. The three men lifted Burnett and kept her walking until an ambulance arrived and transported her to the emergency hospital.

Stahl informed Flesh and Murray that he came to Buffalo to talk with Hattie Burnett since he had acted as her guardian. When the two went out that evening, the young woman declared to Chick that she wished to travel to Europe to study painting and become an artist. Stahl told the police officers that he denied her request. Stahl felt Hattie's disappointment over his stance on the subject caused her to drink something that had the effect of poison to scare him. Detectives Flesh and Murray confirmed that the bottle she drank from contained four ounces of laudanum. Chick informed police that Charles Burnett maintained a status as a phenomenally successful businessman in Buffalo, and his daughter also possessed great wealth. Upon the officers informing Stahl that Hattie would recover, he grabbed the next train for Fort Wayne. At the hospital, Hattie told doctors she used clove oil. Martha Stephens declared the whole incident a misunderstanding and that her granddaughter had partaken in a prescription to alleviate pain caused by sore teeth.

"It was all a mistake; Hattie did not take the poison with the intention of killing herself," stated Mrs. Stephens. "For some time Hattie has been troubled with her mouth and gums and the doctor prescribed a painkiller for her. She always carried it with her, and mistaking the poison for the painkiller, swallowed a quantity of the liquid. She was not at the depot unaccompanied, as it was reported, but was with a party of friends whom she was seeing to a train."[73]

The grandmother did not know the entire story, when declaring a party of friends accompanied Hattie Burnett to the Erie Railroad Depot rather than Chick Stahl. Mrs. Stephens also did not explain to the press why her granddaughter happened to be carrying a vial of poison. Hattie insisted from her hospital bed that she did not wish to commit suicide and only drank the concoction to eliminate a toothache. On the morning of October 13, hospital surgeons said the young woman would be well in one or two days.[74] During her arraignment in the courtroom of Buffalo Police Justice Thomas Murphy on the charge of attempting to commit suicide, Burnett received a suspended sentence from the judge.[75] The fact that Hattie's grandfather had committed suicide the previous spring added a bizarre connection to the story. Isaac Stephens, who suffered from insanity, died after drinking carbolic acid.[76]

On October 17, a *Boston Herald* article declared that the Americans would name Chick Stahl as their manager for the 1907 campaign. The publication cited a story that leaked during the recently completed World Series regarding a meeting between Stahl and Ban Johnson, which had occurred when Boston played in Chicago between September 24 and 26. At this conference, Johnson affirmed that Jimmy Collins would not return to his old post, and offered the player-manager job to Chick. During the exchange, Ban assured Stahl he had reached a satisfactory settlement with Collins. When the Americans returned to Boston on October 5 to play their season's final series against New York, Chick talked to Jimmy and found that no such agreement existed with his friend. Stahl immediately traveled to club headquarters and told ownership he did not intend to manage the squad until they squared things with Collins.

Chick mentioned to club officials the diamond success and pennants won with Jimmy at the helm while also admitting to owing all financial success as a baseball player to his friend, who had exhibited faith in the outfielder's ability. Stahl demanded they broker a monetary settlement with Collins. An anonymous Americans player stated Jimmy had intervened and squelched a rebellion, imploring his team not to go out on strike after ownership suspended him. Regarding any potential trade to another club, Collins refused to consent to a move until he received back pay for his disbarment at the end of the 1906 season.[77] Stahl, always popular with Boston's fans, received a tempting salary offer to permanently succeed Jimmy. Loyal to a fault, financial inducements proved secondary compared to a longtime friendship.

"Do right by Collins and then I'll talk business," Stahl told the Americans' ownership. "Pay him for the time he was laid off. Tender him the management again. Then, if he doesn't accept, perhaps I will talk business with you."[78]

A more important matter in Chick Stahl's life took center stage, placing baseball in the background. On October 20, 1906, the *Boston Journal* printed a story about Stahl's upcoming nuptials. The previous week, Chick announced his engagement to twenty-seven-year-old Julia Harmon, from Boston's Roxbury neighborhood. Harmon, the daughter of John and Mary Maher Harmon, lived with her parents near Huntington Avenue Baseball Grounds. Julia loved baseball and had frequently attended games at the ballpark for many years. Harmon and Chick started cultivating an intimate friendship when he played for the Boston Beaneaters. Raised in Roxbury and a graduate of the local high school, Julia excelled as an accomplished musician of prominent ability.[79] On the morning of November 10, Stahl arrived in Boston and registered at the Copley Square Hotel. Americans team treasurer Hugh McBreen escorted Chick to city hall, where the ballplayer applied for a marriage license.[80]

Chick Stahl and Julia Harmon's wedding occurred on November 14 at Saint Francis de Sales Church in Boston. Reverend John H. Harrigan, a close friend of the bride and groom whom Chick came to know when he first arrived in Boston in 1897, officiated the ceremony. Miss Harmon wore a blue traveling suit and a large picture hat adorned with ostrich plumes. Timothy J. Bresnahan of South Boston stood as Stahl's best man, while Margaret E. McKenna performed maid of honor duties. When the ceremony concluded in the church rectory, the newly married couple exited and walked down the cathedral's steps amid a shower of rice and confetti, courtesy of Julia's friends and family. They entered a waiting carriage that whisked them to the railroad station, where the newlyweds grabbed a train bound for the South.

Mr. and Mrs. Stahl intended to make their permanent residence in the husband's hometown of Fort Wayne. Before heading to Indiana, the newlyweds planned to spend time in Hot Springs, Arkansas, before traveling to Buffalo to visit Jimmy Collins for a few weeks. Julia Harmon Stahl was one of the most highly esteemed young ladies living in Roxbury. She frequently engaged in social and charitable events at Saint Francis de Sales Church. According to the *Boston Daily Post,* Chick met his future wife four years earlier when he attended one of these church functions with some Americans teammates. This contradicted the *Boston Journal*'s claim that they became acquainted when Stahl played for the Beaneaters. During the summer months, Stahl regularly attended Sunday mass at that church while in Boston. The happy couple received many warm congratulations and handsome presents from friends. Americans team president John I. Taylor gave the Stahls a beautiful silverware set as a wedding gift.[81]

Chick Stahl added another town to his winter itinerary since Boston's team president invited the player to join him at the American League's December meetings in Chicago. This gesture strongly suggested Chick would manage the Americans in 1907. Although Chick appeared anxious to upgrade the club's third base position, he preferred that all parties patch up their differences so Collins could return to his former hot corner station during the upcoming campaign.

"I certainly believe that Collins would like to play again in Boston next season," said Stahl, "and no one would like to see him come back better than I, and I fully believe that this feeling is shared by other members of the club."[82]

On the afternoon of December 4, John I. Taylor announced Chick Stahl would manage Boston in 1907. Taylor closed the deal over the previous two days when he stopped off in Fort Wayne during his travels and spent Sunday and Monday talking to Stahl. Upon hearing the news, many fans reasoned this move a natural progression since Chick always helped Jimmy Collins and deserved more credit for the club's success than he received. The owner offered his expectations regarding Chick running the club's baseball operations.

"I have great faith in Stahl making good," said Taylor, "as the players will work their hands off for him. Stahl will maintain discipline and, when burdened with a duty, is one of those players who rise to the occasion. He is familiar with every man in the American League, and has suggested several trades that I will try to make and give him the men he wants to work with."[83]

John I. Taylor's comment about Chick Stahl rising to the occasion when burdened with duty proved apocalyptic as events dictated that nothing could be further from the truth. This added responsibility supplied the final stress point for a conflicted individual who had battled an inner demon's beckoning since his teenage years.

Boston started preparations for the upcoming season by holding the first phase of spring training at Little Rock, Arkansas. Prominent "Royal Rooters" member Michael "Mike" McGreevy accompanied the club to Little Rock.[84] McGreevy, who owned the Third Base Saloon in Boston, earned the nickname "Nuf Ced" since he used that phrase when ending all baseball arguments at the establishment.[85] Upon returning to Boston following this spring journey, Mike offered his impressions on how Stahl's mood and demeanor quickly changed once the train reached its destination.

> "Chick" was his old self all the way south on the trip. On the train he was in fine spirits, chatted and joked with the boys as he has always done; was interested in how they had been spending the winter, and seemed full of enthusiasm for the coming season and all that he expected it to bring.
>
> At Little Rock, however, there was a change. It was gradual, but nevertheless it developed within a very few days. Almost from the moment we reached Little Rock there seemed to be something on Stahl's mind. He grew moody and morose. He worked like a trojan on the ball field when the team was actually practicing, but before and after the team had worked, he seemed almost in a trance.
>
> On the way to the grounds he sat alone in the team's private trolley car, and said hardly a word to anyone. It was the same when the boys rode back to their hotel. Evenings at the hotel Stahl seemed to want to be alone, and even his old friend, Jimmy Collins, was not with him much of the time.
>
> Even when he was on the field, it seemed to be an effort for him to work; but he stuck to it and drilled the players thoroughly, keeping a watch over them and always offering suggestions.

According to Mike McGreevy, while talking with some Americans players one night, a veteran team member offered a poignant remark about his boss's state of mind.

"Well, this being the manager has lost us the 'Chicken,' hasn't it?" queried this veteran. "He takes hold of business like a veteran, and just the responsibility given him has put real years on his shoulders."

McGreevy noticed that Chick, in excellent condition when they arrived in Little Rock, grew thin as the days passed and seemed to suffer tremendous strain. Mike offered this interview to the *Boston Daily Globe* one day after Stahl made a huge decision surrounding his baseball career.[86] On the evening of March 25, while Boston conducted a leg of their spring training exhibition tour in Louisville, Kentucky, John I. Taylor announced Chick had resigned as the club's manager and planned to assume some of the job's responsibilities. Following dinner, Chick approached the owner and told him he needed to give up the task since it interfered with his performance as a player and upset him in other ways. Chick added he could not eat or sleep and that worry over club affairs caused the sickness he suffered that afternoon.

Although stunned over Stahl's candid admission, Taylor assured the player he would assume responsibility for outside affairs if Chick agreed to oversee the squad as captain on the field. Stahl consented since this arrangement eliminated the duty of releasing players that he found unpleasant. Boston's president had detected Chick's worry, but he never realized things had reached such a terrible point to convince the longtime star to tender his resignation. That evening, Stahl sent a telegram to his wife, Julia, in Roxbury, telling her about his decision. Chick offered a basis for walking away while talking to *Boston Daily Globe* sportswriter Tim Murnane.

"Why, I found myself actually wasting away," said Stahl. "Handling a bunch of players both on and off the field is no cinch, and the one thing I could not stand for was the release of the men that comes almost daily at this time of year."[87]

While the Americans stayed in Louisville, Stahl and Bill Dinneen roomed together. One morning, as he rubbed his face with a carbolic acid solution, Chick offered a cryptic statement to his teammate.

"I wonder if this stuff would kill a man," remarked Stahl.

"Would it!" quickly responded Dinneen. "Why, a spoonful will kill a dozen men."

"Then I have a good mind to take a good drink of it," continued Stahl.

Dinneen briefly stared at his roommate before replying to this eerie suggestion. "How would your mother or your wife like that kind of news?"

"That's so, Bill," answered Chick, after shaking his head. "It would kill my mother."

Dinneen later stated he watched Stahl throughout their entire time rooming together in Louisville. Bill also revealed that Chick lay on his bed and moaned in great pain, complaining about how his head busted from headaches and wishing everything would be over with. Fearing Stahl may attempt to harm himself, Dinneen secured his razor in a safe place. According to Bill, Chick sometimes snapped out of this despondent trance, saying he wished the season would start so he could forget things and once again sleep and eat.[88] A doctor had prescribed the carbolic acid because Stahl contracted a sore on his foot from suffering a stone bruise while on the diamond. The foot healed slowly since Chick practiced every day, so the physician recommended washing the sore with a mixture of carbolic acid and water.[89] After Dinneen related details of his conversation with Stahl, some players took the bottle of carbolic acid away from their troubled teammate.[90]

On another occasion in Louisville, Chick Stahl told William Cahill, an East Boston resident who traveled with the squad, that he would go and shoot his head off but for his mother. During the trip thus far, Stahl preferred talking to recruits rather than confiding in veterans. Although he rarely discussed religion, Chick appeared more attentive to that aspect of his life while in Little Rock, attending to his Lenten duty by going to mass one Sunday and receiving Holy Communion. Stahl talked more about his faith while there and particularly enjoyed conversing with youngster John "Jack" Hoey, who had attended the College of the Holy Cross. Chick confided in Hoey that he should practice in center field since the team captain did not figure on playing much baseball in 1907. Stahl once told Jack he wished to know how to die. The former collegian always attempted to talk continuously about other things to keep Chick's mind off such topics.[91] One night in Little Rock, Stahl offered a powerful pronouncement to players and sportswriters in the hotel lobby.

"You can't imagine how this job is affecting me," said Stahl. "I wish I had never taken it. I don't like it. I would like to make good as a manager, but I have done nothing but worry."[92]

Roberts, a photographer from Memphis, Tennessee, who snapped photos of Boston's players while they trained in Little Rock, noticed Chick's unusual moods. The photojournalist took several negatives of Stahl. After snapping a final photo of Stahl and Jimmy Collins together, Stahl replied, "Well, I guess that will be the last picture ever taken of me." He laughed while saying it and never considered the comment's bizarre nature.[93] After embarking from Louisville for the next part of their spring exhibition tour in West Baden Springs, Indiana, Chick discussed the suicides of former teammate Marty Bergen and one-time Washington hurler Win Mercer with comrades on the train.[94] Collins, understanding that pressure's burden weighed heavily on Stahl's mind, advised his friend to walk away from baseball obligations and take a break to rest.

"I can't, Jim," said Stahl. "I must stick to the club."

"Send for your wife," suggested Collins, "and she can comfort you. Don't keep all your troubles to yourself, or they will bother you a hundred times more."[95]

Chick Stahl arose early on the morning of March 28, 1907. He appeared in good health and spirits, commenting to some of his teammates that he believed it would be a fine day for them to have a game of ball. At 8:30 A.M., Chick arrived at the private office of Lee W. Sinclair, owner of the West Baden Springs Hotel where the Boston Americans lodged. The two men talked for fifteen minutes regarding bathhouse tickets for team members. At that time, Sinclair noticed nothing strange about Stahl's mental state or behavior.[96] Chick also ran an errand at a nearby drugstore when it opened, purchasing a replacement bottle of carbolic acid and placing it in his pocket. He sat next to Jack Hoey at breakfast but only drank from his coffee cup before leaving a generous tip for the waitress. Stahl then checked out the ballpark, found the grounds satisfactory, returned to the hotel, engaged the players in their rooms, and ordered them out for a practice session.

When Chick walked down to the hotel lobby at 9:45 A.M., pitcher George Winter stood at the desk when the Americans' team captain asked the clerk for his room key. Taking Winter by the hand, Stahl said, "Goodbye, George," then waved as he walked to the elevator. Although George felt Chick acted rather oddly, he gave no further thought to this ominous farewell.[97] In the company of Jimmy Collins, Stahl went to his third-floor accommodations, where the two shared adjoining rooms, to dress for morning practice.[98] Alone in his room at 9:50 A.M., Chick put on his baseball uniform and finally committed a deed he had contemplated for some time. Stepping into Collins's room, Stahl swallowed three-quarters of the liquid left from a four-ounce bottle of carbolic acid. Tossing the container into a corner, Chick staggered back into the adjoining room as Jimmy passed by and drank a large quantity of ice water. Collins became concerned when Stahl started swaying about the room.[99]

"What is the matter with you?" Collins asked.

"Nothing," replied Stahl, before he collapsed, prostrate on the bed.

Detecting the scent of carbolic acid when he ran to where Chick landed, Jimmy sounded the alarm and yelled for help.[100] Once on the bed, Stahl experienced body spasms.[101] After a few minutes, he started writhing in great agony as the deadly potion began working.[102] Boston first baseman Robert "Bob" Unglaub, passing the room when Collins issued his distress call, arrived first on the scene. He rushed over to the bed where Stahl lay, conscious. Noticing a little white froth on the side of Chick's mouth and smelling the odor of carbolic acid, Unglaub took hold of his teammate's hands.

"Chick, you have been drinking carbolic acid," said Bob.

"Yes, Bob, it drove me to it," replied Stahl, uttering his final words.

"Where is the bottle?" demanded Unglaub.

Chick Stahl turned slightly and feebly pointed toward the other room, where Bob found the empty bottle with the label nearly torn off, although enough of the sticker remained to reveal Chick had purchased the deadly poison in West Baden Springs. Unglaub continued attempting to assist Stahl until the West Baden Springs Hotel's house physician, Dr. Chauncey W. Dowden, arrived eleven minutes after Chick swallowed the carbolic acid. Dr. Dowden recommended forcing alcohol down Stahl's throat, but this proved futile. Twenty minutes after drinking the poison, Chick died, decked out in the Boston Americans uniform he proudly wore for six years. He remained lying on the bed until a coroner arrived that afternoon to conduct an inquest.[103] Some newspaper accounts claimed that when several players arrived on the scene following Jimmy Collins's cry for help, Stahl uttered, "Boys, I couldn't help it; it drove me to it."[104]

Information about Chick Stahl committing suicide reached Fort Wayne shortly after noon on March 28. A journalist from a local newspaper related the shocking news to Barbara Stahl, who was devastated. The fact that her favorite son took his own life placed Barbara Stahl in a state of shock that proved serious because of her advanced age.[105] Upon hearing the first accounts, people on the street did not believe the news' veracity, feeling the wire services made a mistake when issuing their reports. These individuals hoped it was just the jovial Stahl playing a practical joke and sending out a fake story about his death.[106] Although Chick's closest hometown friends regretted his tragic death, some of them expressed no surprise over his suicide. One boyhood chum, employed as a Fort Wayne city official, expected such news because of Stahl's recent turmoil.

> I looked for it when I heard he was worrying about the management of his team. "Chick" talked about killing himself several times when he was discouraged about his affairs, and I recall one time when he was in a barber's chair, about five years ago, I heard him tell the barber who was shaving him that it would be a good thing for him to put the razor through his neck.
>
> "If you would just push that blade in and cut my head about half off, so I would never feel it I'd be rid of my troubles," said Stahl to the barber. That was about five years ago. But more than once before that time and more than once afterwards he was heard to say things that indicated a suicidal tendency.

According to his Fort Wayne friends, Chick Stahl even suffered bouts of mental depression years ago while playing amateur baseball. When the future looked bleak, Stahl talked about taking his own life. During one moment of discouragement when performing for the Pilsener squad managed by M. F. Belger, Chick expressed a wish to experience death. Although Stahl's friends considered the ballplayer a cheerful soul, his ready laughter partially repressed a concealed despondent spirit. His closest chums reasoned Chick forced his carefree nature to hide his true emotions.[107] In a letter received at the Ohio city one day after Chick died, a Cincinnati man who had traveled through West Baden Springs and knew of the situation regarding Stahl's troubles predicted the ballplayer would take the suicide route.[108]

On the night of March 28, Stanley Kennison, a shoemaker from Lynn, Massachusetts, also committed suicide by drinking carbolic acid. While conversing with a group of friends at the Ward 6 Democratic Party Club in that municipality near Boston, the copycat briefly excused himself, exited to another room, returned, and announced, "I've done what 'Chick' Stahl did." An ambulance rushed Kennison to a hospital, where he died shortly after arriving.[109] Following a series of practice games in West Baden Springs, Boston had planned to travel to Fort Wayne and play two exhibition contests against the Shamrocks, managed by Stahl's childhood friend, Mart Cleary. When hearing the news regarding his buddy's death, Cleary announced the probable cancelation of those dates. Weeks before the scheduled exhibitions, when asked to predict the outcome of a contest, seeress and prophetess Anna Ray declared these teams would not play the game.[110]

After witnessing the tragic demise of his dear friend, Jimmy Collins sent out telegrams to Chick Stahl's family members. Collins received a response from Julia Stahl that she, her father, her brother-in-law, and a group of relatives would leave Boston that evening and travel to Fort Wayne. Jimmy and others sent numerous wires to inform team president John I. Taylor about the unfortunate situation. Taylor had boarded a train in Omaha, Nebraska, that morning.[111] Immediately after receiving the sad news, Chick's brother Perry Stahl, left Fort Wayne in the company of James Goodfellow, the baseball player's good friend, to bring the body home. The family still had not determined if the burial would happen there or in Roxbury at Julia's request.[112] Mrs. Stahl; her father, John Harmon; and sister, Margaret, made the trip to Fort Wayne. News of her husband's death emotionally shattered Julia.[113] She had just wired Stahl at noon the previous day, asking about his health.[114] She regretted not joining her husband on the spring training excursion before this tragedy occurred.[115]

"This is terrible," moaned Julia before leaving for Fort Wayne. "He was the last person in the world I thought would kill himself. I know he had worried over the responsibilities of managing the Boston Americans, but in a letter he told me that he was happy to give up the place and felt he would become much better now that these things were off his mind. His letter was bright. There did not seem to be any thread of moodiness in it."

The evening before Chick committed suicide, Julia received a telegram from her husband that read, "Cheer up, little girl, and be happy. I am all right now and able to play the game of my life."[116] While the Boston Beaneaters trained in Thomasville, Georgia, and someone announced Chick Stahl had committed suicide, they discontinued their practice game in the sixth inning. Many players, exhibiting disbelief, responded, "You're kidding." Stahl's former Beaneaters teammate Fred Tenney scarcely believed the news, declaring that a merrier fellow never existed, who constantly laughed and had fun while engaging in his life's passions. Fred also crowned Chick as one of the game's best players. Second baseman Claude Ritchey, Stahl's ex-teammate on the Buffalo Bisons and 1903 World Series opponent as a member of the Pittsburgh Pirates, echoed Tenney's sentiment.

"I never saw a more jolly, cheery, pleasant chap in my life than 'Chick,'" said Ritchey. "Everybody on the team liked him. He did not seem to have a care or a sorrow on earth."[117]

On March 28, 1907, shocked Boston Americans team members gathered that evening at the West Baden Springs Hotel. After much discussion, they agreed something other than baseball affairs had weighed heavily on Chick Stahl's mind.[118] Tears streamed down pitcher Cy Young's face while addressing some teammates as he said, "It is mighty tough, boys. I never dreamed of such a thing."

Jimmy Collins offered his solemn comment to fellow team members. "It's awful, boys. I knew he had been worrying a bit, but I would no more believe he would do such a deed than I would anything in the world."

"Poor Chick Stahl. For six years I have known him intimately, and he has always stood for the best in baseball."[119]

One of the largest turnouts for a funeral in Fort Wayne occurred on Saturday, March 30, for Chick Stahl's burial. Thousands of people from the city arrived for the viewing, which began at 2 P.M. in the Stahl residence. Although the suicide component prohibited a church mass, the Benevolent and Protective Order of Elks and Fraternal Order of Eagles conducted a religious ceremony at the home. Hundreds of friends traveled on foot when undertaker Henry H. Schone transported the casket to Lindenwood Cemetery, Chick's final resting place.[120] Former Indiana Congressman James M. Robinson gave a stirring eulogy at the gravesite.[121] The *Buffalo Commercial* received a dispatch stating Jimmy Collins needed to walk away from the grave during Robinson's tribute to Stahl, extremely distraught and overcome with grief and sorrow.[122] Chicago's *Inter Ocean* reported that Collins did not attend the funeral.[123]

That same morning, Chick's intimate friend David P. Murphy, a thirty-three-year-old engineer for the Grand Rapids & Indiana Railroad, ended his life. At 9 A.M., in a room at the Aveline Hotel (Aveline House) in Fort Wayne, Murphy committed suicide by drinking carbolic acid. David admitted to a traveling salesman at breakfast in the hotel's dining room beforehand that he had been drinking heavily the previous night and never went to bed. Murphy remained up, waiting for the arrival of Stahl's body at the Schone Undertaking Rooms. While visiting the deceased, he wept bitterly, expressing deep sorrow and regret. Around 7:30 A.M. on March 30, after purchasing some cigars at L. S. Soest Drugstore, David bought a bottle of carbolic acid. Upon handing it to him, prescription clerk A. W. Koehn advised Murphy not to do what Chick did. David quickly replied, "Well, I should think not." Stahl's distraught friend left a brief note regarding burial for his brother, Francis "Frank" Murphy.

"Frank—Place me next to 'Chick,'" wrote David Murphy. "Goodbye. Best wishes to all. Pay what I owe. Dave."[124]

Following the funeral, Julia Stahl lovingly agreed to live with her mother-in-law in Fort Wayne for a period before returning to Boston after Barbara

Stahl requested that the young lady remain in town. Julia also dreaded going back home due to her residence's proximity to Huntington Avenue Baseball Grounds.[125]

Months before embarking on the fateful spring training trip, Chick Stahl had confided to a friend that he would never accept playing minor league baseball again. Fear over such a downgrade because of the realization he could not manage a baseball club preyed on Chick's mind and consumed him. Outliving his usefulness proved unacceptable, especially if fans who adored and cheered him turned when the downslide started. Stahl could not bear losing that popularity or being branded a failure due to incapability within the manager's role.[126] Although extreme sorrow and mentally debilitating worry destroyed Chick on earth, he hopefully achieved everlasting peace, playing the game of his life in the afterlife.

Chick Stahl burst onto the scene in a big way in 1897, batting .354 for the Boston Beaneaters. After establishing himself as one of the National League's top ballplayers, Stahl joined teammate and friend Jimmy Collins by jumping to the American League's Boston Americans in 1901. In 1903, the club, managed by third baseman Collins, won the pennant and defeated the Pittsburgh Pirates in the World Series. The franchise fell on tough times in 1906, finishing in last place as Chick temporarily took over for Jimmy as the squad's skipper. Boston owner John I. Taylor named Stahl as a permanent replacement for 1907. During spring training, Chick resigned from the post, citing extreme stress as a reason. On March 28, 1907, while the club trained at West Baden Springs, Indiana, Stahl committed suicide by drinking carbolic acid. (Courtesy of the Michael T. "Nuf Ced" McGreevy Collection, Boston Public Library).

CHAPTER 8

The 1908 National League Pennant Race

Chaos, Protests, and Bribes

Besides casting the entire Boston Americans' organization under a deep, depressing pall, Chick Stahl's suicide caused negative repercussions on the diamond. While in Omaha, Nebraska, Boston president John I. Taylor wired Cy Young in West Baden Springs, Indiana, ordering the star pitcher to temporarily take charge of the club.[1] After departing West Baden Springs, the squad arrived in Cincinnati, Ohio, on March 30, 1907, where the Americans had three exhibition games scheduled against the Reds. Amidst rumors of calling off these contests because of Stahl's death, both baseball organizations that afternoon announced they planned to hold them as previously agreed.[2] Taylor's prior arrangement with Chick, also stipulating Young run the club on the field, did not garner Ban Johnson's approval. The American League president unequivocally stated he would not permit the team president to manage Boston in 1907. John responded harshly to Johnson's edict.

> One thing is certain and that is that the manager of the Boston team will be selected by officials of the club, and not by Mr. Johnson, who has absolutely nothing to do with the case, unless his advice should be asked.
> Before Chick Stahl's death I went to Chicago and consulted with Mr. Johnson as to a suitable captain for the team in case Stahl should resign the position, which I feared he would do. Mr. Johnson declined to advise me in the matter, stating that he could not name any man on the team for the position.

When Taylor talked with Johnson on the telephone about his remarks, the league's president denied ever saying he would not allow Boston's owner to assume some of the club's managerial responsibilities.[3] Although Cy Young agreed to oversee the team under dire circumstances, he expressed unhappiness over ownership thrusting him into a management role.[4] The Americans' team president believed he had found a permanent replacement for Chick Stahl upon announcing George Huff's hiring. After debuting as Boston's skipper in a game against the New York Highlanders on April 20, Huff only lasted thirteen days at the job. George resigned, returning to his former occupation as Director of Athletics at the University of Illinois. Taylor immediately appointed club captain Bob Unglaub to manage the Americans. Amid shock and surprise among Boston's fans that he gave up so quickly, Huff made a brief statement.

"I have come to the conclusion that I would not like professional baseball as well as I did college work," said Huff, "and I believe that no one can make a success unless his heart is in it. Furthermore, I doubt whether my temperament is suited for professional baseball."[5]

Front office dysfunction partially impacted another rough season in Boston, as the Americans held down seventh place in 1907 with a 59–90 record. After performing as one of the American League's elite contenders when the organization achieved major status in 1901, Boston did not raise another pennant flag until 1912 as the Red Sox. The power paradigm continued to shift in the Junior Circuit throughout the remainder of the twentieth century's first decade. In 1906, the Chicago White Sox claimed the American League pennant and defeated the crosstown Chicago Cubs in the World Series, four games to two. One year later, the Detroit Tigers secured their first league crown before the Cubs swept them in the 1907 World Series.

Following five seasons where the Pittsburgh Pirates and New York Giants dictated championship terms in the National League from 1901 through 1905, Chicago rose above their two rivals as the new dominant power. On July 28, 1905, Cubs president James Hart granted manager Frank Selee an indefinite leave of absence because of poor health after physicians recommended a change of climate and a long rest period for Chicago's skipper. In a letter to Selee, the Cubs' president commended him for his dedication as a faithful employee and a proficient manager. Hart wished Frank a speedy recovery, allowing him to resume his post once again as pilot in the future.[6] Chicago's front office selected first baseman Frank Chance to succeed Selee. Chance, who became known as the "Peerless Leader," had been an organization member since debuting as a catcher for the Orphans in 1898.

As the 1905 campaign wound down, Cubs vice president Charles Murphy offered his opinion on Frank's continuation within that position for the club.

"If Frank Selee's health is not improved enough for him to manage the team next season, Frank Chance is my choice to lead the players on the field," said Murphy before leaving Cincinnati to travel back to Chicago at the end of September. "Chance has been keeping the club up where Selee left off, and I see no reason why he could not do it next season without affecting his playing or batting."[7]

Murphy purchased the club from Hart and quickly became the deciding factor in Chicago's fortunes. Albert Spalding, the former Chicago White Stockings pitcher, manager, and magnate, congratulated the new team president while offering wishes for continued diamond success.[8] Charles immediately named Chance the Cubs' permanent manager for 1906. Frank wasted no time bolstering his club. On December 15, 1905, Chicago shipped pitcher Herbert "Buttons" Briggs; outfielders John "Jack" McCarthy and William "Billy" Maloney; third baseman James "Doc" Casey; and cash to the Brooklyn Superbas for star outfielder Jimmy Sheckard. Sheckard's addition in left field gave Chance a solid outfield combination that included James "Jimmy" Slagle in center and Frank Schulte in right.[9]

The Cubs destroyed all National League competition in 1906, going 116–36, before falling to the White Sox in the World Series. Following their repeat in 1907, things looked promising for a third consecutive pennant in 1908. The races in both the American and National leagues that year evolved as the most exciting pennant battles since the two organizations secured a peace accord before the 1903 season. In the American League, Detroit prevailed with a 90–63 record. The Cleveland Naps finished second, ½ game back at 90–64, while the White Sox secured third with a mark of 88–64, leaving them 1 ½ games behind the pace-setting Tigers. Such razor-thin margins paled in comparison when discussing the 1908 National League race. The organization's heavy hitters, Pittsburgh, New York, and Chicago, engaged in one of the fiercest and tightest fights in baseball history to gain the privilege of appearing in another World Series.

When the National League schedule reached September 1, New York held a scant 3-percent point advantage over second-place Chicago. Throughout the month, the Giants maintained the top spot except for one day as the Cubs and Pirates nipped at their heels like angry dogs. When league play closed on September 2, New York maintained a 4-percent point lead over Pittsburgh. The Giants hit their peak after all games concluded on September 18, leading the Cubs by 4 ½ games, while the Pirates held down third place, five games back. The standings four days later showed Chicago pared that margin to a mere 6 percent edge. When diamond play closed on October 1, New York possessed a 94–54 record while Chicago and Pittsburgh breathed down their neck with

95–55 marks. Once games concluded on October 2, Pittsburgh jumped into first place, leading each rival by ½ game.

The quest to represent the National League in the 1908 World Series rested on the outcomes and unique events surrounding four contests involving these three clubs during the season's final five weeks. With margin for error slight, these various moments in baseball history defined the outcome of this exciting pennant race. When Chicago played Pittsburgh on September 4 at Exposition Park, the Pirates held second place with a 74–47 record, while the Cubs breathed down their neck, ½ game back in third at 74–48. The two clubs treated the 8,306 fans to an exhilarating contest, as the game remained scoreless through nine innings. Pittsburgh's Vic Willis and Chicago's Mordecai "Three Finger" Brown pitched brilliantly for their respective teams. Willis set the stage for a grand finale by retiring the Cubs in the tenth frame.[10] Up to this point, Vic and Brown had each only surrendered four hits.

Fred Clarke stroked a single past Cubs third baseman Harry Steinfeldt to start off the Pirates' half of the tenth. Tommy Leach laid down a beautiful sacrifice bunt that moved Clarke to second. Honus Wagner stepped up to the plate and blasted the baseball over Chicago second baseman John "Johnny" Evers's head for a clean hit. Wagner moved up to the keystone sack when Evers made a wild throw toward home plate, hoping to keep Pittsburgh's manager from scoring the winning run. Rookie Warren Gill stepped in to bat for the Pirates. Brown plunked Gill in the ribs to load the bases. Chicago's hurler then fanned Edward "Ed" Abbaticchio for the second out. First-year outfielder John Owen "Chief" Wilson sent the patrons home happy, smacking a single to center field that drove in Clarke with the game's only run.

The *Pittsburgh Press*'s article chronicling this game noted that Fred Clarke should have already scored the winning tally when Johnny Evers committed an error by throwing wildly to the dish after Honus Wagner singled.[11] Instead, utility infielder Charles "Charlie" Starr, coaching at third base, opted for caution and held Clarke.[12] Had Starr taken an aggressive approach following Wagner's hit, the foundation and groundwork for one of the most famous incidents in baseball history would never have occurred. Following the period's standard protocol, Warren Gill did not completely run from first base to second when he saw his manager cross home plate, but rather started heading for the clubhouse. When Chicago center fielder Jimmy Slagle fielded Chief Wilson's clean hit, he fired the baseball to Johnny Evers, who stepped on second base for an apparent force-out of Gill that ended the inning, the game still scoreless.

After Fred notched the deciding run for Pittsburgh, umpire Hank O'Day, working the game alone, headed to the Pirates' dugout. Many players from both squads started walking off the field. Once Evers held the baseball and touched second base, he yelled at O'Day to get the umpire's attention. Failing to hear him, Johnny ran to the home team's bench and called Hank's attention to what transpired before the arbitrator remarked, "Clarke has crossed the plate."[13] Evers persisted complaining, leading O'Day to tell the ballplayer to desist since the game had officially ended, before walking away. Johnny continued badgering Hank as he left, declaring the game not over until Gill touched second base. Evers shouted that the umpire should wait until the contest concluded before leaving the diamond. He then called O'Day a fathead.[14] Such an approach appeared counterproductive since Hank could stand any vicious name like crook, burglar, or blind man but detested someone referring to him as a fathead. O'Day usually ejected ballplayers from the ballpark for utilizing this moniker.[15]

That evening, Johnny Evers discussed this play with anybody willing to listen, believing he correctly understood the rule. Evers engaged owner Charles Murphy, who appeared very attentive and interested in the subject. As somebody who championed a two-umpire system in baseball, Murphy saw an opportunity to make a point.[16] That night, Charles lodged a protest with National League president Harry Pulliam. Murphy alleged that if two umpires had been on duty for that afternoon's contest at Exposition Park, one of the arbitrators would have declared Warren Gill out, thus wiping Clarke's run off the board. The telegram Chicago's owner sent to Pulliam laid out the case supporting his contention.

"Chicago protests Friday's game here," wrote Murphy. "With the bases full and two outs, Wilson hit safely to center. Gill, of Pittsburgh, failed to run to second base from first. He ran a few feet down the line, then turned out and went to the clubhouse. Evers, who covered second base, received the ball from Slagle and called the attention of the umpire to the force-out. The umpire simply said: 'Clarke has crossed the plate.' Chicago claims Gill should have touched second base before he ran to the clubhouse, and will prove by the affidavits of a number of persons that he failed to do so. This protest is filed by Chicago despite the fact that you have never yet allowed one, because Clarke's run should not count, as Gill was plainly forced at second base on the play."

Charles Murphy readily admitted he believed the league would reject his protest. When talking to reporters, Murphy affirmed the National Pastime had now progressed to the point where the league needed to commission two umpires to officiate every game.[17] Harry Pulliam denied this request, ruling that Hank O'Day did not witness Warren Gill's gaffe of not touching second base. This point proved critical since the league president never indicated that a requirement did not exist for Gill to proceed to the next bag when a run scored.[18] Knowledge of the rules and established precedent proved crucial for future events.

Although Warren only engaged in a customary practice of rushing for the clubhouse when a game ended, he tended to commit baserunning blunders. In the first game of a doubleheader against the Philadelphia Phillies on September 16 at National League Park, Gill attempted to steal second base in the fourth inning. Unfortunately, teammate Ed Abbaticchio already occupied that bag, leading the Phillies to catch Warren in a rundown, which resulted in them tagging out the Pirates' first baseman. An opportunity for a big inning ended in a contest Pittsburgh lost, 5–2.[19] Johnny Evers, a smart, cerebral, argumentative player who had debuted for the Cubs on September 1, 1902, started a debate regarding the laxness of enforcing baseball rules. Individuals who followed the events involving Evers, Gill, and O'Day at Exposition Park on September 4 never dreamed the same situation would arise so quickly before the 1908 season ended.

On September 22, Chicago started a series against New York with a doubleheader at the Polo Grounds, trailing the first place Giants by two games in the standings. The Cubs experienced a grand day at the ballpark, sweeping the twin bill by securing 4–3 and 3–1 victories. Excitement and enthusiasm pulsated within the Polo Grounds as these two teams locked horns on September 23 in a contest where the outcome impacted which club held an edge in the tight National League pennant race. New York pitcher Christy Mathewson and Chicago hurler John "Jack" Pfiester engaged in a thrilling mound duel throughout the afternoon.

The Cubs struck first in the fifth inning when Joseph "Joe" Tinker blasted a home run beyond center field ropes used to contain the overflow crowd.[20] New York evened the score in the sixth frame. Charles "Buck" Herzog smashed a single past third baseman Harry Steinfeldt, whose wild throw to first allowed the runner to reach second. After Roger Bresnahan sacrificed Herzog to third, Buck scored the game's tying run on Mike Donlin's single to center field.[21] The score remained knotted until the Giants batted in the bottom of the ninth inning. Chicago secured the frame's first out when Cy Seymour grounded out to Johnny Evers at second base. Arthur "Art" Devlin stepped up to the plate and got a potential winning rally going when he drilled a single to center field. Harry McCormick then forced Devlin at second for out number two on a ground ball, fielder's choice, recorded in the scorebook as Evers to shortstop Joe Tinker. Angry over the aggressive manner with which Art slid into the keystone sack, Tinker brushed up against his competitor as the two exchanged heated words.

Nineteen-year-old utility player Carl Frederick Rudolph "Fred" Merkle walked up to the plate to face Pfiester.[22] New York manager John McGraw placed Merkle in the lineup since veteran first baseman Fred Tenney could not play due to his legs bothering him for some time.²³ Fred had suffered a serious medical issue earlier in the campaign that limited his ability to participate on the diamond. In July, Merkle's plan to travel to Pittsburgh with his teammates following a series in Cincinnati changed because of dire circumstances. Instead, Fred entered Cincinnati's Good Samaritan Hospital as a patient. On July 11, physicians announced they had performed two operations on the ballplayer's right foot due to serious blood poisoning. The doctors also announced they would not discharge Merkle from the hospital for quite some time.

These physicians feared that if things did not improve, it might force them to amputate Fred Merkle's foot, which had ballooned to the size of a pumpkin. Swelling moved into his lower right leg up to the knee. Breakage of the skin between the big and second toes on his foot from a spiking caused Merkle's condition. Doctors believed blood poisoning resulted from the dye of his baseball hose seeping into the wound. Realizing the injury's severity, Fred wanted to keep information about it from becoming public since he did not wish to worry his family.²⁴ Later that day, manager John McGraw received word from Good Samaritan Hospital authorities that the press exaggerated this grim report. Fred happened to be progressing as well as expected.²⁵ On July 15, the infirmary discharged Merkle, who went home to Toledo for a recuperation period. Fred's condition continued improving under the watchful eyes of his parents, Ernest and Amalie Thilghman (Thielman) Merkle.²⁶

Given an opportunity to contribute at a critical juncture against the Cubs on September 23, Merkle delivered, driving a single to right field that moved Harry McCormick to third base. Giants shortstop Albert "Al" Bridwell sent the Polo Grounds' fans into a frenzy when he lashed a single to center field and pushed McCormick across home plate with the game's winning run. Guaranteeing legitimacy, Bridwell properly ran out his hit by touching first base.²⁷ Ecstatic fans rushed onto the field as players from both teams attempted to navigate their way to the clubhouse.²⁸ Although New York's shortstop did his job by officially reaching first base, a question arose as to whether Fred Merkle had continued to second to eliminate a force-out, or did he cut short his route and instead trot toward the clubhouse?²⁹

After incorrectly complaining to umpires Bob Emslie and Hank O'Day that Al did not touch first base, a group of Chicago's players turned their attention toward Fred reaching second base, although half of their teammates had left the diamond following the game-winning hit.³⁰ As he did weeks earlier in Pittsburgh when the Pirates' Warren Gill committed a similar blunder, Johnny Evers, while standing at second base, signaled for center fielder Arthur "Solly" Hofman to throw him the baseball. At the same time, he frantically gestured toward Emslie, who worked as the base umpire for this contest, to watch the play because Merkle had not run to second base. Although O'Day, the man at the center of the Pittsburgh controversy from a ruling standpoint, also officiated this game as the home plate umpire, the final decision rested with his counterpart.[31]

Some fans jostled Evers as he attempted to catch Hofman's toss, causing the baseball to bounce off his back to teammate Jack Pfiester, who tried to throw the sphere toward the bag.[32] Before Johnny could execute a definitive play, the Giants' Joe McGinnity, who started heading to the clubhouse after working the coaching lines, charged over in that direction and either grabbed the baseball or intercepted Jack's toss. Evers and Tinker tackled McGinnity and attempted to retrieve the ball. This effort proved unsuccessful, as Joe succeeded in firing the baseball toward the left-field bleachers. Another Cubs team member rescued the sphere and carried it back to the infield.[33] While all this chaos played out in front of delirious, celebratory fans, Christy Mathewson hustled after Fred Merkle and told him to retrace his steps and touch second base.[34]

Sensing Fred's intentions, two or three Chicago players desperately grabbed him and hung on to prevent the young New York first baseman from rectifying a blatant mistake. Merkle later claimed he did touch second base before journeying to the clubhouse, while others on the field challenged that contention.[35] According to Chicago's *Inter Ocean*, Johnny Evers completed the putout at second base with a baseball in hand, and Bob Emslie declared Fred out on the play. Evers then shared that decision with umpiring crew chief Hank O'Day. Around five thousand belligerent fans surrounded the arbitrator as Johnny awaited a response. Amid catcalls and threats of violence, Hank stood his ground until police officers escorted him to a little pen under the grandstand for his own protection. While sequestered against his will, O'Day ordered the game to resume and told police to perform the impossible task of clearing people from the grounds.

Frank Chance attempted to reach Hank, but the mob pushed him back and thwarted that effort.[36] During this mayhem on the Polo Grounds' diamond, Cubs catcher Patrick "Pat" Moran became involved in a fiery argument with a group of New York rooters and struck one of the individuals. Law enforcement rushed to the scene before any further harm occurred.[37] Regular New York police officers, dispatched by Commissioner Theodore A. Bingham to restore order at the ballpark, saved Hank O'Day and Bob Emslie from suffering severe injury or even death. Before police ushered the two umpires from the field, Chance yelled to O'Day that Fred Merkle had made the third out; thus, Harry McCormick's run did not count.[38] Once escorted off the diamond, Hank and Bob sequestered themselves for thirty minutes in a room with biased New York newspaper scribes. An *Inter Ocean* article reported that when this conference ended, the two arbitrators declared they had reached no conclusive decision. For now, the score stood 2–1 in New York's favor, under protest.[39]

Confusion prevailed over the true outcome of this important baseball game. In their article, New York's *The Sun* related that when Chicago owner Charles Murphy came down from his box in the upper grandstand and inquired about a final judgment on the matter, O'Day responded, "Emslie says he didn't see the play at second base, and it's no game, I suppose." That evening, when the New York Stock Exchange attributed Harry Pulliam with declaring the contest a tie that the two clubs needed to replay, the National League president called the statement unauthorized since he had not yet made any decision. Pulliam added that no ruling would occur until addressing the situation using proper organizational protocols.[40] After the game, Giants manager John McGraw offered his opinion regarding the ludicrous notion that today's battle between these clubs qualified as "no game."

"How can umpires decide it is no game?" asked McGraw. "Umpires can't go out on the field and make rules. Either the game should be declared forfeited on account of the crowd overrunning the field and preventing further play, or it was won by us. The Chicago club can protest of course, but they wouldn't have any grounds for a protest. The play in the ninth inning wasn't a question of interpretation of the rules, which is the only ground on which protest can be made. Emslie swears he didn't see the play at second base, and Merkle swears he touched the bag."

A baseball scholar agreed with McGraw's premise. This knowledgeable individual stated that since the September 4 game at Exposition Park went in Pittsburgh's favor on the grounds the umpire had not witnessed a disputed play, the same should hold true for New York on September 23 because Emslie could not verify whether Fred Merkle touched second base. Murphy sent a long statement to Pulliam that night, alleging he should award the contest to the Cubs by virtue of a forfeit.[41] Charles demanded this action, based on New York's players leaving the field while his men remained prepared to continue until dragged and carried off by police officers. At 10 A.M. on September 24, the league president and his two umpires conferred at the New York league offices in the St. James Building. For the first time during this meeting, Hank O'Day offered that he stopped the previous day's game on account of darkness when a riot happened following the disputed play. At 11 A.M., Pulliam issued a statement regarding his decision.

> In the matter of the New York-Chicago game September 23 I have received the written reports of the umpires in charge of the game, Messrs. O'Day and Emslie. They report that the game resulted in a tie score, 1 to 1, and that it was impossible to continue the game after the ninth inning.

Without entering at this time into the merits of the controversy that has arisen over this game or, passing upon the legality of any decision, the game will be recorded as reported, namely, a tie score.

Many powerful New York politicians attempted to use their influence and sway Harry Pulliam to rule in the Giants' favor despite the report filed by umpires Hank O'Day and Bob Emslie. The Cubs' faithful rejoiced over the outcome since a tie proved every bit as good as a victory.[42] Pulliam's statement did not address the necessity for these two teams to replay this game. According to some accounts, Harry declared New York need not play off the tie if unwilling to do so, thus leaving the game from September 23 in limbo. After meeting with Pulliam that morning, New York owner John T. Brush, when interviewed by newspaper reporters, believed no requirement existed for his club to continue the contest. Otherwise, Brush said, he would have opened the Polo Grounds at 1:30 P.M. for that purpose. Harry ordered no afternoon game that day, beginning until the regularly scheduled time of 3:30 P.M.

These statements proved critical since Frank Chance brought his squad to the ballpark early, although neither league nor Giants officials had announced playing a doubleheader.[43] Once there, Chance ordered his men to take the field amid a heavy police presence in case any trouble occurred. Hurler Andy Coakley walked out to the mound and fired three pitches toward home plate before departing, causing those already in attendance to howl. While getting in preliminary work on the diamond, New York utility player David "Dave" Brain threw his bat at one of Coakley's offerings. Pulliam ordered umpires Hank O'Day and Bob Emslie not to appear until the regularly scheduled game that afternoon. When New York did not take the diamond to oppose Chicago, Charles Murphy mailed the National League president a forfeiture claim.

The Cubs reasoned that since the National League constitution stipulated replaying a tie or postponed game, the previous afternoon's affair should have resumed before the regularly scheduled contest. If deemed an actual forfeit since Chicago appeared on the field to participate in a game, New York needed to pay a $1,000 fine and damages to the Cubs' organization. Under the bylaws, Giants manager John McGraw and magnate John T. Brush remained suspended until the organization paid this penalty. The rules also stipulated that the day's second game qualified as illegal if New York did not fork over $1,000.[44] The fact that the two umpires did not arrive on the diamond until 3:30 P.M. indicated Harry Pulliam gave no consideration to this action on the part of Chicago's baseball organization.[45] On the other hand, Cubs manager Frank Chance reasoned that since no umpires appeared earlier when they wanted to finish the tied game, he decided to award the contest in favor of his club, 9–0, through forfeit. The organization believed Section 55 of the league constitution entitled them to this remedy.

Several thousand people arrived at the Polo Grounds early to witness the Cubs pull their stunt. When the regularly scheduled game started, over 25,000 fans packed the ballpark. After the Giants built up a 5–0 lead, Christy Mathewson saved the day when starter George "Hooks" Wiltse wilted in the seventh inning.[46] Mathewson entered the contest after a triple by Chicago catcher John "Johnny" Kling plated two runs and cut the lead to 5–3. Following a single by pinch hitter George Elmer "Del" Howard that scored Kling, Christy shut the door, as the Giants held on for a 5–4 victory.[47]

Sportswriter Bozeman Bulger of *The World* felt Harry Pulliam's decision to declare the September 23 Polo Grounds game a tie purposely did not produce finality. Bulger argued Pulliam did this as a matter of standard order, so the two baseball clubs involved had a basis from which to lodge protests. Bozeman believed that the National League's Board of Directors could settle this or any decision regarding the event. Manager John McGraw exhibited no concern over a negative outcome since he could not comprehend any fair-minded individual ruling against New York.[48]

Two correspondents, one covering each team for the *Sporting News*, also weighed in on the controversy. In his column, Joe Vila, who covered both New York major league clubs for the publication, ruled Fred Merkle out in the September 23 game for two reasons. The writer deemed Merkle was forced out for not touching second base when Al Bridwell sent a safety to center field, while Joe McGinnity's action constituted interference regarding the efforts of Cubs players to retrieve the baseball so Johnny Evers could complete the play. Vila declared the game should have continued since plenty of daylight still existed. When the contest could not resume because the crowd saturated the diamond, Joe felt umpires should have declared Chicago the winner by forfeit, 9–0.[49]

Irving "Sy" Sanborn also chronicled the exploits of Chicago's two teams for the *Sporting News*. Consequently, Sanborn was fully aware of what happened between Chicago and Pittsburgh on September 4. Irving affirmed that he never believed the same play might recur so quickly. Sanborn blamed New York's newspapers for the events surrounding Warren Gill's blunder. The scribe stated publications only chastised the Cubs' organization for protesting the decision and failed to mention the particulars behind the failure to uphold a league rule. Sanborn further criticized New York's broadsheets for ignoring to report baseball news not directly impacting either the Giants or Highlanders. Irving reasoned that if more printed pages in the Big Apple contained stories on this subject, Fred Merkle may have been smart and cognizant enough not to commit such a costly gaffe.[50]

A continued skin-tight pennant race raised the stakes when an unresolved game still hung in the balance. All three teams battling to represent the National League in the World Series had been involved in identical disputed plays that added more spice to an exhilarating race to the finish line. Near the end of September, a loyal Giants fan declared to Pirates manager Fred Clarke that the final game between his squad and the Cubs on October 4 at West Side Grounds could well determine the pennant winner.

"There is a chance that it will turn out that way," replied Clarke, "and I would like to see it come about. If the pennant depended on that game in the Windy City, we would win it. We are always good in Chicago on Sunday, and we would beat the Cubs. In such a case, I would have four or five pitchers warmed up all the time, and the minute the Cubs began to look a wee bit dangerous, I'd yank out one and shove in another."[51]

Fred Clarke's Pirates remained in the hunt due to a brilliant September hot streak. After New York swept them in a doubleheader at the Polo Grounds on September 18, Pittsburgh went 13–1 in the next 14 games leading up to the Sunday afternoon finale against Chicago on October 4 at West Side Grounds. For the Pirates and the Cubs, help remaining relevant in the race came courtesy of the Philadelphia Phillies. From September 28 through October 3, the Giants played eight contests against Philadelphia in home-and-home four-game sets at each club's ballpark. New York went 5–3 in the eight games, as southpaw hurler Harry Coveleski won all three contests for the Phillies, going the distance in each and allowing only four runs over 27 innings. After Pittsburgh defeated St. Louis on October 3 at League Park, 3–2, the Pirates held a ½ game lead over Chicago heading into the decisive clash.

On the evening of October 2, Harry Pulliam ruled that Cubs management possessed no claim in equity for a forfeited game on September 24 against the Giants, and they alleged the previous afternoon's tie contest should have resumed. Pulliam based this decision on the very fabric of having originally declared the game from September 23 a tie. Because he reiterated this stance regarding a stalemate, Giants ownership appealed the verdict. The league's Board of Directors would finally decide the matter during a meeting at Cincinnati's Hotel Sinton on Monday, October 5. According to Pulliam, he based his decision on the question of upholding an umpire's ruling.

"The playing rules say that the decision of the umpire on a question of fact is final," said Pulliam. "The whole question hinges on a simple question: Was Merkle forced out at second base? Umpire-in-chief O'Day says he was. O'Day is no novice and there is no reason to doubt his accuracy in this decision."[52]

On behalf of the Chicago Cubs, Charles Murphy also filed a protest over Harry Pulliam's verdict, which the National League's Board of Directors planned to address at their conference.⁵³ Before the board considered such disputes, the Pirates and Cubs engaged in the biggest game thus far on the National League docket. In Pittsburgh, thousands of enthusiastic baseball patrons traveled to the city's downtown district to watch the contest's progress on bulletin boards at various newspaper offices. A large crowd packed Fifth Avenue from Grant Street all the way to Market Street while a huge throng gathered in front of the building housing the *Pittsburgh Press*.⁵⁴ The mass populace of baseball rooters was so dense that the heat coming off their bodies made things unbearable, especially when considering the cosmopolitan nature of the group, not accustomed to this type of discomfort. An individual holding a megaphone out a window shouted the game's events to the crowd shortly after they occurred in Chicago.⁵⁵

The Cubs, playing in front of a West Side Grounds record 30,347 patrons, immediately obliterated any enthusiasm held by Pirates fans by scoring single runs in both the first and fifth innings.⁵⁶ One of Honus Wagner's two errors that day aided Chicago in placing their fifth-frame tally on the scoreboard. Pittsburgh's *Gazette Times* categorized Wagner's performance in the field all afternoon like a cheese sandwich without mustard. Hope temporarily emerged for Smoky City baseball fans when the Pirates evened the score in the top of the sixth inning.⁵⁷ While watching one of the bulletin boards in Pittsburgh, mill worker Martin Argo, from the nearby city of McKeesport, went berserk when the Pirates tied the score, knocking several people down before being subdued and escorted home.⁵⁸ Joy did not last long in Pittsburgh, as Chicago reclaimed the lead in the bottom of the sixth. A tactical error by Pirates starter Vic Willis proved fatal when he purposely passed Johnny Kling after Joe Tinker doubled. This strategy backfired when Mordecai Brown drove home Tinker with a single to right field.⁵⁹

As Brown's bat connected against Willis's pitch, a commotion occurred in the grandstand. A woman fell forward in her seat, leading those sitting around the female patron to believe she fainted because of the tightly packed spectators. As the crowd moved back to give her some air, another woman nearby raised her head to explain a would-be mother was giving birth to a child, a baby boy. Shortly after the birth, ballpark officials escorted both mother and newborn son to the clubhouse to receive medical attention. An ambulance arrived and took them to a nearby hospital. Wanting to remain anonymous, press members failed to gain any information regarding her identity and that of the "baseball baby" when inquiring at different West Side Chicago hospitals.⁶⁰

Pittsburgh's hopes dwindled when the Cubs added single tallies in the seventh and eighth innings. Honus Wagner started a potential Pirates rally in the top of the ninth frame by blasting a single to center field. Ed Abbaticchio stepped in to take his turn at the plate and smashed an apparent double into right field's overflow crowd. Regrettably, home plate umpire Hank O'Day ruled the blast a foul ball. Although every Pittsburgh team member argued that the baseball landed in fair territory, O'Day held firm in his decision.[61] The Pirates' players also appealed to base umpire Charles "Cy" Rigler. An article in the *Pittsburgh Press* intimated that since Hank could lick Rigler in a fight, Cy concurred that Abbaticchio's blast landed foul.[62]

When Ed returned to the batter's box, Three Finger Brown fired a fastball that he took for a called third strike. First baseman Alan Storke then forced Honus at second on a groundball to shortstop Joe Tinker. The Tinker-Evers duo finished off the game as Brown induced Chief Wilson to hit a grounder to short, retiring Storke at the keystone sack. The Cubs clinched a 5–2 victory that eliminated Pittsburgh from pennant contention.[63] After the contest ended, Fred Clarke declared the long, hard fight left his men tired and that all the luck broke with the Cubs. Pittsburgh owner Barney Dreyfuss joined the people gathered in Charles Murphy's office as Chicago's president celebrated his club's victory. Dreyfuss possessed a cheerful smile despite the Pirates' loss, prompting Murphy to exclaim, "You are a better loser than I am, you are the best loser in the league."[64]

Clarke stated the 1908 pennant race involving his team had been the warmest he ever experienced. While rooting for a tie at season's end between the Cubs and New York Giants, thus necessitating an exciting playoff series, Fred picked Chicago to win the pennant.[65] The Pirates' magnate commended his squad for playing remarkable baseball throughout 1908 and applauded home fan support during the campaign's final month. Like his manager, Dreyfuss selected the Cubs to grab the flag and offered impressions on his club's last game of the season.

"Only one team could win and it wasn't us," said Dreyfuss. "It's too bad. Willis was in grand form and the other members of the team played the game of their lives, but against Brown and the support given him by the Cubs, chances were indeed slim for the Pirates taking the crucial game. If it develops that New York and Chicago must meet in three games to decide the supremacy in the National League, I hope the series can be staged in Pittsburgh, especially as our fans at home are to be denied a glimpse of the world's championship battles."[66]

Barney Dreyfuss and Fred Clarke alluded to a special playoff clash since the National League constitution stipulated playing a three-game series to decide the pennant race in the event two teams tied atop the standings at season's end. Charles Murphy remarked that his squad would play out the string regarding a potential tie before adding the Giants could still lose one of their three remaining contests against the Boston Doves.[67] The Cubs' record stood at 98–55, while the Giants held third place at 95–55. The Pirates finished the campaign with a

98–56 mark. New York maintained relevance in the pennant battle, defeating Boston in the first two games between the squads at the Polo Grounds. The Giants breezed to an 8–1 victory on October 5 and won a day later, 4–1. These triumphs added even more importance to the Board of Directors' meeting on October 5, tackling two complaints surrounding the disputed contest between Chicago and New York on September 23.

For nearly two full days and one night, the board heard testimony regarding these protests. The Giants objected to Harry Pulliam's ruling that the game on September 23 ended in a tie, while the Cubs appealed the decision where they did not deserve a win through forfeit as decreed in the National League's constitution. In both instances, the Board of Directors upheld Pulliam's verdicts. Regarding the question on a deadlocked score, the ruling body stated New York should have won that game if not for a reckless, careless, inexcusable blunder by Fred Merkle. In demanding enforcement of a league rule, the board found they should not penalize Chicago for trying to gain a victory through a technicality, because other teams did not possess the foresight to challenge a flawed common diamond practice where players quickly left the field at a contest's conclusion to avoid converging spectators. They also declared umpires Hank O'Day and Bob Emslie correctly followed league rules when deciding on the questionable play.

In ruling against the Cubs on the forfeiture request, the Board of Directors determined they should not consider this protest. The baseball body asserted that when Chicago's baseball organization petitioned Harry Pulliam to award a victory by forfeit on the night of September 23, this tied his hands on the matter of continuing the suspended contest the following afternoon before a scheduled meeting that day between the two teams. In offering this ruling, the board cited evidence of Pulliam informing John T. Brush on September 24 that he would not require the Giants to play off the tie game.

Lastly, league leadership offered a remedy for dealing with an unfinished tie game that impacted a pennant race. The Board of Directors ordered the two clubs to replay the disputed contest on October 8 at the Polo Grounds or soon thereafter, if weather conditions interfered with this plan.[68] Once the board announced their decision to the press, people connected to and rooting for the New York club initially believed staging the game as an optional endeavor. John McGraw had stated for weeks he did not intend to play off the disputed contest under any circumstances.[69]

Brooklyn Superbas owner Charles Ebbets, who presided over the board meeting, eliminated ambiguity on the voluntary assumption, affirming that replaying the game was mandatory, even if Boston defeated New York in their final meeting. Upon hearing the news, Cubs owner Charles Murphy declared, "We will play Thursday and we'll lick 'em, too." Giants magnate John T. Brush left Cincinnati for New York before the Board of Directors announced their rulings.[70] Upon arriving back in New York, Brush expressed bitter disappointment over the outcome. Following a brief discussion with McGraw, the owner stated he planned to abide by the credo. Brush added that the board seemed resolute in robbing his Giants of that game. He also stated that the ruling body accepted Harry Pulliam's testimony as irrefutable gospel. When questioned on October 7 about the huge contest the following afternoon, New York's manager simply said, "Yes, we are going to play, and we are going to beat them, too."[71]

This decision breathed life back into the Pittsburgh Pirates' season. If the Doves defeated New York on October 7 and the Giants then knocked off Chicago in the playoff game, all three teams would end up tied for first place.[72] Such a scenario could prove a logistical nightmare for the league because many of Pittsburgh's players had disbanded and embarked for their off-season homes throughout the United States.[73] Another issue related to a three-team playoff series surrounded the number of days required to crown a National League champion. Given the unpredictable nature of weather at this time of year, the prospect of delaying the World Series so late into the autumn might make it impossible to hold the event.[74] Such problems became moot as New York crushed the Pirates' spirit for the second time in three days, defeating Boston, 7–2, on October 7 and eliminating them from the race.

On that day in Chicago, manager Frank Chance expressed outrage over the Board of Directors selecting the Polo Grounds as the playoff game site. Chance viewed this decision as tainted since he felt Charles Ebbets should have recused himself from the proceeding. Frank alleged that before Brooklyn's September series against New York started, a biased Ebbets told his players he hoped the Giants prevailed, winning the pennant. Although angry, Chance expressed optimism and confidence over capturing the league flag.

"We have to accept the decision, we suppose," said Chance, "but it is an outrage.

"Since we have to, we'll go to New York and we'll win that pennant too, don't you forget that. Pfiester probably will pitch for us, as he is in especially great form now and likely to be effective against the Giants who did not like the left handers."

The Cubs participated in their final practice that morning.[75] On the evening of October 7, they left the Windy City aboard the Twentieth Century Flyer, bound for the Big Apple.[76] The train pulled into New York's Grand Central Station at 9:25 A.M. on October 8. During their time in the city, Chicago's squad set up headquarters at the Hotel Somerset. Some newspaper commentaries claimed a large crowd of baseball enthusiasts, reporters, photographers, and waiting passengers greeted them with cordial cheers.[77] Local sportswriter Joe Vila vouched for this account's falseness. According to Vila, around five thousand men and boys adorned the train platform, insulting the ballplayers with vile and obscene language when they arrived at 5:30 A.M. Joe alleged that strong police efforts averted serious and dangerous consequences. Officers escorted team members to waiting transportation, which took them to the safety of their hotel.[78]

For days before the game, Mordecai Brown received letters threatening his life if he pitched against the Giants and won. Brown showed Frank Chance and Charles Murphy the murderous correspondence, begging them to let him take the mound to show such threats could not intimidate him.[79] Several of Mordecai's teammates also received similar warnings. The night before the game, hundreds of patrons attempted to slip into the ballpark. A security guard on duty hindered those efforts. By 6 A.M., a huge crowd gathered at the Polo Grounds' ticket office, hoping to purchase duckets for the game. Five thousand people stood in line when ticket windows opened around 10:30 A.M. These pasteboards made available for the general public's benefit sold out in about an hour, resulting in fights among unhappy rooters unable to gain admission.[80]

Craziness, mayhem, and chaos defined the most important baseball game of the twentieth century's first decade. An unmanageable crowd of fifty thousand people witnessed this titanic clash. Forty thousand devoted patrons crammed into the Polo Grounds while another ten thousand found vantage points at Coogan's Bluff, the Viaduct, and by clinging to the nearby elevated subway platform.[81]

Henry T. McBride, a firefighter in his fifties from Engine Company No. 71, had reached the Polo Grounds after police and team officials closed the gates. McBride ventured with hundreds of other people to the platform so they could view the game over a tall fence. The firefighter and two other individuals wedged into a tight spot, clutching one of the structure's pillars. McBride somehow lost his grip and tumbled twenty-five feet to the ground below before his companions could grab him. Henry died by splitting his skull on the cobblestone pavement. A doctor, summoned from Washington Heights Hospital, examined the body and declared the fall killed the firefighter instantly. McBride had a wife and four children and had worked as a firefighter for thirty-four years.[82]

Law enforcement and team officials closed the Polo Grounds' gates at 1 P.M. Between four hundred and five hundred undaunted souls climbed up to the grandstand roof so they could watch the ballgame. Others navigated the narrow edges of signboards near the clubhouses and held that uncomfortable vantage point for the entire contest. Early in the afternoon, somebody tore a board loose from the ballpark fence adjacent to Eighth Avenue, allowing men and boys ages six to sixty to traverse through the opening, climb over the visiting dressing quarters' roof, and then reach the field by making a perilous jump from shaky, narrow, wooden planks. Some became entangled in barbed wire. Suffering torn clothing and bruises was a small price to pay for getting an opportunity to watch this pennant-deciding contest.[83]

Many affluent fans, exhibiting great foresight by purchasing their box seat tickets in advance, exhibited no haste in reaching the ballpark. This decision proved misguided since when these individuals reached 155th Street and Eighth Avenue at 2 P.M., they found the Polo Grounds' route blocked by a line of police officers. With box seat admissions in their pockets, disappointed rooters of high social standing turned around and trekked back downtown. Those exhibiting a bolder mentality marched south toward nearby Manhattan Field to secure entry. Police officers and Pinkerton detectives attempted to push the surging crowd away from the ballpark's gates. Some maddened patrons demolished a fence near 155th Street and attempted to set it on fire. Law enforcement ordered one hundred reinforcements to the grounds for the contest's start time at 3:30 P.M.[84]

Before the game commenced, the loudest cheer went out to New York manager John McGraw when he appeared on the field. Although Chicago skipper Frank Chance received the harshest abuse of any player, the Peerless Leader calmly forged onward, head erect, exhibiting pride for this great moment.[85] Each Cubs player needed to fight through the hostile crowd to gain entrance to the diamond. Rooters subjected these baseball warriors to hoots, catcalls, jeers, hisses, and obscene epithets. Hundreds of men also threatened to inflict bodily harm upon Chicago's team members.[86] For Chance, fans occupying the right field bleachers howled, "Robber! Bandit! Quitter!" before patrons throughout the ballpark joined this chorus.[87]

A confrontation occurred between players from both clubs during the pre-game practice session. While Cubs team members participated in hitting practice, the Giants' Joe McGinnity stepped up to the plate, claiming Chicago had exceeded their allotted preparation time.[88] McGinnity wanted to smack groundballs to his New York teammates, but the Cubs' players complained and refused to leave the field.[89] Chicago's manager and Joe exchanged heated words and brushed up face-to-face against each other. Before the two combatants threw any punches, other players pulled McGinnity and Chance apart.[90] John McGraw acted as a peacemaker, dispersing the ballplayers gathered around Joe and Frank.[91] Police drove back curious spectators wanting to lend a helping hand to the home team. During the protracted debate, Johnny Evers unsuccessfully attempted to goad McGraw into some fisticuffs. McGinnity returned to the Giants' bench and the Cubs finished practicing.[92]

New York's supporters immediately had a reason to applaud once the game started. Jack Pfiester started the bottom of the first frame by plunking Fred

Tenney and walking Buck Herzog. When Roger Bresnahan struck out, catcher Johnny Kling gunned down Herzog on a steal attempt as Tenney retreated to second base. Mike Donlin's two-out double into the right-field overflow crowd drove home the contest's first run. Umpire Jim Johnstone rebuked the claim by Chicago's players that Donlin's drive landed foul. Down 1–0 at this early juncture, Chance called on staff ace Three Finger Brown to replace Pfiester.[93] When the Giants scored their first run, Brooklyn restaurant keeper Edward Wheeler fell backward in the grandstand's top row while celebrating. When ballpark attendants reached him, they found Wheeler had fractured his left leg in the fall. Edward received treatment at Harlem Hospital before being placed in a cab to take him home, although he insisted on returning to the Polo Grounds to watch the game's conclusion.[94]

Feelings of elation and joy proved fleeting as the Cubs scored four runs off Christy Mathewson in the third inning.[95] Mathewson did not execute his mound duties in prime condition, having awakened with a sore arm that morning.[96] During the third frame, a group of spectators attempted to scale a fence at the ballpark's northwest corner. Police suppressed this rabble using fire hoses to blast a steady stream of water that knocked them back to the ground. One young man needed medical attention for a broken wrist.[97]

Sensing an opportunity to make up ground on the scoreboard, John McGraw sent Lawrence "Larry" Doyle up to pinch hit for Christy with the bases loaded and none out in the seventh inning. Doyle mustered nothing better than a pop foul that Chicago catcher Johnny Kling grabbed. Art Devlin scored on Tenney's long fly to right fielder Frank Schulte to cut the Cubs' lead to 4–2. That score stood to the end, allowing Chicago to win their third consecutive National League pennant.[98]

Once the contest concluded, it became every man for himself, navigating the large group of outraged, jilted rooters on the field. As umpires Jim Johnstone and William "Bill" Klem hurriedly made their escape, individuals with nefarious intent rushed the Cubs' players. Police officers, prepared for such a riot, quickly surrounded the team members. Disenchanted Giants fans called Frank Chance filthy names and threatened his life. One miscreant reached around Frank's shoulder and connected against his throat with a powerful punch. As Chance angrily turned around to grab his assailant, the man had already disappeared, blending in with the massive throng of people. When Chicago's players reached their dressing room, outraged patrons hurled brickbats at the clubhouse windows before police suppressed them.[99]

The severe blow to Frank's neck broke cartilage in his windpipe, and he could barely speak that night. Every Cubs player suffered bruises while performing their getaway. Fans knocked down Jack Pfiester and beat him, while a group of people gave winning pitcher Mordecai Brown a rough time. Johnny Evers, while escorted to the clubhouse by police officers, dealt with various unsavory interactions involving bad actors.[100] Thomas Walsh, an innocent bystander, received a wound to his scalp when someone in the mob hurled a pop bottle and struck him on the head. Walsh received treatment at Harlem Hospital.[101] After checking out of the Hotel Somerset, the National League champions ventured to the station and boarded a train at 8 P.M., which whisked them to Detroit for the first World Series game scheduled at Bennett Park on October 10.[102] The Cubs won their second title in a row, cruising over the Tigers in the World Series, four games to one.

More than a month after the season ended, Fred Merkle admitted he had lost fifteen pounds since his infamous mistake.[103] On October 16, an editorial in Washington's *Evening Star* sports page suggested Merkle should receive boosts rather than knocks over his blunder. This newspaper column realized censure was a natural reaction, although he had only done something older ballplayers had engaged in for several years. The writer charged these individuals got away with following such a practice without pushback since they happened to be veterans. The newspaper affirmed that Fred had learned a hard lesson and paid dearly for his mistake. Why not give him a chance to show he profited from the experience?[104] In late December, when new St. Louis Cardinals manager Roger Bresnahan, recently traded by New York, expressed interest in acquiring Merkle, John McGraw rebuffed this silly notion.

> They all seem to want Merkle. As I said before, I made the trade letting Bresnahan go, I am willing to do business if I can strengthen the New York team. At the same time I have decided to keep Merkle. Nobody can get him. Any idea Merkle may have or that others may try to put in his head, that the supporters of the Giants are opposed to him on account of the mix-up that lost us the pennant, is ridiculous.
>
> You will remember I put him in to bat the day Harry Coveleski beat us at the Polo Grounds in the last series with Philadelphia. I didn't hear anybody roast him. He came through with a two-base hit that put us in a position to win the game.[105]

When asked to express his thoughts on the Chicago defeat, McGraw told reporters, "I do not feel badly about the game; we merely lost something we had won before."[106] While the Giants' skipper spoke diplomatically in this instance, a strong sentiment existed among fans and some club members that the National League's legal apparatus cheated them. Those searching for retribution by participating in illicit behavior, believing detractors unjustly stole something away from them, helped justify that conduct. Newspapers across the country reported a bombshell, unearthed when National League owners held their December winter meetings in New York. On December 12, 1908, the league's magnates revealed somebody made unsuccessful efforts to bribe the two umpires scheduled to work the October 8 game between Chicago and New York.

That morning, umpires Bill Klem and Jim Johnstone held a long conference with league president Harry Pulliam at his St. James Building office. While addressing press members, Pulliam stated he could not offer any concrete information surrounding the case. One leaked piece of news alleged that an individual had offered each umpire $5,000 to render decisions in that game against the Cubs. Most diligent reporters understood New York's gambling syndicate had bet over $100,000 on the Giants to win the league pennant. The bookmakers' concern arose over this fact rather than any bets on the playoff game. These parties initiated the bribery gambit as a final, desperate attempt to prevent taking a financial bath.[107] For years, wagering on baseball had been prominent in Pittsburgh. Smoky City bookies reaped a large windfall on the Pirates' final contest versus the Cubs because of loyalty to the local team. Pittsburgh's gamblers hedged their action for both clubs participating in the playoff matchup on October 8, while New York bettors wagered heavy wads of cash on a Giants victory.[108]

Although newspapers pondered various rumors about who bribed the umpires, a favorite unnamed suspect emerged, who possessed a connection to baseball and had ties to horse racing. New York County District Attorney William Travers Jerome planned to investigate criminal activity and prosecute any offenders. John T. Brush expressed displeasure over the news becoming public after fighting to keep the case's facts hidden.[109] Pirates owner Barney Dreyfuss marveled over Brush's absence from league business days earlier due to a health issue until a powder keg beckoned on his doorstep.

"John T. Brush was at yesterday's session of the league," said Dreyfuss upon returning to Pittsburgh on December 12. "He had remained away from all the others, but when he was told about what was coming up, he was on hand. He didn't have any rheumatism after he got to the meeting rooms. Perhaps he had it all knocked out of him."

Dreyfuss declared no doubt existed regarding the identity of the attempted briber. Barney then sarcastically said it was a shame that the National League president could not even leave a pass at the Polo Grounds, but New York ownership welcomed prize fighters as honored guests every day during the season.[110] National League owners also appointed a four-member committee to further explore this blemish that tarnished the organization's reputation. Three of the men on this committee included Garry Herrmann, Charles Ebbets, and Harry Pulliam. The league selected John T. Brush as the committee chairman.[111] Within that capacity, the Giants' magnate retained supreme control over the situation and could steer things in his desired direction.

On December 21, 1908, when Washington's *Evening Star* carried a story about the bribery scandal, their article also pointed out that National League officials currently investigated alleged attempts by seedy individuals to influence Philadelphia Phillies team members with monetary inducements. During the Phillies' final series in New York at season's end, tin-horn gamblers approached various players and offered them money for laying down against the Giants. The gambling agents continually harassed Philadelphia's team members at their hotel, making veiled insinuations and specific threats. When approached by reporters on December 20, Phillies president Bill Shettsline and manager Billy Murray refused to discuss the allegations. Some players who happened to be in New York offered that they had moved on and forgotten about the incident. Phillies catcher Charles "Red" Dooin, in talking about the matter, did not directly accuse any person of approaching him.

Although these charges could be readily proven, National League owners did not seem intent on searching for answers regarding gamblers blatantly working to influence diamond outcomes. Magnates appeared satisfied that the Phillies' team members speculators approached adamantly refused to listen to these opportunists, hoping to bribe them. Ironically, about forty people connected to New York's gambling syndicate submitted affidavits that Fred Merkle had touched second base in the game against Chicago on September 23. Since these sworn statements so greatly contradicted the facts in the case, baseball's National Commission threw them out after receiving the written proclamations. While in New York, Johnny Evers discussed this point about the Merkle incident.

"Merkle never came near second base," said Evers, "and he so testified and admitted afterwards. Yet, in the face of that, those men in New York swore they saw him run to second and touch the bag before I received the ball."[112]

A murky conclusion quickly resulted from one of these bribery cases, while the second drifted out of consciousness for more than a decade. Thanks to *Chicago Daily Tribune* sportswriter and editor Harvey Woodruff's diligent efforts in uncovering the mysterious umpire briber's name, the public found out his identity.[113] On April 24, 1909, each major league team received a bulletin from the National Commission, ordering them to deny admission to their ballparks for Dr. Joseph M. Creamer, who performed duties as the New York Giants' team physician in 1908. This banishment resulted from the commission finding Dr. Creamer guilty of attempting to bribe the umpires involved in the playoff game between the Giants and Cubs on October 8, 1908.

Bill Klem and Jim Johnstone had offered written testimony to National League president Harry Pulliam. Both umpires filed affidavits detailing their interactions with New York's team physician. Within his sworn statement, Klem stated that Dr. Creamer attempted to conduct a transaction with him under the Polo Grounds' grandstand before the playoff contest started, holding a wad of bills in his right hand.

"Here's $2,500," said Dr. Creamer, "which is yours, if you give all the close decisions to the Giants, and see that they win sure. You know who is behind me, and you needn't be afraid of anything. You will have a good job the rest of your life."[114]

According to accounts, Dr. Creamer and other cohorts attempted over two days to induce Klem and Johnstone to accept a payment in exchange for giving New York favorable decisions in that game versus Chicago.[115] Shady characters approached Jim at a train station, requesting that he cheat. At the same time, a seedy associate extended a previous proffer to Bill after the game he officiated between the Giants and Boston concluded on October 7. Both arbitrators, exhibiting the highest moral standards, rejected these bribes while also declaring the National League had not yet made a final determination on that assignment. Upon receiving word from league secretary John Heydler that they indeed would work the game, Klem and Johnstone begged him to excuse them.[116] Since the two umpires already happened to be in New York, having participated in the just-completed series involving the Doves, this proved impossible logistically.[117] Bill reported the incident to Harry Pulliam and other league officials.[118]

In his endeavors to bribe these umpires over two days, Dr. Joseph Creamer offered each man $2,500 before raising the ante to $3,000. In one instance, Dr. Creamer thrust a roll of bills into Bill Klem's hands. Before becoming the Giants' team physician, Joseph worked as a doctor at the Broadway and Lenox Athletic clubs, attending to the medical needs of many noted boxers. Dr. Creamer's father once held the city coroner position. Joseph inherited his dad's thriving practice when the elder Creamer died. A longtime East Side resident, Dr. Creamer had previously enjoyed a sterling reputation in his field, although one newspaper article referred to him as a henchman for former state senator and Tammany Hall politician Timothy D. "Big Tim" Sullivan. The physician's friends claimed he planned to sue the New York Giants' organization, the National Commission, Klem, and Johnstone if the edict banishing him from Major League Baseball for life stood.

Some reporters affirmed that, in his affidavit, Bill Klem alleged the man who approached him to offer a bribe stated he acted on behalf of three New York Giants players. Although that sworn statement included the names of these three accused ballplayers, they remained unknown since the investigation committee headed by John T. Brush found no evidence to substantiate this charge. Hoping to follow a lowkey approach, the National Commission did not release Dr. Creamer's first name or any initials when issuing the disbarring edict. His full identity, revealed to select baseball correspondents in confidence months prior, finally leaked out.[119] The *Washington Herald* wrote that when bribing Bill before the big game, Dr. Creamer mentioned a prominent politician's name, who claimed to only know the medico casually.[120]

Early the previous summer, the physician, a close friend of John McGraw, expressed interest in spending his vacation accompanying the Giants on their western trip. Club secretary Fred Knowles heartily invited Dr. Creamer to join the entourage as the organization's guest. While playing in the West, McGraw asked the physician to examine pitcher Red Ames, who had been dealing with an illness. Over time, the Giants sanctioned Dr. Creamer to administer medical attention to other players, either injured or suffering from some malady.[121] New York's manager requested his friend assume the position as the club's regular doctor. When the season concluded, a disagreement occurred between John T. Brush and Dr. Creamer after McGraw told the physician to offer an accounting for services rendered and then bill the team. When the doctor sent Brush an itemized list of expenses totaling $2,840, Brush refused to pay because of surprise over finding out Joseph worked for the club.

Dr. Creamer answered this refusal by saying he expected either payment or denial in writing. After consulting his manager, the Giants' owner settled with the doctor, while John McGraw informed Joseph the organization had stricken him from the payroll forever.[122] When offering a statement to the press, Dr. Creamer, with tears streaming down his face, adamantly denied any involvement in the scandal.[123] The physician declared that during his twenty years showing interest and participating in sports, nobody ever accused him of any misconduct. While talking to reporters about his dispute with John T. Brush, Dr. Creamer asserted he had earned the money legitimately, giving up free time to be on duty each day within his role as team physician. The doctor appeared excited and agitated while speaking to the press.

"It is a job to ruin me," said Dr. Creamer. "I never saw Klem or Johnstone to speak to that day or any other day. I did not go outside the grandstand to meet them before the game in question, and I never tried to bribe anybody in my life. I have not decided what I shall do yet, but I have been advised to seek legal redress."[124]

In the end, Dr. Creamer's bark proved worse than his bite when it came to lawsuits, and he never sought vindication in the courts.[125] While the good doctor believed individuals perpetrated a conspiracy to damage him, friends determined that the real conspirators had used him as a scapegoat.[126] Many people, assuming Dr. Creamer lacked the financial means to pull off such an operation, wanted to know the identity of a supposedly well-known baseball figure who gave him the necessary capital to bribe Bill Klem and Jim Johnstone.[127] When probed by fellow magnates at the National League meetings back in December, John T. Brush disavowed all knowledge of the doctor or his activities. John then shifted blame and responsibility for Dr. Creamer's hiring to Fred Knowles before informing his colleagues he likely would not retain the club secretary in 1909.[128]

When asked on May 14, 1909, how things had progressed regarding unearthing the physician's accomplices, investigative committee chairman Brush replied, "I have nothing to say." Cartoonist and New York sportswriter Thomas Aloysius Dorgan, who used the pen name "Tad" for articles, presented some interesting questions and theories in his column after the Giants' owner offered the terse response. Dorgan, alluding to the distribution of fifty tickets to gambling syndicate goons stationed at various points of the Polo Grounds for the playoff game on October 8, 1908, wanted to know why somebody had assaulted Frank Chance. Did one of these hoodlums, employed as muscle, punch Chance? Tad pondered whether Johnny Evers might know the identities of those men who caused him trouble after that game since the second baseman's Big Apple relative recognized them. Dorgan wondered if the true perpetrators would continue to use Dr. Creamer as a duped tool to cover up their crimes.[129]

Dorgan's queries went unanswered, as John T. Brush correctly gauged that by offering only snippets of information, fans and press members would eventually lose interest once the 1909 pennant races commenced.[130] On July 29, 1918, Dr. Joseph Creamer died from heart failure. Dr. Creamer's obituary in *The Sun* did not mention his connection to bribing two umpires, only writing that he closely followed the New York Giants' fortunes.[131] Over two years later, former sportswriter and Philadelphia Phillies president Horace Fogel resurrected the other facet of the 1908 bribery scandal. On September 29, 1920, while discussing a compromised Rube Waddell in 1905, Fogel also commented about archived, secret National League records regarding attempts to bribe Phillies team members when they played New York at the end of the 1908 campaign.

According to Horace, these records revealed that a former Giants player, currently engaged as a minor league magnate for a western team, had attempted to bribe Philadelphia team members Red Dooin, Kitty Bransfield, Franz Otto Knabe, Michael "Mickey" Doolin, and Sherwood "Sherry" Magee. Fogel declared that the emissary offered each player between $1,000 and $5,000 not to participate in the second series between these clubs at National League Park. Horace also alleged that American League president Ban Johnson and Cincinnati owner Garry Herrmann, both National Commission members, wagered on the World Series each year.[132] Former New York pitcher Joe McGinnity fell under Fogel's criteria as a recent western minor league magnate for those pondering the briber's identity.

Unlike his accusation against Waddell, Horace's 1908 charge received immediate substantiation from two retired Phillies. Kitty Bransfield, now an Eastern League umpire, backed up Fogel's claim, declaring that somebody approached him before Philadelphia played a doubleheader at home against St. Louis on September 26, 1908 (while sharing his tale, Bransfield erroneously said his club played in Pittsburgh that day). With rumors of Phillies players planning to throw the two series already abounding, Kitty recalled his teammates realized they needed to avoid committing errors in the eight games to avert any hint of impropriety or crookedness.[133]

> On the Saturday before the series was opened in New York, while we were practicing before the game in Pittsburgh [Philadelphia], word came to me that a doctor from New York wanted to see me outside. I went out and met a man I had never seen before. He wanted me to go to New York that night, but I did not know him and refused. Later I found out he was the head of a clique of New York gamblers. Other players on our team were approached by him, but refused to have anything to do with him.
>
> When we reached our hotel in New York on Sunday, this same man was hanging around on the opposite side of the street. He hung around all Sunday and Monday, trying to get to some of our fellows, but the talk about throwing the series was so great at the time we purposely avoided him. As a result of the talk about throwing the series, we determined to win at all costs, and we played better ball than we ever did in our lives before, setting back the Giants and causing them to lose the pennant.[134]

Former Phillies catcher Red Dooin, now selling real estate in Atlantic City, New Jersey, corroborated Bransfield's recollection.[135] Dooin proclaimed that Philadelphia's players never mentioned the matter to league officials because they believed it benefited baseball's self-interest to remain silent. Team members reasoned that since some people already viewed baseball as dishonest, revealing a seedy matter like this would only give naysayers more ammunition to whine. Red alleged that after the series in New York against the Giants started, hoodlums kidnapped him and locked the catcher in a room. He escaped and continued playing in the series. Following one of these contests, an assailant struck Dooin in the head with a blackjack. Red did not regain consciousness until some teammates took him to the hotel. Dooin also stated the currently married man with a family, who approached Phillies team members, became quite prosperous.[136] If a physician, as Kitty Bransfield claimed, this fact eliminated Dr. Joseph Creamer from suspicion since he had died over two years ago.

Red added that while attempting to orchestrate the fix, the gambling syndicate agents that approached them did not request a pledge to throw games but only desired a promise to remain out of the lineup in the two series versus New York.[137] Although he had not witnessed this transaction, Dooin alleged gamblers laid out $150,000 on the table in a Philadelphia café in front of three Phillies hurlers and told them to take all or any amount of it if agreeing to cooperate. When discussing the current scandal involving eight members of the White Sox and their nefarious behavior in the 1919 World Series, Red said, "These fellows in Chicago were pikers to what we passed up." Dooin shared the offer an agent made to him in 1908.[138]

"In 1908 every member of the Philadelphia team was approached with offers of fabulous sums." Dooin said to reporters. "All any of us had to do was to name our price. A member of the Giants was one of those who tried to buy us off. A man approached me after the first game in New York and handed me a package containing $8,000. I was told there was $40,000 more in the bank awaiting me. He was a big fellow and I called 'Kitty' Bransfield, our first baseman. 'Kitty' threw him down the steps of our clubhouse."[139]

Red Dooin also revealed he later regretted not accepting the money and then turning it over to National League officials.[140] Law enforcement authorities intimated on October 1, 1920, they may investigate Dooin's charges.[141]

Regarding baseball's league jurisprudence, ancient history proved insignificant as details surrounding the Chicago Black Sox World Series scandal broke. The 1908 National League pennant race was one of the greatest in baseball history. Regrettably, wagers, bribes, and despicable people reveling in their own selfish schemes showed no concern for the game and almost brought about its ruination.

*In 1908, the Chicago Cubs, New York Giants, and Pittsburgh Pirates engaged in a thrilling National League pennant race. Cubs second baseman **Johnny Evers** became involved in critical plays from two games that impacted the race. On September 4, during a contest between Pittsburgh and Chicago at Exposition Park, Evers lost an argument with umpire Hank O'Day. Johnny claimed the two-out winning run Fred Clarke scored should not count since he executed a force play at second when the Pirates' Warren Gill failed to touch that bag before heading to the clubhouse. Weeks later when the same situation occurred in a contest against the Giants at the Polo Grounds September 23, umpires O'Day and Bob Emslie sided with Evers after he executed a force-out to end the ninth inning when New York's Fred Merkle did not continue to second base as Harry McCormick scored the deciding marker. (Courtesy of the Library of Congress).*

CHAPTER 9

Ty Cobb

Fearless Grit and Determination, with a Confrontational Mindset

After losing to the Chicago White Sox in the 1906 World Series, Frank Chance's Chicago Cubs achieved dynasty status, claiming two more National League pennants and easily dispatching the Detroit Tigers in the 1907 and 1908 World Series. Through their postseason dominance, Chicago only suffered one defeat in nine decisions against Detroit, while Game One of the 1907 World Series on October 8 at West Side Grounds ended tied, 3–3, after twelve innings. Although the Tigers could not gain any traction against the Cubs in two consecutive Octobers, the club possessed a youngster destined to become the Deadball Era's most proficient hitter and one of the greatest ballplayers in the game's history. Detroit outfielder Tyrus Raymond "Ty" Cobb left his huge imprint on baseball in 1907, winning the American League batting title as a twenty-year-old, with a .350 average. Cobb followed that up by wearing the crown a year later, pacing the circuit, hitting .324.

As young Ty Cobb gained a strong foothold establishing new batting standards and utilizing a diverse approach to the game, he proved a complex enigma plagued by adversity while reaching glory and fame's pinnacle. At times, Ty's actions and decisions caused his hardship, while in other instances, unfortunate circumstances victimized the young man. Blessed with raw diamond talent, Cobb possessed a strong will, desire, and drive to succeed at baseball's highest level. His passion and a combative personality that sometimes rose to the surface led to unfortunate encounters with teammates and opposing ballplayers. While Ty's physical prowess aided his growth as a performer, the future star's mental approach and a willingness to go against standard diamond orthodoxy allowed him to stand out alongside his peers.

Assuming the mantle as a trailblazing pioneer did not suit everybody connected to the game. Players comfortable with the status quo regarding strategy and things evolving on the field did not take kindly to a young wonder bucking tradition. Ty revolutionized baseball in 1907, introducing bold base running and a fresh style of hitting to all fields at the plate. Others started copying his methods. Batting, fielding, and base running experienced a metamorphosis because of Cobb's innovative measures. Most American League players, including many Tigers teammates, considered Ty a "morning glory" or "flash in the pan." Some explained Cobb's sudden success as the "luck of a crazy man." Baseball veterans disliked his playing style and could not understand why fans embraced it. As Ty achieved stardom, individuals jealous of his success belittled him and discounted any achievements. After the 1907 campaign concluded, Detroit pitcher Bill Donovan classified Cobb as a one-year wonder.

"He won't finish in the league next year," said Donovan, one of the Tigers' players who befriended Cobb. "He plays contrary to all baseball law and he won't last. He can't. He's a wild man. Next year they will just throw the ball to the home plate and wait for him to dash around to it. These freak players never last because they go contrary to the law."

Like many others, Bill Donovan did not understand the transformation before his eyes. Rather than going contrary to diamond law, Ty transformed the game into a new and exciting version through his daring style that challenged his opponents.[1] Cobb's road to becoming a big-league icon started years earlier in Georgia. Ty was born on December 18, 1886, in Narrows, Georgia, located in Banks County near the South Carolina border, to parents William Herschel and Amanda Chitwood Cobb. Following the birth of first son, Tyrus, brother John Paul and sister Florence soon joined the family dynamic.[2] The Cobbs enjoyed a comfortable life in the Narrows due to William's college education and the successful business interests of Amanda's family.[3] After teaching in various small farming communities near their home, Ty's father moved the family to Royston, Georgia, in 1893, where William became a local school's principal. Previously, he had gained prominence and a sterling reputation as an educator.[4]

A highly intelligent and brilliant man, William Cobb gave an address in 1883 at a state convention for Georgia educators. William's speech led to the development of new schools throughout the state and the implementation of his educational reforms. Four decades later, an individual who attended this convention sent a copy of the transcript to Ty Cobb in 1923, calling it the finest address ever delivered before such a body. This speech raised the elder Cobb's profile as one of the top schoolmasters in Georgia.[5] Besides achieving the lofty status of a distinguished professor, William also became mayor of Royston, represented that district as a state senator, and functioned as a county school commissioner. Cobb also worked as an editor for the *Royston Record*, a local newspaper.[6]

Growing up in Royston, Ty, a skinny, gangly, spindle-legged boy, engaged in ordinary activities like other kids. He rode a bicycle, fished, played baseball, and eventually learned to swim. While growing up, Ty deeply admired his paternal grandmother, Sarah, a woman Cobb believed possessed the most remarkable mind he ever experienced. He found no person franker while at the same time more diplomatic than her. Ty felt his grandmother exhibited uncanny insight regarding human nature.[7] Once, as the school year concluded, Cobb looked forward to summer vacation with great anticipation, yearning to enjoy himself playing baseball, fishing, and swimming. William Cobb had other ideas. One evening, William pulled his son aside and told him he needed to work during summer vacation. Although Ty expressed discontent over the idea, his father remained firm.

The younger Cobb found this entire concept displeasing. Ty had eagerly awaited summer vacation and longed to join the other boys on ballfields and at swimming holes. William believed the time had arrived for his eldest son to experience earning a livelihood while learning something about the demands of work and the inherent pleasure derived through reaping benefits from that hard labor.

> I have ten acres near here. This ten acres I have been holding for several years until you grew old enough to work it. The soil will produce cotton and I want you to produce ten acres of cotton.
>
> We will go about the thing in a regular manner, the same as if you owned the land and were a cotton planter. You will keep books and supervise everything. It will be up to you entirely; I am putting the whole thing in your hands.
>
> Tomorrow morning we will go out, you and I. We will make all the necessary purchases, acquire all necessary equipment. We will put down the cost of everything. Then you must keep in mind the cost and learn to make up all the cost and get the investment to earn money.

The following morning, Ty Cobb and his father bought the necessary tools for this project. They purchased a plow at a hardware store, went to a harness shop for a harness, and bought seed at a seed store. Knowing that the family owned numerous horses, Ty asked William Cobb's permission to use one of them to plow the ten-acre farm.

"You can't have any of them," replied his father. "That would be borrowed equipment. I want you to be entirely on your own. A horse is too expensive. It would raise the investment too high. We cannot afford to buy a horse to pull the plow on the ten acres. A mule is less expensive and it will do the work required out there. We will buy a mule."

After acquiring all necessary materials, William took the supplies, equipment, mule, and his son to the small plot of land and told Ty to start working. At first, the youth showed little interest in laboring on his farm since it proved a difficult and distasteful task. He initially loafed on the job, dreaming of smacking hits on a baseball field. Ty quickly grew to hate plows, mules, cotton, and farming. Despite his son's disdain when beginning to cultivate the land, William Cobb took him out each morning to the ten-acre farm. Slowly, over time, Ty's attitude changed. When the cotton stalks started growing, he better appreciated the daunting task, realizing that his sweat and arduous work produced something. It gave Ty a powerful feeling of self-worth as a valuable person contributing to the world.

Whereas rain clouds previously meant a boring day for him since it prevented engaging in fun activities, this type of weather took on new meaning. When the cotton fields needed nourishment from drenching rain, Cobb enthusiastically wished for an impending storm while watching clouds move across the sky. Ty also started speculating on how much cotton the land might produce and calculated potential earnings when taking the product to market. Decades later, after making his imprint on Organized Baseball, Cobb commended his father for using this approach to supply a crucial life's teaching moment.

"That was the most valuable lesson I ever received," said Tyrus. "I learned to produce, I learned that money had to be earned. I learned the value of the dollar, the joy of earning it. I could not have learned it in any better way."[8]

This valuable lesson did not eradicate Ty Cobb's thirst for athletic endeavors. He played shortstop for one of Royston's sandlot baseball teams. As Ty's diamond performance improved, he hooked up with the area's supreme town club. Although possessing skill as one of Royston's diamond elites, he had not gained recognition for being the town's ultimate ballplayer.[9] As a lad, Cobb's big athletic ambition centered on becoming a college sprinter. The youngster constantly practiced, hoping to someday experience success as a track athlete. He checked out Royston's library books dealing with sprinting. Ty conscientiously absorbed information, reading the techniques and practices shared on these pages by college coaches and sprinters. Many of the experts stressed stride over speed. After memorizing this data, Cobb applied it every morning before breakfast, running one to two miles. The concept of stride while running holding so much importance later helped him achieve greatness as one of baseball's finest baserunners.[10]

At sixteen, Ty determined he wanted to attend the University of Georgia and study to become a surgeon. William Cobb heartily endorsed this plan, expressing joy over his son choosing such an upstanding profession. The younger Cobb also hoped to play baseball and football at Georgia. Fostering this vision mapped out for years, Ty rejected accepting money playing sandlot baseball to preserve his purity as an amateur. A new call beckoned when a Royston teammate and friend received an opportunity to play professional baseball for a team in the Southern League. To follow his buddy's career, Cobb began reading baseball news for the first time. Observing box scores daily, Ty became interested in the professional leagues. When the season ended, Cobb's friend returned to Royston and offered a romantic overview of life as a professional baseball player.

Ty's former teammate told him it was simple to make the grade by playing baseball at the next level. After listening to these positive tales each day, Cobb committed himself to following that same path into professional baseball. In the spring of 1904, Ty wrote letters to two clubs in the South Atlantic League, requesting a trial. Management from the Augusta Tourists responded, informing Ty that they would give him a tryout if he paid his own traveling expenses.[11] Although William Cobb stressed to his son the importance of a college education and minimized playing baseball, he acceded to his son's wishes. Understanding that the teenager refused to waver from following his dream despite fatherly advice, William gave him the necessary money to make the trip by train to Augusta.[12] Upon arriving in the city, Ty wasted little time trekking to the Tourists' headquarters to see manager John Cornelius "Con" Strouthers. Cobb immediately got to the point regarding his intentions.[13]

"Well, young man, what can I do for you?" asked Strouthers.

"I'd like to play on your team," answered Cobb.[14]

Realizing no financial risk existed through giving Ty Cobb a trial, Strouthers told the youngster to report to Warren Park and request a uniform. Ty followed Con's instructions and worked out with the squad. With the season opener beckoning, Strouthers was in a bind since the South Atlantic League hierarchy had ruled regular outfielder Harry Bussey ineligible. Bussey received a suspension for participating in an outlaw league. Con told Cobb to practice in the outfield, and if the South Atlantic League did not reinstate Harry, he would start Ty on opening day. Cobb realized his dream of playing professional baseball on April 26, 1904, when Strouthers placed him in the lineup against the Columbia Skyscrapers. The recruit experienced a marvelous debut, smacking a double and a home run, although Columbia secured an 8–7 victory.

Ty also played the following afternoon and registered a single as Augusta gained revenge by defeating the Skyscrapers. That evening, Con walked over to Ty in the clubhouse and asked him to come to his office the following morning.

Believing the organization planned to offer him a contract containing a good salary, Cobb enthusiastically anticipated this meeting. Ty arrived at team headquarters on April 28 and anxiously waited for Strouthers. When the manager arrived, Cobb followed him into the office. Without exhibiting common courtesy by asking Ty to take a seat, Augusta's manager delivered devastating news.

"You're released," said Strouthers.

Cobb stood in stunned silence for a moment before responding. "You mean I'm let out here?" Ty asked. "You're letting me go?"

"Yes," replied Strouthers. "I'm letting you go. You're a free agent. I can't use you. My regular outfielder has been reinstated and I'm going to use him. You can join any club you like because you're a free agent now."[15]

Although extremely disappointed, an opportunity presented itself to play for a team from Anniston, Alabama, in the Tennessee-Alabama League. Realizing he faced a dilemma since his father opposed baseball as a profession, Cobb pondered his future. Ty had traveled to Augusta against William Cobb's wishes and quickly lost that job. Cobb finally decided to call his father on the telephone, believing William would tell him to return home. Ty received straightforward advice after informing the elder Cobb that the Tourists had released him and that he could sign with a lower-level club.

"All right, take the job," responded William Cobb. "Don't come home a failure. You've decided on professional baseball and now show that you can be a success at it. Try and do your best, but don't come home until you succeed."

Uplifted by his father's blunt, honest guidance, Ty Cobb signed an Anniston contract and quickly became the league's sensation. In his first 22 games with the club, Ty batted .370. This outraged Augusta's fans following Cobb's exploits. They criticized management and severely lamented the talented outfielder's release when the team spiraled into a horrendous slump. Patrons reasoned that the club might be higher in the standings if Ty still patrolled the outfield. Tired of receiving harsh blowback, Con Strouthers attempted to bring Cobb back into the fold. Ty made his feelings quite clear when Strouthers wired him a contract offer to rejoin the Tourists.

"I won't play for you in Augusta and I'll never play for you anywhere else," replied Cobb in his message to Con.

Weeks after attempting to rectify this big mistake, Con cut his ties to the club. Since Augusta's fans still demanded Cobb's return, the organization continued their courtship with the teenage outfielder. Consequently, with Harlan Wingard now at the helm and Strouthers gone, Ty gladly agreed to rejoin the Tourists.[16] Cobb participated in 37 games for Augusta in 1904 and batted .237.[17] Ty received a break while preparing for the 1905 season. That spring, Detroit trained in Augusta and used the Tourists' facility for their practice sessions. Francis J. "Frank" Navin served as bookkeeper and business manager in the Tigers' organization for the past three years and had just purchased an interest in the franchise, making him part-owner. He decided to travel south and observe his ballplayers during spring training.

Detroit lodged at the Albion Hotel while spending time in Augusta. After Navin arrived at the hotel, two players greeted him upon entering the lobby. Second baseman and team captain William "Germany" Schaefer and hurler Bill Donovan immediately beckoned for Frank to join them on the other side of the foyer. Once together, Schaefer informed the new magnate about a hilarious young outfielder playing for the Augusta Tourists who uniquely approached baseball.

"We've got the richest joke in the world for you out here," said Schaefer. "There's a kid playing on the local nine who thinks he's a ballplayer. He's just a nut but a scream. Wait till you see this baby run bases. You'll laugh yourself sick. But don't let him know he's a joke. We've been having a swell time just kiddin' him along. If you talk to him, tell him you think he's a great ballplayer. Whatever you do, don't let him get wise to what we think about him or you'll spoil the best laugh we ever had."

The following day, Navin ventured to the ballpark to scout the young recruit Germany had talked about, Ty Cobb. Navin immediately noticed Cobb possessed extreme speed and a quick start when running from the batter's box to first base. After watching Ty for some time, Navin concluded that despite his immense ability and potential, rough spots in his game needed smoothing. Frank assessed how Cobb ran freely on the bases like a wild colt. That afternoon, while talking with Tourists outfielder George Leidy, the two discussed Ty. Leidy admitted Cobb needed a little polish. He told Navin that once Cobb became used to the bridle of instruction, the world would witness one of baseball's greatest players.

Before Detroit left Augusta to start their exhibition game tour, the club needed to settle accounts for using Warren Park. Rather than handing over money for rent, Tigers management offered to farm out a player to the Tourists. Since Augusta needed a pitcher, Detroit decided to turn over recruit Edgar "Eddie" Cicotte. Besides not needing to pay for using their grounds, handing over Cicotte proved fiscally prudent since it saved on train fare required to send the hurler to another minor league team for more seasoning. A clause in this agreement stipulated that if the Tigers wanted a player from Augusta's roster near season's end, they could secure the individual for $750. When Detroit broke camp and headed north, their players laughed and joked about the Tourists' odd nut for a while before forgetting about him as the campaign approached.[18]

Ty Cobb's development received a boost when George Leidy replaced Andrew "Andy" Roth as Augusta's pilot partway through the 1905 season. Leidy decided that firing up Cobb's imagination and allowing the youngster to figure things out for himself offered the best way to nurture him. George felt that interceding in his diamond education might hinder Ty's progress. Realizing Cobb's resolute personality made him unlikely to accept advice, Leidy instead offered suggestions by telling yarns about past players, feeling the youngster would absorb this baseball wisdom and adapt in a way that best suited his goals and needs. Following such instruction, George noticed Ty spending more time at the ballpark than his teammates. He had already started working on the field when team members showed up each day and remained after they departed.

Leidy stressed to Ty that talented players like Honus Wagner and Christy Mathewson practiced for many hours each day to achieve star status. Cobb likewise followed this blueprint. Having primarily played shortstop for years before becoming a professional ballplayer, Ty worked diligently each day in the outfield, learning the nuances of proper positioning, how to measure flyballs hit to his right or left, and perfecting going in or out on a direct line chasing the sphere. Teammates swatted flyballs to Cobb for hours each day.[19] Years after Ty reached the major leagues, George explained his methodology behind cultivating the outfielder's talent and ability.

"Of course, he was the kind of youngster that a lot of managers would pass up," said Leidy. "But I figured him like a fine thoroughbred racehorse. I said to myself: 'Now, you wouldn't give a snap for a horse that acted like a plow horse at the barrier. This kid is high-strung and he can't be bullied. He's got to be nursed along. He's got the fire and the thing to do is break him to bridle. He's got to be handled like a prancing colt and that's how I'll handle him.'"[20]

Ty Cobb experienced a grand season for Augusta in 1905, appearing in 103 games and batting .326. Just as his baseball career exhibited boundless possibilities, Cobb suffered a personal tragedy involving the person he revered most in life, whose guidance and influence molded him into the man he was destined to become. Back in Royston, around midnight on August 8, 1905, Amanda Cobb accidentally shot and killed her husband. While in bed, after hearing a noise near the window, Amanda saw a man moving outside on the veranda. Grabbing a pistol hidden under her pillow, Ty's mother fired two shots to defend herself. One bullet hit William in the head, while the other penetrated his abdomen.[21]

Law enforcement officials arrested Mrs. Cobb for murder shortly after her husband's funeral and burial. Authorities surmised that on the night of his death, William Cobb spied on his wife, who he suspected of infidelity. Leading Amanda to believe he traveled to Atlanta, Georgia, on business, William remained behind after receiving a tip from a close friend that his wife entertained a gentleman whenever he went out of town. When Mr. Cobb returned to the house close to midnight and suffered his cruel fate, a man whose identity authorities did not release happened to be in the bedroom when Amanda fired the weapon.[22] On March 31, 1906, a jury acquitted Ty Cobb's mother of manslaughter in the esteemed schoolmaster's death.[23] Sadly, the man who had told Tyrus not to return home a failure would not experience his son's outstanding success looming on the horizon.

As the 1905 season progressed, Augusta's ownership pressed Detroit to select a player as per their previous agreement. The club initially showed no interest in bringing back Eddie Cicotte because he happened to be too small. During discussions, some organizational members offered that the Tourists' Arthur Clyde Engel appeared promising, but dissenters pointed out he lacked speed. Someone then suggested Cobb. Although ownership favored Engel, Tigers manager William "Bill" Armour recommended purchasing Ty. George Leidy and future National League umpire William "Lord" Byron, who worked in the South Atlantic League that year, sold Armour on Cobb's merits by constantly praising Augusta's outfielder. If the Tigers did not move on Ty, another major league club would draft him. Following days of internal discussions, Detroit purchased Cobb from Augusta on August 19, 1905.[24]

According to American League umpire William "Billy" Evans, in 1907, the Tigers only made a down payment of $250 for Cobb, with a contingency that the Tourists receive any remaining amount if he made good and remained with the club. The Tigers' manager exhibited so much commitment to adding Ty that Bill offered to pay the $250 installment out of his own pocket to secure the eighteen-year-old player.[25] Although still a babe, Cobb held a distinct advantage upon joining Detroit. Since Armour had fought hard for this purchase, the skipper needed to justify his confidence in the player and a commitment to ownership by playing Ty.

In a game against the New York Highlanders in front of 1,200 fans at Bennett Park on August 30, 1905, Bill inserted Cobb into the lineup to replace ill, regular center fielder Duff Cooley, who the club released six days later. Star hurler Jack Chesbro worked on the hill for New York. Ty batted fifth in the batting order behind icon Sam Crawford. In the bottom of the first inning, Tigers leadoff hitter Matty McIntyre stroked a double. First baseman Christian "Chris" Lindsay's single drove home McIntyre with the game's first run. Germany Schaefer laid down a sacrifice bunt that moved Lindsay to second base. Chris reached third when Crawford tapped back to Chesbro in the box, who then threw to first base. Cobb stepped up to the plate for his first major league at bat.

A murmur went through the crowd as patrons glanced at their scorecards, hoping to identify this newcomer. Realizing most minor league players were high-ball hitters, Jack followed that scouting report and blazed an enticing pitch past Ty for a swinging strike. Cobb had never experienced a high pitch quite so fast while playing for Augusta. Chesbro wound up again and tossed a beautiful curveball. Although Ty did not offer, umpire Silk O'Loughlin yelled "strike tuh" in his standard vibrant manner. Ahead in the count, Jack figured he had gained the upper hand against this neophyte. Guessing Cobb would be looking for another high, hard pitch, Chesbro crossed him up by throwing a fastball at the waist. Ty connected against the offering and tagged the ball to center field. The Highlanders' William Edgar "Ed" Hahn gazed quickly at the baseball before running toward the fence. Streaking to first, Cobb did not break stride, making the turn and heading for second base. He slid safely into the bag with a double that drove home Lindsay.[26]

Ty Cobb only collected that one safety as the Tigers defeated New York, 5–3. Cobb appeared in 41 games for Detroit in 1905 and batted .238. One year later, Ty saw action in 98 contests and hit .316. Cobb did not find it easy to transition from the minors to big-time baseball. According to Billy Evans, one day, Ty looked like a diamond in the rough, while in other instances, he performed horribly. Cobb's fiery Southern disposition turned many veteran Detroit players against him. Ty also exhibited open animosity over only earning a bush-league salary of $1,200 in 1906. Many problems emerged, and fights with teammates commonly occurred. This strained atmosphere caused the Tigers to finish in sixth place that year with a 71–78 record, resulting in Bill Armour losing his job when the season ended.[27]

Veteran baseball players loathed young recruits possessing boundless promise when joining a club and possibly taking their jobs. Such was the case when Cobb joined Detroit. Many team members bullied the youngster and ridiculed him unmercifully. They resented his appearance and hated that he received a starting job without paying dues sitting on the bench. Few Tigers players spoke to Ty other than to insult him. One day after he experienced going 3-for-4 at the plate in 1906, Cobb arrived at the ballpark and found his two favorite black bats, brought with him to Detroit from Augusta, missing. Upon inquiring as to their whereabouts, a teammate told Ty he could locate the bats on the other side of the outfield fence. When Cobb reached that area, he found them reduced to splinters.

Some of Detroit's players had used a hatchet to destroy Ty Cobb's favorite bats. These team members believed that no longer possessing the crucial pet cudgels would be a detriment to Cobb's hitting ability. The loss of these bats that had supplied so many base hits devastated the nineteen-year-old rising star. When Ty entered the clubhouse, he sat down and slouched to one corner of the locker room in deep despair. Catcher Charles "Charlie" Schmidt witnessed the destruction of Cobb's beloved willows. Schmidt, weighing two hundred pounds, built like a boxer and referred to as "Boss" by other players, walked over to Ty and offered him one of his favorite bats.

"There's just as many hits in this one as the bats they broke up for you," Schmidt told Cobb. "Use it. If anybody tries to break up that bat they'll reckon—with me."[28]

Fellow outfielder Matty McIntyre rose to the forefront as Cobb's prime antagonist, loathing the young player after he joined the club. This feeling stemmed from Ty poaching into Matty's left-field territory from center to grab a flyball in the second game of a doubleheader against Chicago at Bennett Park on September 5, 1905.[29] McIntyre did not speak to Cobb. Pitcher Edwin "Ed" Killian followed suit, not because he necessarily expressed jealousy or animosity toward Ty, but due to his close friendship with Matty.[30] McIntyre's poor attitude and occasional deliberate lethargic play resulting from his dislike of Cobb brought about repercussions in the summer of 1906. On June 23, manager Bill Armour suspended Matty indefinitely for indifferent play. In the game that afternoon versus the White Sox at South Side Park, Ty, who recently had been playing right field, shifted to left. McIntyre expressed anger over the punishment and threatened to jump to an outlaw baseball league.[31]

Armour affirmed that he suspended Matty for loafing on flyballs hit in his direction, while Matty claimed that the club had made him the victim of a conspiracy intended to belittle and smear him. Bill seemed intent on eliminating any malcontents from his squad. Problems arose resulting from two team cliques firmly establishing themselves when the Tigers held spring training at Augusta. Although suspended without pay, Matty remained in Detroit. A trade appeared imminent, with McIntyre willing to go to Cleveland, New York, or Boston. Matty blamed hurler Edward "Ed" Siever for his trouble. Siever complained to Armour during the game against Chicago on June 22 when McIntyre failed to catch a drive off the bat of White Sox catcher William "Billy" Sullivan, which Matty claimed was a physical impossibility.[32] According to Frank Navin, this festering problem occurred because of the way Ty Cobb had put it over on McIntyre. The Tigers' manager shared with the press part of a conversation between him and Matty before he issued the suspension.

"I asked McIntyre if he wouldn't ginger up his work in Chicago," said Armour. "He said he would not hustle, and I told him he had put on a Detroit uniform for the last time."

Matty McIntyre also made sure sportswriters and baseball fans knew his side of the story, feeling management persecuted him.

"As long ago as in Boston they told me they would get me," said McIntyre. "What sort of spirit could I put into my work with that hanging over my head."[33]

Hoping to garner sympathy, Matty attempted to drag teammates within his circle as fellow dissatisfied players. McIntyre named Sam Crawford, George Mullin, Jack Warner, and Ed Killian. His claim lacked any truth. The fact that Warner and Bill Armour shared a close friendship at the time proved the absurdity of Matty's contention. McIntyre had previously stated he refused to give his best efforts on the diamond if Ty Cobb played on the same team. Fans overwhelmingly agreed with Armour's and Frank Navin's decisions.[34] Bill stating Matty had put on a Detroit uniform for the last time proved to be a huge understatement. McIntyre's punishment only lasted a week, as he returned to the starting lineup against the St. Louis Browns on June 30.

Following Armour's dismissal, Navin hired former Baltimore Orioles great Hughie Jennings to manage the club in 1907. An astute judge of baseball talent, Jennings's addition proved a stroke of genius by Frank regarding Ty's continued growth as a player.[35] Although the person who suspended him the previous season no longer managed the Tigers, Matty refused to go South with the team for spring training in 1907. McIntyre received no satisfaction following a meeting with Detroit's owner in late February. Navin rejected Matty's trade request, declaring Jennings insisted on retaining the outfielder. McIntyre countered that he planned to remain a holdout.[36] For the third consecutive season, the Tigers held spring training in Augusta. Before a practice session started on March 16, Hughie needed to deal with an ugly situation that presented a baptism under fire for him at the outset of overseeing Detroit's squad.

When team members arrived at Warren Park that afternoon, Henry "Bungy" Cummings, a Black man employed at the ballpark as a groundskeeper and partially under the influence of liquor, approached Ty Cobb on the field. A presumed acquaintanceship between the two existed from when Cobb played for Augusta. Cummings stepped up near the player, held out his hand, and said, "Hello, Ty, old boy." Whether peeved about something unrelated, unhappy over smelling alcohol on this man's breath, dissatisfied with the diamond's condition, or feeling such action from a perceived inferior individual insulting, Ty responded harshly. Cobb did not accept Bungy's greeting. Cobb drew back the hand the groundskeeper had reached for and, instead of extending it for a handshake, struck him with great force before chasing Bungy off the grounds into the nearby clubhouse behind the third-base bleachers reserved for Black patrons.

The groundskeeper's house stood close to the one-story cabin clubhouse.[37] As Cummings ran toward the cabin, Ty followed, demanding an apology.[38] Reacting to the commotion, Bungy's wife arrived from the clubhouse area to rescue her husband. She frantically hurled epithets at Detroit's outfielder. Turning toward the woman, a further angered Ty grabbed Cummings's spouse and started choking her.³⁹ The team members who gathered around the scene suggested Cobb leave. Catcher Charlie Schmidt offered his opinion on the matter.

"A man who would abuse a woman that way, white or black, is no good," said Schmidt.⁴⁰

Schmidt, through presenting his view about abusing a woman, further infuriated Ty, who, according to Southern tradition, believed nobody should interfere in another man's business. Cobb suggested that Charlie go to hell. Schmidt responded by viciously swinging his right hand and connecting with Ty's jaw. Cobb quickly retaliated, and the two ballplayers exchanged punches. Teammates separated them before any damage occurred. Many of Detroit's players sided with Charlie, whom they revered, and condemned Ty for his behavior. Throughout that afternoon practice session, Cobb appeared meek as a lamb. On the other hand, Schmidt continued expressing his feelings on such a violent act, while Hughie Jennings looked distraught.

That night, Jennings sent a wire to Macon, Georgia, where the Cleveland Naps trained. In the message to Cleveland manager Napoleon "Nap" Lajoie, Hughie proposed trading Ty Cobb for dissatisfied Naps outfielder Elmer Flick. When approached by reporters, Jennings refused to deny or confirm the possibility. His players deemed the report true, declaring the club would trade Cobb. Hughie offered a general statement regarding the incident.

"Harmony in a ball team is absolutely essential to success, and I intend to prevent dissensions among the players at all costs, no matter who is effected," said Jennings.

That same evening, Ty denied choking or touching the groundskeeper's wife, claiming he only scolded her for intervening. He also declared Charlie Schmidt needlessly interfered and punched him first.

"I am in the right," said Cobb, "and so long as I know that fact, I don't care what is done or said."⁴¹

Cleveland president Charles Somers responded to Jennings's request, stating he did not plan to trade Flick. New York manager Clark Griffith expressed interest in acquiring Cobb and offered outfielder Frank Delahanty to the Tigers.⁴² Ty's continued presence with Detroit was why Matty McIntyre refused to join his teammates in Augusta. Matty informed Hughie that he would report as soon as the Tigers removed Ty from the club.⁴³ On March 18, Jennings and Cobb engaged in a long conference. Although the two sides reached no satisfactory resolution during this discussion, Hughie believed the main problem could be partially rectified. Admitting he now had no friends on the team, Ty accepted none of the blame but placed it all on the other players. Jennings also wired McIntyre to travel to Augusta so they could talk things over.⁴⁴

Matty joined the club when they reached Charleston, South Carolina, and played left field in that afternoon's exhibition game. After Hughie Jennings stressed to McIntyre that team harmony and cohesion would exist on his squad, Matty appeared happy over this proclamation and promised to give his best diamond effort. On March 29, 1907, before the Tigers engaged in a contest at Meridian, Mississippi, Ty Cobb and Charlie Schmidt participated in Round Two of their bout that started almost two weeks earlier in Augusta. When the squad stopped in Atlanta for an exhibition game, Ty's friend boasted to a writer that Detroit's outfielder could lick Schmidt or any other team member in a fight. The newspaper employing this journalist foolishly printed the declaration. Although Cobb disavowed all responsibility for his friend's comment, Charlie felt it a swell idea to settle things. The skirmish between the two ballplayers only lasted about one minute before Ty declared he had enough and stopped the one-sided bout.

Cobb returned to his hotel room to have wounds around a black eye dressed. George Mullin played right field in that afternoon's contest. A club correspondent reported that this scrap helped clear the atmosphere between Ty and his teammates. Some players respected that Cobb proved willing to tangle with a much bigger man. They also acted more friendly toward him, willing to forget past indiscretions and start with a clean slate.[45] From that day forward, Ty and Schmidt engaged in a friendship that lasted for many years.[46] As the season opener beckoned, Boston Red Sox president John I. Taylor sounded out Frank Navin and Hughie Jennings about the prospect of dealing Cobb or Matty McIntyre to his club in exchange for holdout shortstop Freddy Parent.[47] Taylor desperately needed an outfielder to fill the void left by Chick Stahl's death.

Following a meeting with his players on April 8, Jennings announced he planned to keep his young firebrand in the fold as insurance in case Claude Rossman, purchased from Cleveland in the off-season, proved inadequate at first base. If Claude failed, Hughie intended to move Sam Crawford to first base and plug Ty into his outfield spot. Team members aired their grievances related to Ty during the confab. Charlie Schmidt expressed his complete satisfaction to the manager and told him he bore no ill will toward Cobb.[48] With Rossman securing the starting job at first base, Jennings changed his outfield configuration to instill harmony and placate McIntyre. Hughie moved Crawford to center field and shifted Ty to right to keep Matty and the Georgian separated in the outer garden. This shift worked marvelously for Jennings. Unfortunately, McIntyre did not remain part of this unit for long, suffering a season-ending injury.[49] In a game against the Boston Americans at Bennett Park on May 9, 1907, Matty broke his right ankle while sliding into first base.[50]

When Hughie Jennings took control of Detroit during spring training, he observed Ty Cobb on the diamond for about a week and then completely ignored him. Noticing this slight, Cobb confided to a newspaper reporter that Jennings hurt his feelings by overlooking him each day. The sportswriter then went to Hughie, informed the pilot of Ty's distraught and perplexed demeanor, and asked Jennings why he did not pay more attention to this youngster possessing so much untapped potential. Hughie assured the pundit he did not intentionally ignore Cobb. That evening, Jennings took Ty aside and alleviated the young player's apprehension.

"My boy," said Jennings, "you may think I've been overlooking you. I have been watching you closely and I want to tell you this: There isn't a thing about baseball that I can teach you. Anything I might say to you would simply hinder you in your development. The only thing for you to do is to go ahead and do as you please. You just use your own judgment. You can teach yourself better and get along faster than by the aid of any man I know. Now just go ahead and work things out in your own way and do what you think is best, and I'll back you."

The following morning, when Hughie saw this sportswriter before leaving for Warren Park, the journalist asked the Tigers' manager if Cobb possessed the tools to be a good ballplayer. Jennings took the reporter by the arm and gave him a measured response.

"Listen to me!" exuded Hughie. "He has the making of the greatest ballplayer that ever lived and that's exactly what he will be within the next three years. Mark my word and play that as strong as you like. You can't go wrong."

In the future, Hughie allowed Cobb to make his own game decisions. Jennings exempted Ty from following signals that might impede his scientific assessment of a diamond situation. Hughie reasoned he could not mold Cobb into conforming with how his teammates played and analyzed the game because none of them approached his level regarding mechanical ability or tactical aptitude.[51] Jennings displayed astute accuracy about Ty during his three-year period. The pennant-winning seasons of 1907 and 1908 provided a prelude to the young outfielder's magnificence. In 1909, Cobb captured the American League's Triple Crown in hitting by exceeding all others in batting average (.377), home runs (9), and RBIs (107). Ty also paced the circuit with 76 stolen bases. Detroit secured their third consecutive pennant, outdueling Philadelphia in a vigorous battle and finishing 3 ½ games ahead of the Athletics with a 98–54 record. The Pittsburgh Pirates then defeated the Tigers in a World Series that went the full seven games.

In a season where Ty Cobb etched his name among the greatest to ever pull on a uniform in baseball history, his profile raised in other areas for all the wrong reasons. Although never intentionally injuring an opponent when running from one bag to another, Cobb staunchly believed the basepath fell within his domain and always belonged to the runner. Any clumsy or foolish fielder who did not understand this principle challenged such a basic concept at their own peril and deserved blame for any incident. One such confrontation occurred when Detroit played Philadelphia at Bennett Park on August 24. The Athletics started the game grandly by scoring two runs off Tigers pitcher Oren Edgar "Ed" Summers in the top of the first inning.

In the bottom of that frame, Ty, batting third in the lineup, drew a walk against southpaw hurler Harry Krause and promptly stole second base. Exhibiting his daring on the paths as Sam Crawford started jogging down to first base when Krause issued another free pass, Cobb bolted for third.[52] Philadelphia catcher Patrick "Paddy" Livingston made a low throw down to the hot corner, hoping to catch Ty. Third baseman John Franklin "Frank" Baker plucked the baseball inches from the ground in his glove. As Baker shifted and then lunged for the runner with ball in hand, Cobb's spikes tore into his right arm while executing a hook slide into third base. With Frank's arm bleeding, the two players came close to delivering blows, as Baker accused Ty of cutting him on purpose. Later in the contest, Athletics second baseman Edward "Eddie" Collins deliberately blocked Cobb's path running to the keystone sack for an apparent double. Charging with the force and speed of a freight train, Ty slid into Collins with so much velocity that he tossed his opponent into the air.[53] Detroit won the exciting game, 7–6.

Philadelphia's team members adamantly felt Cobb spiked Baker on purpose. Those who played devil's advocate and pondered the possibility of inadvertent contact scratched their heads upon realizing Ty had spiked Frank up high on the arm near his elbow. This meant Cobb flashed airborne spikes when penetrating flesh. *North American* sportswriter James Isaminger, traveling with the club on their road trip for the Philadelphia newspaper, witnessed Ty's stunt. The writer stated Cobb deliberately threw his foot into the air once he realized Baker would tag him out. Isaminger condemned Cobb for unwisely rebuffing responsibility by quantifying it as an accident. Following the collision, Frank required a bandage to cover an ugly gash. Athletics manager Connie Mack bitterly complained to league president Ban Johnson about the unnecessary tactic.[54]

On the morning of August 25, Mack severely denounced Ty Cobb's behavior. While admitting Cobb surpassed all others as the world's greatest player, he also referred to the Tigers' outfielder as one of the dirtiest diamond participants. Connie charged Ty with boasting before the previous day's game that he planned to get some of the Athletics. Mack then declared he would not allow Cobb on his team even if the Georgian agreed to play for free. Connie felt American

League officials should act, compelling Ty to treat opponents with decency.[55] Mack later elaborated while sharing his feelings on the matter with reporters.

> I'm not going to prolong my arguments why Cobb is too aggressively inclined on the ball field. Personally, I am not very well acquainted with the young man. I think it is just his second nature to act mean on the ball field. He probably gets up in the morning with a grouch on and it sticks to him all day. Then when the game is on he gives vent to this feeling by making trouble. Such tactics ought to be looked into by the American League, and I intend to see to it that the matter is taken up. Other players have rights as well as Cobb. He should not be permitted to vent his spite upon them. I know that Cobb had threatened to get Baker, [Athletics shortstop John "Jack"] Barry, and Collins. He did spike Baker and knocked Collins heels overhead yesterday trying to do the same to him. He may be a great player, but he is a pinhead in this respect. Organized Baseball ought not to permit such a malefactor to disgrace it. You can take this straight. I am going to take steps to stop it.[56]

Never one to quietly submit when someone criticized his style or attitude as a ballplayer, Ty Cobb responded with venom to Connie Mack's accusatory remarks.

> It was most ungentlemanly of Mack to run to the newspapers knocking me. He goes around with the salve in one hand and a piledriver in the other and expects to get by with everything. Mack knows I never spiked a man deliberately, and he also knows that the runner is entitled to the line, and if the baseman gets in the way he is taking his own chances. When I slid I made for the bag. If the man with the ball is in the way he is apt to get hurt. But that is his lookout, he has no business on the line.
>
> It is a plain case of squeal with Mack, and I'm going to tell him so. Look at what they did to us in Philadelphia, when they were seven runs to the good and we hadn't a chance to win. Both Barry and Collins dove into Schaefer and tried to put him out. And Collins did get [Detroit catcher Oscar] Stanage and put him out of the game for a week. But we didn't holler.
>
> That is baseball, and if we get hurt we take our medicine and don't go around crying over it. Collins is all right. He tried to block me off Tuesday, but I dumped him. He didn't say a word, because he knew that I was right. He goes into the bases the same way that I do, and he has hurt as many men as I have.

When asked by reporters to reply to Connie Mack's comments, Hughie Jennings refused to answer what he qualified as an absurd charge. Jennings then declared that Cobb, one of baseball's cleanest players, never injured an individual intentionally and always used proper sliding technique.[57] Although Connie decided against filing a formal protest with Ban Johnson, this did not prevent the league president from weighing in on the spiking affair. Ban condemned the entire Tigers' organization for condoning such practices and called Ty the chief offender. Threatening to make an example of someone if such dirty methods continued, Johnson exclaimed Cobb must cease resorting to such tactics or risk expulsion from baseball.[58]

Everybody held an opinion on whether Ty Cobb acted within diamond etiquette or executed a dirty play. Many Philadelphia scribes demanded Cobb's removal from baseball.[59] A newspaper photographer stationed near third base on August 24 fortunately snapped a picture of the disputed play. When people viewed the photo, those predisposed to believe fault solely rested with Ty remained firm, while the same held true for individuals who reasoned Frank Baker displayed clumsiness while attempting to make the play. Cobb contended Baker purposely got in the way and remained in his path so the third baseman could get spiked.[60]

Ty graciously sent a copy of this photograph by messenger to Boston sportswriter Tim Murnane while he was in Detroit to cover a series between the Red Sox and Tigers that began on August 31. After perusing the picture, Murnane agreed with Connie Mack's assessment of the incident. Tim stated that he had heard of spiking a fielder in the foot, but something seemed amiss when a runner with spikes a foot off the ground committed this act on a fielder's arm after pulling away to give the opposing player a clear path to the base.[61] Cleveland sportswriter Tip Wright did not think Ty intentionally spiked Frank, adding he believed Detroit's star performer would never purposely injure another ballplayer. Wright characterized Cobb as a peppery kid who carried a full head of steam on the baselines. Tip's solution for these occurrences suggested finding a viable alternative to metal spikes.[62]

Bob Unglaub of the Washington Senators defended Ty, saying that although the play may have appeared dirty to some individuals, he felt the Tigers' player never considered deliberately spiking those who blocked a bag. Unglaub stated that Cobb's focus always centered on reaching that base safely.[63] Germany Schaefer, who Detroit had just traded to Washington on August 13, along with Wade "Red" Killefer, for James "Jim" Delahanty, also sided with his former teammate.

> Cobb is a game, square fellow. He never cut a man with his spikes intentionally in his life and anyone who gets his by his spikes knows it.

When Cobb joined the team he was a fast, rather awkward fellow and he didn't know how to slide. Jimmie Ryan [a former nineteenth century outfielder who primarily played for Chicago] had taught me how to make the old Chicago slide, twisting away from the baseman and hooking the feet on the bag. I showed Cobb how it was done and he slides that way. He never slides feet first into a baseman, but hooks around, and if anyone gets cut it is for trying to block Cobb as he reaches for the base with his foot.

This Baker case I know nothing about, but Baker is a rough, awkward fellow who doesn't know how to protect himself and he probably could not shift his feet and get out of Cobb's way.[64]

Athletics fans sent threatening letters to Ty Cobb on the eve of a return meeting between these two squads, beginning at Shibe Park on September 16. Rain showers decorated the field before and during the game as Philadelphia defeated Detroit, 2–1.[65] Hughie Jennings implored Athletics part-owner Benjamin "Ben" Shibe to secure extra police officers at the ballpark due to threats against Cobb. Philadelphia Assistant Superintendent of Police Timothy "Tim" O'Leary dispatched officers from every district in the city to the new grounds and surrounding neighborhood known as "Bloody Angle." As 24,710 fans filled the baseball arena, 180 bluecoats protected Ty and his teammates throughout Shibe Park. Athletics team management did not permit concessionaires to sell soda pop since enthusiastic patrons might use the empty bottles as projectiles. The sole items fans tossed in Cobb's direction while playing right field were a handful of straw hats.[66]

The only incident throughout the afternoon requiring law enforcement's attention occurred when Philadelphia's Daniel "Danny" Murphy attempted to strike David "Davy" Jones after accusing the player of making a derogatory remark from Detroit's bench.[67] In the series' final contest on September 20, Ty became the center of attention in another spiking incident for which he bore no responsibility. While attempting to steal second base as Athletics pitcher Edward "Eddie" Plank fanned the Tigers' Sam Crawford, Cobb spiked shortstop Jack Barry. Few Shibe Park patrons roasted Ty over the incident since many savvy baseball spectators realized that public enemy number one did so unintentionally. Cobb immediately apologized to Barry before the injured ballplayer limped off the field and informed other Philadelphia team members that his opponent's action was purely accidental. John "Stuffy" McInnis replaced Jack at shortstop.[68]

On this fourth-inning play, Ty's spikes ripped open a two-inch long and a half-an-inch wide gash in Barry's left ankle. Jack had unnecessarily blocked Cobb's path to the bag since Philadelphia catcher Paddy Livingston's throw easily beat the runner to second base. Barry only needed to wait at the keystone sack and execute a standard tag. Instead, Jack attempted to record the out by moving in front of the bag as Cobb slid in feet first. Ty and other players immediately rushed to his fallen foe's aid. Individuals from both teams concurred Barry's injury was the result of an accidental collision.[69] Barry yelled to Cobb before he left the game, "Don't mind, Ty. It was not your fault." Although understanding he accidentally spiked the Athletics' shortstop, it bothered Ty since he hurt Jack worse than any other player during his major league career.

Cobb felt so terrible over the situation that he refused to eat dinner with teammates that night after traveling by train to Washington for a series against the Senators. Coaxing and cheerful words from Hughie Jennings failed to persuade Ty to change his mind. Team members and employees at the Aldine Hotel, where the Tigers lodged while in Philadelphia, confirmed to newspaper reporters that this incident deeply affected Cobb, who eventually addressed the press on the matter.

"I would not have this happen for all the money I ever made in baseball," he said. "And to think that it came at a time when the Baker affair was almost forgotten. But it was an accident, and I am sure that the fans, particularly the good class who go to see a game and look for the best team to win, will bear me out that it was an unfortunate affair and absolutely unavoidable."[70]

Spiking incidents did not exclusively prey on Ty Cobb's mind. A confrontation away from the diamond placing Cobb in legal peril occurred in Cleveland, sandwiched between his troubles connected to incidents involving Philadelphia Athletics players. On September 3, umpires called the game at League Park between Detroit and the Naps on account of darkness, with the score tied 1–1 after nine innings.[71] That night, Ty and other team members attended the theater. After the show, he dined with actor Vaughan Glaser and actress Fay Courteney. When Cobb returned to the Hotel Euclid, where the club lodged, he found a note in his mailbox at the desk asking to call on a person in a second-floor room. According to Ty, he could not find the room, went up to the third floor, and rang for the elevator.

Cobb asked the elevator boy the location of that second-floor room. Rather than lower the elevator one floor, the operator returned it to the lobby. When Ty told the employee to take him to his fifth-floor room, he refused. The loud commotion caught the attention of hotel watchman, or house detective, George Stanfield, who intervened. Cobb told Stanfield he wanted the elevator operator to take him to his room, but the young man had strongly declined. The watchman started insulting Ty, who protested that, as a hotel guest, he did not deserve such treatment. Stanfield threatened Cobb, who responded that he could always take care of himself. When Ty stepped toward the elevator,

George struck him from behind on the head. Cobb turned around and immediately started fighting Stanfield. Ty pushed the house detective to the floor and punched him. George responded by sinking his fingernails into one of Cobb's eyelids.

Cobb yelled in pain, demanding his adversary release the grip on his precious eye that held immense importance, performing as an elite batter. As Stanfield dug deeper into the eye, Ty pulled a knife from his pocket and slashed the watchman across the hand. This maneuver caused George to release his hold on Cobb's face. Stanfield stumbled toward the first-floor grillroom entrance, drew a gun, and covered his antagonist. As the nightwatchman held the weapon in one hand, he walked up to Ty and smacked him numerous times with his billy club. Stanfield then asked the hotel desk clerk if he could identify his combatant. The clerk did not recognize Cobb, who returned to his room battered, bruised, scratched, and containing fingernail imprints around his eye.[72] Detroit's trainer Harry Tuthill tended to both Ty's and the nightwatchman's injuries. The bandages Tuthill wrapped around the wounds on Cobb's head remained throughout the beginning of the following day. Ty removed that dressing before he left to appear in the doubleheader versus Cleveland that afternoon at League Park.[73]

Although the Naps defeated Detroit, 4–0, in the initial tilt on September 4, Cobb kept up his torrid hitting pace, going 3-for-4 at the plate. Ty had now hit safely in 14 straight games, going 31-for-51 for a .608 average over that span of sensational batting.[74] Cleveland hurler Cy Young held Ty hitless in the twin bill's nightcap and defeated the Tigers, 4–3. Since Detroit needed to make a tight train connection for a Sunday game in St. Louis, Naps management graciously allowed Hughie Jennings's boys to share their locker room facilities. A problem arose after the second game concluded when Tigers team members berated Cleveland's players for losing all four games of a recent series against Philadelphia. Naps manager Deacon McGuire and his club thought the Tigers made these comments in jest but quickly realized their scathing remarks contained a serious tone.

When some Detroit team members accused Cleveland of deliberately playing poorly against the Athletics, trainer James "Doc" Payne threatened to toss Bill Donovan and several other Tigers outside. McGuire and Jennings utilized their utmost persuasive powers to alleviate the tension.[75] Hughie also needed to deal with the hotel issue regarding Ty Cobb. Jennings and team secretary Charles "Charlie" Schumm received credible information that police would issue a warrant for Ty's arrest over assaulting George Stanfield. To evade law enforcement constables keeping watch on special transportation taking Detroit's ballplayers to the train station, Cobb and Schumm boarded a common streetcar that whisked them to the depot. Constables never detected Ty's whereabouts.

This plan worked after Hughie failed to secure a taxicab to take Cobb to the city's outskirts so he could board the train at a different depot.[76]

On September 7, Stanfield's lawyer, J. J. Klein, secured a warrant from Justice William Brown, charging Cobb with intent to kill. Claiming injuries from the ordeal made him too weak to leave his bed, the Hotel Euclid's nightwatchman signed a sworn statement in his room at that establishment.[77] Detective Jake Mintz, from a private law enforcement agency, received the warrant and left that night for Detroit to serve Ty. An effort would then proceed for extradition back to Ohio. Friends and Tigers fans charged such despicable action as a ploy to sabotage the club's pennant chances. Detroit's players expressed disgust over Stanfield's bedridden claim. Some team members had seen George moving around nicely following the attack, including traveling to the city's downtown area, talking to friends about his encounter with baseball's supreme player. Teammates believed Stanfield played a role in a plot to keep Cobb sidelined during the pennant race's most crucial time. The nightwatchman also planned to file a lawsuit against Ty to collect $5,000 in damages for his injuries.[78]

Hughie Jennings exhibited no concern over that city's legal apparatus rightly or wrongly issuing an arrest warrant for his star player since the Tigers' manager considered it nothing more than a spectacular maneuver that did not deserve sincere consideration. Cobb fervently denied he committed any crime.

"The thing is a joke," said Cobb. "Why, I struck that fellow in Cleveland in self-defense, and only after he had hit me a wallop. And at that, I didn't give him what he deserved. The whole thing is a 'frameup' to get me out of the game for a few days. I don't believe they'll even serve the warrant. I don't see how it was ever issued, for I have broken no law."[79]

When Detective Mintz reached Detroit, he attended two conferences on the morning of September 8 with Detroit owner Frank Navin. The second of those two meetings brought about a resolution. Navin telephoned Hotel Euclid proprietor Fred Avery, the employer for George Stanfield, whose condition had markedly improved. Avery promised to handle the matter. The Tigers' magnate agreed to pay George's doctor bills, while also writing out a check to rectify the damages situation. Stanfield's lawyer, J. J. Klein, requested $500 from Frank. George and his counsel dropped the assault charge hanging over Ty as part of this agreement.[80] Although all parties reached a satisfactory outcome, this did not mean Cobb's legal problems ended. Cuyahoga County Prosecutor John Cline commissioned a grand jury in Cleveland to examine evidence related to the event and return an indictment.[81]

As the World Series between Detroit and Pittsburgh commenced, rumors abounded that an indictment and arrest appeared imminent.[82] Worried over law enforcement officials detaining him while the Tigers challenged for a championship, Ty and his wife, Charlotte "Charlie" Lombard Cobb, traveled in a roundabout manner between the two cities throughout the postseason clash.[83] To avoid Ohio, Cobb and his wife made the trip utilizing a longer railroad route, traveling from Detroit through Canada to Buffalo, and then making the trek to Pittsburgh. The decision took its toll on Ty, who appeared worn down as the World Series progressed.[84] Cobb batted .231 in the seven games, while star shortstop Honus Wagner hit .333, leading his Pirates to victory. Prosecutor Cline planned to indict Ty on October 9 after the grand jury decided to charge him. He intended to arrest Cobb if present when the Tigers' train entered Ohio on its jaunt toward Detroit after the club played Game Two of the World Series that afternoon at Forbes Field. Cline changed his mind when someone leaked that objective to the press.

On October 15, the criminal court indictment against Ty on a charge of stabbing to wound became official. Prosecutor Cline instructed Cuyahoga County Sheriff A. J. Hirstius to travel to Detroit and arrest Cobb after handling extradition proceedings.[85] Sheriff Hirstius wired his counterpart in Wayne County, Michigan, Sheriff Jeremiah Collins, explaining authorities wanted Ty back in Cleveland, before requesting he place the ballplayer under arrest.[86] A delay occurred since the requisition papers needed to conduct this apprehension edict required Ohio Governor Judson Harmon's signature. Governor Harmon happened to be touring the South for at least another week. Cobb's lawyer, former Cleveland mayor Robert E. McKisson, offered to produce the player without process on October 21, but authorities rejected this suggestion.[87] On October 20, Ty surprised A. J. Hirstius by arriving at the sheriff's office to surrender on the charge.[88]

McKisson and Frank Navin accompanied Cobb as he turned himself in to Cuyahoga County authorities. Ty appeared in Common Pleas Court that day, pleaded not guilty, and secured his release on $500 bail.[89] Judge George H. Schwan set Cobb's trial for November 22.[90] Ty's friend E. S. Burke Jr. posted the $500 bail. Before the case went to trial, Ty explained the course of events involving his encounter with George Stanfield.

> On the evening the trouble happened I took dinner with my friend, E. S. Burke Jr. After the theater, I had supper with Vaughan Glaser and Miss Fay Courteney, of his company. After that I sat and talked with Mr. Glaser and at 1:30 A.M. I left the Hollenden [Hotel] and went straight to Hotel Euclid.
>
> I do not drink except an occasional glass of beer, and do not drink while I am playing ball. I had not had a drop that evening. When I got to the Euclid, I found in my box a note to go to a room. Several members

of the Detroit team were playing cards there. I started to go to the room, which was on the second floor, and asked the elevator boy to show me the room. He asked me if it was mine, and I said it was not. The boy said he would not show me the way and we argued about it.

As he turned away I seized his coat sleeve and said: "Hold on, here; I'm a guest of the hotel, and it's your business to do what I ask you."

Then the watchman or house detective came up, and wanted to know what I was doing. I told him. An argument started between us, which ended in the watchman striking me behind the ear. We grappled and fell to the floor of the lobby. The other fellow had his fingers in my left eye, and I could not get away. I was afraid he was going to ruin my eye. I had one hand free, and finally got out my silver penknife and raked him across the back of the hand with it. Then I got loose.

I didn't stab him. I did cut my own finger so that it had to be bandaged for several days while I was playing. I didn't cut him in the shoulder, as people said I did. The knife was too dull to go through the coat he was wearing, and my own hand was cut as badly by the knife as his was.

Cobb expressed worry and appeared visibly upset over this allegation as when accused of spiking Frank Baker on purpose. In rebutting the contention that Cobb appeared intoxicated when he attacked George Stanfield, E. S. Burke Jr. declared his friend had remained perfectly sober that night and Vaughan Glaser would substantiate this fact.[91] On November 22, 1909, Ty appeared in the criminal courtroom of Judge Willis Vickery. After Cobb pleaded guilty to assault and battery, Judge Vickery rendered punishment, fining the ballplayer $100 and ordering him to pay court costs for attacking George Stanfield. Since Ty did not possess the entire $100, the judge continued the execution of judgment until he obtained the funds.[92] Had the court found Cobb guilty on the initial charge, it carried a penalty of one to fifteen years in an Ohio penitentiary.[93]

Ty Cobb continued his proficiency over American League hurlers, hitting .382 in 1910. Even today, statistical barometers split over whether Cobb or Cleveland's Nap Lajoie claimed the batting title that year. Shenanigans regarding St. Louis manager Jack O'Connor ordering his third baseman, John "Red" Corriden, to play back in a doubleheader between the Browns and Naps at Sportsman's Park on the season's final day on October 9 so Lajoie could bunt his way on base and beat Ty for the title, muddies hitting indicators.[94] Cobb dominated league hitting categories in 1911, topping the circuit in batting average (.419), runs scored (148), hits (248), doubles (47), triples (24), RBIs (127), slugging percentage (.620) and stolen bases (83). Although he secured another batting title in 1912, recording a .409 average, Ty engaged in another confrontation that brought about condemnation from the organization's top official.

On May 11, Detroit started a series versus New York at Hilltop Park. The Tigers won the first game that Saturday afternoon, 9–5. The two clubs then split the contests they played on Monday and Tuesday. Detroit secured the final game, 8–4, on Wednesday, May 15. In previous years, Cobb had experienced confrontations with teammates, opponents, a hotel detective, and a groundskeeper. As tensions became strained in this final matchup, Ty, fuming and disgusted over receiving constant heckling this entire series, took matters into his own hands and entered the stands to teach one patron a harsh lesson.

In an article covering the contest between these two squads, New York's *The World* offered how events progressed. When the Highlanders took their turn at the plate in the second inning, Cobb fumbled a single that Albert "Cozy" Dolan hit to center field. A group of fans in the left-field seats razzed Ty over his miscue. A New York club official later claimed that reputable patrons in attendance stated Cobb responded to the hecklers using obscene language. Other reliable witnesses claimed one spectator brutally roasted the Tigers' outfielder. When Detroit came in from the field to bat in the fourth inning, Ty, ballcap pulled over his eyes and wearing a fierce expression, jumped into the stands, ran up the row of seats, and landed a solid right hand on the offender's jaw. The patron clinched to avoid further punishment and prevent receiving a severe mauling.

Umpires Frederick Westervelt and Silk O'Loughlin, police officers, and security officials rushed to the scene. Police officer Tom O'Neil separated the two men and escorted the fan to the back of the grandstand. Another law enforcement official detained Cobb. As police restored order, some patrons roasted Ty while others implored officers to throw the player's antagonist out of the ballpark. In accordance with American League rules, O'Loughlin banished Cobb from the game and ordered him to the clubhouse. League president Ban Johnson happened to attend the contest and witnessed the entire scuffle. Johnson initially refused to indicate what action his office might take against Ty, but he added that he did not know of any provocation that justified ballplayers going into the stands to thrash a spectator.[95]

The man Ty Cobb attacked, Claude Lucker (sometimes erroneously referred to as Claude Lueker in newspaper articles), looked after law offices in a building that also contained former sheriff Thomas "Tom" Foley's headquarters.[96] Lucker originally hailed from Georgia, in a town near Cobb's boyhood home. A press operator by trade, Claude had lost all of one hand and most of the other a year earlier in an accident when working for a New York newspaper. While talking to reporters after the incident, Lucker stated a problem developed between him and Ty during Tuesday's game. As he had done for most Highlanders contests that season, Lucker sat behind the visitors' bench on a line with third base. When someone shouted a derisive remark at Cobb after he made a poor play, the Tigers' outfielder singled out Claude for attack and insulting comments.[97]

On the evening of May 18, Lucker called New York's *The Sun* on the telephone to utilize the print medium to tell his story. In this interview, Claude said he always kidded opposing players from his accustomed seat in the left field seats' paddock area. Lucker alleged he and Ty had previously been on good terms with one another. Claude claimed Cobb took the ribbing good-naturedly and joked back at him. For some reason during Wednesday's game, Ty acted testily dealing with such exchanges and started to walk toward where he sat when another patron shouted, "Go out and play ball, you coon." Claude told the newspaper that he never considered referring to Cobb as a "coon" due to likewise hailing from Georgia. Lucker explained that he had lost the use of one hand and three fingers from the other in an accident and could not defend himself. Injuries currently confined Claude to his home under a physician's care.[98]

The day after the incident occurred, Claude Lucker stated that Ty Cobb stood at first base when someone in the crowd shouted, "Oh, you dope!" According to Lucker, as Cobb returned to the visitors' dugout, the player turned toward him and said, "Yes, I'm dopey again and you know what made me dopey—the same thing that made me dopey yesterday."[99] On May 18, *The World* printed a story that included Claude's most detailed account of his confrontation with Ty while sharing he still belonged to the Pressmen's Union.

> I did not get up to the game until after the first inning. When the Detroits came on the field there was a good deal of "kidding" and "booing" of Cobb. I did not hear anyone make a remark that was out of the way. It all seemed good natured. With some friends I was sitting in the open stand back from third base, just where the grandstand comes up.
>
> When the Detroits were in the field in the third inning, the boys kept it up on Cobb. Still there was no harm in what was said. I had on an alpaca coat and he seemed to single me out once, for he yelled back, "Oh, go back to your waiter's job." But that did not harm. Then someone near me hollered out to Cobb, "Oh, you're dopey anyway." With that Cobb turned and replied: "Yes, I'm dopey because I was out with a member of your family last night."
>
> He followed this up with some vile talk. The crowd seemed taken aback at this, but then there was louder "booing." I suppose I joined in with the rest, but there was nothing said back at Cobb half as bad as what he said himself—and he said it first.

In the middle of the yells, a man near me called out, "Oh, go on and play ball, you half-coon." I forget just what Cobb said back at this, but he quieted down before the inning was through and the Detroits started to go back to the bench. In other games with the Detroits, I have seen Cobb, who generally gets a good deal of ragging, walk in by the stands across from third base and keep up his talk with the crowd as he went along. Wednesday after the third inning it was different. He circled around over by first base and then went to the bench of the Detroit players.

We noticed that he seemed excited and was telling the players something, and the Detroit rooters who were behind the Tigers' bench also seemed to go up in the air. Then we saw Cobb, followed by a half dozen or more Detroit players, each with a bat in his hand, start for the section of the stand where we were. Cobb ran over to just in front of where I was and vaulted over the fence. I was sitting in the third row and he made straight for me.

He let out with his fist and caught me on the forehead, over the left eye. You can see the big lump over there now. I was knocked over and then he jumped me. He spiked me in the left leg and kicked me in the side. Then he booted me behind the left ear. I saw that the Detroit players were wading into the crowd with their bats, but I did not see anybody hit. I was down and couldn't see much, anyway. Then the fuss was broke up.

While I was down and Cobb was kicking me someone in the crowd shouted: "Don't kick him. He is a cripple and has no hands!" Then I heard Cobb say: "I don't care if the [blank] has no feet!"

Claude Lucker concluded by saying Ty Cobb's attack left him bruised and covered in blood. Lucker's friends at the baseball game wanted Cobb arrested, but Claude felt this useless. The player would only pay a ten-dollar fine. Lucker hired attorney Michael N. Delagi, who planned to act the same day Claude's interview appeared in *The World*, requiring Ty to pay damages.[100] In response to Ty's dastardly attack against a paying customer at an American League ballpark, Ban Johnson suspended the player indefinitely, pending further investigation.[101] Answering Johnson's punishment and Lucker's version of events, Cobb intended to make his feelings known about the situation. Detroit's players appeared committed to standing behind their teammate until the end, engaging in an unprecedented maneuver challenging the American League president's power and authority.

As the Deadball Era evolved, **Ty Cobb** *eventually became baseball's supreme diamond performer when he joined the Detroit Tigers in 1905. After claiming two American League batting titles, Cobb left his huge imprint on the game by winning hitting's Triple Crown in 1909. Besides possessing boundless talent and relentless drive, Ty also experienced unfortunate issues because of his personality and demeanor. This led to confrontations with teammates, a spiking incident involving Philadelphia Athletics third baseman Frank Baker in 1909, and a fight with Cleveland hotel detective George Stanfield that same year. On May 15, 1912, after enduring heckling throughout a series against the New York Highlanders at Hilltop Park, Cobb entered the stands and attacked his abuser, Claude Lucker. (Courtesy of the Library of Congress).*

CHAPTER 10

Tigers Solidarity, Carl Mays, and Ban Johnson

Players Strike, a Deserter, and Baseball's Czar

Whenever challenged throughout his illustrious diamond career, Ty Cobb never yielded an inch of ground when responding to accusations, believing he diligently followed a proper course of action. Regarding his attack against Claude Lucker, Cobb believed he reacted in a justified manner. Ty offered his version of what happened in the game against the New York Highlanders at Hilltop Park on May 15, 1912. Cobb explained that Lucker started heckling him the minute this antagonistic individual arrived at the ballpark, making his voice heard when the Detroit Tigers held batting practice. The verbal barrage continued once the contest started.[1] Ty offered a full account for the benefit of newspaper reporters covering the story.

> The New York rooter who got after me Wednesday is the same man who made it unpleasant for me on other trips to that city. He has continually picked me out as the object of his insulting remarks. One day last summer I remonstrated with the man. I pointed out to him that I was out there on the field earning my livelihood and that there was no sense in his getting after me. I told him that he had better lay off. As soon as this man came into the park Wednesday he got after me. He didn't wait for the game to begin but during batting practice he started to warm up.
>
> As soon as the game began he cut loose for fair. In order to avoid the man I walked to the right side of the field toward the New York club's bench in coming off the field. Still the rooter kept up his tirade. [Detroit

shortstop Owen "Donie"] Bush asked the fellow to keep quiet, but it did no good. Finally I went to the man and told him to lay off. As soon as I spoke the man cut loose with a flow of bad language. Then I lost my temper and jumped into the stand and punched him three or four times.

I am sorry for what I did, but I simply could not help myself. I am sorry for the effect such an incident has upon the game and because of my family. A ballplayer, though, should not be expected to take everything. We have some self-respect, and human nature will not stand for everything. If a man insults another when he is walking on the street, that man is supposed to resent the insult. Of course, ballplayers are expected to exercise self-restraint and not take the law into their own hands, but—well, I'm sorry it happened.[2]

Many players from other American League teams supported Ty Cobb's action dealing with a rowdy and belligerent fan. St. Louis Browns veterans Barney Pelty, John "Jack" Powell, and George Stovall gave favorable impressions regarding Cobb's behavior. Walter Johnson and Jesse Clyde Milan of the Washington Senators believed Ty had right on his side acting in this manner.[3] Team members from New York and the Cleveland Naps also sympathized with Cobb. Harry Wolverton, a former player who witnessed the incident as the Highlanders' manager, offered his opinion.

It's part of the game for ballplayers to submit to personal abuse by spectators. It's hard to keep one's temper under such trying circumstances. Certain fans believe that because they pay to get into a ballpark they have a right to insult players and umpires.

The best way to square accounts is to pick out the tormentors and then nail them outside the grounds. If it were possible to print some of the things said to players the public would not condemn a man like Cobb for his recent assault. But as it is there is no way to show how players must bear the cowardly insults heaped upon them.[4]

Important political and religious figures in Detroit also backed Ty's necessary recourse following Claude Lucker's abusive heckling. These individuals felt the autocratic Ban Johnson overstepped his authority by suspending Cobb and should have instead issued a fine. Detroit Mayor William Barlum Thompson believed Ty was perfectly warranted in answering insulting remarks with his fists. Judge James Phelan stated Johnson should have afforded Cobb a hearing before passing judgment. Southern Michigan League president James Bowen declared he would have presented Ty with the best gold medal money could buy while not suspending him.⁵ In the nation's capital, senators and congressmen representing Georgia heartily stood by their home state's favorite son. These politicians sent the Tigers' star outfielder a telegram offering their admiration and support.

"As Georgians we commend your action in resenting an uncalled-for insult," wrote Georgia's political leaders. "We hope for your complete exoneration and speedy restoration to a place in the clean sport of baseball. We are proud of your record as a leader."⁶

Ty Cobb certainly considered strong backing from fellow diamond competitors, politicians, citizens of Georgia and Detroit, and enthusiastic baseball fans vital in his dispute with Ban Johnson. More importantly, the reaction of Cobb's teammates to Johnson's arbitrary decision quickly became the big story surrounding the Lucker incident. Following their series in New York, the Tigers traveled to Philadelphia to play the Athletics. Detroit's players squarely stood behind Ty in solidarity. Team members threatened to strike unless Johnson canceled his order indefinitely suspending Cobb. Tigers players and colleagues from other clubs, who readily admitted Ty made a mistake reacting in such a manner to Claude's taunts, insisted the American League afford every diamond artisan the same protection given any other professional performer on a public stage.

Ballplayers committed to improving safety cited that if theater-goers violated the conditions on tickets, it resulted in a threat of expulsion from the premises for breaking those provisions. They alleged that Major League Baseball organizations followed no such practice, allowing ignorant patrons to roast and insult ballplayers beyond the point of human endurance. Such a mutiny against league authority rivaled any other baseball story for its sensational nature covered by publications in recent years. Manager Hughie Jennings classified Ban's punishment as unwarranted, adding that the league president should reconsider the matter, fine Ty, or issue a definitive suspension length.⁷ Jennings further stated that his players took their stance on the grounds that Johnson unfairly mistreated Cobb and should have only penalized him monetarily for responding to an unwarranted outburst.

Hughie also pointed out that his men agreed to stand together under rules from the old Protective Association of Professional Baseball Players (established in 1900) to safeguard a fellow member from injustice. Jennings wired the American League president on May 17, asking him not to take any hasty action on the matter until the Tigers' organization presented evidence, which included numerous affidavits from people who witnessed the incident. That same day, Ty's teammates sent the following message to Johnson in Cincinnati, informing him of their ultimatum:

"To Ban Johnson: Feeling Mr. Cobb is being done an injustice by your action in suspending him, we, the undersigned, refuse to play in another game after today until such action is adjusted to our satisfaction. He was fully justified in his action, as no one could stand such personal abuse from anyone. We want him reinstated for tomorrow's game, May 18, or there will be no game. If players cannot have protection, we must protect ourselves."

All eighteen club members signed their official notification to Ban Johnson.[8] On May 17, Detroit defeated Philadelphia at Shibe Park, 6–3. The following day, Johnson issued a response to the message from the Tigers' players. Always firm in his convictions and unflappable when confronted, Ban strongly reinforced Ty Cobb's verdict.

"Cobb's suspension stands," said Johnson. "He remains on the ground, as it were, till the whole case can be thoroughly investigated and all sides of the matter heard. I wired Hugh Jennings last night from Cleveland, telling him that Cobb must stay out till every angle of the case can be reviewed. As far as I am concerned, that is all. I stand pat, and that is the last word in the matter."

Johnson added he would consider any extenuating circumstances if presented, although allegations pointed toward Cobb never requesting relief from umpires because of Claude Lucker's behavior. Devoid of such evidence coming to the forefront, Ban reasoned that Ty entered the stands without waiting for authorities to address the matter and took the law into his own hands. Johnson also vehemently declared that a strike threat by Cobb's teammates would not alter his decision.

"I will not condemn him until I get the fullest details," reiterated Johnson, "but no threats, no uproar, can budge me. Cobb's suspension stands, no matter what the players may demand, and will not be lifted till the proper time."[9]

Hughie Jennings prepared for the worst if his team decided not to participate in the contest versus the Athletics on May 18. Realizing that the American League would fine the Tigers' organization $5,000 if the game ended in a forfeit due to not fielding a team, Jennings scoured Philadelphia and Jersey City, New Jersey, hoping to procure twelve amateur diamond performers to suit up for Detroit. When discussing his players' determined resolve sticking up for Ty, Hughie told the press that the teammates' decisions to challenge an adverse atmosphere at ballparks supplied a good lesson for club owners, who should realize they must protect diamond performers from insult-hurling patrons.[10] Initial rumors related to Connie Mack's Athletics squad members following their Detroit counterparts' lead proved unfounded.[11]

The Tigers' players held a meeting at noon on May 18 at the Aldine Hotel, where they lodged, before their scheduled game that afternoon against Philadelphia. Team members unanimously decided to travel to the ballpark in full uniform and that all the regulars, including Ty Cobb, take their accustomed positions on the field. If umpires Bill Dinneen and Frederick "Bull" Perrine did not permit Cobb to play, the players planned to walk off the diamond and initiate their strike. Before conferring in the hotel's council room, team members told reporters they intended to stick together and live up to the sentiment expressed in their telegram to Ban Johnson. Detroit shortstop Donie Bush, while talking with sportswriters, touched upon the men considering a barnstorming tour that could prove quite lucrative.

"It is time the players had some rights as well as the club owners," said Bush. "We consider that we could make a lot of money by going on a trip and touring the country. We have offers from many places and we may accept one to go to Japan. Cobb has not yet signed an agreement to go on tour with us. From what he has said, however, Ty is certain to go with us."

After taking the field and holding practice for a few minutes, the umpires informed Hughie Jennings's players that Johnson's suspension of Cobb still stood. The players, reaching a quick decision, gathered up their gloves and sweaters and walked off the diamond. Fans in the right-field bleachers cheered as they left the field while Athletics team members gazed at the empty diamond, waiting to take their turn engaging in pre-game practice. When the strikers notified Jennings that Detroit refused to participate in that afternoon's contest, he ordered them to go to the dressing room and take off their uniforms.[12] Amid rumors that Hughie needed players, amateur, semi-professional, and college athletes gathered near Detroit's dugout.[13] When Jennings finally assembled his junior varsity squad, these rookies put on the spangles immediately after Tigers team members discarded them. Many of the individuals slated to make their major league debuts played for Pennsylvania's St. Joseph's College baseball team that had defeated Philadelphia in a preseason exhibition game.

Hughie promised each replacement player $50 for their afternoon's work.[14] Detroit scout and coach Deacon McGuire and Philadelphia native Joseph "Joe" Sugden, both former major leaguers, and several members of St. Joseph's squad played for the Tigers against the Athletics. Some newspapers reported that the amateur players only received $10 for receiving the opportunity of a lifetime to wear a big-league uniform.[15] Boxer William "Billy" Maharg, who hailed from the City of Brotherly Love, started at third base for Detroit. Maharg later gained fame in baseball circles by helping to orchestrate the 1919 World Series gambling scandal involving eight members of the Chicago White Sox. Philadelphia pounded the Tigers, 24–2, as hurler Aloysius "Allan" Travers pitched the entire game, allowing 26 hits and 7 walks. Around three thousand spectators attending the game became disgusted with the diamond product they witnessed and requested refunds. After Athletics representatives denied this appeal, the mob, cheering loudly and voicing their displeasure, rushed the box office before returning to their seats.[16]

Ty Cobb felt bitter over the entire ordeal and considered quitting baseball. Cobb wished no harm to employer Frank Navin, and his pride made the star outfielder reticent to becoming the object of charity.[17] Ty's teammates sat in Shibe Park's grandstand and witnessed the spectacle perpetrated by their substitutes. Although they talked amongst themselves, the Tigers' club members put no tentative plan to restart a Protective Association of Professional Baseball Players into place. Cobb believed such an entity should rise again for its own protection and to meet the current emergency. Ty also exhibited no reservations in offering his opinion regarding Ban Johnson. Cobb declared he wished Johnson had been the person who heckled him on Wednesday, before giving the league president a stinging rebuke.

> I think Johnson has treated me most unfairly. He is trying to be a Czar. He won't give the players a fair chance of fair treatment. He was there and he should have judged the incident at once instead of suspending me and waiting a long time before giving his decision.
>
> I do not feel that I should have been suspended for what I did, or even fined. The players for many years have been treated unfairly. My treatment in New York was only an instance. The league has policemen at the parks to recover the balls that fly into the audience, to protect spectators from annoyance and, in short, to protect and save everything and everybody except the players.[18]

Ty also remarked that he appreciated his teammates' support, who were standing by him in this matter.[19] Tigers squad members intended to organize two baseball nines and travel across the United States on a barnstorming tour. These individuals reasoned they did not need Ban Johnson's or the American League's protection to earn a living playing baseball. According to a telephone message Hughie Jennings received from Johnson before leaving to go to the ballpark on May 18, the league president planned to travel to Philadelphia and meet with Detroit's players at the Aldine Hotel.[20] Ban certainly did not need rogue diamond performers, under contract to play within his organization, usurping his authority and assuming they possessed rights as free agents to offer their services to the highest bidder. A Milwaukee, Wisconsin, syndicate wired Tigers team members, asking them to name their collective price to play for a club in that city. Holding an option on a franchise for the outlaw United States League, this group of magnates hoped to enter a team in that organization stocked with Detroit's ballplayers.[21]

The Tigers' and Athletics' organizations agreed to postpone their May 20 game. If all parties reached no settlement regarding Ty Cobb's suspension, the league might also reschedule games for Detroit's next series against Washington until later in the season.[22] Although Ban Johnson threatened to suspend and blacklist the strikers, the Tigers' players remained firm in their convictions. When some baseball officials suggested an impartial third party arbitrate the dispute, Johnson rejected such a notion. Within his ultimatum to Detroit's team members, Ban declared he must uphold American League authority and discipline, even if needing to propose retaliatory measures to achieve that goal. When informed of this demand, Cobb's teammates responded, "Let them go ahead." League magnates also planned to meet on May 21 and discuss a proposition where every club in the organization other than Cleveland each donated two or more players to Hughie Jennings so he could field a competitive team if reaching no agreement with the strikers.[23]

On the afternoon of May 20, Ty implored his teammates to return to the diamond the following day for their game against the Senators at National Park. That morning, Detroit owner Frank Navin arrived in Philadelphia at 9:30 and traveled directly to the hotel where Johnson stayed for a conference. The previous evening, Ban had affirmed he suspended the Tigers' players that refused to play one day earlier, prompting a team member in the Aldine Hotel corridor to say, "Well, I see we are probably blacklisted." Johnson offered that the strikers, who he never personally engaged, automatically suspended themselves due to their actions. Before Navin talked to the league president, Ban met with manager Hughie Jennings, who then remained at the hostelry, anticipating the arrival of his boss. Following his interaction with Johnson, Frank made a brief statement to reporters before trekking to the Aldine Hotel so he and Jennings could confer with Detroit's players.

"I have been in the American League for ten years and hope to be in it for ten years more," said Navin. "It is now a question whether the club owners are to run the league or the players are to run it."

During the conclave with his employees, which lasted until 1:30 P.M., Navin reiterated Johnson's refusal to budge on reinstating Cobb. Frank urged them to discontinue their strike and offered to pay any fines incurred resulting from league suspensions. When later interviewed by sportswriters, Hughie alleged Navin promised them the league would thoroughly investigate Ty's suspension if they returned to work without their star teammate. Frank then told them, "I am getting the worst of it, and I want you back in uniforms." His players expressed sorrow over the situation for their boss but told Navin they planned to see this stand through to a satisfactory conclusion. The Tigers' team members then met privately to further discuss the matter. When their conference broke up at 2 P.M., they handed Frank a document containing a compromise proposal. Since Ban did not lodge at the Aldine Hotel, Navin quickly traveled to the temporary residence, where the president was conducting league business, to share this latest proposition.[24]

Late in the afternoon on May 20, Detroit's players aborted their strike and agreed to play the next day's scheduled contest versus Washington without Ty Cobb. They cited not wanting to see Frank Navin suffer any further financial consequences because of their actions as the reason behind this decision. In the end, the players received no concessions from Ban Johnson. On the other hand, Navin promised to work tirelessly to have Cobb reinstated as quickly as possible and would handle any economic loss on their part regarding fines. Frank also agreed to find ways, as an American League club owner, to insure better protection for them on the field against unsportsmanlike conduct by spectators.[25] Johnson did agree to swiftly expedite Ty's case. Although league rules stipulated players held the responsibility for paying their own fines, Navin planned to work around that regulation through a pledge to give each man $100 to use when forking over their monetary penalty.

On May 22, Cobb formulated his official statement surrounding the Claude Lucker incident as requested by Ban. Players throughout the organization hoped the united front exhibited by their Tigers compatriots, who placed their professional careers in jeopardy, struck a blow against rowdyism, and magnates now held a deep respect for serious concerns regarding them receiving fair treatment.[26] When the two sides negotiated on May 20, hoping to reach a compromise, former major league player and lawyer David "Dave" Fultz weighed in on the controversy. Fultz, posturing to head a prospective resurrected Protective Association of Professional Baseball Players, or pseudo players' union, which became a reality later that year, criticized both Johnson and baseball's National Commission while disclosing a piece of information during an interview with a *Brooklyn Daily Eagle* reporter.

"The entire attitude of the National Commission in cases of this kind is unfair," said Fultz. "Ban Johnson showed the commission's attitude when after receiving a telegram from the Detroit players to the effect that unless Ty Cobb was reinstated they would refuse to play their scheduled game, he telegraphed orders that every player whose signature appeared on the telegram should be fined. He thus imposed the punishment even before the deed was actually committed."[27]

After reviewing all the evidence supplied through sworn statements, Ban Johnson ruled Cobb responsible for what occurred at Hilltop Park on May 15 and that he had been the first person to use vicious language before the encounter. Johnson punished Ty by suspending him for ten days and issuing a $50 fine.

Ban hoped this discipline dissuaded Cobb and others from behaving this way in the future. For those who decided to function as judge and avenger, Johnson threatened severe retribution. Detroit's team members gained something out of their one-game strike, as Ban promised to give all American League players fair protection at ballparks against patron abuse or attacks. Cobb's suspension called for Ty to be eligible once again to play on May 26.[28] Ty returned to the lineup that afternoon against Chicago at White Sox Park, going 1-for-4 and drawing two walks as the Tigers claimed a 6–2 victory.[29]

Throughout this battle of wills, Johnson weathered the storm and maintained his scope of absolute power over league affairs. At the same time, Detroit's players earned a small victory by flexing their collective bargaining power by striking. Consequently, this established an early precedent of challenging the owners' ideals regarding them existing as nothing more than property to trade, sell, or release on a whim. The die of Ban coming out on top was cast by that period's existing climate. Dealing with players entailed simplicity since they possessed minimal rights. Tangling with magnates proved another matter, as the behavior exhibited by one individual seven years after Ty Cobb's assault against Claude Lucker resulted in Johnson receiving another challenge to his authority. While Boston Red Sox hurler Carl Mays initially stood in the forefront when this incident occurred in 1919, he soon became pushed to the background as bigger fish entered the pond and attempted to chop Johnson's power at the knees.

Carl William Mays was born to parents William and Louisa Callie Land Mays on November 12, 1891, in Liberty, Kentucky. At four, Carl looked into the face of his father, a traveling Methodist minister, and remarked that upon growing up, he wanted to become a baseball player. Although not finding baseball an objectional profession, William entertained other designs and plans for the lad when he reached young adulthood.[30] The Mays family eventually settled down in Mansfield, Missouri, in Wright County.[31] Sadly, Carl's father died in 1905, leading the teenager to grow up quickly and assume responsibility, helping to put much-needed food on the family's kitchen table. Mays developed excellent throwing accuracy by killing rabbits and squirrels with rocks to supply meat so his mother, brothers, and sisters could eat.[32] To earn cash, Carl and younger brother Wesley traveled on horseback to the nearby town of Olathe, Missouri, to sell their mother's farm eggs for seven cents per dozen. One brother handled the reins while the other held the eggs.[33]

Carl Mays first gained notice as a baseball player in Mansfield and Kingfisher, Oklahoma, where the family later briefly lived. Every boy who chased a diamond dream hoped to reach the major leagues, and the youngster, whose accuracy developed so impeccably that he did not need a gun while hunting, proved no different. Naysayers from Wright County and nearby Douglas County held an opposing view. While gathering at the post office or village store, these cynics commented that a boy whose mother happened to be a widow should not waste his time with baseball.[34] In an effort to realize his aspiration to play the game, Mays entered the realm of professional baseball under unusual circumstances.

Edward Black "Ed" Johnstone discovered Carl in 1911. A former guard at the Utah State Capitol building in Salt Lake City, Johnstone gained fame as a law enforcement officer when he killed outlaw Clarence "Gunplay" Maxwell in Southern Utah two years earlier. In 1911, Ed worked as an undersheriff for Carbon County, stationed in Price, Utah. Since the town featured a baseball team, Johnstone expressed an interest in the diamond game. That June, Ed offered his services to help the Denver & Rio Grande Western Railroad deal with hobos gaining a free ride at the company's expense. Through diligent efforts, Johnstone and a group of deputies captured thirty to forty railroad tramps. Authorities took these disreputable men into custody and lined them up at the county jail for processing. Ed eventually questioned a young man, close to twenty years old, regarding his identity.

"What's your name?" Johnstone asked this hobo.

"Mays," responded the young man.

"Where ya from?" queried Ed.

"Kansas," replied Carl Mays, although he hailed from Missouri.

"What's your business?" asked Johnstone.

"Ballplayer," declared Mays. "I'm a pitcher."

A thought entered Ed Johnstone's mind. Price's baseball team had a game scheduled against Kenilworth in two days. Since Price happened to be short on pitchers, Johnstone reasoned Carl Mays could prove an adequate recruit. The lawman separated Carl from the others, who ended up jailed on vagrancy charges or received floaters for transfer to another facility. Dressed in a nice suit, Mays exhibited his pitching ability in the jail office. Johnstone immediately signed Carl and promised to pay him $125 a month to pitch for Price. In his first start, Mays limited Kenilworth to one hit as Price claimed a 2–1 victory. Carl's mound dominance led to his feats of fame garnering attention in the Northwest. Price manager Harry Good recommended Mays to owner Duff Cooley of the Union Association's Salt Lake City Skyscrapers, but he passed on the pitcher. Good then suggested to skipper John "Dad" Gimlin, of the Western Tri-State League's Boise Irrigators, that he take a chance securing Carl. Gimlin signed Mays to a Boise contract for the 1912 campaign.[35]

Mays pitched magnificently for Boise in 1912, posting a 22–9 record, supported by a 2.08 ERA. Impressed with Carl's fine work, the Pacific Coast

League's Portland Beavers drafted the young hurler. After finishing first in that organization in 1910 and 1911, Portland, managed by former major league player Walter "Walt" McCredie, came home fourth in 1912. Walter and his uncle William Wallace "Judge" McCredie also owned the club. To further Mays's development, the McCredies farmed him out to a lower minor league affiliate. The two magnates turned Carl over to Richard "Nick" Williams, manager of the Portland Colts, their feeder club in the Northwestern League.[36]

Although he had only played one professional baseball season, Mays exhibited strong resolve as a tough negotiator regarding the price for his services. When the McCredies mailed Carl a contract early in 1913, the pitcher initiated a holdout after ownership rejected his counteroffer to receive $110 per month more than Boise paid him in 1912. Mays remained in Portland for a few weeks, declaring he refused to agree to a contract unless the organization acceded to his salary demand. Carl eventually acquiesced and signed a document at the end of February to play for Nick Williams. An article in a Spokane, Washington, newspaper reported Mays received $40 a month more over his salary from last season.[37] A story in a Pendleton, Oregon, publication placed that increase at $60 per month.[38]

Walter McCredie never took the trouble to personally scout or watch Carl Mays before turning him over to Williams. Mays exhibited solid stuff working on the mound during spring training. Unfortunately, when the 1913 campaign started, wildness plagued the young hurler. Nick expressed faith and confidence in Carl, although the sturdy, blond-haired twirler lost eleven out of his first twelve games.[39] Another source placed Mays's early-season misfortune at one victory in his first ten decisions. Despite tough times, Williams remained committed to the young man, whose pitching and hitting improved as the campaign progressed. Nick ignored the cold, stark figures, clinging to intangibles while supporting Carl.

"I knew he was a pitcher," said Nick. "He was losing close games when it seemed that the only thing needed to make us all go on a batting slump was to put him into the box. I don't think we made more than two runs in two of those first ten games. Still, nothing hurt his nerve. He kept improving right along, and nobody could beat him in the last part of the season."[40]

Mays rallied like a true champion in 1913, going 10–15 for Portland with a 2.45 ERA. As the season progressed, Judge McCredie implored his nephew to add Carl and outfielder Harry Heilmann to the Portland Beavers' squad within the eligibility date to not risk exposing them to the minor league draft. Instead, Walter McCredie transferred a group of non-descript individuals to the Pacific Coast League Club. This gaffe proved consequential when current Northwestern League president and former Chicago White Sox manager and outfielder

Fielder Jones, while scouting on Detroit's behalf, arrived in Portland to look over Mays and Heilmann.[41] On September 23, John H. Farrell, secretary of the Minor League Association, conducted the Class AA draft in his Auburn, New York, office. The International League's Providence Friars drafted Carl from the Portland Colts.[42] Jones had instructed the Tigers to directly draft Harry for the major league squad, while the Providence minor league club owned by Detroit selected Carl. The Tigers paid $1,200 for Heilmann and, through the Friars, secured Mays for $750.[43]

Detroit's baseball officials believed Carl needed another year's seasoning pitching at the minor league level. For the second consecutive campaign, Mays started out poorly on the mound, leading some within Providence's management hierarchy to question whether they should retain him. Carl quickly put such fears to rest as he became one of the International League's top pitchers, finishing the season with a 24–8 record. That summer, Boston Red Sox owner Joseph Lannin purchased the Friars and their home facility, Melrose Park, to utilize Providence as a minor league affiliate for his club. Because other major league teams expressed an interest in drafting Mays from the Friars, Boston protected their rights by purchasing the hurler before August 26 and circumventing all competitors wishing to place a claim for his services.[44]

Those beyond the reaches of Organized Baseball also coveted bringing Carl Mays into the fold. On January 27, 1915, Federal League president James A. "Jim" Gilmore sent a telegram to Mays in Portland from his Chicago, Illinois, office. Gilmore sounded out Carl about playing for his organization, which had presented an alternative to the National and American leagues in 1914. The Federal League president stated in the message that if free to do business, Mays should wire him terms regarding a two-year contract. When pressed by a *Boston Daily Globe* sportswriter, Carl declined to divulge further information about ongoing negotiations before revealing he requested Boston pay him $3,600 to pitch in 1915.[45] Although some newspaper reports suggested Carl accepted the Federal League's terms, he mailed a signed contract to Red Sox offices on February 17.[46]

Boston manager William "Bill" Carrigan used Mays primarily in a relief role in 1915, as the club finished first in the American League with a 101–50 record. Carl made 38 appearances and posted a 6–5 mark supported by a 2.60 ERA. Mays finished a league high 27 games for relievers and later received credit retroactively for 7 saves. Carl did not see any action in the World Series, as Boston claimed the title by beating the Philadelphia Phillies, four games to one. During a critical game against Detroit at Fenway Park on September 16, as the two squads battled for the pennant, Mays, after entering the fray in relief of Ray Collins, established his credentials using headhunting tactics to gain an advantage over batters.

When Ty Cobb stepped up to the plate to face him in the eighth inning, Carl buzzed two beanballs near the Tigers' outfielder's head. After Mays delivered the third pitch, Cobb swung and missed, allowing his bat to fly toward the hill at him. As Ty walked out to retrieve his cudgel, he gave the hurler a blistering rebuke. Carl responded to this verbal lambasting by plunking Cobb on the elbow with his next offering. Although Detroit won the game, 6–1, Ty needed to make a mad dash for the clubhouse once the contest ended. Quickly surrounded by furious patrons, an individual hurled a bottle that struck Cobb in the shoulder. Teammates helped before police intervened just as a free-for-all seemed ready to break out.[47] Before the 1916 season started, Mays admitted during an interview with a Western newspaper that he had deliberately attempted to bean Ty, feeling throwing at Cobb's head qualified as a commendable and noble deed.[48] Unlike the previous year, Mays wasted no time reaching a salary agreement for 1916 by accepting terms before he left Boston following the World Series.[49]

Carl Mays worked as both a starter and a reliever for Bill Carrigan in 1916, posting an 18–13 record and a 2.39 ERA. The Red Sox claimed their second consecutive American League pennant and then defeated the Brooklyn Robins in the World Series, four games to one. Although Mays recorded the final out in Boston's 6–5 victory in Game One on October 7 at Braves Field, he started Game Three at Ebbets Field on October 10 and suffered the club's only loss, allowing four runs in five innings of work as Brooklyn secured the contest, 4–3. Carl achieved star status at the major league level in 1917, going 22–9 for Boston and fashioning a 1.74 ERA. During that season, players from other teams charged Mays with using the beanball to intimidate opposing batters.

Athletics outfielder Frank "Buck" Thrasher accused Carl of engaging in this tactic against him in a contest at Shibe Park on April 19. Frank dodged numerous attempts by Mays to bean him until the Red Sox' pitcher finally achieved his goal, smacking Thrasher in the head with a pitch in the eighth inning, which forced him to leave the game. New York Yankees outfielder Leo "Lee" Magee also charged Carl with trying to hurt him early in the season by headhunting. Boston manager Jack Barry declared that no truth existed surrounding the complaints that Mays and other Red Sox hurlers threw at batters' heads. He believed such accusations a conspiracy on the part of the other seven American League teams dedicated to getting his players at all costs. League president Ban Johnson, who abhorred such tactics, promised to eliminate this type of maneuver from the game. Johnson told his umpires to keep a sharp eye out for any pitcher purposely throwing at a batter's head and to banish all guilty parties.[50]

The stocky, sandy-haired, right-armed throwing Boston pitcher could be an intimidating figure due to his submarine delivery. In executing this sweeping, underhand motion, Carl Mays's right hand swung down while holding the baseball, missing the ground by inches, and shot it upward to the catcher, sending the sphere breaking sharply as it approached home plate. By utilizing this delivery, Carl's arsenal included speed, a good curveball, and an excellent change of pace. Batters struggled with his delivery because they were unaccustomed to seeing it regularly. In the summer of 1917, Mays explained to sportswriter Paul Purman that he battled managers at all levels, wishing to convert him from a submarine pitcher to a more conventional style hurler.

> Jack Barry is the only manager who did not try to break me of the underhand delivery. Even Bill Carrigan, as smart a manager as ever lived, thought I should drop the underhand and adopt the sidearm or overhand delivery. I had quite a time convincing him otherwise.
>
> In the minor leagues I was always having arguments with managers who believed the underhand delivery was to be tabooed because it was scarcely ever used.
>
> That was the best reason, to my notion, for keeping on using it. A batter is less likely to hit the kind of pitching he seldom sees than that he runs across every day.
>
> I believe many managers make mistakes in trying to tell their pitchers how to pitch. Of course, there are many faults which a manager can correct, but when it comes to changing a pitcher's whole delivery, I believe it is radically wrong. There have been many pitchers ruined by having a manager interfere with their pitching style.[51]

Carl played for his third manager in the past three years as Ed Barrow took control running Boston in 1918. Barrow came aboard because Jack Barry had joined the Naval Reserve as a yeoman in support of the Great War effort the previous July and became an active member when the 1917 campaign ended.[52] Changes had also come to the front office dynamic when Joseph Lannin sold his interest in the club in November 1916 to a consortium headed by New York Broadway producer and theater mogul Harry Frazee. The Red Sox claimed the American League pennant during the war-shortened season of 1918, posting a 75–51 record. The campaign in both major leagues ended on September 2. Ban Johnson received fierce opposition from magnates in both organizations when he suggested pushing the season's close date back thirteen days earlier.

On August 3, Johnson attended a meeting in Cleveland that included American League owners and the other two members of the National Commission who served with Ban: National League president John Heydler and Cincinnati magnate Garry Herrmann. Secretary of War Newton Baker issued an order that all ballplayers eligible for the draft must be prepared to work or fight after September 1. Johnson desired to change the final day of the regular season to August 20 so the two competing World Series squads completed their games by September 1. National League owners declared they planned to play regular season games until September 2 as originally scheduled. When Ban reached Cleveland, he found an antagonistic sentiment against his plan by a group of American League magnates.

Some owners cited that Western clubs on the circuit happened to be drawing better than ever in the East, and it would prove foolish to cancel games before Secretary Baker's date. Regarding the World Series, these baseball titans argued that few players from participating squads would immediately become eligible for the draft. Lastly, the magnates wanted to make as much money as they could during a shortened season. Johnson appeared annoyed when he discovered that the organization's owners he presided over refused to agree to his demand that league operations cease on August 20. When reporters asked Ban to explain the magnates' sentiment, he offered a curt response.

"If the club owners wish to take a chance with the government, that is their own business," responded Johnson.

Numerous owners did not appreciate Johnson's comment or attitude. They countered that it was not their intention to defy the War Department nor antagonize Secretary Baker. These magnates called Ban's statement unwarranted, accused him of botching league affairs, and declared the league president's "rule or ruin" policy would soon end. One unnamed magnate offered his feelings about Johnson's conduct.

"He has tried to close our gates several times this season, but from now on he is through spending our money," said the anonymous American League owner.[53]

Carl Mays pitched brilliantly for the pennant-winning Boston Red Sox in 1918, going 21–13, supported by a 2.21 ERA. Mays crowned off a glorious campaign by winning two games in the World Series against Chicago, allowing only two earned runs in 18 innings as Boston secured the championship over the Cubs, winning the postseason affair four games to two. Carl tossed a three-hitter in the clinching Game Six on September 11 at Fenway Park, defeating Chicago, 2–1. Following another superb moment in his baseball career, Mays remained in Boston.[54] On September 18, he consummated the beginning of a grand journey related to his personal life.[55] At noon that day, Carl married Marjorie Fredericka Madden, who hailed from Philadelphia, Pennsylvania, at the New Old South Church. Reverend W. B. Butler, the church's assistant pastor, officiated the ceremony, while friend and former Tufts College outfielder Ralph McDonald, from Burlington, Massachusetts, stood as Mays's best man.

Marjorie, a huge baseball fan and incredibly talented student at the New England Conservatory of Music for the past few years, met Carl shortly after he joined the Red Sox in 1915. Because the former Miss Madden exhibited a bright future as a vocalist and aspiring actress, her parents envisioned their daughter someday becoming an opera singer. Throughout the 1918 campaign, Mays's teammates wondered why, after removing his uniform or pitching the first game of a doubleheader at Fenway Park, the star hurler immediately left the clubhouse and headed for the grandstand. The nuptials later explained Carl's behavior over why he sat many rows behind Boston's bench with a pretty, petite young lady. Mays only revealed her identity and his wedding intentions to a few close friends.[56]

Besides baseball leading to this courtship blossoming, Carl also lived at Putnam's Hotel, a residential establishment where many Red Sox players resided during the season, accessible to the New England Conservatory of Music located within proximity. Mays always carried a picture of Marjorie sitting on Boston's dugout roof.[57] Following their wedding ceremony, the couple rushed to Trinity Place Station and boarded a Western train departing at 2 P.M. for Mansfield, where Carl owned a sizable farm. Once there, Mays planned to auction off the ranch's cattle and furnishings so he could join the Army. Two months prior, Carl had an opportunity to receive a commission within the Aviation Corps but opted to remain with Boston and help them win a pennant and a world championship.[58] Mays decided to become an Army member for another important reason.

Back in June, when Boston played a series in New York, Carl visited younger brother Franklin "Frank" Mays for a few days during his furlough from Fort Slocum in New Rochelle, New York.[59] While later en route to France, a German Navy destroyer torpedoed Frank's transport ship. The explosion caused severe injuries to Frank's right ear and left eye.[60] Angry over what occurred and possessing a burning desire to seek revenge, Carl abandoned thoughts of becoming an Aviation Corps member and joined the Army.[61]

In early November, Mays traveled to Ava, Missouri, for his medical examination.[62] Once admitted and sworn in on November 6, that branch of the military service appointed Carl to oversee a group of eighteen men as they traveled from Mansfield to St. Louis by train. Sadly, many of these soldiers never received an opportunity to serve their country. Several from this group died after becoming ill with Spanish influenza as servicemembers fighting in Europe brought back a stronger strain of the virus when they returned to the United States. Five days after Carl officially became an Army soldier, fighting nations signed the Armistice on November 11, 1918, ending the Great War.[63]

Carl Mays had volunteered for special training to help with the war effort. Once Mays arrived in St. Louis, he attended the Washington University division of the Army. Marjorie Mays joined her husband at the learning institution near the end of November.[64] Carl and 1,200 other soldiers were members of the Student Army Training Corps, taking courses at the government's expense. Although he appreciated an opportunity to receive a free education in a specific course, Mays hoped to be one of the first soldiers discharged after January 1, 1919, since the need for young men to fight in Europe no longer existed. Carl did not mind studying but hated certain duties, like an assignment as "kitchen police." While tasked with this job, Mays had just finished washing the dishes used by four hundred hungry soldiers following a dinner shift before peeling potatoes so the next group of four hundred men could eat their meal.[65]

On December 19, Carl returned to Mansfield from St. Louis after receiving his Army discharge. Mays's wife immediately traveled to Pittsburgh, Pennsylvania, to visit her sick mother, Minnie Madden.[66] When Carl left his home in March and trekked to Tampa, Florida, to participate in Boston's spring training session, Marjorie remained in Pittsburgh.[67] After only playing four seasons of major league baseball, Mays had reached the pinnacle of success in his profession. Unfortunately, the 1919 campaign tested the hurler's resolve and resilience facing adversity from the outset as the Red Sox prepared to defend their title. On March 26, while Carl trained with teammates in Tampa, a fire destroyed his elegant country home in Mansfield.[68]

Carl Mays's house, just south of town, burned with all its contents inside. Mays had spared no expense, utilizing the plans of expert architects and decorators in erecting this grand home. The dwelling included the best and most elaborate furnishings in that part of the country. The fire's origin appeared unknown, and the loss from this tragedy looked to be several thousand dollars. The residence, empty of the family members who lived there, only possessed partial insurance coverage. Marjorie Mays remained in Pennsylvania when the fire occurred, while Carl's mother and sisters had recently traveled to Kansas City, Missouri. Frank Mays and his wife, Ruby, had made a trip to visit his mother-in-law. While building a cobblestone fence along the grounds and making other improvements to the property, contractor Frank Barnes discovered the building burning, but flames had already done too much damage to save the structure.[69]

Carl suspected arson.[71] Someone had torched the house he built for his devoted mother and Mays had been involved in contentious negotiations with Red Sox management in his effort to earn a yearly salary of at least $8,000 before signing a contract.[72] Bad things continued to happen to Carl. When Boston played a four-game series at the end of May against the Athletics at Shibe Park, Mays became involved in an incident with a fan during one of the Memorial Day doubleheader contests. A patron in the crowd vociferously heckled Carl and baited the hurler into throwing a baseball at his oppressor.[73]

When the Red Sox arrived in Philadelphia on July 1 to start their next road series versus the Athletics, a constable greeted manager Ed Barrow at the train station. This detective possessed a warrant for Carl Mays's arrest on the charge of assaulting a spectator back in May. After fellow players tipped Carl off about a constable intending to take him into custody, the pitcher dodged arrest by immediately purchasing a ticket and boarding a train to New York, where he made another railroad connection and returned to Boston. Mays planned to remain there until the Red Sox returned home on July 4. The attacked fan, a noted athlete in the Philadelphia area named Byron Hayes, had sworn out a warrant for Carl's arrest after Boston departed that city in May. When Mays chucked a baseball into Shibe Park's crowd, it struck Hayes in the head, damaging his hat and leaving a bump on his noggin. Before leaving for Washington, Red Sox management reimbursed Byron for his hat.[74]

More than a month after this incident occurred, Ban Johnson became aware of the situation because of the circumstances surrounding Carl's return to Boston. The league president swiftly fined Mays $100 and suspended him until the hurler paid that penalty. Mays immediately declared he did not intend to pay the fine and would not tolerate the Boston club docking his salary while suspended. Barrow and owner Harry Frazee maintained that Carl indeed would pay the $100 and not receive his salary during the suspension. Ed also added that intervening with Johnson and explaining extenuating circumstances related to Mays throwing a baseball at Byron Hayes prevented a more severe punishment. Carl responded to the drama by stating he planned to go fishing.[75] Mays also threatened to quit the team if forced to reach into his pocket and dole out the money owed for the fine.[76] As Red Sox correspondent James C. O'Leary for the *Sporting News* pointed out, somebody paid that fine and Carl traveled with the club on their western road trip, which started in St. Louis on July 9 at Sportsman's Park.[77]

Thus far, Boston had failed miserably in their effort to repeat as league champions. When the Red Sox reached St. Louis, they occupied sixth place with a 30–34 record. Carl Mays pitched the series' first game against the Browns on July 9 and lost 3–0. This defeat dropped his record to 5–10. Carl took the mound versus Chicago on July 13 at Comiskey Park and received heavy doses of punishment in the first inning, allowing the White Sox to score four runs. Carl became distressed over some inadequate fielding by his teammates behind him that might have prevented such a brutal start to the contest.[78] Mays received another physical and mental jolt in the second frame when catcher Walter "Wally" Schang's throw to second base, attempting to cut down Eddie Collins stealing, struck the hurler in the back of his head.[79] After retiring Chicago that inning without allowing a run, Carl decided he could no longer take the strain or pressure.

When Mays reached the dugout, he did not say a word to any team members and headed straight for the clubhouse.[80] After Chicago hurler Urban "Red" Faber set down Boston in the top of the third, manager Ed Barrow sent pitcher Samuel "Sad Sam" Jones to the locker room, hoping to locate Carl.[81] Barrow wanted his messenger to tell Mays to resume his place on the mound. When Jones reached the clubhouse, he found Carl weeping and changing into his street clothes, intending to leave the ballpark.[82] Mays's behavior forced Ed to rush hurler George Dumont into the game as a replacement. When the Red Sox reached their hotel after losing to the White Sox, 14–9, they found Carl had departed the premises with his luggage.[83]

In establishing damage control, Boston's baseball organization released conflicting information regarding Mays deserting the club. Initially, the team stated that Carl traveled to Cleveland so he could rest in preparation for the Red Sox' next series against the Indians. Another report claimed Mays returned to Boston. Vagueness also existed surrounding Schang hitting Carl in the head while throwing to second base, as one story alleged a serious injury while another declared the impact did not hurt the hurler.[84] To add to the confusion, Ed Barrow announced Mays left the squad because of a family illness.[85] Sportswriter James C. O'Leary surmised a nervous breakdown might explain Carl's decision to abandon his team. O'Leary saw a note written by Mays before he left Chicago on the afternoon of July 13, which helped expose the hurler's state of mind. Although the sportswriter maintained a level of confidentiality regarding the message's discreet contents, he stated that factors other than baseball caused Carl to become despondent and discouraged.[86]

Carl Mays returned to Boston after leaving Chicago. As he exited the train, Carl told reporters he planned to quit playing baseball. On the morning of July 15, Mays also contacted Red Sox manager Ed Barrow to inform him of his intentions. People within the baseball world doubted Carl's sincerity since they felt he would struggle to walk away from a job that paid him between $8,000 and $9,000 per year.[87] Minutes after exiting the Chicago-Boston express train that brought him back to his in-season base city on the evening of July 14, Mays spoke to camped-out reporters hoping to interview the twirler.

"I'll never pitch another ball for the Red Sox," declared Mays. "I intend to fix up my affairs here tomorrow and then go on a fishing trip in upper Pennsylvania."

Carl told the press he left the club in Chicago on Sunday afternoon as quickly as he could change out of his uniform. Mays also affirmed he had decided against rejoining the squad.

> I want to say right here, and I cannot make it too strong, Ed Barrow is a gentleman and a fine fellow. But I am convinced that it will be impossible

for me to preserve my confidence in myself as a ballplayer and stay with the Red Sox as the team is now handled.

So far this year I have won five games and lost 11. I have pitched better ball than ever. But I never have known where I was at. The entire team is up in the air and things have gone from bad to worse. The team cannot win with me pitching, so I am getting out. And that is all there is to it.

I do not say that I will not play any more ball. Maybe there will be a trade or a sale of my services. I do not care where I go in that event. I have enough confidence in my ability as a pitcher to believe that I could finish over the .500 mark in wins and losses, even if I went to the Athletics [the American League's last-place club].

Don't make it appear as if I were throwing down the team. That would be putting it wrong. I believe the team ought to be up there fighting for the lead right now, but there is not a chance of this the way things are being handled.

While admitting to earning $50 a day during the baseball season, Carl Mays declared he preferred to go fishing and collect no salary rather than maintain the status quo. When asked by a reporter why the pitcher did not inform Barrow of his intention to leave the team during the game on July 13, Mays responded that such a step would have been futile since he had already reached a decision and nobody could change his mind. Carl also added that the other club shut out Boston in seven of his eleven defeats, an embellishment on his part since it only happened five times. Mays denied his action resulted from the Red Sox' organization attempting to force him to pay the $100 league fine over attacking a patron in Philadelphia on Memorial Day. The loss of their star pitcher came at a juncture where team morale sunk following numerous defeats.[88] Problems over club management had been bubbling near the surface regarding Mays and a group of Boston teammates. The organization had already shipped out some malcontents while others wanted to join that parade.[89]

Following a stopover in Boston, Carl and his wife traveled to Pennsylvania to spend some relaxing time with Marjorie's parents.[90] Red Sox baseball fans feared Mays's desertion might act as an example for other unhappy team members hoping to obtain a transfer to another club. In response to the hurler's interview, manager Ed Barrow sent a wire to a Boston sports editor offering his impression of the situation.

"A big surprise," wrote Barrow in his message. "The player gave entirely different reason for going home. He will positively not be traded or sold. Will make no further statement until I know just what player has actually said regarding the matter."[91]

Ed Barrow's words about positively not trading or selling Carl Mays rang hollow. Red Sox players and fans appeared mystified and upset when Barrow, at owner Harry Frazee's behest, started opening negotiations with other American League clubs interested in acquiring Mays. These angry individuals believed Boston's manager should suspend Carl to maintain team discipline and did not want the pitcher rewarded because he was at odds with the pilot or expressed displeasure over teammates committing errors while pitching. Some Red Sox players threatened mutiny over the report, especially since the contending New York Yankees entered the Mays sweepstakes. One scribe stated that if Ban Johnson did not take a stand against such a despicable deserter by punishing him, the league president should become a farmer and allow someone else to oversee that organization.[92]

Fans and sportswriters also expressed outrage since Barrow had displayed a lousy record regarding trades since taking control of the club. A group of fans threatened to boycott Fenway Park if management did not force Carl to rejoin the squad, while newspaper journalists criticized Ed for his failure in the player procurement department. *Boston Post* sports editor Howard G. Reynolds offered a scathing critique of Barrow's work in this sphere in an article titled "Barrow Responsible for Red Sox Downward Slide."

"When it comes to making trades it would make David Harum [a fictional character in a literary work who labored as a banker and a horse trader] groan to think Barrow was in baseball instead of horse trading," wrote Reynolds.

Other complaints about Ed's managing capabilities included his inability to develop inexperienced players, his failure to maintain discipline, and that Barrow's players exhibited no respect for him because they believed he did not understand the game any better or as well as them. Fans feared Ed dealing Mays due to his poor past performance making trades.[93] These patrons also disapproved of Carl's behavior, sanctioning a long suspension over rewarding his misconduct by allowing the pitcher to join another club.[94] On July 29, 1919, the first-place Chicago White Sox obtained an option to purchase Mays from Boston for $40,000. White Sox owner Charles Comiskey sanctioned manager Kid Gleason to offer that sum, and then raise it to a higher amount if necessary so Chicago could outbid other suitors hoping to acquire the star hurler. Unfortunately, Barrow and Harry Frazee wanted a couple of pitchers as well for Carl, and the White Sox were only willing to offer cash in any transaction. The Cleveland Indians also wished to secure the hurler but likewise appeared only inclined to exchange money for Mays.

While holding discussions with the Yankees' organization when New York arrived in town to start a series against the Red Sox on July 24, Ed Barrow insisted upon outfielder Frank "Ping" Bodie's inclusion in any deal between the two clubs. Bodie immediately announced his refusal to play for Boston if shipped there. The Yankees finally made an offer to Frazee that the Red Sox' owner found so appealing he did not even contact Comiskey to allow him to make a counterproposal. Following New York's doubleheader split with Chicago on July 30 at the Polo Grounds, owners Jacob Ruppert and Tillinghast "Til" Huston announced the club had completed a deal with Harry Frazee for Carl Mays. New York traded pitchers Robert "Bob" McGraw and Allen Russell, a player to be named later, and cash to the Red Sox for Mays.

Initial reports placed the sum of money thrown into the pot as close to $25,000.[95] Negotiations, which had been ongoing for four or five days, reached a satisfactory conclusion when Ruppert, Huston, and Frazee finalized the agreement in New York. Harry declared he planned to use the money secured in this transaction to purchase a topflight pitcher. A potential deal with Chicago stagnated since Charles Comiskey was unwilling to part with the two hurlers Frazee coveted.[96] All three players were expected to report to their new teams at once. Harry also declared his club could select one of six individuals on the Yankees' roster agreed upon as the player to be named later.[97]

As it turned out, Boston received $40,000 from New York along with Russell and McGraw, valued at $15,000. Sportswriters speculated that Yankees second baseman Derrill "Del" Pratt might be the third player in the trade. Frazee then hoped to include Pratt, another individual, and $15,000 in a pending deal for disgruntled Athletics pitcher Herbert Scott Perry.[98] Although no unknown player mentioned in this deal ever joined the Red Sox, Del became a team member on December 15, 1920, as part of a package sending hurler Waite Hoyt to New York. After not addressing the Carl Mays situation for over two weeks, American League president Ban Johnson shocked all the major participants connected to this case. From his Chicago office on July 31, Johnson announced Carl Mays's indefinite suspension for deserting Boston's team during their game in the Windy City on July 13. Ban pointed out that when Mays abandoned the club, he broke the terms of a recently signed three-year contract.[99]

An adverse reaction quickly resulted over Johnson's decision. Just as the Detroit Tigers did in 1912 supporting Ty Cobb, Yankees team members declared they might consider striking if the league president refused to allow Carl to join them on the field. These players reasoned that such punishment was not only unfair to Mays but proved a hardship on them since adding the hurler bolstered their chances in the league pennant race, resulting in earning more money as World Series participants. This action never went beyond clubhouse discussion. New York's players did not plan to issue a demand pending the outcome of a hearing held by Ban in that city on August 4.[100]

On Sunday, August 3, Johnson arrived in New York and conducted a secret meeting with Jacob Ruppert and Til Huston. The three convened that evening at the Holland House to discuss the Yankees' newest acquisition. New York's two magnates received no satisfaction during the stormy session, as Ban vehemently refused to reinstate Carl Mays. After emerging from the conference, Ruppert and Huston expressed defiance against the league czar, declaring they intended to go to court and gain an injunction stopping Johnson from interfering with their baseball franchise's affairs. The two partners believed Ban waged a personal vendetta against them and desired to wreck their property, valued at over one million dollars. Following the meeting, Johnson retired to a cellar room at the Holland House and remained sequestered, avoiding curious reporters. Ruppert eagerly offered a statement for the press detailing the partners' meeting with Ban.

> We met Mr. Johnson at the Holland House tonight (Sunday) and requested he lift the suspension on Mays. Mr. Johnson refused, claiming that five clubs in the league had requested that Mays be suspended for the balance of the season. These clubs are supposedly Detroit, Cleveland, St. Louis, Washington, and Philadelphia.
>
> We both know that two, possibly three, of the clubs Mr. Johnson states requested Mays's suspension are clubs which were negotiating for Mays's services up to the very time that New York secured him.
>
> Mr. Johnson, throwing the blame on these clubs, said he would have to consult them, and is calling a meeting of the league in New York on Tuesday next, which we refuse to attend, inasmuch as the five protesting clubs would form a majority of the meeting.
>
> We will proceed at once to protect our rights by enjoining Johnson from interfering with the club. We feel that if it was a mere matter of discipline in the case of Mays New York would be the first club to back up Mr. Johnson, but Mr. Johnson's whole action in this matter seems to have been actuated by a desire to give Mr. Frazee the worst of it and the Cleveland club the best of it. His negligence in not acting promptly has precipitated this action.

Jacob Ruppert and Til Huston felt Ban Johnson discriminated against them through this decision. The owners alleged Johnson made no protest to other clubs hoping to acquire Carl Mays and only acted once he found out New York secured the pitcher. Ruppert and Huston also declared Ban's past rulings had adversely affected their franchise. Ultimately deciding to strike on August 5 if Johnson did not reinstate Mays, the Yankees' magnates persuaded their players to refrain from this type of demonstration and allow things to proceed through the courts. Jacob and Til vowed to give Johnson a rough ride much like the defunct Federal League did through litigation when the league president's czar-like remarks substantiated that organization's anti-trust charge and cost the American League thousands of dollars.[101]

Ban Johnson offered a statement to the press, explaining his decision to finally suspend Carl Mays. After rehashing the events related to Mays abandoning the club that legally owned his rights through a contract, Johnson stated it had been incumbent for Boston to suspend the player and notify league headquarters of the situation. Ban declared the Red Sox' organization never did so, and nobody filed a report regarding the incident. In punishing Carl, Johnson said he did it through the strong response from many American League owners, prompted by a determination to preserve baseball's integrity and a keen sense of upholding the entire organization's welfare.

According to Ban, when Chicago, Cleveland, and New York opened negotiations with Boston's Ed Barrow and Harry Frazee, hoping to secure Mays, this prompted vigorous protests from the Washington, St. Louis, and Detroit clubs. The ownership groups for these three franchises felt that transferring a player to another contending club lowered baseball's standards and placed a premium on flagrant violations of team discipline. Connie Mack's Philadelphia Athletics quickly joined the three other protesting clubs. Ban claimed that after talking with Indians owner James "Jim" Dunn, Cleveland's baseball magnate agreed to stop conducting discussions with the Red Sox over Carl. Ban also declared that when engaging earlier with Tillinghast Huston about each team standing down pursuing Boston's star hurler, New York's owner agreed to do so on the condition that all his cohorts followed that directive. When Chicago declined to uphold this pledge, Huston believed the Yankees had no alternative but to act by acquiring Mays.

Johnson had also sent a telegram to Ed Barrow on July 23, asking why that organization did not act disciplining Carl.

"Please explain why the Boston club has neglected to suspend Mays," wrote Johnson. "This must be done immediately, or American League will be forced to take action."

Ban Johnson announced that since Tillinghast and Jacob Ruppert refused to attend the American League's special meeting at his suggestion, he canceled a conference, which he now deemed unnecessary. Huston declared that the league president had brought this fight upon himself and that he and Ruppert proposed to use every means possible to go after Ban and retain their rights. During an interview with a reporter, Huston revealed a bombshell, accusing Johnson of giving Cleveland's baseball organization favorable treatment because he owned a large block of stock in the club.

"The trouble is fundamental," said Huston. "We believe the president of the American League is interested in the Cleveland club. We are not going to try to attempt to prove this, but that is our belief, and we believe it is the conviction of every club owner in the American League. Until this carbuncle is removed there can be no health in our league."

Til Huston alleged that since James Dunn's consortium purchased Cleveland's baseball franchise from Charles Somers in 1916, rumors abounded that Ban possessed a large stake in the club. Somers, in deep financial trouble and facing bankruptcy at the time, needed to liquidate his interest in the team as creditors threatened to sell it at auction if they did not receive the money he owed them. Johnson found a group from Chicago to purchase the club, with the league president securing a large bulk of the stock. Responding to Ban's comment about Dunn pulling out of negotiations with the Red Sox following their discussion, Huston offered that he believed the Indians' owner called Harry Frazee long distance on the telephone about acquiring Carl Mays shortly before they closed their deal with Boston's magnate.[102]

In issuing this decree, Johnson added that he may not permit Mays to play for the remainder of the 1919 season unless objecting parties showed extenuating circumstances existed. Ban wanted to send a message to other players who felt they could disregard contractual obligations on a whim, hoping to gain free agency through a sale or a trade to another squad.[103] Johnson certainly had allies lined up in this fight. Ban could count on Connie Mack since the two had been together as league figureheads since the organization shifted from minor to major status in 1901. Jim Dunn, Washington owner Clark Griffith, and St. Louis magnate Philip "Phil" Ball supported Johnson. All three men would never have obtained their positions within the American League if not for Ban. Dunn, a contractor from Davenport, Iowa, had an office in the same Chicago building with Johnson before the league president solicited his help to save Cleveland's baseball franchise.

Phil Ball and Otto Stifel had owned the Federal League's St. Louis Terriers. When that organization folded, they stood to suffer heavy financial losses. Ban allowed them to join the American League in 1916 by purchasing Robert Hedges's stake in the St. Louis Browns. Ball had no intention of opposing his overlord. Although he had bitterly fought with Johnson on many occasions in the past, Chicago owner Charles Comiskey realized the American League could find no better leader than him at the present time. Comiskey stood by Ban when the president made his incendiary statement in Cleveland one year earlier, after American League magnates refused to follow his directive of shutting down the season on August 20. Johnson never afforded Harry Frazee a very warm welcome when he purchased the Boston Red Sox from Joseph Lannin in

1916. Lannin's failure to confer with Ban before selling his franchise miffed the league head. Exhibiting an independent spirit and quarreling with Johnson on some issues prevented Frazee from entering the good old boys club.

In the past, Jacob Ruppert and Til Huston had usually backed Ban Johnson. Tired of hemorrhaging cash through losing baseball in New York, that atmosphere morphed into a desire to extricate Johnson from his position following the Carl Mays ruling. Huston alleged Johnson only suspended Mays after Boston's owner rejected Cleveland's proposal to obtain the hurler.[104] Til and Ruppert followed through with their threat to utilize the courts to gain relief from Ban's dictatorial power. On August 6, New York's baseball club gained a temporary injunction, preventing Ban and his umpires from interfering with Carl suiting up to play for the Yankees. This edict also ordered the St. Louis and Cleveland clubs to play against Mays.[105]

New York Supreme Court Justice Robert L. Luce's decree stated that under the protection of this injunction, he permitted Mays to play versus St. Louis on August 7 at the Polo Grounds. The judge also included umpires Tommy Connolly and Clarence "Brick" Owens in this writ, whom Yankees ownership had adjoined in the suit since they currently worked a series involving Cleveland against Boston at Fenway Park. Serving Browns manager James "Jimmy" Burke with a copy of the order restrained him from refusing to take part in their game at the Polo Grounds. Justice Luce's mandate also stipulated that Ban Johnson appear in court on August 12 to show just cause why Carl could not pitch for the Yankees.[106] After New York manager Miller Huggins selected Mays to start the second game of a doubleheader that afternoon, the recently acquired pitcher tossed a complete game and defeated St. Louis, 8–2. Although he had yet to receive marching orders from Johnson, Phil Ball commented on the Yankees' owners' tactics.

"Personally I think Ruppert's action in the Mays case is decidedly detrimental to baseball and my support will be given to President Johnson," said Ball.[107]

Justice Luce based his decision on affidavits from Carl Mays, Ed Barrow, and Harry Frazee. Mays's statement offered a chronological order of events from the time he left the team in Chicago leading up to his New York trade.

"When the Boston team was in Chicago I went to Pennsylvania because of trouble in my personal affairs," said Mays in his statement. "Manager Barrow sent me a telegram in regard to my return. I telegraphed him in effect that I could pitch with my arm, but that I could not pitch with my heart and soul, which every person has got to do if he pitches winning games. I then received a telegram from Mr. Frazee requesting me to meet him in New York. I did so, and explained to him at length the reason, purely personal to myself, that had necessitated my going to Pennsylvania. He was satisfied with my explanation.

He then asked me if I desired to continue with the Boston club; that I would lose nothing by it; that my salary would be paid and that they wanted me. I stated that I did not think I could give them my best services."

Carl further stated Frazee told him he could offer the pitcher to any club in the league he preferred to join. Mays gave New York as his choice. Carl also declared he never received a notice of suspension or termination of his contract from either the Yankees' or Red Sox' organizations. Mays concluded that the business of playing baseball was his livelihood, and such a suspension, without any hearing, prevented him from earning a living. In conjunction with the court victory, Jacob Ruppert sent out notices to each of the other seven league owners, requesting they attend a meeting at the Biltmore Hotel in New York on August 11 to consider ways to oust Ban from his post and resolve the situation related to Carl.[108] Johnson immediately declared he would not attend that conference to discuss the Mays case.[109] On August 8, Phil Ball tersely responded to Ruppert's initial telegram invitation to participate in the meeting.

"Answering telegram," wrote Ball in his message, "your business sagacity and acumen in Mays case does not appeal to us. Your sportsmanship smells to heaven. We decline your invitation."

Taken aback by Ball's attitude, Jacob Ruppert replied on August 9: "Refusal not unacceptable in view of your gratuitous response to polite invitation."[110]

The entire issue involving Carl Mays had morphed into something much larger than a player deserting his team. Mays no longer functioned as a focal point in the matter. A battle between owners and a league president over who possessed the organization's true power pushed Carl's behavior to the background. A rancorous atmosphere resulted as rhetoric escalated and court proceedings grabbed headlines that newspapers should have reserved for a tight race to see who represented the American League in the 1919 World Series.

*In his rookie season with the Boston Red Sox in 1915, hurler **Carl Mays** primarily performed as a reliever for manager Bill Carrigan. Carl's career blossomed in 1917 when he posted a 22-9 record, supported by a 1.74 ERA. Although Boston claimed their third World Series title over the past four years in 1918, the club performed horribly the following season. After Carl deserted the team during a game against the Chicago White Sox at Comiskey Park on July 13, 1919, Red Sox management traded him to the New York Yankees on July 30. One day later, Ban Johnson tardily decided to suspend Mays for his original desertion, leading to a protracted court battle between the American League president and Yankees owners Til Huston and Jacob Ruppert. (Courtesy of the Library of Congress).*

CHAPTER 11

Mayhem and Tragedy in the Deadball Age

Coinciding with the Yankees' court victory, president Jacob Ruppert and vice president Til Huston called for a meeting in New York on August 11, 1919, involving all American League magnates to discuss Carl Mays's case. Before leaving for that city, Ban Johnson declared he would not attend the conference. Johnson planned to travel to New York to appear at a second hearing regarding an injunction preventing him from interfering with the Yankees allowing Mays to pitch. According to Ban, only Ruppert, Huston, Charles Comiskey, and Harry Frazee intended to show up for that unauthorized meeting since the other five American League magnates declined to attend.[1] One of those dissenting owners, the Detroit Tigers' Frank Navin, hinted that the organization's other seven clubs should boycott taking the field against New York if Carl suited up for their squad. This suggestion prompted a terse response from Huston.

"That is dangerous talk," responded Huston, "especially in view of the fact that baseball got a pretty hard bump in court recently on just such a charge. It doesn't behoove a club owner to speak of boycotting one of his fellow clubs."[2]

Both sides became firmly entrenched in bickering and posturing to protect their interests. When pressed by newspaper journalists to respond to Til Huston's allegation that Johnson controlled a large stake in the Cleveland Indians' ownership, magnate James Dunn initially appeared evasive. Dunn responded while fielding reporters' questions that they ask Ban directly about owning stock in Cleveland's baseball club.[3] James carefully selected his words when issuing a statement about the matter on August 9.

Since taking over the Cleveland baseball club in 1916, with my associates, I have been in complete control of the policies and business affairs of the club.

At the time we made the purchase we assumed certain obligations, all of which have been met when due or prior to maturity. I do not believe the people of Cleveland are very much concerned as to who holds the stock in the club, so long as I remain in complete control of the policies of the organization and continue my efforts to give Cleveland a winning club.

However, those who are asserting that B. B. Johnson is interested in the Cleveland baseball club are treading on very dangerous ground.[4]

Concerns over entering dangerous territory abounded as Dunn tiptoed around the issue. As Boston's, New York's, and Chicago's owners prepared to hold their conference on August 11, rumors flourished that discussed business might include removing Johnson or stripping him of power, forming a new league, and filing suit for dissolving the National Commission since it violated the United States' Sherman Antitrust Act, enacted in 1890 to curtail business monopolies and trusts.[5] At this meeting held at New York's Biltmore Hotel, Charles Comiskey, Harry Frazee, and Jacob Ruppert, within their capacity as three members of the American League's Board of Directors, rescinded Ban Johnson's suspension of Mays. The fourth associate on that board, James Dunn, did not attend the conference.[6] Attorneys for the Board of Directors ordered Johnson to appear before a referee on August 14 and explain his alleged connection to the Cleveland Indians while also offering a detailed account related to punishing Carl.[7]

Ban arrived in New York on August 10 for his appearance in Justice Robert L. Luce's courtroom in two days.[8] Johnson ended up waiting to have his day in court, as both the referee's hearing and the Supreme Court appearance ended up postponed until August 19.[9] Further delays prevented the public from discovering if Ban truly acted as Cleveland's majority owner, and finding out new information regarding his mindset when suspending Carl. The hearing before Referee George J. Gillespie finally commenced on September 4.[10] Attorney Charles H. Tuttle represented New York's baseball club. When Tuttle cross-examined Johnson regarding Mays's suspension, the league president admitted that he ordered that punishment two days after the Yankees acquired the hurler (although he issued the order the following day). Ban added he had notified Boston Red Sox manager Ed Barrow about the prospect of a suspension. Charles found this response unsatisfactory.

"Now, Mr. Johnson, you answer my question," replied Tuttle, waving his finger in the witness's face.

This elicited a contentious response from Johnson's counsel, Stephen C. Baldwin.

"If Mr. Tuttle threatens you, Mr. Johnson," shouted Baldwin, "you are perfectly justified in punching him in the nose."

Tuttle declared that he did not threaten Ban. After the court stenographer read the previous testimony, Referee Gillespie agreed that the Yankees' lawyer possessed no threatening intent, leading Baldwin to apologize to the court.[11] New York owners Jacob Ruppert and Tillinghast Huston attended the hearing. During the trial, their lawyer hammered the league president with one hundred questions about Carl's desertion and subsequent suspension. When Charles asked Johnson to explain why he did not send a letter of notification to Harry Frazee, baseball's czar replied it was not incumbent upon him to follow such a course while also not wanting to interfere with a baseball organization's responsibility.

Opposition from Stephen Baldwin on behalf of those he represented resulted in the quashing of an attempt by Ruppert and Huston to introduce the Cleveland baseball club's constitution. Ban testified that the Indians' franchise currently possessed $500,000 in capital and bonded indebtedness of $60,000. In 1916, when five bankers seized control of the club, Cleveland's organization owed the American League $22,000. Johnson admitted under oath that to assist in finalizing the sale, he put up $100,000 in cash and gained $50,000 in club stock, equal to the total obtained by Jim Dunn when his group purchased the franchise. Ban confessed he now held $58,000 in Cleveland stock options.[12] Johnson further added that he attended all the organization's stockholder meetings but never saw the record of what occurred at those conferences. Ban admitted appearing at these meetings to represent the interests of former league secretary Robert "Bob" McRoy, who had died in 1917. Johnson concluded by stating he held no proxy at these councils, could not remember if he ever voted, and had never seen a stock book.[13]

Upon adjourning the hearing, Referee George J. Gillespie scheduled the next installment for September 11. Besides testifying, Ban Johnson also identified telegrams and copies of letters entered as evidence he had sent out to five league club presidents, telling them not to entertain the idea of acquiring Carl Mays from Boston.[14] In his piece for the *Birmingham News* on September 5, 1919, sports columnist Henry Vance wrote that this revelation could mean Ban's downfall as the American League's top executive. Vance argued that a league president should oversee the organization's affairs in an unbiased manner. The columnist felt that since Johnson held ownership in Cleveland's franchise as a stockholder, this circumvented any appearance of impartiality when he ruled on league matters.[15]

In the winter of 1915–16, baseball looked bleak in Cleveland. A group of bankers decided owner Charles Somers should sell his holdings in the club because of financial problems. Unable to find interested parties in Cleveland to purchase the team, Ban and American League owners held a conference on the eve of spring training beginning for squads to resolve the problem. The Indians lacked the necessary funds to send players to participate in the training session. A Chicago group headed by James Dunn happened to be short by $100,000, raising the necessary $400,000 to purchase the club. White Sox magnate and current Johnson insurgent Charles Comiskey offered critical help during this emergency. Although Comiskey's fellow moguls declined to assist when Ban asked, Chicago's owner lent a helping hand.

Charles endorsed a loan for half the difference needed to place Cleveland's organization on firm financial ground and acquired stock in the club as security, in tandem with Johnson's investment to insure eight American League teams took the field when the upcoming campaign opened. Through this venture, Cleveland continued operating and possessed enough money to acquire a drawing card like Tristram "Tris" Speaker from Boston on April 9, 1916. Business boomed to a point where Comiskey quickly received repayment on his note. Charles had demanded restitution once money became available to sell his stock when originally agreeing to offer aid to the Indians' organization. Ban decided to defer reimbursement.[16]

Following his inquisition on September 4, 1919, Ban Johnson appeared in Supreme Court Justice Robert Wagner's New York courtroom the following day for Part I of the hearing regarding showing just cause for reinstating Carl Mays's suspension. Attorney Joseph Auerbach joined Charles Tuttle on the team representing Yankees ownership for this round. During the proceeding, the two lawyers referred to Johnson as an "unmolested despot." The lead attorney started off his case by showing sworn statements regarding Red Sox catcher Wally Schang hitting Mays in the head with a baseball in the game versus Chicago on July 13. Auerbach immediately minimized umpire George Hildebrand's sworn declaration stating he perceived the blow to Carl's head a glancing one, leading the lawyer to declare a beaned party the best judge of velocity and impact from a ball smacking his cranium. Readily admitting to rooting for the Yankees, Joseph hammered home the point that Mays did not commit his offense on the field.

"Did he spit tobacco juice in the eye of the umpire?" Auerbach demanded to the court. "Did he hurl a pop bottle at a spectator? He did not. He merely broke down after being struck on the head and was found later in the clubhouse crying."

Near the end of the hearing, Joseph Auerbach declared Johnson had become so isolated he commandeered a league constitution unto himself, leaving him as sole judge of its provisions and supreme administrator issuing verdicts. Auerbach also condemned Ban's practice of directing his umpires to snoop around dugouts at American League ballparks so they could listen for scandalous comments and then report back to baseball's czar. The relentless lawyer concluded by proclaiming Johnson had established a dictatorship over the organization.

"I am the Great Mogul, says Johnson," according to Mr. Auerbach. "As Mr. Johnson has a college education, I will put it in the words of Shakespeare. This man says in effect, 'I am Sir Oracle, and when I open my mouth let no dog bark.'"[17]

Auerbach and Charles Tuttle explained that Harry Frazee, sympathetic to Carl's distress over family and financial difficulties, agreed to his pitcher's request for a trade to New York. Tuttle also read the American League's constitution to Justice Wagner before maintaining the document contained nothing that allowed Ban to suspend Mays. The lawyer contended the league's Board of Directors acted as an appellate court when a club suspended a player, and Johnson held no jurisdiction in disciplinary matters.[18] After Johnson's rough morning in court ended, Martin A. Schenck, a New York Yankees' legal team member, served the league president with a subpoena and handed him a dollar bill as a mocking endeavor for defraying litigation costs.[19] The subpoena called for Ban to produce to the court copies of all letters he wrote regarding Carl's case, particularly the one to Hildebrand asking him how Boston's players felt about Mays's desertion when it happened.[20]

Meanwhile, because the wheels of justice moved slowly, Carl Mays remained active to pitch throughout the season, going 9–3 for New York, supported by a 1.65 ERA. Chicago claimed the American League pennant with an 88–52 record. Cleveland finished second, 3 ½ games behind by posting an 84–55 mark, while the Yankees came home third, 7 ½ games off the pace, at 80–59. On September 16, under their purview as Board of Directors members, Charles Comiskey, Harry Frazee, and Jacob Ruppert held an executive session where they agreed to conduct a thorough investigation regarding the American League's finances. James Dunn did not attend the conference, due to pressing business. The other two magnates present authorized Comiskey to proceed with the inquiry. The three owners also discussed gambling at league ballparks and criticized Ban Johnson for failing to supply requested information on the subject.[21]

Yankees ownership gained another victory on September 24 when Justice Robert Wagner granted their injunction prohibiting Ban from using the league's diminishing funds to defend against the suit brought by New York's baseball institution. Justice Wagner also granted Ruppert and Til Huston another application to file a supplementary complaint to restrain Johnson, and the St. Louis and Cleveland clubs, from interfering with Carl Mays.[22] On October 9, 1919, a report leaked from Chicago stated the National Commission might consider holding back paying the Yankees their World Series share for finishing in third place. Detroit owner Frank Navin protested New York receiving the money since he considered any game Mays pitched illegal because Johnson had handed down a suspension.[23]

This setback for New York proved trivial in the scheme of the bigger picture. Different learned jurists on New York's Supreme Court heard various arguments before the case finally came up for determination by Justice Wagner. On October 25, 1919, Justice Wagner issued his ruling, deciding to permanently enjoin Ban Johnson, as an individual and head of the American League, from interfering with Carl Mays in his capacity as a Yankees pitcher. The judge also cited monetary damages that New York's organization might accrue through the interference toward that franchise's property rights relevant to Mays. While weighing the rights of a player and a baseball organization, Justice Wagner reasoned Ban arbitrarily suspended Carl based on paper facts rather than conducting a thorough investigation before rendering punishment.[24] Following the court's decision to grant New York's baseball club a permanent injunction, Johnson remained uncharacteristically silent. Some baseball experts believed the league president might be quietly calculating his next move, fighting this decision.[25]

Jacob Ruppert and Til Huston gained another victory four days later when the National Commission shifted the responsibility for deciding if the Yankees received their third-place share of World Series money back to Ban. Newspapers printed the finding, signed by National League president John Heydler and chairman Garry Herrmann, stating the commission lacked jurisdiction since the American League possessed sole authority in this affair. New York's owners immediately demanded the National Commission hand over their cut of the postseason spoils.[26] At the last possible moment on December 11, Johnson filed his appeal of Justice Robert Wagner's ruling in the New York Appellate Court, Part I. Since it usually took eighteen days before a case reached the docket, and because of the Christmas holiday, the appellate court would not hear arguments until January. On December 12, Harry Frazee declared that the entire ordeal had escalated beyond Carl Mays.

"People should get it out of their heads that this fight is all over the Mays case," said Frazee. "The Mays case now is only an incident, and it only served to bring the feeling that had been engendered against Johnson in the league to the surface. As a matter of fact a rebellion against Johnson's domineering, autocratic power had been smoldering for some time."

Although five club owners sided with Ban on the Mays case, Frazee revealed some of these same magnates admitted the league president ran things to suit his own needs. Harry declared he and his counterparts wanted the club owners to operate the American League as fellow magnates did in the Senior Circuit.[27] Some National League moguls also did not like the power Johnson wielded through his insidious relationship with Garry Herrmann on the National Commission. The two constantly stood in tandem together on decisions, leading John K. Tener, when he presided over the senior organization, to officially announce his unwillingness to sit on the commission. Tener remained firm in that conviction until replaced by John Heydler in 1918.[28] Mistrust and animosity caused the warring American League factions to dig in and begin behaving like petulant little children.

On November 30, New York Supreme Court Justice Joseph E. Newburger granted a court injunction requested by Jacob Ruppert and Til Huston, preventing Ban Johnson from holding the annual American League winter meetings in Chicago on December 10. Justice Newburger required Ban and representatives from Cleveland's and St. Louis's baseball organizations to appear in court and offer testimony showing justification why this order should not become permanent.[29] On December 4, Supreme Court Justice Samuel Greenbaum conducted a hearing on the matter. As lawyers for both parties presented their cases, a sizable portion of the hearing involved the judge making decisions on technical legal points. Johnson, Ruppert, Harry Frazee, and Charles Comiskey did not attend the court proceeding. Although he put off issuing a verdict on the injunction until the following afternoon, Justice Greenbaum stated during the hearing that he felt no question existed over the Board of Directors possessing superior power above the league's president.[30]

A pending decision from Justice Greenbaum proved moot. New York's baseball organization withdrew its application for an injunction against Ban, meaning the league president could now hold the winter meetings in Chicago on December 10, as he did in the past. The three opposing members of the league's Board of Directors still planned to conduct their own conference that same morning in New York.[31] Jacob Ruppert and Til Huston cited legal points that arose as the reason for renouncing their desire to gain an injunction stopping the Chicago meeting. The two owners declared that the New York conclave still functioned as the true legal proceeding, meaning their five fellow magnates planned to participate in an unlawful gathering. Ruppert, Frazee, and Comiskey wanted to deem the Chicago conference illegal in case attendees initiated efforts to vote on selecting a new Board of Directors.[32]

On January 23, attorney Marvin W. Wynne, representing Ban Johnson, and the Yankees' legal counsel, Charles Tuttle, presented arguments in the first phase of the Appellate Division trial. Supreme Court Justice John Proctor Clarke presided over the initial hearing brought forth through Johnson appealing Justice Robert Wagner's decision regarding Carl Mays.[33] A week later, on January 30, the New York Supreme Court's Appellate Division rejected Ban's application to have the preliminary injunction set aside, pending litigation to resolve this matter. By rendering their decision, the court did not express an opinion on the controversy's merits. The legal body offered some relief by giving leave to the defendants to vacate the injunction if the plaintiffs did not quickly move the case forward to trial.[34]

With the joint session of the two major leagues in Chicago to finalize schedules for the upcoming season on the horizon, Jacob Ruppert, Harry Frazee, and Charles Comiskey filed a $500,000 lawsuit against Ban Johnson.[35] The two organizations scheduled that conference for February 10, 1920. The following day, baseball's sixteen owners planned to vote on a new National Commission chairman, since Garry Herrmann had resigned from the post.[36] Some parties suggested that Chicago federal judge Kenesaw Mountain Landis replace Herrmann.

Constantly fighting among themselves and engaging in continuous court litigation certainly did not enhance the American League's image in baseball. A compromise finally arose from a meeting involving the league's magnates that began on the night of February 10. The following morning, the owners reached an agreement related to all the fallout from the Carl Mays affair. American League secretary William "Will" Harridge announced the fruit of these negotiations to the press. The first point in Harridge's statement declared that all litigation instituted by New York's baseball organization would cease or suffer a dismissal. According to Will, the second aspect of this resolution officially reinstated Carl Mays as a Yankees team member. The third point stated organizational officials would recommend the National Commission pay New York their third-place prize money.

Lastly, this compromise established a two-man arbitration committee, including Jacob Ruppert and Washington owner Clark Griffith, to act as a reviewing board tasked with undertaking cases where a player's fine exceeded $100 or if an individual received a ten-day suspension.[37] Following the conciliation ending this round of league strife, Johnson's supporters denied rumors regarding the league president resigning. On February 11, magnates from both leagues decided against naming Herrmann's successor.[38] Although Ban remained in office, New York's, Chicago's, and Boston's owners had chiseled away at some of the baseball czar's absolute power. That foundation and granite bedrock of Johnson's strength further eroded when information about eight 1919 Chicago White Sox members having conspired to throw the World Series reached the public square. This led owners from both circuits in November 1920 to select Judge Landis as baseball's first commissioner and new absolute czar.

Johnson achieved two victories once the 1920 campaign started. On June 21, Clark Griffith announced during a league session in Chicago that the organization would reimburse Ban for all legal fees regarding court costs accrued in his prior litigation battles. Griffith happened to reside on the recently elected American League Board of Directors, including Connie Mack, Phil Ball, and Frank Navin. Rebellious owners Harry Frazee, Jacob Ruppert, and Charles Comiskey, whose fight over the Carl Mays affair did harness some of Johnson's power, offered no objection to the change.[39] Years after deserting the Boston Red Sox, Mays recollected that he acted this way through being young, impetuous, hot-tempered, discouraged, and frustrated over debt incurred by the fire that destroyed his mother's home and the cost of rebuilding the structure. Carl declared that in the summer of 1919, his entire world crumbled around him.[40]

During his moment of mental anguish, Mays ran away from a part of his life that supplied a great deal of pressure. Not to minimize what Carl felt in 1919, he did nothing more extreme than deserting his baseball club and embarking on a fishing trip. Sixteen years earlier, Pittsburgh Pirates hurler Eddie Doheny, farther along in a depreciating mental state, experiencing paranoia, physically attacked the physician and nurse tasked with helping him to regain his health. Consequently, doctors declared Doheny insane and committed him to an asylum in Danvers, Massachusetts.[41] On October 12, 1903, one day before Pittsburgh played the Boston Americans in the eighth and final game of the World Series at Huntington Avenue Baseball Grounds, Pirates manager Fred Clarke visited Ed's wife following the hurler's institutionalization.[42] Months after Doheny suffered his mental breakdown, Pirates outfielder Jimmy Sebring penned a letter to the *Pittsburgh Press*'s sports editor, which included a comment on his teammate's health.

"I have not heard how Eddie Doheny is getting along," wrote Sebring, "but I sincerely hope the poor fellow is coming out all right."[43]

In 1904, Pittsburgh traded Sebring to the Cincinnati Reds. The following season, when Cincinnati traveled to Boston for a series against the Beaneaters that started on May 13, 1905, Jimmy took advantage of an idle Sunday the following day to visit Doheny in Danvers. Sebring immediately realized the stark reality regarding this establishment housing the violently insane. While waiting to see Ed, an emergency call went out for two guards to help with a patient. When officials finally permitted Jimmy to visit his old comrade, Doheny's face lit up with intelligent eyes upon recognizing the outfielder when he entered the room.

"Hello, there, Jim; how's the folks?" greeted Doheny.

"Did you know I'd left the Pittsburgh Club and gone to Cincinnati?" Sebring asked the former hurler.

"So they ran you out of there just as they did me!" exclaimed Doheny.

Following an initial moment of sanity, the unfortunate soul quickly sunk into his inner darkness.

"They threw it into me good," growled Ed before turning to Jimmy and shouting, "and you were one of those who gave it to me, too!"

Deeply saddened over his former teammate's condition, Jimmy Sebring left the sanitarium, a tomb for the living where Eddie Doheny remained for the rest of his life.[44] Could alleged ostracization from Doheny's New York teammates while pitching for the Giants have contributed to him developing a paranoid state of mind? Although this is a question better left to mental health professionals, it deserves reflection while searching for the reasons behind Ed's later behavior. Seeking answers also holds true when pondering motives that drove pitcher Win Mercer to commit suicide earlier in 1903. Win's mother, Maggie Mercer, family members, and others from East Liverpool, Ohio, believed somebody murdered him.[45] Friends refused to comprehend that any potential motivation offered could cause Mercer to kill himself. Such sentiment from those who knew the pitcher appeared plausible.

Instead, could the cumulative stress and pressure of getting married shortly, gambling issues, problems with women drawn to his alluring beauty, and health concerns because his brother suffered from tuberculosis collectively have pushed Win to commit suicide? Washington's baseball fans adored Mercer, while female patrons attended games on Ladies' Day to catch a glimpse of the handsome hurler. When placed on a pedestal, the desire to maintain the fragile façade of a good-boy-next-door persona certainly could cause extreme anxiety. Senators baseball owners and brothers George and Earl Wagner admired Win so much and appreciated his work for the club that they always refused to entertain trade offers from other teams for their star diamond performer.[46]

Following the 1906 campaign's conclusion, Cleveland Naps hurler Addie Joss worked in the off-season as sports editor for the *Toledo Times-Bee*.[47] In February 1907, Joss paid tribute to Win Mercer in a column. Addie praised Mercer's uncanny control and ability as a stellar pitcher while also bestowing accolades on him for his work as a fine fielder, a corking hitter, and a speedster running the bases. Joss then shared a story that exhibited how much the Wagner brothers appreciated having Win on their club.

> While at his best, when a member of the Washington team during the regime of the Wagner brothers, he was the matinee idol of the city, and to show the high esteem in which he was held by his employers the following from one of the Wagner's is quoted: "I will sell anything I have with the exception of my family or Mercer." Off the field Mercer's conduct was

second only to his ability to be a thorough gentleman in every sense of the word.

When the grim reaper took "Win" Mercer into his fold he took with him one of baseball's most precious gems.[48]

Four years after Win Mercer committed suicide, the baseball world mourned once again over the death of popular Boston Americans outfielder Chick Stahl, by his own hands through drinking carbolic acid. Pressure and stress over managing Boston in 1907 appeared to be the main reason behind Stahl's decision to end his life, although he had talked of committing suicide as a young man years earlier while breaking into baseball playing in his hometown of Fort Wayne, Indiana. Did things unrelated to baseball influence Chick's decision? After Stahl died, *Boston Post* sports editor Frederic P. O'Connell wrote that domestic problems may have contributed to Chick killing himself, and many people knew the true cause. Unfortunately, O'Connell did not receive an opportunity to elaborate on this point in future articles.[49]

While traveling with the Americans as they held spring training in 1907, rainy weather at West Baden Springs, Indiana, led Frederic to contract rheumatism from getting his feet wet. The affliction caused the need to use crutches that same night. While doctors treated the twenty-six-year-old O'Connell for rheumatism, the journalist caught pneumonia. When Chick Stahl committed suicide, the shock caused Frederic's immune system to weaken, and typhoid fever developed.[50] O'Connell died in West Baden Springs on April 21, 1907.[51] Although Frederic's secret regarding Stahl went to the grave with him, baseball historian and author Glenn Stout considered the domestic trouble O'Connell spoke about might have occurred due to a rumor that a woman claiming to be pregnant because of a recent dalliance with the ballplayer demanded from Chick financial support for her child and a marriage pledge.[52] If true, this unfaithfulness could have led to marital problems between a womanizing Stahl and his wife, Julia.[53]

Years before Stout offered his opinion, baseball historian Harold Seymour identified this blackmailer as residing in Chicago. In his book about Boston baseball before Babe Ruth, author Donald Hubbard contended that no evidence existed in newspaper articles to corroborate this theory, leading him to ponder an interesting question. If true, why did this pregnant woman not file a claim against Chick Stahl's estate after he committed suicide?[54] On June 13, 1907, news leaked from Buffalo, New York, that Stahl's former teammate and best friend Jimmy Collins, now a third baseman for the Philadelphia Athletics, had secretly wed six months earlier. This revelation occurred when Jimmy and his bride, Boston native Sadie Murphy Collins, visited Buffalo to attend his sister's wedding.[55] Sadie happened to be good friends with Chick's widow, Julia Harmon Stahl.[56]

Sadly, as mystery prevailed surrounding Stahl's demise, the tragic tale did not end with his death. Months after the outfielder committed suicide, the Americans' baseball organization held "Chick Stahl Day" at Huntington Avenue Baseball Grounds. The club turned over a decent amount of money raised from this benefit game to Julia Stahl, who had returned to her Roxbury home and remained out of the public limelight.[57] In the fall of 1908, Julia took a trip with her father, John Harmon, to visit Great Britain and France.[58] They also spent some time in Ireland. Shortly after returning from this vacation, Mrs. Stahl left her home on November 15 to go out for the day.[59] Relatives who shared the residence with Julia later stated the young lady did not tell them her destination.[60]

Family members affirmed that she appeared in good spirits and declared that the young woman had left the home wearing several diamond rings worth more than $2,000. One of the rings, belonging to Julia's husband before they wed, held a $1,500 value. She also carried an engagement ring and another finger ornament containing diamonds originally belonging to a pair of Chick's cufflinks.[61] That night, two male teenagers discovered a dead woman's body in the doorway of a tenement house in South Boston. These two young men, sixteen-year-old Michael Quinn and his friend, eighteen-year-old John O'Toole, found the female lying on the floor, her head resting on the stairway's bottom step, with a coat, hat, and muff draped over the banister. The two lads sent a young man named John Joy to get assistance from Councilman John D. McGivern of Ward 16 in nearby Andrew Square. When McGivern arrived on the scene, immediately realizing the woman had expired, he advised the teenagers to notify police.

Law enforcement officials identified the female as around thirty-two years old, five feet, four inches tall, and weighing about 140 pounds. Stylishly dressed, the deceased wore a lavender skirt, white-lace waist, a large silk-covered lavender hat with three ostrich plumes, a fawn-colored underskirt, and black shoes and stockings. She also had on a silk-lined, three-quarter length mink coat marked Brown, Thomas, Co., Dublin, and a mink muff. The woman possessed a wedding ring on her finger and a silver chain around the neck. Her pocketbook contained a one-dollar bill and a fifty-cent piece, along with $1.25 in loose change.[62] Immigrants from Poland populated that neighborhood, located in a poorer section of town.[63] Three Polish families lived at this three-story tenement located on Ellery Terrace. While waiting for the undertaker's wagon to take the body to the Boston City Hospital morgue, five young men viewing the deceased woman agreed, recognizing her as Chick Stahl's widow. The following morning, Frank Fay, a Harmon family friend, positively identified the body at the morgue as Julia Stahl.

When questioned by police, the group of teenagers who discovered Julia's body stated it had been in the building's hallway for less than fifteen minutes. The lads said they witnessed a young man walking with Mrs. Stahl along Southampton Street from Andrew Square. Michael Quinn told police officers that while standing with a companion at the corner of Southampton Street and Dorchester Avenue, near Andrew Square, he witnessed a woman leaning against a nearby brick building. A man then approached Julia and spoke to her before the two started walking together on Southampton Street and then turned down Ellery Street. Quinn and his companion followed the couple. The woman and her escort then entered the dark, secluded area known as Ellery Terrace, which abruptly ended with a fence over the Midland Division of the New York, New Haven & Hartford Railroad, and walked into a building.

After waiting for about ten minutes, Michael and his friend, John O'Toole, opened the house's door, which struck Mrs. Stahl's limp body lying on the hallway entrance's floor.[64] The dark corridor lacked lighting, no evidence existed of anybody striking a match, and Julia's companion had disappeared. Without Quinn or O'Toole seeing him, the gentleman's only means of escape would have required climbing the fence over the railroad tracks. Division 6 of South Boston's Police Department investigated the case in earnest on November 16. Although Sergeant Thomas Keane, one of the officers probing Mrs. Stahl's death, believed Michael Quinn's friend, John O'Toole, gave him a straightforward and honest eyewitness statement, he questioned some of the teenager's account. Regarding Julia standing on the corner at the time O'Toole and Quinn alleged, Sergeant Keane would have noticed the victim due to the stylish clothing she wore, including a mink coat and the ostrich plumes in her hat, since he happened to be standing on the opposite corner.

While canvassing Andrew Square on the morning of November 16, hoping to discover Mrs. Stahl's male companion's identity, police officers found no individuals from that area claiming to know her. Clerks employed at three drugstores in that vicinity stated no woman fitting Julia's description had visited their establishments the previous night. This information led police to believe Mrs. Stahl had traveled on foot in the opposite direction, over Southampton Street from Roxbury.[65] Law enforcement also interviewed friend Abbie Foley in her home and found she had accompanied Julia leaving the deceased woman's residence the previous afternoon.[66] Police anxiously awaited the medical examiner's report, scheduled for 10 A.M. on November 16.[67] Upon completing the autopsy, medical examiner William G. MacDonald concluded Julia Stahl died from natural causes and that no marks existed on the body suggesting foul play.[68]

However, MacDonald did not issue a final report, pending the results from sending Julia's vital organs to forensic experts at Harvard Medical School. The medical examiner based this on police information that someone might have drugged the woman, hoping to commit a robbery. Apparently, a male followed Mrs. Stahl after she exited a drinking establishment on Eliot Street. The man then offered Julia alcohol, allegedly laced with a drug intended to render the young woman powerless to prevent him from stealing her valuables.[69] This angle appeared logical since, in his findings, MacDonald cited exhaustion from drugs and alcohol, coinciding with natural causes.[70]

Mrs. Stahl's relatives believed an individual murdered her, with robbery as a motive.[71] Julia's brother-in-law declared she never left the house without wearing valuable jewelry Chick Stahl gave her when they married. A robbery motive certainly eliminated the suicide theory police considered through a group of Mrs. Stahl's friends confiding she never fully recovered from the shock of Chick's tragic death.[72] Some people, including John Harmon, suspected his daughter met a violent death at someone's hands. According to Harmon, black and blue marks on Mrs. Stahl's throat indicated strangulation, while her disheveled clothing suggested a criminal searched the body for valuables.

> Julia was murdered for her jewels. Nobody can make me believe that my daughter committed suicide or died of heart disease. What more evidence do the police need? Are not the marks of violence on her throat and the fact that she was robbed conclusive? She left here laughing and in fine spirits at 2 o'clock Sunday. We know she spent the afternoon calling on friends and at 7 P.M. left the house of an intimate acquaintance.
>
> Where she was after 7 P.M. we do not know. But my daughter has been foully slain. I'll never rest until I clear up this terrible mystery—for her good name and ours.
>
> Julia was not keeping company with any man, as a morning paper stated. She was not thinking of marrying again.[73]

Chick Stahl's brother Perry, stated his family found out about Julia's death through press dispatches rather than her relatives. He said his sister-in-law had received a letter from Julia about a week ago, talking about returning from the trip abroad and feeling in good health and spirits despite gaining weight during her travels. Upon hearing the story about Julia's death, Chick's family dismissed notions of foul play, believing a heart problem arising from becoming "fleshy" appeared plausible. Perry stated that since his brother's death, Julia did not frequently correspond with the family. Regarding a theft involving jewelry, Perry Stahl said Julia could not wear one of the diamond rings previously belonging to Chick, valued between $700 and $800, unless she had it remounted because it would prove too bulky for a woman to put on her finger.[74]

On November 18, 1908, the *Boston Daily Globe* reported South Boston police from Station 6 held four people in connection with Julia Stahl's death three days earlier. Officers arrested two individuals, the untruthful Michael Quinn (now identified as eighteen years old by that newspaper) and John O'Toole. Following further questioning requested by Captain Forrest Hall of Division 6, the pair admitted they spent three hours with Julia that night, along with two other men, before she died at the tenement building on Ellery Terrace. Sergeant Thomas Keane, Sergeant James P. Smith, and special officer John Hughes arrested the other two accomplices at midnight on November 18.[75] Law enforcement had brought Quinn and O'Toole in for more questioning on the morning of November 17. These two teens appeared in court for arraignment, along with thirty-one-year-old James (Joseph) M. McSweeney and twenty-seven-year-old John F. Cook, charged with larceny of rings and other jewelry belonging to Mrs. Stahl.

Each of the four defendants effectively told police the same story when questioned about what happened regarding Julia on the night of November 15. They met her at 8 P.M. near Andrew Square and started walking on Southampton Street until reaching a bridge on the roadway. All five then traversed under the bridge when McSweeney and Cook pulled out bottles of whiskey, which everyone consumed, including Mrs. Stahl. The accused men stated that, later in the evening, Julia appeared helpless and unable to walk. The four males needed to drag Mrs. Stahl into the doorway of the building located on Ellery Terrace. They intended to leave her there until they secured help, but she died at 10:20 P.M. before summoning an individual to assist. Each of the four defendants claimed Julia possessed neither rings nor other jewelry when they met her, and they denied stealing anything from the young woman.[76] On the same day these four suspects made their court appearance, Reverend Dennis J. O'Farrell, pastor at Saint Francis de Sales Church, officiated Mrs. Stahl's heavily attended funeral mass at 9 A.M.[77]

Family friends cleared up the mystery surrounding $3,000 worth of jewelry allegedly stolen from Julia Stahl upon finding the gems in a bureau drawer at her father's home.[78] This discovery occurred three days after her funeral.[79] Out on bail since their arraignment, Michael Quinn, John O'Toole, James McSweeney, and John Cook appeared in court before Judge Joseph D. Fallon on November 24. After Officer John Hughes told Judge Fallon police desired to drop larceny charges since a family member had found Julia's missing jewels, the magistrate talked with the males before exonerating and discharging them.[80] When originally discussing the arrest of these four individuals, *The Tribune*, a newspaper in Hicksville, Ohio, twenty-five miles from Fort Wayne, stated Mrs. Stahl had gone on a drunk with these sports. The publication claimed they took Julia to different rough joints and then subjected her to treatment likely to shame a brute. The newspaper maintained some people from Fort Wayne offered an opinion that the shock of having such a female brute for a wife caused Chick Stahl to commit suicide.[81]

While covering Mrs. Stahl's death, the *Buffalo Evening Times* revealed a nugget of information. In their article from November 16, 1908, the publication exposed something about Hattie Burnett, the young woman Chick previously alleged he accepted responsibility for as her guardian. The *Buffalo Evening Times* reported Stahl had cultivated a relationship with Burnett, and the two became engaged. When Miss Burnett later learned Chick also secured an engagement to Julia Harmon, she attempted to harm herself.[82] Two days after Stahl committed suicide on March 27, 1907, the *Fort Wayne-Journal Gazette* affirmed that domestic difficulties did not influence the player to end his life. On the evening of March 28, Mary Schneider, wife of Fort Wayne cigar manufacturer Frederick "Fred" Schneider, stated the couple seemed entirely devoted to each other while attending a party at their home five weeks earlier. Mrs. Schneider declared that after witnessing Chick and Julia together, she could not conceive of two happier people at that moment.

"I never saw a man and wife more devoted to each other than were Mr. and Mrs. Stahl," said Mary Schneider after learning Chick killed himself.[83]

Chick Stahl's and Win Mercer's suicides, Ed Delahanty's accidental death, and Eddie Doheny's mental breakdown stand out as some of the most prominent tragic moments during the Deadball Era. While these sad misfortunes profoundly affected other people and events connected to baseball, individuals engaging in scandalous behavior followed a similar path affecting the game. Madcap Philadelphia Athletics hurler Rube Waddell certainly riveted fans with his natural diamond ability and crazy antics throughout the first decade of the twentieth century. Regarding sinister intent on his part in 1905, two questions arise. Did Rube injure his arm tripping over a valise at a train station in Providence, Rhode Island, while attempting to grab teammate Andy Coakley's straw hat? Or, had New York gamblers paid off Waddell not to appear in a World Series matchup against the Giants, leading the pitcher to fake his injury? Different events in 1906 helped substantiate considering either scenario.

On September 29, 1920, as people discussed the scandal surrounding eight Chicago White Sox players conspiring to throw the 1919 World Series, former Philadelphia sportswriter and Phillies owner Horace Fogel declared gamblers had gotten to Rube in 1905. Fogel alleged Tammany Hall politician and bettor Little Tim Sullivan offered Waddell a generous sum of money not to participate in the 1905 World Series against New York. According to Fogel, despite Organized Baseball possessing evidence of this indiscretion, they permitted Rube to remain with the Athletics.[84] News shortly after the 1906 baseball campaign opened offered further proof to individuals at that time supporting a theory of New York gamblers compromising Waddell because he needed the money.

On May 10, 1906, Philadelphia's desertion court decreed Rube must give his estranged wife, May Waddell, half his salary for playing baseball that season. Waddell produced a copy of his contract, proving Philadelphia paid him $1,200 to pitch for their club in 1906. Rube appeared melancholy after the legal proceeding, not due to losing the money but because May trampled on his tender and trusting nature. Waddell also claimed he had saved $1,200 in 1905 to tide the couple over for the winter. Rube alleged his wife, responsible for holding the bundle of cash, took all the money when the baseball campaign closed and headed to Peabody, Massachusetts, leaving him with nothing. Although he felt betrayed, Waddell still held deep feelings for his spouse.

"Say," sighed Rube as he lit a cigarette while speaking to reporters after the hearing. "If I didn't love her so much I would almost wish she would jump to the outlaw league."[85]

Throughout his life, Rube Waddell never considered his long-term financial security, although sinking into dire monetary shortfalls did cause people to make bad decisions if a proposition guaranteed a big payday. However, while this court decision showed Waddell might have welcomed cash from any source, other incidents in 1906 indicated the pitcher was just as likely to engage in foolish stunts, displaying no regard for his health or well-being. As the team traveled by train through New Jersey for an early May series versus New York, Rube decided to consume peanuts while passing the time. Inexplicably, Waddell ate three quarts of peanuts, forgetting to remove the shells. When the locomotive reached a ferryboat and the squad waited for the ship to take them across the water on their journey, Rube became ill, his face turning dill-pickle green as he doubled over with stomach cramps while sitting on his suitcase.

Athletics catcher Michael "Doc" Powers, a licensed physician, suggested a few simple remedies to Waddell to help alleviate his pain. None worked, as the stricken athlete played an invalid role until the club reached their New York hotel. Upon coming across a group of actors in the lobby, Rube became fascinated when one of the performers related a story of recently losing $6,000 worth of diamonds in the San Francisco earthquake and fire. The abject shock over hearing the tale caused Waddell to forget about the ossified peanuts raging within his system.[86] On July 30, 1906, while gallantly helping fight a fire in Philadelphia, Rube suffered another mishap. That evening, Waddell assisted a company of National Guard soldiers from the Sixth Regiment, leading horses and pulling wagons out of a burning stable. Y. W. Ralph & Co. owned the stable housing one hundred horses.

Although the blaze destroyed several wagons, Rube and the soldiers saved every horse. Waddell happened to be in the neighborhood at the time and naturally followed the sound of fire bells. When he arrived on the scene, Rube shouted to the guardsmen, "Come on, comrades," as they disregarded the danger perpetrated by flames and thick smoke and bravely entered the burning structure. Waddell also helped a group of firefighters struggling to hook up a hose. A moment after successfully securing the firehose, a stream of water burst forth, striking Rube on the chest and face. Following a brief rest and a change into dry clothes, the hero continued saving the day.[87]

In December 1907, while Athletics owner Ben Shibe attended the American League's winter meetings, some people suggested Rube Waddell belonged in a padded cell rather than a baseball uniform. Shibe, talking at great length about his star southpaw twirler, defended Rube.

"He doesn't need any cell," said Ben, "he is as cunning a man as ever lived. He's erratic, yes. He's just a great big boy with the body of a man. And he's a bright boy, at that."

Shibe offered that on three previous occasions, manager Connie Mack told him he had tired of Waddell's antics and no longer wanted to deal with the eccentric hurler. In each instance, Ben convinced Mack to allow Rube's return to the squad. Shibe, who stated Waddell referred to him as "Uncle Ben," shared one of those occurrences. Connie had announced that he parted ways with Rube for good because the pitcher went fishing and did not return in time to join his teammates to travel with them to New York. After receiving a call from Waddell at the train station, Ben embarked to meet him there. When Shibe arrived, he witnessed Rube sitting on the depot's steps, crying, as his wife wiped away those tears with her handkerchief. As Waddell sobbed, stating he wanted to square things with Mack, Ben informed him that Philadelphia's manager wanted nothing to do with the pitcher.

Rube continued crying, pleading his case. Shibe finally asked Waddell if he promised to be a good boy, leading the hurler to respond, "Yes, Uncle, honest." Ben purchased a railroad ticket for Rube and shipped him to Connie. When he arrived in New York, the reformed pitcher shut out the Highlanders.[88] This lovefest between Waddell and Philadelphia's baseball organization finally ended on February 7, 1908, when Connie Mack sold Rube to the St. Louis Browns. After finalizing the transaction with Browns manager James "Jimmy" McAleer, Mack wired Waddell, who currently resided down South, telling him to report to St. Louis's club. Upon making the announcement, reporters questioned Connie over the reason for dealing Rube.

"Simply for the good of the Athletics as a team," replied Mack. "I think the team will play better without him."

Although he still considered Waddell a winning pitcher, Mack moved the hurler for the entire team's benefit since friction existed in the past. Connie did not reveal how much McAleer paid to acquire Rube, but he stated that the price fell well below market value considering his reputation as a pitcher and a ballpark drawing card.[89] Fans and sportswriters reasoned Mack sold Waddell because his career had started a downward slide and he needed to work out a deal while the hurler still held some value. In the summer of 1912, former Athletics shortstop Montford "Monte" Cross shared a story offering the true reason behind Rube's exit from Philadelphia.

> During the fall prior to Waddell's sale by Mack, we were out on a barnstorming trip under the leadership of [Philadelphia first baseman and captain] Harry Davis. The Rube was in the crowd. It was customary for Davis to give Rube $2 each night with which to buy a little false courage. Well, Waddell became so boisterous that Davis decided to cut off this allowance and give him his share of the proceeds in bulk at the close of the trip. He told the Rube about the scheme and George said it would be O. K. with him.
>
> One night, though, Waddell reported at the hotel, tanked to the ears, and demanded two iron men [two dollars]. Davis refused. Then Rube began to abuse Davis and everybody else on the club. He used vile language and when the hotel proprietor interfered, Rube tossed him over the counter. That was the climax.
>
> [Athletics outfielder] Topsy Hartsel spoke up and said he would refuse to continue on a trip with such a man as Waddell. All the other players chimed in with the same threat. So Davis called a meeting of the players and we proportioned off Waddell's share of the receipts, paid his bills and told him to vanish. That ended Waddell as a member of the Athletics. The players swore they never again would associate with him and the next spring seven regulars demanded that Waddell be fired off the club. The seven stood solid and refused to sign unless Mack got rid of the Rube. So Connie shipped him to St. Louis.[90]

Horace Fogel later declared Organized Baseball possessed evidence that Rube Waddell had accepted money from gamblers in 1905 and did nothing about it.[91] In the end, internal justice by his teammates, through threatening to strike, brought about Rube's exodus from the City of Brotherly Love in 1908. Although Waddell and Connie Mack parted ways, the Athletics' manager helped the old hurler in 1910. On February 10, St. Louis Circuit Court Judge C. B. Allen granted Rube a divorce from his wife, May, which had been pending for a year. Waddell accused his wife, who did not contest the divorce request, of nagging and harassing him. Although May Waddell did not appear at the hearing, lawyer George E. Mix represented her interests, which included a still unsettled abandonment charge. Mack offered a deposition to the court, testifying to Rube's general character and May's temper.[92]

Besides accusing Waddell in 1920 of conspiring with gamblers fifteen years earlier, Fogel also levied other charges against New York bettors attempting to bribe Philadelphia Phillies team members in 1908, hoping to entice them to offer a substandard effort in two late-season, home-and-home series versus the Giants.[93] Horace's comments in 1920 corroborated reports from December 1908 that the gambling apparatus had approached Phillies players about laying down or not playing in those contests against New York.[94] Coinciding with this gambit, Giants team physician, Dr. Joseph M. Creamer, attempted to bribe umpires Bill Klem and Jim Johnstone to give New York favorable calls in the playoff game against the Chicago Cubs on October 8, 1908. This involvement led to his banishment from admission to all major league ballparks.[95]

Giants owner John T. Brush blamed team secretary Fred Knowles for hiring Dr. Creamer. Regarding the doctor bribing two National League umpires, Knowles knew nothing about this fraud and intended no harm to the organization when placing Joseph on the payroll. This did not matter to Brush since Fred shared a close friendship with the bombastic Andrew Freedman. In his February 5, 1910, column, New York sportswriter Joe Vila discussed false rumors about John planning to retire as team president, with Knowles succeeding him in that position. According to Vila, upon hearing this fabricated information about his baseball demise, Brush rushed to club headquarters, appearing in excellent health. John immediately announced he had given Fred a leave of absence due to a nervous breakdown and appointed William M. Gray, prominent within the theater apparatus, to succeed him as the organization's secretary. Sources claimed the move on Brush's part to sever ties with Knowles was permanent, while manager John McGraw had experienced a recent disagreement with the former employee.

This decision to release Fred Knowles was a small phase of John T. Brush's grand plan. In 1902, Andrew Freedman closed a deal with Brush, selling stock in the New York baseball club, which elevated John to the organization's presidency. At the time, Brush purchased 30 percent of the 65 percent of stock Freedman controlled. Although many believed Andrew no longer enjoyed any connection to the club, he lurked in the shadows, earning the same $10,000 per year salary as John, agreed upon by these two largest shareholders. Unbeknownst to Freedman, Brush started purchasing minority stakeholders' stock over several years when an opportunity presented itself, including a $20,000 option owned by Bert Dosher, who had secured it from former Chicago Colts player Cap Anson.

In 1909, John brokered a deal acquiring minority club stock that gave him supreme control of the organization, leading Brush to immediately eliminate Andrew's yearly salary. Freedman only discovered his partner's calculating maneuvers when he agreed to sell a perceived controlling interest in the Giants' club to a wealthy Tammany Hall man willing to pay any price. While the buyer mulled over this offer, people knowing the secret behind who held a substantial portion of the team stock alerted that rich individual, leading him to conduct a secret investigation. The potential purchaser pulled out of the deal since Andrew could not fulfill his promise. Joe Vila declared John fired Freedman confidant Fred Knowles to show people Andrew no longer held any power within the organization. Brush declared he had not seen Freedman for a year and planned to direct New York's baseball affairs for the remainder of his life.[96]

Individuals other than Dr. Joseph Creamer and New York's gambling underworld perpetrated a baseball scandal in 1908. The foul stench of potential corruption engulfed the championship Chicago Cubs organization, related to the World Series. On November 11, 1908, baseball's National Commission held an inquiry on the charge that Cubs management had worked with scalpers to sell tickets for the World Series against the Detroit Tigers.[97] Over the next few weeks, this body heard testimony about gross irregularities regarding how Chicago's front office oversaw distributing tickets for the big event. One scalper offered a sworn statement claiming the club sold tickets directly to him. Hundreds of fans had stood in long lines for hours, hoping to purchase duckets when they became available, only to find the team possessed none to sell.

In one instance, a club agent departed the organization's offices in the Corn Exchange Bank building with tickets bound for the A. G. Spalding & Brothers Sporting Goods Store since they functioned as a seller for this purpose. On his journey, the employee stopped various times and gave blocks of tickets to scalpers before reaching his destination. Upon arriving at A. G. Spalding's, the agent no longer possessed any pasteboards. Fifteen minutes after the store announced to waiting fans they had no tickets for home games at West Side Grounds, scalpers and speculators started selling their duckets in hotels throughout Chicago for double the standard admission price.

A patron, appearing before the National Commission, stated he traveled to the ballpark on the morning of October 11, hoping to purchase tickets for Game Two of the World Series that afternoon. As happened with others, workers at the ticket window turned him down. This individual vouched to the commission that while standing at the window, he saw a ticket seller hand a bundle wrapped in paper to another person. The testifying fan offered that he could clearly see the package contained duckets, which the scalper immediately started selling near the ballpark. Cubs president Charles Murphy sent National Commission chairman Garry Herrmann numerous letters, asking him to call off the investigation and exonerate his organization of any blame or culpability. Herrmann ignored this request.[98]

The front office's botched effort at distributing tickets peeved manager Frank Chance and his players. Chicago's team members figured the poor job handling ticket sales cost them about $8,000 in postseason proceeds. Because of this lost revenue, the ballplayers demanded Murphy pay them a cash bonus, offer contract increases for 1909, or investigate and punish those responsible for keeping so many fans away from the ballpark.[99] The National Commission finally released its report from Ban Johnson's office on December 18, 1908. Major League Baseball's governing body exonerated Chicago's club of conspiring with ticket scalpers. However, the commission condemned the Cubs' organization for their sloppy and careless manner of managing ticket sales, and criticized their general business practices.[100]

Chicago management had testified they made ticket sales available to the public. The National Commission disagreed, affirming the team only initiated this function at club offices before Game One of the World Series. Team officials admitted they permitted one individual to purchase 630 tickets, while a well-known ticket broker testified he bought around six hundred pasteboards. As punishment for this mismanagement, the National Commission revoked the organization's right to sell tickets if the Cubs reached another World Series in the future.[101] The report stated that while scalpers gained possession of tickets through the regular mail order process, club officials did not work out any deal to receive a cut of the profits when delivering them. Through their finding, the commission determined establishing a definitive, regulated plan for all major league teams selling World Series tickets.[102]

In response to the National Commission's verdict, Chicago's assistant treasurer Rutherford B. Cook issued a statement. Cook said that he and team secretary Charles Thomas did their best under trying and strenuous circumstances. Rutherford added that it proved impossible for two men to handle the entire proposition, and they could not gain assistance from outside parties due to not having enough time.[103] President Charles Murphy returned to Chicago on November 27 after vacationing in Cuba for three weeks.[104] One day before the commission released their findings to the public, Murphy offered a comment while predicting the report would prove satisfactory for his baseball club.

"The charges of mismanagement will always be made," said the Cubs' executive, "against clubs which have charge of the sale of tickets for World Series. It is absolutely impossible to guard against it. I understand the commission is to take over the sale next year. The same charges will go the rounds against their work even under the best of conditions."[105]

The ticket scandal, bribery charges, and his ruling on the deciding playoff game between New York and Chicago on October 8, 1908, necessitated by a tied outcome he decreed when these two teams met on September 23, caused consternation for National League president Harry Pulliam. Hounded by different parties, Harry's already fragile psyche suffered while dealing with situations that exacerbated prior stress. Before league magnates appointed Pulliam president on December 12, 1902, he had spent many years connected to baseball. Harry was born in Scottsburg, Kentucky, on February 9, 1869. After graduating from Virginia University with a law degree, he worked as a successful reporter and city editor for the *Louisville Commercial*. Pulliam eventually became president of the Louisville Colonels' baseball organization and later team secretary when Barney Dreyfuss gained total control of the club. Harry also worked as Dreyfuss's secretary for the Pittsburgh Pirates from 1900 through 1902.[106] Pulliam served one term in the Kentucky Legislature after being elected by constituents in 1897.[107]

During the winter league meetings at New York's Waldorf-Astoria Hotel on December 9, 1908, National League owners re-elected Pulliam as president by a 7–0 tally, with no New York Giants representative attending the meeting. Since John T. Brush voted against retaining Harry in the past, fellow magnates believed his absence inconsequential.[108] Although Charles Murphy voted in favor of Pulliam, an intense feud developed between the two gentlemen. Murphy wanted to make Harry's job as unpleasant as possible, while the Kentuckian planned to fight the Cubs' magnate with every fiber of his strength. Pulliam became particularly irked over Charles's idea to appoint Cap Anson as supervisor of umpires if the league president ever decided to eliminate that job from his responsibilities. While Harry agreed with rewarding Anson for his years of service within the National League, the body's executive had already selected umpire Bob Emslie to someday succeed him, a fact known by the organization's eight owners.

The two men did not correspond or speak to each other. Murphy exhibited animosity toward Pulliam because the league president publicized the ticket scalping scandal report. When Harry traveled to California to mediate a salary problem between Frank Chance and Charles, and obtained a successful compromise, the Cubs' owner referred to the president as "Mr. Buttinsky." Upon returning to New York following the California trip, Murphy started a habit of writing to Pulliam using another person's name. When responding, Harry addressed his letters to team secretary Charles Thomas, requesting he give them to his boss for inspection. Garry Herrmann strongly urged Pulliam not to engage in controversy with Murphy.[109] In January, Harry also announced umpire Brick Owens, who officiated games at season's end in 1908, would never work in the National League again. Pulliam based his decision on Owens jumping to the American Association and declaring the National League held no claim to his services.[110]

No National League magnate seemed exempt from Harry Pulliam's erratic behavior. During a joint session of owners from both major leagues on February 17, 1909, in Chicago, somebody in the hotel corridors leaked the story about an incident where, in a fit of rage, Pulliam recently ordered Pittsburgh owner Barney Dreyfuss and Brooklyn mogul Charles Ebbets out of his New York office. Although Dreyfuss and Ebbets both complied with this demand, they vowed to retaliate against the league president.[111] In opposition, Pittsburgh's owner refused to attend the Chicago meeting and declared he would not involve himself in another league function if Harry remained in charge.[112] When confronted by press members about the story surrounding him expelling the two owners from his office, Harry admitted to committing the act and vowed he would do it again if similar circumstances arose.

Upon learning someone divulged this incident, Pulliam, exhibiting paranoia, declared he had tired of warfare and, after traveling to California the following Monday, would not be surprised to hear news of the antagonistic league magnates firing him.[113] While owners held their session on February 17, Harry, overwrought from stress, moved about the hotel lobby, issuing incoherent typewritten statements to press members every few minutes. Pulliam distributed one bulletin that read, "I most emphatically deny that I ever said Barney Dreyfuss was a shrimp," although no newspaper correspondent had accused him of making such a comment.[114] That evening, Charles Comiskey hosted a dinner for attendees at the Chicago Automobile Club. Owners from both leagues remained in the city since the American League had not yet announced its schedule for the upcoming season, while National League leaders planned to gather the following day before adjourning. Although Comiskey issued a no-speech-making rule for the banquet, Harry rose and delivered a tirade, excoriating his organization's magnates.

"My days as a baseball man are numbered," said Pulliam. "The National League doesn't want me for president anymore. It longs to go back to the days of dealing from the bottom of the pack, hiding the cards under the table, and to the days when the trademark was the gumshoe. Because I am for dealing above board and playing in the open, my days are numbered. I can't afford to quit or I would resign now from my position, which pays $9,000 a year. But I will have to quit at the end of this year, for the club owners of the National League want to revert to the old methods."

As Harry Pulliam delivered this harsh verbal attack about his desire to exhibit transparency, which he claimed National League owners rejected, host Charles Comiskey, sitting at the head table, became more shocked as the words spewed from his colleague's mouth.

"How did this get started?" Comiskey kept asking his neighbors at the table.[115]

On the afternoon of February 18, National League owners relieved Harry Pulliam of his duties, granting an indefinite leave of absence to improve his physical and mental health. Magnates appointed secretary-treasurer John Heydler as acting president with full powers, including a seat on the National Commission. Later that day, Pulliam responded to this action through a statement.

"I will not resign the presidency of the National League," stated Pulliam. "I never will quit under fire. My motto is the motto of another Kentuckian, Abraham Lincoln: 'We cannot all win, but we can all be true, and we can all live in the light, pray and trust that right makes might.'"

A group of magnates telegraphed Harry's brother and other relatives to come to Chicago to care for him. Following a long automobile ride, Pulliam appeared calmer that evening, but still insisted on treating the owners as his enemies. After Harry decided to travel to St. Louis, Garry Herrmann, Ban Johnson, and other friends implored him to go to Muldoon's Sanitarium in White Plains, New York, as he did the previous spring, to rest and recuperate from his nervous condition.[116] Pulliam stated he happened to be madly in love with a St. Louis divorcée and desperately needed to see her.[117] A group of owners took measures to prevent Harry from traveling to that city, concocting a delay tactics plan with a cabman (possibly Boston Doves owner George Dovey in disguise) commissioned to drive him to the train station. This guise of not reaching the depot on time worked until Pulliam suddenly bolted from the conveyance, leaving behind his topcoat and luggage. This caused him to become soaked from rain while running for his train and barely reaching the locomotive before it departed.

Pirates team secretary William Locke telephoned Planter's Hotel proprietor Johnny Ryan to request that he meet Harry's train at St. Louis's Union Station. Ryan did so, escorted Pulliam to the hotel, gave him a room, and the league president retired to bed. On February 19, Harry visited different people in St. Louis and then departed for Cincinnati, still without any luggage. Due to talking with some individuals at Union Station's midway, a tardy Pulliam needed to run across half a length of the platform to catch his train.[118] In early June, newspapers reported that Harry's health had improved while relaxing in Oshkosh, Wisconsin.[119] His brother, John P. Pulliam, lived in Oshkosh and worked as a superintendent for the Wisconsin Electric Railway Company and the Eastern Wisconsin Electric Railway and Light Company.

Pulliam arrived in his brother's hometown, immediately making new friends and spending the better part of his time for two weeks fishing and resting. Harry then traveled to Eagle River, Wisconsin, and remained there for ten days before returning to Oshkosh. He stayed in that town for one more day, and left for Cincinnati, seemingly recovered to his former health after being away from work's daily grind.[120] On June 4, 1909, National League owners conducted a conference at Cincinnati's Sinton Hotel to tackle whether they should allow Pulliam to return to his post as league president. While the caucus included dissenters, Gary Herrmann and George Dovey stood behind their friend.[121] Following a rousing four-hour session on June 7, a 6–2 vote decreed Harry could resume his duties around June 19. Charles Murphy and John T. Brush voted against Pulliam. The owners called a meeting for June 16 to officially rescind John Heydler's authority and once again bestow it upon Harry.

A requirement for his return stipulated Harry Pulliam visit various owners while their clubs played out West to prove he had fully recovered his health. Herrmann, Dovey, Barney Dreyfuss, and St. Louis Cardinals owner Stanley Robison did not require a confab with the reinstated league president since they realized his outburst last winter resulted from a serious illness.[122] The *St. Louis Globe-Democrat* confirmed that while making the rounds with magnates before returning to his job, Harry stopped in St. Louis to meet with the woman he loved. They also affirmed Pulliam had seen her while visiting the city in February. The newspaper speculated a love affair with this woman, a member of a family holding interests in an area brewing business, may have contributed to his nervous breakdown.[123] On June 28, Harry returned to his New York office and resumed the duties as National League president.[124]

Sadly, Pulliam's deep depression and anxiety still existed despite his resting period. On July 28, 1909, while reading some mail, Harry stopped and stared out his office window. Pulliam then abruptly told his stenographer, Lenore Caylor, that he did not feel well and intended to leave.[125] Harry appeared to be in good spirits when he exited his office on Broadway Avenue. Nobody knew where Pulliam went before returning to his apartments at the New York Athletic Club, where he had lived for several years.[126] Since arriving back in the city, Harry portrayed a recluse, never seen by other club members.[128] The league executive did partake in an evening meal on July 28 in the facility's dining room.[129] Pulliam returned to his rooms around 8:30 P.M. and locked the doors behind him. Shortly after 9 P.M., while only wearing his undergarments, Harry, holding a pistol, shot himself in the head.[130]

While standing in the center of his room, Pulliam fired one shot with the revolver into his right temple. The bullet, which came out seven inches away on the left side of his head, destroyed the right eye and passed through the upper part of the left. Nobody throughout the club heard the shot, but while falling to the floor, Harry dislodged the receiver of a telephone resting on a nearby table.[131] The pistol round also severed the optic nerve in one of Pulliam's eyes. A few minutes after committing this fatal deed, the telephone operator noticed a light flickering on the switchboard, indicating a phone call from Harry's room. Upon answering and receiving no response, the telephone operator heard a crash on the other end that sounded like an individual falling. Club officials sent bellhop Thomas Brady to investigate. When the employee arrived at Pulliam's apartment, he peered through the transom and noticed a body on the floor with blood pouring from his head. The bellhop immediately summoned the New York Athletic Club's physician.[132]

Dr. J. J. Higgins quickly arrived on the scene at Harry's room. Following a hurried examination, Dr. Higgins advised calling Manhattan coroner Dr. George Schrady and then started carefully dressing Pulliam's wounds. Although still conscious, Harry appeared too confused to answer the doctor's questions. When Dr. Schrady arrived, he assisted his fellow physician in attending to Pulliam's needs. Both men continued trying to find out the reason Harry had attempted to kill himself, but the wounded man remained too dazed to offer cognitive responses.

"Why did you shoot yourself?" the coroner asked twice as he leaned close to Pulliam.

"Why, who's shot?" replied Harry following the second inquiry.

When Dr. Schrady repeated the query, Pulliam asked, "What shot?" The two doctors decided any further questioning might hamper recovery and, with the help of club employees, carried him to a bed. They also diagnosed the bullet had destroyed both eyes and appeared to have at least entered the brain's covering.[133] The medicos reasoned blindness would prevail if Harry miraculously survived his suicide attempt. At one point, Pulliam requested someone to rub his head since it hurt. Following that appeal, Harry offered no more lucid words. Dr. Schrady also placed Pulliam under technical arrest for attempting to commit suicide. On July 29, 1909, Harry died at 7:30 A.M. from his injuries.[134]

Upon receiving notification of his brother-in-law's death, George W. Cain, of Nashville, Tennessee, before leaving to travel to New York that day because of the calamity, stated Pulliam had sent a letter to his wife about a week ago. According to George, the letter Harry wrote to his sister, Elizabeth Pulliam Cain, contained no hint of discontent or despondency. Mr. Cain could not comprehend any plausible explanation for why Pulliam killed himself.[135] As had occurred when Win Mercer and Chick Stahl committed suicide, Harry's devastated family members and friends sought answers over what triggered such a tragic act.

Harry Pulliam, Garry Herrmann, and Ban Johnson – *Already suffering from a fragile psyche, events from the 1908 baseball season further compounded the issues regarding National League president Harry Pulliam's state of mind. Needing to deal with various situations regarding the pennant race and World Series further increased Harry's stress level. After exhibiting erratic behavior during joint major league meetings in Chicago, National League owners temporarily relieved Pulliam of his duties on February 18, 1909. Following a rest period, Harry resumed his duties on June 28. On the evening of July 28, in his room at the New York Athletic Club, Pulliam shot himself in the head with a pistol. He died the following morning. On this photo from the cover of a 1906 World Series program, the* **National Commission members** *from left to right are Harry Pulliam, Garry Herrmann, and Ban Johnson. (Photo in the Public Domain).*

CHAPTER 12

Baseball's Dawn Turns to Morning

Sadly, National League president Harry Pulliam joined the fraternity of individuals like Win Mercer and Chick Stahl, who committed suicide because of pressure related to baseball and everyday life. Regarding suffering a breakdown through job stress, working as an executive for a major sports league consisting of eight diverse owners espousing personal agendas to guarantee success for their franchises functioned as a catalyst. For Pulliam, the 1908 season alone, dealing with contested games, bribes, a World Series ticket scalping scandal, and magnates turning angry when they received unfavorable decisions, wore him down physically and mentally. When reporting on Harry's death in his *Sporting Life* article, Francis C. Richter believed temperament and poor health in recent years caused the league president to end his life.

The baseball writer declared that a decline in Pulliam's nervous condition became very noticeable over the past year. A combination of anxious temperament and finding any criticism unbearable regarding running the National League led to a fatal outcome for Harry. Richter also stated Pulliam had recently stayed in a sanitarium for a week. Francis had spent time with Harry when the Pittsburgh Pirates played their inaugural game against the Chicago Cubs at owner Barney Dreyfuss's new baseball palace, Forbes Field, on June 30, 1909. The two men then traveled together to Philadelphia to attend Phillies owner Israel Durham's funeral. Richter declared Pulliam exhibited a melancholy demeanor on both occasions. Tending to National Commission work in Cincinnati while Garry Herrmann attended the Elks Convention in California, these bouts of depression continued as Harry spent silent hours staring into space. Francis also alleged that Pulliam had announced his engagement to a

St. Louis woman while visiting that city following his February outburst in Chicago at Charles Comiskey's banquet.[1]

Those who interacted with Harry Pulliam at Forbes Field's grand opening expressed no surprise over his death. After receiving news of Harry's suicide, close Pittsburgh friend Henry Feuchtwanger revealed that while extending good-byes to a group of people as he departed the game, Pulliam lingered a long time shaking his hand before offering a parting comment.

"Henry don't fail to come down to New York when anything happens," said Pulliam in a strained voice.

Since that encounter, Feuchtwanger expected to hear sad news regarding his friend. Barney Dreyfuss expressed horror but not surprise when informed on the morning of July 29 that his dear friend shot and killed himself.

"Oh, it's awful," Dreyfuss later told the press. "It's awful, but I expected it. Poor, old boy."

Over the past two years, Harry had talked openly about suicide. The famous executive, who staunchly supported clean and fair baseball and aided in the organization's growth throughout the twentieth century's first decade, repeated a mantra foreshadowing the intent to someday end his life.

"If a man is of no more use to his friends and feels that he is in even his own way it's a sin for him to stick," frequently repeated Pulliam.[2]

On August 2, 1909, Reverend T. M. Hawes, pastor of the Highland Presbyterian Church in Louisville, Kentucky, conducted Harry's funeral service at the Cave Hill Cemetery's chapel. Following the service, pallbearers laid Pulliam's body to rest at that cemetery in the family vault.[3] Out of respect for the deceased, National and American League officials canceled all games scheduled for August 2. That afternoon, National League magnates elected secretary-treasurer John Heydler to succeed Harry.[4] In this tragedy's aftermath, theories and suppositions explaining why Pulliam killed himself rose to the forefront. Back in March, former league umpire Brick Owens, whom Pulliam had criticized in January, claimed he had the goods on the organization's executive. Owens did not go into detail out of respect for Harry's attempts to regain his health during an imposed leave of absence. Brick claimed to possess something earthshattering about Pulliam that he planned to later share. Although Owens vowed to disclose information once Harry recovered, the umpire never followed through with his threat.

What dark secret about Harry Pulliam remained hidden due to Brick Owens's silence? Despite stories about a relationship with a St. Louis woman, could it have been related to a perception that Harry might be gay? Known to dress ostentatiously at league functions, this may have led some people to believe he could be gay since males wearing gaudy clothing during that period caused individuals to reach such a conclusion. Owens may also have known about Pulliam's opulent lifestyle, which Garry Herrmann and Cincinnati Reds stockholder Thomas Logan had disclosed to the other National League magnates.[5] In searching for answers, Harry may have been emotionally devastated by the recent deaths of Israel Durham and Boston Doves owner George Dovey, whom he considered good friends and staunch allies.[6] Some outlandish stories also gained prominence in the wake of Pulliam's suicide.

A report from Pittsburgh on August 1 contended Harry Pulliam had expressed worry over a disabled man placing a curse on the league president and two friends four years earlier. The incident occurred while Pulliam and chums Harry K. Thaw and Dr. Walter S. Bingaman stood in front of Pittsburgh's Hotel Henry in 1905. As the three men talked amongst themselves, they each laughed loudly when one individual shared a funny remark.[7] While they chuckled, a disabled man passing the group lost his balance and fell onto the pavement. This individual believed Pulliam, Thaw, and Dr. Bingaman laughed because of his tumble. The man rose to his feet, cursed the three gentlemen, and vehemently predicted everyone in the group would meet an awful death. Unnerved over this bleak forecasting of their demise, the league president ran after the man to offer his apologies and attempt to clear things up by stating the disabled individual's fall did not precipitate their laughter. The angry man refused to accept Pulliam's explanation. Upon rejoining his friends, Harry expressed concern over the man's curse.

"I don't know what you fellows think of this," said Pulliam, "but I don't like it. It makes me feel queer; as if something would really happen to us."[8]

On June 25, 1906, millionaire Harry Thaw, the product of a wealthy Pittsburgh family, shot and killed architect Stanford White at Madison Square Garden's roof theater in New York. Following his arrest, police escorted Thaw to The Tombs for booking and detention.[9] When Harry Pulliam heard the news, he immediately recalled the disabled man's venomous curse. One week before Harry committed suicide, Dr. Walter S. Bingaman's relatives placed him in the Dixmont Insane Asylum in Western Pennsylvania. This further fulfilled the tragic outcome prophecy. The National League president became so worried over the curse after the White murder that he hired private detectives to search for the disabled man. This effort failed. One time, while on an automobile outing in Pittsburgh with some friends, Pulliam thought he recognized the disabled person on a city street. Risking injury, Harry jumped from the moving vehicle and approached the man, only to find it was not the same individual.[10]

A Louisville press dispatch sent out a sensational story on August 5, 1909, which considered the possibility that Harry Pulliam and a group of friends had entered a suicide pact almost two decades earlier. When Pulliam committed suicide, he became the sixth and final member of this clique to end his life. Although unconfirmed, this article suggested these six men might have entered such an agreement while they dined at the Seelbach Hotel in 1891. The friends had gathered to wish Horace Brown, who resigned as city editor of the *Louisville Commercial*, a fond farewell. Harry succeeded Brown in that position. Horace killed himself in 1894 by taking morphine. At 2 A.M. on March 6, Pulliam answered a call at the *Louisville Commercial*'s office. A frantic voice on the other end shared a dire message.

"Come quick," said the caller. "Horace Brown is dying in a Brook Steet house."

Harry and several friends commandeered a carriage and rushed to that Brook Street address. They ran upstairs and found Brown barely conscious. Horace begged them not to allow him to die in that place. His friends carried Horace down to the carriage, where he died as they rushed him to the hospital. That same year, Dr. Dudley Reynolds Jr. shot and killed himself. Reynolds, a prodigy from one of Kentucky's oldest and richest families, came home one afternoon, immediately went to his room, and turned a gun on himself. The sound of Dudley's body hitting the floor alerted other family members, who discovered him before he passed away.

In 1895, *Louisville Commercial* reporter Harry Wilson became the third person from this group to end his life. At the time, Wilson happened to be studying medicine at Louisville Medical College. Engaging in advanced studies at the university, Harry had access to laboratories and drug rooms. One morning, an individual found Wilson slumped over dead in the drug room, his hand in the neck of a large jar containing an antidote for morphine poisoning. A coroner's report found that Harry's stomach contained ninety grams of morphine. The medical examiner surmised that Wilson collapsed as he reached for the jar containing an antidote. The story surrounding the fourth member of this group's demise may have been most tragic due to its truly Shakespearean nature.

William Preston Thornton committed suicide in 1897 by shooting himself. Referred to by his middle name, the young man's lineage included Kentucky's prestigious Thornton, Breckinridge, and Preston families. Preston exhibited outstanding ability working within the railroad industry.[11] This high society individual fell in love with Nettie Smith, the daughter of his employer, Milton H. Smith, millionaire president of the Louisville & Nashville Railroad.[12] On May 16, the handsome, twenty-six-year-old Thornton arrived at the Smith residence, intending to take Nettie for Sunday mass at a nearby church.[13] The couple had hoped to get married until recently ending their engagement.[14] When Preston entered the mansion's parlor, the doorman noticed the young man transfer a revolver from his trousers pocket to the inside pocket of his coat. Once Miss Smith joined him in the room, Thornton posed a question from the heart.

"Will you marry me?" asked Thornton.

"Not as long as my father withholds his consent," replied Nettie.[15]

Preston Thornton quickly grabbed the revolver from his coat pocket and fired a shot directly into his chest. The bullet entered his body near the heart.[16] Initially believing Thornton intended to murder her, Nettie started running from the room, screaming. Once Miss Smith realized Preston had attempted suicide, she reversed course and rushed toward the prostrate body lying on the floor. By the time Nettie's father and a group of servants reached the pair, her clothing had become saturated in Thornton's blood from hugging him and attempting to elicit any words. Miss Smith only allowed Preston to enter the home after rejecting his first two requests before assuring her mother it would be unkind to turn him away. Thornton had worked for four years as a clerk in Milton's office before the owner dismissed Preston for showing affection toward his daughter. When Nettie urged her father to reconsider, he initially refused but changed his mind and rehired the young man as a traveling agent to keep him away from Louisville.[17] Milton H. Smith dispatched a special train to Lexington, Kentucky, so Preston Thornton's mother, Caroline, and father, Colonel Robert A. Thornton, could be by their son's side.[18] Preston never regained consciousness and died about ten hours later on May 17.

In 1900, traveling salesman Stanley Lyons became the fifth member of the 1891 dinner party at the Seelbach Hotel to commit suicide. Like every other individual from this group, Lyons came from a prominent, wealthy family background in Kentucky.[19] Stanley shot himself in the head while in Paducah, Kentucky.[20] Lyons killed himself in the fall of 1900 as he lodged at Paducah's Richmond House. Stanley checked into a room, wrote several letters, mailed them, and then prepared to retire for the night before committing his fatal act. Hotel employees found Lyons dead in bed the following morning.[21]

When Harry Pulliam shot and killed himself in his New York Athletic Club room in 1909, he became the final person from this circle of friends to commit suicide. The Louisville newspaper dispatch from August 5, 1909, admitted nobody could confirm if these six friends entered a suicide pact and all the incidents only added up to a strange set of coincidences.[22] Still, the similar instruments of destruction used by these men to achieve their end substantiated at least probing such a theory. When Pulliam offered a blistering rebuke at Charles Comiskey's dinner on February 17, 1909, he also eulogized himself, months before committing suicide.

"After I am dead and gone I hope the world will say of me: 'Well, Harry Pulliam was a good fellow,'" said Harry at the Chicago banquet. "That's the only tribute I want them to pay me, for 'good fellow' means everything. One thing is certain, my enemies will have to join with my friends and say: 'Harry Pulliam was on the level. He never played any man a dirty trick. He was as honest as the day is long.'"[23]

During Harry Pulliam's tenure overseeing the National League, numerous scoundrels attempted dirty tricks that threatened baseball's integrity. Sadly, the Deadball Era also saw its share of morbid tragedies, challenging the resolve of even the toughest individuals. Conversely, some of baseball's greatest players, such as Nap Lajoie, Honus Wagner, Ty Cobb, Tris Speaker, Christy Mathewson, and Walter Johnson, performed at an elite level throughout the epoch's two decades, aiding in the sport's growth. That period in the game's history emerged as a beacon for future baseball generations to remember fondly. The Deadball Era functioned as baseball's dawn before it turned to morning, as influential diamond performers like Cobb, Johnson, and Babe Ruth, along with managers Connie Mack and John McGraw, maintained their commanding stature and influence in the new era of the 1920s.

Throughout the Deadball Era, civic pride existed in a player's hometown when he made the grade as a major leaguer. Sometimes, as it turned out with Cobb, different areas of the country claimed an individual's humble beginnings. In 1911, native North Carolinians disputed the notion that Ty spent his entire childhood living in Georgia.[24] While in Murphy, North Carolina, in Cherokee County, R. N. Murphy, an Asheville native from that state, talked in August 1911 with Cobb's great-uncle Harrison Taylor Cobb about the iconic ballplayer's roots. According to the great-uncle, his brother and Ty's grandfather, John F. Cobb, at one time bought land and moved to Moccasin Creek in Cherokee County. Harrison declared that Ty's father, William Herschel Cobb, lived in Moccasin Creek, received his education at the Bellview village school, and married Amanda Chitwood in that town.

According to his great-uncle, Ty Cobb also claimed Moccasin Creek as a birth home and attended the Bellview learning institution before the family moved to Georgia.[25] In 1913, veteran sportswriter and editor William Arlie "W. A." Phelon offered information regarding a stormy relationship between two competitive youngsters precipitating the incident involving Ty and Claude Lucker on May 15, 1912. Phelon, who worked in 1913 as a sports editor for the *Cincinnati Times-Star* and authored articles for *Baseball Magazine*, declared in his February 27 *Sporting News* column that he knew Claude and had talked to him. William affirmed Lucker still had not forgotten the incident and remained angry over Cobb's behavior that afternoon at Hilltop Park. Phelon then revealed how Cobb and Lucker had built up animosity toward each other years earlier while competing as athletes in rival Georgia communities. According to

William, this Southern feud resulted in strong contempt and disdain between the two youngsters, which led to numerous fights.[26]

Besides a desire to settle old scores, when it came to one of the greatest players in baseball history, states and communities drew battle lines regarding a devout, proud spirit over lineage origin. Ty continued displaying diamond dominance when baseball transformed into a fresh style in the 1920s. New York manager John "Muggsy (Mugsy)" McGraw dominated throughout that decade as his Giants claimed four consecutive National League pennants from 1921 through 1924 and two World Series titles. With his pugnacious personality, McGraw certainly created his share of chaos and mayhem during the Deadball Era. Whether rattling president Ban Johnson's cage while briefly managing the American League's Baltimore Orioles or insulting and ridiculing Pirates owner Barney Dreyfuss and declaring Pittsburgh's baseball club public enemy number one, John willingly embraced all battles.

In the summer of 1904, an anonymous Giants ballplayer well acquainted with McGraw admitted that New York's skipper happened to be a composite character and a diamond fiend. According to the individual, John did anything to win and utilized foul language against umpires and opposing ballplayers to achieve that goal. This diamond competitor added that McGraw functioned as a crafty politician off the field whenever dealing with magnates from both major leagues before sharing a story exhibiting a softer, kinder side to the Giants' field leader.

> McGraw's kindness, charity, and sympathetic nature, on the other hand, are but little known for Mugsy never parades his good points. I have seen instances, however, which show that the little pepper-pod is as big-hearted as he is sinful when in battle. One day, a certain broken-down ballplayer—long out of the game, and a man famous as a mighty slugger in his time—came to see McGraw. With him he brought a bat, a famous bat, which had cracked out hits by the hundred in a bygone day. He told McGraw a pitiful—and perfectly truthful—story of his poverty and illness, and asked Mugsy to buy the bat. He asked no charity—the old-timer was still proud—but he thought McGraw might prize the historic hickory, and would give him something for the club.
>
> Did McGraw buy the bat? Yes—and for $100. When the veteran protested to such kindness, Mugsy stuffed the money in the old man's pocket and threatened to throw him out of the clubhouse if he made any further kicks. And, furthermore, McGraw, knowing how the old fellow loved the bat he had just sold, insisted he should act as its custodian till the stick might be called for.

That's only one case of dozens I know of, but Mugsy doesn't go round advertising his charity.²⁷

Although mayhem, bedlam, scandal, and tragedy prevailed at times throughout the Deadball Era, that period boasted outstanding players and nail-biting pennant battles. The era deftly combined a good and bad side before baseball's dawn turned to morning. Nobody represented the complex necessary mix which helped baseball thrive better than John McGraw, a diamond demon who, on occasion, also personified sympathy and kindness.

*As a player, **John McGraw** always exhibited a strong commitment to winning when performing on a baseball diamond. While managing the Baltimore Orioles in 1901 and 1902, he constantly butted heads with American League president Ban Johnson. This pugnacious attitude continued when he embarked on a long and successful managerial career with the New York Giants. When it came to hurling insults, McGraw exempted no individual, not even Pittsburgh Pirates owner Barney Dreyfuss. Although an anonymous Giants player in 1904 referred to John as a composite character and a diamond fiend who utilized any methods to achieve victory, this individual offered up a heartwarming story that revealed a softer, kinder side to New York's skipper. (Courtesy of the Library of Congress).*

Notes

Chapter 1: Mike Donlin

1. David L. Fleitz, *The Irish in Baseball: An Early History* (Jefferson, NC: McFarland, 2009), 136.
2. "A Terrible Fall: Four Persons Thrown from a Trestle Eighty Feet High," *Conneautville Courier*, July 3, 1885, 1.
3. "A Frightful Accident," *Weekly Wisconsin*, July 8, 1885, 6.
4. "A Terrible Fall," 1.
5. "Two Women Badly Injured," *Harrisburg Telegraph*, July 1, 1885, 1.
6. "Under the Wheels: A Veteran Conductor Killed at Conneautville Station," *Conneautville Courier*, August 14, 1890, 5.
7. "Of Local Interest," *Conneautville Courier*, January 11, 1894, 1.
8. "Fatal Accident," *Lake Shore Visitor*, March 20, 1875, 8.
9. Fleitz, *The Irish in Baseball*, 136.
10. Patrick R. Redmond, *The Irish and the Making of American Sport, 1835-1920* (Jefferson, NC: McFarland, 2014), 70.
11. Fleitz, *The Irish in Baseball*, 136.
12. "Signed a Player in Jail," *Buffalo Enquirer*, March 28, 1900, 4.
13. "Donlin Got Break Through Editor of Sporting News," *The Sporting News*, January 25, 1945, 9.
14. "Signed a Player in Jail," 4.
15. "Donlin Got Break through Editor of Sporting News," 9.
16. "The World of Base Ball: The League Race – Games Played Wednesday, July 19," *Sporting Life*, July 29, 1899, 2.
17. "Visit of Mike Donlin Revives Memories of Baseball Triumphs: A Dashing Gossoon Was Broth of a Boy, Who Started Glorious Career with Pat Tebeau's National Leaguers," *St. Louis Star*, November 10, 1922, 22.
18. Dick Connally, "On 'the Trail' of Sport," *Hamilton Evening Journal*, April 8, 1926, 12.
19. "Mike Donlin a Scrapper: Engages in a Fistic Engagement with a Catcher of His Team," *Evening Sentinel*, August 14, 1899, 4.
20. "Base Ball Briefs," *Evening Star*, August 11, 1899, 9.
21. "Base Ball Briefs," *Evening Star*, August 12, 1899, 9.
22. "Gossip of the Ball Players: Ten of the Cuban Tourists Return Home on the Yucatan from Havana," *Brooklyn Daily Eagle*, November 17, 1900, 12.
23. "Little Joe Quinn: He Won the Last Two Games for the Cincinnati Reds," *St. Louis Post-Dispatch*, June 25, 1900, 5.
24. "Mike Donlin Cut: Guyed an Old Gentleman and Was Attacked by a Young One," *St. Louis Globe-Democrat*, June 25, 1900, 9.
25. "Mike Donlin Was Severely Stabbed: Young Ball Player Badly Slashed about Face and Neck by a Stranger," *St. Louis Republic*, June 25, 1900, 5.

26. "Mike Donlin in Trouble: Exuberance of Spirits Leads to Rather Disastrous Results," *Evening Sentinel*, June 26, 1900, 1.
27. "Mike Donlin Was Severely Stabbed," 5.
28. "Mike Donlin in Trouble," 1.
29. "Little Joe Quinn," 5.
30. "Mike Donlin Cut," 9.
31. "Mike Donlin Was Severely Stabbed," 5.
32. "Base Ball Notes," *Evening Star*, June 28, 1900, 9.
33. "The National Game," *Sunday State Journal*, July 1, 1900, 16.
34. "Heidrick Is Out: Center Fielder May Not Play Again This Season," *St. Louis Globe-Democrat*, June 27, 1900, 11.
35. "Brooklyn Closes Series in West with Credit: Took One More Game Than They Lost, but Were Twice Beaten by Pirates – Notes of the Diamond – Tebeau's Resignation," *Brooklyn Daily Times*, August 20, 1900, 6.
36. "McGraw Says He Isn't: Directly Contradicts President Robison's Official Announcement," *St. Louis Globe-Democrat*, August 21, 1900, 11.
37. Fred Stein, *And the Skipper Bats Cleanup: A History of the Baseball Player-Manager, with 42 Biographies of Men Who Filled the Dual Role* (Jefferson, NC: McFarland, 2002), 79.
38. "McGraw Says He Isn't," 11.
39. "Brooklyn Closes Series in West with Credit," 6.
40. "McGraw Says He Isn't," 11.
41. "Base Ball News and Gossip: Betting on the Races by Ball Players Having a Bad Effect on the National Game," *Brooklyn Daily Eagle*, August 26, 1900, 10.
42. "The True Story of the Day Mike Donlin Tried to Drown Manager of Cardinal Club: Titanic Thumper of Baseball Spheres Made His Debut with St. Louis Club and Still Holds Record for Longest Drive Ever Seen at Cardinal Field," *St. Louis Star*, February 10, 1919, 13.
43. "Donlin May Not Return: Has a Chance to Become a California League Magnate," *St. Louis Globe-Democrat*, November 9, 1900, 10.
44. "McGraw Laughs at Hanlon: Returns to Baltimore with Signed Contracts of Williams, Donlin, Sheckard and Others," *Boston Daily Globe*, March 29, 1901, 11.
45. "Donlin Signs with McGraw: Cardinals' Superfluous Fielder Yielded to 'Muggsy's' Blandishments," *St. Louis Globe-Democrat*, March 26, 1901, 10.
46. "Base Ball Notes," *Evening Star*, March 30, 1901, 7.
47. "McGraw Laughs at Hanlon," 11.
48. Burt Solomon, *Where They Ain't: The Fabled Life and Untimely Death of the Original Baltimore Orioles, the Team That Gave Birth to Modern Baseball* (New York: Doubleday – Random House, 2000), 220.
49. Richard Scheinin, *Field of Screams: The Dark Underside of America's National Pastime* (New York: W.W. Norton, 1994), 123.
50. Solomon, *Where They Ain't*, 220.
51. "'Rowdy Mike' Released: Baltimore Club Officials Take Prompt Action with Donlin," *Inter Ocean*, March 15, 1902, 4.
52. "Actress Knocked Down: Miss Minnie Fields Beaten on Baltimore Street – Warrant Out for Mike Donlin of the Ball Club of That City," *Boston Daily Globe*, March 14, 1902, 11.
53. "Chorus Girl Beaten in Baltimore Street: Miss Fields, of the Ben Hur Company, Assailed," *Washington Times*, March 14, 1902, 1.
54. Scheinin, *Field of Screams*, 123.
55. "Chorus Girl Beaten in Baltimore Street," 1.
56. "Ballplayer Mike Donlin Assaulted an Actress: His Friends Put Up a Flimsy Excuse for the Brutal Act," *Buffalo Evening Times*, March 15, 1902, 8.

57. "A Dastard's Deed: A Most Brutal Act Charged to Mike Donlin," *Sporting Life*, March 22, 1902, 11.
58. "Donlin Is Expelled," *Buffalo Evening Times*, March 15, 1902, 8.
59. "Donlin Thrown Out by Orioles: Ball Player Who Assaulted Actress Is Expelled by the Baltimore Club," *Philadelphia Inquirer*, March 15, 1902, 10.
60. "Johnson's Plain Talk: American League President Tells Some Base Ball Truths," *The Times* (Philadelphia), March 16, 1902, 8.
61. Solomon, *Where They Ain't*, 221.
62. Charles C. Alexander, *John McGraw* (Lincoln: First Bison Book – University of Nebraska Press, 1988), 87.
63. "'Rowdy Mike' Released," 4.
64. "Donlin Arrested Here: Held in $1,000 Bail for Alleged Assault on Miss Fields," *Evening Star*, March 17, 1902, 10.
65. "Donlin Under Arrest," *Sporting Life*, March 22, 1902, 11.
66. "Donlin Arrested Here," 10.
67. "'Rowdy Mike' Arrested: Ball Player Who Assaulted a Chorus Girl Captured," *St. Paul Globe*, March 18, 1902, 5.
68. "Donlin Arrested Here," 10.
69. "To Locate Miss Fields: Detective Hogan Comes to Washington for the Purpose," *Washington Times*, March 18, 1902, 10.
70. "Case Goes to Grand Jury: Michael Donlin to Answer to Two Charges of Assault," *Evening Star*, March 18, 1902, 5.
71. "Indicted on Two Counts: Grand Jury's Action in Case of Michael Donlin," *Evening Star*, March 19, 1902, 16.
72. "Mike Donlin Ungrateful: Fooled Frank Robison, Who Kept His Brother Out of Prison," *Pittsburg Press*, March 19, 1902, 12.
73. "Will Release Donlin: Managers of Baltimore Club Decide to Act at Once," *Washington Times*, March 15, 1902, 7.
74. "Will Reopen the Case: Wilhelmina A.E. Von Olsen Desires to Answer Certain Charges," *The Times* (Washington, DC), September 11, 1898, 10.
75. "Makes Reply to Mr. Fields: Defendant's Answer in the Suit to Annul Marriage," *Evening Times*, September 21, 1898.
76. "Crushed by Walls: Thousands in Property and Three Lives Lost by Fire," *Evening Star*, July 25, 1894, 7.
77. "Death in the Flames: Three Firemen Lose Theirs Lives in a Fire at Washington," *Record-Union*, July 26, 1894, 1.
78. "Wilhelmina A. Von Olsen Not Thomas Fields' Wife," *Washington Times*, April 8, 1903, 4.
79. "Six Months in Jail: Fielder Donlin Must Also Pay a Fine of $250," *Baltimore Sun*, March 20, 1902, 12.
80. "Fine and Imprisonment: Penalty Imposed Upon Michael Donlin by a Baltimore Judge," *Evening Star*, March 20, 1902, 6.
81. Alexander, *John McGraw*, 86.
82. "Six Months in Jail," 12.
83. "Donlin in Jail: The Former Santa Cruz Baseball Player Must Serve Six Months," *Santa Cruz Morning Sentinel*, March 25, 1902, 3.
84. "A Dastard's Deed," 11.
85. "Would Get Donlin Out: Baltimore Fans Seek Pardon of Rowdy Ball Player," *St. Paul Globe*, April 17, 1902, 5.
86. "Baseball: Mike Donlin Out of the Game," *Fall River News*, May 9, 1902, 5.
87. "Mike Donlin Signs in Jail," *Fort Wayne Journal-Gazette*, May 21, 1902, 2.
88. "Donlin Out of Jail, to Join Reds," *Philadelphia Inquirer*, August 21, 1902, 10.

89. "Baseball Notes," *Brooklyn Citizen*, May 24, 1902, 6.

90. "Mike Donlin in Jail Hospital: Unfortunate Ball Player Is Reduced to 125 Pounds," *Pittsburg Press*, June 24, 1902, 12.

91. "Donlin Out of Jail, to Join Reds," 10.

92. "Mike Donlin Says He Will Not Touch Whisky," *Pittsburgh Press*, July 29, 1902, 12.

93. "Donlin Joins Reds: Says He Is in Condition and Asks for a Trial," *St. Louis Globe-Democrat*, August 26, 1902, 13.

94. "Donlin Again Suspended by Manager Kelly: Persisted in Getting Drunk and Reported for a Game in That Condition," *Dayton Daily News*, July 6, 1904, 8.

95. "Mike Donlin's Case: The Penitent Ball Player Says He Will Drink No More," *Topeka State Journal*, July 14, 1904, 2.

96. "A Triangular Deal: Sebring, McCormick and Donlin Change Teams," *Wilkes-Barre Leader*, August 9, 1904, 10.

97. "Mike Donlin in Trouble at Albany: Ball Player Became Engaged in Altercation with Railroad Conductor and Was Locked Up," *Scranton Republican*, February 9, 1906, 2.

98. "Albany Police Nab Ballplayers: Mike Donlin Charged with Pulling Loaded Revolver on Porter on Train," *Buffalo Morning Express*, February 9, 1906, 1.

99. "Mrs 'Mike' Donlin Is Dead of Cancer: Mable Hite, Actress-Wife of Ball Player, Dies in New York," *Pittsburgh Post*, October 23, 1912, 2.

100. "Mike Donlin Quits Diamond for Stage," *Meriden Morning Record*, April 5, 1907, 1.

101. "Mrs 'Mike' Donlin Is Dead of Cancer," 2.

102. "Balking at Giants' Offer Mike Took to Vaudeville," *The Sporting News*, January 25, 1945, 9.

103. "Donlin Punches a Lawyer: E.N. Danforth Bumped into Mabel Hite on Street," *The Sun*, September 12, 1909, 1.

104. "Donlin, Discharged, Says He Was Hit First," *Boston Daily Globe*, September 13, 1909, 4.

Chapter 2: Win Mercer

1. "Winifred B. Mercer," *The Sporting News*, January 17, 1903, 1.

2. "The Sunlit Road," *East Liverpool Review*, September 30, 1933, 4.

3. Sid Mercer, "Death of Winnie Mercer Ends a Remarkable Career: Had Been a Baseball Pitcher for Eight Years – Fear of Consumption Thought to Be the Cause of His Suicide - Incidents of His Career and Some of His Characteristics – Story of Famous Pitchers' Battle in Which He Participated," *St. Louis Republic*, January 18, 1903, 20.

4. "Winifred B. Mercer," 1.

5. "Realm of Sports: Winnie Mercer's First Manager – Frank Leonard, of Columbus, Claims the Credit of Introducing Him," *Evening News Review*, February 3, 1903, 2.

6. John H. Gruber, "Old Time Players – Winnie Mercer," *The Sporting News*, April 9, 1914, 4.

7. "Mercer's Name: How the Famous Twirler's Name of 'Winnie' Originated," *Evening Star*, April 20, 1901, 7.

8. "William Barclay Mercer: How the Famous Base Ball Twirler Got His Name," *Evening News Review*, April 8, 1901, 2.

9. "Mercer's Name," 7.

10. "The Sunlit Road," 4.

11. "Players in Training: Pitcher Win Mercer Reported at National Park Yesterday," *Morning Times*, April 1, 1896, 3.

12. "Baseball: News of the Game Indoor and Outdoor – Meeting of the Local League – President Franklin Dickering with a New Man," *Buffalo Morning Express*, December 26, 1895, 10.

13. "Dr. Probst's View: He Visited Winnie Mercer This Morning," *Evening News Review*, December 19, 1895, 1.

14. "Players in Training," 3.

15. "Senators at Home: Will Open with the Cincinnatis Today," *Evening Star*, May 26, 1896, 10.

16. "General Sporting Gossip: Great Event of This Week Will be the National League Baseball Men's Convention – Win Mercer the Lucky Pitcher," *Sunday Post*, November 8, 1896, 19.

17. "M'Nichol Has Started: He Had a Good Game with Toledo Yesterday," *Evening News Review*, May 27, 1897, 5.

18. "Diamond Dust," *Evening Times*, July 17, 1897, 6.

19. "Dr. James Loses the Game: The Young Physician Gave Four Successive Bases on Balls," *The Times* (Washington, DC), September 14, 1897, 6.

20. "He Forgot the Rule: Umpire Carpenter Victim of a Case of 'Rattles,'" *Evening Star*, September 14, 1897, 7.

21. "Reds Win a Close Game: But for McJames's Wildness the Score Might Have Been 1 to 1," *Indianapolis Journal*, September 14, 1897, 3.

22. "He Forgot the Rule," 7.

23. "Dr. James Loses the Game," 6.

24. "Reds Win a Close Game," 3.

25. "Dr. James Loses the Game," 6.

26. "The Orioles' Strike: Current Sensation in Base Ball Circles," *Evening Star*, March 19, 1898, 11.

27. "Our Own Win Mercer: May Not Be a Member of the Senators," *Evening News Review*, September 10, 1898, 2.

28. "To Report March 19: Washington Players Notified to Be Here," *Evening Star*, March 2, 1900, 9.

29. "Eight Clubs in the League: Baltimore, Washington, Cleveland and Louisville Dropped," *Pittsburg Press*, March 9, 1900, 5.

30. "Base-Ball Situation Cleared: Retiring Clubs Come to Agreement with National Body," *St. Louis Globe-Democrat*, March 10, 1900, 7.

31. "Patsy Donovan Secured: Pirates' Great Right Fielder Joins the Tribe of Tebeau," *St. Louis Globe-Democrat*, March 10, 1900, 7.

32. "William Barclay Mercer," 2.

33. Sid Mercer, "Death of Winnie Mercer Ends a Remarkable Career: Had Been a Baseball Pitcher for Eight Years – Fear of Consumption Thought to Be the Cause of His Suicide – Incidents of His Career and Some of His Characteristics – Story of Famous Pitchers' Battle in Which He Participated," 20.

34. "Mercer to Play Here: Manager Manning Signs the Popular Ladies' Day Twirler," *The Times* (Washington, DC), March 24, 1901, 8.

35. "Diamond Dust," *St. Paul Globe*, May 2, 1901, 5.

36. Mercer, "Death of Winnie Mercer Ends a Remarkable Career," 20.

37. "Mercer Not Released," *Bloomington Evening World*, August 28, 1901, 2.

38. "Baseball: Addition of New York Would Greatly Strengthen American League," *St. Louis Globe-Democrat*, November 10, 1901, 6.

39. "Gossip of the Latest Happenings in Sport: Fans Shocked by the Tragic Death of 'Win' Mercer – Mystery in It," *Buffalo Evening Times*, January 14, 1903, 8.

40. "Base Ball Notes," *Evening Star*, December 13, 1901, 9.

41. "In a Bad Wreck: Win Mercer's Base Ball Team in a Serious Accident Out West," *Evening News Review*, December 20, 1901, 1.

42. "In the Great West: Local Ball Player Receives a Flattering Offer," *Evening News Review*, December 27, 1901, 1.

43. "Detroit Staff of Pitchers: Manager Dwyer Completed the Same by Signing Win Mercer," *Buffalo Enquirer*, January 29, 1902, 4.

44. "Mathewson's Success Due to Mercer's Teaching: Catcher Frank Bowerman Gives the East Liberty Adonis Credit for Splendid Showing Made by Christy Last Season," *Pittsburg Press*, March 3, 1902, 10.

45. "Pittsburg Club Raided?: Win Mercer Says President Dreyfuss Will Lose Two-Thirds of His Men," *Pittsburg Post*, August 30, 1902, 6.

46. "Winnie Mercer Ends His Life in Hotel Room: Famous Baseball Pitcher Committed Suicide by Asphyxiation," *Pittsburg Press*, January 13, 1903, 1.

47. "Pitcher Win Mercer to Manage Detroit Team Next Season: Frank Dwyer Will Be Shipped from the City of the Straits to Some Other American League City," *Buffalo Courier*, October 8, 1902, 9.

48. "Win Mercer's Plans: Do Not Include the Management of the Detroit Club Next Season," *Evening News Review*, October 8, 1902, 5.

49. "American to Enter Pittsburg," *Beacon Journal*, October 15, 1902, 5.

50. "Mercer's Luck: The Treasurer of the Base Ball Tourists Narrowly Escapes Being Mulcted of All the Velvet," *Sporting Life*, December 20, 1902, 1.

51. Mercer, "Death of Winnie Mercer Ends a Remarkable Career," 20.

52. "Gossip of the Latest Happenings in Sport," 8.

53. "Base Ball: Caught on the Fly," *The Sporting News*, October 11, 1902, 5.

54. "Gossip of the Latest Happenings in Sport," 8.

55. "Bunko Men Attempt a Trick at a Hotel: Effort to Obtain the Money of a Baseball Player Narrowly Frustrated," *San Francisco Call*, December 1, 1902, 3.

56. "Mercer's Luck: The Treasurer of the Base Ball Tourists Narrowly Escapes Being Mulcted of All the Velvet," 1.

57. "Bunko Men Attempt a Trick at a Hotel," 3.

58. "Win Mercer's Luck: Served Him in Good Stead – Came Near Losing $5,000 in Cold Cash," *Evening News Review*, December 9, 1902, 7.

59. "Bunko Men Attempt a Trick at a Hotel," 3.

60. "Win Mercer's Luck: Served Him in Good Stead – Came Near Losing $5,000 in Cold Cash," 7.

61. "Bunko Men Attempt a Trick at a Hotel," 3.

62. "Play Clever Game, but Don't Get Money: Ruse of Clever Schemers That Have Serious Designs on the Funds of Two Well-Known Baseball Players," *San Francisco Examiner*, December 1, 1902, 9.

63. "Mercer's Luck: The Treasurer of the Base Ball Tourists Narrowly Escapes Being Mulcted of All the Velvet," 1.

64. "Play Clever Game, but Don't Get Money," 9.

65. "Win Mercer Offers to Join Reds: Message to President Herrmann from 'Frisco Conveys Important News," *Pittsburg Press*, December 28, 1902, 19.

66. Ren Mulford Jr., "Life in Redland: Studying the Problem of Peace Settlement," *Sporting Life*, January 3, 1903, 2.

67. "Detroit Will Lose Mercer," *St. Louis Globe-Democrat*, June 24, 1902, 13.

68. C.G. Wellington, "Detroit Doings: Win Mercer Slated to Manage the Tigers Next Season – Messrs. Angus and Postal Deny New York Rumors," *Sporting Life*, January 17, 1903, 2.

69. "Hoodoo Hovers over Players from the Big Eastern Leagues: Winnie Mercer's Tragic End Is the Climax of a Host of Misfortunes Which Have Haunted the Ball Tossers," *San Francisco Call*, January 15, 1903, 8.

70. "Big Hospital List: Many of Cantillon's Touring Stars Are Unable to Play," *The Sporting News*, January 10, 1903, 6.

71. "Hoodoo Hovers over Players from the Big Eastern Leagues," 8.

72. "Baseball Star Puts End to Life: Winnie Mercer Commits Suicide in Occidental Hotel," *San Francisco Call*, January 13, 1903, 14.

73. "Untimely Death of 'Win' Mercer Ends Career of Great Promise: Brilliant Young Baseball Player and Manager Leaves Many Friends to Mourn His Passing – His Accounts Show He Was True to His Trust," *San Francisco Call*, January 14, 1903, 3.

74. "Sporting News of the World: Suicide's Grave for Mercer – American League Star Pitcher Takes His Own Life," *Salt Lake Herald*, January 14, 1903, 7.

75. "Baseball Star Puts End to Life," 14.

76. 'Untimely Death of 'Win' Mercer Ends Career of Great Promise," 3.

77. "Baseball Star Puts End to Life," 14.

78. "Untimely Death of 'Win' Mercer Ends Career of Great Promise," 3.

79. "Sporting News of the World," 7.

80. "Pitcher Win Mercer's Romance," *Buffalo Morning Express*, January 16, 1903, 11.

81. W.A. Calhoun, "Vale, Winnie Mercer: The Dead Player Laid to Rest Amid Impressive Surroundings – No Shadow Now on His Name," *Sporting Life*, January 31, 1903, 2.

82. "Was Mercer Murdered?: All of East Liverpool in Mourning for Mercer – A Grave Suspicion of Foul Play," *Sporting Life*, January 24, 1903, 2.

83. "Gossip of the Latest Happenings in Sport," 8.

84. "Was Mercer Murdered?" 2.

85. "Was Win Mercer Murdered? East Liverpool Friends of Dead Ball Player Scout Theory of His Suicide," *Pittsburg Post*, January 17, 1903, 6.

86. "A Little of the All Sorts: Not a Murder," *Lima Times-Democrat*, January 17, 1903, 5.

87. "Verdict Was Suicide: Coroner's Jury Reports on Death at San Francisco of Win Mercer, the Baseball Player," *Boston Daily Globe*, January 22, 1903, 4.

88. Gossip of the Latest Happenings in Sport," 8.

89. Sid Mercer, "Death of Winnie Mercer Ends a Remarkable Career: Had Been a Baseball Pitcher for Eight Years – Fear of Consumption Thought to Be the Cause of His Suicide – Incidents of His Career and Some of His Characteristics – Story of Famous Pitchers' Battle in Which He Participated, 20.

90. "Believe Mercer Was Demented: Players Claim He Had Not Acted Naturally for Some Time," *St. Paul Globe*, January 19, 1903, 5.

91. "Late News: En Route for Burial – All That Is Mortal of Mercer," *The Sporting News*, January 17, 1903, 1.

92. "Pitcher Mercer Squandered Funds: Story That He Had Spent Several Thousand Dollars of Other Players' Money," *Evening Mail*, January 28, 1903, 4.

93. "Mercer's Friends Talk about Him: Generous Tributes from His Baseball Associates," *Evening News Review*, January 21, 1903, 4.

94. "Pitcher Mercer Squandered Funds," 4.

95. "Gossip of the Players," *The Sporting News*, January 24, 1903, 2.

96. "Untimely Death of 'Win Mercer' Ends Career of Great Promise," 3.

97. "Mercer Was Not Murdered," *Evening Star*, January 21, 1903, 9.

98. "Late News," 1.

99. "Greatest Pitcher in the Business: What Dick Harley Says of His Dead Friend, Winnie Mercer," *Evening News Review*, January 20, 1903, 2.

100. "Trip Was Big Success: Baseball Players Have Returned Home, Enthusiastic over Their Long Journey," *Buffalo Morning Express*, January 26, 1903, 9.

101. "Winnie Mercer's Death a Lesson to Players," *Pittsburgh Press*, January 19, 1903, 10.

102. B.F. Wright, "Tigers' Manager: Barrow Will Have Charge of Detroit Team," *The Sporting News*, January 24, 1903, 5.

103. "Win Mercer's Funeral: Floral Tributes Finest Ever Seen in East Liverpool," *Pittsburgh Press*, January 22, 1903, 12.

104. "Last Honors Are Paid to Loved Winnie Mercer: The Church Crowded and Many Who Desired to Do So Unable to Gain Admission," *Evening News Review*, January 21, 1903, 1.

105. "'Win' Mercer's Funeral," *St. Joseph Gazette*, January 24, 1903, 5.

106. "Magnificent Floral Designs for Win Mercer's Funeral," *Pittsburgh Press*, January 19, 1903, 10.

107. "Last Honors Are Paid to Loved Winnie Mercer," 1.

108. "Last Honors Are Paid to Loved Winnie Mercer," 4.

109. "Lessons Drawn from Mercer's Life: An Elegant, Forcible Sermon by Dr. Pratt," *Evening News Review*, January 21, 1903, 4.

110. "Last Honors Are Paid to Loved Winnie Mercer," 1.

111. "Comments of the Day in Realm of the Rooter," *Pittsburg Press*, February 11, 1903, 12.

112. Clarence L. Cullen, "Tales of the Turf: Ball Playing and Backing Ponies," *Sunday Star*, August 4, 1907, 4.

113. "Ornament's Handicap: Piloted by Sloan, He Wins the Big Brooklyn Race Easily," *The Sun*, May 29, 1898, 5.

114. "Turned the Trick: Patriots Sent Winnie Mercer to the Bench in Disgrace," *Pittsburg Press*, May 29, 1898, 12.

115. "General Sporting Gossip," 19.

116. "Rubbed Mercer Out," *Buffalo Evening News*, January 29, 1903, 10.

117. "Rogers May Soon Be Put On the Retired List: News from the Quaker City Points to the Sale of the Phillies to Barney Dreyfus, Reach and Others," *Washington Times*, January 16, 1903, 5.

118. "Trip Was Big Success," 9.

Chapter 3: Ed Delahanty

1. Steven K. Wagner, *The Four Home Runs Club: Sluggers Who Achieved Baseball's Rarest Feat* (Lanham, MD: Rowman & Littlefield, 2018), 12.

2. Harry Grayson, "Ed Delahanty Led Both Major Leagues," *Daily Times* (New Philadelphia, Ohio), June 2, 1943, 5.

3. "Story of Delehanty: One of Three Greatest Ball Players Ever in the Game – Wonderful Left Fielder," *Salt Lake Herald*, July 30, 1903, 7.

4. "Sporting Notes," *Philadelphia Inquirer*, October 11, 1894, 3.

5. "National League: Delahanty Played Chicago and Came Near Beating the Colts," *The Times* (Philadelphia), July 14, 1896, 8.

6. Grayson, "Ed Delahanty Led Both Major Leagues," 5.

7. "National League," 8.

8. "Sports and Athletics: Baseball," *Waterbury Evening Democrat*, July 6, 1903, 10.

9. "National League," 8.

10. Joel Stashenko, "The Puzzling Saga of Ed Delahanty," *Salina Journal*, September 20, 1992, 35.

11. "Napoleon Lajoie's Case Is Heard: The Philadelphia National Base Ball Club Tries to Restrain Baseman," *Scranton Tribune*, April 20, 1901, 1.

12. Stashenko, "The Puzzling Saga of Ed Delahanty," 35.

13. John A. Wood, *Beyond the Ballpark: The Honorable, Immoral, and Eccentric Lives of Baseball Legends* (Lanham, MD: Rowman & Littlefield, 2016), 279.

14. "New Men Engaged: One Result of Manager Manning's Recent Efforts," *Evening Star*, August 13, 1901, 7.

15. "American League Forms New Plans: National League Stars to Be Signed to Kill Off Interest," *The Times* (Philadelphia), August 22, 1901, 10.

16. "American League after the Reds: Delahanty Said to Have Approached Cincinnati Players with Offers," *The Times* (Philadelphia), September 3, 1901, 8.

17. Arthur D. Hittner, *Honus Wagner: The Life of Baseball's "Flying Dutchman"* (Jefferson, NC: McFarland, 1996), 93.
18. "Comments of the Day in Realm of the Rooter," *Pittsburg Press*, August 27, 1902, 10.
19. "Colonel Rogers an Agnostic: So Declares Himself in Reference to Reported Loss of Players," *Philadelphia Inquirer*, December 3, 1901, 10.
20. Grayson, "Ed Delahanty Led Both Major Leagues," 5.
21. "Ban Johnson and Comiskey Own Senators: President of American League Admitted to Be Stockholder in Washington Baseball Club," *Pittsburg Press*, November 6, 1901, 8.
22. Angelo J. Louisa and David Cicotello, eds., *Mysteries from Baseball's Past: Investigations of Nine Unsettled Questions* (Jefferson, NC: McFarland, 2010), 13.
23. "Loftus' Large Loss: Three Stars Reported as Deserting Washington," *Sporting Life*, December 6, 1902, 6.
24. "Denials and Affirmations: Delehanty and Orth Say They Have Not Yet Signed with New York While McGraw Insists That They Have Done So," *Sporting Life*, December 13, 1902, 3.
25. "Orth's Statement: The Crack Pitcher Says That He Has Not Signed with New York, Not Having Even Been Approached," *Sporting Life*, December 13, 1902, 3.
26. "Townsend Also Denies," *Sporting Life*, December 13, 1902, 3.
27. "Brush Says He Has 'Del,'" *Sporting Life*, December 13, 1902, 3.
28. "Denials and Affirmations," 3.
29. "Won't Play with New York: Delahanty Says He Turned Down McGraw's Offer," *Topeka Daily Capital*, December 6, 1902, 2.
30. "Fred Postal Shocked: Will Never Again Trust Any Ball Player If Delehanty Has Broken Faith with Him, Says the Washington Club Owner," *Sporting Life*, December 13, 1902, 3.
31. Wm. F.H. Koelsch, "New York Nuggets: President Brush Acts While Manager McGraw Rests – Delehanty Undoubtedly Signed to a New York Contract – The American League Invasion," *Sporting Life*, December 13, 1902, 3.
32. "'Del' Doesn't Care: He Will Get His Money Although His Fellow-Players May Suffer Through His Act, Which Hastened Peace," *Sporting Life*, December 27, 1902, 3.
33. "Harmony Prevails in League: By Unanimous Vote the Magnates Adopt Peace Agreement," *Pittsburg Press*, January 22, 1903, 12.
34. Francis C. Richter, "Settlement Secured; Peace Proclaimed!: The Popular Double League System Scores a Splendid Triumph," *Sporting Life*, January 17, 1903, 4.
35. "Delahanty Has Funny Ideas: Star Player Says He Will Never Return the $2,500 He Accepted from New York," *Buffalo Enquirer*, January 14, 1903, 8.
36. "Sporting Gossip," *Buffalo Enquirer*, January 14, 1903, 8.
37. Louisa and Cicotello, eds., *Mysteries from Baseball's Past*, 14.
38. "Gossip of the Players," *The Sporting News*, January 17, 1903, 2.
39. "Aleck Smith's Verdict: Broadway Says Peace Is Good for Everybody Save Players," *Pittsburg Press*, January 16, 1903, 16.
40. "Delahanty Decides to Play in New York: Big Fielder Says He Will Retire from the Game if Compelled to Go to Washington," *Buffalo Courier*, February 28, 1903, 11.
41. "Fred Postal's Turn to Smile: Has Stopped Payment on the Advance Money Check He Sent to Delahanty," *Buffalo Evening Times*, January 22, 1903, 12.
42. "Wants a Substitute: Postal Will Part with Del If He Can Get Another Man," *Pittsburg Press*, January 26, 1903, 10.
43. "Delahanty Is Evidently Becoming Worried," *Philadelphia Inquirer*, March 21, 1903, 10.
44. "Loftus Expects Delahanty to Report to Him," *Philadelphia Inquirer*, March 21, 1903, 10.
45. "Hot Shot for Davis and Del: Johnson and Pulliam Confer on the Players and Settle the Question," *Philadelphia Inquirer*, March 21, 1903, 10.
46. "Gossip of Base Ball and Other Sports: Delahanty and Davis," *Daily Albuquerque Citizen*, March 26, 1903, 6.

47. "Johnson's Hot Shot: Scores New York Lawyer Reported to Have Advised Davis to Break His Contract," *Buffalo Evening Times*, April 11, 1903, 8.
48. "Gossip of Base Ball and Other Sports: Loftus Talks to Delahanty," *Daily Albuquerque Citizen*, March 27, 1903, 6.
49. "Gossip of Base Ball and Other Sports: $200,000 to Build Grounds," *Daily Albuquerque Citizen*, March 27, 1903, 6.
50. "The Old Sports Musings: If You Can't Boost Don't Knock," *Philadelphia Inquirer*, March 23, 1903, 10.
51. John F. Luitich, "Are at Practice: Senators Hustling to Get in Shape," *The Sporting News*, April 4, 1903, 5.
52. "M'Closkey Fails to Show Up: Not Known Whether Ike Francis Succeeded in Changing Homesteader's Mind," *Buffalo Courier*, April 5, 1903, 29.
53. "Base Ball," *Daily Standard*, April 14, 1903, 5.
54. John F. Luitich, "Has Surrendered: Delahanty Will Be with the 1903 Senators," *The Sporting News*, April 18, 1903, 5.
55. John F. Luitich, "Too High in Flesh: Delahanty Starts Season with Big Handicap," *The Sporting News*, April 25, 1903, 3.
56. "'Del.' Reinstated: The American League's Champion Batter in Good Standing," *Sporting Life*, May 2, 1903, 4.
57. "Gossip in the World of Sport of Local Interest: Why Delahanty Didn't Jump," *Buffalo Evening Times*, May 1, 1903, 10.
58. "'Del.' Reinstated," 4.
59. "Gossip in the World of Sport of Local Interest," 10.
60. "'Del.' Almost Went West," *Sporting Life*, May 2, 1903, 4.
61. Tom Deveaux, *The Washington Senators, 1901-1971* (Jefferson, NC: McFarland, 2001), 12.
62. "Notes of the Game," *Evening Star*, May 8, 1903, 9.
63. John F. Luitich, "Loftus' Cripples: Several of the Senators in Poor Shape," *The Sporting News*, June 6, 1903, 4.
64. Deveaux, *The Washington Senators*, 12.
65. John F. Luitich, "Faults Forgotten: Delahanty's Remains Rest in Cleveland Cemetery," *The Sporting News*, July 18, 1903, 7.
66. Paul W. Eaton, "From the Capital: The Western Trip – The Fourth Made Glorious – Senators Lose a Pitcher and Sign a Catcher – Delehanty's Last Bad Break," *Sporting Life*, July 11, 1903, 11.
67. John F. Luitich, "Disgusted Fans: Senators' Slump Has Caused Cranks to Roast," *The Sporting News*, June 20, 1903, 5.
68. "Loftus Suspended by President Johnson: Washington Manager Under the 'Ban' for Five Days – Burkett Fined $50 and Umpire Connolly Reprimanded," *Washington Times*, June 23, 1903, 8.
69. Deveaux, *The Washington Senators*, 13.
70. "Delehanty Comes to an Untimely End: Mystery Envelops Noted Ball Player's Death," *Washington Times*, July 8, 1903, 2.
71. Patrick R. Redmond, *The Irish and the Making of American Sport*, 71.
72. Eaton, "From the Capital: The Western Trip – The Fourth Made Glorious – Senators Lose a Pitcher and Sign a Catcher – Delehanty's Last Bad Break," 11.
73. Paul W. Eaton, "From the Capital: Delehanty Dead – The Great Player Falls from a Railroad Bridge at Fort Erie, Ont. – The Body Went Over Niagara Falls – Interment at Cleveland," *Sporting Life*, July 18, 1903, 3.
74. "Three=Cornered Baseball Battle Over George Davis: Pulliam's Position," *St. Louis Globe-Democrat*, June 27, 1903, 15.

75. "Late News: Davis Restrained by U.S. Court – George Davis Enjoined," *The Sporting News*, July 18, 1903, 1.

76. Redmond, *The Irish and the Making of American Sport*, 71.

77. Eaton, "From the Capital: Delehanty Dead – The Great Player Falls from a Railroad Bridge at Fort Erie, Ont. – The Body Went Over Niagara Falls – Interment at Cleveland," 3.

78. "Delehanty Comes to an Untimely End," 2.

79. Luitich, "Faults Forgotten," 7.

80. Jerrold I. Casway, *The Culture and Ethnicity of Nineteenth Century Baseball* (Jefferson, NC: McFarland, 2017), 113.

81. Redmond, *The Irish and the Making of American Sport*, 71-72.

82. Eaton, "From the Capital: The Western Trip – The Fourth Made Glorious – Senators Lose a Pitcher and Sign a Catcher – Delehanty's Last Bad Break," 11.

83. "Delehanty Comes to an Untimely Death," 2.

84. Casway, *The Culture and Ethnicity of Nineteenth Century Baseball*, 113.

85. Redmond, *The Irish and the Making of American Sport*, 72.

86. B.F. Wright, "Delehanty Dazed: Death Due to Accident Not Design," *The Sporting News*, July 18, 1903, 5.

87. Deveaux, *The Washington Senators: 1901-1971*, 13.

88. "Delehanty Comes to an Untimely Death," 2.

89. John F. Luitich, "Left His Uniform: Delahanty Jumped Tom Loftus' Team," *The Sporting News*, July 11, 1903, 5.

90. Eaton, "From the Capital: The Western Trip – The Fourth Made Glorious – Senators Lose a Pitcher and Sign a Catcher – Delehanty's Last Bad Break," 11.

91. Eaton, "From the Capital: Delehanty Dead – The Great Player Falls from a Railroad Bridge at Fort Erie, Ont. – The Body Went Over Niagara Falls – Interment at Cleveland," 3.

92. Deveaux, *The Washington Senators*, 13.

93. Eddie Mitchell, *Baseball Rowdies of the 19th Century: Brawlers, Drinkers, Pranksters and Cheats in the Early Days of the Major Leagues* (Jefferson, NC: McFarland, 2018), 127.

94. Louisa and Cicotello, eds., *Mysteries from Baseball's Past*, 17.

95. Eaton, "From the Capital: Delehanty Dead: The Great Player Falls from a Railroad Bridge at Fort Erie, Ont. – The Body Went Over Niagara Falls – Interment at Cleveland," 3.

96. "Delehanty Dead: The Famous Player Finds His End in Niagara River," *Sporting Life*, July 18, 1903, 3.

97. Mitchell, *Baseball Rowdies of the 19th Century*, 127.

98. Louisa and Cicotello, eds., *Mysteries from Baseball's Past*, 17.

99. "Delehanty Dead," 3.

100. "Delehanty Comes to an Untimely End," 2.

101. Louisa and Cicotello, eds., *Mysteries from Baseball's Past*, 18.

102. Eaton, "From the Capital: Delehanty Dead – The Great Ball Player Falls from a Railroad Bridge at Fort Erie, Ont. – The Body Went Over Niagara Falls – Interment at Cleveland," 3.

103. "Delehanty May Have Been Pushed Off Bridge: Story Comes from Buffalo That Looks Very Suspicious on the Face," *Wilkes-Barre Leader*, July 8, 1903, 7.

104. Eaton, "From the Capital: Delehanty Dead – The Great Ball Player Falls from a Railroad Bridge at Fort, Erie, Ont. – The Body Went Over Niagara Falls – Interment at Cleveland," 3.

105. "Lost, Strayed or Stolen; Big Edward Delehanty: Anyone Ascertaining His Whereabouts Will Inform Loftus and Oblige," *Washington Times*, July 5, 1903, 4.

106. "'Del' Still Missing," *Evening Journal*, July 7, 1903, 2.

107. "Looking for Delahanty: Officials in Michigan Trying to Find the Base Ball Player," *Wilkes-Barre Leader*, July 8, 1903, 7.

108. "Did Delahanty Jump Overboard?: Supposed That the Famous Ball Player Plunged into the Niagara River," *Philadelphia Inquirer*, July 9, 1903, 10.

109. "Delehanty Comes to an Untimely End," 2.
110. "Delehanty May Have Been Pushed Off Bridge," 7.
111. "Ed Delahanty Drowned: The Great Ball Player Supposed to Have Committed Suicide," *York Dispatch*, July 8, 1903, 3.
112. "Frank Delahanty Visits Buffalo," *Wilkes-Barre Leader*, July 8, 1903, 7.
113. "Delehanty's Folks Say Accident; Deny Suicide and Murder: Famous Ballplayer's Relatives after Investigating His Disappearance Say They Are Convinced He Accidentally Fell from Bridge – They Blame Conductor," *Buffalo Courier*, July 9, 1903, 6.
114. "Delahanty Dead," 3.
115. "Delehanty's Folks Say Accident; Deny Suicide and Murder," 6.
116. "Body Taken from the River: Remains Believed to Be Those of Ed. Delehanty," *Evening Star*, July 9, 1903, 5.
117. Eaton, "From the Capital: Delehanty Dead: The Great Player Falls from a Railroad Bridge at Fort Erie, Ont. – The Body Went Over Niagara Falls – Interment at Cleveland," 3.
118. "The Finding of Delehanty's Body: Put Off the Train, He Walked Through Open Draw of Bridge Over the Niagara River," *Butte Miner*, July 14, 1903, 5.
119. "Delahanty Dead," 3.
120. "Widow in Want," *Sporting Life*, July 25, 1903, 18.
121. Eaton, "From the Capital: Delehanty Dead: The Great Player Falls from a Railroad Bridge at Fort, Ont. – The Body Went Over Niagara Falls – Interment at Cleveland," 3.
122. Louisa and Cicotello, eds., *Mysteries from Baseball's Past*, 25-26.
123. "Widow in Want," 18.
124. "Says 'Del' Was Murdered: Brother of Dead Ball Player Declares Gems Are Missing," *Semi-Weekly Gazette and York Democratic Press*, July 18, 1903, 2.
125. "Delehanty a Swimmer: Billy Hallman Cannot Account for 'Del's' Death in the Water Considering His Ability in Swimming," *Sporting Life*, July 25, 1903, 18.

Chapter 4: Eddie Doheny

1. Eaton, "From the Capital: Delehanty Dead – The Great Player Falls from a Railroad Bridge at Fort Erie, Ont. – The Body Went Over Niagara Falls – Interment at Cleveland," 3.
2. B.F. Wright, "Delahanty Dazed: Death Due to Accident Not Design," *The Sporting News*, July 18, 1903, 5.
3. Clarence L. Cullen, "Tales of the Turf: Ball Playing and Backing Ponies," *Sunday Star*, August 4, 1907, 4.
4. Louis P. Masur, *Autumn Glory: Baseball's First World Series* (New York: Hill and Wang, 2003), 137.
5. "Death of Ed Doheny: Once Famous Ball Player Dies in Massachusetts Hospital," *Montpelier Evening Argus*, January 1, 1917, 2.
6. "E.R. Doheny," *The Sporting News*, October 23, 1897, 2.
7. "How Doheny Joined the League," *Northfield News*, January 9, 1917, 8.
8. "E.R. Doheny," 2.
9. "Death of Ed Doheny," 2.
10. Sid Mercer, "Death of Winnie Mercer Ends a Remarkable Career: Had Been a Baseball Pitcher for Eight Years – Fear of Consumption Thought to Be the Cause of His Suicide - Incidents of His Career and Some of His Characteristics – Story of Famous Pitchers' Battle in Which He Participated," *St. Louis Republic*, January 18, 1903, 20.
11. J.B. Sheridan, "Money, Just Money, Makes the Baseball World Move, Stirs Strife and 'Outlawry,': The Very Human Desire to Be One of the Inner Ring Inspired the Brotherhood Revolt, Roused Ban Johnson and His Horde of 'Sandlotters,' and Now Drives the Federals at the Throat of the Organization, Determined to Gain Admittance to the El Dorado That the Old Leagues Are Pleased to Call Theirs," *St. Louis Globe-Democrat*, March 8, 1914, 2.

12. "Northfield," *Northfield News*, February 2, 1897, 8.
13. "Shower Spoils the Game: New Yorks and Washingtons Open the Ball with a Draw," *The Sun*, April 27, 1897, 4.
14. "Sporting: Vermont's Noted Base Ball Twirlers," *Vermont Phoenix*, April 30, 1897, 8.
15. "Doheny's First Victory: He Pitches Fine Ball and the New Yorks Win Easily," *The Sun*, May 5, 1897, 4.
16. "Doheny Is a Wonder: Joe Campbell Describes the Southpaw Twirler's Delivery," *Pittsburg Press*, May 6, 1897, 5.
17. W.F.H. Koelsch, "New York Nuggets: The Giants Now Give Signs of a Brace-Up," *Sporting Life*, June 5, 1897, 10.
18. "Easy Win for Giants: The St. Louis Team a Stepping Stone to Third Place," *The World*, June 13, 1897, 12.
19. "Town Affairs," *St. Albans Daily Messenger*, June 14, 1897, 6.
20. W.F.H. Koelsch, "New York Nuggets: Things Not Working Smoothly in the Metropolis," *Sporting Life*, June 19, 1897, 8.
21. "Base Ball Gossip: Notes of Interest About the National Game – Doheny's Dodge," *New Hampton Herald*, August 5, 1897, 8.
22. "Barre Bundle," *Argus and Patriot*, July 7, 1897, 3.
23. "Northfield Notes," *Argus and Patriot*, July 21, 1897, 3.
24. "Hard Week for Joyce: New Yorks Have Seven Games Scheduled with the Bostons," *The World*, August 9, 1897, 9.
25. W. F.H. Koelsch, "New York Nuggets: Not Hopeful Now of Better than Third Place," *Sporting Life*, August 28, 1897, 7.
26. "Northfield," *Vermont News*, December 21, 1897, 8.
27. "Doheny Struck Out Twelve," *Indianapolis Journal*, June 10, 1898, 6.
28. "Northfield," *Northfield News*, August 2, 1898, 8.
29. W. F.H. Koelsch, "New York Nuggets: The Memorable Series with the Erstwhile Leaders – The Giants Set Too Fast a Pace – Some Individual Tributes," *Sporting Life*, August 27, 1898, 11.
30. "'Giants' Demoralized: Joyce's Warriors in a State of Insurrection," *Brooklyn Citizen*, September 3, 1898, 4.
31. "Scrappy Joyce's Men Refuse to Pitch Ball: Meekin and Seymour Decline to Take Rusie's Place on the Rubber," *Pittsburg Post*, September 3, 1898, 6.
32. "'Giants' Demoralized," 4.
33. "Scrappy Joyce's Men Refuse to Pitch Ball," 6.
34. "'Giants' Demoralized," 4.
35. "Scrappy Joyce's Men Refuse to Pitch Ball," 6.
36. "'Giants' Demoralized," 4.
37. "Knocking Doheny: Giants Do Not Like the Young Twirler," *Buffalo Courier*, September 19, 1898, 8.
38. W. F. Koelsch, "What Koelsch Says: Nothing in Reports of Mutiny – The Giants' Defeats the Result of the Crippled Condition of the Team and Continual Newspaper Hammering," *Sporting Life*, September 24, 1898, 8.
39. W.F.H. Koelsch, "New York Nuggets: A Plea for Harmony among the Giants," *Sporting Life*, March 25, 1899, 2.
40. "Death of Ed Doheny," 2.
41. "Base Ball Notes," *Wilkes-Barre Daily News*, March 16, 1900, 1.
42. "New York Club Troubles," *Standard Union*, March 16, 1900, 9.
43. "Two Hits All Hughey Allowed: 'Coldwater Jeems' Was in Excellent Form and Had Wonderful Speed," *St. Louis Republic*, July 1, 1900, 12.
44. "Donovan at Pittsburg: Cardinal's Commander Tarries on His Way West – Burkett with Him," *St. Louis Globe-Democrat*, March 26, 1901, 10.

45. "Baseball: New-York Loses Another Game at Cincinnati and Drops Back into Third Place," *New-York Tribune*, July 10, 1901, 8.
46. "Baseball Comment," *St. Louis Republic*, July 14, 1901, 5.
47. "Baseball: New-York Beaten and Back in Fifth Place – Mills, the New Pitcher, Hit Freely," *New-York Tribune*, July 18, 1901, 4.
48. "Ely Released, Doheny Signed: Pittsburg Club Parted with Its Veteran Shortstop," *Pittsburg Press*, July 26, 1901, 8.
49. "Sporting Notes," *Pittsburg Post*, July 29, 1901, 6.
50. "Sporting Notes," *Pittsburg Post*, July 30, 1901, 6.
51. "Pirates Curb the Ambition of the Red Caps from the Mound City: Powell Tries it Once Too Often," *Pittsburg Post*, August 8, 1901, 6.
52. "Baseball Chatter," *Pittsburg Post*, August 18, 1901, 2.
53. "Diamond Chips," *Brooklyn Daily Eagle*, September 14, 1901, 10.
54. "Clarke Stands Guard over the Champions: Not a Single Member of 1901 Team to Be Allowed to Escape – Manager Fred Has Served Notice on the Other Clubs," *Pittsburg Press*, January 12, 1902, 18.
55. Robert Peyton Wiggins, *The Deacon and the Schoolmaster: Phillippe and Leever, Pittsburgh's Great Turn-of-the-Century Pitchers* (Jefferson, NC: McFarland, 2011), 108.
56. A.R. Cratty, "Pittsburg Points: Champs Not Able to Win So Readily as in Seasons Gone By – Wagner's Suspension Not Relished – Bits of News," *Sporting Life*, May 16, 1903, 13.
57. "Pirates Beat Giants: Doheny and Wagner Use Rough Tactics – Later Disciplined," *New-York Tribune*, May 19, 1903, 5.
58. "In the Baseball World: New York Nationals Lose Game and Also First Place," *The Sun*, May 19, 1903, 5.
59. "Champions Win and Pull New York Giants into Second Place, Chicago Going to First: Doheny Outpitches Iron Man M'Ginnity," *Pittsburg Post*, May 19, 1903, 10.
60. "In the Baseball World," 5.
61. "Champions Win and Pull New York Giants into Second Place, Chicago Going to First," 10.
62. "In the Baseball World," 5.
63. "M'Graw's Team Is Outclassed: Eddie Doheny Pitched Rings Around Iron Man McGinnity," *Pittsburg Press*, May 19, 1903, 14.
64. "In the Baseball World," 5.
65. A.R. Cratty, "Pittsburg Points: Pitcher Doheny's Desertion of the Team a Singular Move – New England Twirler Is a Sensitive Man – Team Wins Regardless of the Absence of Regulars," *Sporting Life*, August 8, 1903, 6.
66. "Captain Clarke Emphatically Denies That His Health Is Breaking Down: Champions Beaten by a Single Run," *Pittsburg Post*, May 20, 1903, 8.
67. "Baseball Elections: Harry Pulliam Chosen as President, Secretary and Treasurer by the National," *Brooklyn Daily Times*, December 13, 1902, 14.
68. "Captain Clarke Emphatically Denies That His Health Is Breaking Down," 8.
69. "President Pulliam Sprang Big Surprises," *Pittsburg Press*, May 21, 1903, 18.
70. "The Four Games between the New Yorks and Pittsburgs Attracted 55,000 People: Sam Leever Is Just a Little Unsteady," *Pittsburg Post*, May 21, 1903, 12.
71. "Baseball Notes," *Pittsburg Press*, May 21, 1903, 18.
72. "The Four Games between the New Yorks and Pittsburgs Attracted 55,000 People," 12.
73. Fred W. Veil, *Bucky: A Story of Baseball in the Deadball Era* (Tucson: Wheatmark, 2013), 99.
74. Veil, *Bucky*, 101-102.
75. A.R. Cratty, "Pittsburg Points: The Champions Still Keep Up Their Fast Pace – No Friction between Club Officials – Comment upon Visiting Teams and Local Players," *Sporting Life*, July 18, 1903, 2.

76. "Doheny Insane," *Buffalo Evening News*, March 3, 1904, 12.
77. Wiggins, *The Deacon and the Schoolmaster*, 128.
78. "Eddie Doheny Deserts Team: Clever Southpaw's Mind Is Affected and He Goes Home," *Pittsburg Press*, July 29, 1903, 12.
79. "Doheny Went Home to Rest: Says He Will Report to the Pittsburg Team for Duty, on August 10," *Dayton Evening Herald*, August 1, 1903, 6.
80. "Eddie Doheny Deserts Team," 12.
81. "No Rest Now for Clarke: Pirate Leader Is Busily Looking for Men to Fill Holes on Crippled Team," *The Pittsburg Press*, July 29, 1903, 12.
82. "Johnson May Not Be Sick: Pat Powers Declares That Foxy Ban Wants No National Agreement Now – Dreyfuss on Doheny Case," *Pittsburg Press*, July 29, 1903, 12.
83. "Donovan Postponed the Game: National League Grounds at St. Louis Too Wet for Yesterday's Contest," *Pittsburg Press*, August 2, 1903, 19.
84. A.R. Cratty, "Pittsburg Points: Break-Up of Champs' Pitching Staff Helped the Race," *Sporting Life*, August 15, 1903, 2.
85. "Doheny Went Home to Rest," 6.
86. Ralph S. Davis, "Doheny to Return: Pirates' Southpaw Sorry That He Deserted," *The Sporting News*, August 8, 1903, 4.
87. A.R. Cratty, "Pittsburg Points: Pitcher Doheny's Desertion of the Team a Singular Move – New England Twirler Is a Sensitive Man – Team Wins Regardless of the Absence of Regulars," 6.
88. Cratty, "Pittsburg Points: Break-Up of Champs' Pitching Staff Helped the Race," 2.
89. "Doheny Will Rejoin Team: Physician Writes Manager Clarke about the Famous Pitcher's Condition," *Pittsburg Press*, August 9, 1903, 19.
90. Ralph S. Davis, "In Better Shape: Pirates' Disabled List Grows Smaller," *The Sporting News*, August 15, 1903, 6.
91. "Doheny Has Joined Team: Clever Southpaw Again Returned to the Pirate Fold," *Pittsburg Press*, August 16, 1903, 18.
92. "Players Down on Doheny," *Buffalo Morning Express*, August 18, 1903, 11.
93. "Kennedy Knew It," *Pittsburg Press*, August 3, 1903, 10.
94. "Money and Jewels Gone: The Sensational Story Told by a Tourist," *Saturday Bee*, August 18, 1894, 2.
95. "Kennedy Knew It," 10.
96. "Win One Each: Boston and Pittsburg Break Even," *Boston Sunday Globe*, August 16, 1903, 4.
97. "The Pirates Are Downed by Chicago: Chicago Gave the Champions a Terrific Walloping in First Labor Day Game – Doheny Knocked Out of the Box and Thompson Was Hit Hard," *Pittsburg Press*, September 7, 1903, 1.
98. "A World's Series: May Not Be Played This Fall After All," *Sporting Life*, September 19, 1903, 5.
99. Andy Dabilis and Nick Tsiotos, *The 1903 World Series: The Boston Americans, the Pittsburg Pirates, and the "First Championship of the United States"* (Jefferson, NC: McFarland, 2004), 2.
100. Diabilis and Tsiotos, *The 1903 World Series*, 54-55.
101. "Will Bet on Boston," *Wilkes-Barre Times*, September 22, 1903, 5.
102. A.R. Cratty, "Pittsburg Points: Champs Ready for the Fray with American Banner Bearers – One Star Pitcher Ailing but He May Be Brought Around – New Men Have Been Getting an Opportunity," *Sporting Life*, October 3, 1903, 3.
103. A.R. Cratty, "Pittsburg Points: Ambitions of Premier Managers in the Games for World's Honors – Hope to Excel Boston in Field and Gate – Local Patrons Enthused," *Sporting Life*, October 10. 1903, 7.
104. John H. Gruber, "Champions of National and American Leagues on Even Terms: Dineen Too Much for the Pirates," *Pittsburg Post*, October 3, 1903, 12.

105. "Boston Again Lowers Colors of Pirates: Dineen Pitches American Leaguers to Victory, Placing Collins' Team on Even Footing in Championship Race," *Buffalo Courier*, October 9, 1903, 11.

106. "Dineen Beat the Pirates: Boston Took Sixth Game of the World's Championship Series," *Pittsburgh Press*, October 9, 1903, 24.

107. "Fred Clarke Roasted by Jimmy Collins: For Refusing to Play Yesterday's Scheduled Game in the Smoky City – Declared Off it Is Said to Save Phillipi's Arm," *Buffalo Enquirer*, October 10, 1903, 8.

108. Ralph S. Davis, "Title Is Yet to Be Claimed: Fight between Boston and Pittsburg Has Proved Bitter One," *Pittsburg Press*, October 11, 1903, 19.

109. Masur, *Autumn Glory*, 205.

110. Roger I. Abrams, *The First World Series and the Baseball Fanatics of 1903* (Boston: Northeastern University Press, 2003), 163-164.

111. Masur, *Autumn Glory*, 205.

112. "Eddie Doheny Insane: Assaulted His Doctor and Nurse at Home in Andover," *Fall River Daily Globe*, October 12, 1903, 1.

113. "Ed. Doheny Fells Nurse with Poker: Pittsburg Baseball Club's Pitcher Holds Score of People at Bay for an Hour," *Pittsburg Post*, October 12, 1903, 1.

114. "Eddie Doheny Insane," 1.

115. "Ed. Doheny Fells Nurse with Poker," 1.

116. "Eddie Doheny Insane," 1.

117. "Ed. Doheny Fells Nurse with Poker," 1.

118. "Eddie Doheny Insane," 1.

119. "Doings of Doheny: His Mad Outbreak the Result of Pittsburg's Defeat by Boston – The Patient Certain to Recover His Reason," *Sporting Life*, October 24, 1903, 12.

120. Dabilis and Tsiotos, *The 1903 World Series*, 163.

121. "Doheny's Last Sane Thoughts Were of a Small Debt," *Buffalo Evening Times*, October 15, 1903, 14.

122. "No Winter Sports for the Pirates: Barney Dreyfuss Refuses to Let Any of His Players Take Chances of Being Hurt," *Buffalo Evening News*, December 24, 1903, 8.

123. "Late News: Players' Share of Receipts – Doheny Included in Division," *The Sporting News*, October 17, 1903, 1.

124. A.R. Cratty, "Pittsburg Points: Captain Clarke Coming East to Coach Princeton Lads," *Sporting Life*, February 27, 1904, 8.

125. "Doheny Insane," 12.

126. "National League News," *Sporting Life*, March 26, 1904, 4.

127. "Base Ball Notes," *Waterbury Evening Democrat*, May 21, 1904, 9.

128. "National League News," *Sporting Life*, February 25, 1905, 3.

129. "Death of Ed Doheny," 2.

130. Ralph Davis, "Ralph Davis' Column – The End of Eddie Doheny," *Pittsburg Press*, January 3, 1917, 24.

Chapter 5: A Heated Rivalry

1. Edward F. Balinger, "Sports World Mourns Death of Dreyfuss: Pirate Owner Succumbs in N.Y. Hospital," *Pittsburgh Post-Gazette*, February 6, 1932, 14.

2. "Pneumonia after Operation Causes Dreyfuss' Death: Noted Baseball Club Owner Settled in Paducah after Coming from Germany," *Sun-Democrat*, February 5, 1932, 9.

3. Balinger, "Sports World Mourns Death of Dreyfuss," 14.

4. "Pneumonia after Operation Causes Dreyfuss' Death," 9.

5. Balinger, "Sports World Mourns Death of Dreyfuss," 14.

6. "Pneumonia after Operation Causes Dreyfuss' Death," 9.

7. Balinger, "Sports World Mourns Death of Dreyfuss," 14.

8. "Pneumonia after Operation Causes Dreyfuss' Death," 9.

9. Pirate, "Gigantic Deal: Star Colonels Sold to Pittsburg Club," *The Sporting News*, December 16, 1899, 3.

10. "Late News: Dreyfus Elected President – Will Control Pittsburg Club," *The Sporting News*, December 16, 1899, 1.

11. A.R. Cratty, "Pittsburg Points: Barney Dreyfuss Blocks the Effort to Sidetrack Him – Kerr and Auten May Go into Court – Bits of News," *Sporting Life*, January 19, 1901, 7.

12. Francis C. Richter, "Dreyfus Dumped: Pittsburg's Club Can't Let Well Enough Alone," *Sporting Life*, December 29, 1900, 7.

13. A.R. Cratty, "Angry Owners: Col. Dreyfus' Bed in Pittsburg Evidently Not One of Roses – What the Gossips Say about Pittsburg Club Affairs," *Sporting Life*, December 29, 1900, 7.

14. Francis Richter, "Dreyfuss Wins Out: Secures Control of Pittsburg Through Purchase," *Sporting Life*, February 23, 1901, 8.

15. "Muggsy M'Graw Has Been in Game Long Time: Giant Manager Started Playing When but Seventeen Years of Age," *Sunday Times*, June 4, 1905, 19.

16. "Scribbled by Scribes: John McGraw as a Boy," *The Sporting News*, August 18, 1938, 4.

17. Westbrook Pegler, "As Westbrook Pegler Sees It," *Park City Daily News*, June 18, 1953, 4.

18. "Scribbled by Scribes," 4.

19. "Muggsy M'Graw Has Been in Game Long Time," 19.

20. "M'Graw's Action Commented Upon: Opinions Differ as to Result of Player's Latest Move," *Philadelphia Times*, July 14, 1902, 8.

21. "Muggsy M'Graw Has Been in Game Long Time," 19.

22. "A Slap at McGraw," *Sporting Life*, January 13, 1900, 8.

23. "M'Graw's Action Commented Upon," 8.

24. "Muggsy M'Graw Has Been in Game Long Time," 19.

25. "McGraw and Party Depart: Talk of American League Invading St. Louis Regarded as 'Moonshine,'" *St. Louis Globe-Democrat*, February 25, 1901, 7.

26. "Mugsy M'Graw in New York: He May Manage the Giants in the Race the Coming Season," *Pittsburg Post*, January 3, 1901, 6.

27. "M'Graw Talks of Court: Orioles' Manager Thinks He Will Enjoin President Ban Johnson," *The Times* (Philadelphia), June 18, 1901, 10.

28. "M'Graw Attacks Johnson: Fight May Result in a Split in the American League," *Houston Daily Post*, June 20, 1901, 5.

29. "Comiskey on Jennings Case: Chicago Magnate Upholds American League Officials against McGraw," *The Times* (Philadelphia), June 18, 1901, 10.

30. "M'Graw Attacks Johnson: Fight May Result in a Split in the American League," *Topeka State Journal*, June 19, 1901, 2.

31. "Dropping M'Graw: Talk of Supplanting Baltimore in American League," *Evening Star*, July 31, 1901, 9.

32. "Spalding Will Save League: Baltimore Magnates Say His Election Was a Wise Move," *Pittsburg Press*, December 19, 1901, 8.

33. Hotspur, "Sporting News of the Day: Punishment of Rowdy Baseball Players Is All Right, but the Presidents of Leagues Who Engage Incompetent Umpires Should Also Be Blamed for Much of the Trouble – Johnson Has His Troubles," *Buffalo Enquirer*, August 26, 1901, 4.

34. Alexander, *John McGraw*, 88-89.

35. "'Mugsy's' Way: Back in Game Again, He Is Ordered Out," *Boston Sunday Globe*, June 29, 1902, 4.

36. "M'Graw and Kelley Put Out of Running: Ban Johnson Severely Scores Baltimore Players," *Washington Times*, July 1, 1902, 4.

37. "McGraw Leaves the American League," *Buffalo Enquirer*, July 8, 1902, 4.

38. Hotspur, "Sporting Gossip: M'Graw Leaves the American League to Accept the Position of Captain-Manager of the New York Club in the National League – Refused to Stand Longer for Ban Johnson's Suspensions – M'Graw's Friends Predict the Fight of Johnson's Life Is Now On," *Buffalo Enquirer*, July 8, 1902, 4.

39. "M'Graw's Action Commented Upon," 8.

40. "Base Ball Notes," *Evening Star*, July 9, 1902, 9.

41. "Why McGraw Jumped: Facts Regarding the Move of the Famous Oriole," *Evening Star*, July 9, 1902, 9.

42. "M'Graw's Action Commented Upon," 8.

43. "Baltimore to Have Another Ball Team: Franchise Forfeited If No Game Is Played Today," *Evening Times*, July 17, 1902, 3.

44. "Sporting News: The Sale of the Cincinnati Ball Team Completed," *Topeka State Journal*, August 11, 1902, 2.

45. "Freedman Turns Over the Giants to John T. Brush: Without Warning Andrew Cuts Loose a Bit of Sensation," *Philadelphia Inquirer*, September 30, 1902, 11.

46. "Baseball Stars Had Lively Scrap: Big Bowerman of New York and Little Clarke of Pittsburg the Principals," *Buffalo Evening News*, June 27, 1903, 8.

47. "Bowerman and Clarke Fought," *St. Louis Globe-Democrat*, June 27, 1903, 15.

48. "Baseball Players Slug Each Other in New York: Catcher Bowerman Knocked Fred Clarke Down in the Office of the National League Club," *Buffalo Enquirer*, June 27, 1903, 8.

49. "Baseball Stars Had Lively Scrap," 8.

50. "Clarke Cowardly Attacked: Knocked Down by Captain Bowerman and Taken Unawares – Conspiracy Is at the Bottom," *Pittsburg Post*, June 27, 1903, 8.

51. "Bowerman and Clarke Fought," 15.

52. "Baseball Stars Had Lively Scrap" 8.

53. "Baseball Players Slug Each Other in New York," 8.

54. "Mathewson a Real Hoodoo: Once More the Lucky Giant Twirler Downed the Champs," *Pittsburg Press*, June 27, 1903, 10.

55. "Minor Leaguers May Take a Hand: Are Expected to Rise in Support of Pulliam against the American League Robbers," *Pittsburg Press*, June 27, 1903, 10.

56. Ralph S. Davis, "Battle Opened Afresh: Horizon of the Baseball World Is Obscured by Dark Warclouds," *Pittsburg Press*, June 28, 1903, 18.

57. Ralph S. Davis, "Refuses to Talk: Dreyfuss Declines to Discuss Pulliam's Action," *The Sporting News*, July 4, 1903, 1.

58. "Champions in the Metropolis: Most of Them Remain Indoors on Sunday – President Dreyfuss Joins the Team and Refuses to Discuss the Assault on Clarke," *Pittsburg Post*, June 29, 1903, 6.

59. "Ha! Ha!: There'll be Blood on the Face of the Moon," *Philadelphia Inquirer*, June 28, 1903, 14.

60. "Catcher Bowerman Fined $100," *Philadelphia Inquirer*, July 16, 1903, 4.

61. "Bowerman Fined $100 for Assault: Giants' Catcher Severely Dealt with by National League for Hitting Fred Clarke at Polo Grounds Last Month," *The World*, July 15, 1903, 8.

62. "Police Protect Pugilistic Catcher: Bowerman Escapes Wrath of Pittsburg Crowd, Caused by Assault on Clarke," *St. Louis Post-Dispatch*, July 16, 1903, 3.

63. Ralph S. Davis, "Giants Downed Again: Roscoe Miller Pitched Good Ball, but the Champions Won in the Ninth," *Pittsburg Press*, July 19, 1903, 19.

64. "Bowerman's Nerve Gone: Unwilling to Stand Jeers He Refused to Catch Yesterday," *Pittsburg Press*, July 19, 1903, 19.

65. "M'Graw Put Life into Team: Made the Offended Bowerman Square Matters with Fred Clarke," *Inter Ocean*, November 27, 1904, 4.

66. "The Bowerman-Clarke Feud," *St. Louis Globe-Democrat*, June 18, 1905, 3.

67. "Echoes of the Game," *Boston Daily Globe*, October 3, 1903, 8.

68. "True Facts Disclosed: Enemies of Barney Dreyfuss Making Desperate Efforts to Injure Him," *Pittsburg Press*, March 3, 1904, 14.

69. "M'Graw Has Settled It: Pittsburg Cannot Possibly Win the Pennant This Season," *Pittsburg Press*, March 3, 1904, 14.

70. Ralph S. Davis, "Have Fighting Chance Yet for That Pennant: The New York Team, However, Must Be Beaten Rather Frequently by Some Clubs If We Would Pull to the Front Row," *Pittsburg Press*, August 21, 1904, 20.

71. "Baseball Notes," *Pittsburg Press*, August 24, 1904, 8.

72. "Why: Reason for the McGraw and Dreyfuss Battle," *Chattanooga Sunday Times*, June 11, 1905, 32.

73. "Fred Clarke Adopts New Plan on the Field: Intends to Report to President Pulliam Every Violation of the League Rules Not Punished Immediately by the Umpires," *Pittsburg Press*, May 19, 1905, 22.

74. Ralph S. Davis, "Strenuous Series: Hot Times for Pirates in New York," *The Sporting News*, May 27, 1905, 2.

75. "Why: Reason for the McGraw and Dreyfuss Battle," 32.

76. "Conduct of M'Graw Will Cause Trouble: Magnate Barney Dreyfuss Files Formal Protest against Actions of Pugnacious New York Manager," *Washington Times*, May 23, 1905, 8.

77. "Why: Reason for the McGraw and Dreyfuss Battle," 32.

78. "Pirates Are Having a Scrappy Time with McGraw and His Champion Giants: West Just Holding Its Own in East," *Pittsburg Post*, May 22, 1905, 6.

79. "Captain Clarke Threatens to Trim Manager McGraw," *Washington Times*, May 23, 1905, 8.

80. "Why: Reason for the McGraw and Dreyfuss Battle," 32.

81. "Washington: It's a Good Ball Town, Says Tim Murnane," *Chattanooga Sunday Times*, June 11, 1905, 32.

82. Joseph Vila, "Knows No Better: M'Graw Has Always Played Rowdy Ball," *The Sporting News*, May 27, 1905, 1.

83. "Conduct of M'Graw Will Cause Trouble," 8.

84. "M'Graw Is Suspended and Fined by Pulliam: Forfeits All Privileges of the Ball Field for Fifteen Days and Fined $150 for Insulting Remarks Made to President Barney Dreyfuss," *Pittsburg Press*, May 28, 1905, 22.

85. Ralph S. Davis, "President Pulliam Made a Popular Move: His Desire to Remit Fines Collected from Players Convicted of Rowdy Conduct on the Ball Field Is Generally Approved," *Pittsburg Press*, June 18, 1905, 19.

86. "McGraw Indignant: Claims President Pulliam Is Favoring Barney Dreyfuss," *Evening Star*, May 29, 1905, 9.

87. "McGraw Criticizes Pulliam," *Sporting Life*, June 3, 1905, 3.

88. "The Presidential Punishment," *Sporting Life*, June 3, 1905, 3.

89. Alexander, *John McGraw*, 114.

90. "M'Graw Is Suspended and Fined by Pulliam," 22.

91. "McGraw to Be Squelched," *Sporting Life*, June 3, 1905, 3.

92. "A Complication: Will the National Board of Directors Be Eligible to Act in the McGraw Case?," *Sporting Life*, June 3, 1903, 1.

93. "McGraw to Be Squelched," 3.

94. "Rain Prevents the Game with Chicago: Both Teams Compelled to Loaf, but Will Meet This Afternoon," *Pittsburg Post*, June 3, 1905, 8.

95. "M'Graw Wins Case: Barney Dreyfuss Fails to Substantiate Charges Which He Made," *Galveston Daily News*, June 11, 1905, 14.

96. "Pulliam Besieged: McGraw's Friends Waylay Him," *Boston Daily Globe*, June 2, 1905, 5.

97. "Rain Prevents the Game with Chicago," 8.
98. "M'Graw Wins Case," 14.
99. "Pulliam Besieged," 5.
100. Alexander, *John McGraw*, 114.
101. "Why: Reason for the McGraw and Dreyfuss Battle," 32.
102. "M'Graw Wins Case," 14.
103. "Brush after Pulliam: New York Magnate Says He Supported League Construction," *Evening Star*, June 8, 1905, 9.
104. "M'Graw Is Suspended and Fined by Pulliam," 22.
105. "Pulliam Besieged," 5.
106. "Barney Dreyfuss Home: The President Is Not at All Sore over the Action of the Board of Directors," *Pittsburg Post*, June 4, 1905, 2.
107. A.R. Cratty, Pittsburg Points: Club Owner Is Satisfied with Make-Up of Team," *Sporting Life*, June 10, 1905, 8.
108. "Barney Dreyfuss Home," 2.

Chapter 6: Rube Waddell

1. "Pulliam Besieged," 5.
2. "M'Graw Goes to Court: Asks for Injunction Restraining President Pulliam from Collecting a Fine of $150," *Pittsburg Post*, June 3, 1905, 8.
3. "M'Graw Vindicated: Massachusetts Court Renders Null and Void Pulliam's Ruling," *New-York Tribune*, June 6, 1905, 10.
4. Ralph S. Davis, "Outcome of Big Tangle Is Still Uncertainty: Constitution of the National League May Be Changed at the Annual Meeting of the Organization Next Fall," *Pittsburg Press*, June 11, 1905, 19.
5. "May Remit Fines: Must Be One Law for All in Baseball, Says Pulliam," *New-York Tribune*, June 13, 1905, 4.
6. Ralph S. Davis, "President Pulliam Made a Popular Move: His Desire to Remit Fines Collected from Players Convicted of Rowdy Conduct on the Ball Field Is Generally Approved," *Pittsburg Press*, June 18, 1905, 19.
7. "Brush after Pulliam: New York Magnate Says He Supported League Construction," *Evening Star*, June 8, 1905, 9.
8. Barney Dreyfuss, "Clubs Must Line Up to Base Ball Law," *Philadelphia Inquirer*, June 7, 1905, 10.
9. "Brush Extends Glad Hand: Says Barney - - - 'So Sizzle,'" *Philadelphia Inquirer*, June 12, 1905, 10.
10. J.W. M'Conaughy, "Is Pride or Prudence between Giants and American Champions?: President Brush Coolly Disqualifies Highlanders as Members of Minor League, but it Is Not So Certain His Men Could Vanquish Them," *St. Louis Post-Dispatch*, October 2, 1904, 9.
11. "We Are Not Required to Contest Championship with Minor League – Pres. John T. Brush," *St. Louis Post-Dispatch*, October 2, 1904, 9.
12. "Afraid of 'Hey Barney' Signs," *Sunday Star*, November 5, 1905, 3.
13. "Giants Awarded World's Honors: Defeat Athletics in Last Game 2 to 0, Mathewson Outpitching Bender – Immense Crowd Gives Ovation to the Victors," *Inter Ocean*, October 15, 1905, 1.
14. J.G. Taylor Spink, "Waddell: Madcap Mound Marvel – Rose to Fame under Mack's Kindly Hand," *The Sporting News*, October 9, 1946, 10.
15. "Rube Waddell Loses Battle for His Life: Hero of Many Queer Exploits on the Diamond Dies of Tuberculosis," *The Sun*, April 2, 1914, 8.
16. Spink, "Waddell," 10.

17. John M. Graham, "Rube Waddell Sprung into Fame from Volant: Strikes Out Five Men in Two Innings in His First Game – Is under Contract by Louisville Colonels within Eight Weeks after Making Debut at Volant College – He Couldn't Bat Well but He Poled Out the Longest Hit Ever Seen on Slippery Rock Normal Field – Was Popular with Small Boys and Would Go Wading in Creek with Youngsters," *New Castle News*, April 17, 1914, 17.

18. "Baseball Yarns: Rube Waddell Was Once Kidnapped, Commandeering a Pitcher," *Winnipeg Tribune*, March 2, 1906, 5.

19. "Waddell Ways: A New Story on the Eccentric Twirler," *Sporting Life*, February 10, 1906, 10.

20. Alan H. Levy, *Rube Waddell: The Zany, Brilliant Life of a Strikeout Artist* (Jefferson, NC: McFarland, 2000), 15.

21. Spink, "Waddell," 10.

22. "Some New Stories on Rube Waddell: Eccentric Pitcher's Arrival and Departure with Pittsburg Club," *Wilkes-Barre Record*, March 3, 1910, 16.

23. John H. "Honus" Wagner, "Third Story in Wagner Series: The 'Nuts' of the National Pastime," *Pittsburg Press*, July 4, 1915, 1.

24. "Some New Stories on Rube Waddell," 16.

25. "Waddell Faces the Champions," *Pittsburg Post*, September 9, 1897, 6.

26. Levy, *Rube Waddell*, 24.

27. "Comedian Waddell: Louisville's Famous Rube Is the Arlie Latham of the National League," *Buffalo Enquirer*, October 1, 1897, 8.

28. Levy, *Rube Waddell*, 25.

29. Levy, 26.

30. Levy, 29.

31. "When Waddell Pitched in Chatham, Ont.: It Was on the Queen's Birthday and He Struck Out Twenty-Seven Men and Won the Game Single-Handed," *Buffalo Enquirer*, February 10, 1906, 8.

32. "Sporting Notes: Some Afterclaps of the Dunnville-Chatham Game – Other Notes," *The Expositor*, June 24, 1898, 6.

33. "Sporting Notes," *Pittsburg Post*, June 25, 1898, 6.

34. "Sporting Notes: Some Afterclaps of the Dunnville-Chatham Games – Other Notes," 6.

35. "Additional Local," *Advance Argus*, August 11, 1898, 7.

36. "Additional Local," *Advance Argus*, September 8, 1898, 7.

37. "Additional Local," *Advance Argus*, August 11, 1898, 7.

38. "Waddell Quick to Retort: A Ball Player Who Has a Lively Sense of Humor," *Philadelphia Inquirer*, October 29, 1899, 13.

39. Spink, "Waddell," 10.

40. "Base Ball Briefs," *St. Paul Globe*, August 7, 1899, 5.

41. "Another New Pitcher: Rube Waddell of Grand Rapids Likely to Join the Brooklyns This Week," *Brooklyn Daily Eagle*, August 7, 1899, 6.

42. Spink, "Waddell," 10.

43. Pirate, "Gigantic Deal: Star Colonels Sold to Pittsburg Club," *The Sporting News*, December 16, 1899, 3.

44. "Baseball Chatter," *Pittsburg Post*, July 8, 1900, 6.

45. Circle, "Pittsburg Points: High-Class Work by the Buccaneers Results in the Development of Enthusiasm – Excellent Financial Returns – Big Rube Suspended," *Sporting Life*, July 14, 1900, 10.

46. "Waddell's Lay-Off: Clarke Angered by Rube's Statement That He Wasn't Properly Supported," *St. Louis Republic*, July 9, 1900, 3.

47. Spink, "Waddell," 10.

48. Spink, "Waddell," 12.

49. "Rube Waddell Joins the Pirates Again," *Pittsburg Press*, September 3, 1900, 5.

50. "Clarke Defends Waddell: Bad Weather Effects Eddie as Much as Other Players," *Pittsburg Press*, April 24, 1901, 8.

51. "Final Practice: Pirates Put in a Busy Day at the Pittsburg College Park," *Pittsburg Press*, April 27, 1901, 7.

52. Levy, *Rube Waddell*, 76.

53. "Rube Waddell Wild and Erratic: Loses the Game to the Chicago Orphans in the First Inning," *Pittsburg Post*, May 2, 1901, 6.

54. Levy, *Rube Waddell*, 77.

55. "Some New Stories on Rube Waddell," 16.

56. Spink, "Waddell," 12.

57. "Rube Is Protected: Ban Johnson Issues Order to Save the Erratic Twirler," *Pittsburg Press*, August 31, 1902, 18.

58. "Waddell Suspended; 'I'm Done,' Says Mack: Athletics' Twirler Meets His Just Deserts," *Washington Times*, August 26, 1903, 4.

59. "'The Stain of Guilt,'" *Public Daily Ledger Maysville Republican*, September 25, 1903, 1.

60. "Sports: Base Ball," *Wilkes-Barre Record*, August 26, 1903, 9.

61. "Rube Waddell Takes unto Himself a Wife," *Pittsburg Press*, June 4, 1903, 15.

62. "The Wedding of the Ruben and the Maid: George Edward Waddell, Light of the Diamond, Dons Glad Rags and Takes a Bride," *Philadelphia Inquirer*, June 4, 1903, 10.

63. "Rube Waddell's Freak: Assaulted Father-in-Law and Mother-in-Law," *Fall River Daily Globe*, February 10, 1905, 2.

64. "Dog Used Teeth: Drove 'Rube' Waddell from Ross Home," *Boston Daily Globe*, February 9, 1905, 1.

65. "Rube Waddell's Freak," 2.

66. "Dog Used Teeth," 1.

67. "Rube Waddell Wanted: Assaulted Wife's Parents in Quarrel over Board Bill," *Daily Times* (New Philadelphia, Ohio), February 9, 1905, 4.

68. "Rube Waddell Goes Wrong: Baseball Pitcher Accused of Assaulting Father-in-Law," *Weekly State Journal*, February 10, 1905, 1.

69. "'Rube' Waddell Skips the State: Pitching Hand Injured in the Mix-Up at His Wife's Home in Peabody," *Daily Evening Item*, February 10, 1905, 8.

70. "'Rube' Waddell's Erratic Record: Eccentric Twirler Not in Favor with His Wife's Massachusetts Relatives," *Scranton Republican*, February 26, 1905, 3.

71. "Baseball Notes," *Pittsburg Press*, February 23, 1905, 12.

72. "Sport Gossip," *Butte Inter Mountain*, February 27, 1905, 7.

73. "'Rube' Waddell a Fire Hero: 'Spit' Ball Twirler Shows His Nerve," *Daily Evening Item*, February 6, 1905, 5.

74. "Peculiar Actions of Rube Waddell: As a Butcher," *Oakland Tribune*, March 30, 1905, 6.

75. "Rube Waddell a Hero: Pitcher Pitches a Hot Stove into the Snow," *Oakland Tribune*, February 13, 1905, 4.

76. Veteran, "Four Contracts: Received by Shettsline within a Week," *The Sporting News*, February 18, 1905, 3.

77. "Sporty Paragraphs: Interesting Items Gathered Chiefly from the Baseball Diamond," *Fall River Daily Globe*, January 10, 1906, 2.

78. "Waddell Discharged: No One Appears against Rube at Peabody on Complaint of Assault on Father-in-Law Ross," *Boston Daily Globe*, January 8, 1906, 9.

79. "New Yorkers Win Two Games: Philadelphia Puts the Kibosh on Boston – Rube Waddell Receives Injury to Pitching Hand and Retires," *Salt Lake Tribune*, July 8, 1905, 8.

80. "Waddell Pitches in Country," *Los Angeles Express*, July 28, 1905, 10.

81. "Keep an Eye on Rube Waddell: Big Pitcher Is Watched Carefully by Connie Mack's Special Emissary," *Minneapolis Journal*, September 20, 1905, 12.

82. "Mack Fears Rube Has Been Tampered With," *Los Angeles Record*, September 26, 1905, 6.

83. Veteran, "Big Lead Reduced: Athletics Have No Cinch on '05 Pennant," *The Sporting News*, September 30, 1905, 1.

84. "Rube Waddell: Denies the Many Rumors Concerning His 'Sale' to Gamblers," *Dayton Evening Herald*, September 23, 1905, 13.

85. "Reuben Says He Is Not a Quitter," *Minneapolis Journal*, September 23, 1905, 28.

86. "Mack Fears Rube Has Been Tampered With," 6.

87. "'Rube' Waddell's Case Worries Connie Mack," *Buffalo Evening Times*, September 29, 1905, 10.

88. "'Rube' Waddell Out: Pitching Days of the Great Southpaw Are Probably Over," *Evening Star*, September 28, 1905, 9.

89. Francis C. Richter, "Quaker Quips: A Record-Breaking Week in Philadelphia Base Ball – The Case of Pitcher Waddell," *Sporting Life*, October 7, 1905, 2.

90. "May Investigate Waddell's Conduct: Rumored That President Johnson of the American League Will Probe Nasty Rumors Concerning Rube's Actions in Post-Season Series," *Inter Ocean*, January 8, 1906, 8.

91. "Why Rube Didn't Pitch: Was Injured in Horse Play with Coakley," *Buffalo Courier*, December 22, 1905, 10.

92. R.S. Davis, "Seven Clubs Are after Scalps of the Giants: Aim of All the Managers in the National League in Strengthening Teams Is to Conquer the Boastful New Yorkers," *Pittsburg Press*, January 14, 1906, 18.

93. Bozeman Bulger, "'Rube' Waddell Crooked? The Idea Is Ridiculous: Absolutely Nothing in Rumor That He Was Disloyal to His Team," *The World*, January 18, 1906, 14.

94. "Wild Pipe by Setley," *Salt Lake Herald*, April 6, 1906, 8.

95. "Says Waddell Was Bought by Gamblers," *Los Angeles Express*, April 16, 1906, 10.

96. Veteran, "Are at Practice: Athletics and Phillies in the South," *The Sporting News*, March 10, 1906, 3.

97. "Waddell to the Front: Must Put Up Half of Year's Salary for Support of Spouse," *Spokane Daily Chronicle*, May 11, 1906, 13.

98. Veteran, "Big Lead Reduced," 1.

99. "$350,000 Paid for Philadelphia National Club to Beat Heydler: Syndicate, Headed by Horace Fogel, Buys Quaker Stock, and it Is Said Vote for League Presidency Will Be Thrown to John M. Ward," *Buffalo Courier*, November 27, 1909, 8.

100. "Horace Fogel Denies Charges: Also Questions Right of the National League to Try His Case," *Wilkes-Barre Record*, October 29, 1912, 20.

101. "Horace Fogel Resigns: President of Philadelphia Club of National League Quits under Fire," *Boston Evening Transcript*, November 26, 1912, 14.

102. "Gamblers Tried to Buy Local Players: Fogel Cites Two Instances When New York Offered Money for Victories," *Philadelphia Inquirer*, September 30, 1920, 5.

103. "Rube Waddell Loses Battle for His Life," 8.

104. "Gamblers Tried to Buy Local Players," 5.

Chapter 7: Chick Stahl

1. "Fort Wayne Friends Shocked: Suicide of Ballplayer Could Not at First Gain Credence," *Fort Wayne Sentinel*, March 28, 1907, 2.

2. "The Motive Unknown: Stahl and His Wife Lived Happily Since Their Marriage," *Fort Wayne Journal-Gazette*, March 29, 1907, 2.

3. Frederic P. O'Connell, "Worried to Death: Care Caused Chick Stahl to End Life," *The Sporting News*, April 6, 1907, 1.

4. "The Motive Unknown," 2.
5. "Fort Wayne Friends Shocked," 2.
6. "A Player Here 10 Years: Charles S. Stahl with Boston Teams Since 1897 – Married Only Five Months – 17 Years in Baseball," *Boston Daily Globe*, March 29, 1907, 9.
7. "The Motive Unknown," 2.
8. "Fort Wayne Friends Shocked," 2.
9. "The Motive Unknown," 2.
10. "Fort Wayne Friends Shocked," 2.
11. "Charles Stahl Boston's New Player," *Sunday Post*, October 25, 1896, 19.
12. "Fort Wayne Friends Shocked," 2.
13. "Charles Stahl Boston's New Player," 19.
14. "Sporting," *Buffalo Enquirer*, July 8, 1896, 8.
15. "Sporting," *Buffalo Enquirer*, July 9, 1896, 8.
16. "Sporting," *Buffalo Enquirer*, November 11, 1896, 8.
17. "Charles Stahl Boston's New Player," 19.
18. "A Player Here 10 Years," 9.
19. "Many at Grounds: Disappointment Because There Is No Game – Comment at Washington," *Boston Daily Globe*, May 4, 1897, 5.
20. "Baseball Notes," *Boston Daily Globe*, August 24, 1897, 2.
21. "The Daily News-Democrat," *Daily News-Democrat*, October 7, 1897, 5.
22. "Slapped His Face: Sensational Incident at the Southern Hotel," *The Sporting News*, October 15, 1898, 2.
23. "'Chick' Stahl as a Catcher," *Buffalo Commercial*, October 31, 1898, 5.
24. "Just Three Hits: All That Lewis Issued to the Cincinnatis," *Boston Sunday Globe*, June 4, 1899, 4.
25. "Sporting World: Notes," *Fort Wayne Sentinel*, October 16, 1899, 5.
26. "Goes to Notre Dame: Chick Stahl Will Coach the University Boys in Base Ball Tactics," *Fort Wayne News*, January 15, 1900, 6.
27. "Bergen Tragedy: Terrible Deed of the Demented Catcher," *The Sporting News*, January 27, 1900, 3.
28. "Chick Stahl Home: Boston Player to Spend the Winter in the City," *Fort Wayne Journal-Gazette*, October 26, 1900, 1.
29. "'Chick' Stahl at Home," *Fort Wayne Sentinel*, October 26, 1900, 1.
30. "Chick Stahl Home," 1.
31. "By U.S. Grand Jury: Two Fort Wayne Men Are Indicted at Indianapolis – Sues Chick Stahl," *Fort Wayne News*, December 3, 1900, 4.
32. "'Chick' Stahl Deserts," *Evening Star*, March 5, 1901, 9.
33. "Chick Stahl Takes a Jump," *Pittsburg Post*, March 5, 1901, 6.
34. Long Shot, "The Sporting World: Boston's American League Is Reporting Here Today – 'Chick' Stahl, the Ex-Bison, Is Here and Declares He Will Stick to Jimmy Collins," *Buffalo Evening Times*, March 30, 1901, 8.
35. Hotspur, "Sports of All Sorts: Jimmy Collins and Chick Stahl Had a Conference Yesterday in This City and Will Leave Tonight for Their Training Quarters – Chick Stahl in Buffalo," *Buffalo Enquirer*, March 30, 1901, 4.
36. "'Chick' Stahl Is Going to Stick," *Topeka State Journal*, April 23, 1901, 2.
37. "Are after Chick Stahl: National League Offers Ex-Buffalonian $10,000 and a Three Years' Contract," *Buffalo Enquirer*, September 2, 1901, 4.
38. "Chick Stahl Wanted: A National Agent Spends Two Hours Trying to Land Him," *Topeka State Journal*, August 29, 1901, 2.
39. "Baseball on the Shelf: Last Games for This Season Have Been Played," *Buffalo Morning Express*, October 14, 1901, 12.

40. "Baseball Gossip," *Fall River Daily Herald*, April 5, 1902, 2.
41. "Tries to Shoot Him: Fort Wayne Girl Draws a Revolver on Fielder 'Chick' Stahl," *Indianapolis Journal*, January 27, 1902, 2.
42. "Shot at Stahl Famous Fielder," *Meriden Daily Journal*, January 27, 1902, 1.
43. "Tries to Shoot Him," 2.
44. "Gunning for Stahl: Fort Wayne Girl Tries to Shoot the Boston Baseball Player," *Boston Daily Globe*, January 27, 1902, 1.
45. "Jilted Girl Tried Murder: Timely Arrival of Policeman Saved Stahl, the Base Ball Star," *The Times* (Philadelphia), January 28, 1902, 2.
46. "Shot at Stahl Famous Fielder," 1.
47. "Tries to Shoot Him," 2.
48. "Tried to Kill 'Chic' Stahl: Miss Lulu Ortman Made Attempt on the Life of the Boston Ball Player," *Fort Wayne Journal-Gazette*, January 27, 1902, 1.
49. "Gunning for Stahl," 1.
50. "The Motive Unknown," 2.
51. "Ortman Case Causes Confusion: Girl Not the Father of Henry Ortman, of 'Pearl' and 'H.O.' Fame," *Fort Wayne Journal-Gazette*, January 29, 1902, 8.
52. "Indiana Notes: Fort Wayne," *Indianapolis Journal*, January 28, 1902, 6.
53. "The Motive Unknown," 2.
54. "Chick Stahl Coming Back: He Should Be Able, It Is Thought, to Get into the Game Again in a Few Days," *Boston Daily Globe*, June 15, 1903, 5.
55. "American League Notes," *Sporting Life*, May 30, 1903, 9.
56. "Young Shuts Out Chicago: Told in a Nutshell," *Boston Post*, May 25, 1903, 8.
57. "American League Notes," *Sporting Life*, June 6, 1903, 5.
58. "American League Notes," *Sporting Life*, June 13, 1903, 9.
59. "Chick Stahl Coming Back," 5.
60. "New England News: The Base Ball Situation in the Hub of the Universe," *Sporting Life*, June 27, 1903, 1.
61. "Collins' and His Secret Methods: 'Chick' Stahl, One of Buffalo's Old Reliables, Stops Off in This City," *Buffalo Courier*, November 30, 1903, 11.
62. "Chick Stahl Is in Town: Chick Stahl on the Street," *Buffalo Morning Express*, March 9, 1905, 9.
63. "Dineen in the Box: Boston's Great Pitcher Shows Up Well in His First Game," *Boston Daily Globe*, April 11, 1905, 8.
64. "Gets the Pinch Hit: Selbach Bats for Stahl," *Boston Daily Globe*, May 24, 1905, 8.
65. "Selbach Will Replace Chick Stahl While the Latter Is Mending," *Boston Daily Globe*, May 24, 1905, 8.
66. "'Chick' Stahl Would Be a Magnate, but Must Wait," *Boston Daily Globe*, July 18, 1905, 2.
67. "News from the Baseball World: Boston's Once-Famous Manager Is Suspended," *Salt Lake Tribune*, September 9, 1906, 2.
68. "Indefinitely Suspended: Action Taken in Case of Jimmy Collins," *Boston Daily Globe*, August 29, 1906, 5.
69. "Collins Is Out: Manager of Boston Americans Suspended for Absence without Leave," *Fall River Daily Globe*, August 29, 1906, 7.
70. "Indefinitely Suspended," 5.
71. "Capt Jimmy Collins No Longer at Helm: Indefinitely Suspended by Boston American League Club," *Boston Daily Globe*, August 29, 1906, 14.
72. "Indefinitely Suspended," 5.
73. "Girl Would an Artist Be; Ballplayer Don't Agree, So Girl Takes Poison: Hattie Burnett of No. 140 Carlton Street, after Telling Her Artistic Yearnings to 'Chick' Stahl, the Boston Americans' Manager, Swallows a Big Sup of Laudanum," *Buffalo Courier*, October 13, 1906, 6.

74. "Said She Didn't Try to Commit Suicide: Miss Hattie Burnett Claims She Took Medicine to Stop Attack of Toothache," *Buffalo Enquirer*, October 13, 1906, 3.
75. "Miss Burnett Gets Suspended Sentence: Young Woman Who Took Poison in Company of 'Chick' Stahl," *Buffalo Courier*, October 16, 1906, 6.
76. "Girl Would an Artist Be; Ballplayer Don't Agree, So Girl Takes Poison," 6.
77. "'Chick' Stahl for Manager: Offered the Boston Berth, but Wants Collins Fixed Up First," *Fall River Daily Globe*, October 17, 1906, 9.
78. The Little Old Man, "Loyalty of Stahl to Collins: Refuses Boston Managership until Owners Treat His Old Friend Right," *Oklahoma News*, November 22, 1906, 3.
79. "Baseball: 'Chick' Stahl's Coming Wedding," *Fort Wayne News*, October 20, 1906, 4.
80. "'Chick' Stahl Given Marriage License," *Pittsburg Press*, November 11, 1906, 22.
81. "Stahl-Harmon: Ball Player Wedded to Roxbury Girl," *Boston Daily Globe*, November 15, 1906, 2.
82. "Looks Good for 'Chick,'" *Fall River Daily Globe*, November 13, 1906, 9.
83. "'Chick' Stahl to Be Manager: Pres John I. Taylor of Boston Americans Announces His Appointment," *Boston Daily Globe*, December 5, 1906, 20.
84. "Incomprehensible to All: Even Those Intimate with Stahl Cannot Account for His Act – Change Came at Little Rock," *Boston Daily Globe*, March 29, 1907, 9.
85. Alan E. Foulds, *Boston's Ballparks & Arenas* (Lebanon, NH: Northeastern University Press – University Press of New England, 2005), 36.
86. "Incomprehensible to All," 9.
87. T.H. Murnane, "Chick Stahl Resigns Position as Manager: Finds Himself Worrying Too Much over Duties - - - Will Captain Team," *Boston Daily Globe*, March 26, 1907, 1.
88. T.H. Murnane, "Stahl Talked Suicide Often: Meditated Yesterday's Act for Many Days," *Boston Daily Globe*, March 29, 1907, 1.
89. O'Connell, "Worried to Death,"1.
90. "'Chick' Stahl Ends His Life with Carbolic Acid: Noted Ballplayer Commits Suicide," *Fort Wayne Sentinel*, March 28, 1907, 2.
91. Murnane, "Stahl Talked Suicide Often," 1.
92. O'Connell, "Worried to Death," 1.
93. "'Last Picture,' Said Stahl: Memphis Photographer Remembers Unusual Statements," *Fort Wayne Journal-Gazette*, March 30, 1907, 2.
94. "Stahl a Victim of Nervousness: He Suffered a Breakdown as a Result of Worry over Club's Affairs," *Fort Wayne News*, March 29, 1907, 4.
95. O'Connell, "Worried to Death," 1.
96. "Stahl a Victim of Nervousness," 4.
97. Murnane, "Stahl Talked Suicide Often," 1.
98. "Stahl a Victim of Nervousness," 4.
99. Murnane, "Stahl Talked Suicide Often," 1.
100. "Stahl a Victim of Nervousness," 4.
101. "Ball-Player 'Chick' Stahl Commits Suicide in Hotel at West Baden: Famous Athlete Ends His Own Life without Warning - - - Drank Carbolic Acid after Talking to Team Mates - - - Was a Product of Fort Wayne," *Fort Wayne Journal-Gazette*, March 29, 1907, 1.
102. "'Chick' Stahl Ends His Life with Carbolic Acid," 1.
103. Murnane, "Stahl Talked Suicide Often," 1.
104. "Ball-Player 'Chick' Stahl Commits Suicide," 1.
105. "Caused Shock in Fort Wayne: News of Stahl's Death a Blow to His Friends at Home," *Fort Wayne Journal-Gazette*, March 29, 1907, 2.
106. "Fort Wayne Friends Shocked," 2.
107. "Meditated Self-Slaying: 'Chick' Stahl Had Often Talked about Suicide," *Fort Wayne Journal-Gazette*, March 30, 1907, 1.

108. "Stahl's Death Foretold," *Fort Wayne Journal-Gazette*, March 30, 1907, 2.
109. "'I've Done What "Chick" Stahl Did': Said Lynn Shoemaker, Who Took Carbolic Acid and Died after His Arrival at Hospital," *Fort Wayne Journal-Gazette*, March 29, 1907, 2.
110. "The Motive Unknown," 2.
111. T.H. Murnane, "Mrs. Stahl on Way West: Goes to Home of Dead Husband – Team Unable to Notify Pres Taylor – Collins Practically in Charge," *Boston Daily Globe*, March 29, 1907, 9.
112. "Caused Shock in Fort Wayne," 2.
113. "Graver Trouble Than Baseball the Cause: Boston People Believe Stahl's Rash Act Was Due to a Strain on the Mind from Worry but Not Connected with the Diamond," *Fort Wayne Journal-Gazette*, March 30, 1907, 2.
114. Murnane, "Mrs. Stahl on Way West," 9.
115. "The Bride's Lament," *Fort Wayne News*, March 29, 1907, 4.
116. "Graver Trouble Than Baseball the Cause," 2.
117. "Dovey's Players Stunned: Refused to Believe at First That Stahl Had Killed Himself – Game Comes to End with News," *Boston Daily Globe*, March 29, 1907, 9.
118. T.H. Murnane, "Stahl Insured for $5,000: Policy Made Out to Mother, Says Collins – Funeral May Be Held Tomorrow," *Boston Daily Globe*, March 29, 1907, 9.
119. O'Connell, "Worried to Death," 1.
120. "Last Rights for Stahl: Remains Laid to Final Resting Place in Lindenwood," *Fort Wayne Journal-Gazette*, April 1, 1907, 1.
121. "Last Rights for Stahl," 5.
122. "'Chick' Stahl's Funeral," *Buffalo Commercial*, April 1, 1907, 5.
123. "Funeral of Chick Stahl Held at His Fort Wayne Home: Star Player of Boston Americans Is Buried – Thousands Follow His Body to Lindenwood Cemetery," *Inter Ocean*, April 1, 1907, 9.
124. "Dies by His Own Hand: David P. Murphy Swallows Acid in Aveline Hotel Apartment," *Fort Wayne Journal-Gazette*, March 31, 1907, 10.
125. "Stahl's Widow: Will Henceforth Make Her Home with 'Chick's' Old Mother," *Sporting Life*, April 13, 1907, 2.
126. "Meditated Self-Slaying," 1.

Chapter 8: The 1908 National League Pennant Race

1. "Team Leaves for Cincinnati: 'Cy' Young Is Ordered to Take Charge Temporarily," *Fort Wayne Sentinel*, March 30, 1907, 2.
2. "Games Will Be Played: No Postponement on Account of the Death of Stahl," *Fort Wayne Sentinel*, March 30, 1907, 2.
3. "Ban Johnson Denies: Statement That He Wouldn't Let Taylor Act as Manager," *Fall River Daily Globe*, April 2, 1907, 7.
4. O'Connell, "Worried to Death," 1.
5. "Under Unglaub: Are Now the Boston American Club Players," *Sporting Life*, May 11, 1907, 2.
6. "Manager Selee Retires Through Ill Health," *Philadelphia Inquirer*, July 29, 1905, 13.
7. "Baseball Notes," *Chattanooga Sunday Times*, October 1, 1905, 32.
8. "Spalding Hopes for Double Win: Former Magnate Sees Possibility of Murphy's Cubs Winning Both Championships," *Buffalo Morning Express*, November 17, 1905, 12.
9. John H. Gruber, "Frank Schulte Made Good from the Start with the Cubs: As a Batsman He Always Has Been Held in High Esteem, and as a Fielder Ranks among the Choicest," *Evening Star*, April 12, 1915, 15.
10. "Willis Whitewashes World's Champs and Wilson's Wallop Wins in Tenth: Brown Pitches Brilliant Ball for Nine Innings, Then Pirates Get Busy," *Pittsburgh Post*, September 5, 1908, 7.

11. "Miner Brown Is Beaten by the Pirates: Buccaneers Win Great Game from World's Champions in Tenth Inning," *Pittsburg Press*, September 5, 1908, 7.

12. John H. Gruber, "Wilson Bats in the Winning Run against Cubs: Pirates Beat the Cubs in Ten Long Innings," *Gazette Times*, September 5, 1908, 7.

13. Ralph S. Davis, "The Cubs Protest Yesterday's Game: Murphy Claims Gill Failed to Advance on Wilson's Hit, and Was Forced at Second in Tenth Inning," *Pittsburg Press*, September 5, 1908, 7.

14. Dennis Snelling, *Johnny Evers: A Baseball Life* (Jefferson, NC: McFarland, 2014), 72.

15. Billy Murphy, "Hank O'Day Will Fight for His Rights on the Field, Says Tebeau: New Cincy Manager Umpired Many a Game for Former Cardinal Boss," *St. Louis Star*, December 27, 1911, 5.

16. Snelling, *Johnny Evers*, 72.

17. Davis, "The Cubs Protest Yesterday's Game," 7.

18. Snelling, *Johnny Evers*, 72.

19. Edward F. Ballinger, "Even Break for Pirates in Double-Bill at Philadelphia: Camnitz Fails to Stop Quakers and They Get Away with the First Game by score of 5 to 2," *Pittsburgh Post*, September 17, 1908, 9.

20. Bozeman Bulger, "Bridwell's Hit Wins for Giants; Riot Follows at Polo Grounds: Chance Protests to Umpire Because Batter Failed to Run the Bases, but Emslie Answers with a Grin," *The World*, September 23, 1908, 1.

21. Bulger, "Bridwell's Hit Wins for Giants; Riot Follows at Polo Grounds," 2.

22. "Chaos at the Ball Game: Stormy Times Attend New York's Run in the Ninth," *The Sun*, September 24, 1908, 1.

23. Bulger, "Bridwell's Hit Wins for Giants; Riot Follows at Polo Grounds," 1.

24. Red Perkins, "News and Notes of the Diamond," *Los Angeles Herald*, July 23, 1908, 7.

25. "Brief Baseball Bits," *Pittsburg Press*, July 12, 1908, 20.

26. "Merkle Goes Home," *The Star*, July 16, 1908, 6.

27. "Chaos at the Ball Game," 1.

28. Bulger, "Bridwell's Hit Wins for Giants; Riot Follows at Polo Grounds," 1.

29. "Chaos at the Ball Game," 1.

30. Bulger, "Bridwell's Hit Wins for Giants; Riot Follows at Polo Grounds," 1.

31. "Chaos at the Ball Game," 1.

32. "Pulliam Awards Game to Giants; Champs Protest: National League Head Gives the Disputed Contest to New York, 2 to 1, in Face of Facts," *Inter Ocean*, September 24, 1908, 4.

33. "Chaos at the Ball Game," 1.

34. Joe Vila, "Margin Is Small: Giants Hard Pressed for First Place," *The Sporting News*, October 1, 1908, 1.

35. "Chaos at the Ball Game," 1.

36. "Pulliam Awards Game to Giants; Champs Protest," 4.

37. Bulger, "Bridwell's Hit Wins for Giants; Riot Follows at Polo Grounds," 1.

38. Vila, "Margin Is Small," 1.

39. "Pulliam Awards Game to Giants; Champs Protest," 4.

40. "Chaos at the Ball Game," 1.

41. "Chaos at the Ball Game," 8.

42. "Chicago Cubs Profit by Big Tangle over Disputed Decision," *Mattoon Morning Star*, September 25, 1908, 1.

43. "Pulliam Declares Game Was a Tie: Says Umpires O'Day and Emslie Report That Contest Resulted in a 1 to 1 Score," *Scranton Republican*, September 25, 1908, 8.

44. "Chicago Cubs Profit by Big Tangle over Disputed Decision," 1.

45. "Pulliam Declares Game Was a Tie," 8.

46. Bozeman Bulger, "Wiltse Knocked Out, 'Matty' Saves Game: Cubs' Batting Rally in Seventh Inning Scares Manager McGraw and Star Hurler Quickly Relieves the Southpaw," *The World*, September 24, 1908, 1.

47. Bulger, "Wiltse Knocked Out, 'Matty' Saves Game," 2.

48. Bulger, "Wiltse Knocked Out, 'Matty' Saves Game," 1.

49. Vila, "Margin Is Small," 1.

50. I.E. Sanborn, "Backed Off Board: National Politics Sidetracked for Base Ball," *The Sporting News*, October 1, 1908, 1.

51. Ralph S. Davis, "President Harry C. Pulliam, of National League, Lauds Manager Fred Clarke of the Pirate Team: Fred Clarke Has Proved One of Baseball's Great Leaders," *Pittsburg Press*, September 27, 1908, 19.

52. "Pulliam Declares Game a Tie," *Evening Mail*, October 3, 1908, 4.

53. "Pirates Deserve Great Credit for Their Remarkable Fight: Clarke's Warriors Have Shown Gameness That Could Hardly Be Surpassed," *Pittsburgh Post*, October 5, 1908, 7.

54. "Bulletin Boards Attracted Crowds: Local Fans by the Thousands Besieged Newspaper Office during Game at Chicago," *Pittsburg Press*, October 5, 1908, 12.

55. "Moving Pictures of Joy and Grief on Streets: Wildly Excited Fans about the Bulletin Board Show Confidence and Hope and Doubt as Messages Come In," *Gazette Times*, October 5, 1908, 2.

56. "Pirates Finally Eliminated from Great Race for Pennant: Succumb to Cubs in Final Contest of Season in Presence of Crowd of More Than 30,000 Fans," *Pittsburg Press*, October 5, 1908, 12.

57. "Cubs Snatch the Pennant from Our Pirates' Grasp; Score, 5 to 2: Brown Too Much for Home Team," *Gazette Times*, October 5, 1908, 7.

58. "Moving Pictures of Joy and Grief on Streets," 2.

59. "Cubs Snatch the Pennant from Our Pirates' Grasp; Score, 5 to 2," 7.

60. "Base Ball Baby: Born at Chicago Park during the Deciding Game with Pittsburg," *Sporting Life*, October 17, 1908, 2.

61. "Cubs Snatch the Pennant from Our Pirates' Grasp; Score, 5 to 2," 7.

62. "Pirates Lose to Champions: Chance's Men Win Last Game of the Season," *Pittsburgh Post*, October 5, 1908, 7.

63. "Cubs Snatch the Pennant from Our Pirates' Grasp; Score, 5 to 2," 7.

64. "Pirates Lose to Champions," 7.

65. Fred Clarke, "Barney and Fred Choose the Cubs: Pittsburg Moguls Think Chicago Will Win the National League Championship – Manager Pittsburg Baseball Club," *Pittsburg Press*, October 5, 1908, 12.

66. Barney Dreyfuss, "Barney and Fred Choose the Cubs: Pittsburg Moguls Think Chicago Will Win the National League Championship – President Pittsburg Baseball Club," *Pittsburg Press*, October 5, 1908, 12.

67. "Pirates Lose to Champions," 7.

68. "Three-Cornered Tie Possible in National: Cub-Giant Tie Game Must Be Played Off – National Directors Rule That Teams Meet and Play Contest Over," *Minneapolis Tribune*, October 7, 1908, 10.

69. "Three-Cornered Tie Possible in National: Will New York Consent to Play Off Tie? – McGraw Opposed to Meeting Cubs as Directors Rule," *Minneapolis Tribune*, October 7, 1908, 10.

70. "Three-Cornered Tie Possible in National: Cub-Giant Tie Game Must Be Played Off – National Directors Rule That Teams Must Play Contest Over," 10.

71. "Pennant between Cubs and Giants: Game in New York Today Will Settle National League Title for Season," *St. Louis Globe-Democrat*, October 8, 1908, 4.

72. "Three-Cornered Tie Possible in National: Will New York Consent to Play Off Tie? – McGraw Opposed to Meeting Cubs as Directors Rule," 10.

73. "Tigers Win the Pennant: Chicago Is Shut Out in the Deciding Contest – One Lost, Other in Jeopardy," *Boston Daily Globe*, October 7, 1908, 1.

74. "Three-Cornered Tie Possible in National: Will New York Consent to Play Off Tie? – McGraw Opposed to meeting Cubs as Directors Rule," 10.

75. "Angry, but Will Play: Cubs Left Chicago for New York Today," *Pittston Gazette*, October 7, 1908, 1.

76. "Three-Cornered Tie Possible in National: Cub-Giant Tie Game Must Be Played Off – National Directors Rule That Teams Meet and Play Contest Over," 10.

77. "The Chicago Cubs Arrive in New York," *Birmingham News*, October 8, 1908, 3.

78. Joe Vila, "Fans Were Unfair: Crowds Bully Cubs at Polo Grounds," *The Sporting News*, October 15, 1908, 1.

79. Jason Cannon, *Charlie Murphy: The Iconoclastic Showman Behind the Chicago Cubs* (Lincoln: University of Nebraska Press, 2022), 131.

80. Jonathan Weeks, *The Umpire Was Blind!: Controversial Calls by MLB's Men in Blue* (Jefferson, NC: McFarland, 2020), 58.

81. "Incidents of the Record-Breaking Giants-Cubs Game: Hundreds of Fans with Tickets in Pockets Turned Back – Men Fall from Insecure Perches – Rooters Clash with the Police," *The World*, October 8, 1908, 2.

82. "Baseball Fan Falls to Death Watching Game: Fireman McBride Unable to Get in Polo Grounds, Tumbles from 'L,'" *The World*, October 8, 1908, 1.

83. "Chicago Wins Pennant Game: Playoff of National League Baseball Tie Makes Cubs Three Time Champions," *The Sun*, October 9, 1908, 1.

84. "Incidents of the Record-Breaking Giants-Cubs Game," 2.

85. "Chicago Wins Pennant Game," 1.

86. Vila, "Fans Were Unfair," 1.

87. "And the Crowd Cheered: Heartily for New York; Ironically for Chicago," *The Sun*, October 9, 1908, 2.

88. "Cubs Take Pennant by Beating Giants, 4-2, in Great Game: Win the Third Successive National League Championship by Perfect Play," *Inter Ocean*, October 9, 1908, 2.

89. "Chicago Wins Pennant Game," 2.

90. "Cubs Take Pennant by Beating Giants, 4-2, in Great Game," 2.

91. "Chicago Wins Pennant Game," 2.

92. "Cubs Take Pennant by Beating Giants, 4-2, in Great Game," 2.

93. Bozeman Bulger, "'Hoodoo' Brown Beats Giants in Final Contest: Chicago Earns Victory by Timely Hitting in the Third, When Four Runs Were Scored off 'Matty,'" *The World*, October 8, 1908, 2.

94. "Cubs Take Pennant by Beating Giants, 4-2, in Great Game," 2.

95. Bulger "'Hoodoo' Brown Beats Giants in Final Contest," 2.

96. Weeks, *The Umpire Was Blind!*, 58.

97. "Cubs Take Pennant by Beating Giants, 4-2, in Great Game," 2.

98. Bulger, "'Hoodoo' Brown Beats Giants in Final Contest," 2.

99. Vila, "Fans Were Unfair," 1.

100. "Cubs Champions for Third Time: Despite Heavy Handicaps Chicago Defeated the Giants in Final Game for the Championship of the National League," *Winnipeg Tribune*, October 9, 1908, 6.

101. "Chance Slugged by Excited Fans after Giants-Cubs Game: Chicago Captain Punched Twice in the Jaw before the Police Arrive and Chase the Mob from the Field," *The World*, October 8, 1901, 1.

102. Vila, "Fans Were Unfair," 1.

103. "Sport Notes," *Dayton Herald*, November 14, 1908, 6.

104. "Fodder for the Fans," *Evening Star*, October 16, 1908, 19.

105. "Merckle Best Baseman Will Be Retained: McGraw Claims He Will Not Trade Merckle, Best First Baseman in National," *Daily State Journal*, December 23, 1908, 2.

106. "Cubs Take Pennant by Beating Giants, 4-2, in Great Game," 1.

107. "Charge of Bribery Excites Baseball Fans of New York: District Attorney Jerome Agrees to Investigate Case against 'Man' Accused of Tampering with Umpires in Cub-Giant Series," *Inter Ocean*, December 13, 1908, 1.

108. "Charge of Bribery Excites Baseball Fans of New York," 2.

109. "Charge of Bribery Excites Baseball Fans of New York," 1.

110. "Name of Would Be Briber Is Known, Declares Dreyfuss," *Inter Ocean*, December 13, 1908, 2.

111. "To Probe Bribery Charge: It Is Alleged Umpires Were Approached during New York-Chicago Game," *Daily News*, December 12, 1908, 2.

112. "Allege Attempts to Bribe Phillies: 'Sure Thing' Bettors said to Be after the Quaker Nationals," *Evening Star*, December 21, 1908, 13.

113. Harold Seymour, *Baseball: The Golden Age* (New York: Oxford University Press, 1971), 284.

114. "Baseball Scandal: Dr. Creamer Tried to Bribe Umpire, Is Claim," *Washington Herald*, April 25, 1909, 1.

115. "Dr. Creamer Under Ban: Charged with Having Attempted to Bribe Umpires Klem and Johnstone," *The Sporting News*, April 29, 1909, 2.

116. Cannon, *Charlie Murphy*, 131.

117. Weeks, *The Umpire Was Blind!*, 58.

118. "Dr. Creamer Under Ban," 2.

119. "Rumor Names Dr. Creamer in Umpire Bribing Case: New York Reports Have It That Well-Known Athletic Physician Is Man Barred from Baseball by National Commission – Dr. Creamer Says He Will Begin Suit," *Minneapolis Sunday Tribune*, April 25, 1909, 47.

120. "Baseball Scandal," 1.

121. "Umpires Name Dr. Creamer: Giants' Physician Last Year Involved in Bribery Charges," *The Sun*, April 25, 1909, 5.

122. "Rumor Names Dr. Creamer in Umpire Bribing Case," 47.

123. "'Dr. Creamer' Will Start Suit against National Commission," *Inter Ocean*, April 25, 1909, 1.

124. "Further Light on the Umpire Bribery: New York Clubs Ordered to Bar 'Dr. Creamer;' other Names Mentioned," *San Francisco Examiner*, May 16, 1909, 36.

125. Seymour, *Baseball: The Golden Age*, 284.

126. "Baseball Scandal," 1.

127. Tad, "New York Eager to Know Identity of Man Higher Up: Rumor That Real Culprit in Attempt to Bribe Klem and Johnstone Is a Well Known Figure in Baseball," *Pittsburg Press*, April 26, 1909, 8.

128. "Umpires Name Dr. Creamer," 5.

129. Tad, "Brush Has Nothing to Say Now: New York National Head Won't Talk on Bribery Question," *Butte Inter Mountain*, May 14, 1909, 8.

130. Seymour, *Baseball: The Golden Age*, 284.

131. "'Doc' Creamer Dead: Physician Was Well Known Figure in Local Boxing Circles," *The Sun*, July 30, 1918, 13.

132. "Gamblers Tried to Buy Local Players: Fogel Cites Two Instances When New York Offered Money for Victories," *Philadelphia Inquirer*, September 30, 1920, 5.

133. "Gamblers Offered Philadelphia Players $140,000 to 'Lay Down' in Series and Permit the Giants to Defeat the Cubs for the National League Pennant in 1908 – Kitty Bransfield, Now Eastern League Umpire, Thrashed Man Who Endeavored to Bribe Dooin – Herzog Stabbed by Fan in Joliet, Ill.: Bransfield's Story," *Berkshire Evening Eagle*, October 1, 1920, 1.

134. "Bransfield Gives Version," *Evening Star*, October 1, 1920, 30.

135. "1920 Baseball to Be Probed: Cook-co Grand Jury Will Widen Investigations," *Sacramento Star*, October 1, 1920, 1.

136. "Gamblers Offered Philadelphia Players $140,000: Dooin Confirms Story," 1.

137. "Gamblers Tried to Bribe Phils in 1908, Says Dooin," *Philadelphia Inquirer*, October 1, 1920, 18.

138. "$150,000 Offered Phillies, Dooin Charges, in 1908: Former Manager Recalls Promise of Bribe and Refusal of Players to Touch It," *New York Herald*, October 1, 1920, 1.

139. "Phils Offered Bribes: Dooin, Manager of 1908 Team, and Bransfield Corroborate Charges of Fogel," *Evening Star*, October 1, 1920, 30.

140. "$150,000 Offered Phillies, Dooin Charges, in 1908," 1.

141. "1920 Baseball to Be Probed," 1.

Chapter 9: Ty Cobb

1. H.G. Salsinger, "Ty Cobb – Remaker of Base Ball: Revolution – Studying the Leaders – New Batting Stance – Hits to All Fields," *Evening Star*, November 14, 1924, 31.

2. Dan Holmes, *Ty Cobb: A Biography – Baseball's All-Time Greatest Hitters* (Westport, CT: Greenwood Press, 2004), 1.

3. Holmes, *Ty Cobb: A Biography*, 1-2.

4. Holmes, *Ty Cobb: A Biography*, 2.

5. H.G. Salsinger, "Cobb Wanted to Be Regular Ball Player Left His Home 1904: Ty's Idea of One of Greatest Women in the World Was His Grandmother," *Winnipeg Evening Tribune*, November 5, 1924, 14.

6. Howell Foreman, "When Ty Cobb Was a Boy: Early Chapters from the Most Remarkable Career in the Records of the National Game," *Baseball Magazine*, March 1912, 1.

7. Salsinger, "Cobb Wanted to Be Regular Ball Player Left His Home 1904," 14.

8. H.G. Salsinger, "Ty Cobb: His Father's Orders – A Shattered Outlook – Ty Goes to Work," *Buffalo Evening News*, December 3, 1924, 30.

9. H.G. Salsinger, "Ty Cobb – Remaker of Baseball: Ty's Father – A Schoolmaster's Address – Cobb Praises Grandmother – The Boy Leaves Home," *Evening World-Herald*, November 5, 1924, 19.

10. H.G. Salsinger, "Ty Cobb: Remaker of Baseball," *St. Louis Globe-Democrat*, November 30, 1924, 15.

11. H.G. Salsinger, "Ty Plunges: A Skinny Lad of 17 – First Opening Day – The Boy's Chagrin," *Virginian Pilot and Norfolk Landmark*, November 6, 1924, 9.

12. Holmes, *Ty Cobb: A Biography*, 7.

13. Salsinger, "Ty Plunges," 9.

14. Salsinger, "Cobb Wanted to Be Regular Ball Player Left His Home 1904," 14.

15. Salsinger, "Ty Plunges," 9.

16. H.G. Salsinger, "Ty Cobb – Remaker of Base Ball: Ty Jobless – A Laconic Father – Ty Gets Contract – His Real Discover," *Evening Star*, November 7, 1924, 31.

17. H.G. Salsinger, "Ty Cobb: Learning to Slide – And How to Field – Cobb's Worst Season," *Buffalo Evening News*, December 10, 1924, 32.

18. H.G. Salsinger, "Ty Cobb – Remaker of Baseball: 'The Nut' – Schaefer's Joke – Navin Watches Him – Cobb's Average Jumps," *Evening World-Herald*, November 10, 1924, 10.

19. Salsinger, "Ty Cobb: Learning to Slide," 32.

20. Salsinger, "Ty Cobb – Remaker of Base Ball: Ty Jobless – A Laconic Father – Ty Gets Contract – His Real Discoverer," 31.

21. "By His Wife: Who Mistook Him for a Burglar, the Somnambulist Georgia Senator Was Shot Dead," *Cairo Bulletin*, August 11, 1905, 1.

22. "Charged with Murder: Mrs. Cobb Mistook Her Husband for a Burglar, Is Arrested," *Waterbury Evening Democrat*, August 11, 1905, 5.

23. Joe S. Jackson, "Cold Shoulder for Tiger Brigade: Weather Man Refused Our Boys Farewell Augusta Game – Detroiters Bid Good-Bye to Training Camp Today – Visit Has Been Fairly Satisfactory – Players All in Pretty Fair Condition – Cobb's Mother Acquitted of Murder," *Detroit Free Press*, April 1, 1906, 13.

24. H.G. Salsinger, "Ty Cobb: 1200 Fans See Debut – A Nervous Substitute – Two Strikes and a Hit," *Buffalo Evening News*, December 11, 1924, 36.

25. Umpire Billy Evans, "Umpire Billy Evans Considers Tyrus Cobb Wonderful Player: Augusta Youngster Had Hard Time When He First Came with Detroit, but His Success This Season Places Him in Enviable Position," *St. Louis Globe-Democrat*, October 30, 1907, 14.

26. Salsinger, "Ty Cobb: 1200 Fans See Debut – A Nervous Substitute – Two Strikes and a Hit," 36.

27. Evans, "Umpire Billy Evans Considers Tyrus Cobb Wonderful Player," 14.

28. H.G. Salsinger, "Ty Cobb: The Recruit Bullied – A Youth in Despair – His Only Pinch-Hitter," *Buffalo Evening News*, December 12, 1924, 44.

29. Holmes, *Ty Cobb: A Biography*, 17.

30. "Matty McIntyre: Former Augusta Player Booked for Sale or Release," *Daily Kennebec Journal*, June 29, 1906, 4.

31. "Matty M'Intyre Ready to Jump," *Buffalo Evening News*, June 27, 1906, 8.

32. "Shake-Up for Detroit Team: Armour Starts to Weed Out Clique to Get Harmony – Matty McIntyre Incident," *Buffalo Evening Times*, June 26, 1906, 8.

33. "Matty McIntyre: Former Augusta Player Booked for Sale or Release," 4.

34. "M'Intyre Getting Little Sympathy: Has Long Been Quietly Breeding Dissension among Tigers," *Washington Times*, June 28, 1906, 10.

35. H.G. Salsinger, "Ty Cobb: Hughie Jennings' Tact – Cobb's Turning Point – Envy and Jealousy," *Buffalo Evening News*, December 13, 1924, 10.

36. "Amendments to Rules by Baseball Magnates: National League Adopts Schedule and Dissatisfied Players Bob Up," *Fall River Daily Globe*, February 27, 1907, 7.

37. "Manager Jennings Is in a Fine Pickle: Tyrus Cobb Beat Negro, a Colored Woman and Then Mixes with Charlie Schmidt – Cobb May Be Traded," *Buffalo Evening Times*, March 18, 1907, 8.

38. "Base Ball Notes," *Evening Star*, March 20, 1907, 9.

39. "Manager Jennings Is in a Fine Pickle," 8.

40. "Base Ball Notes," *Evening Star*, March 20, 1907, 9.

41. "Manager Jennings Is in a Fine Pickle," 8.

42. "Ty Cobb May Be Swapped for Flick," *Dayton Herald*, March 20, 1907, 4.

43. "Cobb Released Fighting Player," *Meriden Daily Journal*, March 18, 1907, 8.

44. "Jennings Wires for M'Intyre: Ty Cobb Will Probably Be Forced to Quit the Tiger Bunch," *Buffalo Evening Times*, March 19, 1907, 8.

45. B.F. Wright, "Cobb Had Enough: Lasted One Minute in Fight with Schmidt," *The Sporting News*, April 6, 1907, 2.

46. Harry Jones, "Baseball's Immortal Madcaps," *Chattanooga Daily Times*, April 27, 1962, 23.

47. "Parent Coming Home: Fails to Reach Agreement with Taylor and Is Sent Back to Maine," *Daily Kennebec Journal*, April 3, 1907, 4.

48. "Ty. Cobb Will Stick with Tigers," *Dayton Herald*, April 3, 1907, 4.

49. Evans, "Umpire Billy Evans Considers Tyrus Cobb Wonderful Player," 14.

50. "American: The Pilgrims Trim Detroit Team, 3 to 2," *Daily Kennebec Journal*, May 10, 1907, 4.

51. Salsinger, "Ty Cobb: Hughie Jennings' Tact – Cobb's Turning Point – Envy and Jealousy," 10.

52. Holmes, *Ty Cobb: A Biography*, 45.
53. "Mack Fathers Charge: Says Cobb Deliberately Spiked Baker and Upset Collins in Sliding to Bases in Tuesday's Game," *Boston Daily Globe*, August 26, 1909, 5.
54. "Athletics Say Cobb Uses Rough Tactics," *St. Louis Globe-Democrat*, August 29, 1909, 1.
55. "Mack Fathers Charge," 5.
56. "Connie Mack after Cobb," *Philadelphia Inquirer*, August 27, 1909, 6.
57. "'Must Take Chances' - - - Cobb," *Philadelphia Inquirer*, August 27, 1909, 6.
58. "May Bar Ty Cobb from the League: Is Accused of Dirty Ball Playing and Johnson Expresses Himself," *Butte Inter Mountain*, August 30, 1909, 6.
59. "Last Day for Red Sox in West This Season," *Boston Daily Globe*, September 2, 1909, 9.
60. H.G. Salsinger, "Ty Cobb – Remaker of Baseball: Ty Accused – Spiking Players – Cobb's Contention – Cutting Down Baker," *Night Journal*, December 10, 1924, 9.
61. T.H. Murnane, "Red Sox Still Have Chance: Murnane Figures on Luck Changing," *Boston Sunday Globe*, September 5, 1909, 44.
62. Tip Wright, "Tip Wrights Talk on Cobbs Doing: Baseball Sage Believes Remedy for These Cases is to Find a Substitute for Spikes," *Pittsburg Press*, September 2, 1909, 16.
63. "Rain Prevents the Nationals Playing: Will Hook Up with White Sox in Double-Header Today," *Evening Star*, August 28, 1909, 9.
64. "Schaefer Comes to Defense of Ty Cobb," *Wichita Sunday Eagle*, September 19, 1909, 1.
65. "First One Goes to Philadelphia: Wins from Detroit by Score of 2 to 1, the Tigers Making Costly Errors," *Nashville Banner*, September 17, 1909, 16.
66. "Crowd of 24,710 Sees Athletics Win First Game: Detroit Tigers' Tails Twisted in First Clash," *Philadelphia Inquirer*, September 17, 1909, 6.
67. "First One Goes to Philadelphia," 16.
68. "Athletics Defeat Detroit; Now Only 2 Games Behind Leader: Another Grand Crowd Sees Mackmen Win Final Game 4 to 3," *Philadelphia Inquirer*, September 21, 1909, 10.
69. "Athletics Took Last Game of Series from Detroit; Barry Spiked by Ty Cobb: Victory Places Mack's Team within 14 Points of Tigers - - - Plank Outpitched Summers - - - Barry Out of Game for Season," *Wilkes-Barre Times-Leader*, September 21, 1909, 17.
70. "Jennings Feels Sure of Pennant: 'Ty' Cobb Deplores Spiking of Barry, Who Has Ugly Cut in Leg," *Philadelphia Inquirer*, September 21, 1909, 10.
71. "American League: The Official Record of the 1909 Pennant Race with Tabulated Scores and Accurate Accounts of All Championship Games Played – Games Played Friday, September 3," *Sporting Life*, September 11, 1909, 11.
72. "Ty Cobb Wanted: Detroit Star in Trouble for Assaulting Watchman," *Evening Star*, September 8, 1909, 14.
73. "Night Watchman Pounds Ty Cobb," *Sunday Star*, September 5, 1909, 1.
74. "Base Ball Notes," *Evening Star*, September 8, 1909, 14.
75. "Tigers Sore on Naps: Players Nearly Come to Blows after Yesterday's Double-Header," *Sunday Star*, September 5, 1909, 1.
76. "Night Watchman Pounds Ty Cobb," 1.
77. "Ty Cobb Wanted," 14.
78. "Detroit Says It's a Plot to Hurt Team: Ty Cobb Threatened with Arrest on Very Serious Assault Charge," *Boston Daily Globe*, September 8, 1909, 5.
79. "Warrant Out for 'Ty' Cobb: Noted Ball Player Charged with a Serious Offense at Cleveland – Cobb Says It's 'Frameup,'" *Davenport Democrat*, September 8, 1909, 6.
80. "Pres Navin Settles It: Assault Complaint against Cobb to Be Dropped by Agreement Reached Yesterday," *Boston Daily Globe*, September 9, 1909, 5.
81. "Ty Cobb Indicted by Cleveland Grand Jury," *St. Louis Globe-Democrat*, October 16, 1909, 10.
82. "Ty Cobb May Be Indicted; Arrest Is Threatened," *Pittsburg Press*, October 9, 1909, 2.

83. Charles Leerhsen, *Ty Cobb: A Terrible Beauty* (New York: Simon & Schuster, 2015), 225.

84. David Finoli and Bill Ranier, *When Cobb Met Wagner: The Seven-Game World Series of 1909* (Jefferson, NC: McFarland, 2011), 95.

85. "Ty Cobb Indicted by Cleveland Grand Jury," 10.

86. "Ty Cobb's Case: The Detroit Star Wanted in Cleveland for That Hotel Scrape," *Sporting Life*, October 23, 1909, 2.

87. "Later – Cobb Safe for a Time," *Sporting Life*, October 23, 1909, 2.

88. Hotspur, "Sporting Chat of the Town," *Buffalo Enquirer*, October 21, 1909, 10.

89. "Ty Cobb Surrenders; Will Stand Trial in Cleveland," *St. Louis Post-Dispatch*, October 20, 1909, 4.

90. "Ty Cobb to Stand Trial: Will Return to Cleveland, Ohio, for Trial in November," *Wilmington Morning Star*, October 22, 1909, 1.

91. "Ty Cobb's Coming Trial at Cleveland," *Evening Mail*, November 6, 1909, 7.

92. "Ty Cobb Fined: And Tells Cleveland Court He Has Not the Requisite $100," *Sporting Life*, November 27, 1909, 2.

93. "Warrant Out for 'Ty' Cobb," 6.

94. Mark S. Halfon, *Tales from the Deadball Era: Ty Cobb, Home Run Baker, Shoeless Joe Jackson, and the Wildest Times in Baseball History* (Lincoln: Potomac Books – University of Nebraska Press, 2014), 12-13.

95. "Jennings Picks Up Amateur Players: American League Clubs Are in Sympathy with Ty Cobb – How the Scrap Started," *Daily Times* (Davenport, Iowa), May 18, 1912, 17.

96. "Lucker Tells How Cobb Assaulted Him at Yankee Game," *The World*, May 18, 1912, 2.

97. "Detroit Baseball Team May Strike: Mutiny against Johnson's Order Suspending Ty Cobb – Victim Is a Cripple," *Kenosha Evening News*, May 18, 1912, 3.

98. "Says Cobb Hit a Cripple: Man the Great Fielder Hit Insists That It Was All a Mistake," *The Sun*, May 19, 1912, 2.

99. "Detroit Baseball Team May Strike," 3.

100. "Lucker Tells How Cobb Assaulted Him at Yankee Game," 2.

101. "Head of Big League Says He Stands Pat, Strike or No Strike," *The World*, May 18, 1902, 2.

Chapter 10: Tigers Solidarity, Carl Mays, and Ban Johnson

1. "Detroit Tigers to Go on Strike: If President Johnson Doesn't Cancel Cobb's Suspension," *Champaign Daily Gazette*, May 18, 1912, 1.

2. "Strike Is Threatened by Ty Cobb's Detroit Mates: Tigers Will Refuse to Take the Field To-Day Unless Their Champion Is Reinstated by Johnson," *San Francisco Examiner*, May 18, 1912. 14.

3. "Tigers Refuse to Play until Ty Is Reinstated: Entire Detroit Baseball Team Goes on Strike – Players Notify Ban Johnson They Will Quit – Griff Makes Statement," *Washington Herald*, May 18, 1912, 10.

4. "Jennings Picks Up Amateur Players: American League Clubs Are in Sympathy with Ty Cobb – Other Teams in Sympathy," *Daily Times* (Davenport, Iowa), May 18, 1912, 17.

5. "Detroit Fans Uphold Cobb: From the Mayor Down They Unite in Blaming Ban Johnson," *The Sun*, May 19, 1912, 2.

6. "Georgia Congressmen All for Cobb," *The Sun*, May 19, 1912, 2.

7. "Detroit Baseball Team May Strike: Mutiny against Johnson's Order Suspending Ty Cobb," *Kenosha Evening News*, May 18, 1912, 3.

8. "Tigers Refuse to Play until Ty Is Reinstated," 10.

9. "Head of League Says He Stands Pat, Strike or No Strike," *The World*, May 18, 1912, 2.

10. "Jennings Picks Up Amateur Players: American League Clubs Are in Sympathy with Ty Cobb," *Daily Times* (Davenport, Iowa), May 18, 1912, 17.

11. "Detroit Baseball Team May Strike," 3.
12. "Tigers Walk Off Field on Strike; Spectators Cheer: Entire Team Refuses to Play When Ty Cobb Is Not Reinstated," *St. Louis Post-Dispatch*, May 18, 1912, 1.
13. "Detroits to Go on Tour: Striking Players to Form Two Nines to Play Here and Abroad," *The Sun*, May 19, 1912, 2.
14. "Tigers Walk Off Field on Strike; Spectators Cheer," 1.
15. "No Sign of Break in Baseball Strike: Jennings Washes Hands of Entire Affair and Scouts for a Team," *Lincoln Daily Star*, May 19, 1912, 7.
16. "Detroits to Go on Tour: Striking Players to Form Two Nines to Play Here and Abroad," 2.
17. "Tigers Walk Off Field on Strike; Spectators Cheer," 1.
18. "Detroits to Go on Tour," 2.
19. "No Sign of Break in Baseball Strike," 7.
20. "Detroits to Go on Tour," 2.
21. "Detroit Team Gets Offer: Milwaukee Syndicate Would Enter it in U.S. League," *York Dispatch*, May 20, 1912, 1.
22. "Cobb Requests His Teammates to Back Down: Advises Them to Play Tomorrow, Detroit Club President Urges Return," *York Dispatch*, May 20, 1912, 1.
23. "Tigers Steadfast in Support of Ty Cobb; Ban Johnson Worried: Czar Wants to Draw Players from Other Clubs to Take the Place of Detroiters – Syndicate Baseball Shown by the Attitude of 'Big-Head Ban'," *St. Louis Star*, May 20, 1912, 10.
24. "Cobb Requests His Teammates to Back Down," 1.
25. "Strike of the Detroit Tigers Is Called Off by the Players: Athletes Are Forced to Give in to Save President Navin from Suffering Financially as the Result of Their Actions," *Buffalo Evening Times*, May 21, 1912, 12.
26. "Cobb Promised Quick Justice," *Dayton Evening Herald*, May 22, 1912, 12.
27. "Ban Johnson Fined Striking Tigers before They Actually Walked Out: Dave Fultz Makes Interesting Disclosure While Discussing Proposed Protective Association, of Which He Is the Moving Spirit – Says Present Rule Regarding Rowdy Spectators Is a Joke – Attitude of National Commission Unfair," *Brooklyn Daily Eagle*, May 21, 1912, 20.
28. Percy H. Whiting, "Crackers Take on Doughty Barons for Four Games: If They Keep Their Stride They Should Win Three," *Atlanta Georgian*, May 27, 1912, 9.
29. "Ty Cobb's Suspension Ends; He Plays Again," *Atlanta Georgian*, May 27, 1912, 9.
30. John J. Ward, "The 'Pinch Pitcher' of the World's Champions: Carl Mays, the Man with the Underhand Delivery, and How He Broke into the World's Series," *Baseball Magazine*, December 1916, 41-42.
31. "Home Town Proud of Pitcher Mays: Missourians Take Pride in Ball Player Who Has Built Fine Home for His Mother," *Lincoln Daily Star*, May 23, 1918, 9.
32. Mansfield Area Historical Society, *Around Mansfield: Images of America* (Charleston: Arcadia Publishing, 2013), 8.
33. Mansfield Area Historical Society, *Around Mansfield*, 87.
34. "The Widow's Boy," *Mansfield Mirror*, May 30, 1918, 2.
35. "Carl Mays, Eccentric Pitcher, Started in Utah – Dick Cooley and McCredie Passed Him Up: Price, Utah, Place Where Mays Really Got His Start to Fame and Big Money," *Salt Lake Telegram*, August 7, 1919, 8.
36. "Carl Mays Eccentric Pitcher, Started in Utah – Dick Cooley and McCredie Passed Him Up: Portland Pulled Prize Boob Play of Baseball in Losing Pitching Star to Providence, *Salt Lake Telegram*, August 7, 1919," 8.
37. "Holdout Pitcher Signs Contract: Carl Mays Comes to Terms to Pitch for the Portland Lineup," *Spokane Daily Chronicle*, February 27, 1913, 18.
38. "Mays Signs Up with the Beavers," *East Oregonian*, February 27, 1913, 2.

39. "Carl Mays Eccentric Pitcher, Started in Utah – Dick Cooley and McCredie Passed Him Up: Portland Pulled Prize Boob Play of Baseball in Losing Pitching Star to Providence," 8.

40. "Hero of the Northwestern '13 Season," *Spokesman=Review*, October 5, 1913, 4.

41. "Carl Mays Eccentric Pitcher, Started in Utah – Dick Cooley and McCredie Passed Him Up: Portland Pulled Prize Boob Play of Baseball in Losing Pitching Star to Providence," 8.

42. "Carl Mays Is Lost to Colts: Portland Coast League Club Does Not Fare Well in AA Drafts," *East Oregonian*, September 24, 1913, 6.

43. "Carl Mays Eccentric Pitcher, Started in Utah – Dick Cooley and McCredie Passed Him Up: Portland Pulled Prize Boob Play of Baseball in Losing Pitching Star to Providence," 8.

44. "Carl Mays Goes to the Boston Red Sox," *Evening Capital News*, September 5, 1914, 5.

45. "Federals after Carl Mays, Red Sox Recruit," *Boston Daily Globe*, February 5, 1915, 7.

46. "Carl Mays Signs," *Salt Lake Herald-Republican*, February 18, 1915, 8.

47. "Jennings' Tigers Land First Game from Sox: Detroit Returned Winner by 6 to 1 in Roughest Game Ever Seen in Boston," *Washington Herald*, September 17, 1915, 14.

48. "Carl Mays Tried to Bean Ty Cobb," *Bakersfield Californian*, February 8, 1916, 9.

49. "Carl Mays Signs His Contract with Boston," *Daily News-Advertiser*, December 19, 1915, 16.

50. "Carl Mays Is Accused of Hurling 'Beaner' in Big Bean Ball Probe," *Akron Beacon Journal*, May 5, 1917, 14.

51. Paul Purman, "Carl Mays Masters the Submarine Ball Despite Doubt of His Managers," *Chattanooga News*, August 31, 1917, 8.

52. "Manager 'Jack' Barry Joins Naval Reserve," *San Francisco Examiner*, July 29, 1917, 11.

53. Edward Tranter, "Sport Review," *Buffalo Enquirer*, August 5, 1918, 10.

54. Allan Wood, *Babe Ruth and the 1918 Red Sox* (Lincoln: Writers Club Press – iUniverse, 2000), 345.

55. "Carl Mays of Sox Married: Famous Boston Pitcher Is Wedded to Miss Marjorie Madden of Philadelphia," *Fall River Evening News*, September 19, 1918, 4.

56. "Carl Mays, Red Sox Pitcher, Returns with Bride," *Douglas County Herald*, October 3, 1918, 7.

57. Wood, *Babe Ruth and the 1918 Red Sox*, 345.

58. "Carl Mays, Red Sox Pitcher, Returns with Bride," 7.

59. "Carl Mays Going to Enter Army to Avenge Brother," *Pittsburg Press*, September 26, 1918, 26.

60. "The War Is Over!" *Mansfield Mirror*, November 21, 1918, 3.

61. "Carl Mays Going to Enter Army to Avenge Brother," 26.

62. "Tersely Told Town Tales," *Mansfield Mirror*, November 7, 1918, 7.

63. Wood, *Babe Ruth and the 1918 Red Sox*, 345-346.

64. "Local Happenings," *Douglas County Herald*, November 21, 1918, 5.

65. "He Doesn't Care How Soon," *The Sporting News*, December 5, 1918, 1.

66. "With Our Soldier Boys," *Mansfield Mirror*, December 19, 1918, 8.

67. "Local Happenings," *Douglas County Herald*, March 27, 1919, 5.

68. "Home of Carl Mays Is Destroyed by Fire," *Douglas County Herald*, April 3, 1919, 1.

69. "Carl Mays Home Is Burned," *Mansfield Mirror*, March 27, 1919, 6.

70. Mansfield Area Historical Society, *Around Mansfield*, 8.

71. Wood, *Babe Ruth and the 1918 Red Sox*, 374.

72. Daniel R. Levitt, *Ed Barrow: The Bulldog Who Built the Yankees' First Dynasty* (Lincoln: University of Nebraska Press, 2008), 153.

73. James C. O'Leary, "Barrow's Life One Round of Problems to Be Settled: Now Its Mays' Turn to Act Up," *The Sporting News*, July 10, 1919, 1.

74. "Mays Dodges Warrant Issued in Philadelphia," *Boston Daily Globe*, July 2, 1919, 14.

75. James C. O'Leary, "Barrow's Life One Round of Problems," 1.

76. "Mays Won't Pay," *Evening Herald*, July 15, 1919, 12.

77. James C. O'Leary, "Brain Storm as an Alibi for Carl Mays: Pitcher Disturbed in Mind When He Quit Red Sox," *The Sporting News*, August 7, 1919, 1.

78. Thomas J. Whalen, *When the Red Sox Ruled: Baseball's First Dynasty, 1912-1918* (Chicago: Ivan R. Dee – Rowman & Littlefield, 2011), 180-181.

79. "Rumbles from Chicago," *Boston Daily Globe*, July 14, 1919, 4.

80. James C. O'Leary, "Brain Storm as an Alibi for Carl Mays," 1.

81. Levitt, *Ed Barrow*, 153.

82. James C. O'Leary, "Brain Storm as an Alibi for Carl Mays," 1.

83. "Carl Mays Is Finished with Red Sox: Star Mound Man Peeved over Actions of Men and Resigns from Club," *Davenport Democrat*, July 16, 1919, 7.

84. "Notes from Chicago," *Boston Daily Globe*, July 15, 1919, 11.

85. "Is Mays Quitting?," *Boston Evening Globe*, July 15, 1919, 16.

86. James C. O'Leary, "Brain Storm as an Alibi for Carl Mays," 1.

87. "Carl Mays Is Finished with Red Sox," 7.

88. "Mays Says He's Through with Sox: Leaves the Team and Declares He Will Not Return While the Team Is Handled Such as it Is at the Present Time," *Evening Herald*, July 15, 1919, 12.

89. "Carl Mays Is Finished with Red Sox," 7.

90. Levitt, *Ed Barrow*, 153-154.

91. "Pitcher Mays, Who Deserted Red Sox, Will Not Be Sold Says Barrows: Chicago, New York and Cleveland Clubs Would Buy," *Pittsburgh Post*, July 16, 1919, 13.

92. "Mutiny Redsox Threat," *Pittsburgh Press*, July 22, 1919, 32.

93. Louis A. Dougher, "Boston Fans and Writers Slam Barrow," *Washington Times*, July 22, 1919, 14.

94. James C. O'Leary, "Needs of Red Sox to Save Mays' Scalp: Frazee Will Trade Him for Best That Is Offered," *The Sporting News*, July 24, 1919, 1.

95. "Kid Gleason Stunned over 'Loss' of Mays," *Evening Star*, July 31, 1919, 26.

96. James C. O'Leary, "Yankees Get Mays in Red Sox Deal: Russell and McGraw and One Other in Exchange," *Boston Daily Globe*, July 31, 1919, 1.

97. James C. O'Leary, "Yankees Get Mays in Red Sox Deal," 4.

98. "Carl Mays Traded: Mansfield Player Brings a Record Price of $55,000," *Mansfield Mirror*, August 7, 1919, 1.

99. "Carl Mays Suspended for Deserting Boston," *Evening Star*, July 31, 1919, 26.

100. "Strike Suggested to Get Carl Mays Back on Payroll: Yankee Players Said to Be Discussing Plan to Force Reinstatement of Hurler," *Sunday St. Louis Post-Dispatch*, August 3, 1919, 8.

101. W.O. McGeehan, "Ban Johnson Refuses to Reinstate Mays – Yankee Owners Will Fight in Courts: Ruppert and Huston Start Fight against League Czar," *New York Tribune*, August 4, 1919, 11.

102. "Johnson Owns Cleveland Stock Declares Huston," *Meriden Daily Journal*, August 5, 1919, 8.

103. James C. O'Leary, "Brain Storm as an Alibi for Carl Mays," 1.

104. Louis A. Dougher, "Looking 'Em Over," *Washington Times*, August 10, 1919, 22.

105. "Browns Ordered by Court to Play if Mays Pitches: Injunction Obtained to Prevent Johnson, St. Louis or Cleveland from Interfering," *St. Louis Post-Dispatch*, August 7, 1919, 26.

106. "Yanks Get Injunction against Circuit Boss," *Washington Times*, August 7, 1919, 18.

107. "Ball Has Received No Word from B. Johnson; Will Stand by 'Czar'" *St. Louis Post-Dispatch*, August 7, 1919, 26.

108. "Yanks Get Injunction against Circuit Boss," 18.

109. "Ban Heard from; Will Not Attend Yankees' Meeting," *New York Tribune*, August 10, 1919, 21.

110. "Insult Ball's Retort to Ruppert Invitation," *New York Tribune*, August 10, 1919, 21.

Chapter 11: Mayhem and Tragedy in the Deadball Age

1. "Ban Heard from; Will Not Attend Yankees' Meeting," 21.
2. "Yanks Get Injunction against Circuit Boss," 18.
3. "'Ask Johnson,' Says Indian Leader," *Washington Times*, August 7, 1919, 18.
4. "Does Ban Johnson Own Cleveland Stock? Dunn Answers, but Sidesteps," *Sunday St. Louis Post-Dispatch*, August 10, 1919, 8.
5. W.O. McGeehan, "Mays Controversy May Result in Formation of New League: Either That or Removal of Johnson Expected; Ban in Court Tuesday," *New York Tribune*, August 10, 1919, 21.
6. "The Old Sport's Musings: If You Can't Boost Don't Knock," *Philadelphia Inquirer*, August 18, 1919, 12.
7. "Ban Johnson on Trial," *Evening Record*, August 14, 1919, 1.
8. McGeehan, "Mays Controversy May Result in Formation of New League," 21.
9. "Johnson Hearing for Next Tuesday: Referee Postpones Trial of League Head on Carl Mays Case – Injunction Proceedings Also Postponed," *Evening Herald*, August 16, 1919, 6.
10. "Ban Johnson Is Put on 'Grill': Little Information Out of Him as to Mays Incident – Has Stock Cleveland Club," *Tampa Morning Tribune*, September 5, 1919, 10.
11. "Ban Johnson Owns Big Block of Stock in Cleveland Club: American League President Values His Present Holdings at $58,500," *St. Louis Star*, September 5, 1919, 16.
12. "Ban Johnson Is Put on 'Grill,'" 10.
13. "Ban Johnson Owns Big Block of Stock in Cleveland Club," 16.
14. "Ban Johnson Is Stockholder in Cleveland Club," *Birmingham News*, September 5, 1919, 8.
15. Henry Vance, "On the Level," *Birmingham News*, September 5, 1919, 9.
16. Denham Thompson, "Comiskey, Like Johnson, Gave Aid to the Cleveland Club: Both Made Loans on Indians' Stock to Keep Team Going – Other Magnates Aware of Dealings in Winter of 1915-16," *Evening Star*, August 15, 1919, 12.
17. W.O. McGeehan, "Ban Johnson Called 'Unmolested Despot' in Supreme Court: Attorneys for Yankees Give 'Czar' Bad Afternoon," *New York Tribune*, September 6, 1919, 14.
18. "Counsel Claims Ban Picked on Fired Twirler: Looks Like Torrid Spell for High-Handed President," *Edmonton Journal*, September 6, 1919, 18.
19. McGeehan, "Ban Johnson Called 'Unmolested Despot' in Supreme Court," 14.
20. "Counsel Claims Ban Picked on Fired Twirler," 18.
21. "Inquiry Ordered into A.L. Finances; Comiskey in Charge," *New York Tribune*, September 17, 1919, 12.
22. "Johnson Can't Use Any American League Cash," *New Castle Herald*, September 25, 1919, 10.
23. "Yankees' Share of Series Is Held Up: Navin, Detroit President, Protests Games Won by Mays," *The Sun*, October 10, 1919, 20.
24. "New York American League Baseball Club Obtains Permanent Injunction in Mays Case from Justice Wagner: Ban Johnson Loses in Carl Mays Case," *The Sun*, October 26, 1919, 3.
25. "Karpe's Comment on Sport Topics," *Buffalo Evening News*, October 30, 1919, 26.
26. "Shift Buck to Ban Johnson: Heydler and Herrmann Say Third Place Money Up to His League," *Buffalo Evening News*, October 30, 1919, 26.
27. Frederick G. Lieb, "Johnson Appeals Carl Mays Case: Ban's Attorney Asks Appellate Court to Reverse Justice Wagner's Decision," *The Sun*, December 13, 1919, 17.
28. Louis A. Dougher, "Looking 'Em Over," *Washington Times*, November 6, 1919, 21.
29. "Ban Johnson Is Again Enjoined by Court: Must Not Hold American League Meeting at Chicago," *Wilkes-Barre Record*, December 1, 1919, 25.

30. "Favor Insurgents," *Washington Herald*, December 5, 1919, 8.

31. "Johnson Is Free to Convene His Cohorts in West: New York Club Withdraws Application for Injunction – Another War Move," *Brooklyn Daily Times*, December 7, 1919, 13.

32. "League Lifts its Ban on Johnson: Withdraws Application for Injunction, but Holds Only N.Y. Meeting Is Legal," *Spokesman=Review*, December 7, 1919, 1.

33. Frederick G. Lieb, "Learned Jurists Asked to Decide Whether Ban Johnson Is 'The Man Who Made Baseball,' or Only a Chief Umpire: Appellate Division Hears Mays Case," *The Sun*, January 24, 1920, 15.

34. "Ban Johnson Bothered in Carl Mays Lawsuit," *Knoxville Sentinel*, January 30, 1920, 20.

35. Louis A. Dougher, "Looking 'Em Over," *Washington Times*, February 6, 1920, 18.

36. "Magnates in Big Meetings: American and National Leagues with Minors and Commission in Session," *Washington Herald*, February 9, 1920, 8.

37. Louis A. Dougher, "Looking 'Em Over," *Washington Times*, February 11, 1920, 14.

38. "Deny That Johnson Wants to Resign: Herrmann Presided at Joint Baseball Commission Meeting," *Fall River Evening News*, February 12, 1920, 10.

39. Louis A. Dougher, "Ban Johnson Gets Cash for Legal Expenses," *Washington Times*, June 21, 1920, 12.

40. Daniel R. Levitt, *Ed Barrow*, 154.

41. "Eddie Doheny Insane," *Fall River Daily Globe*, October 12, 1903, 1.

42. "Doings of Doheny," 12.

43. "Bransfield Has Been Ill: Pirates' First Baseman Was Confined to Bed for Three Weeks," *Pittsburgh Press*, January 10, 1904, 20.

44. "Ed Doheny Is in Sad Plight: Jimmie Sebring Calls on Former Pirate in Danvers Sanitarium," *Pittsburg Press*, May 20, 1905, 10.

45. "Was Win Mercer Murdered?," 6.

46. "Mercer to Play Here," 8.

47. "Cy Young, Grandest Twirler in the Game: Glowing Tribute Paid Boston Veteran by Pitcher-Editor Addie Joss, of Cleveland," *Scranton Republican*, February 16, 1907, 9.

48. "Addie Joss Praises Win Mercer," *Evening Star*, February 25, 1907, 9.

49. Louisa and Cicotello, *Mysteries from Baseball's Past*, 33.

50. "Died Doing His Duty: Fred O'Connell Made Game Fight for His Life," *The Sporting News*, May 4, 1907, 3.

51. "Mass for Frederic P. O'Connell," *Boston Sunday Globe*, May 26, 1907, 2.

52. Louisa and Cicotello, *Mysteries from Baseball's Past*, 33-34.

53. Louisa and Cicotello, *Myseries from Baseball's Past*, 36.

54. Donald Hubbard, *The Red Sox Before the Babe: Boston's Early Days in the American League, 1901-1914* (Jefferson, NC: McFarland, 2009), 104.

55. "Collins Was Married Over Six Months Ago," *Pittsburg Press*, June 13, 1907, 14.

56. Charlie Bevis, *Jimmy Collins: A Baseball Biography* (Jefferson, NC: McFarland, 2012), 166.

57. "Identified by Relatives: No Further Doubt of Mrs. 'Chick' Stahl's Death," *Boston Daily Globe*, November 16, 1908, 1.

58. "Widow of Ball Player Found Dead: Relatives Say Wife of 'Chick' Stahl Was Murdered," *Fall River Evening News*, November 16, 1908, 1.

59. "Identified by Relatives," 1.

60. "Stahl's Widow Found Dead: Autopsy Shows That Death Resulted from Natural Causes – No Indications of Robbery," *Boston Evening Transcript*, November 16, 1908, 8.

61. "Identified by Relatives," 1.

62. "Body Found in Hallway: 'Chick' Stahl's Widow, Viewers Assert," *Boston Daily Globe*, November 16, 1908, 1.

63. "South Boston Police: Inclined to Think Mrs. Stahl Came Over Southampton Street from Roxbury – Their Investigations," *Boston Daily Globe*, November 16, 1908, 2.

64. "Body Found in Hallway," 1.

65. "South Boston Police," 1-2.

66. "No Evidence of Foul Play: Mrs. Stahl's Death Due to Natural Causes," *Boston Daily Globe*, November 17, 1908, 9.

67. "Widow of Ball Player Found Dead," 1.

68. "Identified by Relatives," 1.

69. "Mrs. Stahl Possibly Drugged: Organs of Woman Found Dead in South Boston Sent to Harvard Medical School," *Boston Evening Transcript*, November 17, 1908, 1.

70. "Friends of Mrs. Stahl: Of Opinion That She Was Murdered," *Biddeford Daily Journal*, November 16, 1908, 1.

71. "Stahl's Widow Found Dead," 8.

72. "Mrs. Stahl's Diamonds Gone: And Her Body Found Huddled in Hallway of a Cheap Building," *Fort Wayne News*, November 16, 1908, 1.

73. "Mrs. Stahl's Diamonds Gone," 9.

74. "Were Not Advised: Relatives Here Learned of Death Through Press Dispatches," *Fort Wayne News*, November 16, 1908, 9.

75. "Four Held in Stahl Case: Admit They Were with Woman on Sunday," *Boston Daily Globe*, November 18, 1908, 1.

76. "Deny Taking Her Jewelry: Four Men Charged with Larceny from Mrs. Stahl," *Boston Daily Globe*, November 18, 1908, 1.

77. "Mrs. Stahl's Funeral: Every Seat in St. Francis de Sales' Church, Roxbury, Taken – Many Beautiful Floral Tributes," *Boston Daily Globe*, November 19, 1908, 16.

78. "Mrs. Stahl's Jewelry Found at Father's Home," *Meriden Daily Journal*, November 20, 1908, 2.

79. J.C. Morse, "Boston Briefs: Little Likelihood of Shortstop Dahlen Being Traded to the Brooklyn Club – Current Hub News, Gossip and Comment," *Sporting Life*, November 28, 1908, 8.

80. "Four Are Exonerated: Accused of Larceny of Mrs Stahl's Jewels," *Boston Daily Globe*, November 24, 1908, 3.

81. "Ft. Wayne: Bunch of Interesting Events from over the Hoosier Line," *The Tribune*, November 26, 1908, 1.

82. "Mystery in Death of 'Chick' Stahl's Widow: Wife of Late Baseball Player Found Dead in South Boston Doorway – Police Are Making Investigation," *Buffalo Evening Times*, November 16, 1908, 1.

83. "The Motive Unknown: Stahl and His Wife Lived Happily Since Their Marriage," *Fort Wayne Journal-Gazette*, March 29, 1907, 2.

84. "Gamblers Tried to Buy Local Players," 5.

85. "Waddell to the Front," 13.

86. "A Story of Rube Waddell: How He Happens to Be 'Off His Feet,'" *Leavenworth Post*, May 29, 1906, 6.

87. "Reuben, the Rescuer, Gets Ducking at Fire," *Washington Times*, August 1, 1906, 6.

88. M.W. Bingay, "Rube Waddell's Eccentricities: President Shibe of the Philadelphia Club Tells a Few Stories of the Crazy Twirler – Has a Soft Head but a Softer Heart," *Buffalo Enquirer*, December 18, 1907, 8.

89. "Mack Says Rube Was Sold to Avoid Friction on Team: Athletics' Manager Declares, However, That He Is Still Great," *St. Louis Post-Dispatch*, February 8, 1908, 6.

90. "Cross Tells Why Mack Released 'Rube' Waddell: The Rube Got Boisterous on a Trip and Athletics Went on Strike," *Buffalo Evening Times*, June 1, 1912, 11.

91. "Gamblers Tried to Buy Local Players," 5.

92. "Waddell Gets Divorce without Any Contest: Wife Fails to Appear, but Is Represented by Attorney – Abandonment Case Still Stands," *St. Louis Globe-Democrat*, February 10, 1910, 16.

93. "Gamblers Tried to Buy Local Players," 5.

94. "Allege Attempts to Bribe Phillies," 13.

95. "Dr. Creamer Under Ban," 2.

96. Joseph Vila, "Vila's Chat about Sports: No Doubt Now Who Owns the Giants," *Boston Sunday Globe*, February 6, 1910, 54.

97. "Ticket Scandal to Be Investigated," *La Crosse Tribune*, November 11, 1908, 2.

98. "Cubs Sold Tickets for Series to Scalpers: National Commission Is Now Ready to Fix the Blame," *Fort Wayne Sentinel*, November 28, 1908, 7.

99. "Cubs Sore at Murphy for Bungling Tickets," *San Francisco Call*, December 1, 1908, 4.

100. Richard G. Tobin, "Cubs Officials Not in Collusion with Scalpers, Verdict: National Commission Decides Chicago National League Club Officers Did Not Aid 'Outside' Sale of Tickets for World Series," *Inter Ocean*, December 18, 1908, 4.

101. "Censured the Cubs in Report on Tickets: Carelessness Charged in the Report of the Commission," *Fort Wayne Sentinel*, December 19, 1908, 7.

102. Tobin, "Cubs Officials Not in Collusion with Scalpers, Verdict," 4.

103. "Commission Report on Scalping Bears Out Its Forecast: Gives Cub Officials Whitewash on Collusion Charge, but Issues Reprimand on Bad Business Methods Used in Handling Tickets," *Inter Ocean*, December 19, 1908, 4.

104. "Cubs Sold Tickets for Series to Scalpers," 7.

105. Tobin, "Cubs Officials Not in Collusion with Scalpers, Verdict," 4.

106. "Harry A. Pulliam Dies from Bullet Wound: Self Inflicted Injury Proves Fatal – Ill Health Said to Be the Cause," *Topeka Daily Capital*, July 30, 1909, 8.

107. "Pulliam Attempts Suicide in New York: National League President Shoots Himself Through Head, Destroying Both Eyes and Injuring Brain – Had Just Resumed Office after Long Illness," *St. Louis Globe-Democrat*, July 29, 1909, 9.

108. "Pulliam Re-Elected National League President – Opposition Fades Away to Lonesome Brush: John Heydler Goes in with Chief as Secretary," *Evening Star*, December 9, 1908, 17.

109. "Pulliam Threatens to Open Warfare with Murphy Soon: National League Men Are Expected to Clash in Epistolary Battle in the Near Future, as President Is Tiring of Attacks," *Inter Ocean*, January 26, 1909, 4.

110. "In the Sporting World," *Racine Daily Journal*, January 13, 1909, 7.

111. "Pulliam Tired of it All: Will Not Be Surprised if He Is Deposed, and Wouldn't Regret Such Action, He Declares," *Boston Daily Globe*, February 18, 1909, 4.

112. "Pulliam in Tirade Berates Magnates: In Fiery Peroration National League Executive Denounces Conferees at Length," *St. Louis Globe-Democrat*, February 18, 1909, 10.

113. "Pulliam Tired of it All," 4.

114. "Worry Makes Harry Pulliam Kill Himself: President of National League Ends Life in New York Club," *St. Louis Post-Dispatch*, July 29, 1909, 3.

115. "Pulliam in Tirade Berates Magnates," 10.

116. Hugh S. Fullerton, "President Pulliam Nervous Wreck; Relieved from Place: Secretary Heydler Is Made Acting President until Such a Time As Pulliam Recovers His Mental Poise and Is Able to Attend to His Duties One More with Usual Success," *Inter-Mountain Republican*, February 19, 1909, 7.

117. "Worry Makes Harry Pulliam Kill Himself," 3.

118. "Doubtful Outlook Confronts Pulliam: National League President Pays Hurried Trip to St. Louis and Says He Will Not Resign Unless He Is Assured of Better Job," *St. Louis Globe-Democrat*, February 20, 1909, 11.

119. "Will Pulliam Be Recalled?: National Baseball Board to Take Up Warm Controversy," *Birmingham News*, June 4, 1909, 9.

120. "Blow to His Brother: J.P. Pulliam and Friends in Oshkosh Thought League President Had Recovered His Health," *Boston Daily Globe*, July 29, 1909, 5.

121. "Will Pulliam Be Recalled?," 9.

122. "Pulliam the Victor!: The Young Chief of the Senior League Will Resume His Presidential Duties on or About," *Sporting Life*, June 12, 1909, 1.

123. "Pulliam Attempts Suicide in New York," 9.

124. "Pulliam Redivivus: The Young National League President Resumes His Duties," *Sporting Life*, July 3, 1909, 2.

125. Louisa and Cicotello, *Mysteries from Baseball's Past*, 70.

126. "Pulliam Attempts Suicide in New York," 9.

127. "Harry C. Pulliam Commits Suicide: League President Found in Is Room with Bullet Hole Through His Head," *La Crosse Tribune*, July 29, 1909, 6.

128. "Pulliam Attempts Suicide in New York," 9.

129. William A. Cook, *August "Garry" Herrmann: A Baseball Biography* (Jefferson, NC: McFarland, 2008), 109.

130. "Harry C. Pulliam Commits Suicide," 6.

131. "Pulliam Attempts Suicide in New York," 9.

132. "Harry C. Pulliam Commits Suicide," 6.

133. "Pulliam Attempts Suicide in New York," 9.

134. "Harry C. Pulliam Commits Suicide," 6.

135. "No Sign of Despondency: Pres Pulliam Wrote to His Sister in Nashville about a Week Ago, Seemingly Well," *Boston Daily Globe*, July 29, 1909, 5.

Chapter 12: Baseball's Dawn Turns to Morning

1. Francis C. Richter, "Passing of Pulliam!: The Young Chief of the Venerable National League Shocks the Great Base Ball World," August 7, 1909, *Sporting Life*, 3.

2. "Expected Suicide," *Philadelphia Inquirer*, July 30, 1909, 10.

3. Richter, "Passing of Pulliam!," 3.

4. "Heydler Heads National League: Was Secretary-Treasurer under Late Harry Pulliam," *Tampa Weekly Tribune*, August 5, 1909, 12.

5. Louisa and Cicotello, *Mysteries from Baseball's Past*, 68.

6. Louisa and Cicotello, *Mysteries from Baseball's Past*, 69.

7. "Cripple's Curse on Thaw True in Pulliam's Case," *Newark Star*, August 2, 1909, 2.

8. "Death of Harry Pulliam Recalls Strange Incident: Dr. Bingaman, Harry Thaw and Himself Have Met Fates Such as Cripple Pronounced on Them Four Years Ago – Curse Remembered," *New Castle Herald*, August 9, 1909, 2.

9. "Thaws Defense Is to Be Based on Insanity: Millionaire Slayer of Stanford White Held for Trial," *Altoona Times*, June 27, 1906, 1.

10. "Harry Pulliam's Suicide Recalls Strange Curse: Cripple with Evil Eye Predicted Fate of Thaw, Pulliam and Another," *Warren Mirror*, August 13, 1909, 1.

11. "Pulliam Suicide Was Sixth in a Weird Sequence: Six Members of Dinner Party 18 Years Ago Have Died by Their Own Hands," *St. Louis Post-Dispatch*, August 5, 1909, 1.

12. "Officer Shot Filipino Dead: Now Lieut. Brown Is under Sentence of Dismissal," *St. Louis Post-Dispatch*, October 25, 1901, 5.

13. "Pulliam Suicide Was Sixth in a Weird Sequence," 1.

14. "Shot Himself for Love: Preston Thornton Attempts Suicide," *New-York Tribune*, May 17, 1897, 1.

15. "Pulliam Suicide was Sixth in a Weird Sequence," 1.

16. "Shot Himself for Love," 1.

17. "Thornton Buried: More about Louisville's Latest and Most Pathetic Story," *Owensboro Weekly Messenger*, May 22, 1897, 3.

18. "Shot Himself for Love," 1.
19. "Pulliam Suicide Was Sixth in a Weird Sequence," 1.
20. "Pulliam Suicide Was Sixth in a Weird Sequence," 2.
21. "Lyons Killed Self in Paducah, Ky.," *St. Louis Post-Dispatch*, August 5, 1909, 2.
22. "Pulliam Suicide Was Sixth in a Weird Sequence," 1.
23. "Here's a Little Speech: Harry Pulliam Made at the Comiskey Banquet," *Butte Inter Mountain*, August 7, 1909, 6.
24. "South at War over 'Ty' Cobb's Birthplace," *Evening Star*, August 14, 1911, 10.
25. "'Ty' Cobb Is Native North Carolinian: Famous Baseball Player Was Born in Cherokee County, Later Going to Ga.," *Asheville Gazette News*, August 11, 1911, 3.
26. W.A. Phelon, "Base Ball Odds and Ends: Fitted Up by W.A. Phelon," *The Sporting News*, February 27, 1913, 4.
27. "Other Side of McGraw: A Player Says He Is Kindness and Sympathy Personified," *Pittsburg Press*, August 18, 1904, 10.

Bibliography

Books

Abrams, Dennis. *Ty Cobb*. New York: Chelsea House – Infobase Publishing, 2007.

Abrams, Roger I. *The First World Series and the Baseball Fanatics of 1903*. Boston: Northeastern University Press, 2003.

Alexander, Charles C. *John McGraw: A Giant in His Time*. Lincoln: University of Nebraska Press, 1988.

Anderson, David W. *More Than Merkle: A History of the Best and Most Exciting Baseball Season in Human History*. Lincoln: University of Nebraska Press, 2000.

Bevis, Charlie. *Jimmy Collins: A Baseball Biography*. Jefferson, NC: McFarland, 2012.

Billheimer, John. *Baseball and the Blame Game: Scapegoating in the Major Leagues*. Jefferson, NC: McFarland, 2007.

Cannon, Jason. *Charlie Murphy: The Iconoclastic Showman Behind the Chicago Cubs*. Lincoln: University of Nebraska Press, 2022.

Casway, Jerrold I. *The Culture and Ethnicity of Nineteenth Century Baseball*. Jefferson, NC: McFarland, 2017.

Cava, Pete. *Indiana-Born Major League Baseball Players: A Biographical Dictionary, 1871- 2014*. Jefferson, NC: McFarland, 2015.

Cook, William A. *August "Garry" Herrmann: A Baseball Biography*. Jefferson, NC: McFarland, 2008.

Dabilis, Andy and Nick Tsiotos. *The 1903 World Series: The Boston Americans, the Pittsburg Pirates and the "First Championship of the United States."* Jefferson, NC: McFarland, 2004.

Deveaux, Tom. *The Washington Senators, 1901-1971*. Jefferson, NC: McFarland, 2001.

Ellis, William Arba, ed. *Norwich University 1819-1911: Her History, Her Graduates, Her Roll of Honor*. Montpelier: The Capital City Press, 1911.

Faber, Charles F. *Major League Careers Cut Short: Leading Players Gone by 30*. Jefferson, NC: McFarland, 2011.

Felber, Bill. *A Game of Brawl: The Orioles, the Beaneaters & the Battle for the 1897 Pennant*. Lincoln: University of Nebraska Press, 2007.

Finoli, David and Bill Ranier. *When Cobb Met Wagner: The Seven-Game World Series of 1909*. Jefferson, NC: McFarland, 2011.

Fleitz, David L. *More Ghosts in the Gallery: Another Sixteen Little-Known Greats at Cooperstown*. Jefferson, NC: McFarland, 2007.

———. *The Irish in Baseball: An Early History*. Jefferson, NC: McFarland, 2009.

Foulds, Alan E. *Boston's Ballparks & Arenas*. Lebanon, NH: Northeastern University – University Press of New England, 2005.
Halfon, Mark S. *Tales from the Deadball Era: Ty Cobb, Home Run Baker, Shoeless Joe Jackson, and the Wildest Times in Baseball History*. Lincoln: Potomac Books – University of Nebraska Press, 2014.
Hernández, Lou. *Manager of Giants: The Tactics, Temper, and True Record of John McGraw*. Jefferson, NC: McFarland, 2018.
Hittner, Arthur D. *Honus Wagner: The Life of Baseball's "Flying Dutchman."* Jefferson, NC: McFarland, 1996.
Holmes, Dan, *Ty Cobb: A Biography – Baseball's All-Time Greatest Hitters*. Westport, CT: Greenwood Press, 2004.
Hubbard, Donald. *The Red Sox Before the Babe: Boston's Early Days in the American League, 1901-1914*. Jefferson, NC: McFarland, 2009.
Jordan, David M. *Closing 'Em Down: Final Games at Thirteen Classic Ballparks*. Jefferson, NC: McFarland, 2010.
Kerr, Roy, *Sliding Billy Hamilton: The Life and Times of Baseball's First Great Leadoff Hitter*. Jefferson, NC: McFarland, 2010.
Kimberly, Chuck. *The Days of Wee Willie, Old Cy and Baseball War: Scenes from the Dawn of The Deadball Era, 1900-1903*. Jefferson, NC: McFarland, 2014.
Leerhsen, Charles. *Ty Cobb: A Terrible Beauty*. New York: Simon & Schuster, 2015.
Levitt, Daniel R. *Ed Barrow: The Bulldog Who Built the Yankees' First Dynasty*. Lincoln: University of Nebraska Press, 2008.
Levy, Alan H. *Rube Waddell: The Zany, Brilliant Life of a Strikeout Artist*. Jefferson, NC: McFarland, 2000.
Louisa, Angelo A. and David Cicotello, eds. *Mysteries from Baseball's Past: Investigations of Nine Unsettled Questions*. Jefferson, NC: McFarland, 2010.
Macht, Norman L. *Connie Mack and the Early Days of Baseball*. Lincoln: University of Nebraska Press, 2007.
Mansfield Area Historical Society. *Around Mansfield: Images of America*. Charleston: Arcadia Publishing, 2013.
Martin, Brian. *Barney Dreyfuss: Pittsburgh's Baseball Titan*. Jefferson, NC: McFarland, 2021.
Masur, Louis P. *Autumn Glory: Baseball's First World Series*. New York: Hill and Wang, 2003.
Matthews, George R. *When the Cubs Won It All: The 1908 Championship Season*. Jefferson, NC: McFarland, 2009.
Mitchell, Eddie. *Baseball Rowdies of the 19th Century: Brawlers, Drinkers, Pranksters and Cheats in the Early Days of the Major Leagues*. Jefferson, NC: McFarland, 2018.
Nash, Bruce and Allan Zullo. *The Baseball Hall of Shame: The Best of Blooperstown*. Guilford, CT: Lyons Press – Globe Pequot Press, 2012.
Redmond, Patrick R. *The Irish and the Making of American Sport, 1835-1920*. Jefferson, NC: McFarland, 2014.
Scheinin, Richard. *Field of Screams: The Dark Underside of America's National Pastime*. New York: W.W. Norton, 1994.
Segrave, Kerry. *Ticket Scalping: An American History, 1850-2005*. Jefferson, NC: McFarland, 2007.

Seymour, Harold. *Baseball: The Golden Age*. New York: Oxford University Press, 1971.
Smiles, Jack. *"Ee-Yah": The Life and Times of Hughie Jennings, Baseball Hall of Famer*. Jefferson, NC: McFarland, 2005.
Snelling, Dennis. *Johnny Evers: A Baseball Life*. Jefferson, NC: McFarland, 2014.
Solomon, Burt. *Where They Ain't: The Fabled Life and Untimely Death of the Original Baltimore Orioles, the Team That Gave Birth to Modern Baseball*. New York: Doubleday – Random House, 2000.
Stein, Fred. *And the Skipper Bats Cleanup: A History of the Baseball Player-Manager, with 42 Biographies of Men Who Filled the Dual Role*. Jefferson, NC: McFarland, 2002.
Swift, Tom. *Chief Bender's Burden: The Silent Struggle of a Baseball Star*. Lincoln: University of Nebraska Press, 2008.
Veil, Fred W. *Bucky: A Story of Baseball in the Deadball Era*. Tucson: Wheatmark, 2013.
Wagner, Steven K. *The Four Home Runs Club: Sluggers Who Achieved Baseball's Rarest Feat*. Lanham, MD: Rowman & Littlefield, 2018.
Waldo, Ronald T. *Characters from the Diamond: Wild Events, Crazy Antics, and Unique Tales From Early Baseball*. Lanham, MD: Rowman & Littlefield, 2016.
———. *Deadball Trailblazers: Single-Season Records of the Modern Era*. Mechanicsburg, PA: Sunbury Press, 2022.
———. *Fred Clarke: A Biography of the Baseball Hall of Fame Player-Manager*. Jefferson, NC: McFarland, 2010.
Weeks, Jonathan. *The Umpire Was Blind!: Controversial Calls by MLB's Men in Blue*. Jefferson, NC: McFarland, 2020.
Whalen, Thomas J. *When the Red Sox Ruled: Baseball's First Dynasty, 1912-1918*, Chicago: Ivan R. Dee – Rowman & Littlefield, 2011.
Wiggins, Robert Peyton. *The Deacon and the Schoolmaster: Phillippe and Leever, Pittsburgh's Great Turn-of-the-Century Pitchers*. Jefferson, NC: McFarland, 2011.
Wood, Allan. *Babe Ruth and the 1918 Red Sox*. Lincoln: Writers Club Press – iUniverse, Inc., 2000.
Wood, John A. *Beyond the Ballpark: The Honorable, Immoral, and Eccentric Lives of Baseball Legends*. Lanham, MD: Rowman & Littlefield, 2016.
Zimniuch, Fran. *Shortened Seasons: The Untimely Deaths of Major League Baseball's Stars And Journeymen*. Lanham, MD: Taylor Trade – Rowman & Littlefield , 2007.

Newspapers and Magazines
Advance Argus (Greenville, PA), August 14, 1890–September 8, 1898.
Akron Beacon Journal (Akron, OH), August 9, 1913–October 29, 1918.
Albuquerque Morning Journal, August 14, 1910.
Altoona Times (Altoona, PA), June 27, 1906–December 11, 1909.
Anaconda Standard (Anaconda, MT), January 4, 1910.
Argos Reflector (Argos, IN), March 26, 1908.
Argus and Patriot (Montpelier, VT), July 7, 1897–July 21, 1897.
Asheville Gazette News (Asheville, NC), August 11, 1911.
Atlanta Georgian, May 27, 1912.
Bakersfield Californian (Bakersfield, CA), February 8, 1916.
Bakersfield Morning Echo (Bakersfield, CA), October 3, 1920.
Baltimore Sun, January 9, 1901–March 29, 1902.

Barre Daily Times (Barre, VT), April 14, 1913.
Baseball Magazine, March 1912–December 1916.
Beacon Journal (Akron, Ohio), October 15, 1902.
Bedford Weekly Mail (Bedford, IN), May 17, 1907.
Berkshire Evening Eagle (Pittsfield, MA), October 1, 1920.
Biddeford Daily Journal (Biddeford, ME), November 16, 1908.
Birmingham News (Birmingham, AL), October 8, 1908–September 5, 1919.
Bloomington Evening World (Bloomington, IN), August 28, 1901.
Boston Daily Globe, *Boston Sunday Globe*, and *Boston Evening Globe* May 4, 1897–October 1, 1920.
Boston Evening Transcript, March 8, 1906–November 26, 1912.
Boston Post and *Sunday Post*, October 26, 1896–June 28, 1921.
Bristol Herald (Bristol, VT), August 5, 1897.
Brooklyn Citizen, September 3, 1898–January 24, 1903.
Brooklyn Daily Eagle, August 7, 1899–November 19, 1926.
Brooklyn Daily Times, August 20, 1900–December 7, 1919.
Buffalo Commercial, October 31, 1898–April 1, 1907.
Buffalo Courier, January 14, 1898–December 27, 1914.
Buffalo Enquirer, June 1, 1895–August 5, 1918.
Buffalo Evening News, January 27, 1902–December 13, 1924.
Buffalo Evening Times and *Buffalo Sunday Times*, March 30, 1901–June 4, 1913.
Buffalo Morning Express, December 26, 1895–March 24, 1908.
Buffalo Review, May 20, 1903.
Burlington Daily News, February 3, 1908.
Butte Inter Mountain (Butte, MT), February 27, 1905–August 30, 1909.
Butte Miner (Butte, MT), July 14, 1903.
Cairo Bulletin (Cairo, IL), August 11, 1905.
Calgary Daily Herald (Calgary, Alberta, Canada), August 8, 1919.
Carbondale Leader (Carbondale, PA), April 7, 1904.
Champaign Daily Gazette (Champaign, IL), May 18, 1912.
Chattanooga News, August 31, 1917.
Chattanooga Sunday Times and *Chattanooga Daily Times*, June 11, 1905–April 27, 1962.
Coalville Times (Coalville, UT), September 6, 1901.
Colorado Statesman (Denver, CO), July 4, 1908.
Conneautville Courier (Conneautville, PA), July 3, 1885–January 11, 1894.
Daily Albuquerque Citizen, March 26, 1903–March 27, 1903.
Daily Evening Item (Lynn, MA), January 5, 1905–April 1, 1910.
Daily Industrial News (Greensboro, NC), April 1, 1906.
Daily Kennebec Journal (Kennebec, ME), June 29, 1906–May 10, 1907.
Daily News (Mount Carmel, PA), December 12, 1908.
Daily News-Advertiser (Vancouver, British Columbia, Canada), December 19, 1915.
Daily News-Democrat (Huntington, IN), October 7, 1897.
Daily Review (Decatur, IL), March 20, 1902.
Daily Standard (Hazelton, PA), April 14, 1903.
Daily State Journal (Ogden, UT), December 23, 1908.
Daily Times (Davenport, IA), May 18, 1912.

Daily Times (New Philadelphia, OH), February 5, 1905–June 2, 1943.
Davenport Democrat (Davenport, IA), March 29, 1907–July 16, 1919.
Dayton Daily News, July 6, 1904.
Dayton Evening Herald and *Dayton Herald*, August 1, 1903–May 22, 1912.
Detroit Free Press, March 24, 1895–April 1, 1906.
Detroit Times, April 2, 1908–November 15, 1912.
Douglas County Herald (Ava, MO), October 3, 1918–April 3, 1919.
East Oregonian (Pendleton, OR), February 27, 1913–September 24, 1913.
Eastern Utah Advocate (Price, UT), August 26, 1909.
Edmonton Journal (Edmonton, Alberta, Canada), September 6, 1919.
El Paso Herald, October 15, 1920.
Elyria Republican (Elyria, OH), July 22, 1909.
Evening Bee (Sacramento, CA), January 28, 1903.
Evening Call (Lead, SD), December 26, 1899.
Evening Capital News (Boise, ID), September 5, 1914.
Evening Herald (Fall River, MA), January 11, 1906–August 16, 1919.
Evening Journal (Wilmington, DE), July 7, 1903.
Evening Mail (Stockton, CA), January 28, 1903–November 6, 1909.
Evening News Review, *Evening Review*, and *East Liverpool Review* (East Liverpool, OH),
    December 18, 1895-July 10, 1936.
Evening Record (Greenville, PA), August 14, 1919.
Evening Star and *Sunday Star* (Washington, DC), July 25, 1894–November 14, 1924.
Evening Telegram (Elyria, OH), December 10, 1910.
Evening World-Herald (Omaha, NE), November 5, 1924–November 10, 1924.
The Expositor (Brantford, Ontario, Canada), June 24, 1898.
Fall River Daily Globe (Fall River, MA), July 1, 1902–May 20, 1912.
Fall River Daily Herald (Fall River, MA), April 5, 1902.
Fall River Evening News (Fall River, MA), November 16, 1907–May 21, 1921.
Fall River News (Fall River, KS), May 9, 1902.
Fort Scott Monitor (Fort Scott, KS), July 8, 1903.
Fort Wayne Journal-Gazette (Fort Wayne, IN), October 26, 1900–May 23, 1919.
Fort Wayne News (Fort Wayne, IN), January 15, 1900–April 23, 1912.
Fort Wayne Sentinel (Fort Wayne, IN), July 11, 1891–June 2, 1913.
Franklin Press (Franklin, NC), April 4, 1906.
Galveston Daily News, June 11, 1905.
The Gazette (Montreal, Quebec, Canada), March 7, 1904–September 25, 1919.
Gazette Times (Pittsburgh, PA), September 5, 1908–October 5, 1908.
Greenwood Gazette (Greenwood, NE), June 2, 1926.
Hamilton Evening Journal (Hamilton, OH), April 8, 1926.
Harrisburg Star Independent, July 8, 1903.
Harrisburg Telegraph, July 1, 1885.
Hattiesburg News (Hattiesburg, MS), September 11, 1908.
Herald Advance (Milbank, SD), April 8, 1904.
Herald and News (Randolph, VT), August 11, 1898.
Houston Daily Post, June 18, 1901.
The Independent (Santa Barbara, CA), March 9, 1901.

Indiana Daily Times (Indianapolis, IN), February 28, 1922.
Indianapolis Journal, September 14, 1897–January 28, 1902.
Inter-Mountain Republican (Salt Lake City, UT), March 29, 1907–February 19, 1909.
Inter Ocean (Chicago, IL), March 15, 1902–April 25, 1909.
Journal and Tribune (Knoxville, TN), October 1, 1920.
Kenosha Evening News (Kenosha, WI), May 18, 1912.
Knoxville Sentinel, September 8, 1909–January 30, 1920.
La Crosse Tribune (La Crosse, WI), November 11, 1908–July 29, 1909.
Lake County Times (Hammond, MN), September 29, 1910.
Lake Shore Visitor (Erie, PA), March 20, 1875.
Lancaster Intelligencer (Lancaster, PA), March 30, 1907–July 22, 1909.
The Leader (Freemont, NE), August 23, 1901.
Leavenworth Post (Leavenworth, KS), May 29, 1906.
Lima Citizen (Lima, OH), July 12, 1962.
Lima News-Democrat (Lima, OH), January 17, 1903.
Lincoln Daily Star, May 19, 1912–May 23, 1918.
Los Angeles Evening Express and *Los Angeles Express*, December 17, 1900–April 16, 1906.
Los Angeles Herald, June 23, 1907–July 23, 1908.
Los Angeles Record, September 26, 1905.
Mansfield Mirror (Mansfield, MO), May 30, 1918–August 7, 1919.
Mattoon Morning Star (Mattoon, IL), September 25, 1908.
Meriden Daily Journal (Meriden, CT), January 27, 1902–August 5, 1919.
Meriden Morning Record (Meriden, CT), April 5, 1907.
Minneapolis Journal, September 20, 1905–September 23, 1905.
Minneapolis Tribune and *Minneapolis Sunday Tribune*, December 13, 1902–April 25, 1909.
Montgomery Times (Montgomery, AL), April 27, 1909.
Montpelier Evening Argus, January 2, 1917.
Montreal Daily Star, May 25, 1905.
Nashville Banner, September 17, 1909–March 3, 1913.
New Castle Herald (New Castle, PA), February 8, 1906–September 25, 1919.
New Castle News (New Castle, PA), April 17, 1914.
New Hampton Herald (New Hampton, MO), August 5, 1897.
New York Herald, October 1, 1920–April 30, 1922.
New York Times, July 26, 1894–May 18, 1945.
New-York Tribune and *New York Tribune*, May 17, 1897–September 30, 1920.
News Scrimitar (Memphis, TN), September 30, 1920.
Newark Star (Newark, NJ), August 2, 1909.
Night Journal (Lincoln, NE), December 10, 1924.
Northfield News (Northfield, VT), February 2, 1897–January 9, 1917.
Oakland Tribune, February 13, 1905–March 30, 1905.
Oklahoma News (Oklahoma City, OK), November 22, 1906.
Omaha Daily Bee, November 11, 1914.
Owensboro Inquirer (Owensboro, KY), August 3, 1909.
Owensboro Weekly Messenger (Owensboro, KY), May 22, 1897.
Park City Daily News (Bowling Green, KY), June 18, 1953.

Philadelphia Inquirer, October 11, 1894–September 30, 1920.
Philadelphia Times, July 14, 1902.
Pittsburgh Commercial, March 17, 1875.
Pittsburg Dispatch, July 4, 1891–April 26, 1892.
Pittsburg Gazette, July 16, 1905.
Pittsburg Post, Pittsburgh Post, and *Pittsburgh Sunday Post*, September 9, 1897–September 30, 1920.
Pittsburgh Post-Gazette, February 6, 1932.
Pittsburg Press, December 4, 1895–July 22, 1919.
Pittston Gazette (Pittston, PA), October 7, 1908.
Ponca City Daily Courier (Ponca City, OK), September 4, 1901.
Portsmouth Daily Times (Portsmouth, OH), August 4, 1909.
Potter Review (Potter, NE), June 4, 1926.
Public Daily Ledger Maysville Republican (Maysville, KY), September 25, 1903.
Racine Daily Journal (Racine, WI), January 13, 1909.
Reading Times (Reading, PA), April 6, 1903.
Record-Union (Sacramento, CA), July 26, 1894.
Richmond Dispatch, May 16, 1902.
Rutland Daily Herald (Rutland, VT), May 19, 1943.
Sacramento Star, October 1, 1920.
St. Albans Daily Messenger (St. Albans, VT), June 14, 1897.
St. Albans Weekly Messenger (St. Albans, VT), April 23, 1903.
St. Joseph Evening Herald (St. Joseph, MO), May 18, 1912.
St. Joseph Gazette (St. Joseph, MO), January 24, 1903.
St. Louis Globe-Democrat, February 17, 1893–June 3, 1937.
St. Louis Post-Dispatch and *Sunday St. Louis Post-Dispatch*, April 1, 1892–August 10, 1919.
St. Louis Republic, June 25, 1900–January 18, 1903.
St. Louis Star, December 27, 1911–November 10, 1922.
St. Paul Globe, August 7, 1899–January 19, 1903.
Salina Journal (Salina, KS), September 20, 1992.
Salt Lake Herald and *Salt Lake Herald-Republican*, January 14, 1903–February 18, 1915.
Salt Lake Telegram and *Evening Telegram*, April 29, 1911–August 7, 1919.
Salt Lake Tribune, July 8, 1905–April 25, 1911.
San Francisco Call, November 22, 1901–December 1, 1908.
San Francisco Examiner, December 1, 1902–July 29, 1917.
Santa Cruz Evening Sentinel and *Evening Sentinel* (Santa Cruz, CA), August 14, 1899–March 25, 1902.
Saturday Bee (Sacramento, CA), August 18, 1894.
Savannah Morning News, May 25, 1904–September 25, 1904.
Scranton Republican, October 21, 1899–November 21, 1908.
Scranton Tribune, April 20, 1901.
Sedalia Democrat-Sentinel (Sedalia, MO), August 25, 1907.
Sedalia Evening Democrat (Sedalia, MO), April 29, 1902.
Semi-Weekly Gazette and York Democratic Press (York, PA), July 18, 1903.

Sioux City Journal (Sioux City, IA), April 20, 1902–July 28, 1907.
Southwest News (Dodge City, KS), June 10, 1926.
Spokane Daily Chronicle (Spokane, WA), May 11, 1906–February 27, 1913.
Spokesman=Review (Spokane, WA), October 5, 1913–December 7, 1919.
Sporting Life, June 5, 1897–December 27, 1909.
The Sporting News, October 23, 1897–October 9, 1946.
Standard Union (Brooklyn, NY), March 16, 1900.
The Star (Newark, NJ), July11, 1908–July 16, 1908.
Stark County Democrat (Canton, OH), March 3, 1903.
The Sun (New York, NY), April 27, 1897–January 24, 1920.
Sun-Democrat (Paducah, KY), February 5, 1932.
Sunday State Journal (Lincoln, NE), July 1, 1900–April 3, 1904.
Sunday Times (Minneapolis, MN), June 4, 1905.
Tampa Morning Tribune, September 5, 1919–October 2, 1920.
Tampa Weekly Tribune and *Weekly Tribune*, April 9, 1903–August 5, 1909.
The Times (Philadelphia, PA), July 14, 1896–March 16, 1902.
Times=Democrat (New Orleans, LA), March 7, 1894.
Topeka Daily Capital, December 6, 1902–August 11, 1909.
Topeka State Journal and *Weekly State Journal*, September 4, 1897–November 7, 1905.
The Tribune (Hicksville, OH), November 26, 1908.
True Northerner (Paw Paw, MI), January 4, 1901.
Tulsa Democrat (Tulsa, OK), October 13, 1918.
Vermont News (Northfield, VT), December 21, 1897.
Vermont Phoenix (Brattleboro, VT), April 30, 1897.
Virginian Pilot and Norfolk Landmark (Norfolk, VA), November 6, 1924.
Warren Mirror (Warren, PA), August 13, 1909.
Washington Herald (Washington, DC), April 25, 1909–February 9, 1920.
Washington Times (Washington, DC), *Evening Times*, *Morning Times*, and *The Times*, April 1, 1896–June 21, 1920.
Waterbury Democrat and *Waterbury Evening Democrat* (Waterbury, CT), May 16, 1902-October 8, 1908.
Weekly Pantagraph (Bloomington, IL), August 24, 1906.
Weekly State Journal (Lincoln, NE), February 10, 1905.
Weekly Wisconsin (Milwaukee, WI), July 8, 1885.
Wichita Sunday Eagle, September 19, 1909.
Wilkes-Barre Daily News, March 16, 1900.
Wilkes-Barre Leader, June 23, 1903-August 9, 1904.
Wilkes-Barre Record, August 26, 1903-December 1, 1919.
Wilkes-Barre Times, September 22, 1903.
Wilkes-Barre Times-Leader, September 21, 1909.
Wilmington Morning Star (Wilmington, NC), October 22, 1909–August 15, 1911.
Winnipeg Tribune and *Winnipeg Evening Tribune* (Winnipeg, Manitoba, Canada), March 2, 1906-November 5, 1924.
Wood County Reporter (Grand Rapids, WI), August 13, 1908.
The World (New York, NY), June 13, 1897–May 18, 1912.
York Dispatch (York, PA), July 8, 1903–May 20, 1912.

Websites

Andover Center for History and Culture, https://andoverhistoryandculture.org
Baseball Almanac, https://www.baseball-almanac.com
Baseball Reference, https://www.baseball-reference.com
Brookline Connection, https://brooklineconnection.com
Buffalo Architecture and History, https://www.buffaloah.com
Cincinnati and Hamilton County Public Library, https://digital.cincinnatilibrary.org
City of St. Louis, MO, https://www.stlouis-mo.gov
Cleveland Historical, https://clevelandhistorical.org
Coney Island History Project, https://www.coneyislandhistory.org
East Liverpool History Society, https://www.eastliverpoolhistoricalsociety.org
Find a Grave, https://www.findagrave.com
Free Library of Philadelphia, https://www.freelibrary.org
Georgia Archives – University System of Georgia Virtual Vault, https://vaultgeorgiaarchives.org
Google Books, https://books.google.com
Google Newspaper Archives, https://news.google.com
Historic Detroit, https://historicdetroit.org
Historic Pittsburgh, https://historicpittsburgh.org
Historical Newspapers – World Collection, https://newscomwc.newspapers.com
Historical Society of Clarendon Vermont, https://www.clarendonvthistory.org
Historical Society of the District of Columbia Circuit, https://dcchs.org
Historical Society of the New York Courts, https://history.nycourts.gov
History, Art & Archives – United States House of Representatives, https://history.house.gov
LA84 Foundation Digital Library, https://digital.la84.org
Library of Congress, https://www.loc.gov
Mass.gov, https://www.mass.gov
Metropolitan Police Washington DC, https://mdpc.dc.gov
Museum of Wayne County History, https://www.waynehistory.org
National Archives, https://www.archives.gov
National Baseball Hall of Fame, https://baseballhall.org
National Governors Association, https://www.nga.org
Northern Illinois University Digital Library, https://digital.lib.niu.edu
Ohio History Central, https://ohiohistorycentral.org
Paper of Record, https://paperofrecord.hypernet.ca
Peabody Police Department, https://www.peabodypd.org
Retrosheet, https://www.retrosheet.org
RootsWeb, https://sites.rootsweb.com
Sacramento History Online, https://www.sacramentohistory.org
St. Louis Union Station, https://www.stlouisunionstation.com
San Francisco Police Department, https://www.sanfranciscopolice.org
Seamheads, https://seamheads.com
Society for American Baseball Research, https://sabr.org
Stats Crew, https://www.statscrew.com

Index

Numbers in **bold** indicate pages with photographs.

A.G. Spalding and Brothers Sporting Goods Store, 295
Abbaticchio, Edward "Ed," 194, 196, 203204
Academy Café, 20, 22
Academy of Music, 16, 20, 22
Adonis (Greek god), 29
Albany, New York, 25
Albion Hotel, 225
Aldine Hotel, 238, 250, 252–54
Algonquin Club, 177
All-Americans, 37–40, 42, 47–48
All-Nationals, 40, 42, 47
Allen. Circuit Court Judge C.B., 293
American, 73
American Association (major league), 108, 110, 145
American Association (minor league), 47, 138, 298
American League (major league), x, 14, 17, 23, 37–41, 48–49, 57–59, 61, 64–68, 70, 81, 91–92, 100, 111–18, 125, 138, 147–48, 152, 154, 156–57, 160, 163, 169–70, 173–77, 181, 191–93, 215, 219–20, 227, 233, 235, 242–43, 245, 248–50, 252–55, 258–61, 267–68, 270–71, 273, 275, 277–82, 292, 298, 304, 309
American League (minor league), 36, 146
American League All-Stars, 92
American League Board of Directors, 276, 279, 281, 283
American League Park (New York), 154
American League Park (Washington), 66–68, 74, 157
American Leaguers, 37
Ames, Leon "Red," 125, 214
Anderson, George W., 131
Andover, Massachusetts, 95, 97–100, 102, 104
Andrew Square, 286–87, 289
Angus, Samuel F., 39, 42, 47–50

Anniston, Alabama, 224
Anson, Adrian "Cap," 32, 55–56, 89, 295, 297
Apollo Belvedere, 30
Appellate Division (New York), 281–82
Aqueduct Racetrack, 59
Arbuckle Building, 108
Argo, Martin, 203
Arkansas, 17
Armistice, 262
Armour, William "Bill," 227–30
Army (United States), 262–63
Asheville, North Carolina, 308
Atkinson, Fred, 143
Atlanta, Georgia, 226, 232
Atlantic City, New Jersey, 216
Atlantic Ocean, 78
Atkinson, Fred, 143
Atlanta, Georgia, 226, 232
Auburn, New York, 258
Auerbach, Joseph, 278–79
Augusta, Georgia, 223–25, 228–32
Augusta Tourists, 223–28, 230
Auten, Philip, 108–109, 124
Ava, Missouri, 262
"Ave Maria," 83
Aveline Hotel (Aveline House), 188
Avery, Fred, 240
Aviation Corps, 262
Avilla, Indiana, 164

Baker, John Franklin "Frank," 234–38, 242
Baker, Secretary of War Newton, 260–61
Baker, Wesley, 139
Baldwin, Stephen C., 277
Ball, Philip "Phil," 271–73, 283
Baltimore, Maryland, 3, 12, 15–19, 23–24, 111–13, 116–17
Baltimore American, 113
Baltimore & Ohio train, 5
Baltimore Orioles (American Association major league), 110
Baltimore Orioles (American League), 14–17, 19, 22–23, 62, 111–18, 309

Baltimore Orioles (National League), 3, 12, 32, 34–36, 57, 87, 89, 110, 112, 131, 142, 166, 170, 230
Baltimore Police Department, 18
Baltimorean, 111
Banks County, Georgia, 220
Barnes, Frank, 263
Barnie, William "Billy," 110
Barre, Vermont, 85
Barrett, James "Jimmy," 38
Barrow, Edward "Ed," 49, 260, 264–67, 270, 272, 276
"Barrow Responsible for Red Sox Downward Slide," 267
Barry, John "Jack," 235, 237–38, 259–60
Baseball Magazine, 308
Beach, Robert W., 22
Becker, Edward C., 12
Beckley, Jacob "Jake," 58
Belger, M.F., 186
Bellview village school, 308
Ben Hur, 16, 18, 21
Bender, Charles "Chief," 152, 155
Benevolent and Protective Order of Elks, 188
Bennett, Walter, 25
Bennett Park, 71, 210, 227, 229, 232, 234
Benning Race Track, 51, 80
Bergen, Florence, 168
Bergen, Harriet (Gaines), 168
Bergen, Joe, 168
Bergen, Martin "Marty," ix, x, 166, 168, 184
Bernhard, William "Bill," 13
Bernheim Brothers, 108
Bierbauer, Louis "Lou," 32
Big Apple, 25, 111, 201, 206, 215
Billings, James B., 170
Biltmore Hotel, 273, 276
Bingaman, Dr. Walter S., 305
Bingham, Commissioner Theodore A., 198
Bingham House Hotel, 58
Birmingham News, 277

the Bison, 174
Black, 230
Blanchard Opera House, 85
Bloody Angle (Philadelphia neighborhood), 237
Blunett, John K., 73–74
Bodie, Frank "Ping," 267
Bogart, Helen, 21
Boise Irrigators, 256–57
Boland, Reverend J.D., 23
Booblsville, 84
Boston, Massachusetts, 18, 42, 82, 95, 98, 101–102, 104, 131, 135–36, 149, 152, 154, 156–57, 160, 166, 168–70, 176–77, 179–81, 183, 186–88, 192, 229, 236, 259, 261, 264–66, 283, 285
Boston Americans, x, 67, 100–105, 113–15, 124–25, 138, 149, 152–53, 155–57, 163, 169–71, 173–88, 191–92, 232, 283, 285–86
Boston Beaneaters, ix, x, 4, 35–36, 82, 85, 99, 131, 135–36, 147, 163, 165–71, 180–81, 187, 283
Boston Daily Globe, 16, 182–83, 258, 289
Boston Daily Post, 180
Boston Doves, 204–206, 213, 299, 305
Boston Herald, 179
Boston Journal, 180–81
Boston Post, 267, 285
Boston Red Sox, x, 5, 192, 232, 236, 255, 258–68, 270–73, 276–79, 282–83
Bostons, 169, 174
Boundary Field, 29–31, 33, 83
Bowen, James, 248
Bowerman, Frank "Brutal," 38, 93, 119–24, 128
Bowker, Margaret (McGraw), 131
Boyton, Paul, 77
Bradford, Pennsylvania, 139
Bradley, District of Columbia Supreme Court Justice Andrew C., 20
Brady, Thomas, 301
Brady, Detective William "Sport," 10
Brain, David "Dave," 200
Brannon, Edward C., 25
Bransfield, William "Kitty," 58–59, 92, 126, 215–17
Breckinridge family, 306
Breitenstein, Theodore "Ted," 84

Bresnahan, Roger, 118, 120, 196, 209–210
Bresnahan, Timothy J., 180
Bridgeburg, Ontario, 72, 78
Bridwell, Albert "Al," 197, 201
Briggs, Herbert "Buttons," 193
Brighton Beach Race Course, 70
Broadway (New York), 260
Broadway (St. Louis), 24
Broadway Athletic Club, 213
Broadway Avenue (New York), 300
Bronx Borough, New York, 117
Brook Street, 306
Brooklyn, New York, 42, 117, 209
Brooklyn Bridegrooms, 142
Brooklyn Daily Eagle, 254
Brooklyn Handicap, 51–52
Brooklyn Robins, 259
Brooklyn Superbas, 13, 15, 23, 35, 57, 81, 89, 91, 98, 112–13, 145, 167, 193, 205–206, 298
Brotherhood of Professional Baseball Players, 55
Brouthers, Dennis "Dan," 32
Brown, Horace, 306
Brown, Mordecai "Three Finger," 194, 203–204, 207, 209–210
Brown, Thomas "Tom," 33, 136–37
Brown, Justice William, 240
Brown, Thomas, Co., Dublin, 286
Brownson Council, 105
Brunswick squad, 164
Brush, John T., 23, 25, 59–60, 62, 64–65, 70–71, 93–94, 118–19, 121, 131–33, 135–38, 200, 205–206, 211–12, 214–15, 294–95, 297, 300
Bruski, Paul, 143–44
Buffalo, New York, 71–72, 74–76, 164, 166, 169–71, 174–75, 178–80, 241, 285
Buffalo Bisons (American League club), 7
Buffalo Bisons (minor league club), 164–65, 169, 171, 175, 187
Buffalo Commercial, 188
Buffalo Courier, 76
Buffalo Enquirer, 61, 169
Buffalo Evening Times, 169, 290
Buffalo Morning Express, 98, 171
Bulger, Bozeman, 158, 201
Burke, E.S. Jr., 241–42

Burke, James "Jimmy," 272
Burke, Theresa Agnes, 19
Burkett, Jesse, 4, 6–7, 32, 68–69
Burleigh, Clarence, 131
Burlington, Massachusetts, 261
Burnet House, 24
Burnett, Charles, 178
Burnett, Hattie, 178–79, 290
Bush, Owen "Donie," 248, 251
Bussey, Harry, 223
Butler, Reverend W.B., 261
Butler County, Pennsylvania, 139
Byron, William "Lord," 227

Cahill, William, 183
Cain, Elizabeth (Pulliam), 301
Cain, George W., 301
Calhoun, W.A., 29
California, 3–4, 14, 37–38, 41–42, 46–48, 148, 297–98, 303
California League, 3, 23, 38, 42, 148
Calvary Cemetery, 77
Camden, New Jersey, 159
Campbell, Dr. A.E., 174
Campbell, Joe, 30–31, 84, 165–66
Campbell, William F., 22
Canada, 72, 85, 143, 241
Canadian, 72–73, 144
Cantillon, Joseph "Joe," 23, 37–38, 42, 47, 114
Canton, Ohio, 176
Carbon County, Utah, 256
Carey, George "Scoops," 45, 68
Carey, James, 18
Carnegie, Pennsylvania, 126
Carpenter, William "Bill," 33–34
Carr, Lewis "Lew," 90
Carrigan, William "Bill," 258–60
Case, Charles "Charlie," 127
Casey, James "Doc," 193
Cassen, Henry, 43
Cassidy, Joseph "Joe," 175
Casway, Jerrold, 57
Catholic, 71, 93, 100
Catholic Church, 105
Catholicism, 164
Cave Hill Cemetery, 304
Caylor, Lenore, 300
Cedar Rapids Canaries, 110
Central League, 176
Central Vermont Railroad, 82
Chance, Frank "Peerless Leader," 192–93, 198, 200, 206–209, 215, 219, 296–97
Charleston, South Carolina, 232
Charlottsville, Virginia, 169–70

Chase, Harold "Hal," ix
Chatham, Ontario, Canada, 143–44
Cherokee County, North Carolina, 308
Cherry Street, 3
Chesbro, John "Jack," 39, 41, 48, 81, 92, 147, 227–28
Chester, West Virginia, 28
Chicago, Illinois, 16, 19–20, 37–38, 42, 111, 113, 119, 123, 142–43, 159, 166, 173, 179, 181, 188, 191, 193, 198, 202–203, 206, 217, 258, 265, 268, 271–72, 278, 280–83, 285, 295, 298–99, 304, 307
Chicago Americans, 147
Chicago Automobile Club, 298
Chicago Black Sox, 217
Chicago-Boston express train, 265
Chicago Colts, 56, 237, 295
Chicago Cubs, 48, 64–65, 81, 99–100, 107, 131–32, 192–206, 208–213, 219, 261, 294–97, 303
Chicago Daily Tribune, 212
Chicago Orphans, 82, 86, 90, 144, 147
Chicago slide, 237
Chicago White Sox, 37–38, 64, 67, 70, 112–14, 126, 138, 148, 152, 156, 159, 170, 173, 175–76, 192–93, 217, 219, 229, 251, 255, 257, 264–65, 267–68, 270–72, 276, 278–79, 282, 290
Chicago White Stockings, 11, 146, 193
"Chick Stahl Day," 286
Christmas, 39, 41, 50, 280
Church of the Immaculate Conception, 77
Cicotte, Edgar "Eddie," 225, 227
Cincinnati, Ohio, 5–6, 8, 24, 35, 41–42, 49, 61, 95, 99, 186, 191, 193, 197, 202, 206, 249, 299, 300, 303
Cincinnati Reds, 5, 11–12, 23–24, 31–33, 41, 50, 58, 64, 90, 95, 99, 118–19, 136, 142, 159–60, 167, 191, 215, 260, 283, 305
Cincinnati Times-Star, 308
Cincinnatis, 61
City Hospital morgue (Boston), 286
City of Brotherly Love, 251, 293
Civil War, 54

Clarke, Fred "Cap," 81, 90–104, 107–108, 119–24, 127–28, 140–43, 146–47, 194–95, 202, 204, 283
Clarke, Justice John Proctor, 281
Clarke, William "Boileryard," 129
Class AA, 258
Cleary, Mart, 187
Cleveland, Ohio, ix, 54–55, 57, 69, 73, 77, 139, 148, 153, 169–70, 229, 236, 238, 240–41, 250, 260–61, 265, 271, 276, 278
Cleveland Blues, 169
Cleveland Broncos, 41, 48
Cleveland Indians, 265, 267, 269–72, 275–79, 281
Cleveland Infants, 55
Cleveland Naps, 67, 69–70, 73, 148, 152, 174, 176–78, 193, 231–32, 238–39, 242, 248, 253, 284
Cleveland Spiders, 11, 31, 36, 110–11
Cline, Prosecutor John, 240
Clogg, Reverend Henry S., 19
Clymer, Otis, 136
Coakley, Andrew "Andy," 156–58, 160, 200, 290
Cobb, Amanda (Chitwood), 220, 226, 308
Cobb, Charlotte "Charlie" (Lombard), 241
Cobb, Florence, 220
Cobb, Harrison Taylor, 308
Cobb, John F., 308
Cobb, John Paul, 220
Cobb, Sarah, 221
Cobb, Tyrus Raymond "Ty," ix, 219–45, **246**, 247–55, 259, 268, 308
Cobb, William Herschel, 220–24, 226–27, 308
the Cobbs, 220
Cole, Conductor John, 72, 74–75
College of the Holy Cross, 184
Collins, Edward "Eddie," 234–35, 264
Collins, James "Jimmy," 101–102, 115, 166, 168–71, 173–82, 184–85, 187–88, 285
Collins, Sheriff Jeremiah, 241
Collins, Ray, 258
Collins, Sadie (Murphy), 285
Columbia Park, 152, 155
Columbia Skyscrapers, 223
Columbus Buckeyes/Senators, 144–45, 167

Comiskey, Charles, 4, 37, 112–13, 267–68, 271, 275–76, 278–79, 281–83, 298–99, 304, 307
Comiskey Park, 264
Common Pleas Court (Cleveland), 241
Conant, William, 170
Coney Island, New York, 70
Conneautville Courier, 2
Conneautville Station, 2
Connolly, Thomas "Tommy," 68–69, 114–15, 272
Conroy, Dr. Edward C., 98, 102
Conroy, William "Wid" 39
Coogan's Bluff, 207
Cook, Frank, 45
Cook, John F., 289
Cook, Rutherford B., 296
Cooley, Duff, 42, 227, 256
Copeland, Constable Fred S., 150
Copeland's Store, 150–51
Copley Square Hotel, 180
Copperfield, Vermont, 83
Copperfield's Catholic church, 83
Corbett, James "Gentleman Jim," 125
Corn Exchange Bank Building, 295
Corning, New York, 85
Corriden, John "Red," 242
Coughlin, William "Bill," 71
Courteney, Fay, 238, 241
Coveleski, Harry, 202, 210
Cratty, A.R., 92–93, 100
Crawford, Samuel "Sam," 48–49, 227, 230, 232, 234, 237
Creamer, Dr. Joseph M., 212–15, 217, 294–95
Croke, J.E., 74–77
Croker, Richard, 82
Cronin, John "Jack," 118
Crooked Creek, 1
Cross, Lafayette "Lave," 156, 160
Cross, Montford, "Monte," 293
Cuba, 110, 296
Cullen, Clarence L., 51–52, 80
Cummings, Henry "Bungy," 230
Cuyahoga County, 240–41
Czar, 252

Dahlen, William "Bill," 56
Danforth, Edward N., 25–26
Danvers, Massachusetts, 103–104, 283
Danvers State Hospital, 103–104
D'Artagnan, 52
Davenport, Iowa, 271

Davidson, Mayor William C., 44
Davis, Alfonzo "Lefty," 39
Davis, George, 64–65, 70–71, 85, 90
Davis, Harry, 160, 293
Davis, Ralph S., 97–98, 102, 105, 121, 158
Day, John, 89
Deadball Era, vii, viii, ix, x, 1, 28, 107, 163, 219, 290, 308–310
Decatur, Indiana, 164
Delagi, Michael N., 245
Delahanty, Bridget (Croker), 54, 71, 75
Delahanty, Edward James "Ed, Big Ed, E.J., Del or King of Swatsville," x, 4, 32, 54–78, **79**, 80, 290
Delahanty, Florence, 71, 77
Delahanty, Frank, 74–76, 231
Delahanty, James Sr., 54
Delahanty, James Jr. "Jim," 236
Delahanty, Norine (Thompson), 56, 62, 67, 69, 71–74, 76–77
Delahanty, Thomas "Tom," 66, 77
Delaware River, 78
Delray (Detroit neighborhood), 143
DeMontreville, Eugene "Gene," 31
Denver, Colorado, 66, 77, 158
Denver & Rio Grande Western Railroad, 256
Denver Grizzlies, 66–67, 77
Detroit, Michigan, 38–39, 44–45, 63, 70–71, 76–77, 143, 173, 210, 228–29, 236, 240–41, 245, 248–49
Detroit City League, 143
Detroit Evening News, 45
Detroit Tigers (major league), 38–39, 41–42, 47–50, 63, 69–71, 95, 114, 155–56, 192–93, 210, 219–20, 224–25, 227–45, 247, 249–55, 258–59, 268–70, 275, 280, 295
Detroit Tigers (minor league), 143–44
Detroit Times, 143
Detroits, 244–45
Devlin, Arthur "Art," 196, 209
Dexter, Charles "Charlie," 42
Diamond Café, 16
DiMaggio, Dom, 54
DiMaggio, Joe, 54
DiMaggio, Vince, 54

Dinneen, William "Bill," 101, 169–70, 177, 183, 251
Director of Athletics at the University of Illinois, 192
District of Columbia, 20,
Division 6 (South Boston Police Department), 287, 289
Dixmont Insane Asylum, 305
Dobbs, John, 58
Doheny, Daniel (Dorney), 83
Doheny, Edward Michael O'Sullivan Jr. "Eddie or Little Eddie" (Dorney), 92, 95
Doheny, Edward Richard "Ed, Eddie or Irish" (Dorney), 81–105, **106**, 283–84, 290
Doheny, James (Dorney), 81
Doheny, Katherine (O'Sullivan) (Dorney), 89, 95, 98, 100, 102–105
Doheny, Kathleen (Dorney), 83
Doheny, Mary (O'Connor) (Dorney), 81
Doheny, Mary (O'Sullivan) (Dorney), 83
Doheny, Reverend Father P.J. (Dorney), 100
Dolan, Albert "Cozy," 243
Donlin, James, 2–3
Donlin, Conductor John, 1–3
Donlin, Maggie, 1–2
Donlin, Michael I, 3
Donlin, Michael "Mike or Turkey Mike," ix, 1–11, 13–26, **27**, 113, 196, 209
the Donlins, 1
Donovan, Patrick "Patsy," 88, 140, 142
Donovan, William "Bill," 48–49, 220, 225, 239
Dooin, Charles "Red," 212, 215–17
Doolin, Michael "Mickey," 215
Dorchester Avenue, 287
Dorgan, Thomas Aloysius (alias Tad), 215
Dosher, Bert, 295
Douglas County, Missouri, 256
Dover, New Hampshire, 28–29
Dovey, George, 299–300, 305
Dowden, Dr. Chauncey W., 185
Doyle, John "Jack," 32, 34, 86–88
Doyle, Lawrence "Larry," 209
Dreyfuss, Bernard "Barney," 35–36, 39, 81, 91, 94–98, 100, 103–105, 107–110, 119, 121–22, 124–25, 127, 129–33, 135–38, 145–47,

204, 211, 297–98, 300, 303–304, 309
Dreyfuss, Samuel (father), 108
Dryden, Charles "Charley," 148, 153–54
Duffy, Hugh, 165, 169
Dumont, George, 265
Dunn, James "Jim," 270–71, 276–79
Dunning, N., 31
Dunnville, Ontario, Canada, 144
Durham, Israel, 303, 305
Dwyer, John Francis "Frank," 38–39, 41
Dygert, James "Jimmy," 153

Eagle River, Wisconsin, 300
East, 42, 113, 261
East Boston, 183
East End (Pittsburgh neighborhood), 97
East Liverpool, Ohio, 28–31, 34, 37–38, 43–45, 48, 50, 284
East River, 117
East Side (New York City neighborhood), 213
East Springfield, Pennsylvania, 1
Eastern League, 49, 126, 132, 164, 216
Eastern Wisconsin Electric Railway and Light Company, 299
Eaton, Paul W., 69, 80
Ebbets, Charles, 91, 205–206, 212, 298
Ebbets Field, 259
Eclipse Park, 142, 144
Eighteenth Street (St. Louis, Missouri), 9–10
Eighth Avenue (New York), 207–208
Elberfeld, Norman "Kid," 49, 69–71
Eliot Street, 288
Elk County, 152
Elks Convention, 303
Ellery Street, 287
Ellery Terrace, 286–87, 289
Elmira, Courtland, and Northern Railroad, 109
Ely, William Frederick "Bones," 90
Emslie, Robert "Bob or Vacillating," 93–94, 126–27, 197–200, 205, 297
Engel, Arthur Clyde, 227
Engine Company No. 71 (New York City), 207

England, 143
English, 139
Erie, Pennsylvania, 1–3
Erie & Pittsburgh Road, 2–3
Erie Lodge No. 42 (Philadelphia, Pennsylvania), 77
Erie Railroad Depot, 178–79
Europe, 108, 178, 262–63
Evans, William "Billy," 227–28
Evans City, Pennsylvania, 140
Evening News Review, 34, 48
Evening Sentinel, 9
Evening Star, 18, 34, 51, 57, 67, 80, 210, 212
Evening Telegraph, 154, 159
Everitt, William "Bill," 32
Evers, John "Johnny," 194–98, 201, 204, 208, 210, 212, 215, **218**
Ewing, James Calvin "Cal," 38
Ewing, William "Buck," 33, 90
Exchange Street, 74, 178
Executive Committee, 118
Exposition Park, 32, 52, 86, 90, 95, 97, 99–102, 119, 122, 126, 129, 137, 147, 194–96, 199

Faber, Urban "Red," 265
Fahey, Thomas, 2
Fall River Indians, 28
Fallon, Judge Joseph D., 289
Farnham, Quebec, Canada, 81
Farrell, Frank "the Pool Room King," 117, 125
Farrell, John H., 67, 258
Fay, Frank, 286
Federal League, 258, 270–71
Feltis, John, 2
Fenway Park, 258, 261–62, 267, 272
Feuchtwanger, Henry, 304
Fields, Minnie "Mamie," (actress), 16–21, 24
Fields, Mrs. Minnie (aliases Wilhelmina A.E. von Olsen or Minnie Roberts – Robert), 19–20
Fields, Thomas M., 19–20
Fifth Avenue (Pittsburgh), 203
Fifth Avenue Hotel, 118
First Avenue (New York), 117
First Presbyterian Church, 50
Flaherty, Patrick "Patsy," 126
Flanner, Alonzo Joseph "Joe," 3–4
Fleischmann clean–ball law, 136
Flesh, Detective Thomas, 178
Flick, Elmer, 231

Fogel, Horace (alias Veteran), 152, 154, 159–61, 215–16, 290, 293–94
Foley, Abbie, 287
Foley, Thomas "Tom," 243
Forbes, Harry, 109
Forbes Field, 241, 303–304
Fort Erie, Ontario, 72, 74, 76
Fort Slocum, 262
Fort Wayne, Indiana, 163–64, 166–69, 171–73, 175–76, 179–81, 185–88, 285, 289–90
Fort Wayne City League, 164
Fort Wayne Journal–Gazette, 172–73
Fort Wayne Railroaders, 176
Fort Wayne Sentinel, 167
Foutz, Frank, 113
Fox, William "Bill," 58
France, 262, 286
France, Joseph C., 118
Frank, Sydney S., 116
Franklin, Pennsylvania, 139
Franklin Street, 20
Fraternal Order of Eagles, 77, 188
Frazee, Harry, 260, 264, 267–73, 275–77, 279–83
Freedman, Andrew, 36, 82, 84–85, 111–12, 116–19, 294–95
Freeman, John "Buck," 35, 175, 177
Freiburg, Baden, 108
Friend, Danny, 84
Frye, Chief of Police William L., 102–103
Fulton County, New York, 131
Fultz, David "Dave," 254

Galveston, Texas, 158
Ganzel, Charles "Charlie," 85
Ganzel, John, 68
Gardner, James "Jim," 87
Gazette Times, 203
George, Thomas H., 139–40
George W. Knox Express Company, 20
Georgia, 65, 220, 243–44, 249, 308
Georgian (Georgians), 232, 234, 249
German, 164
German Navy, 262
Germany, 108
Gilbert, John "Jack," 88
Gill, Warren, 194–97, 201
Gillespie, Referee George J., 276–77

Gilmore, James A. "Jim," 258
Gimlin, John "Dad," 256
Glaser, Vaughan, 238, 241–42
Glasscock, John "Jack or Pebbly Jack," 52
Gleason, William "Kid," 86, 88, 267
Goddard, Mary, 109
Golden Eagle Hotel, 40, 45
Goldman, Police Justice Harry, 17–18
Good, Harry, 256
Good Samaritan Hospital, 197
Good Samaritans, 91
Goodfellow, James, 187
Gordon, Joseph, 65, 70
Gordon's, 21
Gorsline, Police Superintendent Homer A., 171–72
Gould, District of Columbia Supreme Court Justice Ashley, 20
Grady, Michael "Mike," 88
Grady, Police Chief Michael H., 152
Grand Central Depot, 5
Grand Central Station, 25, 71, 206
Grand Hotel, 61
Grand Island, New York, 75
Grand Rapids, Michigan, 145
Grand Rapids & Indiana Railroad, 188
Grand Rapids Furnituremen, 145
Granneman's Drugstore, 172
Grant Street, 203
Graves, Frank, 143
Gravesend Race Track, 52, 117
Gray, William M., 294
Great Britain, 286
Great Mogul, 279
Great War (World War I), 260, 262
Green, M.A., 76
Green Mountain, 84
Greenbaum, New York Supreme Court Justice Samuel, 261
Greensburg, Pennsylvania, 121
Greenville, Pennsylvania, 139
Griffin, Police Chief Richard, 74, 76
Griffith, Clark, 38, 65, 114, 117, 148, 231, 271, 282–83
Grillo, Julius Edgar "J. Ed," 138
Grimshaw, Myron, 175
Griswold Hotel (Griswold House), 38
Griswold House billiard room, 45

Gwilliam, Shad, 128
Hahn, Frank "Noodles," 58
Hahn, William Edgar "Ed," 228
Hall, Captain Forrest, 289
Hallman, William "Bill," 77–78
Hamilton, William "Billy," 165
Hamilton's Fields, 164
Hammerstein's Victoria Theatre, 25
Hancock County, West Virginia, 45
Hanlon, Edward "Ned," 15, 23, 110, 145
Hanna, William B., 130
Harlem Hospital, 209–210
Harlem River, 117
Harley, Richard "Dick," 48–49, 52, 58, 114
Harmon, John, 180, 187, 286, 288
Harmon, Governor Judson, 241
Harmon, Margaret, 187
Harmon, Mary (Maher), 180
Harmon family, 286
Harridge, William "Will," 282
Harrigan, Reverend John H., 180
Harrisonville, Ohio, 44
Harry (Martha C. Porter letter), 44
Hart, James "Jim," 65, 131–32, 192–93
Hartman, Frederick "Fred," 88
Hartsel, Tully "Topsy," 42, 160, 293
Harum, David, 267
Harvard Medical School, 287
Hawes, Reverend, T.M., 304
Hawley, Emerson Pink, 142–43
Hayes, Byron, 264
Hedges, Robert, 68, 271
Heilbroner, Louis "Louie," 12–14
Heilmann, Harry, 257–58
Hell, 72
Herald Square, 111
Hercules, 124
Herndon, Joseph "Joe," 165
Herrman, Magistrate Moses, 26
Herrmann, August "Garry," 24, 41–42, 50–51, 64–65, 118–19, 136, 138, 212, 216, 260, 280–82, 296–97, 299–300, **302**, 303, 305
Herzog, Charles "Buck," 196, 209
"Hey, Barney," 128–29
Heydler, John, 213, 260, 280–81, 299–300, 304
Hicksville, Ohio, 289

Higgins, Dr. J.J., 301
High Street Baptist Church, 149
Highland Presbyterian Church, 304
Hildebrand, George, 278–79
Hill, Bill, 84
Hilltop Park, 243, 247, 254, 308
Hindley, Howard L., 82
Hirstius, Sheriff A.J., 241
Hite, Mabel, 25–26
Hoboken, New Jersey, 83
Hoey, Frederick "Fred," 89
Hoey, John "Jack," 184
Hofman, Arthur "Solly," 197–98
Hogan, Sergeant Thomas, 18
Holland House, 269
Hollenden Hotel, 241
Holy Communion, 184
Homestead, Pennsylvania, 144
Hong Kong, 83
Hooley, Willie, 151
Hoosier, 166
Hot Springs, Arkansas, 15, 17, 19, 91, 111, 113, 129, 180
Hotel Euclid, 238, 240–41
Hotel Henry, 305
Hotel Iroquois, 169
Hotel Marlborough, 121
Hotel Oxford, 65, 77
Hotel Sinton, 202
Hotel Somerset, 206, 210
Hotel Vendome, 103–104
Hotspur, 169–70
Hough, Frank, 58
Howard, George Elmer "Del," 201
Howard Street, 15, 20
Howarth, Oberlin, 102–103
Hoy, William "Dummy," 142
Hoyt, Waite, 268
Hub, 169
Hubbard, Donald, 285
Huff, George, 192
Huggins, Miller, 272
Hughes, Officer John, 289
Hughey, James "Jim," 89
Huntington Avenue Baseball Grounds, 67, 101, 103–104, 125, 149, 153, 174, 176–77, 180, 189, 283, 286
Hurst, Tim, 84
Huser, Justice of the Peace Louis P., 168
Huston, Tillinghast "Til," 268–72, 275, 277, 279–81

Illinois, 19
Illinois-Iowa League, 110

Indiana, 77, 180, 188
Indianapolis, Indiana, 40, 146
Inter Ocean, 16, 166, 188, 198
International League, 258
International Railway Bridge, 72, 74
Ireland, 54, 286
Irish, 1, 3
Irwin, Arthur, 34
Isaminger, James, 234
Isman, Felix, 26
Itha (Mary C. Porter letter), 44

J.M. Strong's grist and saw mills, 1
Japan, 251
Jefferson Market Court (New York), 26
Jennings, Hugh "Hughie," 4, 32, 57, 112–13, 230–33, 236–40, 249–53
Jerome, District Attorney William Travers, 211
Jersey City, New Jersey, 108, 250
Jersey City Skeeters, 132
John (Mary C. Porter letter), 44
John Hancock, 59
Johnny Butt-in, 7
Johnson, Byron Bancroft "Ban or B.B.," x, 17, 36–37, 39–40, 58, 61, 64–66, 69–70, 111–19, 138, 148, 157, 169, 177–79, 191–92, 215, 234, 236, 243, 245, 248–55, 259–61, 264, 267–73, 275–83, 296, 299, **302**, 309
Johnson, M.S., 74
Johnson, Walter, 248, 308
Johnstone, Edward Black "Ed," 256
Johnstone, James "Jim," 119, 128–29, 132, 209, 211, 213–15, 294
Jones, David "Davy," 237
Jones, Fielder, 258
Jones, Samuel "Sad Sam," 265
Joss, Adrian "Addie," 41, 48, 284
Joy, John, 286
Joyce, William, "Bill, Scrappy or Scrappy Bill," 7, 13, 52, 57, 83–89
Junior Circuit, 192

K.T. & K. Pottery, 50
Kahoe, Michael "Mike," 42
Kalamazoo, Michigan, 164
Kansas, 91, 96, 98, 256
Kansas City, Missouri, 263
Karlsruhe, Baden, 108

Keane, Sergeant Thomas, 287, 289
Keazer, Captain John C., 150
Keeler, William "Willie," 32, 42, 47, 166
Keister, William "Bill," 112
Kelley, Joseph "Joe," 24, 41, 50, 115–18
Kelly, "Honest John," 110
Kelly, John "Kick," 142
Kenilworth, Utah, 256
Kennedy, William "Brickyard or Perk," 81, 92, 99, 101
Kennedy Lumber Company, 171
Kennison, Stanley, 186
Kentuckian, 297, 299
Kentucky Legislature, 297
Kerr, William, 108–109, 124
Kilfoyl, John, 169
Killefer, Wade "Red," 236
Killen, Frank "King," 84
Killian, Edwin "Ed," 229
Killilea, Henry, 100, 176
Killilea, Matthew "Matt," 37
Kingfisher, Oklahoma, 255
Kingston, Margaret, 16, 20–22
Kingston, Samuel "Sam," 73–75, 78
Kingston, Ontario, Canada, 77–78
Kittridge, Malachi, 144
Klaw & Erlanger Theatrical Exchange, 18
Klein, J.J., 240
Klem, William "Bill," 209, 211, 213–15, 294
Kling, John "Johnny," 201, 203, 209
Klobedanz, Frederick "Fred," 35
Knabe, Franz Otto, 215
Knickerbocker Hotel, 25
Knowles, Frederick "Fred," 62, 120–21, 130, 214–15, 294–95
Koehn, W.A., 188
Koelsch, William F.H., 60, 85, 89
Koufax, Sanford "Sandy," 149
Krause, Harry, 234

L.S. Soest Drugstore, 188
Labor Day, 58, 99–100
Ladies' Day, x, 32–33, 36, 284
LaForce, Edward "Ed," 101
Lajoie, Napoleon "Nap," 231, 242, 308
Lake Erie, 70
Lakewood, New Jersey, 88
Lambert, William J., 60
Landis, Judge Kenesaw Mountain, 282

Lange, William "Bill," 32, 56
Langham Hotel, 41, 43–44, 48
Lannin, Joseph, 258, 260, 271
Las Vegas, New Mexico, 46
Lauder, William "Billy," 94
Lawrence County, Pennsylvania, 139
Lawson, Al, 110
Leach, Thomas "Tommy," 57, 91, 108, 145, 194
League Park (Cincinnati), 5, 33
League Park (Cleveland), 67, 69–70, 152, 238–39
League Park (St. Louis), 11–13, 24, 89, 147, 202
Leever, Samuel "Sam," 81, 92, 94, 101, 125
Leidy, George, 225–27
Lenox Athletic Club, 213
Lenten, 184
Leonard, Frank, 29
Lewis, Edward "Ted," 167
Lexington, Kentucky, 307
Liberty, Kentucky, 255
Lincoln, Abraham, 299
Lindenwood Cemetery, 188
Lindsay, Christian "Chris," 227–28
Little Rock, Arkansas, 181–84
Livingston, Patrick "Paddy," 234, 237
Locke, William H., 96–97, 120, 122, 299
Loftus, Thomas "Tom," 59, 61–69, 73–74, 77, 145, 147
Logan, Thomas, 305
Long Acre Square, 26
Los Angeles, California, 38, 42, 148
Los Angeles Dodgers, 149
Los Angeles Record, 155
Louisville, Kentucky, 40, 108–109, 130, 145, 168, 182–84, 304–305, 307
Louisville & Nashville Railroad, 306
Louisville Colonels, 29, 35–36, 57, 94, 108, 110, 124, 126, 140–46, 148, 297
Louisville Commercial, 297, 306
Louisville Medical College, 306
Lowe, Mart, 18
Luce, Supreme New York Supreme Court Justice Robert L., 272, 276
Lucker, Claude (Lueker), 243–45, 247–50, 254–55, 308
Luitich, John F., 66

Lush, William "Billy," 165
Lynch, Michael, "Mike," 126–28
Lynch, Thomas "Tom," 83, 159
Lynchburg, Virginia, 59
Lynn, Massachusetts, 149–52, 186
Lynn Woods Road, 150
Lyons, Stanley, 307

MacDonald, Medical Examiner William G., 287–88
Mack, Connie, 112–13, 138, 145–46, 148–49, 152–59, 161, **162**, 169, 175, 234–36, 250, 270–71, 283, 292–94, 308
Macon, Georgia, 175, 231
Madden, Minnie, 263
Madison Square Garden, 305
Magee, Leo "Lee," 259
Magee, Sherwood "Sherry," 215
Maguire, Edward J., 74–76
Maharg, William "Billy," 251
Mahon, John J., 116–17
Mahoney, Sarah "Sadie," 1–2
Maid of the Mist, 76
Maine, 28
Major League Baseball, 85, 140, 161, 213, 249, 296
Maloney, William "Billy," 193
Manhattan Field, 208
Manhattan Island, 117
Mann, Louis, 132
Manning, James "Jimmy," 36–37, 57–59
Mansfield, Missouri, 255, 262–63
Mansfield, Ohio, 55
Market Street, 203
Marlborough Hotel, 160
Mars, Pennsylvania, 142
Marsh, Reverend John Arba, 149
Maryland, 23
Massachusetts, 105, 135–36
Mathewson, Christopher "Christy," 38–39, 121–23, 125–26, 129, 138, 196, 198, 201, 209, 226, 308
Mautner, Isadore "Izy," 176
Maxwell, Clarence "Gunplay," 256
Mays, Carl William, x, 255–73, **274**, 275–80, 282–83
Mays, Franklin "Frank," 262–63
Mays, Louisa Callie (Land), 255
Mays, Marjorie Fredericka (Madden), 261–63, 266
Mays, Ruby, 263
Mays, Wesley, 255

Mays, William, 255
the Mays family, 255
McAleer, James "Jimmy," 292–93
McBreen, Hugh, 177, 180
McBride, Henry T., 207
McCarthy, John "Jack," 193
McCleary, Standish, 114
McCormick, Harry, 24, 196–98
McCredie, Walter "Walt," 257
McCredie, William Wallace "Judge," 257
the McCredies, 257
McDermott, Mike, 29
McDonald, Ralph, 261
McGann, Dennis "Dan," 36, 92, 118, 136
McGinnity, Joseph "Joe or Iron Man," 13, 23, 92–93, 114, 118, 125–26, 128, 198, 201, 208, 216
McGinnity, Stewart, 22
McGivern, Councilman John D., 286
McGrath, Detective John J., 25
McGrath, Thomas "Tom," 10
McGraw, Ellen, 109
McGraw, John Joseph "Jack, Mac, Mack or Muggsy (Mugsy)," 4, 12–17, 19, 25, 59–65, 71, 73, 77, 80, 93, 107, 109–117, 119, 121–33, 135–37, 158, 196–97, 199–201, 205–206, 208–210, 214, 294, 308–310, 311
McGraw, John Sr., 109, 131
McGraw, Robert "Bob," 268
McGreevy, Michael "Mike or Nuf Ced," 181–82
McGuire, James "Deacon," 33–34, 239, 251
McInnis, John "Stuffy," 237
McIntyre, Matthew, "Matty," 155, 227, 229–32
McJames, James "Doc," 32–33
McKean, Edwin "Ed," 4, 7
McKeesport, Pennsylvania, 203
McKenna, Margaret E., 180
McKisson, Robert E., 241
McLane, State Attorney Robert M., 21–22
McPhee, John "Bid," 90
McQuiston, Frank, 100
McRoy, Robert "Bob," 277
McSweeney, James (Joseph) M., 289
Mears, Officer George W., 102–103
Medfield State Hospital, 105

Meekin, George Jouett, 86–89
Melrose Park, 258
Memorial Day, 263, 266
Memphis, Tennessee, 184
Mercer, Pennsylvania, 139–40
Mercer, Clifford, 43, 45–46
Mercer, George Barclay "William Barclay, Winifred B., Win, Winnie, Winifred, Virginia, Virgin, Gin, Apollo of the Potomac or Romeo" (alias George Murray), x, 28, 29–52, 53, 78, 80, 82–83, 95, 166, 184, 284–85, 296, 301, 303
Mercer, Hazel, 43, 45
Mercer, Howard, 43, 45
Mercer, Jacob, 28, 44
Mercer, Margaret "Maggie" (Wells), 28, 43–45, 48, 50, 284
Mercer, Robert, 43, 45
Mercer, Ross, 43, 45
Mercer, Sidney "Sid," 46–47
the Mercer home, 50
the Mercers, 28
Meridian, Mississippi, 232
Merkle, Amalie (Thilghman or Thielman), 197
Merkle, Carl Frederick Rudolph "Fred," 196–99, 201–202, 205, 210, 212
Merkle, Ernest, 197
Methodist, 255
Meyran Avenue, 146
Michigan, 124, 145
Michigan Avenue, 143
Michigan Street, 178
Michigan Central Railroad, 71, 73–74, 77
Michigan Central Railroad Train No. 6, 72
Midland Division, 287
Milan, Jesse Clyde, 248
Miller, Roscoe, 122–23
Mills, William "Willie," 90
Milton, Massachusetts, 149
Milwaukee, Wisconsin, 252
Milwaukee Brewers (major league club), 169
Milwaukee Brewers (minor league club), 47, 146, 148
Milwaukee Brewers/Creams (minor league club), 145
Minor League Association, 258
Mintz, Detective Jake, 240
Missouri, 256
Mrs. O'Connor, 109
Mrs. Pierce, 18

Mrs. Ross, 150
Mrs. Waldron, 151
"Mr. Buttinsky," 297
Mr. Van Horn, 44
Mitchell, Frederick "Fred," 120
Mix, George E., 294
Mobile, Alabama, 110
Moccasin Creek, North Carolina, 308
Monongahela House, 92, 99, 104
Montgomery, Alabama, 159, 175
Montpelier, Vermont, 85
Montreal, Quebec, Canada, 85
Moran, Patrick "Pat," 198
Mount Clemens, Michigan, 67, 73, 168
Muldoon's Sanatorium, 299
Mullin, George, 230, 232
Murnane, Timothy "Tim," 82, 183, 236
Murphy, Charles, 192–93, 195, 199–200, 202, 204–205, 207, 296–98, 300
Murphy, Daniel "Danny," 237
Murphy, David P., 188
Murphy, Francis "Frank," 188
Murphy, Johnnie "Jockey," 9
Murphy, R.N., 308
Murphy, Police Justice Thomas, 179
Murphy, North Carolina, 308
the Murphys, 3
Murray, Detective John, 178
Murray, William "Billy," 132, 212

Nantucket, Massachusetts, 176–78
Narrows, Georgia, 220
Nashville, Tennessee, 301
National Agreement, 85
National Association of Professional Baseball Leagues, 67
National Baseball Club, 31
National Commission, 157–58, 212–14, 216, 254, 260, 276, 280–82, 295–96, 299, 303
National Exhibition Company, 118, 135
National Guard, 291
National League, x, 11–12, 14–15, 23–24, 28–29, 31, 35–36, 39, 41, 48, 51–52, 55–59, 61, 64, 66–67, 69–70, 81–82, 84–85, 89, 91–94, 104, 107–108, 110–11, 113–14, 116–19, 121–22, 124, 127, 129–32, 135–38, 146–47,

159, 163, 165–71, 177, 192–96, 199–200, 202–206, 209–213, 215, 217, 219, 227, 258, 260–61, 280–81, 294, 297–300, 303–305, 308–309
National League Board of Directors, 111, 122, 129–33, 135–36, 201–202, 205–206
National League Park (Philadelphia), 58, 83, 196, 215
National Leaguers, 15, 112
National Park (Washington), 253
National Pastime, 195
the Nationals, 170
Naval Reserve, 260
Navin, Francis J. "Frank," 225, 229–30, 232, 240–41, 252–54, 275, 280, 283
New England Conservatory of Music, 262
New England League, 28, 82
New Jersey, 291
New Old South Church, 261
New Orleans, Louisiana, 60–63, 80
New Rochelle, New York, 262
New York, 25
New York, New York (New York City), 16, 25, 36, 38–39, 59, 61–62, 64, 67, 71, 73, 82–85, 87, 89–92, 94, 96, 98, 105, 111–12, 116–19, 121, 123, 125, 129–32, 136, 138, 142, 153–54, 158–60, 177, 198–201, 206, 211–13, 215–17, 229, 243–44, 247, 249, 252, 260, 262, 264, 268–69, 272–73, 275–76, 278, 281, 290–92, 294–95, 297–98, 300–301, 304–305
New York Appellate Court, Part I, 280
New York Athletic Club, 300–301, 307
New York Baseball Club, 118, 294
New York Club, 62–63, 88, 122
New York County, 211
New York Daily News, 109
New York Giants, ix, 24–25, 38, 51–52, 59–66, 69–71, 73, 77, 80–90, 92–94, 97, 107, 111–12, 116–33, 135–39, 154–55, 157–60, 175, 192–93, 196–202, 204–217, 284, 290, 294–95, 297, 309
New York Herald, 83

New York Highlanders, ix, 39, 65, 68–71, 81, 92, 117, 125, 138, 153–54, 175, 179, 192, 201, 227–28, 231, 243, 247–48, 291–92
New York League, 29
New York Metropolitans, 82
New York, New Haven & Hartford Railroad, 287
New York-Pennsylvania League, 109
New York Press, 83
New York State League, 74
New York Stock Exchange, 199
New York's Supreme Court, 280
New York Supreme Court's Appellate Division, 282
New York Yankees, ix, 259, 267–70, 272–73, 275–82
New Yorkers, 160
Newburger, New York Supreme Court Justice Joseph E., 281
Newfoundland dog, 150
Newhouse, Frank, 153
Niagara Falls, Ontario, Canada, 76
Niagara River, 72–74, 76
Niagara's Horseshoe Falls, 76
Nickel Plate Road, 2
1919 Chicago White Sox, 282
1904 New York Giants, **134**
North, 115
North American, 58, 148, 153, 234
North Brookfield, Massachusetts, 168
North Carolinians, 308
Northern League, 82
Northfield, Vermont, 81, 86
Northfield High School, 81
Northwest, 256
Northwestern League, 257
Northwestern Police Station, 18
Norwich University, 81
Notre Dame University, 168
No. 419 Knights of Columbus, 105

O Street Northeast, 18
Oak Park, 40–41
Oakland, California, 38
Oakland (Pittsburgh neighborhood), 146
Oakland Clamdiggers, 38
Ocala, Florida, 110
Occidental Hotel, 42–43
O'Connell, Frederic P., 285
O'Connor, John "Jack," 6, 39, 242

O'Connor, John D., 109
O'Day, Henry "Hank," 14, 194–200, 202, 204–205
O'Farrell, Reverend Dennis J., 289
Officer Hassenmuller, 25
Ogden, Dr. Charles B., 30
Ohio, 45, 171, 186, 241–42
Ohio State Board of Health, 30
Ohio State League, 54
Ohio Valley, 44
Ohio Valley League, 29
Olathe, Missouri, 255
Olean, New York, 109
O'Leary, James C., 264–65
O'Leary, Assistant Superintendent of Police Timothy "Tim," 237
Olive Street, 10
O'Loughlin, Francis "Silk," 157, 228, 243
Olympic Park II, 164
Omaha, Nebraska, 187, 191
111th Street (New York), 117
155th Street (New York), 208
113th Street (New York), 117
O'Neil, Officer Tom, 243
O'Neill, Norris "Tip," 41–42, 44, 50
Organized Baseball, 109, 157, 160–61, 222, 235, 258, 290, 293
Oriental Hotel, 71
Oriole Park, 24, 114, 118, 170
Ornament, 51–52
Orth, Albert "Al," 59–60
Ortman, Henry, 171, 173
Ortman, Henry W., 173
Ortman (Ortmann), Louise L. "Lulu," 171–73
Oshkosh, Wisconsin, 299–300
Ossian Bedell, 75
O'Toole, John, 286–87, 289
Owens, Clarence "Brick," 272, 298, 304–305

Pacific Coast, 65
Pacific Coast League, 256–57
Pacific National League, 158
Padden, Richard "Dick," 164
Paducah, Kentucky, 108, 164, 307
Palace of the Fans, 95
Paquet, Reverend Joseph, 83
Parent, Alfred "Freddy," 115, 175, 232
Parkside Avenue, 174
Patten, Case "Casey," 68
Patten, Mrs. M.F., 151

Payne, James "Doc," 239
Peabody, Massachusetts, 149–52, 291
Pelty, Barney, 248
Pendleton, Oregon, 257
Pennsylvania, 2, 46, 251, 263, 265–66, 272
Pennsylvania Dutch, 139
Peoria, Illinois, 1
Perrine, Frederick "Bull," 251
Perry, Herbert Scott, 268
Pfiester, John "Jack," 196, 198, 206, 208–209
Phelan, Judge James, 248
Phelon, William Arlie "W.A.," 308
Phelps, Colonel Zachary "Zach," 145
Philadelphia, Pennsylvania, 8, 17, 43, 48, 56, 58, 67, 71, 77, 148, 151–56, 159–60, 216–17, 234–38, 249–53, 261, 264, 266, 290–91, 303
Philadelphia Athletics, ix, 67, 112–13, 121, 138, 148–49, 152–54, 156–61, 169, 173–75, 233–35, 237–39, 249–51, 253, 259, 263–64, 266, 268–70, 285, 290–93
Philadelphia Inquirer, 58
Philadelphia Phillies, 13, 24, 32, 55–59, 61, 77, 81–83, 97, 100, 113, 120, 159, 196, 202, 210, 212, 215–17, 258, 290, 294, 303
Phillippe, Charles "Deacon," 81, 92, 94–95, 97–98, 101–102, 104, 108, 125
Pilsener club, 164, 186
Pinkerton Detective Agency, 148, 208
Pinkney, George, 55
Pittinger, Charles "Togie," 99
Pittsburgh, Pennsylvania, 5, 7, 20, 29, 35, 39–40, 52, 58–59, 86, 88, 90–91, 93–94, 96–100, 105, 108, 119, 121–23, 125, 127–28, 130–31, 133, 137–38, 140, 146–47, 197–98, 203, 211, 216, 241, 263, 304–305
Pittsburgh Club, 283
Pittsburgh College (Duquesne University), 147
Pittsburgh Commercial Gazette, 29
Pittsburgh Daily Dispatch, 100
Pittsburgh Dispatch, 52
Pittsburgh Leader, 110

Pittsburgh Pirates, x, 15, 24, 32, 35, 39–41, 52, 57–59, 81–82, 86–88, 90–105, 107–110, 119–22, 124–32, 135–38, 140, 142–43, 146–48, 174, 187, 192–97, 199, 201–204, 206, 211, 233, 240–41, 283, 297–99, 303, 309
Pittsburgh Press, 18, 23, 49, 98, 102, 105, 121, 125–26, 128, 158, 194, 203–204, 283
Pittsburghs, 61
Plain Dealer, 139
Plank, Edward "Eddie," 237
Planter's Hotel, 299
Players League, 11, 55
Poland, 286
Poland, Philip "Phil," 149, 151
Polish, 286
Polo Grounds, 51–52, 83, 86–87, 89, 92–93, 119, 126–29, 131–32, 138, 157, 196–98, 200–202, 205–211, 213, 215, 268, 272
Poole, Edward "Ed," 91
Porter, Martha C., 43–44, 50
Porter, S.H., 50
Portland, Maine, 29, 52
Portland, Oregon, 52, 257–58
Portland Beavers, 257
Portland Colts, 257–58
Postal, Frederick "Fred," 50, 60, 63
Poughkeepsie, New York, 25
Powell, John "Jack," 248
Powers, Michael "Doc," 291
Pratt, Derrill "Del," 268
Pratt, Reverend Dr. Milton Butler, 50
Pressmen's Union, 244
Preston family, 306
Price, Utah, 256
Probst, Dr. Charles O., 30
Prospect, Pennsylvania, 139, 147
Protective Association of Professional Baseball Players, 15, 249, 252, 254
Providence, Rhode Island, 154, 156, 290
Providence Friars, 258
Pulliam (Pulman), Harry, x, 24, 64, 66, 69–71, 93–94, 108–109, 121–22, 127, 129–33, 135–36, 145, 195, 199–202, 205–206, 211–13, 297–301, **302**, 303–308
Pulliam, John P., 299
Pullman (Pullman Company), 72, 74, 76, 154

Punxsutawney, Pennsylvania, 146
Purman, Paul, 260
Putnam's Hotel, 262

Quakers, 58, 157
Queen Victoria, 143
Queens, New York, 59
Quill, Tom, 104
Quinn, James Aloysius Robert "Bob," 5
Quinn, Michael, 286–87, 289

Rathskeller saloon, 22
Ratty, Michael, 22
Ratty, Thomas, 22
Ray, Anna, 187
the Rayls, 143–44
Raymond, Arthur "Bugs," ix
Reach, Alfred "Al," 57
Reynolds, Dr. Dudley Jr., 306
Reynolds, Howard G., 267
Richmond House, 307
Richter, Francis C., 156, 303
Rigler, Charles "Cy," 204
Ritchey, Claude, 104, 108, 187
Ritchie, Judge Albert, 20–23
Roanoke Magicians, 164
Roberts (photographer), 184
Robinson, Congressman James M., 188
Robinson, Wilbert "Robbie," 12, 16–17, 110–11, 113, 116, 118
Robison, Frank, 3–4, 12–13, 15, 18–19, 50–51, 111
Robison, Martin Stanford "Stanley," 12, 15, 300
the Robisons, 13
Roebke, Fred W., 168
Rogers, Colonel John I., 57, 59, 61
Roman candle, 84
Room 128, 142
Ross, Edward, 149–52
Rossman, Claude, 232
Roth, Andrew "Andy," 226
Rowe, Jack, 171
Roxbury (Boston neighborhood), 180, 183, 187, 286–87
"Royal Rooters," 181
Royston, Georgia, 220–23, 226
Rube, 167
Rueben, 84
Rule 28 (National League bylaws), 136
Ruppert, Jacob, 268–70, 272–73, 275–77, 279–83
Rusie, Amos, 86–88
Russell, Allen, 268
Ruth, Babe, 285, 308

Rutland Herald, 82
Ryan (gambling organization), 160
Ryan, James "Jimmy," 70, 237
Ryan, Johnny, 299

Sacramento, California, 40, 42, 45
St. Albans, Vermont, 82–83, 89
St. Albans Club, 81–82, 85
Saint Francis de Sales Church, 180, 289
St. James Building, 199, 211
St. Joseph's College, 251
St. Louis, Missouri, 4, 9–10, 12–13, 37, 69, 90, 111, 166, 173, 175, 239, 262–64, 293, 299–300, 304
St. Louis Browns (American League), 37–38, 67–68, 118, 174–75, 230, 242, 248, 264, 269–72, 279, 281, 292–93
St. Louis Browns (National League), 55
St. Louis Cardinals, 8–15, 18–19, 24, 50, 89–91, 95, 99, 110–11, 146–47, 202, 210, 216, 300
St. Louis Dispatch, 8
St. Louis Globe-Democrat, 6, 9–10, 12, 37, 124, 300
St. Louis Perfectos, 3–8
St. Louis Post-Dispatch, 10
St. Louis Republic, 3, 9–11, 46, 89
St. Louis Star, 68
St. Louis Terriers, 271
St. Louis's City Hospital, 10
St. Marys, Pennsylvania, 153
St. Vincent de Paul Catholic Church, 23
St. Vincent's Hospital, 3
Salt Lake City, Utah, 256
Salt Lake City Skyscrapers, 256
Salt Lake Herald, 43
San Antonio, Texas, 160
San Diego, California, 14
San Francisco, California, 41–45, 48–49, 291
San Francisco Bulletin, 47
San Francisco Call, 42–43
San Jose, California, 15
Sanborn, Irving "Sy," 201
Santa Cruz, California, 4–5, 9, 14
Santa Cruz Beachcombers/Sand Crabs, 3–4
Scanlan, William "Doc," 125
Schaefer, William "Germany," 225, 227, 235–36

Schang, Walter "Wally," 264–65, 278
Schenck, Martin A., 279
Schmelz, Gustavus "Gus," 28–29, 165
Schmidt, Charles "Charlie or Boss," 228–29, 231–32
Schneider, Frederick "Fred," 290
Schneider, Mary, 290
Schone, Henry H., 188
Schone Undertaking Rooms, 188
Schrady, Dr. George, 301
Schrecongost, Freeman Osse "Schreck," 5–8
Schriver, William "Pop," 33
Schulte, Frank, 193, 209
Schumm, Charles "Charlie," 239
Schwan, Judge George H., 241
Schwartz, Fred, 168
Scottsburg, Kentucky, 297
Sebring, James "Jimmy," 24, 283–84
Section 55 (National League constitution), 201
Section 28 (National League constitution), 121
Seelbach Hotel, 306–307
Seize, 46
Selbach, Albert "Kip," 68, 118, 175
Selee, Frank, 165–66, 192–93
Senior Circuit, 23–24, 66, 111, 175, 281
Setley, William "Wild Bill," 158
Sewell, Joe, 54
Sewell, Luke, 54
Sexton, Michael, 67
Seymour, Harold, 285
Seymour, James "Cy," 82, 85–86, 115, 118, 196
Shakespeare, 279
Shakespearean, 306
the Shamrocks, 187
Sharon, Pennsylvania, 139
Sheckard, Samuel James Tilden "Jimmy," 112, 193
Sheldon, Superior Court Judge Henry Newton, 135–36
Sheridan, John "Jack," 114
Sheridan, John B., 3–4, 82
Sherman Antitrust Act, 276
Shettsline, William "Bill," 57, 59, 212
Shibe, Benjamin "Ben or Uncle Ben," 237, 292
Shibe Park, 237, 250, 252, 259, 263–64
Siever, Edward "Ed," 229

Siler, George, 6
Sinclair, Lee W., 184
Sinton Hotel, 300
Sir Oracle, 279
Sixth Regiment, 291
Slagle, James "Jimmy," 193–95
Slayton, Ernest B., 16, 18, 20–21
Sloan, Ted, 52
Sly Fox, 51–52
Smith, Alexander "Broadway Aleck," 62, 90
Smith, Elmer, 167
Smith, Sergeant James P., 289
Smith, Governor John Walter, 23
Smith, Milton H., 306–307
Smith, Nettie, 306–307
Smoky City, 39, 58–59, 90–91, 203, 211
Snitkin, Leonard, 26
Snowball Farm, 168
Society for American Baseball Research, vii
Soden, Arthur, 131–32, 170
Somers, Charles, 169–70, 176, 231, 271, 278
South, 62, 110, 180, 230, 241, 292
South Atlantic League, 223, 227
South Bend, Indiana, 168
South Boston (Boston neighborhood), 180, 286, 289
South Boston Police Department, 287
South Carolina, 220
South End Grounds, 4, 98–99, 165–67
South Side Park, 148, 173, 175, 229
South Washington, 17
Southampton Street, 287, 289
Southern, 228, 231, 309
Southern California, 38
Southern California Winter League, 15
Southern Hotel, 12, 68, 166
Southern League, 223
Southern Michigan League, 248
Southern Utah, 256
Spalding, Albert "Al," 114, 193
Spanish influenza, 262
Speaker, Tristram "Tris," 278
Speer, George "Kid," 47
Spokane, Washington, 257
Sporting Life, vii, 35, 60, 69, 84, 92, 156, 303
Sporting News, vii, 3–4, 42, 66, 97, 121, 129, 152, 201, 264, 308
Sportsman's Park, 68, 175, 242, 264

Spring Grove Cemetery, 50
Springfield, Illinois, 19
Stahl, Barbara (Stadtmiller), 164, 186, 189
Stahl, Charles Sylvester "Chick, Chic or the Chicken," x, 163–76, 178–89, **190**, 191–92, 232, 285–86, 288, 290, 301, 303
Stahl, Julia (Harmon), 180, 183, 187–89, 285–90
Stahl, Perry, 187, 288
Stahl, Reuben, 164, 173
the Stahl residence, 188
the Stahls, 164, 181
The Stain of Guilt, 148
Stanage, Oscar, 235
Standish, Miles, 82
Stanfield, George, 238–42
Starkloff, Dr. Max C., 173–74
Starr, Charles "Charlie," 194
Stealing Home, 25
Steinfeldt, Harry, 194, 196
Stenzel, Jacob "Jake," 32
Stephens, Isaac, 179
Stephens, Martha, 178–79
Stevens, Harry, 132–33
Stewart, Joe, 6
Stifel, Otto, 271
Stone, Judge Andrew C., 103
Storke, Alan, 204
Stout, Glenn, 285
Stovall, George, 248
Striker, Fred, 143
Strouthers, John Cornelius "Con," 223–24
Student Army Training Corps, 263
Sudhoff, John William "Willie," 4
Sugden, Joseph "Joe," 251
Sullivan, Cornelius, 131
Sullivan, Timothy D. "Big Tim," 213
Sullivan, Timothy P. "Little Tim," 160–61, 290
Sullivan, William "Billy," 229
Summers, Oren Edgar "Ed," 234
The Sun, 25, 83, 116–17, 130–31, 199, 215, 244
Supreme Court of the District of Columbia, 19
Swaim, John "Cy," 167
Sylvester, Major Richard, 74
Syracuse Stars, 29, 74, 126

Tammany Hall, 82, 117, 160, 213, 290, 295
Tampa, Florida, 263

Tannehill, Jesse, 39, 81, 92, 98
Tanner, Governor John R., 19
Taylor, Charles H., 176–77
Taylor, John I., 176, 181–82, 187, 191–92, 232
Taylor, Luther "Dummy," 119
the Taylor ownership, 176
the Taylors, 178
Tebeau, George, 145, 167
Tebeau, Oliver Wendell "Patsy," 3–5, 11–13, 31, 55, 174
Temple Cup, 166
Tenderloin Police Station, 25
Tener, John K., 281
Tennessee–Alabama League, 224
Tennessee River, 108
Tenney, Frederick "Fred," 165, 187, 196, 208–209
Terry, William "Adonis," 56
Thaw, Harry K., 305
Third Base Saloon, 181
Thomas, Charles, 296–97
Thomas, Federal Judge Edward B., 70
Thomasville, Georgia, 144, 187
Thompson, John Gustav "Gus," 100
Thompson, Mayor William Barlum, 248
Thornton, Caroline, 307
Thornton, Colonel Robert A., 307
Thornton, William Preston, 306–307
Thornton family, 306
Thorpe, Monsignor Thomas P., 77
Thrasher, Frank "Buck," 259
The Three Musketeers, 52
Tiernan, Michael "Mike," 32, 88
The Times (Philadelphia), 58
The Times (Washington, D.C.), 34
Tinker, Joseph "Joe," 196, 198, 203–204
Toledo, Ohio, 40, 197
Toledo Mud Hens, 138
Toledo Times-Bee, 284
The Tombs, 305
Toronto, Ontario, Canada, 77
Toronto Maple Leafs, 49
the Tourists, 40–41, 45–48
Townsend, John "Happy," 59–60
Travers, Aloysius "Allan," 251
Travis, George Y., 45
Trew, Marshal Samuel, 73
The Tribune, 289
Trinity Place Station, 262
Triple Crown, 233
Tri-State League, 55

Troy, New York, 25
Truxton, New Jersey, 109
Tufts College, 261
"The Turkey in the Straw," 140
Tuthill, Harry, 239
Tuttle, Charles H., 276–79, 281
Twentieth Century Flyer, 206

Unglaub, Robert "Bob," 185, 192, 236
Union Association, 256
Union Park, 3, 142
Union Station (St. Louis), 9, 299
Union Street, 151
United States, 4, 16, 54, 108, 137, 206, 252, 262, 276
United States League, 252
University of Georgia, 223
University of Michigan, 39
Utah State Capitol, 256

Van, W.H., 43
Van Haltren, George, 94
Vance, Henry, 277
Vanderbeck, George, 143–44
Veil, Frederick "Bucky," 92, 101
Vermont, 83, 85–86
Vermonter, 84
Viaduct, 207
Vickery, Judge Willis, 242
Vila, Joseph "Joe," 125, 129, 201, 207, 294–95
Virginia State League, 164
Virginia University, 297
Volant College, 139–40

Waddell, George Edward "Rube," ix, 108, 121, 138–61, 215–16, 290–94
Waddell, John, 147
Waddell, May (Wynne Skinner, Wyman Skinner or Ross), 149, 151, 159, 291, 294
Wagner, George, 31, 284
Wagner, Jacob Earl, 31, 34–35, 165, 284
Wagner, John "Honus," 93–94, 98, 100, 108, 126, 136–37, 140, 142, 145, 194, 203, 226, 241, 308
Wagner, Phil, 31–32
Wagner, New York Supreme Court Justice Robert, 278–80, 282
the Wagner brothers, 284
the Wagners, 36
Waldorf-Astoria Hotel, 94, 297
Wallace, Roderick, "Bobby," 7

Walsh, Thomas, 210
Waner, Lloyd, 54
Waner, Paul, 54
Ward, John J., 135
Ward 6 Democratic Party Club (Lynn, Massachusetts), 186
Ward 16 (Boston, Massachusetts), 286
Warner, John "Jack," 88, 119–21, 123–24, 230
Warren Park, 223, 225, 230, 233
Washington, D.C., 16–18, 20–22, 30–31, 34–37, 51, 59–60, 62–63, 65–69, 71, 73–74, 76–77, 80, 140–41, 210, 212, 238, 264, 284
Washington Avenue, 9–10
Washington Club, 62–64, 66–67
Washington Heights Hospital, 207
Washington Herald, 214
Washington Nationals, x, 28–37, 40, 51–52, 83, 86, 110, 165–66, 184
Washington Park, 91
Washington Post, 30–31, 49, 84, 165–66
Washington Senators, 36–37, 45–46, 50, 57–71, 73–77, 80, 83, 156, 175, 236, 238, 248, 253–54, 269–71, 282, 284
Washington Times, 16, 18–20, 72
Washington University division (St. Louis, Missouri), 262
Washington's Equity Court, 19
the Washingtons, 83
Wayne County, Michigan, 241
Werden, Perry, 142
West, 38, 96, 214, 300

West Baden Springs, Indiana, 184–86, 191, 285
West Baden Springs Hotel, 184–85, 188
West Coast, 23, 147, 158
West End Park, 28
West Side Chicago, 203
West Side Grounds, 56, 90, 202–203, 219, 295
West Virginia, 29
Western, 259, 261–62
Western League, 66–67, 143–45, 167
Western Pennsylvania, 128, 139, 144, 305
Western Tri-State League, 256
Westervelt, Frederick, 243
Weyhing, August "Gus" (alias John Jones), 9–10
Wheeler, Edward, 209
Wheeling, West Virginia, 28
Wheeling National Citys/Nailers, 55
White, Charley, 6
White, Stanford, 305
White Plains, New York, 299
Whitney Theatrical Company, 25
Wilbur Opera Company, 185
Wilcox, Lewis "Lew," 40–41
Williams, James "Jimmy," 15, 42, 68, 113, 118
Williams, Richard "Nick," 257
Willis, Victor "Vic," 166, 170, 194, 203–204
Wilson, Harry, 306
Wilson, J.W., 40–41
Wilson, John Owen "Chief," 194–95, 204
Wiltse, George "Hooks," 201

"Win Mercer Caprice," 31
Windsor, Ontario, Canada, 143
Windy City, 202, 206, 268
Winfield, Kansas, 91, 96, 98
Wingard, Harlan, 224
Winter, George, 185
Wisconsin Electric Railway Company, 299
Wittman, George, 45
Wolverton, Harry, 248
Woodruff, Harvey, 212
The World, 85, 87–88, 158, 201, 243–45
World Series, ix, x, 100–102, 104–105, 125, 138–39, 145–55, 157–60, 174–75, 179, 187, 192–94, 202, 206, 210, 216–17, 219, 233, 240–41, 251, 258–59, 261, 268, 273, 280, 282–83, 290, 295–96, 303, 309
World's Fair (1893), 56
Wright, Clarence Eugene "Gene," 67
Wright, Tip, 236
Wright, William Henry "Harry," 55–56
Wright County, Missouri, 255–56
Wynne, Marvin W., 281

Y.W. Ralph & Co., 291
Yale University, 15
Young, Denton "Cy," 4, 101, 188, 191–92, 239
Young, Nicholas "Nick," 15, 167

Ziegler, Detective Louis "Louie," 10
Zimmer, Charles "Chief," 90, 146

About the Author

RONALD T. WALDO is a historian and author who has written ten books about baseball history, many devoted to examining the Deadball Era and the 1920s. A resident of Pittsburgh, Pennsylvania, his entire life, he graduated from Point Park University in 1983 with a bachelor's degree in journalism and communications. Following his love and passion for baseball history, Mr. Waldo's first book, *Fred Clarke: A Biography of the Baseball Hall of Fame Player-Manager*, was released in December 2010.

Some of his other books include a biography about Hazen "Kiki" Cuyler, a compilation of stories connected to the life and career of Honus Wagner, and team-related works on the 1902 Pittsburgh Pirates, 1925 Pittsburgh Pirates, and 1938 Pittsburgh Pirates. Mr. Waldo's most recent book, *Days of Reckoning: Players Punching Their Ticket Out of Pittsburgh During the Barney Dreyfuss Era*, was published in October 2023.

He also participated as a contributing author on the 2018 release, *Unlucky 21: The Saddest Stories and Games in Pittsburgh Sports History*, writing the chapter about the 1974–75 Pittsburgh Penguins hockey team titled "History Gone Bad: Chico and His Men Ruin the Pittsburgh Penguins' 1975 Playoff Party."

A longtime member of the Society for American Baseball Research, each of his five books covering baseball's Deadball Era received nominations for the Larry Ritter Book Award by that organization's Deadball Era Committee. The committee selected *Deadball Trailblazers: Single-Season Records of the Modern Era* as a finalist for the award in 2023. Besides being an avid baseball historian, Mr. Waldo also loves following current baseball, college softball, hockey, and soccer.

www.ingramcontent.com/pod-product-compliance
Lightning Source LLC
Chambersburg PA
CBHW011741220426
43665CB00022B/2896